まえがき

— まえがき —

和歌(短歌)は五・七・五・七・七の五つの句から成る三十一文字の言葉の小宇宙、千年以上昔の第一勅撰和歌集『古今集』(905年)でその技巧は確立され、平安時代の終わりの『新古今集』(13世紀初頭)でその文化的頂点に達した。その間、それぞれの時代の[先]帝の命を受けて編まれた八つの主要な勅撰和歌集が存在する — 『八代集』と総称されるこれら和歌集の収載歌総数は約9500首・・・その精髄は、この本に収められた200首の中に見ることができる。本書は、著者が私的に選んだ★ベスト50首★に、さらなる●良歌150首●(外国人や現代日本人に、昔の日本人の季節的・情緒的特性を伝える上で好適な短歌群)を加えたものである・・・長い時代を経て失われたものがどれだけあるか、今なお残るものがどれほどあるか、ありながらかくも長らく見過ごされ続けてきたものがいかに多いことか、この本を通して確認してもらいたいと思う。

「自らの過去(良きも悪しきも)との対話も出来ぬ困った国から日本を救済するために・・・

2016年3月11日

之人冗悟(のと・じゃうご:Noto Jaugo)

合同会社ズバライエ 代表社員

Beneath **U**mbrella of **Z**UBARAIE LLC.

http://zubaraie.com

— PREFACE —

和歌(WAKA＝Japanese 短歌:TANKA) is a 31-letter microcosm composed of 5-7-5-7-7 syllabled phrases, technically established more than a thousand years ago in the first Imperial anthology 古今集(Kokin shuu) in A.D. 905, culturally culminating in 新古今集(Shin-Kokin shuu) at the end of the 平安(Heian) era at the beginning of the 13th century. In the intervening years, there were 8 Great Imperial TANKA anthologies compiled at the order of [ex-]Emperors of the day: these anthologies are collectively called 八代集(Hachidai shuu＝8 great Imperial TANKA anthologies), embracing some **9,500** TANKA poems. You can see their purest essence in the **200** TANKA in this book. It all started from this author's personal ★BEST 50★, supplemented by ●150 good poems● instrumental in telling foreign and modern Japanese people the seasonal and mental characteristics of the ancient Japanese... See how much they have lost, how much they still hold, and how much they have consistently missed all these years.

To help rescue Japan from a sorry nation incapable of
*communication with their own past, **good** and **bad**...*

March 11, 2016

Jaugo Noto(之人冗悟)

representative partner of ***ZUBARAIE LLC.***

短歌索引

―冬～春：Winter～Spring―

●1● ゆきふれば**きごと**にはなぞさきにける　いづれを**うめ**とわきてをらまし(集1 歌337)紀友則
P16【冬】[謎掛]yuki fure-ba ki-goto-ni hana zo saki-ni-keru izure wo ume to waki-te ora-mashi
・・・・・・・・《「唐歌」の栄華の名残り「離合」歌》

●2● をられけりくれなゐにほふうめのはな　けさしろたへにゆきはふれれど(集8 歌41)藤原頼通
P17【冬】[謎掛]ora-re-keri kurenai niou ume-no-hana kesa shirotae-ni yuki wa fure-re-do

―春：Spring―

●3● をりつればそでに**こそ**にほへうめのはな　ありと**や**ここにうぐひすの**なく**(集1 歌32)詠み人知らず
P18【春】[俳諧]ori-tsure-ba sode koso nioe ume-no-hana ari to-ya koko ni uguisu no naku
・・・・・・・・《「俳諧」を俳人子規は憎みけり》

★4★ ひとはいさこころもしらずふるさとは　はなぞむかしのかににほひける(集1 歌42)紀貫之
P20【春】[懐旧]hito wa isa kokoro mo shira-zu furusato wa hana zo mukashi no ka ni nioi-keru

●5● こちふかばにほひおこせようめのはな　あるじなしとてはるをわするな(集3 歌1006)菅原道真
P21【春】[擬人]kochi fuka-ba nioi okoseyo ume-no-hana aruji nashi tote haru wo wasuru-na

●6● ふきくれば**か**をなつかし**み**むめのはな　ちらさぬほどのはるかぜもがな(集6 歌9)源時綱
P22【春】[機知]fuki-kure-ba ka wo natsukashi-mi mume-no-hana chirasa-nu hodo no haru-kaze mogana

★7★ そでひぢてむすびしみづのこほれるを　はるたつけふのかぜ**や**とくらむ(集1 歌2)紀貫之
P22【春】[季題]sode hiji-te musubi-shi mizu no koore-ru wo haru-tatsu kyou no kaze ya toku-ramu
・・・・・・・・《「旧暦」に一月足して「今ごよみ」》

★8★ はるたつといふばかりに**や**みよしのの　やまもかすみてけさはみゆらむ(集3 歌1)壬生忠岑
P23【春】[謎掛]haru-tatsu to yuu bakari-ni-ya mi-Yoshino no yama mo kasumi-te kesa wa miyu-ramu
・・・・・・・・《土地柄に含意ありけり「歌枕」》

●9● よしのやまさくらがえだにゆきちりて　はなおそげなるとしにもあるかな(集8 歌79)西行
P25【春】[謎掛]Yoshino-yama sakura-ga eda ni yuki chiri-te hana osoge-naru toshi ni-mo-aru kana
・・・・・・・・《「俳諧」の三百代言「韜晦(倒壊？)」趣味》

●10● みわたせばやなぎさくらをこきまぜて　みやこぞはるのにしきなりける(集1 歌56)素性
P27【春】[機知]miwatase-ba yanagi sakura wo kokimaze-te miyako zo haru no nishiki nari-keru
・・・・・・・・《大向う唸らす意図の「趣向」歌》

●11● はなのいろはかすみにこめてみせずとも　かをだにぬすめはるのやまかぜ(集1 歌91)遍昭(良岑宗貞)
P28【春】[機知]hana no iro wa kasumi ni kome-te mise-zu-tomo ka wo dani nusume haru no yama-kaze
・・・・・・・・《「出家」してなほ名を求む「歌僧」かな》

★12★ みれどあかぬはなのさかりにか へるかり　なほふるさとのはる**や**こひしき(集3 歌55)詠み人知らず
P29【春】[自然]mire-do aka-nu hana no sakari ni kaeru kari nao furusato no haru ya kohishiki
・・・・・・・・《「字余り」はあれど「字足らず」無かりけり》

●13● はるきて**ぞ**ひともとひけるやまざとは　はな**こそ**やどのあるじなりけれ(集3 歌1015)藤原公任
P30【春】[機知]haru kite zo hito mo toi-keru yama-zato wa hana koso yado no aruji nari-kere

●14● われを**こそ**とふにうからめ**はるがすみ**　はなにつけても**た**ちよらぬかな(集2 歌113)詠み人知らず
P31【春】[願望]ware wo koso tou ni ukarame haru-gasumi hana ni tsuke-te-mo tachi-yora-nu kana
・・・・・・・・《あっち向いてホイ！と不意付く「縁語」かな》

短歌索引

●15●こぞのはるちりにしはなもさきにけり あはれわかれのかからましかば(集6歌402)赤染衛門
P32【春】[慨嘆]kozo no haru chiri-ni-shi hana mo saki-ni-keri aware wakare no kakara-mashi-kaba
·········《本当の名は人知れぬ「女流歌人」》

★16★もろともにをりしはるのみこひしくて ひとりみまうきはなざかりかな(集3歌1039)詠み人知らず
P34【春】[懐旧]morotomoni ori-shi haru nomi koishiku-te hitori mi-mauki hana-zakari kana

●17●こぞみしにいろもかはらずさきにけり はなこそものはおもはざりけれ(集5歌515)秦兼方
P34【春】[擬人]kozo mi-shi ni iro mo kawara-zu saki-ni-keri hana koso mono wa omowa-zari-kere

●18●いにしへにかはらざりけりやまざくら はなはわれをばいかがみるらむ(集7歌1055)藤原基長
P35【春】[擬人]inishie ni kawara-zari-keri yama-zakura hana wa ware wo-ba ikaga miru-ramu

●19●よのなかをおもひすててしみなれども こころよわしとはなにみえける(集4歌117)能因(橘永愷)
P36【春】[機知]yo-no-naka wo omoi-sute-te-shi mi nare-domo kokoro-yowashi to hana ni mie-keru

★20★よのなかにたえてさくらのなかりせば はるのこころはのどけからまし(集1歌53)在原業平
P37【春】[悟り]yo-no-naka ni taete sakura no nakari-se-ba haru no kokoro wa nodokekara-mashi

●21●としをへておなじさくらのはなのいろを そめますものはこころなりけり(集7歌63)藤原公時
P37【春】[悟り]toshi wo he-te onaji sakura no hana no iro wo some-masu mono wa kokoro nari-keri

●22●さくらばなちらさでちよもみてしがな あかぬこころはさてもありやと(集6歌35)藤原元真
P38【春】[機知]sakura-bana chirasa-de chiyo mo mi-te-shigana aka-nu kokoro wa sate-mo ari-ya to

●23●さくらがりあめはふりきぬおなじくは ぬるともはなのかげにかくれむ(集3歌50)詠み人知らず
P39【春】[機知]sakura-gari ame wa furi-ki-nu onajiku-wa nuru tomo hana no kage ni kakure-mu

●24●もろともにあはれとおもへやまざくら はなよりほかにしるひともなし(集5歌510)行尊
P39【春】[擬人]morotomoni aware to omoe yama-zakura hana yori hoka ni shiru hito mo nashi

●25●さけばちるさかねばこひしやまざくら おもひたえせぬはなのうへかな(集3歌36)敦慶親王女
P40【春】[溜息]sake-ba chiru saka-ne-ba koishi yama-zakura omoi tae-se-nu hana no ue kana

★26★はるごとにはなのさかりはありなめど あひみむことはいのちなりけり(集1歌97)詠み人知らず
P40【春】[悟り]haru-goto-ni hana no sakari wa ari-na-me-do ai-mi-mu koto wa inochi nari-keri

●27●やまざとにちりはてぬべきはなゆゑに たれとはなくてひとぞまたるる(集4歌135)源道済
P41【春】[願望]yama-zato ni chiri-hate-nu-beki hana yue ni tare to-wa naku-te hito zo mata-ruru

★28★はなのいろはうつりにけりないたづらに わがみよにふるながめせしまに(集1歌113)小野小町
P42【春】[仮託]hana no iro wa utsuri-ni-keri-na itazurani wa-ga mi yo ni furu nagame se-shi ma ni
·········《仮名漢字異世界つなぐ「懸詞」》

★29★ひさかたのひかりのどけきはるのひに しづこころなくはなのちるらむ(集1歌84)紀友則
P43【春】[自然]hisakata no hikari nodokeki haru no hi ni shizu-kokoro naku hana no chiru-ramu
·········《「言霊」や「枕詞」に宿ける》

★30★さくらちるこのしたかぜはさむからで そらにしられぬゆきぞふりける(集3歌64)紀貫之
P45【春】[機知]sakura chiru ko-no-shita-kaze wa samukara-de sora ni shira-re-nu yuki zo furi-keru

●31●さくらばなちりぬるかぜのなごりには みづなきそらになみぞたちける(集1歌89)紀貫之
P46【春】[機知]sakura-bana chiri-nuru kaze no nagori ni-wa mizu naki sora ni nami zo tachi-keru

●32●さくらちるはなのところははるながら ゆきぞふりつつきえがてにする(集1歌75)承均
P46【春】[謎掛]sakura chiru hana no tokoro wa haru nagara yuki zo furi-tsutsu kie-gate-ni suru

●33●けさみればよるのあらしにちりはてて　にはこそはなのさかりなりけれ(集5歌58)徳大寺実能
P47【春】[機知]kesa mire-ba yoru no arashi ni chiri-hate-te niwa koso hana no sakari nari-kere
●34●さくらいろのにはのはるかぜあともなし　とはばぞひとのゆきとだにみむ(集8歌134)藤原定家
P47【春】[謎掛]sakura-iro no niwa no haru-kaze ato mo nashi towa-ba zo hito no yuki to dani mi-mu
　………《度を超して解けぬ謎々誰々好む♪》
●35●あさぢはらぬしなきやどのさくらばな　こころやすくやかぜにちるらむ(集3歌62)恵慶
P50【春】[擬人]asaji-hara nushi naki yado no sakura-bana kokoro-yasuku ya kaze ni chiru-ramu
●36●いにしへはちるをやひとのおしみけむ　はなこそいまはむかしこふらし(集3歌1279)藤原伊尹
P50【春】[擬人]inishie wa chiru wo-ya hito no oshimi-kemu hana koso ima-wa mukashi kou-rashi
　………《「歌の華」斯くぞ定めし「八代集」》
●37●としをへてはなにこころをくだくかな　をしむにとまるはるはなけれど(集4歌144)藤原定頼
P52【春】[溜息]toshi wo he-te hana ni kokoro wo kudaku kana oshimu ni tomaru haru wa nakere-do
●38●みにかへてをしむにとまるはなならば　けふやわがみのかぎりならまし(集5歌66)源俊頼
P52【春】[機知]mi ni kae-te oshimu ni tomaru hana nara-ba kyou ya wa-ga mi no kagiri nara-mashi
●39●けふのみとはるをおもはぬときだにも　たつことやすきはなのかげかは(集1歌134)凡河内躬恒
P53【春】[季題]kyou nomi to haru wo omowa-nu toki dani-mo tatsu koto yasuki hana no kage kawa
★40★いくかへりけふにわがみのあひぬらむ　をしむははるのすぐるのみかは(集5歌93)藤原定成
P54【春】[季題]iku-kaeri kyou ni wa-ga mi no ai-nu-ramu oshimu wa haru no suguru nomi-kawa
●41●はるのゆくみちにきむかへほととぎす　かたらふこゑにたちやとまると(集5歌90)証観
P54【春】[季題]haru no yuku michi ni ki-mukae hototogisu katarau koe ni tachi-ya-tomaru-to
　………《春ならば斯くは鳴くまじ「郭公」》
●42●みわたせばやまともかすむみなせがは　ゆふべはあきとなにおもひけむ(集8歌36)後鳥羽院
P56【春】[謎掛]miwatase-ba yama-moto kasumu minase-gawa yuu-be wa aki to nani omoi-kemu
　………《門外漢落とす「本節」自滅歌》
●43●てりもせずくもりもはてぬはるのよの　おぼろづきよにしくものぞなき(集8歌55)大江千里
P57【春】[機知]teri-mo se-zu kumori-mo hate-nu haru no yo no oboro-zukiyo ni shiku mono zo naki

―夏：Summer―

●44●ゆふづくよほのめくかげもうのはなの　さけるわたりはさやけかりけり(集7歌140)藤原(三条)実房
P58【夏】[機知]yuu-zukuyo honomeku kage mo u-no-hana no sake-ru watari wa sayakekari-keri
●45●ちりはててはなのかげなきこのもとに　たつことやすきなつごろもかな(集8歌177)慈円
P58【夏】[転季]chiri-hate-ne hana no kage naki ko no moto ni tatsu koto yasuki natsu-goromo kana
★46★さつきまつはなたちばなのかをかげば　むかしのひとのそでのかぞする(集1歌139)詠み人知らず
P59【夏】[懐旧]Satsuki matsu hana-tachibana no ka wo kage-ba mukashi no hito no sode no ka zo suru
●47●あふことのひさしにふけるあやめぐさ　ただかりそめのつまこそみれ(集3歌436)藤原永相女
P60【夏】[慨嘆]au koto no hisashi ni fuke-ru ayame-gusa tada karisome no tsuma to-koso mire
●48●てもふれでをしむかひなくふぢのはな　そこにうつれればなみぞをりける(集3歌87)凡河内躬恒
P61【夏】[機知]te mo fure-de oshimu kai naku fuji-no-hana soko ni utsure-ba nami zo ori-keru
●49●むかしわがあつめしものをおもひいでて　みなれがほにもくるほたるかな(集7歌201)藤原季通
P62【夏】[擬人]mukashi wa-ga atsume-shi mono wo omoi-ide-te minaregaoni-mo kuru hotaru kana

短歌索引

●50● つつめどもかくれぬものはなつむしの みよりあまれるおもひなりけり(集2 歌 209)詠み人知らず
P62【夏】[仮託]tsutsume-domo kakure-nu mono wa natsu-mushi no mi yori amare-ru omoi nari-keri

★51★ なくこゑもきこえぬもののかなしきは しのびにもゆるほたるなりけり(集6 歌 73)藤原高遠
P63【夏】[仮託]naku koe mo kikoe-nu mono-no kanashiki wa shinobi ni moyuru hotaru nari-keri

★52★ ものおもへばさはのほたるもわがみより あくがれいづるたまかとぞみる(集4 歌 1164)和泉式部
P64【夏】[仮託]mono-omoe-ba sawa no hotaru mo wa-ga mi yori akugare-izuru tama ka-to-zo miru

●53● いはたたくたにのみづのみおとづれて なつにしられぬみやまべのさと(集7 歌 221)藤原教長
P65【夏】[叙景]iwa tataku tani no mizu nomi otozure-te natsu ni shira-re-nu mi-yama-be no sato

★54★ やまかげやいはもるしみづおとさえて なつのほかなるひぐらしのこゑ(集7 歌 210)慈円
P65【夏】[叙景]yama-kage ya iwa moru shimizu oto sae-te natsu no hoka naru higurashi no koe

★55★ そらのうみにくものなみたちつきのふね ほしのはやしにこぎかくるみゆ(集3 歌 488)柿本人麻呂
P66【夏】[叙景]sora no umi ni kumo no nami tachi tsuki no fune hoshi no hayashi ni kogi-kakuru miyu

●56● あかなくにまだきもつきのかくるるか やまのはにげていれずもあらなむ(集1 歌 884)在原業平
P67【夏】[俳諧]aka-na-ku-ni madaki-mo tsuki no kakururu-ka yama-no-ha nige-te ire-zu mo ara-namu

●57● なつのよはまだよひながらあけぬるを くものいづこにつきやどるらむ(集1 歌 166)清原深養父
P67【夏】[俳諧]natsu no yo wa mada yoi nagara ake-nuru wo kumo no izuko ni tsuki yadoru-ramu

●58● あひみてもあはでもなげくたなばたは いつかこころののどけかるべき(集3 歌 153)詠み人知らず
P68【夏】[季題]ai-mi-te-mo awa-de-mo nageku tanabata wa itsu-ka kokoro no nodokekaru-beki
………《「七夕」は一年一夜飽かぬ恋》

●59● よられつるのもせのくさのかげろひて すずしくくもるゆふだちのそら(集8 歌 263)西行
P70【夏】[叙景]yora-re-tsuru no-mo-se-no kusa no kageroi-te suzushiku kumoru yuu-dachi no sora

―秋:Autumn―

●60● あきちかきけしきのもりになくせみの なみだのつゆやしたばそむらむ(集8 歌 270)藤原(九条)良経
P71【秋】[機知]aki chikaki Keshiki-no-mori ni naku semi no namida no tsuyu ya shitaba somu-ramu

●61● あさがほをなにはかなしとおもひけむ ひとをもはなはさこそみるらめ(集3 歌 1283)藤原道信
P72【秋】[擬人]asa-gao wo nani-wa kanashi to omoi-kemu hito wo-mo hana wa sa-koso miru-rame

●62● ひぐらしのなきつるなへにひはくれぬと おもへばやまのかげにぞありける(集1 歌 204)詠み人知らず
P72【秋】[叙景]higurashi no naki-tsuru naeni hi wa kure-nu to omoe-ba yama no kage ni-zo ari-keru

●63● なつとあきとゆきかふそらのかよひぢは かたへすずしきかぜやふくらむ(集1 歌 168)凡河内躬恒
P73【秋】[季題]natsu to aki to yuki-kau sora no kayoi-ji wa kata-e suzushiki kaze ya fuku-ramu
………《夏は外秋は内なる心かな》

●64● なにめでてをれるばかりぞをみなへし われおちにきとひとにかたるな(集1 歌 226)遍昭(良岑宗貞)
P74【秋】[俳諧]na ni mede-te oreru bakari zo ominaeshi ware ochi-ni-ki to hito ni kataru-na
………《名引かれて中身など見ぬ和の心》

★65★ あききぬとめにはさやかにみえねども かぜのおとにぞおどろかれぬる(集1 歌 169)藤原敏行
P76【秋】[転季]aki ki-nu to me ni-wa sayakani mie-ne-domo kaze no oto ni-zo odoroka-re-nuru

●66● このまよりもりくるつきのかげみれば こころづくしのあきはきにけり(集1 歌 184)詠み人知らず
P76【秋】[転季]ko-no-ma yori mori-kuru tsuki no kage mire-ba kokoro-zukushi no aki wa ki-ni-keri

●67● やへむぐらしげれるやどのさびしきに ひとこそみえね あきはきにけり(集3 歌140)恵慶
P77【秋】[謎掛]yae-mugura shigere-ru yado no sabishiki ni hito koso mie-ne aki wa ki-ni-keri

●68● いとどしくものおもふやどのはぎのはに あきとつげつるかぜのわびしさ(集2 歌220)詠み人知らず
P78【秋】[転季]itodoshiku mono-omou yado no hagi no ha ni aki to tsuge-tsuru kaze no wabishi-sa

★69★ なくむしのひとつこゑにもきこえぬは こころごころにものやかなしき(集6 歌120)和泉式部
P79【秋】[自然]naku mushi no hitotsu-koe ni-mo kikoe-nu wa kokoro-gokoro-ni mono ya kanashiki

●70● いつとてもこひしからずはあらねども あきのゆふべはあやしかりけり(集1 歌546)詠み人知らず
P80【秋】[溜息]itsu tote-mo koishikara-zu wa ara-ne-domo aki no yuu-be wa ayashikari-keri

●71● ながむればこひしきひとのこひしきに くもらばくもれあきのよのつき(集5 歌384)藤原基光
P80【秋】[溜息]nagamure-ba koishiki hito no koishiki ni kumora-ba kumore aki no yo no tsuki

★72★ ことならばやみにぞあらましあきのよの なぞつきかげのひとだのめなる(集3 歌796)詠み人知らず
P81【秋】[謎掛]koto-nara-ba yami ni-zo ara-mashi aki no yo no na-zo tsuki-kage no hito-danome-naru

★73★ なげけとてつきやはものをおもはする かこちがほなるわがなみだかな(集7 歌929)西行
P82【秋】[謎掛]nageke tote tsuki yawa mono wo omowasuru kakochigaonaru wa-ga namida kana

★74★ つきみればちぢにものこそかなしけれ わがみひとつのあきにはあらねど(集1 歌193)大江千里
P83【秋】[機知]tsuki mire-ba chijini mono koso kanashikere wa-ga mi hitotsu no aki ni-wa ara-ne-do

………《「名引き」芸間引く余所者短歌捨て》

●75● あきかぜにたなびくくものたえまより もれいづるつきのかげのさやけさ(集8 歌413)藤原顕輔
P85【秋】[叙景]aki-kaze ni tanabiku kumo no tae-ma yori more-izuru tsuki no kage no sayake-sa

●76● しらくもにはねうちかはしとぶかりの かずさへみゆるあきのよのつき(集1 歌191)詠み人知らず
P85【秋】[叙景]shira-kumo ni hane uchi-kawashi tobu kari no kazu sae miyuru aki no yo no tsuki

●77● いづくにもこよひのつきをみるひとの こころやおなじそらにすむらむ(集5 歌173)藤原忠教
P86【秋】[季題]izuku ni-mo koyoi no tsuki wo miru hito no kokoro ya onaji sora ni sumu-ramu

●78● はるなつにそらやはかはるあきのよの つきしもいかでてりまさるらむ(集6 歌96)藤原家成
P87【秋】[機知]haru natsu ni sora yawa kawaru aki no yo no tsuki shimo ikade teri-masaru-ramu

●79● こころにもあらでうきよにながらへば こひしかるべきよはのつきかな(集4 歌861)三条院
P87【秋】[溜息]kokoro ni-mo ara-de uki-yo ni nagarae-ba koishikaru-beki yowa no tsuki kana

●80● あきにまたあはむあはじもしらぬみは こよひばかりのつきをだにみむ(集6 歌97)三条院
P88【秋】[溜息]aki ni mata awa-mu awa-ji mo shira-nu mi wa koyoi-bakari no tsuki wo-dani mi-mu

………《「御門」退き「院」に入る世を執るは誰？》

★81★ すだきけむむかしのひとのなきやどに ただかげするはあきのよのつき(集4 歌253)恵慶
P89【秋】[溜息]sudaki-kemu mukashi no hito mo naki yado ni tada kage-suru wa aki no yo no tsuki

★82★ もろともにながめしひともわれもなき やどにはひとりつきやすむらむ(集4 歌856)藤原長家
P90【秋】[溜息]morotomoni nagame-shi hito mo ware mo naki yado ni-wa hitori tsuki ya sumu-ramu

●83● はるはただはなのひとへにさくばかり もののあはれはあきぞまされる(集3 歌511)詠み人知らず
P91【秋】[機知]haru wa tada hana no hitoeni saku bakari mono no aware wa aki zo masare-ru

………《「かたき」どち仲良く遊ぶ「品定め」》

●84● むらさきにうつろひにしをおくしもの なほしらぎくとみするなりけり(集4 歌358)藤原資綱
P92【秋】[機知]murasaki ni utsuroi-ni-shi wo oku shimo no nao sira-giku to misuru nari-keri mi nari-keri

短歌索引

●85●あきくれどいろもかはらぬ**ときは**やま よそのもみぢをかぜぞかしける(集1歌362)坂上是則
P93【秋】[機知]aki kure-do iro mo kawara-nu Tokiwa-yama yoso no momiji wo kaze zo kashi-keru
‥‥‥‥‥《歌詠みの名と技上げし「屏風歌」》

●86●さほやまのははそのもみぢちりぬべみ よるさへみよとてらすつきかげ(集1歌281)詠み人知らず
P94【秋】[機知]Saho-yama no hahaso no momiji chiri-nu-be-mi yoru sae miyo to terasu tsuki-kage

●87●ものごとにあきぞかなしきもみぢつつ うつろひゆくをかぎりとおもへば(集1歌187)詠み人知らず
P95【秋】[溜息]mono-goto-ni aki zo kanashiki momiji-tsutsu utsuroi-yuku wo kagiri to omoe-ba

●88●あきはきぬもみぢはやどにふりしきぬ みちふみわけてとふひとはなし(集1歌287)詠み人知らず
P96【秋】[溜息]aki wa ki-nu momiji wa yado ni furi-shiki-nu michi fumi-wake-te tou hito wa nashi

★89★さびしさにやどをたちいでてながむれば いづこもおなじあきのゆふぐれ(集4歌333)良暹
P96【秋】[悟り]sabishi-sa ni yado wo tachi-ide-te nagamure-ba izuko mo onaji aki no yuu-gure

★90★さびしさはそのいろとしもなかりけり まきたつやまのあきのゆふぐれ(集8歌361)寂蓮
P97【秋】[悟り]sabishi-sa wa so-no iro to-shimo nakari-keri maki tatsu yama no aki no yuu-gure

●91●むらさめのつゆもまだひぬまきのはに きりたちのぼるあきのゆふぐれ(集8歌491)寂蓮
P98【秋】[叙景]mura-same no tsuyu mo mada hi-nu maki no ha ni kiri tachi-noboru aki no yuu-gure

●92●みわたせばはなももみぢもなかりけり うらのとまやのあきのゆふぐれ(集8歌363)藤原定家
P98【秋】[謎掛]miwatase-ba hana mo momiji mo nakari-keri ura no toma-ya no aki no yuu-gure
‥‥‥‥‥《「ののの攻め＆体言止め」の「新古今」》

●93●きりぎりすよざむにあきのなるままに よわるかこゑのとほざかりゆく(集8歌472)西行
P100【秋】[自然]kirigirisu yo-zamu ni aki no naru mama-ni yowaru-ka koe no toozakari-yuku

★94★おくやまにもみぢふみわけなくしかの こゑきくときぞあきはかなしき(集1歌215)詠み人知らず
P100【秋】[溜息]oku-yama ni momiji fumi-wake naku shika no koe kiku toki zo aki wa kanashiki

●95●**あきかぜにあへずちりぬるもみぢばの ゆくへさだめぬ**われぞかなしき(集1歌286)詠み人知らず
P101【秋】[序詞]aki-kaze ni ae-zu chiri-nuru momiji-ba no yukue sadame-nu ware zo kanashiki
‥‥‥‥‥《「序詞」は「絵」から「本音」の橋渡し》

―冬：Winter―

●96●あきのうちはあはれしらせしかぜのおとの はげしさそふるふゆはきにけり(集7歌393)藤原教長
P103【冬】[転季]aki no uchi wa aware shira-se-shi kaze no oto no hageshi-sa souru fuyu wa ki-ni-keri

●97●このはちるやどはききわくことぞなき しぐれするよもしぐれせぬよも(集4歌382)源頼実
P103 冬【謎掛】ko-no-ha chiru yado wa kiki-waku koto zo naki shigure-suru yo mo shigure-se-nu yo mo
‥‥‥‥‥《秋去ぎてひた屋籠もりの「時雨」かな》

●98●たつたがはにしきおりかくかむなづき しぐれのあめをたてぬきにして(集1歌314)詠み人知らず
P104【冬】[機知]Tatsuta-gawa nishiki ori-kaku kamunazuki shigure no ame wo tate-nuki-ni-shi-te

●99●あさぼらけうちのかはぎりたえだえに あらはれわたるせぜのあじろぎ(集7歌420)藤原定頼
P105【冬】[叙景]asaborake Uji no kawa-giri taedaeni araware-wataru seze no ajiro-gi

●100●**おき**あかすしもともともにやけさはみな ふゆのよ**ふかき**つみもけぬらむ(集3歌257)大中臣能宣
P106【冬】[季題]oki-akasu shimo to tomo-ni ya kesa wa mina fuyu no yo fukaki tsumi mo kenu-ramu
‥‥‥‥‥《「仏名」に罪消ち急ぐ「師走」かな》

●101●なにごとをまつとはなしにあけくれて ことしもけふになりにけるかな(集5歌(異本))源国信
P107【冬】[季題]nani-goto wo matsu to-wa nashi-ni ake-kure-te kotoshi mo kyou ni nari-ni-keru kana
●102●けふごとにけふやかぎりとをしめども またもことしにあひにけるかな(集8歌706)藤原俊成
P108【冬】[季題]kyou-goto-ni kyou ya kagiri to oshime-domo mata-mo kotoshi ni ai-ni-keru kana
・・・・・・・《後の代に「歌の徳」説く嘘説話》
●103●ひとりみるいけのこほりに**すむ**つきの やがてそでにもうつりぬるかな(集8歌640)藤原俊成
P109【冬】[溜息]hitori miru ike no koori ni sumu tsuki no yagate sode ni-mo utsuri-nuru kana
●104●ふゆながらそらよりはなのちりくるは くものあなたははるに<u>や</u>あるらむ(集1歌330)清原深養父
P110【冬】[機知]fuyu nagara sora yori hana no chiri-kuru wa kumo no anata wa haru ni-ya-aru-ramu
●105●あさぼらけありあけのつきとみるまでに よしののさとにふれるしらゆき(集1歌332)坂上是則
P110【冬】[叙景]asaborake ariake-no-tsuki to miru made-ni Yoshino-no-sato ni fure-ru shira-yuki
●106●まつひとのいまもきたらば<u>いかがせむ</u> ふままくをしきにはのゆきかな(集5歌284)和泉式部
P111【冬】[願望]matsu hito no ima mo kitara-ba ikaga semu fuma-ma-ku oshiki niwa no yuki kana
●107●さびしさにけぶりをだにもたたじとて しばをりくぶるふゆのやまざと(集4歌390)和泉式部
P112【冬】[溜息]sabishi-sa ni keburi wo dani-mo tata-ji tote shiba ori-kuburu fuyu no yama-zato

―恋愛:Love―

●108●こひしともいはばこころのゆくべきに くるしやひとめつつむおもひは(集8歌1090)近衛院
P112【恋愛】[溜息]koishi to-mo iwa-ba kokoro no yuku-beki-ni kurushi-ya hitome tsutsumu omoi wa
●109●たまのをよたえなばたえねながらへば しのぶることのよわりもぞする(集8歌1034)式子内親王
P113【恋愛】[溜息]tama-no-wo yo tae-na-ba tae-ne nagarae-ba shinoburu koto no yowari-mozo-suru
★110★しのぶれどいろにいでにけりわがこひは ものや<u>おもふ</u>とひとのとふまで(集3歌622)平兼盛
P114【恋愛】[溜息]shinobure-do iro ni ide-ni-keri wa-ga koi wa mono ya omou to hito no tou made
●111●いかでかとおもふこころのあるときは おぼめくさへぞうれしかりける(集3歌693)詠み人知らず
P114【恋愛】[願望]ikade-ka to omou kokoro no aru toki wa obomeku sae-zo ureshikari-keru
★112★おもひつつぬれば<u>や</u>ひとのみえつ<u>らむ</u> ゆめとしりせばさめざらましを(集1歌552)小野小町
P115【恋愛】[溜息]omoi-tsutsu nure-ba-ya hito no mie-tsu-ramu yume to shiri-se-ba same-zara-mashi-wo
●113●うたたねにこひしきひとをみてしより ゆめてふものはたのみそめてき(集1歌553)小野小町
P115【恋愛】[願望]utata-ne ni koishiki hito wo mite-shi yori yume chuu mono wa tanomi-some-te-ki
●114●ゆめよゆめこひしきひとにあひみすな さめてののちはわびしかりけり(集3歌709)詠み人知らず
P116【恋愛】[溜息]yume yo yume koishiki hito ni ai-misu-na same-te no nochi wa wabishikari-keri
●115●**ゆらのとをわたるふなびとかぢをたえ** ゆくへもしらぬこひのみちかも(集8歌1071)曾禰好忠
P116【恋愛】[序詞]Yura-no-to wo wataru funa-bito kaji wo tae yukue mo shira-nu koi no michi kamo
●116●**かぜをいたみいはうつなみの**おのれのみ **くだけて**ものをおもふころかな(集6歌211)源重之
P117【恋愛】[序詞]kaze wo ita-mi iwa utsu nami no onore nomi kudake-te mono wo omou koro kana
●117●**せをはやみいはにせかるるたきがはの** われてもすゑにあはむと<u>ぞ</u>おもふ(集6歌229)崇徳院
P118【恋愛】[序詞]se wo haya-mi iwa ni seka-ruru taki-gawa no ware-te-mo sue ni awa-mu to-zo omou
●118●**みかきもりゑじのたくひの**よるはもえ ひるはきえつつものを<u>こそおもへ</u>(集6歌225)大中臣能宣
P119【恋愛】[序詞]mi-kaki-mori eji no taku hi no yoru wa moe hiru wa kie-tsutsu mono wo-koso omoe

短歌索引

●119●いのちやはなにぞはつゆのあだものを あふにしかへばをしからなくに(集1 歌 615)紀友則
P120【恋愛】[願望]inochi yawa nani-zo-wa tsuyu no ada-mono wo au ni-shi kae-ba oshikara-na-ku-ni

●120●あひみてはしにせぬみとぞなりぬべき たのむるにだにのぶるいのちは(集3 歌 692)詠み人知らず
P121【恋愛】[俳諧]ai-mi-te-wa shini-se-nu mi to-zo nari-nu-beki tanomuru ni-dani noburu inochi wa

●121●おもふひとおもはぬひとのおもふひと おもはざらなむおもひしるべく(集2 歌 572)詠み人知らず
P121【恋愛】[俳諧]omou hito omowa-nu hito no omou hito omowa-zara-namu omoi-shiru-beku

★122★あひみてののちのこころにくらぶれば むかしはものをおもはざりけり(集3 歌 710)藤原敦忠
P122【恋愛】[後朝]ai-mi-te no nochi no kokoro ni kurabure-ba mukashi wa mono wo omowa-zari-keri

..........《「きぬ／こぬ」に千々に乱るる姫心》》

★123★あはざりしときいかなりしものとてか ただいまのまもみねばこひしき(集2 歌 564)詠み人知らず
P124【恋愛】[後朝]awa-zari-shi toki ikanari-shi mono tote-ka tada-ima no ma mo mi-ne-ba koishiki

★124★おもひやるこころにたぐふみなりせば ひとひにちたびきみはみてまし(集2 歌 679)大江千古
P124【恋愛】[後朝]omoi-yaru kokoro ni taguu mi nari-se-ba hito-hi ni chi-tabi kimi wa mi-te-mashi

●125●またもなくただひとすぢにきみおもふ こひぢにまどふわれやなになる(集7 歌 674)藤原伊通
P125【恋愛】[俳諧]mata-mo-naku tada hito-suji-ni kimi omou koi-ji ni madou ware ya nani-naru

..........《誰そ知らむ嘘か真か恋の歌》

●126●あかでこそおもはむなかははなれなめ そをだにのちのわすれがたみに(集1 歌 717)詠み人知らず
P126【恋愛】[悟り]aka-de koso omowa-mu naka wa hanare-na-me so wo-dani nochi no wasure-gatami ni

●127●つらかりこころならひにあひみても なほゆめかとぞうたがはれける(集5 歌 397)源行宗
P127【恋愛】[後朝]tsurakari-shi kokoro-narai ni ai-mi-te-mo nao yume ka-to-zo utagawa-re-keru

★128★きみがためをしからざりしいのちさへ ながくもがなとおもひけるかな(集4 歌 669)藤原義孝
P128【恋愛】[後朝]kimi-ga tame oshikara-zari-shi inochi sae nagaku-mogana to omoi-keru kana

★129★わすれじのゆくすゑまではかたければ けふをかぎりのいのちともがな(集8 歌1149)藤原(伊周母)高階貴子
P128【恋愛】[願望]wasure-ji no yuku-sue made wa katakere-ba kyou wo kagiri no inochi to-mogana

●130●まつよひにふけゆくかねのこゑきけば あかぬわかれのとりはものかは(集8 歌 1191)石清水別当光清女
P129【恋愛】[謎掛]matsu yoi ni fuke-yuku kane no koe kike-ba aka-nu-wakare no tori wa mono-kawa

●131●ありあけのつれなくみえしわかれより あかつきばかりうきものはなし(集1 歌 625)壬生忠岑
P130【恋愛】[謎掛]ariake no tsurenaku mie-shi wakare yori akatsuki bakari uki mono wa nashi

●132●かずかずにおもひおもはずとひがたみ みをしるあめはふりぞまされる(集1 歌 705)在原業平
P131【恋愛】[謎掛]kazukazuni omoi omowa-zu toi-gata-mi mi wo shiru ame wa furi-zo-masare-ru

●133●きみをおきてあだしごころをわがもたば するのまつやまなみもこえなむ(集1 歌 1093)詠み人知らず
P132【恋愛】[謎掛]kimi wo oki-te adashi-gokoro wo wa-ga mota-ba Sue-no-matsuyama nami mo koe-na-mu

―悲恋:Sad Love―

●134●いつはりのなきよなりせばいかばかり ひとのことのはうれしからまし(集1 歌 712)詠み人知らず
P132【悲恋】[謎掛]itsuwari no naki yo nari-se-ba ika-bakari hito no koto-no-ha ureshikara-mashi

●135●いつはりとおもふものからいまさらに たがまことをかわれはたのまむ(集1 歌 713)詠み人知らず
P133【悲恋】[溜息]itsuwari to omou monokara imasarani ta-ga makoto wo-ka ware wa tanoma-mu

★136★ちぎりおきしひともこずゑのこのまより たのめしつきのかげぞもりくる(集5 歌 464)摂政家堀河
P134【悲恋】[溜息]chigiri-oki-shi hito mo kozu...e no ko-no-ma yori tanome-shi tsuki no kage zo mori-kuru

verse INDEX   -10-   http//zubaraie.com

★137★よもすがらものおもふころはあけやらで ねやの**ひま**さへつれなかりけり(集7歌766)俊恵
P134【悲恋】[溜息]yo-mo-sugara mono-omou koro wa ake-yara-de ne-ya no hima sae tsurenakari-keri
★138★**よにふる**はくるしきものをまきのやに やすくもすぐるはつしぐれかな(集8歌590)二条院讃岐
P135【悲恋】[謎掛]yo ni furu wa kurushiki mono-wo maki no ya ni yasuku-mo suguru hatsu-shigure kana
　　　……《パクらずに作り替へてぞ「本歌取り」》
★139★くろかみのみだれもしらずうちふせば まづかきやりしひとぞこひしき(集4歌755)和泉式部
P139【悲恋】[懐旧]kuro-kami no midare mo shira-zu uchi-fuse-ba mazu kaki-yari-shi hito zo koishiki
★140★**なが**からむこころもしらずくろかみの **みだれ**てけさはものを**こそおもへ**(集7歌802)待賢門院堀河
P139【悲恋】[溜息]nagakara-mu kokoro mo shira-zu kuro-kami no midare-te kesa wa mono wo koso omoe
●141●こひすればわがみはかげとなりにけり さりとてひとにそはぬものゆゑ(集1歌528)詠み人知らず
P140【悲恋】[俳諧]koi-sure-ba wa-ga mi wa kage to nari-ni-keri sari-tote hito ni sowa-nu monoyue
●142●**あしひきのやまどりのをのしだりを** ながながしよをひとり**か**もね**む**(集3歌778)柿本人麻呂
P141【悲恋】[序詞]ashihiki-no yama-dori no o no shidari-o no naganagashi yo wo hitori ka-mo ne-mu
●143●**すみのえのきしによるなみ**よるさへ**や** ゆめのかよひぢひとめよくらむ(集1歌559)藤原敏行
P142【悲恋】[序詞]Suminoe no kishi ni yoru nami yoru sae-ya yume no kayoi-ji hito-me yoku-ramu
　　　……《「序詞」の「たたら」踏まぬは「霞懸け」》
●144●きみこふるなみだのとこにみちぬれば **みをつくし**とぞわれはなりぬる(集1歌567)藤原興風
P143【悲恋】[失恋]kimi kouru namida no toko ni michi-nure-ba mi-wo-tsukushi to-zo ware wa nari-nuru
●145●わびぬればいまはたおなじ**なにはなる みをつくし**てもあはむと**ぞおもふ**(集2歌961)元良親王
P144【悲恋】[序詞]wabi-nure-ba ima hata onaji Naniwa naru mi-wo-tsukushi-te-mo awa-mu to-zo omou
●146●いまはただおもひたえなむとばかりを ひとづてならでいふよしもがな(集4歌750)藤原道雅
P145【悲恋】[願望]ima-wa tada omoi-tae-na-mu to-bakari-wo hito-zute-nara-de yuu yoshi mogana
●147●よそながらあはれといはむことよりも ひとづてならでいへと**ぞおもふ**(集6歌196)藤原成通
P146【悲恋】[願望]yoso-nagara aware to iwa-mu koto yori-mo hito-zute-nara-de itoe to-zo omou
●148●おもひやるかたなきままにわすれゆく ひとのこころぞうらやまれ**ける**(集4歌787)中原頼成妻
P147【悲恋】[失恋]omoi-yaru kata naki mama-ni wasure-yuku hito no kokoro zo urayama-re-keru
●149●いまよりはとへともいはじわれぞただ ひとをわするることをしる**べき**(集6歌266)詠み人知らず
P147【悲恋】[願望]ima yori-wa toe to-mo iwa-ji ware zo tada hito wo wasururu koto wo shiru-beki
★150★ちぎりしももろともに**こそ**ちぎりし**か** わすればわれもわすれましかば(集7歌864)藤原為通
P148【悲恋】[願望]chigiri-shi mo morotomoni koso chigiri-shika wasure-ba ware mo wasure-mashika-ba
●151●おもふことなす**こそ**かみのかたから**め** しばしわするるこころつけなむ(集3歌997)詠み人知らず
P149【悲恋】[願望]omou koto nasu koso kami no katakara-me shibashi wasururu kokoro tsuke-namu
●152●いのちをしかけてちぎりしかなれば たゆるはしぬるここち**こそ**すれ(集5歌413)実原
P149【悲恋】[失恋]inochi wo-shi kake-te chigiri-shi naka nare-ba tayuru wa shinuru kokochi koso sure
●153●わすらるるみをばおもは**す**ちかひてし ひとのいのちのをしくもあるかな(集3歌870)藤原季縄女
P150【悲恋】[謎掛]wasu-ruru mi wo-ba omowa-zu chikai-te-shi hito no inochi no oshiku-mo aru kana
　　　……《祈りても恐るに足らぬ「大和神」》
●154●ひたすらにうらみしもせじさきのよに あふまで**こそ**はちぎりざりけ**め**(集7歌775)藤原家通
P152【悲恋】[悟り]hitasurani urami-shimo-se-ji saki-no-yo ni au made koso-wa chigira-zari-keme

短歌索引

……《あるはありなきはなしとて耐ふる民》

●155●うとくなるひとをなにとてうらむらむ しられずしらぬをりもありしに(集8 歌 1297)西行
P153【悲恋】[悟り]utoku-naru hito wo nani-tote uramu-ramu shira-re-zu shira-nu ori mo ari-shi ni

●156●うらみわびほさぬそでだにあるものを こひにくちなむなこそをしけれ(集4 歌 815)相模
P154【悲恋】[失恋]urami-wabi hosa-nu sode dani aru mono-wo koi ni kuchi-na-mu na koso oshikere

●157●よのなかのうきもつらきもしのぶれば おもひしらずとひとやみるらむ(集3 歌 933)詠み人知らず
P155【悲恋】[溜息]yo-no-naka no uki mo tsuraki mo shinobure-ba omoi shira-zu to hito ya miru-ramu

●158●いでていにしあとだにいまだかはらぬに たがかよひぢといまはなるらむ(集8 歌 1409)在原業平
P156【悲恋】[失恋]ide-te ini-shi ato dani imada kawara-nu-ni ta-ga kayoi-ji to ima-wa naru-ramu

★159★こひてしねこひてしねとやぎもこが わがやのかどをすぎてゆくらむ(集3 歌 936)柿本人麻呂
P156【悲恋】[失恋]koi-te shine koi-te shine to-ya wa-gimo-ko ga wa-ga-ya no kado wo sugi-te yuku-ramu

★160★あふことのたえてしなくばなかなかに ひとをもみをもうらみざらまし(集3 歌 678)藤原朝忠
P158【悲恋】[失恋]au koto no taete-shi naku-ba nakanakani hito wo-mo mi wo-mo urami-zara-mashi

……《逢ふべくもあらぬ人見る「宮仕へ」》

●161●きみこふとかつはきえつつほどふるを かくてもいけるみとやみるらむ(集4 歌 807)藤原元真
P159【悲恋】[謎掛]kimi kou to katsu-wa kie-tsutsu hodo-furu wo kakute-mo ike-ru mi to-ya miru-ramu

★162★かたみこそいまはあたなれこれなくば わするときもあらましものを(集1 歌 746)詠み人知らず
P160【悲恋】[失恋]katami koso ima-wa ata nare kore naku-ba wasururu toki mo ara-mashi-mono-wo

●163●わびぬればしひてわすれむとおもへども ゆめてふものぞひとだのめなる(集1 歌 569)藤原興風
P161【悲恋】[溜息]wabi-nure-ba shiite wasure-mu to omoe-domo yume chuu mono zo hito-danome-naru

●164●わすれなむとおもふこころのつくからに ありしよりけにまづぞこひしき(集1 歌 718)詠み人知らず
P162【悲恋】[失恋]wasure-na-mu to omou kokoro no tsuku-kara-ni ari-shi-yori-keni mazu-zo koishiki

……《今昔で蒟蒻ほども違う歌》

★165★かくばかりうしとおもふにこひしきは われさへこころふたつありけり(集3 歌 989)詠み人知らず
P163【悲恋】[失恋]kaku-bakari ushi to omou-ni kohishiki wa ware sae kokoro futatsu ari-keri

●166●よのうきもひとのつらきもしのぶるに こひしきにこそおもひわびぬれ(集8 歌 1424)藤原元真
P163【悲恋】[溜息]yo no uki mo hito no tsuraki mo shinoburu ni koishiki ni-koso omoi-wabi-nure

●167●うきみをばわれだにいとふいとへただ そをだにおなじこころとおもはむ(集8 歌 1143)藤原俊成
P164【悲恋】[失恋]uki mi wo-ba ware dani itou itoe tada so wo dani onaji kokoro to omowa-mu

●168●おもひきやあひみしよはのうれしさに のちのつらさのまさるべしとは(集5 歌 439)徳大寺実能
P166【悲恋】[慨嘆]omoi-ki-ya ai-mi-shi yowa no ureshi-sa ni nochi no tsura-sa no masaru-beshi to-wa

●169●あひみしをうれしきこととおもひしは かへりてのちのなげきなりけり(集4 歌 772)道命
P166【悲恋】[謎掛]ai-mi-shi wo ureshiki koto to omoi-shi wa kaeri-te nochi no nageki nari-keri

●170●いまはただそよそのこととおもひいでて わするばかりのうきこともがな(集4 歌 573)和泉式部
P168【悲恋】[願望]ima-wa tada so-yo so-no koto to omoi-ide-te wasuru-bakari-no uki koto mogana

●171●よもすがらちぎりしことをわすれずば こひむなみだのいろぞゆかしき(集4 歌 536)藤原道隆女定子
P169【悲恋】[慨嘆]yo-mo-sugara chigiri-shi koto wo wasure-zu-ba koi-mu namida no iro zo yukashiki

……《血の涙氷の鏡涙川》

短歌索引

―哀感：Pathos―

★172★ よのなかの**うき**もつらきもつげなくに まづしるものはなみだなりけり(集1歌941)詠み人知らず
P170【哀感】[悟り]yo-no-naka no uki mo tsuraki mo tsuge-na-ku-ni mazu shiru mono wa namida nari-keri

★173★ おもひわびさてもいのちはあるものを うきにたへぬはなみだなりけり(集7歌818)道因(藤原敦頼)
P171【哀感】[悟り]omoi-wabi sate-mo inochi wa aru mono-wo uki ni tae-nu wa namida nari-keri

●174● とまりゐてまつべきみ**こそ**おいに**けれ** あはれわかれはひとのためかは(集5歌344)菅原資忠
P172【哀感】[別離]tomari-i-te matsu-beki mi koso oi-ni-kere aware wakare wa hito no tame kawa

●175● これやこのゆくもか**へ**るもわかれつつ しるもしらぬも**あふ**さかのせき(集2歌1090)蝉丸
P172【哀感】[別離]kore-ya-ko-no yuku mo kaeru mo wakare-tsutsu shiru mo shira-nu mo Ausaka-no-seki

●176● **たちわかれいなばのやまのみねにおふる まつ**としきかばいまかへりこむ(集1歌365)在原行平
P173【哀感】[別離]tachi-wakare Inaba no yama no mine ni ouru matsu to-shi kika-ba ima kaeri-ko-mu

●177● わたのはらやそしまかけてこぎいでぬと ひとにはつげよあまのつりぶね(集1歌407)小野篁
P174【哀感】[別離]wata-no-hara yaso-shima kake-te kogi-ide-nu to hito ni-wa tsugeyo ama no tsuri-bune

●178● **から**ころも**き**つつなれにし**つ**ましあれば **は**るばるきぬる**た**びをしぞおもふ(集1歌410)在原業平
P175【哀感】[懐旧]kara-koromo ki-tsutsu nare-ni-shi tsuma shi are-ba harubaru ki-nuru tabi wo-shi-zo omou

‥‥‥‥‥《「あいうえお作文」の父祖「折り句」歌》

●179● あまのはらふりさけみればかすがなる みかさのやまにいでしつきかも(集1歌406)安部仲麿
P176【哀感】[懐旧]ama-no-hara furi-sake-mire-ba Kasuga naru Mikasa no yama ni ide-shi tsuki kamo

●180● このよにはすむべきほど**や**つきぬ**らむ** よのつねならずもののかなしき(集7歌1094)藤原道信
P177【哀感】[慨嘆]ko-no-yo ni-wa sumu-beki hodo ya tsuki-nu-ramu yo-no-tsune-nara-zu mono no kanashiki

●181● よをすててやまにいるひとやまにても なほうきときは**いづち**ゆく**らむ**(集1歌956)凡河内躬恒
P178【哀感】[溜息]yo wo sute-te yama ni iru hito yama nite-mo nao uki toki wa izuchi yuku-ramu

●182● よのなかよみち**こそ**なけれおもひ**いる** やまのおくにもしかぞなく**なる**(集7歌1151)藤原俊成
P178【哀感】[溜息]yo-no-naka yo michi koso nakere omoi-iru yama no oku ni-mo shika zo naku-naru

●183● よをそむくところかきくおくやまは ものおもひに**ぞ**いるべかり**ける**(集8歌1639)道命
P179【哀感】[悟り]yo wo somuku tokoro to-ka kiku oku-yama wa mono-omoi ni-zo iru-bekari-keru

●184● **たらちめ**はかかれとてしも**むばたまの** わがくろかみをなでず**やありけむ**(集2歌1241)遍昭(良岑宗貞)
P180【哀感】[懐旧]tarachime wa kakare tote-shimo mubatama-no wa-ga kuro-kami wo nade-zu ya ari-kemu

‥‥‥‥‥《上代の「枕詞」の成れの果て》

●185● いとひてもなほしまるるわがみかな ふたたびくべきこのよならねば(集6歌346)藤原季通
P181【哀感】[悟り]itoi-te-mo nao oshima-ruru wa-ga mi kana futatabi ku-beki ko-no-yo nara-ne-ba

●186● ときしもあれあき**やは**ひとのわかる**べき** あるをみるだにこひしきものを(集1歌839)壬生忠岑
P182【哀感】[慨嘆]toki-shimo-are aki yawa hito no wakaru-beki aru wo miru dani koishiki mono-wo

●187● ひとのよのおもひにかなふものならば わがみはきみにおくれましやは(集2歌1399)藤原兼輔
P182【哀感】[慨嘆]hito no yo no omoi ni kanau mono nara-ba wa-ga mi wa kimi ni okure-mashi-yawa

★188★ みなひとのむかしがたりになりゆくを いつまでよそにきかむとす**らむ**(集6歌359)清昭
P183【哀感】[懐旧]mina-hito no mukashi-gatari ni nari-yuku wo itsu-made yoso-ni kika-mu-to-su-ramu

●189● たれを**か**もしるひとにせ**む**たかさごの まつもむかしのともならなくに(集1歌909)藤原興風
P184【哀感】[懐旧]tare wo-ka-mo shiru hito ni se-mu Takasago no matsu mo mukashi no tomo nara-na-ku-ni

http//zubaraie.com　　　-13-　　　verse INDEX

短歌索引

●190●すてはてむとおもふさへこそかなしけれ　きみになれにしわがみとおもへば(集4 歌 574)和泉式部
P184【哀感】[懐旧]sute-hate-mu to omou sae-koso kanashikere kimi ni nare-ni-shi wa-ga mi to omoe-ba
　　　《ほぼ生身和泉捨て身の詩小説》

★191★とどめおきてたれをあはれとおもふらむ　こはまさるらむこはまさりけり(集4 歌 568)和泉式部
P186【哀感】[悟り]todome-oki-te tare wo aware to omou-ramu ko wa masaru-ramu ko wa masari-keri

●192●うたたねのこのよのゆめのはかなきに　さめぬやがてのいのちともがな(集4 歌 564)藤原実方
P187【哀感】[慨嘆]utata-ne no ko-no-yo no yume no hakanaki ni same-nu yagate-no inochi to-mogana

―観念：Finding Out―

●193●ひとのおやのこころはやみにあらねども　こをおもふみちにまどひぬるかな(集2 歌 1103)藤原兼輔
P188【観念】[悟り]hito no oya no kokoro wa yami ni ara-ne-domo ko wo omou michi ni madoi-nuru kana

●194●よもすがらむかしのことをみつるかな　かたるやうつつありしよやゆめ(集8 歌 824)大江匡衡
P189【観念】[懐旧]yo-mo-sugara mukashi no koto wo mi-tsuru kana kataru ya utsutsu ari-shi yo ya yume

★195★みるほどはゆめもゆめともしられねば　うつつもいまはうつつとおもはじ(集7 歌 1234)藤原資隆
P190【観念】[慨嘆]miru hodo wa yume mo yume to-mo shira-re-ne-ba utsutsu mo ima-wa utsutsu to omowa-ji

●196●よのなかをなににたとへむあさぼらけ　こぎゆくふねのあとのしらなみ(集3 歌 1327)沙弥満誓
P190【観念】[悟り]yo-no-naka wo nani ni tatoe-mu asaborake kogi-yuku fune no ato no shira-nami

●197●すめばみゆにごればかくるさだめなき　このみやみづにやどるつきかげ(集7 歌 1224)藤原永範
P191【観念】[悟り]sume-ba miyu nigore-ba kakuru sadame-naki ko-no mi ya mizu ni yadoru tsuki-kage

●198●ながらへばまたこのごろやしのばれむ　うしとみしよぞいまはこひしき(集8 歌 1843)藤原清輔
P192【観念】[悟り]nagarae-ba mata ko-no-goro ya shinoba-re-mu ushi to mi-shi yo zo ima-wa koishiki

★199★うきままにいとひしみこそをしまるれ　あればぞみつるあきのよのつき(集4 歌 263)藤原隆成
P192【観念】[悟り]uki-mama-ni itoi-shi mi koso oshima-rure are-ba-zo mi-tsuru aki no yo no tsuki

★200★つくづくとおもへばやすきよのなかを　こころとなげくわがみなりけり(集8 歌 1774)荒木田長延
P194【観念】[悟り]tsukuzukuto omoe-ba yasuki yo-no-naka wo kokoro-to nageku wa-ga mi nari-keri

…「係助詞―係り結び」及び「を―み」の相関構造には下線を施した

…掛詞／枕詞／序詞／縁語／縁合／折り句／本歌取り
　　　　　　　　　　　　等の短歌修辞法には**太斜字体**＋下線を施した

《一・二・三・四・五　各句ページ索引》P195〜P206

「八代集」概説：Rough sketch of the world of Hachidaishuu P207〜215

「八代集」と本書の関係について：How this book relates to Hachidai shuu P216〜221

（八代集厳選）歌型二百(うたかた)：

日本の四季と心の詩の原型
—千代苔歌(ちょたいか)—
…千代(ちよ)生(む)せば巌(いはほ)と成れり苔(こけ)の華(はな) 言はで身に滲(し)む日(ひ)ノ本(もと)の歌

UTA-KATA 200 (/9500 Hachidai shuu TANKA):

Poetic Molds of Japanese Seasons and Minds
—Millennium Moss—
…Gathering dust ever so long, still so strong in the Japanese psyche

authored by 之人冗悟 (のと・じゃうご: *Jaugo Noto*)

Beneath
Umbrella of
ZUBARAIE LLC.

http://zubaraie.com

ー冬〜春:Winter〜Spring ー

●1● ゆきふればきごとにはなぞさきにける　いづれをうめとわきてをらまし
　　　雪降れば木毎に花ぞ咲きにける何れを梅と分きて折らまし

【冬】[謎掛]『1)古今集:337』紀友則(きのとものり)

雪が降った後だけに、木々の上にはそれぞれに白い雪の花が咲いている・・・
どれが白雪でどれが白梅か、どうやって見分けて折り取ったらよいものやら。

Snow has fallen covering trees in the garden.
Clusters of white here and there on the branch.
Which should I pick to cherish the flowers of plum?

ゆき【雪】〔名〕＜雪｜(n.)snow＞／ふる【降る】〔自ラ四〕＜降る｜(v.)fall＞(ふれ＝已然形)／ば【ば】〔接助〕＜理由｜(conj.)REASON＞／き【木】〔名〕＜木｜(n.)a tree＞／ごと【毎】〔接尾〕＜それぞれに｜(adv.)each＞／に【に】〔格助〕＜場所｜(prep.)PLACE＞／はな【花】〔名〕＜花｜(n.)flowers＞／ぞ【ぞ】〔係助〕＜強調｜(adv.)EMPHASIS＞／さく【咲く】〔自カ四〕＜咲く｜(v.)bloom＞(さき＝連用形)／ぬ【ぬ】〔助動ナ変型〕完了＜すでに〜[し]た｜(aux-v.)PERFECT TENSE＞(に＝連用形)／けり【けり】〔助動ラ変型〕過去＜〜[し]た｜(aux-v.)PAST＞(ける＝連体形係り結び)／いづれ【何れ】〔代名〕＜どちら｜(pron.)which＞／を【を】〔格助〕＜目的格｜(prep.)OBJECT＞／うめ【梅】〔名〕＜梅｜(n.)Japanese apricot＞／と【と】〔格助〕＜資格｜(prep.)as＞／わく【分く】〔他カ四〕＜分別する｜(v.)distinguish＞(わき＝連用形)／て【て】〔接助〕＜順接｜(conj.)and＞／をる【折る】〔他ラ四〕＜折る｜(v.)snap＞(をら＝未然形)／まし【まし】〔助動特殊型〕推量＜〜しようか｜(aux-v.)I wonder＞(まし＝連体形係り結び)

[yuki fure-ba ki-goto-ni hana zo saki-ni-keru izure wo ume to waki-te ora-mashi]

雪も白、梅も白、見分けも付かぬ冬の庭の取り合わせ・・・そもそもこの虚構詩の中では実際梅の花が咲いているのかどうかすら不明。わかっているのは、その「白い花」を愛でるためにわざわざ雪積もる庭に降り立つ平安貴族など実際にはそう多くはなかったということ ─ 彼らが梅を賞美する主な舞台は、紙の上の詩の空想世界。

Snow is white, so is the flower of 梅(ume＝plum, or Japanese apricot) ─ indistinguishable pair in a Winter garden. In fact, we don't even know if that 梅(ume＝plum) has really flourished in this fictional poem. What we do know is that very few Heianese(平安) nobles bothered to go out into a snow-covered garden to cherish the white flower ─ they mostly did so in imaginary poems on paper.

《「唐歌」の栄華の名残り「離合」歌》

『ひとごとにあなづるあせのつひのあか(人類に鑑る吾兄の終の垢＝誰でも彼でもバカにする君のツイッターアカウントは消せない汚点・・・人＋毎→類』((C)之人冗漏:のと・じゃうご 2016)のように部首毎にバラバラにした漢字を歌の中にまぶして遊ぶ知的文字遊戯の「離合」は、「そうひらかなかきたくてんぬき(総平仮名書き濁点抜き)」が基本の「大和歌＝和歌」よりむしろ「唐歌＝漢詩文」の得意技なので、約9500首の八代集全体でも指折り数えるほどしか見られない。ちなみに、同じ音の「あせ」を「吾兄＝貴兄・君」＆「汗」に、「つひのあか」を「終の垢＝消えない汚点」＆「ツイッターのアカ(ウント)」に読み替える「同音異義語のすり替え芸」は、「懸詞」と呼ばれる。さらにその「汗」から「あな(い)づる＝毛穴より出る」＆「垢＝汚れた汗カス」へと(本来の脈絡には無関係の語義つながりで)関連付ける「かくれんぼ連想ゲーム」は、「縁語」と呼ばれる。

―冬～春―

《離合(rigou＝Chinese character mutilation) ― remnant of the past glory of 唐歌(Kara-uta＝Chinese rhymes))》
As in 『ひとごとにあなづるあせのつひのあか(hito-goto ni anazuru ase no tsui no aka：人無に嘲る吾兄の終の垢＝Each person you despise as eternal specks of your Twitter account･･･人＋無→嘲)』((C)之人冗悟：*Jaugo Noto*, 2016), a single 漢字(kanji＝Chinese character) broken into several forming components will make an intellectual wordplay called 離合(rigou), favored in the world of 唐歌(Kara-uta＝Chinese rhymes) but not quite fit for 大和歌(Yamato-uta＝和歌：waka＝Japanese rhymes), which were basically written in ひらがな(hira-gana) with any voiced-consonant marks dropped (総平仮名書き濁点抜き＝そうひらがな**が**き**だ**くてんぬき＞そうひら**か**なかき**た**くてんぬき). Only a handful examples of 離合(rigou) are to be found in the whole 八代集(Hachidai-shuu＝8 great Imperial TANKA anthologies) amounting to some 9,500 rhymes. In case you wonder, homonymous puns like 吾兄(ase＝fellow, chap) and 汗(ase＝sweat, perspiration) from the same sound あせ(ase), and 終の垢(tsui no aka＝stigma of a lifetime) and ツイ[ッター]のアカ[ウント](a Twitter account) from the same sound つひのあか(tsui no aka) are called 懸詞(kake-kotoba＝puns). If you find a hidden semantic link between an apparently irrelevant pair of words ― from 汗(ase＝sweat) to あな[い]づる(穴づる：ana[i]zuru＝exude from pores) or 垢(aka＝scurf, grime) ― such associated words (汗＆穴出る／汗＆垢) lurking behind relevant context are called 縁語(engo).

―――――――――――――――――――――――――――――

●2●をられけりくれなゐにほふうめのはな　けさしろたへにゆきはふれれど
　　　　　折られけり紅匂ふ梅の花今朝白妙に雪は降れれど
　　　　　　　　　【冬】[謎掛]『8)新古今集:41』藤原頼通(ふじわらのよりみち)
真っ白い雪が枝の上に降り積もれば、同じ色した梅の花も埋もれて、折り取ることもできなくなる･･･という古歌の心に反するように、あっさり折られてしまったなぁ ― 色こそ同じ白さでも、薫る匂いは紅の、紛うかた無きこの存在感 ― 梅は香りで聞き分ける花。雪に埋もれど、香は隠れず。

　　　　Morning snow fell as white guise on Japanese apricot.
　　　Despite visual confusion, the flowers got picked, though.
　　Their scent presented themselves as red proof through white veil.

をる【折る】〔他ラ四〕＜折る｜(v.)snap＞(をら＝未然形)／る【る】〔助動ラ下二型〕受身＜～[さ]れる｜(aux-v.)PASSIVE VOICE＞(れ＝連用形)／けり【けり】〔助動ラ変型〕過去＜～[し]た｜(aux-v.)PAST＞(けり＝終止形)／くれなゐ【紅】〔名〕＜真っ赤｜(n.)red＞／にほふ【匂ふ】〔自ハ四〕〔他ハ下二〕〔他ハ四〕＜目・鼻に訴える｜(v.)appeal to smell or vision＞(にほふ＝連体形)／うめ【梅】〔名〕＜梅｜(n.)Japanese apricot＞／の【の】〔格助〕＜の｜(prep.)'s＞／はな【花】〔名〕＜花｜(n.)flowers＞／けさ【今朝】〔名〕＜今朝｜(n.)this morning＞／しろたへ【白妙】〔名〕＜純白｜(n.)pure white＞／に【に】〔格助〕＜様態｜(prep.)like＞／ゆき【雪】〔名〕＜雪｜(n.)snow＞／は【は】〔係助〕＜主格｜(prep.)SUBJECT＞／ふる【降る】〔自ラ四〕＜降る｜(v.)fall＞(ふれ＝已然形・命令形)／り【り】〔助動ラ変型〕存続＜～[し]ている｜(aux-v.)PERFECT TENSE＞(れ＝已然形)／ど【ど】〔接助〕＜～だけれども｜(conj.)although＞

　　　[ora-re-keri kurenai niou ume-no-hana kesa shirotae-ni yuki wa fure-re-do]

一つ前の歌への三百年後の返歌、それもとびきり野心的なやつ･･･だけど、「匂ふ」が嗅覚にも視覚にも解釈され得る語だけに、掴み所のない詩でもある。もし「匂ふ＝色鮮やかに映える」の意に取れば、問題の梅は「紅梅」として周囲の「白雪」と明瞭な対照を成すから、呆気ないほど簡単に折り取れるけど、そうなるとこの詩の面白味は失われる。一方、「紅匂ふ＝赤く香る」の意味だとすれば、かなり奇抜な言い回しながら、

http//zubaraie.com　　　　―Winter～Spring―

—冬〜春—

「目には見えない梅の花の、鼻を突く存在感」の表現としては、面白い。「梅」は臭いも味覚も確かに「赤」っぽいので、もしその「赤みがかった梅の香」が「白い梅の花」から、しかも「白雪の絨毯の下」から漂って来て自らの存在を誇示しているとしたら、「紅梅解釈」よりずっと魅惑的な詩になる…色／香のどちらを取ってもよいけれど、どっちに取るにせよ、この場面、あまり真面目に取らないほうがいい―― 梅花が雪に埋もれたら、どんなに真っ赤に咲こう／臭おうとも、現実にはまずもって識別不能なのだから…雪に埋もれた梅は、そういうちょっぴり哀しい花。咲くのが少々早すぎて、普通の人々には祝ってもらえないから、せめてもの救いに、普通じゃないくらい研ぎ澄まされた想像力の持ち主の平安歌人たちが、その鋭敏な空想的嗅覚を発揮して、雪の中から掘り出してあげてるわけです。

A 300-year-later answer song to the previous TANKA, and that quite an ambitious yet ambiguous one, due to the equivocal nature of the term にほふ (niou) possibly referring both to smell and color: if it does to color, the Japanese apricot flourishes in red, in conspicuous contrast to the white surrounding snow, making it all too easy for us to pick it up, rendering this poem rather flat. If, on the other hand, the expression くれなゐにほふ (kurenai niou) means "smelling red", that's quite an unusual but amusing representation of the pungent presence of an invisible plum. The scent/taste of Japanese apricot is definitely *RED*: if that reddish smell springs from white plum flowers to assert their presence through the white carpet of snow, it will make a far more fascinating poem than the scarlet-colored version. Color or smell, whichever you can take: whichever you take, however, you'll be well-advised *not* to take the scene too seriously — you can hardly discern Japanese apricots buried in snow, however scarlet they may be tinged or smell. A snow-buried plum is such a sad flower, a little too premature to be popularly cherished by ordinary people: only extraordinary imagination of Heianese poets can salvage it with their acute sense of fictional smell.

―春:Spring―

●3● をりつれ ばそでこそにほへ うめのはな ありとやここにうぐひすのなく
折りつれば袖にこそ匂へ梅の花在りとや此処に鶯の鳴く

【春】[俳諧]『1)古今集:32』詠み人知らず

外出先の梅の花を手折って愛でて帰宅した私の着物の袖に、今なお残る移り香に誘われたのか、「梅花ここにあり」とばかり、我が家の庭に鶯が来て鳴いている。

The scent of Japanese apricot I cherished in my hands out there
Still fragrant on my sleeves back here in my residence.
Lured by the phantom presence of the distant flowers,
An oriole came to sing, wondering "Where is the ume?"

をる【折る】[他ラ四]＜折る｜(v.)snap＞(をり＝連用形)／つ【つ】[助動タ下二型]完了＜すでに〜した｜(aux-v.)PERFECT TENSE＞(つれ＝已然形)／ば【ば】[接助]＜理由｜(conj.)REASON＞／そで【袖】[名]＜袖｜(n.)the sleeve＞／こそ【こそ】[係助]＜強調｜(adv.)EMPHASIS＞／にほふ【匂ふ】[自ハ四][他ハ下二][他ハ四]＜におう｜(v.)appeal to smell＞(にほへ＝已然形係り結び)／うめ【梅】[名]＜梅｜(n.)Japanese apricot＞／の【の】[格助]＜の｜(prep.)'s＞／はな【花】[名]＜花｜(n.)flowers＞／あり【あり】[自ラ変]＜存在する｜(v.)exist＞(あり＝終止形)／と【と】[格助]＜内容提示｜(conj.)that 〜＞／や【や】[係助]＜疑問｜(adv.)INTERROGATIVE＞／ここ【此処】[代名]＜ここ｜(adv.)here＞／に【に】[格助]＜場所｜(prep.)PLACE＞／うぐひす【鶯】[名]＜ウグイス｜(n.)an oriole＞／の【の】[格助]＜主格｜

(prep.)SUBJECT＞／なく【鳴く】〔自カ四〕〔他カ下二〕＜鳴く｜(v.)cry＞(なく＝連体形係り結び)
[ori-tsure-ba sode koso nioe ume-no-hana ari to-ya koko ni uguisu no naku]

「梅に鶯」および「梅はその咲く姿より香りを賞美すべき花」というイメージの根強さゆえに成り立つ「俳諧＝シャレ」の歌。

A joking song ― 俳諧(haikai) ― only possible because of the established image of 梅に鶯(ume ni uguisu＝an oriole likes to sing on a plum branch) and of Japanese apricots being cherished not so much for the sight as for the scent.

・・・・・・・・・・・・・・・・・・・・・・・・・・

《「俳諧」を俳人子規は憎みけり》

『梅が香は人糞の如き高き香にあらねばやや遠き処にありてこれを聞くには特に鼻の神経を鋭くせずば聞えず。(中略)元来人の五官の中にて視官と嗅官とを比較すれば視官の刺戟せらるる事多きは論を俟たず。梅を見たる時に色と香といづれが強く刺戟するかといへば色の方強きが常なり。故に「梅白し」といへばそれより香の聯想多少起れどもただ「梅かをる」とばかりにては今梅を見て居る処と受け取れずしてかへつて梅の花は見えて居らで薫のみ聞ゆる場合なるべし。しかるに古よりこれを混同したる歌多きは歌人が感情の言ひ現はし方に注意せざる罪なり。』(『墨汁一滴』より抜粋)・・・正岡子規は明らかにわかっていない ― 暖かい春の野に出てみんなに愛される桜の花と違い、寒さの中で(しばしば雪に埋もれながら)咲いてることさえ見てもらえない哀しい梅の花の愛し方として、大方の人間が発揮してくれない「視官」の代わりに、目に見えずとも発揮し得る「嗅官」を大活躍させることを思い立った「いにしへの歌」の真意が、彼のお粗末な「詩的視官」には映っていないのだ・・・正岡子規のこの愚かな「混同」ぶりは、「写実こそ命！」と叫んでありとあらゆる「詩的放縦(poetic license)＝純然たる虚構世界の中だからこそ可能になる絵空事」の余地を否定し、空想的色彩の濃い平安調短歌を賞美する心の余裕そのものを日本中から抹殺したあの男の罪深さの証拠品・・・出し抜けに「唯一絶対の神聖支配者」としての天皇への問答無用の服従を日本人に強引に押し付けようとした明治時代の急進的空気と同時進行で断行された「廃仏毀釈＝仏教を否定し仏像を破壊する蛮行」を思わせる独善排他的異文化破壊運動＝ヴァンダリズム(vandalism)の悪臭がプンプン漂って来る代物である・・・と同時に、文化の何たるかをまるで認識できもせぬこんな愚か者一匹の戯れ言一つで、いとも簡単に数百年来の伝統美を全否定して平然としていられる明治期以降の日本人の恐るべき文芸音痴ぶりを示すもの・・・そしてさらに恐ろしいのは、「詩的放縦」も許さぬ狭量さと「権威者の放縦」には唯々諾々として従う従順さを奇妙な形で併せ持った日本人が「文明開化＞富国強兵＞挙国一致＞鬼畜米英打倒」へとなし崩し的に流れて行った非人間的全体主義国家体制の歪んだ世の中に於いては、正岡子規の如き「狂ったことを平然と断言して他者に強引に押し付ける独断専行の主」こそが持て囃されるというその事実・・・二十一世紀初頭の日本の姿に照らして、これ以上恐るべき教訓があるだろうか？

《俳諧(HAIKAI＝amusing poems) hated by 正岡子規(Masaoka Shiki), a 俳句(haiku)-maker
of blunt 17 syllables, anything but a 短歌(tanka)-creator of 31-letter fanciful world》

『The smell of Japanese apricots is not as obtrusive as human excrement, making it difficult to discern for anyone but those with excessively acute sense of smell. *(OMISSION)* Thinking of the five human senses, it is needless to say that vision is keener than smell. With Japanese apricots in sight, normal human beings should feel more excited in the eyes than in the nose. The phrase "梅(ume) being white" may suggest the presence of the flowers' smell, but saying "梅(ume) being fragrant" can never be interpreted as seeing the flowers but only smelling their scent. In fact, too many poems from ancient times are in the habit of confusing the two senses, all due to the poets' sinful inattention to the way they express inner feelings.』(excerpt from 墨汁一滴: bokujuu itteki＝a spot of India ink)... The author of the above document 正岡子規(Masaoka Shiki) obviously didn't understand — unlike 桜(sakura＝

cherry flowers) popularly cherished by crowds of folks coming out in the warm Spring fields, 梅(ume＝Japanese apricots) come out in Wintry cold, often buried in snow, barely attracting attention from most folks; as a manner of loving this obscure plum, instead of mostly inoperative sense of "***vision***", "***poems from ancient times***" thought it a good idea to appeal to the sense of "***smell***" that can function where the flower is not in sight ― which fact is totally invisible to 正岡子規's dull sense of "poetic ***vision***"... this foolish "***confusion***" of 正岡子規 is the proof of his ***cardinal sin***: he declared *"photorealistic depiction of things is the essence of art!"*, he denied any room for "poetic license ― something impossible outside pure works of fiction", he purged the whole Japanese of a latitude for appreciating highly imaginative Heianese poems ― a stinking act of vandalism reminiscent of 廃仏毀釈(haibutsu kishaku＝denying Buddhism and destroying images of Buddha) going on in the radical torrents of the Meiji(明治) era which attempted all too abruptly to impose upon the Japanese undoubting obedience to "the Emperor as the sole divine ruler"... which also goes to show how terribly ignorant the Japanese people have been of what art truly is: otherwise how could they have rest satisfied with the total negation of their traditional beauty over centuries just because *a single cultural moron* happened to deny their time-honored treasure? What is still more horrifying is this ― when the eerie combination of the Japanese narrow-mindedness to "poetic license" and their unquestioning obedience to "authoritative license" avalanched into an inhumanly totalitarian system of society leading the Japanese into 文明開化(bunmei kaika＝cultural revolution), thence to 富国強兵(fukoku kyouhei＝a richer nation with stronger armaments), through 挙国一致(kyokoku icchi＝total devotion of all individuals for the good of the nation) to 鬼畜米英打倒(kichiku beiei datou＝fight and conquer the British and American devils), such a morbid trend of a distorted society should desire and admire *someone like* 正岡子規*(Masaoka Shiki) who would assert something crazy with irresponsible assurance and urge others to obey his own version of truth...* this, I believe, is the most terrifying lesson the Japanese folks in the early 21st century should learn from.

──────────────────────────────────────

★4★ひとはいさこころもしらずふるさとは　はなぞむかしのかににほひける
　　　人はいさ心も知らず古里は花ぞ昔の香に匂ひける

【春】[懐旧]『1)古今集:42』紀貫之(きのつらゆき)

人の心は移ろうもの・・・だから、あなたの胸の内はわかりません・・・ただ、馴れ親しんだこの地の花は、今も昔も変わらぬ色と香りで咲いていますね。

What color you wear deep down at your heart
Is not so clear as in old familiar days.
What's still clear to me in this old town
Is the scent of flowers as fragrant as ever.

ひと【人】[名]＜人間｜(n.)a human being＞／は【は】[係助]＜〜に関しては｜(adv.)as for 〜＞／いさ【いさ】[副]＜さておき｜(adv.)aside from＞／こころ【心】[名]＜心｜(n.)heart＞／も【も】[係助]＜意味なし｜(adv.)NO MEANING＞／しる【知る】[他ラ四]＜知る｜(v.)know＞(しら＝未然形)／ず【ず】[助動特殊型]打消＜〜[し]ない｜(adv.)not 〜＞(ず＝終止形)／ふるさと【古里】[名]＜昔馴染みの場所｜(n.)an old familiar place＞／は【は】[係助]＜〜に関しては｜(adv.)as for 〜＞／はな【花】[名]＜花｜(n.)flowers＞／ぞ【ぞ】[係助]＜強調｜(adv.)EMPHASIS＞／むかし【昔】[名]＜昔｜(n.)the past＞／の【の】[格助]＜の｜(prep.)'s＞／か【香】[名]＜香り｜(n.)the scent＞／に【に】[格助]＜様態｜

―春―

(prep.)like＞／にほふ【匂ふ】〔自ハ四〕＜におう｜(v.)appeal to smell＞(にほひ＝連用形)／けり【けり】〔助動ラ変型〕詠嘆＜～だったのだなぁ｜(interj.)REALIZATION＞(ける＝連体形係り結び)

[hito wa isa kokoro mo shira-zu furusato wa hana zo mukashi no ka ni nioi-keru]

この有名な歌は、作者の不実をなじった誰かさんに向けてのしっぺ返しとして贈られたもの・・・「訴えられたら逆に訴え返せ」は現代アメリカ人のみならず平安貴族にも通じる行動原理だったのです(後者は裁判で、前者は戯れ歌で、の違いはあるけど)・・・花の種類は気にせぬこと(アナタが正岡子規みたいな「写実こそ命！」の人でもない限りは、ね) ― 梅でも桜でも橘でも、どんな匂いや咲きぶりでも関係なし。この歌の文脈で大事なことは、せわしなく移り変わる人間関係のムードやモードに染まることなく、花は昔ながらの花のまま、という一点のみ。

This famous poem was given to someone as *a tit for tat*, who accused the poet of faithlessness. When accused, accuse back the accuser – this is as true to Heianese nobles as to modern Americans, this in lawsuits, that in humorous TANKA. Never mind the kind of flower (unless you are something of a 正岡子規:Masaoka Shiki, a die-hard photorealism believer) — plum, cherry or mandarin orange — it's not important how it smelled or flourished: what's important in this context is that it is exactly as it used to be, unaffected by fleeting transition of moods or modes in human relationship.

●5●こちふかばにほひおこせようめのはな あるじなしとてはるをわするな
東風吹かば匂ひ遣せよ梅の花主無しとて春を忘るな

【春】[擬人]『3)拾遺集:1006』菅原道真(すがわらのみちざね)

我が家の梅よ、春を告げる東風が吹いたなら、その風に乗せてお前の懐かしい香りを、遠く離れた私のもとまで届けておくれ。たとえ主人の私がいなくなっても、春を忘れてはいけないよ。

O, plum, when easterly wind blows, bring your scent along with it to me.
Even in a hostless house, never fail to greet Spring each year.

こち【東風】〔名〕＜東風｜(n.)an easterly wind＞／ふく【吹く】〔自カ四〕＜吹く｜(v.)blow＞(ふか＝未然形)／ば【ば】〔接助〕＜仮定｜(conj.)if＞／にほひ【匂ひ】〔名〕＜におい｜(n.)scent＞／おこす【遣す】〔他サ下二〕＜送る｜(v.)bring＞(おこせよ＝命令形)／うめ【梅】〔名〕＜梅｜(n.)Japanese apricot＞／の【の】〔格助〕＜の｜(prep.)'s＞／はな【花】〔名〕＜花｜(n.)flowers＞／あるじ【主】〔名〕＜主人｜(n.)the host＞／なし【なし】〔形ク〕＜存在しない｜(v.)do not exist＞(なし＝終止形)／とて【とて】〔格助〕＜たとえ～でも｜(adv.)even if＞／はる【春】〔名〕＜春｜(n.)Spring＞／を【を】〔格助〕＜目的格｜(prep.)OBJECT＞／わする【忘る】〔他ラ下二〕＜忘れる｜(v.)forget＞(わする＝終止形)／な【な】〔終助〕＜～するな｜(adv.)don't＞

[kochi fuka-ba nioi okoseyo ume-no-hana aruji nashi tote haru wo wasuru-na]

作者の菅原道真は、政治的謀略の犠牲になって京都から日本の南端の太宰府に流罪になりましたが、この歌は旧宅を離れる際に詠まれたものと言われています。梅に向かって「主人の私がいなくとも春を忘れてはいけないよ」と言いながら、道真は自分自身に向かって「私は必ず帰って来る！」と叫んでいたのかもしれません(・・・残念ながら、その願いは叶わずじまいでしたが)

The author, 菅原道真(Sugawara-no-Michizane), got banished from 京都(Kyoto) to 太宰府(Dazaifu) at the southern end of Japan as a victim of a political plot. This poem is said to have been made on departure from his old home. By calling on to plum 主無しとて春を忘るな(aruji nashi tote haru wo wasuru-na=don't forget to greet Spring even though the host is not there), he seems to be declaring to himself "I'll be back!"... sadly, he didn't.

—春—

●6● ふきくればかをなつかしみむめのはな ちらさぬほどのはるかぜもがな

吹き来れば香を懐かしみ梅の花散らさぬ程の春風もがな

【春】[機知]『6)詞花集:9』源時綱(みなもとのときつな)

目に見える所にはなくっても、風が運んで来る香りだけでも心引かれる思いの梅の花…
だから、どうか、花びらを散らさぬ程度の優しい春風が、彼方(かなた)の梅に吹き付けてくれますように。

Sightless perfume is enough to attract me,

Spring breeze, blow through distant apricots

Gently enough not to blow off their petals.

ふきく【吹き来】〔自カ変〕<吹いて来る | (v.)come blowing>（ふきくれ＝已然形）／ば【ば】〔接助〕<理由 | (conj.)REASON>／か【香】【名】<香り | (n.)the scent>／を【を】〔格助〕<主格 | (prep.)SUBJECT>／なつかし【懐かし】〔形シク〕<懐かしい | (adj.)feel nostalgic>（なつかし＝語幹）／み【み】〔接尾〕<理由 | (conj.)REASON>／むめ【梅】【名】<梅 | (n.)Japanese apricot>／の【の】〔格助〕<の | (prep.)'s>／はな【花】【名】<花 | (n.)flowers>／ちる【散る】〔自ラ四〕<散る | (v.)fall>（ちら＝未然形）／す【す】〔助動サ下二型〕使役<～[さ]せる | (aux-v.)CAUSATIVE>（さ＝未然形）／ず【ず】〔助動特殊型〕打消<～[し]ない | (adv.)not ～>（ぬ＝連体形）／ほど【ほど】〔副助〕<程度 | (adv.)to ～ degree>／の【の】〔格助〕<の | (prep.)'s>／はるかぜ【春風】【名】<春風 | (n.)Spring wind>／もがな【もがな】〔終助〕<～があってほしいな | (adv.)hopefully>

[fuki-kure-ba ka wo natsukashi-mi mume-no-hana chirasa-nu hodo no haru-kaze mogana]

遠くの梅の香を運んで来てくれる春のそよ風を喜びつつも、風に吹かれて梅の花が散りはしまいか、と作者は気にしています。春の香(かぐわ)しさ、温かさ、そして優しさに満ちた詩です。

While welcoming Spring breeze as a carrier of plum scent from the distance, the author cares for the unseen flowers lest the wind should blow them off of the branch. A poem full of vernal fragrance, warmth and gentleness.

- -

★7★ そでひちてむすびしみづのこほれるを はるたつけふのかぜやとくらむ

袖沾ちて掬びし水の凍れるを春立つ今日の風や解くらむ

【春】[季題]『1)古今集:2』紀貫之(きのつらゆき)

夏の暑い盛りに袖を濡らして掬(たく)って飲んだあの山川の水…長い冬の間はずっと
氷に閉ざされていただろうが、今日は立春、暖かい東風に氷も解けて、再び流れ出しているだろうか？

The cool water in Summer that quenched my thirst and drenched my sleeves,

Long asleep in Winter locked up under icy cold,

Might today, the first day of Spring, have molten and woken by gentle vernal wind.

そで【袖】【名】<袖 | (n.)the sleeve>／ひづ【漬づ】〔自ダ四〕〔自ダ上二〕<[水に]漬ける | (v.)dip>（ひぢ＝連用形）／て【て】〔接助〕<順接 | (conj.)and>／むすぶ【掬ぶ】〔他バ四〕<手ですくい取る | (v.)scroop [with hands]>（むすび＝連用形）／き【き】〔助動特殊型〕過去<～[し]た | (aux-v.)PAST>（し＝連体形）／みづ【水】【名】<水 | (n.)water>／の【の】〔格助〕<主格 | (prep.)SUBJECT>／こほる【凍る】〔自ラ四〕<凍る | (v.)freeze>（こほれ＝已然形・命令形）／り【り】〔助動ラ変型〕存続<～[し]ている | (aux-v.)PERFECT TENSE>（る＝連体形）／を【を】〔格助〕<目的格 | (prep.)OBJECT>／はる【春】【名】<春 | (n.)Spring>／たつ【立つ】〔自タ四〕<始まる | (v.)start>（たつ＝連体形）／けふ【今日】【名】

―春―

＜今日｜(n.)today＞／の【の】〔格助〕＜の｜(prep.)'s＞／かぜ【風】〔名〕＜風｜(n.)wind＞／や【や】〔係助〕＜疑問｜(adv.)INTERROGATIVE＞／とく【解く】〔自カ下二〕＜溶かす｜(v.)melt＞(とく＝終止形)／らむ【らむ】〔助動ラ四型〕現在推量＜～だろう｜(aux-v.)SUPPOSITION＞(らむ＝連体形係り結び)

[sode hiji-te musubi-shi mizu no koore-ru wo haru-tatsu kyou no kaze ya toku-ramu]

古い中国の故事「東風解凍（とうふうかいとう）＝新年の初日に東風が氷を解かし始める」を足場に、詩人は自らの詩的想像力を駆使して「暑い夏」から「氷れる冬」を経て「新春の初日」への時間旅行を演じています。言葉少なに多くを語る短歌の魔法を見るような詩です。

Based on an old Chinese concept of 東風解凍(toufuu kaitou＝easterly wind will melt ice on the very first day of a new year), the poet travels in time through poetic imagination ― from a hot Summer day through icy Winter to the beginning of a new Spring. See how much is said with so few words in this magical piece of poetry!

・・・・・・・・・・・・・・・・・・・・・・・・・・・

《「旧暦」に一月(ひとつき)足して「今暦(いまごよみ)」》

それまで「太陰暦」だった日本の暦は明治維新（＝めいじ、これ、あらたなりっ！）と共に「太陽暦」に変わり、明治五(1872)年十二月三日が明治六(1873)年一月一日になったので、陰暦に基づく明治以前の文物の季節感を知るには「太陽暦マイナス1ヶ月」の引き算換算が必要。二月初旬の真冬の極みを「立春」と呼ぶ不思議も、1カ月引いて「1月1日」に戻せば、「＜春＞というより＜新年＞の立つ日」と了解できるはず。

《seasons in TANKA based on 旧暦(kyuu-reki＝the lunar calender) ―
add 1 month to the old lunar calendar to get seasons right》

Traditional Japanese calendar until 明治維新(the Meiji Restoration) was the lunar calendar. The beginning of Japanese solar calendar dates back to 明治5年12月3日 on the lunar calendar (=1872/12/3), which became the new solar 明治6年1月1日(1873/1/1) ― in order to grasp the seasonal feelings based on the lunar calendar in pre-Meiji years, "solar -1(one) month conversion" is necessary for modern readers. You may wonder why 立春(risshun＝the first Spring day) should come at the beginning of (solar) February, the depth of coldness in Japan ― just reduce a month to get the date "1/1(January the first)", and you will realize it's not so much the beginning of "Spring" as the start of "a new year".

―――――――――――――――――――――――――――――――――――

★8★はるたつといふばかりにやみよしのの　やまもかすみてけさはみゆらむ
春立つと言ふばかりにや御吉野の山も霞みて今朝は見ゆらむ

【春】[謎掛]『3)拾遺集:1』壬生忠岑(みぶのただみね)

今朝の吉野山は、心なしか、白く霞んで見えるようだ・・・あの霞の正体は、冬の名残りの雪だろうか、それとも春の山肌を埋め尽くす桜だろうか？・・・もしかしたらどちらでもなくて、ただの気のせいなのかもしれないね、時が時だけに・・・あるいはどちらでもいいのかもしれないね、なにせ吉野は名にし負う雪と桜の名所なのだから・・・いずれにせよ、今日は立春、寒い中にも春が立つという特別な一日ゆえの、春霞に見紛う雪か桜の白っぽい何か・・・気の迷いにせよ気が早いにせよ、どっちに転んでも許される、この季節ならではの贅沢(ぜいたく)な錯覚なのだろうね、きっと。

Spring is here, calendar tells me so.
Maybe that's why the white hazy veil ―
Snowy wintry remnant or vernal cherry carpet ―
Seems to wrap around the Holy Mt. Yoshino.

http//zubaraie.com

―春―

はる【春】〔名〕＜春｜(n.)Spring＞／たつ【立つ】〔自タ四〕＜始まる｜(v.)start＞(たつ＝連体形)／と【と】〔格助〕＜内容提示｜(conj.)that ～＞／いふ【言ふ】〔他ハ四〕＜言う｜(v.)say＞(いふ＝連体形)／ばかり【ばかり】〔副助〕＜～[し]たばっかりに｜(conj.)only because＞／なり【なり】〔助動ナリ型〕断定＜～である｜(aux-v.)be＞(に＝連用形)／や【や】〔係助〕＜疑問｜(adv.)INTERROGATIVE＞／み【美】〔接頭〕＜美しき｜(adj.)beautiful＞／よしの【吉野】〔名〕＜[固有名詞]吉野｜(n.)Yoshino＞／の【の】〔格助〕＜の｜(prep.)'s＞／やま【山】〔名〕＜山｜(n.)the mountain＞／も【も】〔係助〕＜～もまた｜(adv.)also＞／かすむ【霞む】〔自マ四〕＜霞む｜(v.)get hazy＞(かすみ＝連用形)／て【て】〔接助〕＜内容提示｜(conj.)that ～＞／けさ【今朝】〔名〕＜今朝｜(n.)this morning＞／は【は】〔係助〕＜～に関しては｜(adv.)as for ～＞／みゆ【見ゆ】〔自ヤ下二〕＜見える｜(v.)appear＞(みゆ＝終止形)／らむ【らむ】〔助動ラ四型〕現在推量＜～だろう｜(aux-v.)SUPPOSITION＞(らむ＝連体形係り結び)

[haru-tatsu to yuu bakari-ni-ya mi-Yoshino no yama mo kasumi-te kesa wa miyu-ramu]

この歌の作者の壬生忠岑は、間違いなく、平安調短歌世界の中でも最上級の技巧を誇る人・・・なので、彼の詩歌と向き合う時は、最大限の詩的注意力が必要。「**山も霞みて今朝は見ゆ**」の表現はクセ者なのでダマされないように ― これ、幻です ― 「霞」なんて実は存在しません(そこにあるのは「雪」だけです)・・・どうしてそう言い切れるか？冒頭句「**春立つと言ふばかりに**(今日が立春の日：太陽暦二月四日だったばっかりに)」をご覧あれ。作者は「**吉野**」の山の白い色を、「冬の雪」ではなく「春の桜」の「白」だと思ってる(というより、そう思いたがっている)のです・・・桜の開花には早すぎる時節だってことは百も承知の上で・・・だから「桜」とも「雪」とも言わずにただ「霞」の白いヴェールに包んでボカしつつ、その「白い霞」の正体が何であるかは、読者の想像に委ねてるわけです・・・ぼーっと読んでるだけの人には、歌に書いてある通りの「霞」でしょう；現実主義者が注意深く読めば、答えは「雪」以外あり得ない、と言うでしょう；「**吉野**」ってどんな場所か、よーく知ってる人が、春を待ち望む気持ちでいっぱいの時には、「白い霞」は「山に居並ぶ桜花」として想像の中で美しく咲き誇ることでしょう・・・読者の想像力の器の程を露呈するとびきり厳しい試薬みたいな詩なので、うかつに反応するとヒドい目見ます。

The author of this poem, 壬生忠岑(Mibu-no-Tadamine), is undoubtedly the greatest technician in the world of Heianese TANKA... be on the keenest poetic alert when face to face with his verse. Don't be taken in by the tricky phrase 山も霞みて今朝は見ゆ(yama mo kasumi-te kesa wa miyu＝the mountain appears to be covered with haze this morning) ― this is an illusion: the haze is *NOT* actually there (there is only snow) ― why can we be sure? Look at the opening phrase 春立つと言ふばかりに (haru-tatsu to yuu bakari-ni＝just because the calendar says this is the first day of Spring＝February 4th on the solar calendar). The author attributes (or *feels inclined to* attribute) the white color of the mountain of 吉野(Yoshino) to 桜(sakura＝cherry blossom of Spring) rather than to 雪(yuki＝snow of Winter), although he knows it's too premature to expect cherry flowers to bloom: so, he refers neither to 桜(sakura＝cherry) nor to 雪(yuki＝snow) but simply blurs it into the white veil of 霞(kasumi＝haze), leaving it up to the reader to imagine what the white haze is... to inattentive readers, it's just "haze" as the poem says; to meticulous realists, it *MUST* be "snow"; in the eyes of those well-acquainted with the nature of 吉野(Yoshino) and hopeful of the arrival of Spring, the white hazy veil can transform itself into "a row of cherry flowers", beautifully blooming in imagination. This is a poetic acid test to reveal the imaginative caliber of the reader... respond with care.

《土地柄に含意ありけり「歌枕」》

古歌の中にたまたま出て来た地名なら何でもかんでも「歌枕」、というのは和歌を知らない大方の日本人の誤解で、「何か具体的なイメージを呼び起こす事物や土地の名」こそが真の意味での「歌枕」。言い換えれば、イメージの広がりをもたらさない地名には「歌枕」の資格なし。「**吉野**」は「雪」と「桜」の歌枕として有名だ

—春—

けど、特に関連付けて語られるべき何の連想も伴わない場合は、単なる「地名」でしかなく「歌枕」ではない。同時にまた覚えておくべきは、「地名」以外の「物事」でも、その名に言及すれば即座に浮かび上がる何らかの連想を伴う場合は「歌枕」になるということ。だから、「満たされぬうちに訪れた別れ」を示唆する「有明[の月]＝明け方の空にぽつんと残る前夜の名残りの月」も、「良かった時期はもう終わり」の感じが伴う「時雨＝晩秋から初冬にかけての通り雨」も、どちらも立派な「歌枕」。

《歌枕(uta-makura＝a poetic pillow) — a name suggestive of some special image》
In spite of the misconception of most Japanese laypersons, 歌枕(uta-makura) does not refer to any given names of places that happened to appear in old poems. The authentic meaning of 歌枕 (uta-makura) is a thing or place suggestive of some specific image. In other words, no place name is worthy of the title of 歌枕(uta-makura) unless it works as an image-enhancer. 吉野(Yoshino) is a famous 歌枕(uta-makura) for both 雪(yuki＝snow) and 桜(sakura＝cherry blossom), but places without anything specifically associated with their names are mere places, no 歌枕(uta-makura). It should also be noted that things other than places are also 歌枕(uta-makura) if they have some notion associated with them, instantly conjured up by the mention of their names. Thus, 有明[の月] (ariake[no tsuki]＝the moon in the morn, suggesting unsatisfied departure) and 時雨(shigure＝ scattered rain from late Autumn to early Winter, suggestive of the passing of a good season) are both 歌枕(uta-makura).

●9●よしのやまさくらがえだにゆきちりて　はなおそげなるとしにもあるかな
吉野山桜が枝に雪散りて花遅げなる年にもあるかな

【春】[謎掛]『8)新古今集:79』西行(さいぎょう)

吉野山の桜の枝の上に白い雪(めいたもの)が散り散りに積もっているところを見ると、今年は例年になく桜の開花が遅い年になりそう···って、おや、よく見ればその白い散り散りの雪は、なぁーんだ、桜の花じゃないか！もう咲いてたんだよ、雪と見間違えてただけで···さすが吉野、雪と桜の名所だけのことはあるね。

On the branches of cherry trees snow has been scattered:.
Flowers seem late coming out this year.
...*Oops!* What did I see but snow-white cherry already!
How nicely I was taken in by the legendary Yosino-yama!

よしのやま【吉野山】[名]＜[固有名詞]吉野山｜(n.)the mountain of Yoshino＞／さくら【桜】[名]＜桜｜(n.)cherry [tree, blossom]＞／が【が】[格助]＜の｜(prep.)'s＞／えだ【枝】[名]＜枝｜(n.)a branch＞／に【に】[格助]＜場所｜(prep.)PLACE＞／ゆき【雪】[名]＜雪｜(n.)snow＞／ちる【散る】[自ラ四]＜散る｜(v.)fall＞(ちり＝連用形)／て【て】[接助]＜順接｜(conj.)and＞／はな【花】[名]＜花｜(n.)flowers＞／おそげなり【遅げなり】[形動ナリ]＜遅そうだ｜(adj.)apparently late＞(おそげなる＝連体形)／とし【年】[名]＜年｜(n.)a year＞／なり【なり】[助動ナリ型]断定＜～である｜(aux-v.)be＞(に＝連用形)／も【も】[係助]＜意味なし｜(adv.)NO MEANING＞／あり【あり】[補動ラ変]＜～である｜(aux-v.)be＞(ある＝連体形)／かな【かな】[終助]＜詠嘆｜(interj.)EXCLAMATION＞

[Yoshino-yama sakura-ga eda ni yuki chiri-te hana osoge-naru toshi ni-mo-aru kana]

短歌世界の伝統芸の「雪」と「桜」の白紛れ。現代の桜(染井吉野)は「薄桃色」だけど、平安時代の桜(山桜)は「真っ白」なので御用心。この歌の作者(西行法師)は、枝の上の「白」を「雪」だと読み手が思い込むよう意図的に誘導しているけど、実際にはこの白いものは「桜」。どうしてこうまで明け透けなダマシの態度を取るのかって？彼の時代にはすでにもうこの「白紛れ」のトリックは見え見えすぎて、大胆な偽装抜きで人前

―春―

に出しても当時の読者は誰も引っ掛かってくれなかったからです・・・同じ道を300年間みんなして踏み均すうちに、ヘンな脇道にそれちゃった感じ・・・こうして年月が流れるほどに、その道を辿ろうとする人達もいなくなっちゃった、って話です。

Traditional white confusion of 雪(yuki＝snow) with 桜(sakura＝cherry flowers). Be advised that Heianese cherry(山桜:yama-zakura) bloomed in white (not cherry-pink as the current 染井吉野: Somei-Yoshino). This author, 西行法師(Saigyou houshi), is consciously trying to mislead readers into believing what is white on the branch is 雪(yuki＝snow), which is actually 桜(sakura＝cherry blossom)... Why is he so blatantly deceptive? Because this white confusion had already been too hackneyed to present without flamboyant disguise to cheat readers of the day. The same old beaten path of 300 years going astray... only to lose followers with advancing years.

・・・・・・・・・・・・・・・・・・・・・・・・・・・

《「俳諧」の三百代言「韜晦(倒壊？)趣味」》

詩歌の世界は、昔から変わらぬ想念を絶えず新たな表現で言い表わす努力の積み重ね。想念そのものは常に古くて変わらないのが当たり前;さもなくば千年も昔の詩が現代人の心に届く道理がない。そんな旧態依然の心の中身を入れる新たな容れ物を探し求めるのが詩人の仕事だが、それが時として「新奇」というより「珍妙」な表現に行き着くこともある。八代集の最後にあたる『新古今集』は、あまりに入り組みすぎて、あまりに曖昧で、内輪にしか通じぬ内奥の深遠さをあまりにも意識的に志向しすぎていて、三百年に及ぶ平安調短歌の目録の全てに精通した博学の持ち主でもない限りは手に負えない歌集として有名(というか、悪名高い)・・・ここに紹介した西行の新古今歌も、基本的には軽い気持ちで詠まれた俳諧(＝冗談)の歌なのだけれど、ナゾナゾ遊びの隠蔽工作が度を越して深すぎるので、平安末期の知識人気取り以外の誰の心にもすんなり届くものではない。それでいてこの歌は、とりあえず読者に紹介しても良さそうな数少ない(まぁまだマトモな)新古今歌の一つ。この歌を見れば、当時の平安調短歌がいかに息詰まる感じで行き詰まっていたかがわかるだろうし、東日本の鎌倉幕府の前に京都と貴族階層が政治的威光を失いつつある世にあって、当時の歌詠み連中が自らの独自性を主張する上で何とも風変わりなやり方を選んだそのさまも覗い知れることだろう。じわじわとコーナーへ追い詰められた時、西欧人ならみんなで力を合わせて押し返して新たな世界への活路を切り開こうとするが、日本人の場合はじわじわ狭まり行く小さな世界の中に自分の居場所を確保しようとして他者を押し退けるべく*部外者お断わり！*と主張するための攻撃的なまでに排他的なチマチマとした専門的知識のひけらかしに活路を見出そうとする・・・そんなことしてるようじゃ、自ら選んだ先細りの道の果てに絶滅したとしても、まぁ当然の話。

《韜晦趣味(toukai shumi＝extreme euphemism) ―
a sickly thick deceptive layer accumulated over 3 centuries trying to pull your leg》

The world of poetry consists of the same old idea expressed in ever fresh ways — the idea itself *MUST* be old and the same (otherwise, how could a millennium-old poem reach our heart?), while poets seek out new bottles to put in old wine... sometimes resulting in stupidity rather than novelty. 新古今集 (Shin-Kokin shuu), the very last of 八代集(Hachidai shuu＝8 great Imperial TANKA anthologies), is famous (or infamous) for being too intricate, too euphemistic, too consciously esoteric, simply too much for anyone but the erudite well-read in the 300-year repertoire of Heianese poetry. This 新古今 -TANKA by 西行(Saigyou), essentially a lighthearted joke, is buried too deep in the camouflage of a riddle to reach the heart of anyone outside the small circle of would-be intellectuals at the end of the Heian era. Still, this is one of the few 新古今調(Shin-Kokinistic) works for me to be able to introduce to you to show the suffocating impasse of Heianese TANKA and the bizarre way the contemporary poets aspired for their own uniqueness, in years when 京都(Kyoto) and the nobles were losing their political

—春—

prestige to the samurai-shogunage in 鎌倉(Kamakura), eastern part of Japan. When pushed to the corner, Westerners try to concentrate their collective efforts to push back and break their way out into a new world; the Japanese try to push others off to claim their place in the dwindling space by resorting to aggressively esoteric technicalities to declare "*Members Only!*"... No wonder they will diminish themselves into extinction.

━━━━━━━━━━━━━━━━━━━━━━━━━━━━━━━

●10● みわたせばやなぎさくらをこきまぜて みやこぞはるのにしきなりける
見渡せば柳桜を扱き混ぜて都ぞ春の錦なりける

【春】[機知]『1)古今集:56』素性(そせい)

山の上から見晴るかす京都の町は、桜花の淡い白と風になびく柳の緑が縦横に入り交じり、自然の織りなす春の錦織のよう。

The capital of Kyoto seen from the distance
Looks like brocade woven with willow-green and cherry-white.

みわたす【見渡す】[他サ四]<見渡す｜(v.)look over>(みわたせ=已然形)/ば【ば】[接助]<〜したところ｜(conj.)when>/やなぎ【柳】[名]<柳｜(n.)willow>/さくら【桜】[名]<桜｜(n.)cherry [tree, blossom]>/を【を】[格助]<目的格｜(prep.)OBJECT>/こきまず【扱き混ず】[他ザ下二]<入り混ぜる｜(v.)mix together>(こきまぜ=連用形)/て【て】[接助]<順接｜(conj.)and>/みやこ【都】[名]<都｜(n.)the capital>/ぞ【ぞ】[係助]<強調｜(adv.)EMPHASIS>/はる【春】[名]<春｜(n.)Spring>/の【の】[格助]<の｜(prep.)'s>/にしき【錦】[名]<錦｜(n.)brocade>/なり【なり】[助動ナリ型]断定<〜である｜(aux-v.)be>(なり=連用形)/けり【けり】[助動ラ変型]詠嘆<〜だったのだなぁ｜(interj.)REALIZATION>(ける=連体形係り結び)

[miwatase-ba yanagi sakura wo kokimaze-te miyako zo haru no nishiki nari-keru]

山の上から眺めた京都の春景色。京都は(南端を除く)周囲を山に囲まれた盆地で、その自然との近接感から、花鳥風月を詠む幾多の詩歌が自然と生まれ、季節の移ろいに深い関心を寄せる日本の伝統的意識も形成されました。

The Spring sight of the city of 京都(Kyoto) surveyed from the top of a mountain. 京都(Kyoto) is a basin, surrounded (except on the southern side) by mountains, which proximity to Nature naturally gave rise to many poems of 花鳥風月(kachoufuugetsu=flowers, birds, wind and the moon), forming traditional Japanese sentiment deeply attached to seasonal transition.

・・・・・・・・・・・・・・・・・・・

《大向う唸らす意図の「趣向」歌》

どうしても言葉にせずにはいられない思いが詩人の内面から溢れ出して形になった詩もあれば、読み手の機転を試す謎掛けとして出てくる歌もある。ここに紹介した短歌のような垢抜けした趣向や気の利いた台詞や万人向けの賛歌をもって満座の拍手を引っさらおうとする歌もまた、平安調短歌の世界には山ほどある ― なぜなら、平安の世にあって「歌を詠む」という営みは基本的に(ちょうど今日のカラオケのように)「芸術創作活動」というよりむしろ「座興芸」だったから。カラオケ熟練者の歌声の殆どが仲間の輪の外では聞くに堪えない代物であるのと同様に、平安の世に誇らしげに謳われた趣向歌のほとんどは、今日の我々の目には「気取った俗物趣味のゴミカス」としか映らない・・・この「春の錦」の歌は明らかに別物だけど。

《stylish poems with a view to impress the whole gallery》

Some poems are born as an embodiment of the poet's feelings crying out for verbal expression; others are given as a riddle to challenge the reader's wit. Songs like this one — an applause-grabber by way of

―春―

sophisticated style, witticism or anthem ― were found in abundance in Heianese TANKA, since it was essentially not so much artistic creation as party entertainment (just like today's KARAOKE). Just as most KARAOKE singers do not merit hearing outside their friendly circles, proudly stylish TANKA of the Heian era were most of them mere trashy snobbery to our eyes... which this Spring brocade song obviously isn't.

●11●はなのいろはかすみにこめてみせずとも かをだにぬすめはるのやまかぜ
花の色は霞に籠めて見せずとも香をだに盗め春の山風

【春】[機知]『1)古今集:91』遍昭（良岑宗貞）(へんじょう(よしみねのむねさだ))

春の霞に封じ込められて見えないけれど、山の上には満開の桜が咲き誇っていることだろう･･･
春風よ吹け、目には映らぬその花の、香りだけでも麓(ふもと)の我々のもとにこっそり届けておくれ。

**Sight and color of cherry unseen beyond the mountain haze
Should at least be ours to smell with a little help from Nature:
Steal, Spring wind, the flowery scent for us.**

はな【はな】〔名〕＜花｜(n.)[especially, cherry] flower＞／の【の】〔格助〕＜の｜(prep.)'s＞／いろ【色】〔名〕＜色｜(n.)color＞／は【は】〔係助〕＜～に関しては｜(adv.)as for ～＞／かすみ【霞】〔名〕＜霞｜(n.)haze＞／に【に】〔格助〕＜手段｜(prep.)by means of＞／こむ【籠む】〔自マ四〕＜閉じ込める｜(v.)envelop＞／こめ＝連用形／て【て】〔接助〕＜状態｜(conj.)while＞／みす【見す】〔他サ四〕〔他サ下二〕＜見せる｜(v.)reveal＞／みせ＝未然形／ず【ず】〔助動特殊型〕打消＜～[し]ない｜(adv.)not ～＞／(ず＝終止形)／とも【とも】〔接助〕＜～だとしても｜(conj.)even if＞／か【香】〔名〕＜香り｜(n.)the scent＞／を【を】〔格助〕＝目的格｜(prep.)OBJECT＞／だに【だに】〔副助〕＜せめて～だけでも｜(adv.)at least＞／ぬすむ【盗む】〔他マ四〕＜盗む｜(v.)steal＞／(ぬすめ＝命令形)／はる【春】〔名〕＜春｜(n.)Spring＞／の【の】〔格助〕＜の｜(prep.)'s＞／やまかぜ【山風】〔名〕＜山の風｜(n.) the wind blowing from the mountain＞

[hana no iro wa kasumi ni kome-te mise-zu-tomo ka wo dani nusume haru no yama-kaze]

「目に見えぬなら、せめて香りだけでも」と、山の霞の帳(とばり)の向こうから桜の芳香を運んで来るよう、詩人は春風に訴えかけています。(世俗時代の)恋愛でも(生涯通してお盛んだった)歌の世界でも共に華麗をもって聞こえた(平安時代最初期の歌人)僧正遍昭(そうじょうへんじょう)らしい趣向の歌。

"If not sight, at least scent" ― the poet appeals to the Spring wind to bring cherry fragrance from beyond the misty curtain over the mountain. A poem of style typical of 僧正遍昭(Henjou the highest ranking Buddhist monk), TANKA-singing bonze of the earliest Heian era who was famous for flamboyance both in love affairs (in his secular years) and poetry (throughout his life).

･････････････････････････

《「出家(しゅっけ)」してなほ名を求む「歌僧(かそう)」かな》

平安時代の日本の坊主(ぼうず)は何とも不思議な非世俗的存在で、建前上(たてまえじょう)は仏道修行(しゅぎょう)に専念しているはずなのだけど、実際には日々歌詠(うた)みに励みつつ、その才芸によって宮廷の高位高官との交流の道を開こうと必死に足掻(あが)いていた人々。俗世での出世の見込みがなくなったら、坊主になって歌詠みの技巧を磨き、あわよくばどこかの歌会(うたかい)で政治力のある有名人と知り合いになってそのご愛顧(あいこ)を求める、というのが当時の世の習い。八代集に登場する約九千五百首の歌の作者総数約千三百人のうち、「歌僧」の数はほぼ千人に達し、そのうち六百人以上が(平安時代の最末期の)『千載集』と(鎌倉時代の最初期の)『新古今集』に集中している･･･雑魚どもが同じ水路に名声と成功を切に求めて群がり出したら、その水路は役立たずとなり、干上が

る時も間近ということ・・・かくて、平安調短歌の優雅な伝統も、公家の時代の終わりと共に息を引き取ったのである:その風変わりな墓碑銘として『新古今集』を後に残して。

《singing bonzes renounced the world and still sought fame》
Heianese Japanese 坊主(bouzu＝bonzes) were a strange breed of non-secular folks, who were supposedly devoted to the way of the Buddha but were still in daily pursuit of making rhymes and tried desperately to mingle with dignitaries of the Imperial Court by virtue of their artistic accomplishment. When worldly success in the secular sector became hopeless, people of the day were in the habit of becoming bonzes to hone their poetic skill and seek favor of people with political power, whom they hoped to get acquainted with at some TANKA reading party. Of about 1,300 poets of some 9,500 poems appearing in 八代集(Hachidai shuu＝8 great Imperial TANKA anthologies), some 1,000 were 歌僧(kasou＝singing bonzes), of which more than 600 were concentrated in the last two anthologies of 千載集(Senzai shuu) and 新古今集(Shin-Kokin shuu), published respectively in the last years of 平安(Heian) and at the break of 鎌倉(Kamakura). When small-timers swarm around the same channel for coveted fame and success, the channel will soon cease to be valid and even drained. The elegant tradition of Heianese TANKA breathed its last at the end of the age of nobles with 新古今集(Shin-Kokin shuu) as its bizarre epitaph.

★12★みれどあかぬはなのさかりにかへるかり なほふるさとのはるやこひしき
見れど飽かぬ花の盛りに帰る雁猶古里の春や恋しき

【春】[自然]『3)拾遺集:55』詠み人知らず

我々としてはいくらでも見ていたい、見飽きることなどあり得ない、見事な桜の満開の時期だというのに、そんな花に背を向けて古里へと帰る渡り鳥の雁の群れ・・・やっぱり、生まれ育った懐かしい土地の春が、恋しいのかな？

Cherry trees in full bloom, endless feast to our eyes
Seem powerless to stop wild geese flying home to their country's Spring.

みる【見る】[他マ上一]＜見る｜(v.)view＞(みれ＝已然形)／ど[ど][接助]＜いくら～しても｜(conj.)no matter how＞／あく【飽く】[自カ四]＜飽きる｜(v.)have had enough of＞(あか＝未然形)／ず[ず][助動特殊型]打消＜～[し]ない｜(adv.)not～＞(ぬ＝連体形)／はな【花】[名]＜花｜(n.)flowers＞／の[の][格助]＜の｜(prep.)'s＞／さかり【盛り】[名]＜最盛期｜(n.)the prime＞／に[に][格助]＜時｜(prep.)TIME＞／かへる【帰る】[自ラ四]＜帰る｜(v.)go back＞(かへる＝連体形)／かり【雁】[名]＜[渡り鳥の]カリ｜(n.)wild geese＞／なほ[猶][副]＜それでもなお｜(adv.)still＞／ふるさと[古里][名]＜故郷｜(n.)the homeland＞／の[の][格助]＜の｜(prep.)'s＞／はる【春】[名]＜春｜(n.)Spring＞／や[や][係助]＜疑問｜(adv.)INTERROGATIVE＞／こひし【恋し】[形シク]＜恋しい｜(v.)feel attached to＞(こひしき＝連体形係り結び)

[mire-do aka-nu hana no sakari ni kaeru kari nao furusato no haru ya kohishiki]

渡り鳥の心境へと詩人が自然に共感の想像の羽を伸ばした「感情移入の詩」 — 概して理知的な平安時代の短歌が「詩人の個人的感情の主観的投影の鏡」としてしか自然の景物に言及しないことを思うと、この短歌は極めて珍しい例外。
A poem of empathy in which the poet naturally extends sympathetic imagination to the heart of migrating birds – quite a rare exception to generally intellectual TANKA of the Heian era which referred to things in Nature only as a subjective mirror of the poets' personal sentiments.

—春—

・・・・・・・・・・・・・・・・・・・・・・・・・
《「字余り」はあれど「字足らず」無かりけり》

この短歌の初句は(本来の五文字より一字多い)六字、こういうのは「字余り」と呼ばれ、短歌世界には山ほどあって、この歌集に含まれる200首の中にも46首あり、八代集の総数約9500首の短歌中にも1750(ほぼ2割)以上の「字余り」歌がある一方で、五・七・五・七・七に満たぬ「字足らず」の例は、ただの一首もありません。

《字余り(ji-amari＝letters too many) are actually so many,
while 字足らず(ji-tarazu＝letters too few) are virtually non-existent》
The opening phrase of this TANKA has 6 letters/syllables (1 letter/syllable too many). Such is called 字余り(ji-amari＝letters too many), which are found in abundance in the world of TANKA ― you can find 46 out of 200 poems included in this book. More than 1,750 excessive-lettered/syllabled TANKA are to be found among some 9,500 poems of 八代集(Hachidai shuu＝8 great Imperial TANKA anthologies) ― nearly ²/₅ of the whole, while there is absolutely NO(＝0) 字足らず(ji-tarazu) one with fewer letters/syllables than the regular 5-7-5-7-7.

●13● はるきてぞひともとひけるやまざとは　はなこそやどのあるじなりけれ
　　　春来てぞ人も訪ひける山里は花こそ宿の主なりけれ

【春】[機知]『3)拾遺集:1015』藤原公任(ふじわらのきんとう)

普段は誰も見向きもしない山里にも、春が来れば人々もやって来る。
まったく、山里の宿の主人は、人ではなく、山桜だねぇ。

It's because it's Spring that people visit this house.
The host is not me but flowers to invite and entertain them in the mountain.

はる【春】[名]＜春｜(n.)Spring＞／＜【来】[自カ変]＜来る｜(v.)come＞(き＝連用形)／て【て】[接助]＜順接｜(conj.)and＞／ぞ【ぞ】[係助]＜強調｜(adv.)EMPHASIS＞／ひと【人】[名]＜人間｜(n.)a human being＞／も【も】[係助]＜～もまた｜(adv.)also＞／とふ【訪ふ】[他ハ四]＜訪れる｜(v.)visit＞(とひ＝連用形)／けり【けり】[助動ラ変型]過去＜～[し]た｜(aux-v.)PAST＞(ける＝連体形係り結び)／やまざと【山里】[名]＜山里｜(n.)the countryside＞／は【は】[係助]＜～に関しては｜(adv.)as for ～＞／はな【花】[名]＜花｜(n.)flowers＞／こそ【こそ】[係助]＜強調｜(adv.)EMPHASIS＞／やど【宿】[名]＜家屋｜(n.)the house＞／の【の】[格助]＜の｜(prep.)'s＞／あるじ【主】[名]＜主人｜(n.)the host＞／なり【なり】[助動ナリ型]断定＜～である｜(aux-v.)be＞(なり＝連用形)／けり【けり】[助動ラ変型]詠嘆＜～だったのだなぁ｜(interj.)REALIZATION＞(けれ＝已然形係り結び)

[haru kite zo hito mo toi-keru yama-zato wa hana koso yado no aruji nari-kere]

人々がこの作者の山荘に来るのは、その主人を訪れるためではなく、花を見るため・・・だが、それを不平がる響きがこの歌にはまるでない・・・・それもそのはず、作者自身もまた自然の景物が面白い時にしかこの山荘を訪ねることはないのだから。「自然は、訪れる幾多の人々をもてなす主人役」というのは、自然物や周囲の環境に対する日本人の伝統的な感覚で、そこには西洋の王や君主のような絶対支配者・所有者は存在しない。天皇さえも、日本の民の全員と喜びを共にする存在であって、国民を支配する神がかった君主ではない・・・権力・富・人気といったものが一部に偏って圧倒的多数がこれになびく時代の日本は常に、混迷の道を辿っている。

People come and visit the mountain villa of this author to see cherry flowers, not to meet the author as their host. There is no blaming tone, though, because the host himself also visits his villa only when the mountain offers him something of Natural interest. Nature being host to a host of visiting guests ― this

—春—

is the traditional Japanese sentiment in their relationship with Nature or their surroundings, with no absolute ruler or owner like the Western kings or lords... even the Emperor of Japan being a co-rejoicer of the whole Japanese folks, not their divine master... when power, wealth and fame polarize and the majority blindly obeys them, the nation was always headed for trouble...

──────────────────────────────────

●14● われをこそとふにうからめはるがすみ　はなにつけてもたちよらぬかな
　　　我をこそ訪ふに憂からめ春霞花に付けても立ち寄らぬかな

【春】[願望]『2)後撰集:113』詠み人知らず

この私に会いに来るのは気乗りがしないかもしれませんが、
せめて我が家に咲き誇る桜の花を目当てにでも、来てくれませんか？

**I may be hardly enough for you to visit here for,
My house is full of flowers, though, come see them, along with me.**

われ【我】〔代名〕＜私｜(pron.)I, myself＞／を【を】〔格助〕＜目的格｜(prep.)OBJECT＞／こそ【こそ】〔係助〕＜逆接｜(conj.)although＞／とふ【訪ふ】〔他ハ四〕＜訪れる｜(v.)visit＞（とふ＝連体形）／に【に】〔格助〕＜仮定｜(conj.)if＞／うし【憂し】〔形ク〕＜気乗りがしない｜(adj.)reluctant＞（うから＝未然形）／む【む】〔助動マ四型〕推量＜だろう｜(aux-v.)SUPPOSITION＞（め＝已然形係り結び）／はるがすみ【春霞】〔名〕＜春霞｜(n.)Spring haze＞／はな【花】〔名〕＜花｜(n.)flowers＞／に【に】〔格助〕＜対象｜(prep.)OBJECT＞／つく【付く】〔他カ下二〕＜かこつける｜(v.)pretext＞（つけ＝連用形）／て【て】〔接助〕＜状態｜(conj.)while＞／も【も】〔係助〕＜意味なし｜(adv.)NO MEANING＞／たち【立ち寄る】〔自ラ四〕＜立ち寄る｜(v.)stop by＞（たちよら＝未然形）／ず【ず】〔助動特殊型〕打消＜〜[し]ない｜(adv.)not〜＞（ぬ＝連体形）／かな【かな】〔終助〕＜詠嘆｜(interj.)EXCLAMATION＞

[ware wo koso tou ni ukarame haru-gasumi hana ni tsuke-te-mo tachi-yora-nu kana]

「長らく御無沙汰の知り合いに送った歌」とされているものの、「溜息交じりの一人言」として聞いたほうが、寂しげな美しい響きが引き立つ歌‥‥春の感情は本来みんなと一緒に催すもの、秋・冬みたいに一人で味わうものではない。

A song said to be a message to someone who hasn't visited the author for a long time. But this song will sound more sadly beautiful as a solitary sigh... the emotion of Spring is innately gregarious, not to be tasted all alone as in Autumn and Winter.

・・・・・・・・・・・・・・・・・・・・・・・・・

《あっち向いてホィ！と不意付く「縁語」かな》

細かい読み手なら、この歌の中の「春霞」が妙に脈絡から浮いて不要っぽいのに気付いただろう。実際、この短歌の論理的解釈は、懸案の「春霞」を除外して初めて成り立つのである‥‥では何故この「春霞」はそこにあるのだろうか？考え得る答えの一つとして、この短歌を次のように書き換えてみよう ── 我をこそ訪ふに憂からめ＜春霞＞＜立ち＞寄らぬかな花に付けても ── この語順なら、「春霞」は後続の動詞「立ち」の「枕詞(まくらことば＝本筋を導く前置き語)」として「縁語(えんご＝意味上関連性のある言葉どうし)」の連環の糸でつながるのである。上記の論理の鎖が断ち切られてしまった原因は、どこかの不注意な写本者が自らの個人的好みに従って(そのもたらす非論理的帰結に思いを巡らすこともなしに)「こっちの方が並びがいい」と感じて行なった恣意的な語順入れ替えによるもの、と考えて間違いあるまい。この種の無責任で身勝手な書き換えの横行も少なからず手伝って、「枕詞」や「縁語」といった短歌世界の専門用語は、いかに緻密な研究者を以てしても論理的理解不可能なほどのひどい混乱状態(あるいは無秩序状態)の中へと雪崩を打って崩壊してしまったのである‥‥これらの用語については、一般読者は無視しておくのがよいだろう：そこに隠されたメッセージを読み取り損ねたとて、失うものはほとんどないのだから。

http//zubaraie.com　　　　-31-　　　　—Spring—

—春—

《縁語(engo=associated words) will take you by surprise in unexpected contexts》
Meticulous readers might have found 春霞(haru-gasumi=Spring haze) in this poem strangely out of context and irrelevant: in fact, this TANKA is logically understandable only when you interpret it without 春霞(haru-gasumi) in question... why, then, is it there? As a possible answer to the question, I'll rephrase it like this — 我をこそ訪ふに憂からめ＜春霞＞＜立ち＞寄らぬかな花に付けても — in this word order, the term 春霞(harugasumi=Spring haze) will have poetic relevance to the following verb 立ち(tachi=rise) as 枕詞(makura-kotoba=a pillow word) in the chain of 縁語(engo=associated words). The logical chain shown above must have been broken by some sloppy transcriber who took the liberty of re-arranging the word order according to his/her own fancy without any thought to the illogical consequence. Thanks largely to such irresponsible tampering, the poetic terms of 枕詞(makura-kotoba=pillow words, introduction to certain nouns) and 縁語(engo=associated words) avalanched into a state of disorder (or even chaos) beyond any logical comprehension of even the most scrutinizing scholar... ordinary readers might just as well ignore them: they'd lose very little by missing their hidden messages.

●15● こぞのはるちりにしはなもさきにけり あはれわかれのかからましかば
　　去年の春散りにし花も咲きにけり哀れ別れの斯からましかば

【春】[慨嘆]『6)詞花集:402』赤染衛門(あかぞめえもん)

去年の春に散った桜の花は、今年また咲きました･･･
あぁ、あんな風に、一度お別れした人とも再び巡り会えたら、どんなにかぃいでしょうに。

Flowers gone last year came back again this Spring.
I wish the same with humans gone once and for all.

こぞ【昨年】[名]＜去年｜(n.)last year＞／の【の】[格助]＜の｜(prep.)'s＞／はる【春】[名]＜春｜(n.)Spring＞／ちる【散る】[自ラ四]＜散る｜(v.)fall＞(ちり=連用形)／ぬ【ぬ】[助動ナ変型]完了＜すでに～[し]た｜(aux-v.)PERFECT TENSE＞(に=連用形)／き【き】[助動特殊型]過去＜～[し]た｜(aux-v.)PAST＞(し=連体形)／はな【花】[名]＜花｜(n.)flowers＞／も【も】[係助]＜～もまた｜(adv.)also＞／さく【咲く】[自カ四]＜咲く｜(v.)bloom＞(さき=連用形)／ぬ【ぬ】[助動ナ変型]完了＜すでに～[し]た｜(aux-v.)PERFECT TENSE＞(に=連用形)／けり【けり】[助動ラ変型]過去＜～[し]た｜(aux-v.)PAST＞(けり=終止形)／あはれ【あはれ】[感]＜あぁ残念｜(n.)a pity＞／わかれ【別れ】[名]＜別れ｜(n.)parting＞／の【の】[格助]＜主格｜(prep.)SUBJECT＞／かかり【斯かり】[自ラ変]＜このような｜(v.)be like this＞(かから=未然形)／まし【まし】[助動特殊型]推量＜だったらいいのに｜(aux-v.)I wish＞(ましか=未然形)／ば【ば】[接助]＜仮定｜(conj.)if＞

[kozo no haru chiri-ni-shi hana mo saki-ni-keri aware wakare no kakara-mashi-kaba]

桜の花は、咲くたびに、かつてはあって今はないものを私たちに思い起こさせます･･･ちなみにこの歌人、前年に夫を失っています･･･愛・友・若さ、何であれ人がひとたび失ったものは二度と戻ってはきません。毎年毎年戻って来る春の特性は、我々の 儚 い(が故にかけがえのない)人生を定期的に思い知らせるよすがなのです。

Whenever it comes again, cherry blossom reminds us of what we used to have but have now lost. Incidentally, this poet lost her husband in the previous year. Whatever you have lost – love, friends or youth – is lost beyond recovery: the reciprocal nature of Spring is the periodical reminder of the pettiness (therefore, preciousness) of our fleeting life.

—春—

《本当の名は人知れぬ「女流歌人」》

この短歌の詠み手は赤染衛門と呼ばれる人で、赤染用時（＜**あかぞめ**＞のもちとき）の娘でお父さんの官職は「右衛門尉（う＜**えもん**＞のじょう）」ということで付いたあだ名が「**赤染衛門**」…「冗談でしょ？」と言われそうだけど、これがホントの話で、平安時代の女性は一般に「本名」で世間に知られることはなかったのです。もちろん女性にだって「本名」はあったけど、それを知り、その名で彼女を呼ぶことができたのは、彼女と特別親しい関係（あるいは肉体関係）にあった人だけ。「言霊（ことだま＝あらゆる語や名に宿る固有の魂）」の存在が信じられていた時代には、人の名前をじかに口にしても許されるのは、その人を支配する立場に身を置く人だけ（女性の場合は、恋人か夫だけ）というのが決まり事だったのです。今日でもなお、日本人は「**両さん、両ちゃん**」といったあだ名や「**お巡りさん、巡査**」といった社会的立場で他人に呼び掛けるのを好み、「**両津、勘吉**」などと本名をじかに呼ぶのを嫌います。本名で呼ばれた時の日本人（特に女性）の反応は二つに一つ — 自らの魂の核の部分に触れがしてその相手に親近感を抱くか、あるいは、自分の精神に過度の影響力を行使する意図をもって図々しくも自分の名を呼び捨てにした相手に対し反感を催すか — だからこそ、根っからの日本人は他人の本名なんて滅多に口にしないのです…が、だからこそまた、英語（＝他人を本名で呼ぶ言語）を話す外国人が、一見よそよそしげな日本人（特に、若い女性！）と親しげな関係（あるいは、ねんごろな関係！）になるのがびっくりするほど簡単だったりもするわけです：だって、ごく自然に「本名」で呼び掛けることで彼らの「魂の核」にじかに触れちゃうことができるのが英語人種の役得なのだから…ぁ、ガイジンさん、これ、乱用しちゃダメですよ…それと、何も知らない日本の（特に女性の）みなさん、上記の事情、どうぞ十分御自覚の上、御用心遊ばせ。

《who ever knows the true name of a woman poet?》

The author of this TANKA was called 赤染衛門(Akazome emon): she was the daughter of 赤染用時 (Akazome-no-Mochitoki) whose official position was 右衛門尉(u-emon no jou), hence her nickname 赤染衛門(Akazome emon). No kidding, you may say, but it's no joke: a woman in the Heian era was not known to the public by her real name. She had her own name, all right, but it was only those especially familiar (or intimate) with her that knew and called her by the real name. Belief in 言霊(kotodama = spirit inherent in any word or name) dictated that the direct mention of someone's name be granted only to those in the position to govern that someone — in the case of a woman, her lover or husband. Even today, the Japanese prefer calling others by their nicknames (両さん:Ryou-san, 両ちゃん: Ryou-chan) or social positions (お巡りさん:omawari-san, 巡査:junsa) to directly calling their real names (両津:Ryoutsu, 勘吉:Kankichi). When called by the real name, the Japanese (especially, women) feel either attracted to the name-caller for touching them at the core of their spiritual existence, or repugnant to having their names called by someone not entitled to do so with conscious intent to exert undue influence on their soul – that is why native Japanese rarely call others by their names... which is also the reason why English-speaking — and real-name-calling — foreigners find it *INCREDIBLY* easy to be on friendly (or even intimate) terms with the apparently distant Japanese (especially, young women!) by quite naturally calling them by the name and directly touching the core of their soul... please don't abuse it, foreigners, and be well-aware and beware, ignorant Japanese (especially, women)!

―春―

★16★もろともにをりしはるのみこひしくて ひとりみまうきはなざかりかな
諸共にをりし春のみ恋しくて一人見まうき花盛りかな

【春】[懐旧]『3)拾遺集:1039』詠み人知らず

誰もがみんな心躍らせる満開の桜の花だけど、かつて一緒にその美を手折って賞美した人が傍に居ないばかりに、昔の春にばかり心奪われて、目の前の桜には気持ちが向かわない今の私。

Cherry flowers come to life again,

Leaving me alone in good old Spring I enjoyed along with my precious one.

How strongly you draw me still more than anything I see around without you.

もろともに【諸共に】[副]＜一緒に｜(adv.)together＞／**(A)をる【折る】[他ラ四]**＜折る｜(v.)snap＞(をり＝連用形)／**(B)をり【居り】[自ラ変]**＜いる｜(v.)stay＞(をり＝連用形)／き【き】[助動特殊型]過去＜～[し]た｜(aux-v.)PAST＞(し＝連体形)／はる【春】[名]＜春｜(n.)Spring＞／のみ【のみ】[副助]＜ばかり｜(adv.)just＞／こひし【恋し】[形シク]＜恋しい｜(v.)feel attached to＞(こひしく＝連用形)／て【て】[接助]＜理由｜(conj.)REASON＞／ひとり【一人】[副]＜一人きり｜(adv.)alone＞／みる【見る】[他マ上一]＜見る｜(v.)view＞(み＝未然形)／まうし【まうし】[助動ク型]＜～したくない｜(aux-v.)don't want to ～＞(まうき＝連体形)／はなざかり【花盛り】[名]＜花盛り｜(n.)the full bloom＞／かな【かな】[終助]＜詠嘆｜(interj.)EXCLAMATION＞

[morotomoni ori-shi haru nomi koishiku-te hitori mi-mauki hana-zakari kana]

「詞書(ことばがき=注釈)」によれば、この歌は前年一緒に花を愛でた誰かさんに送ったものだそうで、そこにはさらに「桜の花を手折って添えた」とまで書いてあるけど、もし本当にそうなら、この歌は近所に住んでる誰かさんに向けて「今年の春も一緒に楽しもう！」と誘ってるだけの催促状になるわけだけど···そんな解釈、あなたはお望みですか？もしそうなら、あなたと私に「詩の話題」は無理そうです。上に紹介した「詞書」を見て「なんて興醒めな！」と呆れ返るような人と一緒にこそ、歌の楽しみは味わいたいもの。出しゃばりな補注抜きでも独り立ち出来るものこそ「詩歌」：文章を補って説明してもらわなきゃ成立しない代物なんて(大部分は)「詩歌」の名に値しません。

Annotation to this poem says it was sent to someone with whom the poet cherished cherry flowers in the previous year; it even says that the poet sent the poem along with a cherry branch. If really so, this is an invitation to someone living in the neighborhood to come enjoy this Spring together... would you like that interpretation? If so, you and I do not speak the same poetic language. I'd rather be with someone who would find the annotation above a total wet-blanket. Poems should stand alone without obtrusive annotations: those requiring supplementary sentences are most of them hardly worth the name of poetry.

●17●こぞみしにいろもかはらずさきにけり はなこそものはおもはざりけれ
去年見しに色も変はらず咲きにけり花こそ物は思はざりけれ

【春】[擬人]『5)金葉集:515』秦兼方(はたのかねかた)

去年見た時と全く変わらず美しく咲くとは、桜の花というものは、

人の世の悲喜にもごもなんてまるで知らないものなのだなぁ。

Immune to human feelings cherry flowers bloom

No less beautifully than last year when we saw it together.

—春—

こぞ【昨年】〔名〕＜去年｜(n.)last year＞／みる【見る】〔他マ上一〕＜見る｜(v.)view＞(み＝連用形)／き【き】〔助動特殊型〕過去＜〜[し]た｜(aux-v.)PAST＞(し＝連体形)／に【に】〔格助〕＜比較｜(prep.)COMPARISON＞／いろ【色】〔名〕＜色｜(n.)color＞／も【も】〔係助〕＜意味なし｜(adv.)NO MEANING＞／かはる【変はる】〔自ラ四〕＜変わる｜(v.)change＞(かはら＝未然形)／ず【ず】〔助動特殊型〕打消＜〜[し]ない｜(adv.)not 〜＞(ず＝終止形)／さく【咲く】〔自カ四〕＜咲く｜(v.)bloom＞(さき＝連用形)／ぬ【ぬ】〔助動ナ変型〕完了＜すでに〜[し]た｜(aux-v.)PERFECT TENSE＞(に＝連用形)／けり【けり】〔助動ラ変型〕過去＜〜[し]た｜(aux-v.)PAST＞(けり＝終止形)／はな【花】〔名〕＜花｜(n.)flowers＞／こそ【こそ】〔係助〕＜強調｜(adv.)EMPHASIS＞／もの【物】〔名〕＜物事｜(n.)a thing＞／は【は】〔係助〕＜目的格｜(prep.)OBJECT＞／おもふ【想ふ】〔他ハ四〕＜感じる｜(v.)feel＞(おもは＝未然形)／ず【ず】〔助動特殊型〕打消＜〜[し]ない｜(adv.)not 〜＞(ざり＝連用形)／けり【けり】〔助動ラ変型〕詠嘆＜〜だったのだなぁ｜(interj.)REALIZATION＞(けれ＝已然形係り結び)

[kozo mi-shi ni iro mo kawara-zu saki-ni-keri hana koso mono wa omowa-zari-kere]

詠み手は最近何か大事なもの(「詞書」によれば、かつてお仕えした後三条天皇)を失ったようです･･･人を取り巻く状況にはまるで左右されない「無情の物」としての自然の景物を見て、感情に支配される人間としての自己存在をより強く意識する･･･詩人の内面世界の主観的投影としての自然描写は、平安調短歌お好みの題材。

The author must have lost something precious recently (his master, the former Emperor 後三条 Go-sanjou, as the annotation says). Things in Nature unaffected by human circumstances — 無情の物 (mujou no mono＝the emotionless) — making us all the more acutely conscious of our emotional existence is a popular theme of Heianese TANKA with depiction of Nature as subjective reflection of the poet's inner world.

●18●いにしへにかはらざりけりやまざくら　はなはわれをばいかがみるらむ
古へに変はらざりけり山桜花は我をば如何見るらむ

【春】[擬人]『7)千載集:1055』藤原基長(ふじわらのもとなが)

昔見た時と何一つ変わらぬ美しさで咲いているなぁ、この山桜は･･･それに引き替え、今の私は･･･(ずいぶんと変わり果てた姿で来ましたねぇ)などと思いつつ、桜花は、私のことを見ているのだろうか？

O, cherry flowers as fresh as ever, never changing in this mountain,
How do I look in your eyes? Do you recognize your old friend in me?

いにしへ【古へ】〔名〕＜昔｜(n.)the past＞／に【に】〔格助〕＜比較｜(prep.)COMPARISON＞／かはる【変はる】〔自ラ四〕＜変わる｜(v.)change＞(かはら＝未然形)／ず【ず】〔助動特殊型〕打消＜〜[し]ない｜(adv.)not 〜＞(ざり＝連用形)／けり【けり】〔助動ラ変型〕詠嘆＜〜だったのだなぁ｜(interj.)REALIZATION＞(けり＝終止形)／やまざくら【山桜】〔名〕＜山に咲く桜｜(n.)cherry blossom in the mountain＞／はな【花】〔名〕＜花｜(n.)flowers＞／は【は】〔係助〕＜主格｜(prep.)SUBJECT＞／われ【我】〔代名〕＜私｜(pron.)I, myself＞／を【を】〔格助〕＜目的格｜(prep.)OBJECT＞／ば【ば】〔格助〕＜強調｜(adv.)EMPHASIS＞／いかが【如何】〔副〕＜どのように｜(adv.)how＞／みる【見る】〔他マ上一〕＜見る｜(v.)view＞(みる＝終止形)／らむ【らむ】〔助動ラ四型〕現在推量＜〜だろう｜(aux-v.)SUPPOSITION＞(らむ＝連体形係り結び)

[inishie ni kawara-zari-keri yama-zakura hana wa ware wo-ba ikaga miru-ramu]

「自然に投影された人間感情」という点では、一つ前の短歌と同じコイン(coin)の裏表の関係にある歌で、これまた「押しつけがましい詞書」抜きで味わうほうが佳い歌･･･それでも知りたい人のために書いておくと、詠み手は仏道に入るべく山に入って髪を下ろして坊主になった直後にこの歌を作った、とのことです。

—春—

Human emotion reflected in Nature, the flip-side of the same coin as the previous TANKA. Just another song that had better be relished without any obtrusive annotation... in case you are still curious, the author made it immediately after he cut off his hair to become a bonze and enter the way of the Buddha in the mountain.

●19● よのなかをおもひすててしみなれども こころよわしとはなにみえける
世の中を思ひ捨ててし身なれども心弱しと花に見えける

【春】[機知]『4)後拾遺集:117』能因(橘永愷)(のういん(たちばなのながやす))

俗世を捨てて仏の道に入ったからには滅多なことに心動かしてはいけないはずの我が身ながら、美しい春の桜を見ると相変わらず心ときめいてしまいます・・・修行が足りないというか、人たる心の根っこの部分だけは変えようがないというか・・・花のおかげで悟らされた次第です。

Worldly emotions I have supposedly given up,
Stirred up by flowers, show how emotional I still am.

よのなか【世の中】〔名〕<世の中│(n.)the world>／を【を】〔格助〕<目的格│(prep.)OBJECT>／おもひすつ【思ひ捨つ】〔他夕下二〕<自らの意志で捨て去る│(v.)desert of one's own free will>(おもひすて=連用形)／つ【つ】〔助動夕下二型〕完了<すでに~した│(aux-v.)PERFECT TENSE>(て=連用形)／き【き】〔助動特殊型〕過去<~[し]た│(aux-v.)PAST>(し=連体形)／み【身】〔名〕<立場│(n.)one's position>／なり【なり】〔助動ナリ型〕断定<~である│(aux-v.)be>(なれ=已然形)／ども【ども】〔接助〕<~ではあるが│(conj.)although>／こころよわし【心弱し】〔形ク〕<精神的に弱い│(adj.)weak at heart>(こころよわし=終止形)／と【と】〔格助〕<内容提示│(conj.)that ~>／はな【花】〔名〕<花│(n.)flowers>／に【に】〔格助〕<原因│(prep.)REASON>／みゆ【見ゆ】〔自ヤ下二〕<見える│(v.)appear>(みえ=連用形)／けり【けり】〔助動ラ変型〕過去<~[し]た│(aux-v.)PAST>(ける=[非文法的]連体形係り結び・・・何の係助詞とも対応しないので、本来なら「けり」)

[yo-no-naka wo omoi-sute-te-shi mi nare-domo kokoro-yowashi to hana ni mie-keru]

「悟り」というよりは「戯れ(ざれ=軽い座興)」の歌。作者は有名な歌僧で、その詩的才芸のおかげで朝廷の高位高官たちとも交流があった人物。そんな人物がどうして「真の世捨て人」たり得るだろうか？日本人の「言うこと」(*世の中を思ひ捨ててし*=私は自らの意志で俗世の地位を捨てました)を決して真に受けてはならない:実際何をしでかすかを見て彼らが何者か判断すべし(この作者はこの歌を朝廷最高位の人物に贈って豪勢な褒美を賜わった、と詞書は語っている)・・・べつにこの作者のことを「看板に 偽りあり」と責めているわけではない:歌僧なんて(あるいは、日本人なんて)そんなもの、ただそれだけの話である。

A song not so much of 悟り(satori=enlightenment) as 戯れ(zare=light entertainment). The author was a famous 歌僧(kasou=a TANKA singing bonze) and would mingle among high-ranking nobles at the Imperial Court of Japan by dint of his poetic accomplishment. How could such a personage be a true recluse? Never trust the Japanese by what they ***say*** — *世の中を思ひ捨ててし*(yo-no-naka wo omoi-sute-te-shi=*I have willingly given up my position in the world*) — judge them by what they actually ***do*** — the author sent this song to the highest ranking official at the Court and was granted quite a gorgeous reward, the annotation tells us... Not that I'm blaming the author for not being what he says he is: that's just what a TANKA-singing bonze (or should I say, ***a Japanese***) is supposed to be.

★20★よのなかにたえてさくらのなかりせば　はるのこころはのどけからまし
　　　世の中に絶えて桜の無かりせば春の心は長閑けからまし

【春】[悟り]『1)古今集:53』在原業平(ありわらのなりひら)
春は気候ものどかで心底安らぐ穏やかな季節・・・でしょうにねぇ、桜の花さえ気にならなければねぇ。

Spring would make our heart rest so easy... without cherry blossom.

よのなか【世の中】〔名〕＜世の中｜(n.)the world＞／に【に】〔格助〕＜場所｜(prep.)PLACE＞／たえて【絶えて】〔副〕＜全く～ない｜(adv.)not at all＞／さくら【桜】〔名〕＜桜｜(n.)cherry [tree, blossom]＞／の【の】〔格助〕＜主格｜(prep.)SUBJECT＞／なし【なし】〔形ク〕＜存在しない｜(v.)do not exist＞(なかり＝連用形)／き【き】〔助動特殊型〕過去＜～[し]た｜(aux-v.)PAST＞(せ＝未然形)／ば【ば】〔接助〕＜仮定｜(conj.)if＞／はる【春】〔名〕＜春｜(n.)Spring＞／の【の】〔格助〕＜の｜(prep.)'s＞／こころ【心】〔名〕＜心｜(n.)heart＞／は【は】〔格助〕＜は｜(prep.)SUBJECT＞／のどけし【長閑し】〔形ク〕＜のどかだ｜(adj.)feel at ease＞(のどけから＝未然形)／まし【まし】〔助動特殊型〕推量＜～だろうに｜(aux-v.)should＞(まし＝終止形)

[yo-no-naka ni taete sakura no nakari-se-ba haru no kokoro wa nodokekara-mashi]

「あぁ、この世に桜の花がなければよかったのになぁ」とこの詩人は言っているけど、それは「もし桜花がなかったら、どうしよう？」の思いの裏返し。とどのつまりは「こんなにも気になる桜木のある世の中を、神様、どうもありがとう」と言ってるわけです。こういう持って回った形で胸の内を明かすのも、平安時代の貴人たちの一特徴・・・私的好き嫌いをズケズケ声高に訴えて恥も外聞もありゃしないやり口に馴らされた現有世代の詩的ならざる日本人には、むしろ不思議と目新しく映るかも。

"O, that there were no cherry blossom in this world!" the poet says as a reversed expression of "What if there were no cherry flowers?" At the end of the day, he says "Thank God there are cherry trees for us to care so much about!" Such a roundabout way of emotional expression is the hallmark of nobles in the Heian era... might appear strangely novel to the current generation of prosaic Japanese accustomed to shamelessly direct declaration of personal likes and dislikes.

●21●としをへておなじさくらのはなのいろを　そめますものはこころなりけり
　　　年を経て同じ桜の花の色を染め増すものは心なりけり

【春】[悟り]『7)千載集:63』藤原公時(ふじわらのきんとき)
年月が経つほどに、今まで何度も見てきた同じ桜の花の美しさが増して来る思いがするのは、それを見る人間の心が添える彩りなんだなぁ。

As my age accumulates, so do colors of flowers
Tinged with experience stored up in my heart.

とし【年】〔名〕＜年齢｜(n.)age＞／を【を】〔格助〕＜目的格｜(prep.)OBJECT＞／ふ【経】〔自ハ下二〕＜経る｜(v.)grow old＞(へ＝連用形)／て【て】〔接助〕＜順接｜(conj.)and＞／おなじ【同じ】〔形シク〕＜同じ｜(adj.)the same＞(おなじ【き】＝連体形)／さくら【桜】〔名〕＜桜｜(n.)cherry [tree, blossom]＞／の【の】〔格助〕＜の｜(prep.)'s＞／はな【花】〔名〕＜花｜(n.)flowers＞／の【の】〔格助〕＜の｜(prep.)'s＞／いろ【色】〔名〕＜色｜(n.)color＞／を【を】〔格助〕＜目的格｜(prep.)OBJECT＞／そむ【染む】〔自マ四〕＜染める｜(v.)tinge＞(そめ＝連用形)／ます【増す】〔他サ四〕＜増す｜(v.)increase＞(ます＝連体形)／もの【物】〔名〕＜物事｜(n.)a thing＞／は【は】〔係助〕＜主格｜(prep.)SUBJECT＞／こころ【心】〔名〕＜心｜(n.)heart＞／なり【なり】〔助動ナリ型〕断定＜～である｜(aux-v.)be＞(なり＝連用形)／けり【けり】〔助動ラ変型〕詠嘆＜～だったのだなぁ｜(interj.)REALIZATION＞(けり＝終止形)

—春—

[toshi wo he-te onaji sakura no hana no iro wo some-masu mono wa kokoro nari-keri]

「自然は鏡に過ぎない ― 人がそこに見るものは、その人自身の反射投影映像だ」という日本の短歌で幾度となく語り尽くされた自明の理を説いた歌・・・いささか陳腐ではあるものの、それでもやはり真実ではある・・・と同時にこれは「同じ桜の花の色を染め増すものは」の部分を変えるだけでほとんど何にでも使える便利なテンプレート(=ひな型)歌でもある(・・・「同じ夜空の月影をいや増すものは」とか「同じ子供の泣き笑い懐かしむるは」とか・・・)

Nature is just a mirror ― what you see in it is the reflected image of yourself. A truism recounted countless times in Japanese TANKA. Hackneyed as it is, true it still is; useful it also is, since you can use it as an almost universal template by changing 同じ桜の花の色を染め増すものは(onaji sakura no hana no iro wo some-masu mono wa=what adds to the colors of the same old cherry blossom) into 同じ夜空の月影を弥増すものは(onaji yozora no tsuki-kage wo iya-masu mono wa=what adds to the brilliance of the same old moonlight) or into 同じ子供の泣き笑い懐かしむるは(onaji kodomo no naki-warai natsukashimuru wa=what makes us more fond of the same old cries and laughs of small kids).

●22●さくらばなちらさでちよもみてしがな あかぬこころはさてもありやと
　　桜花散らさで千代も見てしがな飽かぬ心は然ても有りやと

【春】[機知]『6)詞花集:35』藤原元真(ふじわらのもとざね)

できることなら、千年もの長きに渡ってずっと散ることのない桜の花というものを見てみたいものだ。たとえそうして咲き続けてもなお見飽きることなく桜花を愛でる心持ちが私に残っているかどうか知りたいものだ。

Eternal flowers of cherry unfailing a thousand years
I'd like to see if they still didn't bore me with overjoy.

さくらばな【桜花】〔名〕<桜の花｜(n.)cherry blossom>／ちる【散る】〔自カ四〕<散る｜(v.)fall>(ちら=未然形)／す【す】〔助動サ下二型〕使役<~[さ]せる｜(aux-v.)CAUSATIVE>(さ=未然形)／で【で】〔接助〕<~することなしに｜(prep.)without ~ing>／ちよ【千代】〔名〕<千年｜(n.)a thousand years>／も【も】〔係助〕<ほども｜(adv.)even>／みる【見る】〔他マ上一〕<見る｜(v.)view>(み=連用形)／てしがな【てしがな】〔終助〕<~[し]たいものだ｜(v.)I'd rather>／あく【飽く】〔自カ四〕<飽きる｜(v.)have had enough of>(あか=未然形)／ず【ず】〔助動特殊型〕打消<~[し]ない｜(adv.)not ~>(ぬ=連体形)／こころ【心】〔名〕<心｜(n.)heart>／は【は】〔係助〕<主格｜(prep.)SUBJECT>／さても【然ても】〔副〕<それでもなお｜(adv.)even then>／あり【あり】〔自ラ変〕<存在する｜(v.)exist>(あり=終止形)／や【や】〔終助〕〔疑問〕(adv.)INTERROGATIVE>／と【と】〔格助〕<内容提示｜(conj.)that ~>

[sakura-bana chirasa-de chiyo mo mi-te-shigana aka-nu kokoro wa sate-mo ari-ya to]

「咲いてすぐ散る 儚さこそが、桜花に飽かぬ恋着の元」という言い古された決まり文句を踏まえつつ、この歌人は「決して散ることなき桜の花の千年鑑賞会」にうつつを抜かして見た上で、「なるほど、ずっと見てれば飽きるわな」と証明してみたい(あるいはひょっとしていつまで見ていても飽きることはないと反証してみたい)と戯れ言めかして歌っています。

Our insatiable affection toward cherry blossom springs from their fleeting existence ― based on this truism, this poet jokingly wants to prove it (or possibly *disprove* it) by indulging in a millennium-long viewing of never-falling flowers of cherry.

—春—

●23● さくらがりあめはふりきぬおなじくは ぬるともはなのかげにかくれむ
桜狩り雨は降り来ぬ同じくは濡るとも花の蔭に隠れむ

【春】[機知]『3)拾遺集:50』詠み人知らず

桜の花見の最中(さいちゅう)に、折悪(おりあ)しく降り出した春の雨…どうせ濡れるなら、軒下(のきした)や傘の下ではなく、木の下に宿って桜色の雫(しずく)に濡れることにしよう。

Rain comes to spoil our joy of cherry-viewing outing.
Get wet, yes I will — preferably in the cherry-dew.

さくらがり【桜狩り】〔名〕<花見|(n.)an outing for cherry flower viewing>／あめ【雨】〔名〕<雨|(n.)rain>／は【は】〔係助〕<主格|(prep.)SUBJECT>／ふりき【降り来】〔自力変〕<降って来る|(v.)come falling down>（ふりき＝連用形）／ぬ【ぬ】〔助動ナ変型〕完了<すでに〜[し]た|(aux-v.)PERFECT TENSE>（ぬ＝終止形）／おなじ【同じ】〔形シク〕<同じ|(adj.)the same>（おなじく＝連用形）／は【は】〔係助〕<仮定|(conj.)if>／ぬる【濡る】〔自ラ下二〕<濡れる|(v.)get wet>（ぬる＝終止形）／とも【とも】〔接助〕<〜だとしても|(conj.)even if>／はな【花】〔名〕<花|(n.)flowers>／の【の】〔格助〕<の|(prep.)'s>／かげ【蔭】〔名〕<陰|(n.)the shade>／に【に】〔格助〕<場所|(prep.)PLACE>／かくる【隠る】〔自ラ下二〕<隠れる|(v.)hide>（かくれ＝未然形）／む【む】〔助動マ四型〕意志<〜するつもりだ|(aux-v.)be going to 〜>（む＝終止形）

[sakura-gari ame wa furi-ki-nu onajiku-wa nuru tomo hana no kage ni kakure-mu]

名うての女たらし藤原実方(ふじわらのさねかた)が満座の貴人連を前に気取った態度で言い放(はな)った歌、と言われています…そして実直なライバル(rival)藤原行成(ふじわらのこうぜい)との口論の元となって、最後に実方は身を滅ぼした、との伝説も残っています…興味が沸(わ)いた人は「実方 and 行成」のキーワード(keywords)でネット検索(ググッて)して見てください。

This pompous declaration is said to have been uttered before a crowd of noble folks from the mouth of the notorious womanizer 藤原実方(Fujiwara-no-Sanekata)... and led to his ultimate ruin through quarrels with his scrupulous rival 藤原行成(Fujiwara-no-Kouzei)... If you get interested, just *GOOGLE* it with the keywords "実方 and 行成".

――――――――――――――――――――――

●24● もろともにあはれとおもへやまざくら はなよりほかにしるひともなし
諸共に哀れと思へ山桜花より外に知る人も無し

【春】[擬人]『5)金葉集:510』行尊(ぎょうそん)

人里離れた山奥に、人知れず咲く桜の花を、こうして独り愛でている、私にもまた友はない…わかってもらえる人もない一人孤独な境涯(きょうがい)を、「あぁ、哀しいね」と慰(なぐさ)め合おうか、人に知られぬ山桜よ。

Let's be mutually compassionate, cherry blossom in the mountain.
No one but ourselves know our true colors.

もろともに【諸共に】〔副〕<一緒に|(adv.)together>／あはれ【あはれ】〔感〕<残念|(n.)a pity>／と【と】〔格助〕<内容提示|(conj.)that 〜>／おもふ【思ふ】〔他ハ四〕<思う|(v.)think>（おもへ＝命令形）／やまざくら【山桜】〔名〕<山に咲く桜|(n.)cherry blossom in the mountain>／はな【花】〔名〕<花|(n.)flowers>／より【より】〔格助〕<比較対象|(prep.)than>／ほか【他】〔名〕<他|(adj.)other>／に【に】〔格助〕<限定|(prep.)LIMITATION>／しる【知る】〔他ラ四〕<知る|(v.)know>（しる＝連体形）／ひと【人】〔名〕<人間|(n.)a human being>／も【も】〔係助〕<〜[で]さえも|(adv.)even>／なし【なし】〔形ク〕<存在しない|(v.)do not exist>（なし＝終止形）

[morotomoni aware to omoe yama-zakura hana yori hoka ni shiru hito mo nashi]

http//zubaraie.com　　　　　　　　　　—Spring—

—春—

仏道修行のために一人山奥へと分け入ったこの歌の作者は、そこで人知れず咲く桜の美と鉢合わせします。こうした「私一人のお気に入り」のおかげで救われる人の魂のいかに多いことか･･･親愛なる自然のはからいに、感謝！

The poet went alone deep into a mountain as a Buddhist ascetic and found himself face to face with the unsung beauty of cherry blossom. "My sole favorite flower" like this will often serve to save human soul... thank you, dear Nature!

─ ─

●25● さけばちるさかねばこひしやまざくら　おもひたえせぬはなのうへかな
　　　　咲けば散る咲かねば恋し山桜思ひ絶えせぬ花の上かな
　　　　　　　　　【春】[溜息]『3)拾遺集:36』敦慶親王女(あつよししんのうのむすめ)

咲いた後には散るのが怖い、咲かずにいると開花が待ち遠しい、
どっちに転んでも心穏やかではいられない、山桜の身の上であることよ。

If in full bloom, we'll feel sad to see them fall.
If still in bud, we can hardly wait to see them come out.
The fortune of cherries never cease to stir up our heart.

さく【咲く】〔自カ四〕＜咲く｜(v.)bloom＞(さけ＝連用形)／ば【ば】〔接助〕＜仮定｜(conj.)if＞／ちる【散る】〔自ラ四〕＜散る｜(v.)fall＞(ちる＝終止形)／さく【咲く】〔自カ四〕＜咲く｜(v.)bloom＞(さか＝未然形)／ず【ず】〔助動特殊型〕打消＜～[し]ない｜(adv.)not ～＞(ね＝已然形)／ば【ば】〔接助〕＜仮定｜(conj.)if＞／こひし【恋し】〔形シク〕＜恋しい｜(v.)long for＞(こひし＝終止形)／やまざくら【山桜】〔名〕＜山に咲く桜｜(n.)cherry blossom in the mountain＞／おもひ【思ひ】〔名〕＜心配事｜(n.)worries＞／たゆ【絶ゆ】〔自ヤ下二〕＜終わる｜(v.)end＞(たえ＝連用形)／す【為】〔補動サ変〕＜する｜(v.)do＞(せ＝未然形)／ず【ず】〔助動特殊型〕打消＜～[し]ない｜(adv.)not ～＞(ぬ＝連体形)／はな【花】〔名〕＜花｜(n.)flowers＞／の【の】〔格助〕＜の｜(prep.)'s＞／うへ【上】〔名〕＜身の上｜(n.)circumstances＞／かな【かな】〔終助〕＜詠嘆｜(interj.)EXCLAMATION＞

[sake-ba chiru saka-ne-ba koishi yama-zakura omoi tae-se-nu hana no ue kana]

ただそれだけでも美しい歌･･･先頃亡くしたばかりの我が子の供養に籠もった山寺で生まれたものだと知れば、なおさら心に沁みる詩。
A song beautiful as it is... much more so with the knowledge that the poet gave birth to it at a mountain temple where she stayed to mourn the child she had lost just recently.

─ ─

★26★ はるごとにはなのさかりはありなめど　あひみむことはいのちなりけり
　　　　春毎に花の盛りは有りなめど相見む事は命なりけり
　　　　　　　　　【春】[悟り]『1)古今集:97』詠み人知らず

毎年春が来れば、花は咲き、やがては散って、を繰り返す。その盛衰のさまを見て、人は、花の命の短さや束の間の美の儚さやこの世の無常を感じ、嘆じるけれど、そうした感慨もみな全てこれ「命」あればこそ･･･死んでしまえばもう何も感じず何も動かず、花も人も心もことごとく「無」に帰するのみ･･･いつまでも同じ春の歓喜に浸り続けることは許されないこの世の中で、それでも束の間の生の躍動に心うち震わせることができるのは、花も、自分も、現にこうして生きているからこそ･･･今年もまた巡り会えた、一度限りのこの春に、感謝。

—Spring—　　　　　　　　-40-　　　　　　　http://zubaraie.com

—春—

Flowers bloom and fall each and every Spring,,
From budding to shining to fading day by day.
This year again I exult in seeing them go by.
Thank God I'm alive to feel the passage of time.

はる【春】〔名〕＜春｜(n.)Spring＞／ごと【毎】〔接尾〕＜それぞれに｜(adv.)each＞／に【に】〔格助〕＜時｜(prep.)TIME＞／はな【花】〔名〕＜花｜(n.)flowers＞／の【の】〔格助〕＜の｜(prep.)'s＞／さかり【盛り】〔名〕＜最盛期｜(n.)the prime＞／は【は】〔格助〕＜は｜(prep.)SUBJECT＞／あり【あり】〔自ラ変〕＜存在する｜(v.)exist＞（あり＝連用形）／ぬ【ぬ】〔助動ナ変型〕確述＜きっと～する｜(adv.)EMPHASIS＞（な＝未然形）／む【む】〔助動マ四型〕推量＜だろう｜(aux-v.)SUPPOSITION＞（め＝已然形）／ど【ど】〔接助〕＜～だけれども｜(conj.)although＞／あひ【相】〔接頭〕＜お互い｜(adv.)together＞／みる【見る】〔他マ上一〕＜出会う｜(v.)meet＞（み＝未然形）／む【む】〔助動マ四型〕婉曲＜意味なし｜(adv.)NO MEANING＞（め＝已然形）／こと【事】〔名〕＜ということ｜(n.)the fact that～＞／は【は】〔格助〕＜は｜(prep.)SUBJECT＞／いのち【命】〔名〕＜生きているということ｜(n.)being alive＞／なり【なり】〔助動ナリ型〕断定＜～である｜(aux-v.)be＞（なり＝連用形）／けり【けり】〔助動ラ変型〕詠嘆＜～だったのだなぁ｜(interj.)REALIZATION＞（けり＝終止形）

[haru-goto-ni hana no sakari wa ari-na-me-do ai-mi-mu koto wa inochi nari-keri]

「花の盛り」に殊更言及するのは、花が散って終わるのを意識すればこそ。衰亡よりは隆盛がいいに決まっているけれど、永遠の隆盛なんてあり得ないのもまた事実。春のいいところは、毎年毎年来ては去り、花が咲いては散る姿と共に、世の栄枯盛衰を我々の心にしっかり焼き付けてくれること。盛りを謳歌するのも落ち目になってうなだれるのも、生きている者だけが味わえる特権 ― 去り行くものの姿を見て、生ける我が身を思うべし。

To make special reference to the "prime" of flowers is to be conscious of the "fall" and "end" of them. It's of course better to rise than fall, but it's also true that nothing could ever keep rising forever. What's good about Spring is that it comes and goes with its prime and decline impressed every year on our memories with flowers. To rejoice in prime and to droop at decline are the privilege of the living — feel being alive by seeing things go by.

――――――――――――――――――――――――――――――

●27●やまざとにちりはてぬべきはなゆゑに　たれとはなくてひとぞまたるる
　　　　山里に散り果てぬべき花故に誰とはなくて人ぞ待たるる

【春】〔願望〕『4)後拾遺集:135』源道済(みなもとのみちなり)

誰ぁれも来ない山里で、折角咲いたのにもうじき人知れず散り果ててしまいそうな桜の花を見ると、「あぁ、誰か(誰でもいゝから、誰か!)早く見に来てくれないかなぁ」とか、思わずジリジリしてしまう。

Flowers are about to fall unseen in distant mountains.
Would somebody (*anybody!*) come before they're gone in vain.

やまざと【山里】〔名〕＜山里｜(n.)the countryside＞／に【に】〔格助〕＜場所｜(prep.)PLACE＞／ちりはつ【散り果つ】〔自夕下二〕＜すっかり散る｜(v.)completely fall＞（ちりはて＝連用形）／ぬ【ぬ】〔助動ナ変型〕確述＜きっと～する｜(adv.)EMPHASIS＞（ぬ＝終止形）／べし【べし】〔助動ク型〕推量＜～にちがいない｜(aux-v.)CONVICTION＞（べき＝連体形）／はな【花】〔名〕＜花｜(n.)flowers＞／ゆゑ【故】〔名〕＜原因｜(n.)a cause＞／に【に】〔格助〕＜原因｜(prep.)REASON＞／たれ【誰】〔代名〕＜誰｜(pron.)who＞／と【と】〔格助〕＜内容提示｜(conj.)that～＞／は【は】〔係助〕＜～に関しては｜(adv.)as for～＞／なし【なし】〔形ク〕＜～というわけではない｜(v.)not that～＞（なく＝連用形）／て【て】〔接助〕＜状態｜(conj.)while＞／ひと【人】〔名〕＜客人｜(n.)a visitor＞／ぞ【ぞ】〔係助〕＜強調｜(adv.)EMPHASIS＞／

—春—

まつ【待つ】〔他タ四〕＜待つ｜(v.)wait＞(また＝未然形)／る【る】〔助動ラ下二型〕自発＜[思わず知らず]そうなる｜(adv.)naturally＞(るる＝連体形係り結び)

[yama-zato ni chiri-hate-nu-beki hana yue ni tare to-wa naku-te hito zo mata-ruru]

実際の桜の前で、ではなく、貴人の邸宅内の屏風絵の情景に触発されて詠まれた歌。他者の経験を通じての代償的感覚とはいえ、その心持ちに嘘はない。正岡子規はこういう「作り事」を鼻でせせら笑ったけど、想像世界の中でしか会えない誰かや何かを思い遣る気持ちを失ったら、この世はひどく耐え難いものになる、とは思いませんか？

A song not sung before real cherry blossom but inspired by the scene on a pictorial screen at a nobleman's residence. Though vicarious, the feeling is quite true. Although 正岡子規(Masaoka Shiki) scorned such make-believe, the world would be an intolerable place indeed if we lacked the ability to feel for someone/something we could only meet in our imagination, don't you think?

★28★はなのいろはうつりにけりないたづらに　わがみよにふるながめせしまに
花の色は移りにけりな徒らに我が身世にふるながめせし間に

【春】【仮託】『1)古今集:113』小野小町(おののこまち)

美しかった花の色も、もう色褪せてしまったみたい・・・結局、何もないままに・・・春の長雨が降るうちに・・・ぼんやりと物思いに沈んで日々を過ごしている間に・・・いつの間にか齢をとってしまったこの私みたいに。

Did flowers fade in vain amid vernal rain?
Do people care no more who cheered and stared so much?
Will feminine phase of mine as soon evaporate off...
As I dream away my youth in fruitless hope?

はな【花】〔名〕＜花｜(n.)flowers＞／の【の】〔格助〕＜の｜(prep.)'s＞／いろ【色】〔名〕＜色｜(n.)color＞／は【は】〔係助〕＜主格｜(prep.)SUBJECT＞／うつる【移る】〔自ラ四〕＜色あせる｜(v.)fade away＞(うつり＝連用形)／ぬ【ぬ】〔助動ナ変型〕完了＜すでに～[し]た｜(aux-v.)PERFECT TENSE＞(に＝連用形)／けり【けり】〔助動ラ変型〕過去＜～[し]た｜(aux-v.)PAST＞(けり＝終止形)／な【な】〔終助〕＜詠嘆(interj.)EXCLAMATION＞／いたづらなり【徒らなり】〔形動ナリ〕＜何の意味もなく｜(adv.)in vain＞(いたづらに＝連用形)／わ【我】〔代名〕＜私｜(pron.)I, myself＞／が【が】〔格助〕＜の｜(prep.)'s＞／み【身】〔名〕＜自身｜(n.)[one]self＞／よ【世】〔名〕＜世間｜(n.)the world＞／に【に】〔格助〕＜場所｜(prep.)PLACE＞／**(A1)ふる【古る・旧る】**〔自ラ上二〕＜経る｜(v.)grow old＞(ふる＝連体形)／**(A2)ながめ【眺め】**〔名〕＜うつろな思い｜(n.)wistful thinking＞／**(B1)ふる【降る】**〔自ラ四〕＜降る｜(v.)fall＞(ふる＝連体形)／**(B2)ながめ【長雨】**〔名〕＜降り続く雨｜(n.)continuous rain＞／す【為】〔他サ変〕＜～する｜(v.)do＞(せ＝未然形)／き【き】〔助動特殊型〕過去＜～[し]た｜(aux-v.)PAST＞(し＝連体形)／ま【間】〔名〕＜間｜(n.)while＞／に【に】〔格助〕＜時｜(prep.)TIME＞

[hana no iro wa utsuri-ni-keri-na itazurani wa-ga mi yo ni furu nagame se-shi ma ni]

これはあらゆる時代の短歌の中でおそらく一番有名なものと言っていいでしょう。この歌のおかげで『古今集』の十八の歌を通じて芸術的に創造されたヴァーチュアル・アイドル(現実ならざる理想の女性像)としての「小野小町」の名と実在感は、完全に確立されたのでした。「小町は架空の存在」とどうして言い切れるのか？・・・第一勅撰集でまず18首も一気に登場した彼女の短歌は、第二の『後撰集』ではたった4首だけ、その後の勅撰集には全く登場しない・・・八代集の最後を飾る『新古今集』に至ってようやく(何人かの歌人たちが彼ら自作の短歌でもって各人各様に)この「いにしえの架空の美女」に6首の献歌を捧げるまでは、ね・・・そう、彼女は間違いなく架空の存在;だけど、それが何？もしここに紹介したこの1首があなたに

とって「真実」の響きを持っていたならば、彼女はあなたにとって「実在」の存在・・・もしあなたがこの詩を現実っぽく感じないとしたら、あなたは「詩歌」の世界の住人じゃない・・・ただそれだけのこと。

Arguably the most famous TANKA of all time, which established the name and presence of 小野小町 (Ono-no-komachi), the virtual idol artistically created via 18 songs in 古今集(Kokin shuu). Why can we be sure 小町(Komachi) was virtual, not real? Well, after the initial burst of 18 poems in the 1st Imperial TANKA anthology, her name appeared with only 4 poems in the 2nd anthology 後撰集(Go-sen shuu)... thereafter totally absent, until some poets paid their respective tribute to this ancient imaginary beauty with 6 additional creations of their own in the 8th anthology 新古今集(Shin-Kokin shuu)... fictional she sure is, but what're the odds? If this particular poem sounds real to you, she *is* real to you... and if you don't feel reality in this poem, the world of poetry is no place for you.

・・・・・・・・・・・・・・・・・・・・・・・・・・・・

《仮名漢字異世界つなぐ「懸詞」》

「我が身世にふるながめ」の同じ音から「世に降る長雨(＝外は延々雨続き)」と「我が身世に旧る＋眺め(＝次第に老い行く自分を見て溜息)」へと分岐して行く意味の流れは、この魅惑的な歌の魔法の神髄、そこから「長雨で足が遠のいた人々にその美しさを見てもらえぬままに花盛りも過ぎようとする哀しい桜の風景」と同時に「何人もの男たちが来ては去るのをぼんやり見送りながら女盛りも過ぎようとする哀しい美女の溜息」に同時に言及する・・・こうした同音異義語の多義性を活かした詩的技巧の「懸詞」が日本語の詩文にも散文にも豊富に見られるのは、数が少ない漢字の世界に同音異義語が溢れ返っているからこそ。

《懸詞(kake-kotoba) ― a bridge over different meanings in 漢字(kanji＝Chinese character) via same sound in ひらがな(hiragana＝Japanese cursive syllabary)》

The same flow of sound 我が身世にふるながめ(wa-ga mi yo ni furu nagame) diverging into two semantic streams of 世に降る長雨(yo ni furu nagame＝a long spell of rain in the world outside) and 我が身世に旧る(wa-ga mi yo ni furu＝I advance in years) 眺め(nagame＝I vaguely see) is the magical essence of this charming TANKA, which simultaneously refers to the sad sight of cherry blossom passing its prime as long rain prevents people from coming out to cherish it, and to the sad sigh of a beautiful woman passing her prime as she vacantly watches men come and go through her. This poetic technique of homonymous equivocation called 懸詞(kake-kotoba＝bridging words via same sounds) is found in abundance in verse and prose in Japanese language, due to the nature of 漢字(kanji＝Chinese characters) being so small in number and so profuse with homonyms.

―――――――――――――――――――――――

★29★ひさかたのひかりのどけきはるのひに　しづこころなくはなのちるらむ

久方の光長閑けき春の日に静心無く花の散るらむ

【春】[自然]『1)古今集:84』紀友則(きのとものり)

穏やかな春の日、のどかに流れる時間の中で、桜の花びらだけが、落ち着かぬ心持ちで散るを急ぐのは、いったいどうしてなんだろう。

In the gently restful sunshine on a Spring day,

So restlessly cherry flowers alone are falling down...

I wonder why? Can't you... can't we... stay here more?

—春—

ひさかたの【久方の】【枕詞】＜意味なし｜(adj.)NO MEANING＞／ひかり【光】〔名〕＜光｜(n.)the light＞／のどけし【長閑し】〔形ク〕＜のどかだ｜(adj.)feel at ease＞（のどけき＝連体形）／はる【春】〔名〕＜春｜(n.)Spring＞／の【の】〔格助〕＜の｜(prep.)'s＞／ひ【日】〔名〕＜日｜(n.)a day＞／に【に】〔格助〕＜時｜(prep.)TIME＞／しづこころ【静心】〔名〕＜落ち着いた心持ち｜(n.)peace of mind＞／なし【なし】〔形ク〕＜存在しない｜(v.)do not exist＞（なく＝連用形）／はな【花】〔名〕＜花｜(n.)flowers＞／の【の】〔格助〕＜主格｜(prep.)SUBJECT＞／ちる【散る】〔自ラ四〕＜散る｜(v.)fall＞（ちる＝終止形）／らむ【らむ】〔助動ラ四型〕現在推量＜〜だろう｜(aux-v.)SUPPOSITION＞（らむ＝連体形係り結び）

[hisakata no hikari nodokeki haru no hi ni shizu-kokoro naku hana no chiru-ramu]

あらゆる時代の短歌の中で、ひょっとしたら最も多くの人々に愛された歌かもしれません。すべてが暖かく静かに流れる春に、桜の花だけが(自然界一の人気者なのに)散るを急いでは我々の元から去って行くさまを見て、「もっと、いられないの？」と詩人は問うけれど、花に向けてのその問い掛けは、我々自身へと跳ね返り、散る花を惜しむと同時に、いつかは死すべき我が身の運命を悼んでいる自分自身に気付く‥‥哀しく美しいこだまの歌です。文法的には、この短歌の末尾の推量助動詞「**らむ**」(連体形係り結び)は(省略されている)疑問副詞「**などか**」＝どうして‥‥なのか？」と組み合わせねば意味をなしません‥‥そんな重要な語句を何故省略するのか？ ― 単純なことです：五・七・五・七・七の緊縮字数制限の中ではそんなものを挿入する余地がないからです。この「**らむ**」と「(見えない)**などか**」の組み合わせは、真面目な学生なら「知らなかった」では済まない平安古文の頻出事項です。

Possibly the most popular TANKA of all time. In Spring when all is warm and calm, cherry blossom — the dearest of all Nature — keep busy falling and parting from us. "Why can't you stay?" the poet asks — the question toward the flowers echoes back to ourselves, ending up mourning our own mortality as well as missing the falling flowers... what a sad and beautiful echo. From grammatical point of view, the auxiliary verb of supposition **らむ**(ramu) at the end of this poem makes no sense without being combined with the *omitted* adverb of question **などか**(nado[ka]=why)... why the omission? — simply because there is no space to insert it in the tight stream of 5-7-5-7-7. This combination of **らむ** (ramu) with *invisible* **などか**(nado[ka]) is a frequent phenomenon of Heianese Japanese no serious student could afford to be ignorant of.

・・・・・・・・・・・・・・・・・・・・・・
《「言霊」や「枕詞」に宿りける》

「**久方の**」で始まり「**光**」がそれに続くこの短歌の冒頭部に見られる「**久方の** ― **光**」の取り合わせは、奈良時代から引き継がれた定型表現で、「**久方の**」に実質的な意味はなく、後続の「**光**」を導くだけの役割を担っている。こうした定型的導入語句(通例5字で歌の冒頭に置かれるもの)を「枕詞」と呼ぶ。この種の枕詞の語源は(さらにはその語義さえも！)『古今集』の時代にはすでにもう大方わからなくなっていた ― 枕詞は、言葉や名前に宿る魂としての「言霊」が至る所で意識されていた時代の名残りを神秘的な形で留める過去の遺物だったのである‥‥従って、それに関する理解も平安期以降はデタラメで、冒頭でなく文中に置かれた枕詞だの、直後にあるべき語句と離ればなれの枕詞だのといった「インチキ枕詞もどき」の数々が乱発されて収拾が付かなくなってしまった。真の枕詞は奈良時代のものだけ、と思っておけばよい。

《枕詞(makura-kotoba＝pillow words) ―
remnants of ancient 言霊(kotodama＝spirits inherent in words and names)》

This poem starts with the term **久方の**(hisakata no) followed by **光**(hikari=the sun). This "**久方の** ― **光**" combination is a fixed tradition since the Nara(奈良) era, in which **久方の**(hisakata no) means practically nothing but functions as a formal introduction to the following term **光**(hikari=the sun): such a formal introductory term — usually 5 syllabled and positioned at the top of the song — is called 枕詞(makura-kotoba=a pillow word). The origin (or even the meaning!) of most 枕詞

(makura-kotoba) had already been lost track of in the years of 古今集(Kokin shuu) — they were the mysterious remnants of the years when 言霊(kotodama＝spirits inherent in words and names) made their presence felt in so many ways. It follows from this that the understanding of 枕詞 (makura-kotoba) after the Heian(平安) era left so much to be desired, resulting in such pseudo-枕詞 (makura-kotoba) as would be placed in the middle (not at the top) of a song or would be placed apart from the term to be followed by the 枕詞(makura-kotoba), ending up in total chaos: it is safe to assume that the true 枕詞(makura-kotoba) were only those dating back to the Nara(奈良) era.

─────────────────────────────

★30★さくらちるこのしたかぜはさむからで　そらにしられぬゆきぞふりける
桜散る木の下風は寒からで空に知られぬ雪ぞ降りける

【春】[機知]『3』拾遺集:64』紀貫之(きのつらゆき)

満開だった桜も散る頃になると、木の下に立って惜しみ見送る私に吹き付ける風も
まるで冷たさを感じさせぬ春の気配・・・なのに頭上には季節外れの雪が舞う・・・
深まる春を目にも肌にも鮮やかに印象付ける、桜吹雪の華麗な舞い。

Flowers falling down from cherry trees above
Look just like snow in strangely warm storm.

さくら【桜】〔名〕＜桜｜(n.)cherry [tree, blossom]＞／ちる【散る】〔自ラ四〕＜散る｜(v.)fall＞(ちる＝連体形)／こ【木】〔名〕＜樹木｜(n.)a tree＞／の【の】〔格助〕＜の｜(prep.)'s＞／したかぜ【下風】〔名〕＜下を吹く風｜(n.)the wind underneath＞／は【は】〔係助〕＜主格｜(prep.)SUBJECT＞／さむし【寒し】〔形ク〕＜寒い｜(adj.)cold＞(さむから＝未然形)／で【で】〔接助〕＜～することなしに｜(prep.)without ～ing＞／そら【空】〔名〕＜空｜(n.)the sky＞／に【に】〔格助〕＜場所｜(prep.)PLACE＞／しる【知る】〔他ラ四〕＜知｜(v.)know＞(しら＝未然形)／る【る】〔助動ラ下二型〕受身＜～[さ]れる｜(aux-v.)PASSIVE VOICE＞(れ＝未然形)／ず【ず】〔助動特殊型〕打消＜～[し]ない｜(adv.)not ～＞(ぬ＝連体形)／ゆき【雪】〔名〕＜雪｜(n.)snow＞／ぞ【ぞ】〔係助〕＜強調｜(adv.)EMPHASIS＞／ふる【降る】〔自ラ四〕＜降る｜(v.)fall＞(ふり＝連用形)／けり【けり】〔助動ラ変型〕詠嘆＜～だったのだなぁ｜(interj.)REALIZATION＞(ける＝連体形係り結び)

[sakura chiru ko-no-shita-kaze wa samukara-de sora ni shira-re-nu yuki zo furi-keru]

空に暖かな風が舞う時に、雪が降るなんてあり得ない ― もし風が暖かければ、舞い飛ぶ雪は、春の嵐の中で踊る桜の花びら ― 『古今集』に収められた(その主編者たる紀貫之の手になる)短歌最初期の傑作の一つで、桜花の散るさまを「暖かい春の雪」になぞらえる伝統的イメージは、この歌によって確立された。

No snow falls with warm wind in the sky: if the wind is warm, the snow is cherry flowers dancing in Spring storm. One of the earliest masterpieces in 古今集(Kokin shuu) by its main editor 紀貫之(Ki-no-Tsurayuki) which established the traditional image of falling flowers of cherry as warm snowfall in Spring.

─────────────────────────────

—春—

●31● さくらばなちりぬるかぜのなごりには みづなきそらになみぞたちける
桜花散りぬる風の名残りには水無き空に波ぞ立ちける

【春】[機知]『1)古今集:89』紀貫之(きのつらゆき)

桜の花が散ってしまった後の空には、風に舞う花びらたちが筋を成して、
まるで水もない空に波が立っているように見える。

Cherry flowers have all gone, leaving remnants in the wind:
In the sky where there's no water, cherry-white waves surging in.

さくらばな【桜花】[名]<桜の花 | (n.)cherry blossom>／ちる【散る】[自ラ四]<散る | (v.)fall>（ちり＝連用形)／ぬ【ぬ】[助動ナ変型]完了<すでに～[し]た | (aux-v.)PERFECT TENSE>（ぬる＝連体形)／かぜ【風】[名]<風 | (n.)wind>／の【の】[格助]<の | (prep.)'s>／なごり【名残り】[名]<残ったもの | (n.)remnants>／に【に】[格助]<様態 | (prep.)like>／は【は】[係助]<～に関しては | (adv.)as for ～>／みづ【水】[名]<水 | (n.)water>／なし【なし】[形ク]<存在しない | (v.)do not exist>（なき＝連体形)／そら【空】[名]<空 | (n.)the sky>／に【に】[格助]<場所 | (prep.)PLACE>／なみ【波】[名]<波 | (n.)waves>／ぞ【ぞ】[係助]<強調 | (adv.)EMPHASIS>／たつ【立つ】[自タ四]<立つ | (v.)surge up>（たち＝連用形)／けり【けり】[助動ラ変型]詠嘆<～だったのだなぁ | (interj.)REALIZATION>（ける＝連体形係り結び)

[sakura-bana chiri-nuru kaze no nagori ni-wa mizu naki sora ni nami zo tachi-keru]

風の中を散る桜花の絵画的イメージの確立を目指して紀貫之が行なったもう一つの野心的な試みの成果
(一つ前の歌ほど成功したとは言えないけど)。
Another ambitious attempt (with less success) by 紀貫之(Ki-no-Tsurayuki) to establish picturesque image of falling cherry flowers in the sky.

●32● さくらちるはなのところははるながら ゆきぞふりつつきえがてにする
桜散る花の所は春ながら雪ぞ降りつつ消えがてにする

【春】[謎掛]『1)古今集:75』承均(じょうきん)

桜の花びら舞い散る春の大地は、季節外れの雪が降ってはなかなか消えずにいるような、
不思議な景色だなぁ。

Where the flowers fall down from cherry trees
There also falls snow unmelted in Spring warmth.

さくら【桜】[名]<桜 | (n.)cherry [tree, blossom]>／ちる【散る】[自ラ四]<散る | (v.)fall>（ちる＝連体形)／はな【花】[名]<花 | (n.)flowers>／の【の】[格助]<の | (prep.)'s>／ところ【所】[名]<所 | (n.)the place>／は【は】[係助]<～に関しては | (adv.)as for ～>／はる【春】[名]<春 | (n.)Spring>／ながら【ながら】[接助]<～ではあるが | (conj.)although>／ゆき【雪】[名]<雪 | (n.)snow>／ぞ【ぞ】[係助]<強調 | (adv.)EMPHASIS>／ふる【降る】[自ラ四]<降る | (v.)fall>（ふり＝連用形)／つつ【つつ】[接助]<～し ながら | (conj.)as>／きゆ【消ゆ】[自ヤ下二]<消える | (v.)disappear>（きえ＝未然形)／かつ【かつ】[補動タ下二]<～に堪える | (aux-v.)be able to endure>（がて＝連用形)／ず【ず】[助動特殊型]打消<～[し]ない | (adv.)not ～>（に＝連用形)／す【為】[補動サ変]<する | (v.)do>（する＝連体形係り結び)

[sakura chiru hana no tokoro wa haru nagara yuki zo furi-tsutsu kie-gate-ni suru]

先に紹介した紀貫之の手になる二つの歌が趣向も鮮やかに空高く舞い飛んでいたのと対照的に、この無
名の歌僧の短歌はごくごく真面目に地を這いながら、桜の花びら舞い落ちる地面の上に奇妙に消え残った

—春—

春の雪、という一見辻褄(つじつま)が合わなさそうな情景を説明してくれています。
Unlike the preceding two by 紀貫之(Ki-no-Tsurayuki) that stylishly flew high up in the sky, this TANKA by an obscure 歌僧(kasou＝verse-making bonze) stays sober down on the ground, explaining an apparently incoherent scene of Spring snow strangely remaining on the falling flowers of cherry.

●33● けさみればよるのあらしにちりはてて にはこそはなのさかりなりけれ
今朝見れば夜の嵐に散り果てて庭こそ花の盛りなりけれ

【春】[機知]『5)金葉集:58』徳大寺実能(とくだいじさねよし)
昨日までは木々の上に咲き誇っていた桜の花びらが、夜の嵐ですっかり散らされて、
今朝見てみれば、桜花満開の舞台は、樹上から庭の土の上へと移り変わってしまったなぁ。

I woke up this morning to find cherry flowers in full bloom
Blown by wind at night to flourish again on the garden.

けさ【今朝】〔名〕＜今朝｜(n.)this morning＞／みる【見る】〔他マ上一〕＜見る｜(v.)view＞(みれ＝連用形)／ば【ば】〔接助〕＜～したところ｜(conj.)when＞／よる【夜】〔名〕＜夜｜(n.)the night＞／の【の】〔格助〕＜の｜(prep.)'s＞／あらし【嵐】〔名〕＜嵐｜(n.)the storm＞／に【に】〔格助〕＜原因｜(prep.)REASON＞／ちりはつ【散り果つ】〔自夕下二〕＜すっかり散る｜(v.)completely fall＞(ちりはて＝連用形)／て【て】〔接助〕＜順接｜(conj.)and＞／には【庭】〔名〕＜庭｜(n.)the garden＞／こそ【こそ】〔係助〕＜強調｜(adv.)EMPHASIS＞／はな【花】〔名〕＜花｜(n.)flowers＞／の【の】〔格助〕＜の｜(prep.)'s＞／さかり【盛り】〔名〕＜最盛期｜(n.)the prime＞／なり【なり】〔助動ナリ型〕断定＜～である｜(aux-v.)be＞(なり＝連用形)／けり【けり】〔助動ラ変型〕詠嘆＜～だったのだなぁ｜(interj.)REALIZATION＞(けれ＝已然形係り結び)

[kesa mire-ba yoru no arashi ni chiri-hate-te niwa koso hana no sakari nari-kere]

一つ前の(想像力に欠けた)短歌と同じく、この歌の舞台もまた「地面の上」・・・だが、その情景に「時」の要素をも加えている点で、こちらの歌の方が格段に優れている。実際、桜の花は、一夜明けたら風に散らされて地面を覆う桜色の絨毯(じゅうたん)と化していることも珍しくない。そのさまを「第二の満開が庭に来た」とするこの歌人の趣向は、いかにも『金葉集』好みの「どうだ！」と言わんばかりの華麗さ・・・その華麗さに人が飽きて掃(は)き清めてしまうまで、庭で第二の満開を迎えた桜の花びらたちは、しばらくそこに留(とど)まり続けることだろう。
The stage — on the ground — is the same as in the previous prosaic TANKA, but this one is far superior in that it incorporates the element of "time" into the scene. In fact, cherry blossom will often be swept out of sight overnight, only to be found covering the ground as a cherry-colored carpet, which this poet stylishly calls "the second prime on the garden": with such pompous splendor perfectly fitting to the taste of 金葉集(Kinnyou shuu), stay there it will until humans get tired and sweep it away.

●34● さくらいろのにはのはるかぜあともなし とはばぞひとのゆきとだにみむ
桜色の庭の春風跡も無し訪はばぞ人の雪とだに見む

【春】[謎掛]『8)新古今集:134』藤原定家(ふじわらのていか(さだいえ))
木々を離れた桜の花びらが春風に吹かれて我が家の庭一面を真っ白い雪のように覆い尽くしている・・・のに、その雪のような桜色の絨毯(じゅうたん)には、いまだに訪問客の足跡一つ、付いていない・・・
桜と雪の白紛(しろまぎ)れ、そんな錯覚の面白さも、我が家を訪れて驚いてくれるお客さんあればこその愉悦だというのに・・・寂しいなぁ。

―春―

In the garden tinged with cherry-white
No trace of visitor is left by the Spring wind.
Unless someone comes to tread on the white
Mistake for snow we can't together.

さくらいろ【桜色】〔名〕＜桜の色｜(adj.)cherry-colored＞／の【の】〔格助〕＜の｜(prep.)'s＞／には【庭】〔名〕＜庭｜(n.)the garden＞／の【の】〔格助〕＜の｜(prep.)'s＞／はるかぜ【春風】〔名〕＜春風｜(n.)Spring wind＞／あと【跡】〔名〕＜痕跡｜(n.)a vestige＞／も【も】〔係助〕＜意味なし｜(adv.)NO MEANING＞／なし【なし】〔形〕＜存在しない｜(v.)do not exist＞（なし＝終止形）／とふ【訪ふ】〔他ハ四〕＜訪れる｜(v.)visit＞（とは＝未然形）／ば【ば】〔接助〕＜仮定｜(conj.)if＞／ぞ【ぞ】〔係助〕＜強調｜(adv.)EMPHASIS＞／ひと【人】〔名〕＜客人｜(n.)a visitor＞／の【の】〔格助〕＜主格｜(prep.)SUBJECT＞／ゆき【雪】〔名〕＜雪｜(n.)snow＞／と【と】〔格助〕＜資格｜(prep.)as＞／だに【だに】〔副助〕＜意味なし｜(adv.)NO MEANING＞／みる【見る】〔他マ上一〕＜見る｜(v.)view＞（み＝未然形）／む【む】〔助動マ四型〕推量＜だろう｜(aux-v.)SUPPOSITION＞（む＝連体形係り結び）

[sakura-iro no niwa no haru-kaze ato mo nashi towa-ba zo hito no yuki to dani mi-mu]

庭は「春の雪」(木々から散った桜の花びら)で白く覆われているが、その「雪」には踏みしめられた跡もない；この庭にやって来て「雪と桜の白紛れ」を作者と一緒に楽しんでくれる客人の足跡は、無いのである。ほとんどの読者は「跡も無し」の言い回しを見て「桜の花は跡形も無く散ってしまった」と解釈するだろう・・・が、もし本当に花の痕跡もないならば、そんな庭に(そしてこの詩に)何の面白味があるというのか？そうした思い違いをする読者は、この短歌のカギになる語「庭(の春風)」をうっかり見逃した上で、何も考えずに「春風」がすでに桜花を跡形も無く視界から掻き消してしまったものと決め込んでしまうのである・・・だが、この詩人が「空」ではなく「庭」と言うからには、彼は自らの詩の舞台を「空中」ではなく「大地」に定めているはずだ。そして、平安時代の詩的伝統に照らして言えば、「大地の上の桜の白いじゅうたん」は「不思議に暖かい春の雪」と錯覚してくれなければ話にならない。その由緒ある白紛れの錯覚は、しかし、誰か客人が来て詩人と共にこれを賞美してくれないことには、面白くも何ともないのだ・・・が、彼には客人の一人もいない・・・そのことを示すのが「跡も無し」(桜の花びらの織り成す白い春の雪の上には、客人の付けた足跡の一つも無い)」である ― 桜のじゅうたんの上に人が下り立ったとして、実際そこに雪の上のような足跡が残るか残らないか、という事実性の検証など必要ない。これはそういう詩、第八番目の勅撰和歌集『新古今集』の典型的作品 ― 純然たる想像力の産物であって、事実性など歯牙にも掛けないし、ましてや正岡子規が大騒ぎした「！写実的描写！」になど鼻も引っ掛けぬ短歌なのである・・・子規が烈しく嫌悪し軽蔑したのも当然と言えるこの歌の作者は、藤原定家 ― 『新古今集』の編者の一人であるとともに、もう一つの(第九代)勅撰和歌集『新勅撰集』を単独で撰進し、私撰短歌集としてあの有名な『小倉百人一首』を作り上げた人でもある。明治期の子規が、平安調短歌の高度に洗練された虚構性を徹底的に「クソ！ゴミカス！」呼ばわりして人々に実際そう信じ込ませるのに成功してしまったせいで、この本の中で皆さんに紹介しているような短歌の数々は、もう丸々一世紀以上の長い間まともに顧みられることもないまま放置され続けているわけである・・・モッタイナイ！(・・・まぁ、それにしてもこの定家の短歌はややややこし過ぎだけどね)

The garden is covered white with *Spring snow* – petals of cherry fallen from the trees – but the "*snow*" is still left untrodden, without any footsteps of a visitor coming to relish the confusing view of the garden together with the poet. Most readers will mistake the phrase 跡も無し (ato mo nashi＝there is no trace) as meaning "there is no trace of *cherry flowers*": if there was really no trace of flowers, what fun is there in the garden or in this poem? Such readers simply miss the key term of this TANKA — "庭(の春風)：niwa [no haru-kaze]＝Spring breeze in the garden" and thoughtlessly decide that the 春風 (haru-kaze＝Spring breeze) has already swept cherry flowers completely out of sight... to the extent that

—春—

the poet says 庭(niwa＝the garden) as opposed to 空(sora=the sky), he has set his poetic stage not in the air but on the ground. And the Heianese poetic tradition dictates that the white cherry carpet on the ground should be confused with strangely warm snow in Spring. That time-honored confusion, though, should only be felt interesting with some guest rejoicing with the poet... he's got none, which the poem shows by the phrase 跡も無し(ato mo nashi＝there is no footstep of a visitor left on the Spring snow of cherry flowers) — it doesn't matter if actual trace of human foot may or may not be left on the cherry-carpet as on actual snow. This is such a poem, typical of the 8th great Imperial anthology 新古今集(Shin-Kokin shuu) — a pure product of imagination without any regard to reality, let alone photorealistic depiction 正岡子規(Masaoka Shiki) made so much of... no wonder he vehemently hated and despised this author 藤原定家(Fujiwara-no-Teika), who was one of the co-editors of 新古今集 (Shin-Kokin shuu), the sole editor of another (9th) Imperial TANKA anthology 新勅撰集(Shin-chokusen shuu) and the legendary personal anthology called 小倉百人一首(Ogura hyakunin isshu). Ever since 子規(Shiki)'s successful smear campaign in the Meiji(明治) era against highly sophisticated fictional nature of Heianese TANKA, such works as are picked out and shown you here in this book have been miserably left out of any serious consideration for more than a whole century... what a waste!
(...*Although this TANKA by Teika is a little too complicated to be charming for me*...)
《度を超して解けぬ謎々誰そ好むむ》

「＜桜＞色の＜庭＞の春風」は、300年前に「＜雪＞色の＜木の下＞風」や「＜水＞色の＜空＞の春風」を華麗に吹かせて見せた紀貫之に対抗すべく、藤原定家が試みた想像世界の再構築。平安調短歌世界の全てを知り尽くした名人の中の名人定家ならではの珠玉芸、とも言えるが、それを読み取る読者の側にも平安調短歌世界へのそれなり以上の習熟が求められる「極度に厳しい和歌力審査試験」となっている。見事パスする人の数は極端に少なかろうが、この種の試験に「合格して喜ぶ」人と「落第して不機嫌になる」人々とどちらが多いか、後者が前者をどれほど激しく毛嫌いするか(そして、正岡子規の如く「死ね！」と叫ぶか)、その程度の想像力なら、和歌のイロハも知らぬ現代日本人にも備わっていることだろう・・・その「門外漢の不機嫌さ」と、平安調短歌を支えた「京都の御公家の時代の終わり」を考え合わせれば、優雅なる平安調短歌が(鎌倉最初期の)『新古今集』と共にほぼ死に絶えた理由も、すんなり納得できることだろう。
《who's gonna love insoluble riddles?》

藤原定家(Fujiwara-no-Teika)'s ＜桜＞色の＜庭＞の春風 (＜sakura＞-iro no ＜**niwa**＞ no haru-kaze＝＜cherry-white＞ Spring wind in ＜**the garden**＞) is the re-imagination of ＜雪＞色の ＜木の下＞風 (＜yuki＞-iro no ＜**ko-no-shita**＞-kaze＝＜snow-white＞ wind ＜**under the cherry tree**＞) and ＜水＞色の＜空＞の春風(＜mizu＞-iro no ＜**sora**＞ no haru-kaze＝＜water-colored＞ Spring wind ＜**in the sky**＞) pompously stirred up by 紀貫之(Ki-no-Tsurayuki) 300 years before, only possible by the grand master 定家(Teika) who knew the world of Heianese TANKA inside out, whose correct interpretation requires of its readers more than considerable understanding of the poetic world of the Heian era... an acid test of TANKA literacy very few would ever pass. Even those Japanese who haven't got the slightest idea what TANKA really is would still be able to imagine the ridiculous disparity between the number of "those rejoicing in passing the test" and "those grumbling at failing the test" and the vehement hatred of the former by the latter — and how they would cry "*To hell with it!*" like 正岡子規(Masaoka Shiki) did... such laypersons' tantrum, along with the end of the age of the nobles in 京都(Kyoto) who used to form the background of Heianese poetry, would be enough to convince you of the reason why the elegant verse of the Heian era became virtually extinct with 新古今集(Shin-Kokin shuu) published at the dawn of the Kamakura(鎌倉) era.

—春—

●35● あさぢはらぬしなきやどのさくらばな　こころやすくやかぜにちるらむ
　　　浅茅原主無き宿の桜花心安くや風に散るらむ

【春】[擬人]『3)拾遺集:62』恵慶(えぎょう)

草木もまばらな野原の中の、主人もない宿に寂しく咲いた桜の花が、風に散っている。
見る人もない今、いったいどんな気持ちなのだろう、心穏やかではないだろうに。

On a field where even grass is sparse,
In the garden of a lonely house deserted by its host,
Flowers of cherry trees, are you feeling at ease?
Falling down and whirling in the wind alone.

あさぢはら【浅茅原】[名]<低木もまばらな野原 | (n.)a field with occasional bushes>／ぬし【主】[名]<主人 | (n.)the host>／なし【なし】[形ク]<存在しない | (v.)do not exist>（なき＝連体形）／やど【宿】[名]<家屋 | (n.)the house>／の【の】[格助]<の | (prep.)'s>／さくらばな【桜花】[名]<桜の花 | (n.)cherry blossom>／こころやすし【心安し】[形ク]<落ち着いた心持ちで | (adv.)peacefully>（こころやすく＝連用形）／や【や】[係助]<疑問 | (adv.)INTERROGATIVE>／かぜ【風】[名]<風 | (n.)wind>／に【に】[格助]<原因 | (prep.)REASON>／ちる【散る】[自ラ四]<散る | (v.)fall>（ちる＝連体形）／らむ【らむ】[助動ラ四型]現在推量<〜だろう | (aux-v.)SUPPOSITION>(らむ＝連体形係り結び)

　　　　[asaji-hara nushi naki yado no sakura-bana kokoro-yasuku ya kaze ni chiru-ramu]

この歌人(恵慶法師)は次から次へと哀しい歌ばかり詠んだ人 — いわば「お涙頂戴名人」です…それでもやはり、この歌の情景はほんと寂しげですね…皆さん、どうぞ御用心 — この人の放つ「袖濡らし歌」、これから先にもまだ二つほど登場しますから。

This poet, 恵慶法師(Egyou houshi), made one sad poem after another — a master of tear-squeezers, I should say. Still, the scene is real sad... be prepared, for there'll be two more sleeve-soppers from the same poet coming up later!

——————————————————————————

●36● いにしへはちるをやひとのおしみけむ　はなこそいまはむかしこふらし
　　　古へは散るをや人の惜しみけむ花こそ今は昔恋ふらし

【春】[擬人]『3)拾遺集:1279』藤原伊尹(ふじわらのこれただ)

かつては花が散るのを人が惜しんだものを、今やその人がもういないことを花の方が惜しんで、ありし日のことを懐かしく思い出しているようだ。

How much missed was the cherry blossom in days gone by.
Now the cherry may be missing the one who used to miss it.

いにしへ【古へ】[名]<昔 | (n.)the past>／は【は】[係助]<〜に関しては | (adv.)as for 〜>／ちる【散る】[自ラ四]<散る | (v.)fall>（ちる＝連体形）／を【を】[格助]<目的格 | (prep.)OBJECT>／や【や】[係助]<疑問 | (adv.)INTERROGATIVE>／ひと【人】[名]<人間 | (n.)a human being>／の【の】[格助]<主格 | (prep.)SUBJECT>／をしむ【惜しむ】[他マ四]<惜しく思う | (v.)miss>（おしみ＝連用形）／けむ【けむ】[助動マ四型]過去推量<〜[し]たのだろう | (aux-v.)PAST SUPPOSITION>(けむ＝連体形係り結び)／はな【花】[名]<花 | (n.)flowers>／こそ【こそ】[係助]<強調 | (adv.)EMPHASIS>／いま【今】[副]<今 | (adv.)now>／は【は】[係助]<〜に関しては | (adv.)as for 〜>／むかし【昔】[名]<昔 | (n.)the past>／こふ【恋ふ】[他ハ上二]<懐かしく思い出す | (v.)miss>（こふ＝終止形）／らし【らし】[助動特殊型]推定<〜のようだ | (adv.)it seems that>(らし＝已然形係り結び)

―春―

[inishie wa chiru wo-ya hito no oshimi-kemu hana koso ima-wa mukashi kou-rashi]

大勢の友人たちを前にして、この歌人は、つい最近亡くなった共通の友人の思い出を偲びつつ、この歌を高々と詠み上げます。一同とともにその死者を悼んでくれるその花は、やがて彼らの全員に哀悼を捧げることになるのでしょう・・・彼らの喜び・悲しみを知るたった一人の生存者として。

The poet, in front of lots of his friends, rhymes out this song in memory of their common friend who passed away recently. The same flower that mourns the dead along with the company will soon mourn them all as the sole surviving witness of their joy and sorrow.

・・・・・・・・・・・・・・・・・・・・・・・・・・・

《「歌の華」斯くぞ定めし「八代集」》

平安調短歌がただ単に「花」と言う時、その指し示す花は「桜」である。この事実からも容易に想像が付く通り、日本の短歌世界で最も人気のある花が「桜」であることに議論の余地はなく、八代集約9500首の中で310回も登場する(この数字には単なる「花」として言及される「桜花」は含まれていないことに注意!)・・・以下に示すリストは、八代集に登場する自然界の人気者たちとそれぞれの登場回数である・・・＜花＞「さくら：桜」310／「うめ：梅」148／「をみなへし：女郎花」82／「きく：菊」70／「あやめ：菖蒲」60／「うのはな：卯の花(＝ウツギ)」50／「ふぢ：藤」38＋「ふぢなみ：藤波(＝藤の花が風に揺れるさま)」22＝総数60(参考：「ふぢごろも：藤衣＝喪服の意」20)・・・＜鳥＞「ほととぎす：子規・郭公・時鳥・杜鵑・不如帰」268／「かり：雁」120／「うぐひす：鶯」104・・・＜風＞700超・・・＜月＞900超・・・＜虫＞「むし：虫(全般)」76／「なつむし・ほたる：夏虫(＝蛍)」34／「せみ・うつせみ：蝉・空蝉」27／「ひぐらし：蜩」22／「きりぎりす：蟋蟀(・・・コオロギのこと)」18

《things of poetic interest in Nature popular among
八代集(Hachidai shuu＝8 great Imperial TANKA anthologies)》

When Heianese TANKA simply say 花(hana＝flowers), they refer to 桜(sakura＝cherry blossom). As can be easily inferred from this, the most popular flower in Japanese TANKA is inarguably 桜(sakura), with 310 appearance in some 9,500 poems in 八代集(Hachidai shuu): be advised this does not include those 桜花(sakura-bana＝cherry flowers) which are referred to by the simple name of 花(hana)... The following is the list of the popular things of Natural interest appearing in 八代集(Hachidai shuu) with respective numbers of appearance...＜花：hana＝flowers＞「桜(さくら)：sakura＝cherry blossom」310／「梅(うめ)：ume＝Japanese apricots, or plum」148／「女郎花(をみなへし)：ominaeshi(ladies' flowers)＝patrinia scabiosifolia」82／「菊(きく)：kiku＝chrysanthemum」70／「菖蒲(あやめ)：ayame＝iris」60／「卯の花(うのはな)：u-no-hana＝deutzia crenata」50／「藤(ふぢ)：fuji＝Japanese wisteria」38＋「藤波(ふぢなみ)：fuji-nami... meaning "Japanese wisteria waving in the wind"」22＝60(cf:「藤衣(ふぢごろも)：fuji-goromo... meaning "in mourning"」20)...＜鳥(とり)＝birds＞「郭公(ほととぎす)：hototogisu＝little cuckoos」268／「雁(かり)：kari＝wild geese」120／「鶯(うぐひす)：uguisu＝Japanese nightingales, or orioles」104...＜風(かぜ)：kaze＝wind＞over 700...＜月(つき)：tsuki＝the moon＞over 900...＜虫(むし)：mushi＝insects＞「虫(むし)全般：mushi＝insects (in general)」76／「蛍(ほたる)：hotaru, or 夏虫(なつむし)：natsumushi＝fireflies」34／「蝉(せみ)：semi, or 空蝉(うつせみ)：utsusemi＝cicadas」27／「蜩(ひぐらし)：higurashi＝tanna japonensis, or evening cicada」22／「蟋蟀(きりぎりす)：kirigirisu＝crickets」18

—春—

●37● としをへてはなにこころをくだくかな をしむにとまるはるはなけれど
年を経て花に心を砕くかな惜しむに留まる春は無けれど

【春】[溜息]『4)後拾遺集:144』藤原定頼(ふじわらのさだより)

この世に長らく生きていると、桜の花にひどく心が揺れるようになる･･･つぼんで、開いて、咲き誇って、散って、その移ろいの一つ一つが、切ないほど胸に響くのだ･･･べつに、そうして私が花の行くのを惜しんでみたところで、行かずにずっと春のまま、なんて年はないのだけれど。

The more I advance in years, so does my affection for cherry flowers.
No matter how I miss them, though, there's no stopping Spring from going.

とし【年】[名]<年齢｜(n.)age>／を【を】[格助]<目的格｜(prep.)OBJECT>／ふ【経】[自ハ下二]<経る｜(v.)grow old>（へ＝運用形）／て【て】[接助]<理由｜(conj.)REASON>／はな【花】[名]<花｜(n.)flowers>／に【に】[格助]<理由｜(prep.)REASON>／こころ【心】[名]<心｜(n.)heart>／を【を】[格助]<目的格｜(prep.)OBJECT>／くだく【砕く】[他カ四]<砕く｜(v.)break>（くだく＝終止形）／かな【かな】[終助]<詠嘆｜(interj.)EXCLAMATION>／をしむ【惜しむ】[他マ四]<惜しく思う｜(v.)miss>（をしむ＝連体形）／に【に】[格助]<理由｜(prep.)REASON>／とまる【留まる】[自ラ四]<立ち止まる｜(v.)stop>（とまる＝連体形）／はる【春】[名]<春｜(n.)Spring>／は【は】[係助]<主格｜(prep.)SUBJECT>／なし【なし】[形ク]<存在しない｜(v.)do not exist>（なけれ＝已然形）／ど【ど】[接助]<～だけれども｜(conj.)although>

[toshi wo he-te hana ni kokoro wo kudaku kana oshimu ni tomaru haru wa nakere-do]

その真意、若い読者にはわかるまい、って感じの歌･･･「どういう意味？」なんて聞かないで ― 時がくれば(いやでも)わかっちゃうことだから。

A song whose truth will evade young readers... don't ask what it's like: you'll see in time, like it or not.

― ―

●38● みにかへてをしむにとまるはなならば けふやわがみのかぎりならまし
身に替へて惜しむに留まる花ならば今日や我が身の限りならまし

【春】[機知]『5)金葉集:66』源俊頼(みなもとのとしより)

桜花の散り際の寂しさに、(我が身に替えてもいい、花よ、散るな！)とも思うけど、いくらそうして惜しんだとても、散り行く花は止まらない･･･願いのままに我が命と引き換えになるものならば、私の人生は今日でおしまい、後には桜花だけが散らずに残ることだろうに。

Cherry flowers so dear that I wish I could save in exchange for my life
Would still fall leaving me behind... otherwise, I'd leave this life today.

み【身】[名]<自身｜(n.)[one]self>／に【に】[格助]<対象｜(prep.)OBJECT>／かふ【交ふ】[他ハ下二]<交換する｜(v.)exchange>（かへ＝連用形）／て【て】[接助]<状態｜(conj.)while>／をしむ【惜しむ】[他マ四]<惜しく思う｜(v.)miss>（をしむ＝連体形）／に【に】[格助]<原因｜(prep.)REASON>／とまる【留まる】[自ラ四]<立ち止まる｜(v.)stop>（とまる＝連体形）／はな【花】[名]<花｜(n.)flowers>／なり【なり】[助動ナリ型]断定<～である｜(aux-v.)be>（なら＝未然形）／ば【ば】[接助]<仮定｜(conj.)if>／けふ【今日】[名]<今日｜(n.)today>／や【や】[係助]<疑問｜(adv.)INTERROGATIVE>／わ【我】[代名]<私｜(pron.)I, myself>／が【が】[格助]<の｜(prep.)'s>／み【身】[名]<自身｜(n.)[one]self>／の【の】[格助]<の｜(prep.)'s>／かぎり【限り】[名]<おしまい｜(n.)the end>／なり【なり】[助動ナリ型]断定<～である｜(aux-v.)be>（なら＝未然形）／まし【まし】[助動特殊型]推量<～だろうに｜(aux-v.)should>（まし＝連体形係り結び）

―Spring―

—春—

[mi ni kae-te oshimu ni tomaru hana nara-ba kyou ya wa-ga mi no kagiri nara-mashi]

おそらくは一つ前に紹介した歌にインスピレーションを得たものでしょう、「頼むから、私の命に替えてもいいから、花よ、どうか散らないで！」と叫びつつ、この歌人は知っています ― そんな願い、聞き入れられっこないってことを…もしも望みが叶ったら、彼は今日にも死ぬでしょう；だって現に彼の目の前で、桜の花はその終わりを迎えようとしているのだから…満座の人々の注目をかっさらい大向こうをうならせずにはおかぬ、第五勅撰集『金葉集』の単独編者、平安末期の前衛歌人源俊頼らしい趣向に富んだ短歌です。

Perhaps inspired by the previous song, this poet exclaims "I pray you, flowers, please don't go, in exchange for my life!" while being fully aware that his wishes would never come true... if it did, he would die today, for the life of cherry flowers is coming to its end before him. A stylish TANKA demanding attention and adulation from the whole gallery, typical of 源俊頼(Minamoto-no-Toshiyori), the avant-garde poet of the late Heian era and the sole editor of the 5th Imperial TANKA anthology 金葉集(Kinyou shuu).

●39●けふのみとはるをおもはぬときだにも たつことやすきはなのかげかは
　　今日のみと春を思はぬ時だにも立つ事安き花の蔭かは

【春】[季題]『1)古今集:134』凡河内躬恒(おうしこうちのみつね)

美しく咲く花の下は、ただでさえなかなか立ち去り難いものなのに、暦の上では今日が春の最終日、後ろ髪引かれる思いもまたひとしおだなぁ。

Even at ordinary times when Spring has more days to spare
To turn my back on flowers is no mean feat ― today least of all.

けふ【今日】[名]＜今日｜(n.)today＞／のみ【のみ】[副助]＜唯一～だけ｜(adv.)nothing but＞／と【と】[格助]＜内容提示｜(conj.)that ～＞／はる【春】[名]＜春｜(n.)Spring＞／を【を】[格助]＜目的格｜(prep.)OBJECT＞／おもふ【思ふ】[他ハ四]＜思う｜(v.)think＞(おもは＝未然形)／ず【ず】[助動特殊型]打消＜～[し]ない｜(adv.)not ～＞(ぬ＝連体形)／とき【時】[名]＜時｜(n.)the time＞／だに【だに】[副助]＜～さえ｜(adv.)even＞／も【も】[係助]＜～[で]さえも｜(adv.)even＞／たつ【立つ】[自ハ四]＜立ち去る｜(v.)leave＞(たつ＝連体形)／こと【事】[名]＜～という事｜(n.)the act of ～ing＞／やすし【安し】[形]＜容易だ｜(adj.)easy＞(やすき＝連体形)／はな【花】[名]＜花｜(n.)flowers＞／の【の】[格助]＜の｜(prep.)'s＞／かげ【蔭】[名]＜陰｜(n.)the shade＞／かは【かは】[終助]＜～だろうか？否、そうではあるまい｜(prep.)RHETORICAL QUESTION＞

[kyou nomi to haru wo omowa-nu toki dani-mo tatsu koto yasuki hana no kage kawa]

平安時代の人々の意識では、弥生三月の末が春の終わり ― 太陰暦の三番目の月は、太陽暦では四番目、つまり現在の四月末(＝ゴールデンウィーク)が春の終わりに当たります。この歌の中の「**花**」の種類が何なのか、気にする必要はありません。「四月末には視界内に桜花なし」は真実だけど、それが何？目の前を過ぎ行く春を心底惜しむこの詩人の心の目に映る花と言えば、それは「桜」、それ以外の何物でもないでしょう。

In the Heian era, Spring was felt to terminate at the end of 弥生三月(yayoi san-gatsu＝the lunar March) ― be advised that the third month on the lunar calendar should be converted into the fourth solar month, meaning it's *the end of April today* ― what the modern Japanese call *"the golden week"*. Don't bother to know the kind of flowers in the poem: there'll be no cherry blossom in sight at the end of April, of course, but what does it matter? In the poet's mind's eye that sorely misses this passing Spring, the flower must be cherry, what else?

―春―

★40★いくかへりけふにわがみのあひぬらむ をしむははるのすぐるのみかは
幾返り今日に我が身の会ひぬらむ惜しむは春の過ぐるのみかは

【春】[季題]『5』金葉集:93』藤原定成(ふじわらのさだなり)

花々も散り、寒くもなく暑くもない心安らぐ春爛漫の時を経て、暦の上では明日からはもう夏だという…
あぁ、今年の春も今日限り、惜しいことだなぁ…来年もまた会えるかなぁ…自分はこの先あといくつの春に
巡り会えるのかなぁ…昔なら、新たな季節が巡り来ることなんて当たり前すぎて何も感じなかったのに…
行く春を惜しむのみにとどまらぬこの寂寥感…年を取るって、こういうことなのかなぁ…

From tomorrow it's Summer, so the calendar says.
How many more Springs shall I see go by henceforth?
Which should I miss, the passage of Spring or my life?

いく【幾】[接頭]＜いくつ｜(adv.)how many＞／かへり【返り】[名]＜回｜(n.)times＞／けふ【今日】[名]
＜今日｜(n.)today＞／に【に】[格助]＜対象｜(prep.)OBJECT＞／わ【我】[代名]＜私｜(pron.)I,
myself＞／が【が】[格助]＜の｜(prep.)'s＞／み【身】[名]＜自身｜(n.)[one]self＞／の【の】[格助]＜主
格｜(prep.)SUBJECT＞／あふ【会ふ】[自ハ四]＜出会う｜(v.)meet＞(あひ＝連用形)／ぬ【ぬ】[助動ナ
変型]確述＜きっと～する｜(adv.)EMPHASIS＞(ぬ＝終止形)／らむ【らむ】[助動ラ四型]現在推量＜～
だろう｜(aux-v.)SUPPOSITION＞(らむ＝連体形係り結び)／をしむ【惜しむ】[他マ四]＜惜しく思う｜
(v.)miss＞(をしむ＝連体形)／は【は】[係助]＜目的格｜(prep.)OBJECT＞／はる【春】[名]＜春｜
(n.)Spring＞／の【の】[格助]＜主格｜(prep.)SUBJECT＞／すぐ【過ぐ】[自ガ上二]＜過ぎる｜(v.)go
away＞(すぐる＝連体形)／のみ【のみ】[副助]＜ばかり｜(adv.)just＞／かは【かは】[終助]＜～だろう
か？否、そうではあるまい｜(prep.)RHETORICAL QUESTION＞

[iku-kaeri kyou ni wa-ga mi no ai-nu-ramu oshimu wa haru no suguru nomi-kawa]

これまた「年齢制限あり」の歌で、意味がわかっても溜息出るばかりで嬉しくない短歌。胸にしみじみ沁み
ちゃったら、あなたは人生の春・夏を…ひょっとしたらもう秋さえも…過ぎちゃった人ですね。
Another poem with age restriction, the understanding of which gives you more sigh than joy. If it comes
home to you, you are already past your Spring, Summer... or maybe even Fall.

●41●はるのゆくみちにきむかへほととぎす かたらふこゑにたちやとまると
春の行く道に来向かへ郭公語らふ声に立ちや止まると

【春】[季題]『5』金葉集:90』証観(しょうかん)

暦の上では今日が春の終わり、明日からは夏になるという…あぁ、春はもう行ってしまうのか…
おーい、ホトトギスよ、夏の鳥よ、早いとこ来て鳴いてみておくれ、お前のその声に聞き入って、
去り行く道すがら、春もひょっとして立ち止まるかもしれないから…なぁーんてね。

To the path for Spring to go away
Come, oriole, say hello to Spring
Let's see if it's immune to your pleas
O, Spring, don't go yet, please.

はる【春】[名]＜春｜(n.)Spring＞／の【の】[格助]＜主格｜(prep.)SUBJECT＞／ゆく【行く】[自カ四]＜
行く｜(v.)go＞(ゆく＝連体形)／みち【道】[名]＜道｜(n.)the way＞／に【に】[格助]＜場所｜
(prep.)PLACE＞／きむかふ【来向かふ】[自ハ四]＜来て立ち向かう｜(v.)come and face＞(きむかへ＝
命令形)／ほととぎす【郭公】[名]＜ホトトギス｜(n.)a little cuckoo＞／かたらふ【語らふ】[他ハ四]

―Spring―

—春—

＜語り合ふ｜(v.)have a talk＞(かたらふ＝連体形)／こゑ【声】[名]＜声｜(n.)the voice＞／に【に】[格助]＜原因｜(prep.)REASON＞／たつ【立つ】[自タ四]＜立つ｜(v.)stand＞(たち＝連用形)／や【や】[係助]＜疑問｜(adv.)INTERROGATIVE＞／とまる【留まる】[自ラ四]＜立ち止まる｜(v.)stop＞(とまる＝連体形係り結び)／と【と】[格助]＜内容提示｜(conj.)that ～＞

[haru no yuku michi ni ki-mukae hototogisu katarau koe ni tachi-ya-tomaru-to]

「ほととぎす」は「夏」の鳥だから、「弥生三月(太陽暦では四月)」末の「去り行く春」を惜しむこの短歌の中では少々先走りすぎ…どうしてそんなに急ぐのか？それは、ほととぎすの声に何も感じぬ平安貴族なんて一人もいなかったから ― この鳥の声が聞きたいばかりに一晩中起きてる貴人もいたほどだから、いま目の前を過ぎ行く「春」もまた、「♪テッペンカケタカ♪」の魔法の声に聴き耳立てて、立ち止まってくれるのでは、というわけです。

ほととぎす(hototogisu＝a little cuckoo) is a bird of Summer, a little too premature for this poem, which laments the passing of Spring at the end of 弥生(yayoi＝the third lunar/fourth solar month)... what's the rush? Simply because no poet in the Heian era was immune to the voice of ほととぎす(a little cuckoo) ― they would even spend the whole night waiting for this bird to sing ― this poet wants to see if Spring he sees go away will also stop to listen to its enchanting voice sounding テッペンカケタカ (*teppen kaketaka, meaning "Have you jumped onto the top?"*) to the Japanese ears.

・・・・・・・・・・・・・・・・・・・・・・・・・・

《春ならば斯くは鳴くまじ「郭公」》

まさに「夏の声」とも言うべき「**ホトトギス**」は、平安調短歌世界では断トツの人気を誇る鳥で、約9500首の八代集の中に250回以上登場する。これは秋・冬そして春の空を120回飛ぶ「雁」の倍以上の出現頻度なのだから恐れ入る。この「ホトトギス熱」の原因は何？…って考えてみると、「夏」は外であれこれ楽しい行事がメジロ押しなので、「部屋にこもって短歌詠み」なんてしてる場合じゃない季節だってことに気付く。実際、八代集での「春・夏・秋・冬」の出現頻度を見れば、「秋」と「春」の比重がとっても高い(それぞれ約1300／1100)；これに対し「夏」と「冬」の歌はいずれも500台とまばら ― 外の世界でやることがいっぱいの「夏」は、詩の世界では必然的に不毛な季節なのだ、詩的興趣をそそるものの少ないこの時期にあって、ネタに困った歌人に成り代わって、「時鳥・郭公・杜鵑・不如帰…子規」がひとり気を吐いて「夏の賛歌」を奏でていたのである。春の桜の枝の上で鳴く鳥ならば、こんなに頻出するまいに…英語の格言に言う通り、「appearance(外見／出現度数)にダマされてはならぬ！」のカッコウの例と言えるだろう。

《ほととぎす(hototogisu＝little cuckoos) wouldn't cry so loud
in Heianese TANKA if they were birds of Spring》

ほととぎす(hototogisu) ― *THE* voice of Summer ― is definitely the most popular bird in Heianese TANKA, appearing more than 250 times in some 9,500 poems in 八代集(Hachidai shuu＝8 great Imperial TANKA anthologies) ― more than twice the number of the second popular 雁(kari＝wild geese) flying in the skies of Autumn, Winter and Spring for 120 times. What's the reason for this cuckoo craze? Just think what you're doing in Summer: you'll be so busy happily engaged in so many outdoor activities that rhyming indoors is the last thing you'll do in this season. In fact, the seasonal frequency of 八代集(Hachidai shuu) rhymes is quite heavy in Autumn and Spring (some 1,300 and 1,100 poems respectively) but scarce in Summer and Winter (both in the order of 500) ― Summer is so rich with outdoor activities that the world of Summer poetry must needs be barren: in the absence of things of poetic interest, **ほととぎす**(little cuckoos) sing Summer anthems in place of topic-poor poets. They would never appear so often on paper if they appeared in Spring on popular cherry trees... *appearance is deceptive* indeed.

—春—

●42● みわたせばやまもとかすむみなせがは ゆふべはあきとなにおもひけむ♪
見渡せば山本霞む♪水無瀬川夕べは秋と何思ひけむ♪

【春】[謎掛]『8)新古今集:36』後鳥羽院(ごとばいん)

彼方の山を見渡せば、麓(ふもと)に立つのは春霞(はるがすみ)、目には見えない伏流水(ふくりゅうすい)が、陽気に誘われ空気を揺らす‥‥夕暮れ時の風景は「秋」こそ最高！なんて信じ込んでいたのが悔やまれるほどに、春の夕べのこの光景は(清少納言(せいしょうなごん)＝秋は夕暮れ in『枕草子(まくらのそうし)』に教えてやりたい)見事なものだ。

Looking far over to the mountains, the foot is blurred in mist.
Water coming up from nowhere, running underneath our world
Washes away my preconception that evening is best in Autumn.
Look, old essayist and admirers, at this wonderful Spring eve!

みわたす【見渡す】[他サ四]＜見渡す｜(v.)look over＞(みわたせ＝已然形)／ば【ば】[接助]＜〜したところ｜(conj.)when＞／やまもと【山本】[名]＜山のふもと｜(n.)the foot of the mountain＞／かすむ【霞む】[自マ四]＜霞む｜(v.)get hazy＞(かすむ＝連体形)／みなせがは【水無瀬川】[名]＜[架空の]水の流れていない川｜(n.)a[n imaginary] river with no water running on the surface＞／ゆふべ【夕べ】[名]＜夕方｜(n.)the evening＞／は【は】[係助]＜〜に関しては｜(adv.)as for 〜＞／あき【秋】[名]＜秋｜(n.)Autumn＞／と【と】[格助]＜内容提示｜(conj.)that 〜＞／なに【何】[副]＜どうして｜(adv.)why＞／おもひ【思ふ】[他ハ四]＜思う｜(v.)think＞(おもひ＝連用形)／けむ【けむ】[助動マ四型]過去推量＜〜[し]たのだろう｜(aux-v.)PAST SUPPOSITION＞(けむ＝連体形係り結び)

[miwatase-ba yama-moto kasumu minase-gawa yuu-be wa aki to nani omoi-kemu]

200年前の『枕草子』の著名な一節で「**秋は夕暮れ**」と主張した清少納言への詩的反論を、裏返しの文言で少々ヒネリを加えた「新古今流」で‥‥これを作ったのは、他ならぬ『新古今集』撰進の命を出した後鳥羽上皇その人。(但し、題詠＝現実ならざる想像上の詠歌)

A poetic objection to 清少納言(Sei-shou-nagon)'s famous passage 200 years before asserting **秋は夕暮れ**(aki wa yuu-gure＝Autumn looks best at dusk)(in 枕草子:Makura no soushi) in a little twisted 新古今(Shin-Kokin) manner. The author of this fictional song was none other than 後鳥羽上皇(Go-Toba joukou), the very ex-Emperor who ordered the compilation of 新古今集(Shin-Kokin shuu).

・・・・・・・・・・・・・・・・・・
《門外漢落とす「本節(ほんせつ)」自滅歌》

いかにも「新古今調」のこの短歌の想像世界は、「読み手が当然熟知している筈の著名な古典作品の知識」を前提として成立している。この種の古典への言及を「本説取り」と呼ぶ‥‥もしこの文化的前提が満たされぬ場合、この短歌は不発に終わり、読者はわけもわからず途方に暮れることになる ― 「なんたるややこしさ！なんたる内輪ネタ！なんとまぁ一般読者を小馬鹿にした態度！」と怒り出す読者さえいるかもしれない ― 実際、そうだったのである ― お高くとまった歌人たちの多くは、無知なる門外漢をわざと置き去りにして貴族階層の優位性を声高に賛美するべく殊更難解な歌作りに走り、そうして勿体ぶった貴人どもの尊大なる優雅さは、京都の宮廷の外の世界の一般人の多くに露骨な反感を抱(いだ)かせてしまった‥‥その結果、五・七・五・七・七の「短歌」という文芸様式そのものが自分で自分の首を絞め、12世紀末、平安の世の末の貴族階層の没落と共に、狭苦しい貴族階層の内輪芸としての自滅の道を辿ってしまったのである‥‥19世紀末の明治時代の幕開けに正岡子規が「古今調」短歌にとどめの一撃を加えるよりずっと昔に、短歌の世界は、自分で自分の首を絞めながら滅びて行ったのである。

—春—

《本説取り(honsetsu dori＝re-imagination of classic works),
the overuse of which left laypersons totally cold》

This 新古今(Shin-Kokin) TANKA has as its imaginary basis a famous classic which the readers are naturally supposed to be well aware of: this type of reference to classics is called 本説取り(honsetsu dori)... if this cultural premise is not satisfied, this poem will fall flat leaving readers simply bewildered — or even indignant for finding it too complicated, too esoteric, too much contemptuous of ordinary readers — and yes, they *were* — so many noble poets were consciously trying to exalt themselves by leaving behind ignorant laypersons, and so many folks outside the Imperial Court in 京都(Kyoto) were downright averse to such arrogant elegance of self-important nobles, that the whole genre of 短歌 (TANKA＝5-7-5-7-7 letter/syllable Japanese verse) suffocated itself into cloistered suicide with the downfall of Court nobles in the last years of the Heian era toward the end of the 12th century... long before 正岡子規(Masaoka Shiki) delivered the final blow to elegant TANKA after 古今(Kokin) style at the dawn of the Meiji(明治) era toward the end of the 19th century.

●43● てりもせずくもりもはてぬはるのよの　おぼろづきよにしくものぞなき
　　照りもせず曇りも果てぬ春の夜の朧ろ月夜に如く物ぞ無き
　　　　　　　　　　【春】[機知]『8)新古今集:55』大江千里(おおえのちさと)
照るでもなく曇るでもない、妙なる光のヴェールに包まれた、朧れ夜の春の宵に勝る風情は又と無い。
　　　Neither cloudy nor shiny, the moon is best at hazy Spring night.
てる【照る】〔自ラ四〕＜照る｜(v.)shine＞（てり＝連用形）／も【も】〔係助〕＜意味なし｜(adv.)NO MEANING＞／す【為】〔補動サ変〕＜する｜(v.)do＞（せ＝未然形）／ず【ず】〔助動特殊型〕打消＜〜[し]ない｜(adv.)not 〜＞（ず＝終止形）／くもる【曇る】〔自ラ四〕＜曇る｜(v.)get cloudy＞（くもり＝連用形）／も【も】〔係助〕＜意味なし｜(adv.)NO MEANING＞／はつ【果つ】〔自タ下二〕＜すっかり〜になる｜(adv.)completely 〜＞（はて＝未然形）／ず【ず】〔助動特殊型〕打消＜〜[し]ない｜(adv.)not 〜＞（ぬ＝連体形）／はる【春】【名】＜春｜(n.)Spring＞／の【の】〔格助〕＜の｜(prep.)'s＞／よ【夜】【名】＜夜｜(n.)the night＞／の【の】〔格助〕＜の｜(prep.)'s＞／おぼろづきよ【朧月夜】【名】＜ぼんやり霞む月の夜｜(n.)a night with a hazy moon＞／に【に】〔格助〕＜比較｜(prep.)COMPARISON＞／しく【如く】〔自カ四〕＜勝る｜(v.)excel＞（しく＝連体形）／もの【物】【名】＜物事｜(n.)a thing＞／ぞ【ぞ】〔係助〕＜強調｜(adv.)EMPHASIS＞／なし【なし】〔形〕＜存在しない｜(v.)do not exist＞（なき＝連体形係り結び）

　　　[teri-mo se-zu kumori-mo hate-nu haru no yo no oboro-zukiyo ni shiku mono zo naki]
『新古今集』の収録歌ですが、元々は白楽天の有名な漢詩文 **不明不暗朧々月**（明るくも暗くもなく空に霞む月）」を典拠として『古今集』時代に詠まれたもの。こうした漢籍への言及は、第二勅撰集『後撰集』以降はほぼ完全に姿を消してしまいます…かつては中国重視だった日本文化の潮流が、905年に『古今集』が登場して以降は国風文化中心へと流れを変えたことがうかがえる事実です。

A 新古今(Shin-Kokin) TANKA based on a famous 唐歌(Kara-uta＝Chinese verse) **不明不暗朧々月** (the hazy moon neither too bright nor dark) by 白楽天(Hakurakuten), made in the years of 古今集 (Kokin shuu). Such reference to Chinese classics went into practical extinction after the 2nd great Imperial TANKA anthology 後撰集(Gosen shuu), which goes to show the fact that the former Chinese-oriented cultural trend had been completely reversed toward Japanese by the appearance of 古今集(Kokin shuu) in A.D.905.

—夏:Summer—

●44● ゆふづくよほのめくかげもうのはなの さけるわたりはさやけかりけり
　　　夕月夜仄めく影も卯の花の咲ける辺りはさやけかりけり

【夏】[機知]『7)千載集:140』藤原(三条)実房(ふじわらの(さんじょう)さねふさ)

夏の初めの夜空の月は辺りをおぼろに霞ませる・・・唯一卯の花の周りの空間だけが、くっきり白い別世界。

　　　Early Summer moonlight blurring the scene around
　　　Except around u-no-hana as white as broad daylight.

ゆふづくよ【夕月夜】〔名〕<夕月夜|(n.)the moon towards the evening>/ほのめく【仄めく】〔自カ四〕<ぼんやり光る|(v.)dimly shine>(ほのめく=連体形)/かげ【影】〔名〕<光|(n.)the light>/も【係助】<意味なし|(adv.)NO MEANING>/うのはな【卯の花】〔名〕<ウツギ|(n.)u-no-hana, or deutzia crenata>/の【の】〔格助〕<主格|(prep.)SUBJECT>/さく【咲く】〔自カ四〕<咲く|(v.)bloom>(さけ=已然形・命令形)/り【助動ラ変型】存続<~[し]ている|(aux-v.)PERFECT TENSE>(る=連体形)/わたり【辺り】〔名〕<あたり|(adv.)around>/は【は】〔係助〕<~に関しては|(adv.)as for ~>/さやけし【清けし】〔形ク〕<くっきり明るい|(adj.)lucent>(さやけかり=連用形)/けり【けり】〔助動ラ変型〕詠嘆<~だったのだなぁ|(interj.)REALIZATION>(けり=終止形)

　　　[yuu-zukuyo honomeku kage mo u-no-hana no sake-ru watari wa sayakekari-keri]

「卯の花」は群れ成して咲く白い花ですが、今日ではこの名は「おから(=豆腐の絞りカス)」の異名として有名。花の名としては「卯の花」よりも「空木(ウツギ=茎が中空の木)」の方が一般的です。ちなみに、陰暦四月の「うづき:卯月」の語源は「卯の花が咲く月」です。

卯の花(u-no-hana=deutzia crenata) is a white gregarious floral collective, whose name is less popular today as a flower than as the alias of おから(okara=tofu dreg, or soy pulp). This flower is now more popularly known as 空木(utsugi=empty stem). Incidentally, the name of the lunar 4th month 卯月(uzuki) means "the month when 卯の花(u-no-hana) comes out".

●45● ちりはててはなのかげなきこのもとに たつことやすきなつごろもかな
　　　散り果てて花の蔭無き木の本にたつ事安き夏衣かな

【夏】[転季]『8)新古今集:177』慈円(じえん)

弥生の花もすっかり散り果てて、木の下を立ち去るに何の未練もない卯月の今日、厚い冬物の衣裳を脱ぎ捨てて、ささっと裁縫した蝉の羽のような薄い夏の衣に着替えよう。

　　　Flowers of Spring completely out of sight,
　　　Nothing around to keep me here in thick clothes any more.
　　　Feather-light outfit free as cicadas' wings,
　　　Get me ready for Summer, its heat and lots of fun.

ちる【散る】〔自ラ四〕<散る|(v.)fall>(ちり=連用形)/はつ【果つ】〔自タ下二〕<すっかり~になる|(adv.)completely ~>(はて=連用形)/て【て】〔接助〕<順接|(conj.)and>/はな【花】〔名〕<花|(n.)flowers>/の【の】〔格助〕<の|(prep.)'s>/かげ【影】〔名〕<かすかな姿|(n.)the slightest sight>/なし【なし】〔形ク〕<存在しない|(v.)do not exist>(なき=連体形)/このもと【木の下】〔名〕<木の下|(n.)beneath the tree>/に【に】〔格助〕<原因|(prep.)REASON>/**(A)たつ【立つ】**〔自タ四〕<立ち

—夏—

る｜(v.)leave＞／**(B)たつ【裁つ】〔他夕四〕**＜裁断する｜(v.)cut and sew＞／こと【事】〔名〕＜～という事｜(n.)the act of ～ing＞／やすし【安し】〔形ク〕＜容易だ｜(adj.)easy＞(やすき＝連体形)／なつごろも【夏衣】〔名〕＜夏物の衣服｜(n.)Summer clothes＞／かな【かな】〔終助〕＜詠嘆｜(interj.)EXCLAMATION＞

[chiri-hate-te hana no kage naki ko no moto ni tatsu koto yasuki natsu-goromo kana]

おそらくは『古今集』の「今日のみと春を思はぬ時だにも立つ事安き花の蔭かは」の歌を下敷きにした新古今歌で、「**たつ**」という語が「(桜の木の下を)**立つ**」／「(夏物の着物を)**裁つ**」に分岐する巧みな懸詞がキモになっている歌。昔の京都の貴人たちの「更衣」は(旧暦四月の)「夏」と(旧暦十月の)「冬」の初日に行なわれた。今日の日本でもなお「衣替え」の風習は(女学生の制服の変化を見ればはっきりわかる通り)六月一日と十月一日に行なわれている。

Perhaps based on the 古今集(Kokin shuu) poem 今日のみと春を思はぬ時だにも立つ事安き花の蔭かは(kyou nomi to haru wo omowa-nu toki dani-mo tatsu koto yasuki hana no kage kawa), this 新古今(Shin-Kokin) TANKA hinges on the clever 懸詞(kake-kotoba＝pun) of たつ(tatsu) diverging into 1)立つ(tatsu＝leave cherry trees) and 2)裁つ(tatsu＝cut and make summer clothes). Ancient nobles in 京都(Kyoto) had the custom of 更衣(koromo-gae＝changing clothes) on the first day of Summer (lunar April) and Winter (lunar October).　In today's Japan, this custom ― 衣替え(koromo-gae＝changing seasonal clothes) ― still takes place, notably evident in schoolgirls' uniforms, on the first day of (solar) June and October.

―――――――――――――――――――――――――――

★46★さつきまつはなたちばなのかをかげば　むかしのひとのそでのかぞする
五月待つ花橘の香を嗅げば昔の人の袖の香ぞする

【夏】[懐旧]『1)古今集:139』詠み人知らず

夏も間近の空気に乗せて漂ってくるタチバナの花の香りを嗅ぐと、昔のことを思い出す‥‥懐かしいあの人の袖に焚き込められていたのと、同じ香りがするから。

Mandarin orange fragrantly awaiting May
Invites me back to those amorous days...
The nostalgic scent on her sleeves
Wakes me up to long-lost dreams.

さつき【皐月】〔名〕＜陰暦五月＝新暦六月）｜(n.)the lunar May＝solar June＞／まつ【待つ】〔他夕四〕＜～が間近に迫る｜(adj.)be near at hand＞(まつ＝連体形)／はなたちばな【花橘】〔名〕＜橘｜(n.)a mandarin orange＞／の【の】〔格助〕＜の｜(prep.)'s＞／か【香】〔名〕＜香り｜(n.)the scent＞／を【を】〔格助〕＜目的格｜(prep.)OBJECT＞／かぐ【嗅ぐ】〔他ガ四〕＜臭いをかぐ｜(v.)smell＞(かげ＝已然形)／ば【ば】〔接助〕＜～したところ｜(conj.)when＞／むかし【昔】〔名〕＜昔｜(n.)the past＞／の【の】〔格助〕＜の｜(prep.)'s＞／ひと【人】〔名〕＜あの人｜(n.)that [darling] one＞／の【の】〔格助〕＜の｜(prep.)'s＞／そで【袖】〔名〕＜袖｜(n.)the sleeve＞／の【の】〔格助〕＜の｜(prep.)'s＞／か【香】〔名〕＜香り｜(n.)the scent＞／ぞ【ぞ】〔係助〕＜強調｜(adv.)EMPHASIS＞／す【す】〔補動サ変〕＜～が漂ってくる｜(v.)come floating in the air＞(する＝連体形係り結び)

[Satsuki matsu hana-tachibana no ka wo kage-ba mukashi no hito no sode no ka zo suru]

「**さつき**:皐月・五月(太陰暦の五月／太陽暦では六月)」間近の日本の空気は、この時期ならではの様々な匂いに満ちている‥‥そして思い出の香りにも満ちている‥‥懐かしい香りに誘われて、かつて一緒に過ごした(けど今はもうそばにいない)大事な人との思い出の日々へと、この詩人はタイムスリップしています。

http//zubaraie.com　　　　　　　　　　　　　　　　　　　　―Summer―

—夏—

Japanese atmosphere toward **皐月**:**五月**(satsuki=the lunar fifth/solar sixth month) is thick with seasonal scents... and nostalgic memories... which sends the poet back to good old days spent together with a dear though not near one.

●47●あふことのひさしにふけるあやめぐさ ただかりそめのつまとこそみれ
逢ふ事のひさしに葺ける菖蒲草只かり初めのつまとこそ見れ

【夏】〔慨嘆〕『5)金葉集:436』藤原永相女(ふじわらのながすけのむすめ)

前回の逢瀬からずいぶんと久しいことですね・・・どうやら私、あなたにとってはただのつまみ食い相手のかりそめの妻、端午の節句の時にだけ軒先にぶらさげるショウブみたいなものだったんですね。

**Your absence growing as long as sweet flag hanging from eaves —
Bitter awareness that you loved me in passing as sweet pastime.**

あふ【逢ふ】〔自ハ四〕<[恋人どうしとして]逢う>(v.)have a date>(あふ=連体形)/こと【事】〔名〕<〜という事>(n.)the act of 〜ing>/の【の】〔格助〕<主格>(prep.)SUBJECT>/**(A)ひさし【久し】〔形シク〕**<長らくごぶさたしている>(adj.)have long been absent>(ひさし=終止形)/**(B)ひさし【庇】〔名〕**<軒下>(n.)eaves>/に【に】〔格助〕<場所>(prep.)PLACE>/ふく【葺く】〔他カ四〕<軒下にかざす>(v.)hang from eaves>(ふけ=連用形)/り【り】〔助動ラ変型〕存続<〜[し]ている>(aux-v.)PERFECT TENSE>(る=連体形)/あやめぐさ【菖蒲草】〔名〕<ショウブ>(n.)acorus calamus, or sweet flag>/ただ【只】〔副〕<ただ単に>(adv.)only>/**(A1)かる【刈る】〔他ラ四〕**<刈る>(v.)cut>(かり=連用形)/**(A2)そむ【初む】〔補動マ下二〕**<〜し初める>(v.)start to 〜>(そめ=連用形)/**(B)かりそめ【仮初】〔形動ナリ〕**<ほんの一時の>(adj.)makeshift>(かりそめ=語幹)/の【の】〔格助〕<の>(prep.)'s>/**(A)つま【嬬】〔名〕**<建物の端っこ>(n.)the corner of a building>/**(B)つま【妻】〔名〕**<妻>(n.)a wife>/と【と】〔格助〕<内容提示>(conj.)that 〜>/こそ【こそ】〔係助〕<強調>(adv.)EMPHASIS>/みる【見る】〔他マ上一〕<見る>(v.)view>(みれ=已然形係り結び)

[au koto no hisashi ni fuke-ru ayame-gusa tada karisome no tsuma to-koso mire]

昔の「**あやめ**(菖蒲)」は今で言う「ショウブ」の草であって、今日の「菖蒲」の花とは別物。この「**あやめ草**」は、花は目立たないが、長く張る根と高い香りで名高く、その放つ香気には邪気を払う効き目があるとされたので、人々は初夏になるとこの草を切って軒下に吊るしたり、風呂に浮かべて「菖蒲湯」にしたりした。この短歌にはそうした「**あやめ**」関連の懸詞が満載されていて、あまりにテンコ盛りものだから、本来なら不実な恋人を責めているはずの基調音が、気の利いた台詞の洪水で洗い流されてしまっている・・・けど、ひょっとしたらそれこそこの歌人の狙いなのかもしれない — 平安の世の男女は、現代日本人には信じられないほどドギツいなじり合いを歌の中では平然と演じていたが、実際にはさほどの悪気もなしにゲーム感覚でそれをやっていたのである。

Ancient **菖蒲**(ayame) is not what it is today: it is what we now call ショウブ(shoubu=acorus calamus, or sweet flag). This plant was noted not for its obscure flower but for its widely spreading roots and strong scent supposedly effective against evil spirits, which people cut off and hung from eaves or dipped in bathtubs in early Summer. This TANKA is replete with such **あやめ**(ayame)-related 懸詞(kake-kotoba=puns), so much so that its basic tone of grumble against her faithless lover is drowned off by witticism... maybe that's what she meant: Heianese men and women could blame each other much more blatantly in poems than the modern Japanese could ever believe... without actually meaning it.

―夏―

●48● てもふれでをしむかひなくふぢのはな そこにうつれば なみぞをりける

手も触れで惜しむ甲斐無く藤の花底に映れば波ぞ折りける

【夏】[機知]『3)拾遺集:87』凡河内躬恒(おうしこうちのみつね)

垂れ下がるその繊細な花を折ってしまってはいけないので、手も触れず眺めるばかりの藤の花だったのに、その甲斐もなかったようだ・・・透き通った池の底に映る紫の花を、水面に立つ波紋があっさり折ってしまったよ。

Japanese wisteria hanging from above,
Fragile beauty too delicate for me to touch:
I regret to find it broken on the pond,
Ripple by ripple purple flower ripped apart.

て【手】[名]＜手｜(n.)a hand＞／も[も]〔係助〕＜～[で]さえも｜(adv.)even＞／ふる【触る】〔自ラ下二〕＜触れる｜(v.)touch＞(ふれ＝未然形)／で[で]〔接助〕＜～することなしに｜(prep.)without ～ing＞／をしむ【惜しむ】〔他マ四〕＜大事にする｜(v.)cherish＞(をしむ＝連体形)／かひ【甲斐】[名]＜効き目｜(n.)effect＞／なし【なし】〔形ク〕＜存在しない｜(v.)do not exist＞(なく＝連用形)／ふぢのはな【藤の花】[名]＜藤の花｜(n.)Japanese wisteria＞／そこ【底】[名]＜底｜(n.)the bottom＞／に[に]〔格助〕＜場所｜(prep.)PLACE＞／うつる【映る】〔自ラ四〕＜映る｜(v.)be reflected＞(うつれ＝已然形)／ば[ば]〔接助〕＜～したところ｜(conj.)when＞／なみ【波】[名]＜波｜(n.)waves＞／ぞ[ぞ]〔係助〕＜強調｜(adv.)EMPHASIS＞／をる【折る】〔自ラ四〕＜折る｜(v.)snap＞(をり＝連用形)／けり【けり】〔助動ラ変型〕詠嘆＜～だったのだなぁ｜(interj.)REALIZATION＞(ける＝連体形係り結び)

[te mo fure-de oshimu kai naku fuji-no-hana soko ni utsure-ba nami zo ori-keru]

「水の鏡に映った藤の花が、小波(さざなみ)で折られてしまった」とは、いかにも趣向歌大好きな躬恒らしい歌。『古今集』編者の中では紀貫之(きのつらゆき)に比して評価があまり高くない凡河内躬恒ですが、『金葉集』編者の源俊頼(みなもとのとしより)は「**躬恒をば侮らせ給ふまじきぞ**(あなづ)(=躬恒を軽んじてはいけません)」と言っています：大胆な趣向が好きな人には好まれる(=正岡子規(まさおかしき)には毛嫌いされる)作風ということですね。「**藤**」は初夏を涼しく彩る美しい花。その「紫=藤色(ふじいろ)」はこの上なく高貴な色とされました。最も染(そ)め困難な色だったせいもありますが、同時にまた「**藤**」の字が権勢を誇る「藤原(せんせい)」氏を思い起こさせたからです。実際、宮廷の最高位の貴族の色は「紫」と「青」だったのに対し、最下級貴族のシンボルカラーは「黒」と「緑」(中間は「赤」)・・・八代集編者のほとんどは「いつまで経(かん)っても緑色」の我が身の官途の不遇を嘆く下級役人たちでした。

Flowers of Japanese wisteria reflected on the mirror of the surface of water being broken by the ripple on the pond — quite typical of 躬恒(Mitsune) noted for his love of flamboyant songs of style. Although he is not so much admired as 紀貫之(Ki-no-Tsurayuki), one of the co-editors of the 1st Imperial anthology 古今集(Kokin shuu), another editor of the 5th anthology 金葉集(Kinnyou shuu) 源俊頼(Minamoto-no-Toshiyori) told someone "**You should never underestimate 躬恒(Mitsune)**", which goes to show how much he is favored by poets who love stylish poems — and how much he is despised by 正岡子規(Masaoka Shiki). 藤(fuji=Japanese wisteria) is a cool beauty in early Summer. Its purple color — 藤色(fuji iro) in Japanese — was considered supreme not only because it was the hardest color to dye, but also due to the term 藤(fuji) associated with the powerful clan of the 藤原(Fujiwara)s — in fact, the colors of the highest ranking officers in the Imperial Court were purple and blue, while the lowest colors were black and green (red being in the middle) ... most editors of 八代集(Hachidai shuu=8 great Imperial TANKA anthologies) were low-ranking officials lamenting their hapless career at the Imperial Court which remained "forever GREEN."

—夏—

●49● むかしわがあつめしものをおもひいでて　みなれがほにもくるほたるかな

昔我が集めしものを思ひ出でて見馴れ顔にも来る蛍かな

【夏】[擬人]『7)千載集:201』藤原季通（ふじわらのすえみち）

あぁ、蛍が飛んでいる‥‥懐かしいなぁ、子供の頃、せっせと集めては飽きもせず眺めたっけなぁ‥‥
ぁ、こっちへ飛んで来た‥‥そうか、お前も覚えていてくれたか、昔馴染みのこの私のことを。

Fireflies I used to gather as timeless companions in my youth
Grow fond of old memories and come glowing up to me.

むかし【昔】[名]＜昔｜(n.)the past＞／わ【我】[代名]＜私｜(pron.)I, myself＞／が【が】[格助]＜主格｜(prep.)SUBJECT＞／あつめ【集む】[他マ下二]＜集める｜(v.)gather＞（あつめ＝連用形）／き【き】[助動特殊型]過去＜〜［し］た｜(aux-v.)PAST＞（し＝連体形）／ものを【ものを】[接助]＜〜[だ]というのに｜(conj.)although＞／おもひいづ【思ひ出づ】[他ダ下二]＜思い出す｜(v.)remember＞（おもひいで＝連用形）／て【て】[接助]＜理由｜(conj.)REASON＞／みなれがほなり【見馴れ顔なり】[形動ナリ]＜親しげだ｜(adj.)friendly＞（みなれがほに＝連用形）／も【も】[係助]＜意味なし｜(adv.)NO MEANING＞／く【来】[自カ変]＜来る｜(v.)come＞（くる＝連体形）／ほたる【蛍】[名]＜ホタル｜(n.)fireflies＞／かな【かな】[助助]＜詠嘆｜(interj.)EXCLAMATION＞

[mukashi wa-ga atsume-shi mono wo omoi-ide-te minaregaoni-mo kuru hotaru kana]

概して「虫」を毛嫌いする人でも、ほのかな**蛍**の神秘的な光にはうっとり心奪われるもの。子供たちも大抵この虫が大好きで、自分の手のひらに収まりきらないほどの「蛍の光」を集めようと走り回ったりする‥‥そしてまた蛍の方でも、人の手ですくい取られるのを嫌がったりしない ― たぶん彼らは知っているのだ：世の中全般を吹き荒れる人間たちの残虐性が、彼らの優しい光の前には和らいで消えるということを‥‥そういう無垢な昔、子供らしい聖なる至福の静けさを掻き乱す出来事など何も起こりはしない、と信じきっていた過ぎ去りし日々へと、我々を誘ってくれる素敵な詩。

Even those averse to bugs in general will be enchanted by the faint mysterious glow of glowworms. Many kids will grow so fond of these worms that they will try to see how many they can scoop with their bare hands... and these worms hardly resist being gathered by human hands, perhaps knowing their graceful glow is proof against human cruelty rampant in the world at large. This charming poem brings us back to such innocent old days, when nothing bad could ever happen to disturb the sacred tranquility of childish bliss.

●50● つつめどもかくれぬものはなつむしの　みよりあまれるおもひなりけり

包めども隠れぬ物は夏虫の身より余れる思ひなりけり

【夏】[仮託]『2)後撰集:209』詠み人知らず

袖の内側に包んでもほんのり外へと洩れ出る蛍の光のように、あなたをお慕いする私の恋心も隠しきれずに洩れ出してしまいます‥‥身分違いの卑しい召使いの私には、身の程知らずの恋心なのですが。

However concealed there's something that will reveal itself:
From inside the body of a firefly,
Inner feelings overflow into radiant light,
Which, I'm afraid, is unsuitable for a humble servant-girl like me.

つつむ【包む】[他マ四]＜包み隠す｜(v.)conceal＞（つつめ＝已然形）／ども【ども】[接助]＜〜ではあるが｜(conj.)although＞／かくる【隠る】[自ラ下二]＜隠れる｜(v.)hide＞（かくれ＝未然形）／ず【ず】[助動

特殊型］打消＜～［し］ない｜(adv.)not ～＞(ぬ＝連体形)／もの【物】〔名〕＜物事｜(n.)a thing＞／は【は】〔係助〕＜主格｜(prep.)SUBJECT＞／なつむし【夏虫】〔名〕＜ホタル｜(n.)fireflies＞／の【の】〔格助〕＜の｜(prep.)'s＞／み【身】〔名〕＜身体｜(n.)the body＞／より【より】〔格助〕＜から｜(prep.)from＞／あまる【余る】〔自ラ四〕＜こぼれ出る｜(v.)overflow＞(あまれ＝已然形・命令形)／り【り】〔助動ラ変型〕存続＜～［し］ている｜(aux.-v.)PERFECT TENSE＞(る＝連体形)／おもひ【想ひ】〔名〕＜恋心｜(n.)loving feeling＞／なり【なり】〔助動ナリ型〕断定＜～である｜(aux.-v.)be＞(なり＝連用形)／けり【けり】〔助動ラ変型〕詠嘆＜～だったのだなぁ｜(interj.)REALIZATION＞(けり＝終止形)

[tsutsume-domo kakure-nu mono wa natsu-mushi no mi yori amare-ru omoi nari-keri]

「蛍を捕まえて、袖に入れてごらん」と言われた一人の幼い召使いの少女の口(＆心)から生まれた詩だそうです。自分のお仕えする高貴な女性が逢瀬を重ねていたお相手の若き貴公子に、子供ながらに抱いた恋心を口に出して言っちゃったのがこの歌…その無垢なる光、とくとご鑑賞あれ。

This poem is said to have been born out of the heart and mouth of a small servant girl at the request of catching and gathering fireflies in her sleeves, who rhymed out her childish affection toward the noble young prince with whom her lady master had regular rendezvous... see how innocently it glows!

―――――――――――――――――――――――――

★51★なくこゑもきこえぬもののかなしきは　しのびにもゆるほたるなりけり
鳴く声も聞えぬものの哀しきはしのびに焼ゆる蛍なりけり

【夏】[仮託]『6)詞花集:73』藤原高遠(ふじわらのたかとお)

秋の虫たちの鳴き声もしみじみと哀れだけれど、声も立てずに仄かな光に身を焦がすばかりの蛍のほうが、まるで燃える想いを内に秘めてじぃーっと恋い焦がれている人のようで、見ていて身につまされる。

Men, women, even insects all cry about
Wooing or mourning their covetous love.
Deeper feelings silently grow and
Ultimately glow in speechless fireflies.

なく【鳴く】〔自カ四〕＜鳴く｜(v.)cry＞(なく＝連体形)／こゑ【声】〔名〕＜声｜(n.)the voice＞／も【も】〔係助〕＜意味なし｜(adv.)NO MEANING＞／きこゆ【聞こゆ】〔自ヤ下二〕＜聞こえる｜(v.)be heard＞(きこえ＝未然形)／ず【ず】〔助動特殊型〕打消＜～［し］ない｜(adv.)not ～＞(ぬ＝連体形)／ものの【ものの】〔接助〕＜～ではあるが｜(conj.)although＞／かなし【悲し】〔形シク〕＜悲しい｜(adj.)sad＞(かなしき＝連体形)／は【は】〔係助〕＜主格｜(prep.)SUBJECT＞／しのぶ【偲ぶ】〔他バ四〕〔他バ上二〕＜恋い慕う｜(v.)have affection toward＞(しのび＝連用形、転じて、名詞)／に【に】〔格助〕＜原因｜(prep.)REASON＞／もゆ【燃ゆ】〔自ヤ下二〕＜燃える｜(v.)be on fire＞(もゆる＝連体形)／ほたる【蛍】〔名〕＜ホタル｜(n.)fireflies＞／なり【なり】〔助動ナリ型〕断定＜～である｜(aux.-v.)be＞(なり＝連用形)／けり【けり】〔助動ラ変型〕詠嘆＜～だったのだなぁ｜(interj.)REALIZATION＞(けり＝終止形)

[naku koe mo kikoe-nu mono-no kanashiki wa shinobi ni moyuru hotaru nari-keri]

一つ前の少女の詩に負うところも少なからずと言うべきか、「**蛍**」は「人知れず募る／燃える恋心」の「歌枕(伝統的イメージ)」となりました。「**しのび**」とありますが、この歌の脈絡でのそれは「忍び＝隠れた忍耐」というよりは「**偲び**＝誰か／何かへの恋慕」であるとともに、その**び**の音は「ひ」から「**火**」へと飛び火して、もう一つの「**火**」関連語「**燃ゆ**」との間の密かな連想を呼び起こしつつ、詩的「**縁語**」の火花を散らしている点もおさえておくべきでしょう。ちょっと見には無理があるこの種の「火：**ひ**」と「偲び：しの＜**び**＝火＞」あるいは「思ひ：おも＜**ひ**＝火＞」の連想が、平安調短歌の中には信じ難いほどの頻度で登場するのです…ので、学生の皆さん、知らぬ間に答案用紙が炎上せぬよう、くれぐれも御用心あれ。

—夏—

Thanks not a little to the girl's poem previous to this one, 蛍(hotaru=fireflies) became the 歌枕 (uta-makura=poetic pillow／traditional image) of "silently growing/glowing affection". Note that しのび(shinobi) in this context is not so much 忍び (stealthy patience) as 偲び(affection to someone/something), also igniting the poetic flash by the sound of ひ(び:bi＞ひ:hi＞火=fire) in stealthy association(縁語:engo) with another fire-related term 燃ゆ(moyu=burn). Such apparently impossible association of 火(ひ＜hi=fire) with 偲び(しの＜び＞:shino＜bi＞) or 思ひ(おも＜ひ＞: omo＜hi＞=affection) is found in unbelievable abundance among Heianese TANKA... students, beware lest your ignorance set fire on your answer sheets!

★52★ものおもへばさはのほたるもわがみより　あくがれいづるたまかとぞみる

物思へば沢の蛍も我が身より憬れ出づる魂かとぞ見る

【夏】[仮託]『4)後拾遺集:1164』和泉式部(いずみしきぶ)

苦しい想いに胸焦がし、一人、夏の夜道を歩いていると、水辺に光る儚い蛍の光が、
まるで、肉体から抜け出した私の魂が所在なげに漂っているみたいに見える。

As I wander around mountain streams,

Lost in thought on fruitless love,

Is it my soul evading my body

Glittering in the dark in the form of fireflies?

もの【物】[名]＜あれこれいろいろ｜(n.)one thing or another＞／おもふ【思ふ】[他ハ四]＜思う｜(v.)think＞(おもへ＝已然形)／ば【ば】[接助]＜〜したところ｜(conj.)when＞／さは【沢】[名]＜沼地｜(n.)the swamp＞／の【の】[格助]＜の｜(prep.)'s＞／ほたる【蛍】[名]＜ホタル｜(n.)fireflies＞／も【も】[係助]＜意味なし｜(adv.)NO MEANING＞／わ【我】[代名]＜私｜(pron.)I, myself＞／が【が】[格助]＜の｜(prep.)'s＞／み【身】[名]＜身体｜(n.)the body＞／より【より】[格助]＜〜から｜(prep.)from＞／あくがれいづ【憬れ出づ】[自ダ下二]＜迷い出る｜(v.)wander off＞(あくがれいづる＝連体形)／たま【魂】[名]＜魂｜(n.)one's spirit＞／か【か】[係助]＜疑問｜(adv.)INTERROGATIVE＞／と【と】[格助]＜内容提示｜(conj.)that 〜＞／ぞ【ぞ】[係助]＜強調｜(adv.)EMPHASIS＞／みる【見る】[他マ上一]＜見る｜(v.)view＞(みる＝連体形係り結び)

[mono-omoe-ba sawa no hotaru mo wa-ga mi yori akugare-izuru tama ka-to-zo miru]

この詩の作者は伝説の歌人の和泉式部 ─ 最初の夫に捨てられて途方に暮れた彼女の口から飛び出した歌です。真っ暗闇をあてどなくさまよい飛ぶ蛍の光の散り散りのさまは、どうしていいのかわからない彼女の内面世界のシンボルとして、誰にも真似できぬ異彩を放っています…和泉の心の動きにあまりにも個人的に忠実すぎる表現だったために、凡百の歌詠みたちがおいそれと拝借できるような平安調短歌のスタンダードなイメージにはついにならずじまいでしたが、それこそがまさにこのスゴい詩の時を超えた輝きの光源、現代の我々の心にもスーッと滲み入ってきます。

The author of this poem ─ the legendary 和泉式部(Izumi shikibu) ─ rhymed it out when she found herself at a loss what to do immediately after she had been deserted by her first husband. The scattered glow of fireflies wandering to and fro in the dark is a unique representation of her bewildered inner world... too much personally true to her feelings to become a standard image for any ordinary poets to borrow... which is the very reason for the eternal glow of this superb piece of poetry that still appeals directly to our heart.

―夏―

●53● いはたたくたにのみづのみおとづれて なつにしられぬみやまべのさと
岩叩く谷の水のみ音づれて夏に知られぬ深山辺の里

【夏】[叙景]『7)千載集:221』藤原教長(ふじわらののりなが)

谷川の水が岩を叩く音だけが辺りにこだまして、それ以外は誰一人訪れる者はいない…
夏の暑さもここまではやって来ない…山深い里の静かな情景。

Water in the valley is heard to hit the rocks.
No one seen around in this deep mountain village.
Not even Summer seems to visit here.

いは【岩】[名]＜岩｜(n.)a rock＞／たたく【叩く】[他カ四]＜叩く｜(v.)hit＞(たたく＝連体形)／たに【谷】[名]＜谷｜(n.)a valley＞／の【の】[格助]＜の｜(prep.)'s＞／みづ【水】[名]＜水｜(n.)water＞／のみ【のみ】[副助]＜唯一～だけ｜(adv.)nothing but＞／おとづる【訪る】[自ラ下二]＜訪れる｜(v.)visit＞(おとづれ＝連用形)／て【て】[接助]＜順接｜(conj.)and＞／なつ【夏】[名]＜夏｜(n.)Summer＞／に【に】[格助]＜行為主｜(prep.)by＞／しる【知る】[他ラ四]＜知る｜(v.)know＞(しら＝未然形)／る【る】[助動ラ下二型]受身＜～[さ]れる｜(aux-v.)PASSIVE VOICE＞(れ＝連用形)／ず【ず】[助動特殊型]打消＜～[し]ない｜(adv.)not ～＞(ぬ＝連体形)／みやまべ【深山辺】[名]＜山奥｜(n.)deep in the mountain＞／の【の】[格助]＜の｜(prep.)'s＞／さと【里】[名]＜田舎の村｜(n.)a village＞

[iwa tataku tani no mizu nomi otozure-te natsu ni shira-re-nu mi-yama-be no sato]

自然の姿を絵画的に描いた『千載集』収録歌 ― 十七文字の「俳句」の世界を三十一文字の「短歌」で表現したもの、と言えなくもないこの種の歌が、徐々に詠まれるようになって来たのは第五勅撰和歌集『金葉集』以降のこと…ひょっとしたらそれは、爛熟の極みに達した京都から、それ以前の時代には貴人たちが手つかずのまま放っておいた地方に向けて動き出した政治・経済の大きな流れの一端を示す証拠品と言えるかもしれません。

A pictorial depiction of Nature in 千載集(Senzai shuu)― a snapshot TANKA of 31 letters not unlike 17 version of 俳句(haiku) you might say ― gradually became popular in the years of the 5th Imperial TANKA anthology 金葉集(Kinyou shuu)... possibly a proof of political and economic dynamism away from too much matured 京都(Kyoto) into rural districts that used to be left untouched by nobles of the earlier years.

★54★ やまかげやいはもるしみづおとさえて なつのほかなるひぐらしのこゑ
山陰や岩漏る清水音冴えて夏の外なる蜩の声

【夏】[叙景]『7)千載集:210』慈円(じえん)

山深い木立の中、岩の上を静かに流れる湧き水の音が涼しげに響き渡る…彼方に聞こえるのは物静かなヒグラシの鳴き声…夏の暑さも喧騒も届かない、ここだけまるで別世界。

Deep in mountains in the shade of trees,
Sounds of rocky streams freshly wash my ears,
Deeper still I hear cicadas coolly sing...
Do they really know it's Summer in the world outside?

やま【山】[名]＜山｜(n.)the mountain＞／かげ【陰】[名]＜陰｜(n.)the shade＞／や【や】[感]＜詠嘆｜(interj.)EXCLAMATION＞／いは【岩】[名]＜岩｜(n.)a rock＞／もる【漏る】[自ラ四]＜漏れ出る｜(v.)leak＞(もる＝連体形)／しみず【清水】[名]＜澄んだ水｜(n.)pure water＞／おと【音】[名]＜音｜(n.)the sound＞／さゆ【冴ゆ】[自ヤ下二]＜冴える｜(v.)get sharp＞(さえ＝連用形)／

—夏—

て【て】〔接助〕＜順接｜(conj.)and＞／なつ【夏】〔名〕＜夏｜(n.)Summer＞／の【の】〔格助〕＜の｜(prep.)'s＞／ほか【外】〔名〕＜外｜(adv.)outside＞／なり【なり】〔助動ナリ型〕断定＜～である｜(aux-v.)be＞(なる=連体形)／ひぐらし【蜩】〔名〕＜[セミの]ヒグラシ｜(n.)evening cicadas＞／の【の】〔格助〕＜の｜(prep.)'s＞／こゑ【声】〔名〕＜声｜(n.)the voice＞

[yama-kage ya iwa moru shimizu oto sae-te natsu no hoka naru higurashi no koe]

平安末期の自然派短歌をもう一首・・・松尾芭蕉の有名な俳句 ― 静かさや岩に滲み入る蝉の声 ― の五世紀昔の御先祖様とも呼べそうな短歌です。

Another naturalistic TANKA at the end of the Heian era, arguably a 5-century earlier ancestor of 松尾芭蕉(Matsuo Bashou)'s famous 俳句(HAIKU) ― 静かさや岩に滲み入る蝉の声(shizuka-sa ya iwa ni shimi-iru semi no koe) ― **Tranquility pervades / A cicada's voice permeates / Through silence into rocks.**

★55★ そらのうみにくものなみたちつきのふね ほしのはやしにこぎかくるみゆ
空の海に雲の波立ち月の舟星の林に漕ぎ隠る見ゆ

【夏】[叙景]『3)拾遺集:488』柿本人麻呂(かきのもとのひとまろ)

夜空いっぱいに広がる大海原に、幾重にも立つ雲の波を乗り越えて、まばゆい光を放つ月の舟が漕ぎ進み、星々の森の中へと分け入って行くのが見える。

In the vast oceans of the sky

On waves after waves of clouds

Sail the shiny vessel of the moon

Into the yonder starry forests.

そら【空】〔名〕＜空｜(n.)the sky＞／の【の】〔格助〕＜の｜(prep.)'s＞／うみ【海】〔名〕＜海｜(n.)the ocean＞／に【に】〔格助〕＜場所｜(prep.)PLACE＞／くも【雲】〔名〕＜雲｜(n.)clouds＞／の【の】〔格助〕＜の｜(prep.)'s＞／なみ【波】〔名〕＜波｜(n.)waves＞／たつ【立つ】〔自夕四〕＜立つ｜(v.)surge up＞(たち=連用形)／つき【月】〔名〕＜月｜(n.)the moon＞／の【の】〔格助〕＜の｜(prep.)'s＞／ふね【舟】〔名〕＜船｜(n.)the ship＞／ほし【星】〔名〕＜星｜(n.)stars＞／の【の】〔格助〕＜の｜(prep.)'s＞／はやし【林】〔名〕＜林｜(n.)woods＞／に【に】〔格助〕＜場所｜(prep.)PLACE＞／こぐ【漕ぐ】〔他ガ四〕＜漕ぐ｜(v.)row＞(こぎ=連用形)／かくる【隠る】〔自ラ四〕＜隠れる｜(v.)hide away＞(かくる=連体形)／みゆ【見ゆ】〔自ヤ下二〕＜見える｜(v.)I can see＞(みゆ=終止形)

[sora no umi ni kumo no nami tachi tsuki no fune hoshi no hayashi ni kogi-kakuru miyu]

さらにもう一つ自然の情景、今度の作者は誰あろう、『古今集』より古い時代最大の「歌聖」と呼ばれた柿本人麻呂その人。写実性のかけらもない、とっても空想的な情景ながら、気取った趣向からは程遠く、高尚というより原始的な歌なのに、素朴な中にもグイグイ読み手を引っ張り込むその類推的説得力の力強さは、平安調短歌の中にはちょっと比べ得るものが見当たらない ― 古代メソポタミアの粘土板の上に描かれた星座の絵みたいな、時を超えて永遠に輝き続ける至高の芸術品。

Yet another poem on Natural scene, created by none other than 柿本人麻呂(Kakinomoto-no-Hitomaro), the most sacred of poets in the pre-古今集(Kokin shuu) years. Not at all photorealistic, highly imaginative yet anything but stylistic, more primitive than sophisticated, yet appealing to our mind's eye with unparalleled power of simple but convincing analogy – as timeless a piece of art as constellation pictures on ancient Mesopotamian clay.

―夏―

●56● あかなくにまだきもつきのかくるるか　やまのはにげていれずもあらなむ
　　　飽かなくに未だきも月の隠るるか山の端逃げて入れずもあらなむ

【夏】[俳諧]『1)古今集:884』在原業平(ありわらのなりひら)

まだ飽き足りないのに、早くも月は隠れようというのか・・・
逃げ込めないように、山の端の方がどこかへ逃げてしまえばいいのに。

I've had hardly enough of this wonderful night, and yet
The moon is hiding away — mountains, move, don't let it in.

あく【飽く】〔自力四〕＜飽きる｜(v.)have had enough of＞(あか＝未然形)／ず【ず】〔助動特殊型〕打消＜〜[し]ない｜(adv.)not＞(な＝未然形)／く【く】〔接尾〕＜名詞化成分｜(suffix)[to make n. out of v.]＞／に【に】〔接助〕＜逆接｜(conj.)although＞／まだき【未だき】〔副〕＜早くも｜(adv.)so soon＞／も【も】〔係助〕＜意味なし｜(adv.)NO MEANING＞／つき【月】〔名〕＜月｜(n.)the moon＞／の【の】〔格助〕＜主格｜(prep.)SUBJECT＞／かくる【隠る】〔自ラ下二〕＜隠れる｜(v.)hide away＞(かくるる＝連体形)／か【か】〔終助〕＜疑問｜(adv.)INTERROGATIVE＞／やまのは【山の端】〔名〕＜山の端｜(n.)the edge of the mountain＞／にぐ【逃ぐ】〔自ガ下二〕＜逃げる｜(v.)run away＞(にげ＝連用形)／て【て】〔接助〕＜順接｜(conj.)and＞／いる【入る】〔他ラ下二〕＜入れる｜(v.)let in＞(いれ＝未然形)／ず【ず】〔助動特殊型〕打消＜〜[し]ない｜(adv.)not＞(ず＝終止形)／も【も】〔係助〕＜意味なし｜(adv.)NO MEANING＞／あり【あり】〔自ラ変〕＜〜である｜(v.)behave＞(あら＝未然形)／なむ【なむ】〔終助〕＜〜ならいいのになぁ｜(v.)I hope＞

[aka-na-ku-ni madaki-mo tsuki no kakururu-ka yama-no-ha nige-te ire-zu mo ara-namu]

作者(在原業平)が酒宴の席で詠んだ歌。明け方近くになって彼の御主人様の惟高親王が退席して部屋に引っ込もうとするのを見て、陽気な調子で「まだ引っ込まないで！」とお願いしたものです。
The author, 在原業平(Ariwara-no-Narihira), rhymed out this cheerful desire of his at a banquet when he saw his master Prince 惟喬(Koretaka) about to disappear into his room towards dawn.

―――――――――――――――――――――――――――

●57● なつのよはまだよひながらあけぬるを　くものいづこにつきやどるらむ
　　　夏の夜は未だ宵ながら明けぬるを雲の何処に月宿るらむ

【夏】[俳諧]『1)古今集:166』清原深養父(きよはらのふかやぶ)

夏の夜の明けるのは早くて、まだ宵の口だと思っているうちに、あっという間に朝が来てしまった・・・
こんなせっかちな夜明けには、月が沈む間もあるまいに・・・
おーい、お月さん、雲のどのあたりに隠れているんだい？

This Summer night seems to have broken into dawn,
While we stayed up here thinking it was barely evening.
Behind what clouds in the sky is the moon hiding now?

なつ【夏】〔名〕＜夏｜(n.)Summer＞／の【の】〔格助〕＜の｜(prep.)'s＞／よ【夜】〔名〕＜夜｜(n.)the night＞／は【は】〔係助〕＜主格｜(prep.)SUBJECT＞／まだ【未だ】〔副〕＜まだ｜(adv.)yet＞／よひ【宵】〔名〕＜夜の早い時間｜(n.)early evening＞／ながら【ながら】〔接助〕＜〜ではあるが｜(conj.)although＞／あく【明く】〔自力下二〕＜夜が明ける｜(v.)break into the morning＞(あけ＝連用形)／ぬ【ぬ】〔助動ナ変型〕完了＜すでに〜[し]た｜(aux-v.)PERFECT TENSE＞(ぬる＝連体形)／を【を】〔接助〕＜〜[だ]というのに｜(conj.)although＞／くも【雲】〔名〕＜雲｜(n.)clouds＞／の【の】〔格助〕＜の｜(prep.)'s＞／いづこ【何処】〔代名〕＜どこ｜(adv.)where＞／に【に】〔格助〕＜場所｜(prep.)PLACE＞／つき【月】〔名〕＜月

—夏—

(n.)the moon＞／やどる【宿る】〔自ラ四〕＜宿る｜(v.)stay＞(やどる＝終止形)／らむ【らむ】〔助動ラ四型〕現在推量＜〜だろう｜(aux-v.)SUPPOSITION＞(らむ＝連体形係り結び)

[natsu no yo wa mada yoi nagara ake-nuru wo kumo no izuko ni tsuki yadoru-ramu]

「未だ宵ながら明けぬる」はおどけた矛盾で、夜明けが来たなら宵は当然終わってるはず ─ これと同じくらい陽気な冗談が結句を飾る「雲の何処に月宿るらむ」で、もう夜が明けてるからには月だって当然沈んでるはず。こんな調子で、「夏」の歌の基調音はC調（メージャーの長調）、そこには他の季節の歌にありがちな陰影のかけらも宿らない。

未だ宵ながら明けぬる(mada yoi nagara ake-nuru=it's already dawn though it's still midnight) is a jesting contradiction — when it's dawn, it's already *NOT* midnight — as cheerful as the closing joke 雲の何処に月宿るらむ(kumo no izuko ni tsuki yadoru-ramu=where behind the clouds does the moon hide itself?) – when it's already dawn, the moon has certainly gone. Songs of Summer have a basic tone of C-major without a speck of gloom as in other seasons.

───────────────────────────────

●58●あひみてもあはでもなげくたなばたは いつかこころののどけかるべき
逢ひ見ても逢はでも嘆く織姫は何時か心の長閑けかるべき

【夏】[季題]『3)拾遺集:153』詠み人知らず

晴れて逢瀬が叶っても、共に過ごすは一夜のみ、後に待つのは悲しい別れ・・・曇りや雨に邪魔されれば、逢瀬は流れて翌年待ち・・・逢っても、逢えなくても、いずれにせよ涙に暮れる七夕の哀しきヒロイン織姫の心は、一体いつ安らぎを覚えるのだろう？

Vega meets Altair only once in a year.
If rainy or cloudy, she'll wait another year.
The long-awaited rendezvous ends all too soon.
When will she find her true peace of mind?

あひみる【逢ひ見る】〔他マ上一〕＜(恋人と)逢い引きする｜(v.)have a date＞(あひみ＝連用形)／て【て】〔接助〕＜仮定｜(conj.)if＞／も【も】〔係助〕＜〜でさえも｜(adv.)even＞／あふ【逢ふ】〔自ハ四〕＜(恋人どうしとして)逢う｜(v.)have a date＞(あは＝未然形)／で【で】〔接助〕＜〜することなしに｜(prep.)without 〜ing＞／も【も】〔係助〕＜意味なし｜(adv.)NO MEANING＞／なげく【嘆く】〔自カ四〕＜嘆く｜(v.)grieve＞(なげく＝連体形)／たなばた【棚機】〔名〕＜七夕・織姫｜(n.)Vega＞／は【は】〔係助〕＜主格｜(prep.)SUBJECT＞／いつ【何時】〔代名〕＜いつ｜(adv.)when＞／か【か】〔係助〕＜疑問｜(adv.)INTERROGATIVE＞／こころ【心】〔名〕＜心｜(n.)heart＞／の【の】〔格助〕＜主格｜(prep.)SUBJECT＞／のどけし【長閑し】〔形ク〕＜のどかだ｜(adj.)feel at ease＞(のどけかる＝連体形)／べし【べし】〔助動ク型〕可能＜〜できる｜(aux-v.)POSSIBILITY＞(べき＝連体形係り結び)

[ai-mi-te-mo awa-de-mo nageku tanabata wa itsu-ka kokoro no nodokekaru-beki]

平安時代の貴族たちは大の宴会好き ─ というか、政治的に力のある人々に交じっての社交活動以外、ロクに実務的な仕事もしなかったのが平安の世の御公家たち。その種の社交場面を彩るために、数限りなく価値なき歌が(ここに紹介した七夕関連陳腐短歌150分の1をはじめとして)生まれたのでした・・・マジメな話、八代集の中身なんて、そんなもの・・・だから、普通の読者なら八代集なんて全然読まずに放っておいても(ほとんど)問題はありません ─ この二百首(ぐらいの秀歌選さえ手放さなければ、ね。

Nobles in the Heian era were fond of holding and attending parties — in fact, they had no practical job to do except for social activities among people with political power. Countless worthless songs were made to decorate such social occasions... including this one, one of the 150 七夕(tanabata)-related commonplaces... in fact, the whole contents of 八代集(Hachidai shuu＝8 great Imperial TANKA Anthologies) are such that ordinary readers have little or nothing to lose if they leave them totally unread ─ *so long as they have this 200 (give or take a few) great TANKA anthology in their hands!*

・・・・・・・・・・・・・・・・・・・・・・・・・・

《「七夕」は一年一夜飽かぬ恋》

昔々、天の川の東の岸に織姫(Vega:ヴェガ)という女性がいて、天の衣を四六時中編み続けていました。お年頃の女らしく着飾る暇もなく機織りの天職に励む彼女のことを、天帝は哀れに思い、天の川の東岸の彦星(Altair:アルタイル)に嫁がせてあげました。ところが、女らしい幸せを掴んだ織姫は、天の機織りとしての仕事をサボるようになってしまったので、天帝は怒り、この二人を天の川の両岸に離ればなれにした上で、七月七日の夜が晴れだった場合に限り、年に一度の逢瀬を許すことにしました･･･この古い中国の伝説に従って、平安時代の貴族たちは陰暦の七月七日(太陽暦の八月七日)の夜には毎年祝宴を催し、織姫と彦星が無事に逢えるようお香を焚いてお祈りしました。古代中国の娘たちは、自分が編んだ着物を捧げ物にして、織姫の御加護で自分たちの機織りの腕も上がるようにお祈りしたと言われています。日本の短歌の中には、七夕の夜に織姫が心置きなく機織り仕事をサボれるように、と彼女に織物を貸す歌がいくつも見られます。平安の世の貴人たちは、機織りのみならず染め物や歌詠みの腕も上がるよう織姫にお祈りしました。その後、江戸時代になると、この風習は社会の下々の層にも広まりました･･･今日もなお、七月七日の前後数日間、日本の子供たちは願い事を短冊に書いて笹の葉に吊るしていますが、その風習が陰暦七月(陽暦八月)の「葉月(はづき)」の名の由来と言われています。

《たなばた(tanabata＝midsummer trans-galactic rendezvous) ─
comes once a year and goes without satisfaction》

Once upon a time at the eastern end of the Milky Way, a woman (Orihime＝Vega) was permanently engaged in weaving heavenly dress with hardly any leisure to dress herself up as a young woman should. The Overlord pitied her and allowed her to marry a man (Hikoboshi＝Altair) on the western side. As Vega achieved her womanly happiness, however, she came to neglect her duty as the heavenly weaver. The Overlord got angry and tore the couple apart on both sides of the Milky Way, who were granted an annual rendezvous only when the weather was fine on the night of July 7. In accordance with this ancient Chinese legend, nobles in the Heian era would hold an annual party on the night of lunar July 7/solar August 7, burning incense to hope for a happy rendezvous of Vega and Altair. Ancient Chinese girls are said to have devoted clothing of their own weaving to hope their skill would get better by Vega's favor, while several Japanese TANKA are found to lend clothes to Vega so that she could safely neglect her heavenly duty for the night. Heianese nobles prayed to Vega for improved skill in dying and rhyming in addition to weaving. Later in the Edo(江戸) period, this custom spread lower into the whole society... even today Japanese kids will write down their wishes on a sheet of paper and hang it down from a bamboo leaf several days before and after July 7, which custom is said to have led to the name of 葉月(hazuki＝the month of leaves) for the lunar seventh(solar 8th) month.

―夏―

●59● よられつるのもせのくさのかげろひて　すずしくくもるゆふだちのそら

縒られつる野も狭の草の蔭ろひて涼しく曇る夕立の空

【夏】[叙景]『8)新古今集:263』西行(さいぎょう)

横なびきにサァーッと吹き付ける風に押し流されて、野原一面横倒しになった草木の糸の縒り跡に、涼しい影を落としつつ、空を曇らせ夕立降り注ぐ、夏の終わりの通り雨。

Field-wide blades of grass blown sideways by sudden wind
Offering cool shade under rapidly approaching clouds
Precursor to impending shower from the yonder sky.

よる【縒る】〔他ラ四〕<[糸を]より合わせる｜(v.)weave＞（よら＝未然形）／る【る】〔助動ラ下二型〕受身＜～[さ]れる｜(aux-v.)PASSIVE VOICE＞（れ＝連用形）／つ【つ】〔助動タ下二型〕完了＜すでに～した｜(aux-v.)PERFECT TENSE＞（つる＝連体形）／の【野】[名]＜野原｜(n.)the field＞／も【も】[係助]＜意味なし｜(adv.)NO MEANING＞／せ【狭】[名]＜狭く感じる｜(adj.)feel narrow＞／の【の】[格助]＜の｜(prep.)'s＞／くさ【草】[名]＜草木｜(n.)grass＞／の【の】[格助]＜主格｜(prep.)SUBJECT＞／かげろふ【蔭ろふ】〔自ハ四〕＜影を作る｜(v.)make shadows＞（かげろひ＝連用形）／て【て】[接助]＜順接｜(conj.)and＞／すずし【涼し】[形シク]＜涼しげに｜(adv.)coolly＞（すずしく＝連用形）／くもる【曇る】〔自ラ四〕＜曇る｜(v.)get cloudy＞（くもる＝連体形）／ゆふだち【夕立】[名]＜夕立｜(n.)showers of rain＞／の【の】[格助]＜の｜(prep.)'s＞／そら【空】[名]＜空｜(n.)the sky＞

[yora-re-tsuru no-mo-se-no kusa no kageroi-te suzushiku kumoru yuu-dachi no sora]

驚くばかりのこの短歌の世界には、以下の三つの場面が順を追って展開する：1)野原狭しと生い茂る草木を斜めになぎ倒しつつ、先触れ役の風が吹き抜ける；2)雲が太陽を覆うにつれて、影が大地を走り抜ける；3)横殴りの夕立の矢が、周りの景色を曇らせて、空と大地を灰色一色の単一世界へと融け合わせる･･･これら三つの視覚世界の移行過程に加えて、時間と体表感覚の変化もまた語られる ―「**縒られ＜つる＞**」の完了形助動詞と「**涼しく**」の副詞の取り合わせが、読者の想像世界の中の「**夕立の空**」に、こうした時の流れと肌合いの変化を印象付ける･･･言葉で描く動画の世界、三十一文字の短歌世界が秘めた空間・時間描写の可能性を教えてくれるこの作品の作者は、伝説の放浪歌僧、西行法師。

This incredible TANKA embraces the following three scenes in sequence: 1)the wind blows broadly through the field of oblique grass as the harbinger; 2)the clouds block the sun to cast moving shadows on the ground; 3)oblique arrows of shower dim the scene around to fuse the sky and the ground into a single gray entity... These three visual transition are accompanied by temporal and sensory change ― the auxiliary verb of the present perfect tense in **縒られ＜つる＞**(yorare tsuru＝that ＜have＞ been blown sideways) and the adverb **涼しく**(suzushiku＝coolly) combine to attain these change in time and on the skin in the reader's imagination of **夕立の空**(yuu-dachi no sora＝the showering sky). A verbal moving picture showing spatial and temporal potentiality of 31-lettered TANKA by the legendary wandering bonze of poetic wonder 西行法師(Saigyou houshi).

―秋: Autumn―

—夏〜秋—

●60●あきちかきけしきのもりになくせみの なみだのつゆやしたばそむらむ

秋近き気色の杜に鳴く蝉の涙の露や下葉染むらむ

【秋】[機知]『8』新古今集:270 藤原(九条)良経(ふじわらの(くじょう)よしつね)

秋が近付く気色の杜に、終わりの近い命の限り、声を限りと鳴く蝉たち・・・降る雨露(あまつゆ)が増すほどに色が増すという秋の紅葉(こうよう)は、晩夏(ばんか)に奏でる蝉の挽歌(ばんか)のおびただしい涙で色付くのかもしれないね。

Autumn feels imminent in the woods of Keshiki,

Desperate voices of cicadas make me restless too.

Fall soon they would along with countless tears

To deepen sorrowful colors of changing leaves later.

あき【秋】[名]＜秋｜(n.)Autumn＞／ちかし【近し】[形]＜～が間近に迫る｜(adj.)be near at hand＞(ちかき＝連体形)／(A)**けしき**【気色】[名]＜様子:(n.)feel＞／(B)**けしき**のもり【気色の杜】[名]＜[固有名詞]気色の森｜(n.)the woods of Keshiki＞／に【に】[格助]＜場所｜(prep.)PLACE＞／なく【鳴く】[自カ四]＜鳴く｜(v.)cry＞(なく＝連体形)／せみ【蝉】[名]＜セミ｜(n.)cicadas＞／の【の】[格助]＜の｜(prep.)'s＞／なみだ【涙】[名]＜涙｜(n.)tears＞／の【の】[格助]＜の｜(prep.)'s＞／つゆ【露】[名]＜露｜(n.)dew＞／や【や】[係助]＜疑問｜(adv.)INTERROGATIVE＞／したば【下葉】[名]＜草木の下の方の葉｜(n.)leaves in the lower part of the tree＞／そむ【染む】[他マ下二]＜染める｜(v.)tinge＞(そむ＝終止形)／らむ【らむ】[助動ラ四型]現在推量＜～だろう｜(aux-v.)SUPPOSITION＞(らむ＝連体形係り結び)

[aki chikaki Keshiki-no-mori ni naku semi no namida no tsuyu ya shitaba somu-ramu]

夏に日本を訪れる外国人の多くは、耳をつんざくようなセミの合唱(がっしょう)にびっくり仰天(ぎょうてん)するでしょう・・・蝉の鳴き声は今日の日本では「夏の暑さと活気」の象徴です。しかしながら平安時代の「蝉」は、「騒々しい」よりむしろ「はかない」存在とみなされていました・・・セミの抜け殻を表わす「空蝉:うつせみ」の響きが、「現身:うつしみ＝束(つか)の間の存在」としての自らの人生の儚(はかな)さを強く意識する平安時代の人々の耳に、しんみりと訴(うった)えたからかもしれません。この歌の中の「**気色の森**」は日本の南端にある実際の地名ですが、ここでは「秋近き**気色**」の言い回しを形成するのに便利な「音(もの)」としてのみ用いています。「セミの涙が秋の木の葉の色を濃くする」という発想は、「雨が多く降るほど紅葉の美しさが増す」という当時の俗信にヒネリを加えたものです。

Most foreign people coming to Japan in Summer will be flabbergasted at the deafening noise of 蝉(semi＝cicada)s' harmony: it is a symbol of the heat and energy of Summer in today's Japan. In the Heian era, however, 蝉(semi＝cicadas) were never considered loud but rather pitied for their ephemeral existence, possibly because the name 空蝉(utsu-semi＝the empty shell of a cicada) had a nice ring to it in the ears of people who were only too conscious of their mortality as 現身(utsushi-mi＝temporal entity). **気色の杜**(Keshiki-no-mori) in this TANKA is an actual place name at the southern end of Japan, but is merely used here as a convenient sound to form the phrase 秋近き気色(aki chikaki **keshiki**＝**the feel** of impending Autumn). The idea that the tears of cicadas would deepen the colors of Autumn leaves is a twisted version of the popular belief in those days that the more it rained, the more beautiful 紅葉(momiji＝varicolored leaves) would become.

————————————————————————

―夏～秋―

● 61 ● あさがほをなにはかなしとおもひけむ　ひとをもはなはさこそみるらめ

朝顔を何は悲しと思ひけむ人をも花は然こそ見るらめ

【秋】［擬人］『3)拾遺集:1283』藤原道信（ふじわらのみちのぶ）

早朝に咲いたかと思えば昼過ぎには萎んでしまう朝顔の花の儚さを、
昔は他人事みたいに憐れんでいた私ですが、どうも逆だったようですね・・・
人の世の無常をこそ、きっと花たちは憐れんで見ていることでしょう。

I used to pity morning glory for being ever so transient,
How ignorant it sees humans coming and going like this.

あさがほ【朝顔】［名］＜朝顔｜(n.)morning glory＞／を【を】［格助］＜目的格｜(prep.)OBJECT＞／なに【何】［副］＜どうして｜(adv.)why＞／は【は】［係助］＜強調｜(adv.)EMPHASIS＞／かなし【哀し】［形シク］＜哀れだ｜(adj.)pathetic＞（かなし＝終止形）／と【と】［格助］＜内容提示｜(conj.)that 〜＞／おもふ【思ふ】［他ハ四］＜思う｜(v.)think＞（おもひ＝連用形）／けむ【けむ】［助動マ四型］過去推量＜〜[し]たのだろう｜(aux-v.)PAST SUPPOSITION＞（けむ＝連体形係り結び）／ひと【人】［名］＜人間｜(n.)a human being＞／を【を】［格助］＜目的格｜(prep.)OBJECT＞／も【も】［係助］＜〜もまた｜(adv.)also＞／はな【花】［名］＜花｜(n.)flowers＞／は【は】［係助］＜主格｜(prep.)SUBJECT＞／さ【然】［副］＜そのように｜(adv.)thus＞／こそ【こそ】［係助］＜強調｜(adv.)EMPHASIS＞／みる【見る】［他マ上一］＜見る｜(v.)view＞（みる＝終止形）／らむ【らむ】［助動ラ四型］現在推量＜〜だろう｜(aux-v.)SUPPOSITION＞（らめ＝已然形係り結び）

[asa-gao wo nani-wa kanashi to omoi-kemu hito wo-mo hana wa sa-koso miru-rame]

「しおれ行く花の鏡に反射投影された人間の感情」という手垢の付いたお題ながら、この詩に関して(現代読者には)きっと新鮮に感じられるであろう話題は、我々にとっては間違いなく「夏の花」である「朝顔」が、古歌の世界では「秋」に属する風物だということ・・・移ろいやすいその性質が、万事前向きな「夏」の陽気な空気に不似合いだったから？・・・かもしれません。

A hackneyed human emotion reflected in the mirror of withering flowers. What must be new to modern readers about this TANKA is this ― 朝顔(asa-gao＝morning glory), definitely the flower of Summer for us, happens to belong to early Autumn in the world of old poetry... possibly because its fleeting nature is unbecoming to the cheerful atmosphere of all-positive Summer.

● 62 ● ひぐらしのなきつるなへにひはくれぬと　おもへばやまのかげにぞありける

蜩の鳴きつるなへに日は暮れぬと思へば山の蔭にぞありける

【秋】［叙景］『1)古今集:204』詠み人知らず

肌合いの涼しさに、耳に染み入る清涼感を添えるヒグラシの声が加わり、薄暗い周囲の雰囲気も手伝って、「ああ、もう日暮れ時か」と思ってふと彼方に目をやれば、空はまだ暮れやらず明るいまま・・・
私を取り巻くこの仄暗さは、お日様の光を通せんぼする山の陰影のいたずらだったんだなぁ。

Cicadas sing in soothing voice of Fall
Adding to the feel that the sun has set
In the ambient dark confusingly convincing
Blocking sunshine in this broad daylight.

ひぐらし【蜩】［名］＜[セミの]ヒグラシ｜(n.)evening cicadas＞／の【の】［格助］＜主格｜(prep.)SUBJECT＞／なく【鳴】［自カ四］＜鳴く｜(v.)cry＞（なき＝連用形）／つ【つ】［助動タ下二型］完了＜すでに〜した

｜(aux-v.)PERFECT TENSE＞(つる＝連体形)／なへに【なへに】〔接助〕＜時｜(conj.)while＞／ひ【日】〔名〕＜日｜(n.)the day＞／は【は】〔係助〕＜主格｜(prep.)SUBJECT＞／くる【暮る】〔自ラ下二〕＜日暮れになる｜(v.)get dark＞(くれ＝連用形)／ぬ【ぬ】〔助動ナ変型〕完了＜すでに〜[し]た｜(aux-v.)PERFECT TENSE＞(ぬ＝終止形)／と【と】〔格助〕＜内容提示｜(conj.)that 〜＞／おもふ【思ふ】〔他ハ四〕＜思う｜(v.)think＞(おもへ＝已然形)／ば【ば】〔接助〕＜〜したところ｜(conj.)when＞／やま【山】〔名〕＜山｜(n.)the mountain＞／の【の】〔格助〕＜の｜(prep.)'s＞／かげ【蔭】〔名〕＜陰｜(n.)the shade＞／なり【なり】〔助動ナリ型〕断定＜〜である｜(aux-v.)be＞(に＝連用形)／ぞ【ぞ】〔係助〕＜強調｜(adv.)EMPHASIS＞／あり【あり】〔自ラ変〕＜〜である｜(v.)turn out to be＞(あり＝連用形)／けり【けり】〔助動ラ変型〕詠嘆＜〜だったのだなぁ｜(interj.)REALIZATION＞(ける＝連体形係り結び)

[higurashi no naki-tsuru naeni hi wa kure-nu to omoe-ba yama no kage ni-zo ari-keru]

一つ前の歌の「アサガオ」と同様、**ひぐらし**もまた「晩夏」と「初秋」の境界線上に身を置き、両方の季節に曖昧に熔け入ってしまう自然界の微妙な存在。夏の夕方の暗がりに鳴り響くヒグラシの寂しげな声は、暑さと日射しに一日中さらされた後の人の五感を涼しく癒やしてくれる･･･この生き物を古歌が「夏」ではなく「秋」に組み入れる理由も、このあたりにあるのかもしれない。ここに紹介した短歌は、そうしたヒグラシの「秋、かと思えば実は夏だったりする」性質(あるいは声)を実に見事に表現している。

ひぐらし(higurashi＝tanna japonensis, or evening cicada) is also an obscure thing of Nature with its marginal existence blurred between late Summer and early Autumn. Its forlorn voice ringing in the dusk of Summer evening coolly soothes our senses tired after a day's exposure to heat and sunshine... a possible reason for old poetry to categorize this creature into Autumn, not Summer. This particular TANKA cleverly depicts such ambivalent nature of ひぐらし(higurashi)'s existence (or, voice).

●63● なつとあきとゆきかふそらのかよひぢは かたへすずしきかぜやふくらむ
夏と秋と行き交ふ空の通ひ路は片方涼しき風や吹くらむ

【秋】[季題]『1)古今集:168』凡河内躬恒(おうしこうちのみつね)

夏と秋とが空の上で交じり合う辺りでは、一方の側、秋の向こう側だけ、涼しい風が吹いているのだろうか？

At the crossroad of the heavens where Summer and Autumn come and go,
Is the wind blowing cool on one side, still hot on the other?

なつ【夏】〔名〕＜夏｜(n.)Summer＞／と【と】〔格助〕＜列挙｜(conj.)and＞／あき【秋】〔名〕＜秋｜(n.)Autumn＞／と【と】〔格助〕＜列挙｜(conj.)and＞／ゆきかふ【行き交ふ】〔自ハ下二〕＜行き交う｜(v.)come and go＞(ゆきかふ＝終止形)／そら【空】〔名〕＜空｜(n.)the sky＞／の【の】〔格助〕＜の｜(prep.)'s＞／かよひぢ【通ひ路】〔名〕＜通り道｜(n.)the route＞／は【は】〔係助〕＜〜に関しては｜(adv.)as for 〜＞／かたへ【片方】〔名〕＜片側｜(n.)one side of the way＞／すずし【涼し】〔形シク〕＜涼しい｜(adj.)cool＞(すずしき＝連体形)／かぜ【風】〔名〕＜風｜(n.)wind＞／や【や】〔係助〕＜疑問｜(adv.)INTERROGATIVE＞／ふく【吹く】〔自力四〕＜吹く｜(v.)blow＞(ふく＝終止形)／らむ【らむ】〔助動ラ四型〕現在推量＜〜だろう｜(aux-v.)SUPPOSITION＞(らむ＝連体形係り結び)

[natsu to aki to yuki-kau sora no kayoi-ji wa kata-e suzushiki kaze ya fuku-ramu]

太陰暦の「水無月：みなづき＝6番目の月」の最後の日に詠まれたとされる趣向歌。太陽暦に換算してもこの日はなお「七月末日」だから、まさに暑さの極み･･･それでもなおこの日は「夏の終わり」とみなされて、翌「文月：ふ[み]づき＝陰暦7月／陽暦8月」の初めと共に「**秋**」も始まるとされていました ─ そんなバカな！と言われそうですが、それが昔の日本の約束事。当時の人々は、一年12ヶ月を四等分して各3ヶ月ずつの「四季」に分けたので、「一月(睦月：むつき)・二月(如月：きさらぎ)・三月(弥生：やよい)／新暦2・3・4月」が「春」、「四月(卯月：うづき)・五月(皐月：さつき)・六月(水無月：みなづき)／新暦5・6・7月」が「**夏**」、

—夏〜秋—

「七月(文月：ふ[み]づき)・八月(葉月：はづき)・九月(長月：ながつき)／新暦8・9・10月」が「秋」、残りの「十月(神無月：かんなづき)・十一月(霜月：しもつき)・十二月(師走：しはす)／新暦11・12・1月」は「冬」; その結果、「冬と春」・「夏と秋」の端境期にはどう見てもおかしな季節感の歌があれこれ生まれたのでした。

A song of style allegedly made on the last day of 水無月 (minazuki＝the lunar sixth month). Converted into the solar calendar date, it still is the end of July, the height of Summer heat... still, this was supposed to be the end of Summer, with Autumn beginning with the start of 文月 (fumizuki＝the lunar seventh/solar eighth month) — CRAZY! you might say, but it's the rule of ancient Japan: they just divided the 12 months into 4 seasons with 3 months each, 1st, 2nd and 3rd (solar February, March and April) belonging to Spring, 4th, 5th and 6th (solar May, June and July) to Summer, 7th, 8th and 9th (solar August, September and October) to Autumn, and the rest (lunar 10th, 11th and 12th / solar November, December and January) forming Winter, resulting in apparently queer seasonal poems about *Winter/Spring* and *Summer/Autumn* transition.

....

《夏は外秋は内なる心かな》

色々お目にかけてきた通り、「夏」の短歌は外の世界の自然物に向けられた外向的なもの。一方、これからふんだんにお目にかけることになるが、「秋」の短歌は内向的 — 内なる孤独や悲しみが、「自然の鏡」(大抵は、「月」)に反射投影されたものが多い。

《songs of Summer are extrovert; those of Autumn introvert》

As you have seen, the world of Summer TANKA is directed toward things of Nature in the world outside; while, as you are going to see in abundance, Autumnal TANKA are largely introvert – inner feelings of solitude or sadness reflected in the mirror of Nature... mostly, on the moon.

●64●なにめでてをれるばかりぞをみなへし　われおちにきとひとにかたるな
名に愛でて折れるばかりぞ女郎花我落ちにきと人に語るな

【秋】[俳諧]『1)古今集:226』遍昭(良岑宗貞)(へんじょう(よしみねのむねさだ))

「女郎花：をみなへし・・・美女もタジタジの麗しき花」とは、何とも艶っぽい名前だなあ。そんな妖艶な名を身にまとい、枝も折れんばかりにたわわに咲くその花を見ると、もはや俗界を捨てた僧侶の身である私の心もくずおれて、思わずこの手に手折って愛してやりたい気分になる・・・おっと、「僧正遍昭、オミナエシの色香に堕つ！」などと、人にバラしてくれるなよ。

Your name is to blame — ominaeshi: beautiful lady's flower
For inviting me to stoop to your womanish lure.
If I fell, don't tell of your charming conquest of me.

な【名】[名]＜名前｜(n.)the name＞／に【に】[格助]＜原因｜(prep.)REASON＞／めづ【愛づ】[自ダ下二]＜愛おしく思う｜(v.)feel affectionate｜(めで＝連用形)／て【て】[接助]＜理由｜(conj.)REASON＞／をる【折る】[自ダ下二]＜屈する｜(v.)give in＞(をれる＝連体形)／ばかり【ばかり】[副助]＜〜なほど｜(adv.)to 〜 exent＞／ぞ【ぞ】[終助]＜強調｜(adv.)EMPHASIS＞／をみなへし【女郎花】[名]＜オミナエシ｜(n.)ominaeshi(＝a beautiful lady's flower)＞／われ【我】[代名]＜私｜(pron.)I, myself＞／おつ【落つ】[自ダ上二]＜誘惑に屈する｜(v.)yield to temptation＞(おち＝連用形)／ぬ【ぬ】[助動ナ変型]完了＜すでに〜[し]た｜(aux-v.)PERFECT TENSE＞(に＝連用形)／き【き】[助動特殊型]過去＜〜[し]た｜(aux-v.)PAST＞(き＝終止形)／と【と】[格助]＜内容提示｜(conj.)that 〜＞／ひと【人】[名]＜他人｜(n.)others＞／に【に】[格助]＜対象｜(prep.)OBJECT＞／かたる【語る】[他ラ四]＜語る｜(v.)tell＞(かたる＝終止形)／な【な】[終助]＜〜するな｜(adv.)don't 〜＞

―秋―

[na ni mede-te oreru bakari zo ominaeshi ware ochi-ni-ki to hito ni kataru-na]

この歌の作者の僧正遍昭は、本来なら性的な生臭さを漂わせてはいけないはずの身分ながら、「女郎花
＝美女の花」という名を聞いただけで性的魅惑を覚えてしまう、などとオドケています。名前をネタにして
ただひたすらアソンでるばかりの歌で、現代の読者なら誰もが「バカらしいまでに無意味」と感じる代物・・・
だけど、この種の軽薄な言葉遊びこそが平安調短歌の底辺を形作っていたのでした。大方の平安貴族にと
っての「短歌」は、現代日本人にとっての「カラオケ」みたいなもの ― 軽い社交の口実であって、芸術親交
会ではなかったのです・・・これもまた、短歌が今日の日本ではひどく不人気な理由の一つ・・・だって、
出来合いのカラオケ楽曲を歌って誰もが同じように自分自身に酔える御時世に、わざわざあなたの「個人的
傑作」(あるいは、ゴミカス)ぶつけて他の人たちにバツの悪い思いさせる必要なんて、ないでしょう？

This author, 僧正遍昭(Henjou the highest ranking priest), is making a joke of himself ― a supposedly non-sexual entity ― being sensually tempted by the mere name of おみなへし(**女郎花**: ominaeshi＝the flower of a beautiful lady). A name-play TANKA through and through which most modern readers would find absurdly meaningless... but this type of frivolous play on words formed the basis of Heianese TANKA: TANKA was to most Heianese nobles what KARAOKE is to the modern Japanese ― not so much artistic communion as easy pretext of social intercourse – just another reason why TANKA is pathetically unpopular in today's Japan: when all can equally get intoxicated with ready-made tunes of KARAOKE, why bother to annoy others with your personal masterpiece... or rubbish?

・・・・・・・・・・・・・・・・・・・・・・・・・・・・

《名引かれて中身など見ぬ和の心》

春の花の「桜」と「梅」に次いで三番目に人気のある花は、秋に咲く「**女郎花**」で、八代集約9500の中に82
首登場する。しかしながら「桜」や「梅」に比べれば面白味もまるでなく、花を取り巻く劇的な状況も何一つ
ないこの「**おみなえし**」の唯一の取り柄は、その「女っぽい」名前だけ；だが、日本では、空っぽの中身を
持ち上げるには「名前」さえあればそれで十分。何もないものを取り囲んで80を超える歌が口々にその
「無」への一様の(＝バカの一つ覚えの)賛辞を奏でれば、輪の外から見る人は誰しも、そこには「何か
ある」と信じてしまうもの ― それが、千年昔も今も変わらぬ、日本流の「魔法」の作り方。

《label only, contents notwithstanding ― that's the Japanese way of citation》

Next to 桜(sakura＝cherry blossom) and 梅(ume＝plum, or Japanese apricots) in Spring, **おみなえし**
(**女郎花**: ominaeshi＝patrinia scabiosifolia) in Autumn is the third popular flower appearing 82 times
in some 9,500 poems in 八代集(Hachidai shuu＝8 great Imperial TANKA anthologies). **おみなえし**
(ominaeshi), however, is a flower of much less interest, without any dramatic circumstances, except for
its womanish name – but name alone is more than enough in Japan to commend empty contents.
When eighty-odd galleries make a circle around **nothing**, singing aloud their unanimous
(=*monotonous*) praise of that *nothing*, everybody outside will believe there'll be **something** in it –
that's the Japanese way of creating magic, as valid today as it was a thousand years ago.

—秋—

★65★あききぬとめにはさやかにみえねども かぜのおとにぞおどろかれぬる
秋来ぬと目にはさやかに見えねども風の音にぞ驚かれぬる

【秋】[転季]『1)古今集:169』藤原敏行(ふじわらのとしゆき)

暦の上ではもう秋が来たといっても、見渡せば周りの景色はどれもこれもみな夏模様、はっきりと秋めいた色彩などどこにもない・・・のだが、ふと肌に感じる風だけは微妙に涼しげ・・・もう秋はすぐそこまで来ているのだなぁ。

The first day of Autumn still leaves my eyes cold.
Everything in sight is hot, no sign of Autumn yet.
But wait, the wind is cool... air-mail from coming Fall.

あき【秋】〔名〕<秋 | (n.)Autumn>／く【来】〔自力変〕<来る | (v.)come>(き=連用形)／ぬ【ぬ】〔助ナ変型〕完了<すでに〜[し]た | (aux-v.)PERFECT TENSE>(ぬ=終止形)／と【と】〔格助〕<内容提示 | (conj.)that 〜>／め【目】〔名〕<目 | (n.)the eye>／に【に】〔格助〕<対象 | (prep.)OBJECT>／は【は】〔係助〕<〜に関しては | (adv.)as for 〜>／さやかなり【清かなり】〔形動ナリ〕<はっきりと | (adv.)clearly>(さやかに=連用形)／みゆ【見ゆ】〔自ヤ下二〕<見える | (v.)appear>(みえ=連用形)／ず【ず】〔助動特殊型〕打消<〜[し]ない | (adv.)not 〜>(ね=已然形)／ども【ども】〔接助〕<〜ではあるが | (conj.)although>／かぜ【風】〔名〕<風 | (n.)wind>／の【の】〔格助〕<の | (prep.)'s>／おと【音】〔名〕<音 | (n.)the sound>／に【に】〔格助〕<行為主 | (prep.)by>／ぞ【ぞ】〔係助〕<強調 | (adv.)EMPHASIS>／おどろく【驚く】〔自力四〕<はっと気付く | (v.)suddenly realize>(おどろか=未然形)／る【る】〔助動ラ下二型〕自発<思わず知らず そうなる | (adv.)naturally>(れ=連用形)／ぬ【ぬ】〔助動ナ変型〕完了<すでに〜[し]た | (aux-v.)PERFECT TENSE>(ぬる=連体形係り結び)

[aki ki-nu to me ni-wa sayakani mie-ne-domo kaze no oto ni-zo odoroka-re-nuru]

秋はまだどこにも見えないけれど、風の感触はすでにもう夏のそれではない、とこの詩人は言っています・・・もっとも、彼が実際それを「肌合いで感じた」のか、それとも今日が陰暦七月／陽暦八月の初日だからということで彼の「頭がそう思わせた」だけなのか、実に怪しいところではありますが。正岡子規なら「クソいまいましい観念的なインチキ歌めがっ!」の一言で切り捨てそうな短歌ですが、この歌に確かな実感を抱く日本人は大勢いる ― ただし、詩人の申告より一ヶ月少々遅れての実感、ではありますが。

Though Autumn is nowhere to be seen yet, the feel of wind is not Summer any more, so the poet says... although it is highly doubtful whether he actually felt it on the skin, or in the head at the thought of it being the first day of lunar 7th/solar 8th month. A typical 古今集(Kokin shuu) TANKA 正岡子規 (Masaoka Shiki) would dismiss as naughty notional nonsense, to be sure, but many Japanese find it to be very true ― only a month or so later than the poet says it is.

- -

●66●このまよりもりくるつきのかげみれば こころづくしのあきはきにけり
木の間より漏り来る月の影見れば心尽くしの秋は来にけり

【秋】[転季]『1)古今集:184』詠み人知らず

夏の間は木々の梢を鬱蒼と埋め尽くしていた緑の木の葉のカーテンも今は色褪せ、まばらになって、隙間から漏れ来るこの月明かり・・・あぁ、今年もまた、あれこれ物思う秋がやって来たんだなぁ。

Streak of light coming through fading curtains of Summer leaves
Inviting pensive mood radiating from Autumnal beam of the moon.

—秋—

こ【木】〔名〕＜木｜(n.)a tree＞／の【の】〔格助〕＜の｜(prep.)'s＞／ま【間】〔名〕＜隙間｜(n.)the space＞／より【より】〔格助〕＜〜から｜(prep.)from＞／もりく【漏り来】〔自カ変〕＜漏れて来る｜(v.)leak＞(もりくる＝連体形)／つき【月】〔名〕＜月｜(n.)the moon＞／の【の】〔格助〕＜の｜(prep.)'s＞／かげ【影】〔名〕＜光｜(n.)the light＞／みる【見る】〔他マ上一〕＜見る｜(v.)view＞(みれ＝連用形)／ば【ば】〔接助〕＜〜したところ｜(conj.)when＞／こころづくし【心尽くし】〔名〕＜物思いがつのって心が苦しいこと｜(n.)a wistful state of mind＞／の【の】〔格助〕＜の｜(prep.)'s＞／あき【秋】〔名〕＜秋｜(n.)Autumn＞／は【は】〔係助〕＜主格｜(prep.)SUBJECT＞／く【来】〔自カ変〕＜来る｜(v.)come＞(き＝連用形)／ぬ【ぬ】〔助動ナ変型〕完了＜すでに〜[し]た｜(aux-v.)PERFECT TENSE＞(に＝連用形)／けり【けり】〔助動ラ変型〕詠嘆＜〜だったのだなぁ｜(interj.)REALIZATION＞(けり＝終止形)

[ko-no-ma yori mori-kuru tsuki no kage mire-ba kokoro-zukushi no aki wa ki-ni-keri]

昔の日本人にとって、「秋」は寂しげに美しい「**月の影**（＝光）」と密接に結び付いた季節。この詩人の場合、秋の訪れを、樹木の葉っぱ越しにやってくる月の光に感じ取っています ─ 夏の間は緑に満ちた生命の生い茂っていた木が、今では色も変わり落葉も始まってまばらになりつつあるので「秋だなぁ」と ─ 英語で「Fall：落下」が「Autumn：秋」の別名であるように、日本の陰暦の八月の名は「葉月：はづき」(新暦では九月)、季節の変化が木々の上に顕著な季節らしい名ですね。

To ancient Japanese, Autumn was a season invariably connected with the forlornly beautiful beam of the moon. This poet feels the arrival of Autumn as he sees it coming through the leaves of the tree, which was thick with life full of greenery in Summer, but is now getting bare as the leaves change colors and fall ─ as "**Fall**" is another name for "**Autumn**" in English, 葉月(hazuki＝the month of **leaves**) is the name of Japanese lunar August, when seasonal change is clear to see on the trees.

─────────────────────────────

●67●やへむぐらしげれるやどのさびしきに　ひとこそみえねあきはきにけり
　　八重葎繁れる宿の寂しきに人こそ見えね秋は来にけり

【秋】[謎掛]『3)拾遺集:140』恵慶(えぎょう)

人には見捨てられて雑草ばかりが生い茂る宿なのに、「秋」だけは見捨てずに
今年もまたやって来たのだなぁ。

To a lonely residence hosting weeds alone,

No one ever comes but Autumn didn't forget to come.

やへむぐら【八重葎】〔名〕＜雑草｜(n.)weeds＞／しげる【繁る】〔自四〕＜生い茂る｜(v.)thrive＞(しげれ＝已然形・命令形)／り【り】〔助動ラ変型〕存続＜〜[し]ている｜(aux-v.)PERFECT TENSE＞(る＝連体形)／やど【宿】〔名〕＜家屋｜(n.)the house＞／の【の】〔格助〕＜主格｜(prep.)SUBJECT＞／さびし【寂し】〔形シク〕＜寂しい｜(adj.)lonesome＞(さびしき＝連体形)／に【に】〔接助〕＜理由｜(conj.)REASON＞／ひと【人】〔名〕＜人間｜(n.)a human being＞／こそ【こそ】〔係助〕＜逆接｜(conj.)although＞／みゆ【見ゆ】〔他ヤ下二〕＜見える｜(v.)be seen＞(みえ＝未然形)／ず【ず】〔助動特殊型〕打消＜〜[し]ない｜(adv.)not 〜＞(ね＝已然形係り結び)／あき【秋】〔名〕＜秋｜(n.)Autumn＞／は【は】〔係助〕＜〜に関しては｜(adv.)as for 〜＞／く【来】〔自カ変〕＜来る｜(v.)come＞(き＝連用形)／ぬ【ぬ】〔助動ナ変型〕完了＜すでに〜[し]た｜(aux-v.)PERFECT TENSE＞(に＝連用形)／けり【けり】〔助動ラ変型〕詠嘆＜〜だったのだなぁ｜(interj.)REALIZATION＞(けり＝終止形)

[yae-mugura shigere-ru yado no sabishiki ni hito koso mie-ne aki wa ki-ni-keri]

http//zubaraie.com

—秋—

「侘び歌名人」恵慶法師の手になる虚構歌で、人はもう誰一人寄り付かぬ寂れた家屋を「秋」だけが今なお忘れずに訪れてくれている情景を詠んでいます・・・が、この着想は彼の独創ではなく、100年前の紀貫之の作品をちょちょいのちょいと改変しただけの代物で、『訪ふ人もなき宿なれど来る春は八重葎にも障らざりけり』という貫之のオリジナルが、人はもう誰一人寄り付かぬ寂れた家屋を「春」だけが今なお忘れずに訪れてくれている情景を詠んでいたものを、「春→秋」に改変しただけ・・・英文学の世界ではマトモな詩人なら誰一人ここまで堂々と他人の作品をパクるような芸当はしませんが、こうした真似っこ漫才は平安調短歌の世界では決して珍しいことではありませんでした。このパクリ短歌は、第三勅撰集『拾遺集』に収められているのみならず、藤原定家もこれを採り上げてかの有名な『小倉百人一首』に組み入れています。

A fictional TANKA by "the master of the forlorn", 恵慶法師(Egyou houshi), in which "秋:*Autumn*" doesn't forget to visit the deserted house where no human would come any more. This, however, is not his original but an easy conversion from 紀貫之(Ki-no-Tsurayuki)'s piece 100 years before which ran 「訪ふ人もなき宿なれど来る春は八重葎にも障らざりけり」(=tou hito mo naki nado nare-do kuru haru wa yae-mugura ni-mo sawara-zari-keri), in which "春:*Spring*" doesn't forget to visit the deserted house where no human would come any more. A plagiarism as bold as this would never be attempted by any self-respecting poet in the world of English literature, but such copycats were nothing rare in the world of Heianese TANKA; this *copy &twist &paste* TANKA appeared in the 3rd Imperial TANKA anthology 拾遺集(Shuui shuu) as well as being adopted by 藤原定家(Fujiwara-no-Teika) in the legendary 小倉百人一首(Ogura hyakunin isshu).

●68●いとどしくものおもふやどのはぎのはに あきとつげつるかぜのわびしさ
　　　　いとどしく物思ふ宿の萩の葉に秋と告げつる風の侘びしさ

【秋】[転季]『2)後撰集:220』詠み人知らず

そうでなくても切ない気分のこの私に、庭の萩の葉の上を渡る風の音までもが「もう秋ですよ」と告げているようで、あぁ、ますます侘びしい季節になって行くのだなぁ。

**When I'm already in pensive mood, bush clovers add to my feel;
The wind on their leaves sound sad, telling me Autumn has come.**

いとどし【いとどし】〔形シク〕＜そうでなくてさえ～なのに、ますます一層｜(adv.)all the more so＞（いとどし＜＝連用形）／もの【物】〔名〕＜あれこれいろいろ｜(n.)one thing or another＞／おもふ【思ふ】〔他ハ四〕＜思う｜(v.)think＞（おもふ＝連体形）／やど【宿】〔名〕＜家屋｜(n.)the house＞／の【の】〔格助〕＜の｜(prep.)'s＞／はぎ【萩】〔名〕＜ハギ｜(n.)lespedeza, or bush clover＞／の【の】〔格助〕＜の｜(prep.)'s＞／は【葉】〔名〕＜葉｜(n.)leaves＞／に【に】〔格助〕＜対象｜(prep.)OBJECT＞／あき【秋】〔名〕＜秋｜(n.)Autumn＞／と【と】〔格助〕＜内容提示｜(conj.)that ～＞／つぐ【告ぐ】〔他ガ下二〕＜告げる｜(v.)tell＞（つげ＝連用形）／つ【つ】〔助動タ下二型〕完了＜すでに～した｜(aux-v.)PERFECT TENSE＞（つる＝連体形）／かぜ【風】〔名〕＜風｜(n.)wind＞／の【の】〔格助〕＜の｜(prep.)'s＞／わびしさ【侘びしさ】〔名〕＜わびしさ｜(n.)bleakness＞

[itodoshiku mono-omou yado no hagi no ha ni aki to tsuge-tsuru kaze no wabishi-sa]

「**いとどし**」とは元々の状況を更に悪化させる何らかの出来事があったことを示す表現。この詩人の場合、風に感じる秋の気配に、元々寂しかった思いを一層募らせています・・・ではこの詩人、そもそも最初にどうして寂しかったのでしょうか？・・・理由はわかりません ― 理由なんていくらでも思い付くでしょう？ひょっとしたら「秋だから」、ただそれだけで寂しかったのかもしれません。風に揺れて季節の変わり目を告げる「萩」は、初秋を象徴する花。「花札」の中では、「萩」は「イノシシ」と並んで「七月（陽暦で言えば八月）」を代表する絵柄になっています。

―秋―

いとどし(itodoshi) means some happening aggravating the original situation. This poet feels all the more sad for the feel of Autumn he/she feels in the wind. Why the poet was feeling sad at first is unknown... you could imagine whole lots of reasons for sadness: it may even be simply *because it was Autumn!* 萩(hagi＝a bush clover) is a symbolic plant of early Autumn, waving in the wind to announce the change of seasons. In 花札(hana-fuda：Japanese picture playing cards), 萩(bush clover) represents the lunar 7th month (solar August) along with 猪(inoshishi＝a bore).

★69★なくむしのひとつこゑにもきこえぬは こころごころにものやかなしき
　　鳴く虫の一つ声にも聞こえぬは心々に物や悲しき

【秋】[自然]『6)詞花集:120』和泉式部(いずみしきぶ)

秋の野原を埋め尽くす虫たちの鳴き声はそれはもう賑やかだけれど、
よくよく聞けば、どれもこれもそれぞれ違う声に聞こえるのは、
みな思い思いに何か特別な悲しみを訴えながら泣いているから…なのかしら？

The sounds of Autumnal insects chirp out as many sorrow.
Behind the loud harmony, their cries must all be unique.

なく【鳴く】〔自カ四〕＜鳴く｜(v.)cry＞(なく＝連体形)／むし【虫】［名］＜虫｜(n.)bugs＞／の【の】〔格助〕＜主格｜(prep.)SUBJECT＞／ひとつ【一つ】［名］＜一つだけの｜(adj.)a single＞／こゑ【声】［名］＜声｜(n.)the voice＞／に【に】〔格助〕＜様態｜(prep.)like＞／も【も】〔係助〕＜意味なし｜(adv.)NO MEANING＞／きこゆ【聞こゆ】〔自ヤ下二〕＜聞こえる｜(v.)be heard＞(きこえ＝未然形)／ず【ず】〔助動特殊型〕打消＜〜[し]ない｜(adv.)not 〜＞(ぬ＝連体形)／は【は】〔係助〕＜〜ということは｜(prep.)does it mean that 〜＞／こころごころ【心々】［名］＜それぞれがそれぞれに別の気持ちで｜(adv.)each according to its own mind＞／に【に】〔格助〕＜様態｜(prep.)like＞／もの【物】［名］＜あれこれいろいろ｜(n.)one thing or another＞／や【や】〔係助〕＜疑問｜(adv.)INTERROGATIVE＞／かなし【悲し】［形シク］＜悲しい｜(adj.)sad＞(かなしき＝連体形係り結び)

[naku mushi no hitotsu-koe ni-mo kikoe-nu wa kokoro-gokoro-ni mono ya kanashiki]

「一寸の虫にも五分の魂」とは言うけれど、取るに足らない虫たちの歌声(あるいは、泣き声)の一つ一つに耳を傾けて、「みんな、それぞれなりに、つらいのね」なんて言う人は殆どいない ― 和泉式部はそんな数少ない例外的詩人、他者の立場に身を置いて物事を感じ取る想像力が、人並み外れて強かった女性…なればこそ、彼女の作品は平安調短歌世界の中で際立ち、和泉もまた永遠不滅の生命を保ち続ける ― 人類が死に絶えることなく、古典の中に共感の声を求め続ける限り、永遠に。

Even a worm will turn, but few will turn their ears to individually unique voice of singing (or crying) bugs: 和泉式部(Izumi shikibu) was one of such exceptional poets with extraordinary power of empathic imagination, which makes her works stand out among Heianese TANKA to ensure her survival as long as humanity thrives and seeks out compassionate voice in classics.

—秋—

●70● いつとてもこひしからずはあらねども あきのゆふべはあやしかりけり
何時とても恋しからずは非ねども秋の夕べは怪しかりけり

【秋】[溜息]『1)古今集:546』詠み人知らず

いつだって恋しい思いは常にあるのだけれど、
秋の夕暮れ時はもうヤバい、募る思いに居ても立ってもいられない。

<u>W</u>hen am I not in love?
<u>A</u>lways thinking of you!
<u>N</u>ow, however, it's far too much
<u>T</u>o face this Autumnal eve alone!

いつ【何時】[代名]＜どんな時｜(adv.)anytime＞／とて【とて】[格助]＜たとえ〜でも｜(adv.)even if＞／も【も】[係助]＜意味なし｜(adv.)NO MEANING＞／こひし【恋し】[形シク]＜恋しい｜(v.)feel attached to＞(こひしから＝未然形)／ず【ず】[助動特殊型]打消＜〜[し]ない｜(adv.)not 〜＞(ず＝終止形)／は【は】[係助]＜は｜(prep.)NO MEANING＞／あり【あり】[補動ラ変]＜〜である｜(aux-v.)be＞(あら＝未然形)／ず【ず】[助動特殊型]打消＜〜[し]ない｜(adv.)not 〜＞(ね＝已然形)／ども【ども】[接助]＜〜ではあるが｜(conj.)although＞／あき【秋】[名]＜秋｜(n.)Autumn＞／の【の】[格助]＜の｜(prep.)'s＞／ゆふべ【夕べ】[名]＜夕方｜(n.)the evening＞／は【は】[係助]＜〜に関しては｜(adv.)as for 〜＞／あやし【怪し】[形シク]＜何がなんだかワケわかんない｜(adj.)too strange to be real＞(あやしかり＝連用形)／けり【けり】[助動ラ変型]詠嘆＜〜だったのだなぁ｜(interj.)REALIZATION＞(けり＝終止形)

[itsu tote-mo koishikara-zu wa ara-ne-domo aki no yuu-be wa ayashikari-keri]

秋は、一人ぼっちで過ごすには寂しすぎる季節— 恋する人にとっては特にそう。もし片思いなら、これは恋の拷問の歌。もし相思相愛なら、この歌は「今すぐ来て、今夜は一緒にいて！」と求める緊急SOS…どっちに転んでもメッセージは同じ —「あなたが欲しいっ！」

Autumn is a season too forlorn to spend alone — especially for someone in love. If one-sided, this is a song of love-torture; if mutual, this should be an urgent request to come spend the night together. Whichever it is, the message is the same – "I *WANT* U!"

●71● ながむればこひしきひとのこひしきに くもらばくもれあきのよのつき
眺むれば恋しき人の恋しきに曇らば曇れ秋の夜の月

【秋】[溜息]『5)金葉集:384』藤原基光（ふじわらのもとみつ）

ぼーっと見ているうちに、恋しい人への思いが募るから、
曇るならいっそ曇って見えなくなっちゃえばいいのに、この思わせぶりな秋の夜の月。

Your radiant beam will burn my heart with love,
Why should I be watching you, if my love was here!
Go, moon of Fall, behind the clouds of tears.

ながむ【眺む】[他マ下二]＜ぼんやりと見る｜(v.)vacantly watch＞(ながむれ＝已然形)／ば【ば】[接助]＜仮定｜(conj.)if＞／こひし【恋し】[形シク]＜恋しい｜(v.)feel attached to＞(こひしき＝連体形)／ひと【人】[名]＜あの人｜(n.)that [darling] one＞／の【の】[格助]＜主格｜(prep.)SUBJECT＞／こひし【恋し】[形シク]＜恋しい｜(v.)feel attached to＞(こひしき＝連体形)／に【に】[接助]＜理由｜(conj.)REASON＞／くもる【曇る】[自ラ四]＜曇る｜(v.)get cloudy＞(くもら＝未然形)／ば【ば】[接助]＜仮定｜(conj.)if＞／くもる【曇る】[自ラ四]＜曇る｜(v.)get cloudy＞(くもれ＝命令形)／あき【秋】[名]＜秋

|(n.)Autumn＞／の【の】〔格助〕＜の|(prep.)'s＞／よ【夜】〔名〕＜夜|(n.)the night＞／の【の】〔格助〕＜の|(prep.)'s＞／つき【月】〔名〕＜月|(n.)the moon＞

[nagamure-ba koishiki hito no koishiki ni kumora-ba kumore aki no yo no tsuki]

これは「月前恋:つきぜんのこひ」というお題で詠まれた虚構短歌。詠み人は男性ながら、むしろ女性仮託の歌の響きあり···何故かって？···だって、優しい月の光に導かれて恋人がお部屋まで愛しに来てくれるのをじぃーっとおうちで待ち受けているのは、いつだって女性の方だから(平安時代には「月明かり」以外の街灯はなかった、ってことをお忘れなく)。月が夜空高く昇ると、女性の心は(彼、来てくれるかしら？)と期待に燃える。月が沈み始めると、女性は(今夜はもう来てくれなさそう)との思いに沈み始める。もし月が雲隠れしてしまえば、女性があれこれ胸焦がす理由もなくなる。もし最初から月なんて出ていない夜なら、女性は安心して眠りに就ける。女性にとっての「月」は、恵み深くもあり、残酷でもあるもの···男性にとってはただの「街灯」だけど — これが、平安時代の恋愛模様に関して(その恋が現在進行形の間は)覚えておくべき男女別相関図···その恋愛が過去形になった時には、女も男も同じように月を眺めては、失ったものを悲しく思い浮かべることになるのだけれど、それはこの歌の情況には明らかにそぐわない。そういう次第で、耳の肥えた歌読みには、この歌は男歌より女歌に聞こえるというわけ — なるほどその通り、と感じたらその解釈でどうぞ。さもなくばあっさり無視してください—短歌では、読み手の感じた姿こそが真実なのだから。

A fictional TANKA on the theme of "loving feeling inspired by the moon". Though the poet is a male, this sounds more like a female song. Why? Because it's always the woman that sits at home and waits for her lover to come and love her guided by the benign beam of the moon — remember it's the *only* street light in the Heian era. When the moon rises high, the woman feels her heart burn inside waiting for her man to come. When the moon begins to sink, the woman begins to think her man will not come for the night. If the moon is hidden behind clouds, the woman doesn't have to feel emotionally agitated. If it's a moonless night, the woman can get down to her peaceful sleep. The moon can be at once benign and cruel for the woman: for the man, it's *only a street light* — that's what you should remember about Heianese love affairs while it's going on... after it's gone, both women and men look vacantly at the moon to mourn what they've lost, which is obviously not the case with this particular song. That's why this song sounds not so much male as female to a TANKA connoisseur — if the shoe fits, wear it: otherwise, just ignore it — TANKA sounds as true as you feel it is.

★72★ことならばやみにぞあらましあきのよの　なぞつきかげのひとだのめなる
同ならば闇にぞあらまし秋の夜の何ぞ月影の人頼めなる

【秋】［謎掛］『3)拾遺集:796』詠み人知らず

どうせなら真っ暗闇だったらいいのに、そうしたら「こんな闇夜じゃ、来ようと思っても無理ね」と諦めがつくはずなのに···どうしてこんなに明るく照るのかしら、このお月さま···「これほど月明かりの冴えた晩なら、恋人を訪れずにはいられない(はず)」と私に期待させておいて、結局なんにも起こらない···そんな残酷な結末、どうしても見たいというの？···あぁ何て意地悪な、思わせぶりな、この秋の夜の月！

A night spent alone is already too bleak to bear.
He won't come, I know... but what if he *did* tonight?
If it was totally dark, as dark as my heart was the sky,
No hope would I then get... without this Autumnal moon!

http//zubaraie.com　　　　　　—Autumn—

—秋—

こと【同】〔副〕＜同じ｜(adj.)the same＞／なり【なり】〔助動ナリ型〕断定＜～である｜(aux-v.)be＞(なら＝未然形)／ば【ば】〔接助〕＜仮定｜(conj.)if＞／やみ【闇】〔名〕＜暗闇｜(n.)darkness＞／なり【なり】〔助動ナリ型〕断定＜～である｜(aux-v.)be＞(に＝連用形)／ぞ【ぞ】〔係助〕＜強調｜(adv.)EMPHASIS＞／あり【あり】〔補動ラ変〕＜～である｜(aux-v.)be＞(あら＝未然形)／まし【まし】〔助動特殊型〕推量＜だったらいいのに｜(aux-v.)I wish＞(まし＝連体形係り結び)／あき【秋】〔名〕＜秋｜(n.)Autumn＞／の【の】〔格助〕＜の｜(prep.)'s＞／よ【夜】〔名〕＜夜｜(n.)the night＞／の【の】〔格助〕＜の｜(prep.)'s＞／なぞ【何ぞ】〔副〕＜何故｜(adv.)why＞／つきかげ【月影】〔名〕＜月明かり｜(n.)the moonlight＞／の【の】〔格助〕＜主格｜(prep.)SUBJECT＞／ひとだのめなり【人頼めなり】〔形動ナリ〕＜思わせぶりだ｜(adj.)promising＞(ひとだのめなる＝連体形係り結び)

[koto-nara-ba yami ni-zo ara-mashi aki no yo no na-zo tsuki-kage no hito-danome-naru]

前回お届けした「目利きによる平安調恋愛ガイド」、覚えてますか？この歌のヒロイン(女主人公)(間違っても男ではありません)は、優しい(あるいは、残酷な)月の光に導かれて彼女の恋人がお部屋を訪れるのを(空しく)待っています。おそらくは、問題の男性は「今夜、君を訪ねて行くよ」とは彼女に約束していないはずですが、それでもなお(お月さまがあまりに明るすぎたので)彼女としては彼が来てくれるかも(というか、来るに違いない)と期待せずにはいられなかったのです･･･さもなくば、彼女の恨み言は「月」ではなく「彼」に向けられているはずですからね。月が傾き始め、彼が来てくれそうになくなると、彼女の感覚も変わってきます ―「あぁ、もう、あなたなんて最初からいなければよかったのに、みんなあなたが悪いのよ、この意地悪な(イジワル)お月さま！」･･･これはもちろん八つ当たりだけど、月があまりに優しい光に満ちていれば、女の期待が膨らんじゃうのも仕方ないこと･･･そして、彼女はいくらでも月の冷たさに文句言っちゃって、いいんです ― 何を言われても、月は何も言わず、お礼言う人も恨み言ぶつける人も、同じ光で照らすだけなんだから。

Remember the connoisseur's guide on Heianese love affair offered last time? The heroine (*never a hero*) of this song is waiting (in vain) for her lover to come visit her room, guided by the benign (or, *cruel*) moon. More likely than not, the man in question has *not* promised her to come tonight; still, the moon is so bright that she can't help hoping (or *expecting*) him to come... otherwise, she would be holding a grudge against *HIM*, not the *MOON*. As the moon begins to sink and the man never seems to come, she starts to feel — if only *you* weren't there at all — *you* are all to blame, *this nasty moon!*... It's a false accusation, of course, but the moon is so gently bright that she can expect too much. And she can also say anything against its cruelty because the moon just says nothing, beaming down on the thankful and hateful alike.

★73★なげけとてつきやはものをおもはする　かこちがほなるわがなみだかな
嘆けとて月やは物を思はする託ち顔なる我が涙かな

【秋】〔謎掛〕『7)千載集:929』西行(さいぎょう)

私に悲しい思いをさせようと、月が意地悪(いじわる)しているのだろうか？
私の物思いは、月の光のせいだろうか？そんなことはあるまい･･･
あるまいけど、わけもなく流れる私のこの涙は、いったいどうしたことだろう？お月様のせいみたいにして、恨(うら)みがましい顔で夜空を眺(なが)めてしまうこの気持ちは、いったい何なんだろう？

Is the moon to blame for my moody face and tears?
Though I know it's not, I don't know why it looks so cold.

なげく【嘆く】〔自カ四〕＜嘆く｜(v.)grieve＞(なげけ＝命令形)／と【と】〔格助〕＜内容提示｜(conj.)that ～＞／て【て】〔接助〕＜内容提示｜(conj.)that ～＞／つき【月】〔名〕＜月｜(n.)the moon＞／やは【やは】

〔係助〕＜～だろうか？否、そうではあるまい｜(prep.)RHETORICAL QUESTION＞／もの【物】〔名〕＜あれこれいろいろ｜(n.)one thing or another＞／を【を】〔格助〕＜目的格｜(prep.)OBJECT＞／おもふ【思ふ】〔他ハ四〕＜思う｜(v.)think＞（おもは＝未然形）／す【す】〔助動サ下二型〕使役＜～[さ]せる｜(aux-v.)CAUSATIVE＞（する＝連体形係り結び）／かこちがほなり【託ち顔なり】〔形動ナリ〕＜何か文句でも言いたそう｜(adj.)complaining＞（かこちがほなる＝連体形）／わ【我】〔代名〕＜私｜(pron.)I, myself＞／が【が】〔格助〕＜の｜(prep.)'s＞／なみだ【涙】〔名〕＜涙｜(n.)tears＞／かな【かな】〔終助〕＜詠嘆｜(interj.)EXCLAMATION＞

[nageke tote tsuki yawa mono wo omowasuru kakochigaonaru wa-ga namida kana]

これもまた「月前恋：つきぜんのこひ＝月の光を前にしての恋心」のお題の虚構歌で、詠み手は伝説の歌僧の西行。新古今調の持って回った解釈がお好みなら「私が物思いに沈んで誰かを思って泣くよう仕向けるためにあの月が私の上に照っているはずがない‥‥誰がそうさせているか、あなたならわかるでしょう？ ― あなたのせいですよ」でいいでしょう。秋の月と向かい合った時の何とも言えぬあの感じ、知ってる人なら、郷愁誘うあのムードの背後に「誰か」や「何か」を無理に求める必要も、ないでしょう。

Yet another fictional TANKA on the theme of "loving feeling inspired by the moon" by the legendary singing bonze 西行(Saigyou). If you like 新古今(Shin-Kokin) style of roundabout interpretation, "Why should the moon shine on me to make me brood and cry over someone... you know who is to blame – baby, *it's you!*" will do. If you know how it is when face to face with the Autumnal moon, there is no need for someone or something that is to blame for the nostalgic mood.

★74★つきみればちぢにものこそかなしけれ わがみひとつのあきにはあらねど
月見れば千々に物こそ悲しけれ我が身一つの秋には非ねど

【秋】[機知]『1)古今集:193』大江千里(おおえのちさと)

月を見ると、あれこれ思いが交錯して、物悲しいことだなあ‥‥
べつに、秋の風情は、この私一人を悲しませるためにあるのではないけれど。

The sight of the moon sets me namelessly sad,
As if its radiant gleam were solely for my grief.
Am I alone on earth in selfish wayward sigh?

つき【月】〔名〕＜月｜(n.)the moon＞／みる【見る】〔他マ上一〕＜見る｜(v.)view＞（みれ＝已然形）／ば【ば】〔接助〕＜～したところ｜(conj.)when＞／ちぢなり【千千なり】〔形動ナリ〕＜やたら色々｜(adv.)this way and that＞（ちぢに＝連用形）／もの【物】〔名〕＜あれこれいろいろ｜(n.)one thing or another＞／こそ【こそ】〔係助〕＜強調｜(adv.)EMPHASIS＞／かなし【悲し】〔形シク〕＜悲しい｜(adj.)sad＞（かなしけれ＝已然形係り結び）／わ【我】〔代名〕＜私｜(pron.)I, myself＞／が【が】〔格助〕＜の｜(prep.)'s＞／み【身】〔名〕＜自身｜(n.)[one]self＞／ひとつ【一つ】〔名〕＜のみ｜(adj.)alone＞／の【の】〔格助〕＜の｜(prep.)'s＞／あき【秋】〔名〕＜秋｜(n.)Autumn＞／なり【なり】〔助動ナリ型〕断定＜～である｜(aux-v.)be＞（に＝連用形）／は【は】〔係助〕＜主格｜(prep.)SUBJECT＞／あり【有り】〔自ラ変〕＜である｜(v.)be＞（あら＝未然形）／ず【ず】〔助動特殊型〕打消＜～[し]ない｜(adv.)not ～＞（ね＝已然形）／ど【ど】〔接助〕＜～だけれども｜(conj.)although＞

[tsuki mire-ba chijini mono koso kanashikere wa-ga mi hitotsu no aki ni-wa ara-ne-do]

『古今集』に収められたこの短歌が典拠としているのは、白楽天の有名な漢籍「燕子楼中＊霜月夜秋来只為一人長：えんしろうちゅうそうげつのよしゅうらいただひとりのためにながし＝高い塔の中から霜の降る夜を眺めていると、秋がやって来る ― 私一人に逢うために ― そうして独り明かす秋の夜はひどく長い」。
(＊ここでの「霜月」は「しもつき＝陰暦十一月」ではありません)

―秋―

A poetic reference in 古今集(Kokin shuu) to the famous Chinese classic by 白楽天(Hakurakuten) 燕子楼中霜月夜秋来只為一人長(＝Watching from a tower on a frosty night, Autumn comes to greet me alone, All through this long solitary night) in 『白氏文集(Haku-shi monjuu)』.

・・・・・・・・・・・・・・・・・・・・・・・・・・・・

《「名引き」芸間引く余所者短歌捨て》

この『古今集』の短歌中に見られるような古典作品への言及は、「本説取り」と呼ばれる技巧ですが、時代が下るにつれてその原典は「漢籍」から「日本の作品」へと移って行くようになります。短歌世界でも著名な宗匠格だった藤原俊成は、「『源氏物語』の作中で語られている出来事を十分知らぬようでは、歌詠みとしては困り物である」と言っています‥・「余所からのレファレンス数の多さが、リンク先ターゲットの名声と価値を高めることになる」・・・Google評定システムの平安版みたいなこの「名引き」のおかげで、有名な古典作品のネームバリューは雪だるま式に膨れ上がりましたが、そうしてその「有名な何かを知っている」とひけらかすことによって、人々は自らの文化的洗練度をも誇らしげに主張したのでした。その種のひけらかしに走る人々は、他の人が知らないマイナー作品を引き合いに出すことで、「何のことかわからず途方に暮れる素人ども」に対する自らの優位性を際立たせようとする行動をどんどんエスカレートさせて行きました・・・その結果、「京都のお高くとまったお歴々」の排他的な内輪世界の外にいる日本人は(今日に至るまでずぅーっと)「古典作品を引き合いに出すこと」に対して本能的な反感を抱くようになってしまったのです。西欧人の場合、「聖書」や「ギリシア神話」や「シェイクスピア」等々の世界観をロクに知らないと困ったことになりますが、日本人[ふう]になるのに必要なのは「まぁまぁの日本語力」と「身の回りのすべてに(どんなバカげたことでも)合わせる能力」だけ・・・「日本の伝統文化に対する知識と敬意」？・・・何のことでしょう？そんなの誰も求めやしませんよ！・・・嘘だと思うなら、日本に旅行に来る時にこの本を一緒に持って来て、どれでもいいからお好みの詩を一つ引き合いに出して(あるいは、この本を開いて指差して)ごらんなさい ― 何も知らない日本人、何の反応も興味も示さない日本人、ひどい場合には自らの無知を暴かれて露骨に不機嫌になる日本人の姿に、あなたは、ひどいショックを受けること請け合いですから・・・内輪賛美の武器としての平安調「名引き」は、伝統文化に対する日本人の態度に、修復不能なダメージを与えてしまったのです・・・その犠牲として「短歌」という文芸ジャンルが今日まるで顧みられないのも、自業自得と言うべきでしょう。

《too much name-droppings spoilt the field of TANKA》

A technique seen in this 古今(Kokin) TANKA called 本説取り(honsetsu-dori＝classical reference) would gradually shift its basis from Chinese to Japanese as years went on. The famous TANKA master 藤原俊成(Fujiwara-no-Shunzei) once said "*Those poets will leave so much to be desired who are not well-acquainted with the episodes of* 源氏物語(*Genji monogatari ＝the tales of the Prince Genji*)"... reference from other works enhancing the fame and value of the original target ― a *Google*-like evaluation system in the Heian era went a long way to snowballing the fame of famous classics, at the same time asserting the cultural sophistication of the name-droppers, who were more and more prone to reference to ever-minor works that would serve the purpose of exalting themselves above the ignorantly bewildered laypersons... with the ever-lingering result that the Japanese people outside the esoteric circle of noble folks in 京都(Kyoto) have been traditionally and *instinctively* averse to classical reference. Those Westerners will leave so much to be desired who are not well-acquainted with the world of the Bible, Greek mythology, Shakespeare and suchlike: but you have only to have tolerable command of Japanese language and the adaptable attitude to anything absurd around you in order to be [like] a Japanese... how about knowledge and homage to Japanese traditional culture?... *what are you talking about? There's no such thing needed!* ― if you doubt me, just take this book with you on your trip to Japan and refer to (or point your finger to) some poem to your fancy in front of any given

—秋—

Japanese: you are sure to be shocked by their lack of knowledge or response or interest, or even open resentment to having their ignorance revealed. The Heianese 名引き(na-biki＝name-dropping) as an esoteric weapon caused unrecoverable damage on the Japanese attitude to traditional culture... the literary genre of TANKA is its deserved victim.

●75● あきかぜにたなびくくものたえまより もれいづるつきのかげのさやけさ
　　　秋風に棚引く雲の絶え間より漏れ出づる月の影のさやけさ

【秋】[叙景]『8)新古今集:413』藤原顕輔(ふじわらのあきすけ)

爽やかな秋風に吹かれて、横なびきにちぎれた夜の雲・・・
その切れ間から漏れ出る月の光の、何と明澄な美しさであろうか。

> Sleepless wind creeps through nocturnal skies,
>
> Sweetly cool is its Autumnal feel on the clouds,
>
> Silent radiance of occasionally appearing moon.

あきかぜ【秋風】[名]＜秋風｜(n.)Autumnal wind＞／に[に][格助]＜原因｜(prep.)REASON＞／たなびく【棚引く】[自カ四]＜尾を引く｜(v.)trail＞(たなびく＝連体形)／くも【雲】[名]＜雲｜(n.)clouds＞／の【の】[格助]＜の｜(prep.)'s＞／たえま【絶え間】[名]＜途切れた部分｜(n.)a break＞／より[より][格助]＜～から｜(prep.)from＞／もる【漏る】[自ラ下二]＜漏れる｜(v.)leak＞(もれ＝運用形)／いづ【出づ】[自ダ下二]＜出る｜(v.)come out＞(いづる＝連体形)／つき【月】[名]＜月｜(n.)the moon＞／の【の】[格助]＜の｜(prep.)'s＞／かげ【影】[名]＜光｜(n.)the light＞／の【の】[格助]＜の｜(prep.)'s＞／さやけし【清けし】[形]＜くっきりと明るい｜(adj.)lucent＞(さやけ＝語幹)／さ[さ][接尾]＜～の度数｜(n.)the degree＞

[aki-kaze ni tanabiku kumo no tae-ma yori more-izuru tsuki no kage no sayake-sa]

第六勅撰和歌集『詞花集』によく見られる自然派短歌(この勅撰集を編んだのはこの作者藤原顕輔)。
A naturalistic poem characteristic of the 6th great Imperial TANKA anthology 詞花集(Shika shuu), which was edited by the same author 藤原顕輔(Fujiwara-no-Akisuke).

●76● しらくもにはねうちかはしとぶかりの かずさへみゆるあきのよのつき
　　　白雲に羽打ち交はし飛ぶ雁の数さへ見ゆる秋の夜の月

【秋】[叙景]『1)古今集:191』詠み人知らず

真っ黒い夜空にくっきり浮かび上がる白い雲、
それを背景に群れ成して飛ぶ雁たちの頭数まで数えられそうな、この秋の月の明るさはどうだ。

> White clouds in the sky in contrast to the dark night
>
> Clearly show the number of wild geese on the wing
>
> In the glow of the moon broadly bright in Autumn.

しらくも【白雲】[名]＜白い雲｜(n.)white clouds＞／に[に][格助]＜場所｜(prep.)PLACE＞／はね【羽】[名]＜羽｜(n.)wings＞／うちかはす【打ち交はす】[他サ四]＜交差させる｜(v.)intersect＞(うちかはし＝連用形)／とぶ【飛ぶ】[自バ四]＜飛ぶ｜(v.)fly＞(とぶ＝連体形)／かり【雁】[名]＜[渡り鳥の]カリ｜(n.)wild geese＞／の【の】[格助]＜の｜(prep.)'s＞／かず【数】[名]＜数｜(n.)the number＞／さへ[さへ][副助]＜さえ｜(adv.)even＞／みゆ【見ゆ】[自ヤ下二]＜見える｜(v.)be seen＞(みゆる＝連体形)／あき【秋】[名]＜秋｜(n.)Autumn＞／の【の】[格助]＜の｜(prep.)'s＞／よ【夜】[名]＜夜｜(n.)the night＞／の【の】[格助]＜の｜(prep.)'s＞／つき【月】[名]＜月｜(n.)the moon＞

http://zubaraie.com　　　　　　　　　　　　　　　　　—Autumn—

—秋—

[shira-kumo ni hane uchi-kawashi tobu kari no kazu sae miyuru aki no yo no tsuki]

「黒(夜空)」:「白(雲)」:「焦げ茶(雁)」:「黄金白(月)」の詩的な重ね(襲)の色目の妙は、八代集初代の『古今集』の時代(905年)にはすでにもうこのように、目にも鮮やかな色合いを誇っていました。

The poetic color layers of black (the night sky), white (clouds), brown (wild geese) and golden white (the moon) were this much brilliant to see already in the first great Imperial TANKA anthology 古今集 (Kokin shuu) in A.D. 905.

●77●いづくにもこよひのつきをみるひとの こころやおなじそらにすむらむ

何処にも今宵の月を見る人の心や同じ空にすむらむ

【秋】[季題]『5)金葉集:173』藤原忠教(ふじわらのただのり)

今夜、この見事な月を眺める人たちは、たとえその身は何処にあっても、心だけはみな等しくあの澄み切った月の上に宿っていることだろう。

No matter where, no matter who,

This moon should invite everyone

To dwell on celestial palace up above.

いづく【何処】〔代名〕<どこ | (adv.)where>／に【に】〔格助〕<場所 | (prep.)PLACE>／も【も】〔係助〕<たとえ〜でも | (prep.)no matter 〜>／こよひ【今宵】〔名〕<今夜 | (n.)this evening>／の【の】〔格助〕<の | (prep.)'s>／つき【月】〔名〕<月 | (n.)the moon>／を【を】〔格助〕<目的格 | (prep.)OBJECT>／みる【見る】〔他マ上一〕<見る | (v.)view>(みる＝連体形)／ひと【人】〔名〕<人間 | (n.)a human being>／の【の】〔格助〕<の | (prep.)'s>／こころ【心】〔名〕<心 | (n.)heart>／や【や】〔係助〕<疑問 | (adv.)INTERROGATIVE>／おなじ【同じ】〔形シク〕<同じ | (adj.)the same>(おなじ【き】＝連体形)／そら【空】〔名〕<空 | (n.)the sky>／に【に】〔格助〕<場所 | (prep.)PLACE>／**(A)すむ【澄む】**〔自マ四〕<きれいに澄み渡る | (v.)get serenely clean>(すむ＝終止形)／**(B)すむ【住む】**〔自マ四〕<住む | (v.)live in>(すむ＝終止形)／らむ【らむ】〔助動ラ四型〕現在推量<〜だろう | (aux-v.)SUPPOSITION>(らむ＝連体形係り結び)

[izuku ni-mo koyoi no tsuki wo miru hito no kokoro ya onaji sora ni sumu-ramu]

陰暦八月(陽暦九月)に最も人気のあった旧習といえば、十五夜お月様鑑賞の宴。昔の人々はまた陰暦九月(陽暦十月)廿日の月をも(秋にさよならを言うために)愛でたものでした。この短歌が「八月十五夜／九月二十日の月」のどちらを指すものかは不明ですが、いずれにせよこの詩は、巧みな「懸詞」を用いて、まばゆい光を放って空に「澄む」同じ月が、数知れぬ月見客の心を引き付けて、彼ら全員があたかもその光り輝く天体の表面に「住む」かのように感じられる、と、趣向も鮮やかに謳い上げています。

The most popular ancient custom in the lunar 8th(solar 9th) month was the moon-viewing banquet held on the 15th night; they would also rejoice in the 20th moon in the lunar 9 th (solar 10th) month to say goodbye to Autumn. Whichever this poem refers to, its clever use of 懸詞(kake-kotoba＝pun) stylishly depicts the same radiant (**澄む**:すむ:sumu＝crystal clear) moon drawing the hearts of countless viewers as if they all dwelt (**住む**:すむ:sumu＝lived) on the brilliant surface of the heavenly body.

―秋―

●78●はるなつにそらやはかはるあきのよの　つきしもいかでてりまさるらむ
　　春夏に空やは変はる秋の夜の月しも如何で照り増さるらむ

【秋】[機知]『6)詞花集:96』藤原家成(ふじわらのいえなり)
春や夏と別の空に出るわけでもあるまいに、どうして秋の月だけこうも特別に明るく輝いて見えるのだろう？

Does it appear on a different sky,
A different canvas than Spring or Summer?
Nothing of the sort, but something is special ―
Why does the Autumn Moon shine ever so bright?

はる【春】[名]＜春｜(n.)Spring＞／なつ【夏】[名]＜夏｜(n.)Summer＞／に【に】[格助]＜比較｜(prep.)COMPARISON＞／そら【空】[名]＜空｜(n.)the sky＞／やは【やは】[係助]＜～だろうか？否、そうではあるまい｜(prep.)RHETORICAL QUESTION＞／かはる【変はる】[自ラ四]＜変わる｜(v.)change＞(かはる＝連体形係り結び)／あき【秋】[名]＜秋｜(n.)Autumn＞／の【の】[格助]＜の｜(prep.)'s＞／よ【夜】[名]＜夜｜(n.)the night＞／の【の】[格助]＜の｜(prep.)'s＞／つき【月】[名]＜月｜(n.)the moon＞／しも【しも】[副助]＜意味なし｜(adv.)NO MEANING＞／いかで【如何で】[副]＜どうして｜(adv.)how＞／てる【照る】[自ラ四]＜照る｜(v.)shine＞(てり＝連用形)／まさる【増さる】[自ラ四]＜より一層～になる｜(adv.)increasingly＞(まさる＝終止形)／らむ【らむ】[助動ラ四型]現在推量＜～だろう｜(aux-v.)SUPPOSITION＞(らむ＝連体形係り結び)

[haru natsu ni sora yawa kawaru aki no yo no tsuki shimo ikade teri-masaru-ramu]
同じ空なのに、別物の月・・・このちがいはどこから来るのだろう？　―　短歌の世界で幾度となく繰り返されてきた問答　―　答えはもう御存知のはず　―　月に反射投影された人の「心なりけり」。
The same sky, a different moon... what's the difference?　―　the same old question asked and answered so many times in the world of TANKA　―　the answer, you already know, is 心なりけり(kokoro nari-keri ＝it was human heart that's reflected in the moon).

―――――――――――――――――――――――――――

●79●こころにもあらでうきよにながらへば　こひしかるべきよはのつきかな
　　心にもあらで憂き世に永らへば恋しかるべき夜半の月かな

【秋】[溜息]『4)後拾遺集:861』三条院(さんじょういん)
こんな辛い世の中に、私はもう生きていたくもない・・・が、もし意に反して長生きしてしまったとしたならば、きっと恋しく懐かしく思い出すことになるのだろうなぁ、今夜のこの月のことを。

If I survived long enough against my will in this cruelly unhappy world,
Should I miss with much feeling this moon I'm watching tonight?

こころ【心】[名]＜心｜(n.)heart＞／なり【なり】[助動ナリ型]断定＜～である｜(aux-v.)be＞(に＝連用形)／も【も】[係助]＜意味なし｜(adv.)NO MEANING＞／あり【あり】[自ラ変]＜かなう｜(v.)fit＞(あら＝未然形)／で【で】[接助]＜～することなしに｜(prep.)without ～ing＞／うきよ【憂き世】[名]＜この辛い世の中｜(n.)this cruel world＞／に【に】[格助]＜場所｜(prep.)PLACE＞／ながらふ【長らふ】[自ハ下二]＜長生きする｜(v.)live long＞(ながらへ＝未然形)／ば【ば】[接助]＜仮定｜(conj.)if＞／こひし【恋し】[形シク]＜恋しい｜(v.)feel attached to＞(こひしかる＝連体形)／べし【べし】[助動ク型]推量＜～にちがいない｜(aux-v.)CONVICTION＞(べき＝連体形)／よは【夜半】[名]＜夜間｜(n.)the night-time＞／の【の】[格助]＜の｜(prep.)'s＞／つき【月】[名]＜月｜(n.)the moon＞／かな【かな】[終助]＜詠嘆｜(interj.)EXCLAMATION＞

―秋―

[kokoro ni-mo ara-de uki-yo ni nagarae-ba koishikaru-beki yowa no tsuki kana]

今のこの不幸な「現在」も、「未来」の私にとっては懐かしい贈り物になるのかもしれないな、掛け替えのない私の「過去」の愛しい思い出として・・・不吉な真実の響きを伴って鳴り響くこの歌は、豪腕政治家藤原道長の圧力で退位間近の三条天皇の口から出たものです。

This unhappy *present* of mine may turn out to be a nostalgic present to me in *future* as a fond memory of my precious *past*... a song ringing with a sinister truth born out of the mouth of the unhappy Emperor 三条(Sanjou), who was about to leave the throne under the pressure from the strong-arm politician 藤原道長(Fujiwara-no-Michinaga).

●80●あきにまたあはむ‧あはじもしらぬみは こよひばかりのつきをだにみむ‧
秋に又会はむ‧会はじも知らぬ身は今宵ばかりの月をだに見む‧

【秋】〔溜息〕『6)詞花集:97』三条院(さんじょういん)

来年の秋には果たして巡り会えるかどうか、定かでない我が身としては、今宵限りの見納めのつもりで、この美しい月を目に焼き付けておくことにしよう。

Would I ever see another Autumn?
Unable to answer, I gaze at this moon.
Possibly the last... so the best should it be.

あき【秋】〔名〕<秋│(n.)Autumn>/に【に】〔格助〕<対象│(prep.)OBJECT>/また【又】〔副〕<再び│(adv.)once again>/あふ【会ふ】〔自ハ四〕<出会う│(v.)meet>(あは＝未然形)/む【む】〔助動マ四型〕推量<だろう│(aux-v.)SUPPOSITION>(む＝終止形)/あふ【会ふ】〔自ハ四〕<出会う│(v.)meet>(あは＝未然形)/じ【じ】〔助動特殊型〕打消推量<～ないだろう│(aux-v.)NEGATIVE SUPPOSITION>(じ＝終止形)/も【も】〔係助〕<意味なし│(adv.)NO MEANING>/しる【知る】〔他ラ四〕<知る│(v.)know>(しら＝未然形)/ず【ず】〔助動特殊型〕打消<～[し]ない│(adv.)not ～>(ぬ＝連体形)/み【身】〔名〕<私│(n.)I, myself>/は【は】〔係助〕<～に関しては│(adv.)as for ～>/こよひ【今宵】〔名〕<今夜│(n.)this evening>/ばかり【ばかり】〔副助〕<～限り│(adv.)only>/の【の】〔格助〕<の│(prep.)'s>/つき【月】〔名〕<月│(n.)the moon>/を【を】〔格助〕<目的格│(prep.)OBJECT>/だに【だに】〔副助〕<せめて～だけでも│(adv.)at least>/みる【見る】〔他マ上一〕<見る│(v.)view>(み＝未然形)/む【む】〔助動マ四型〕意志<～するつもりだ│(aux-v.)be going to ～>(む＝終止形)

[aki ni mata awa-mu awa-ji mo shira-nu mi wa koyoi-bakari no tsuki wo-dani mi-mu]

「春」と「秋」の終わりは「ひょっとしたらこれが見納めかも」的感覚を催す定例シーズン。しかしこの短歌は(一つ前の歌と並んで)三条天皇の痛ましいまでの真情を詠んだもの・・・実際、これら二つの悲しい詩を生んだ後で、一年も経たずに詠み手はこの世を去っています。

The end of Spring or Autumn is a regular season for "*Maybe this is it*" type of sentiment. But this TANKA, along with the previous one, represents the painfully true feeling of the Emperor 三条(Sanjou): in fact, he had less than a year to live after he gave birth to these two sad poems.

‧‧‧‧‧‧‧‧‧‧‧‧‧‧‧‧‧‧‧‧‧‧‧‧‧‧‧‧‧

《「御門」退き「院」に入る世を執るは誰？》

明治時代以降の日本の天皇はその死を以て初めて退位することになるが、それ以前の時代、特に平安中期の日本の天皇は、藤原氏の政治的影響力を受けて強制的に退位させられて引退後の住まいである「院」へと押し込められ、以後はこの「院」が「元天皇」の別名となった。かくて「三条天皇」は藤原道長によって強引に退位させられて「三条院」となり、その後を受けた道長の孫(当時まだ8歳！)の「後一条天皇」に代わって

道長が独裁権を揮うこととなった。後代になると、そうした藤原氏の独裁政治を防ぐため、引退して「院」となった「元天皇」はなおもその政治権力を手放さずに若き「天皇」の国政を陰で支えるようになる。この「院政」と呼ばれる政治体制が生まれたのは1086年の「白河院」の時代だが、その後もこの種の「黒幕政治」は生き残り、現代日本の少なからぬ組織が今なお「影の黒幕」によって牛耳られ続けている。

《from 御門(帝・天皇:mikado, or tennou) to 院(上皇:inn, or joukou) ― who's really in charge?》
Japanese Emperors after the Meiji(明治) era would never leave the throne until his (or possibly *her*) death, but in the previous years, especially in the middle of the Heian era, Emperors were forced out of the throne by the political influence from 藤原氏(Fujiwara-shi=the clan of the Fujiwaras) to live in a retiring residence called 院(inn), which became the alias for the former Emperor. Thus, Emperor 三条(Sanjou <u>tennou</u>) was forcibly made to retire by 藤原道長(Fujiwara-no-Michinaga) and became 三条院(Sanjou <u>inn</u>) to give way to Emperor 後一条(Go-Ichijou tennou), 道長(Michinaga)'s *eight-year old* grandson, in the place of whom 道長(Michinaga) wielded dictatorial power. In later years, to prevent such dictatorship by the 藤原(Fujiwara)s, the retired Emperor ― 院(inn) ― would still hold political power to help the young Emperor govern the nation. Such political system called 院政(innsei=wire-pulling politics) began at the time of 白河院(Shirakawa inn) in A.D.1086 and survived into quite a few organizations of the present-day Japan.

★81★すだきけむむかしのひとも なきやどに ただかげするは あきのよのつき
集きけむ 昔の人も 無き宿に 只影するは 秋の夜の月

【秋】[溜息]『4)後拾遺集:253』恵慶(えぎょう)

昔は大勢そこに集まっていた人々も居たろうに、今は誰一人宿すこともない野辺の寂しい古い家を、秋の夜の月だけが今も変わらず訪れては、優しい光に包んでいる…行き交う人々はみな仮の世の旅人、月日もまた百代の過客なれど、変わらぬものは夜の空の月…

A large vacant house with old inhabitants gone
Stands out in silent embrace of the gentle Autumnal moon.

すだく【集く】〔自カ四〕<集まる | (v.)get together＞(すだき=連用形)／けむ【けむ】[助動マ四型]過去推量<～[し]たのだろう | (aux-v.)PAST SUPPOSITION＞(けむ=連体形)／むかし【昔】[名]<昔 | (n.)the past＞／の【の】[格助]<の | (prep.)'s＞／ひと【人】[名]<人々 | (n.)people＞／も【も】[係助]<意味なし | (adv.)NO MEANING＞／なし【なし】[形]<存在しない | (v.)do not exist＞(なき=連体形)／やど【宿】[名]<家屋 | (n.)the house＞／に【に】[格助]<場所 | (prep.)PLACE＞／ただ【唯】[副]<ただ | (adv.)only＞／かげ【影】[名]<光 | (n.)the light＞／す【為】[他サ変]<～を為す | (v.)make＞(する=連体形)／は【は】[係助]<主格 | (prep.)SUBJECT＞／あき【秋】[名]<秋 | (n.)Autumn＞／の【の】[格助]<の | (prep.)'s＞／よ【夜】[名]<夜 | (n.)the night＞／の【の】[格助]<の | (prep.)'s＞／つき【月】[名]<月 | (n.)the moon＞

[sudaki-kemu mukashi no hito mo naki yado ni tada kage-suru wa aki no yo no tsuki]

「侘び歌名人」恵慶法師の描いた、涙なしには見られない秋の情景…「八重葎茂れる宿の寂しきに…」と同じ河原院で作られた歌です。これまた平安調イタダキ歌の事例?…ええ、まぁ、逆の意味でそうですね ― この短歌を便利なテンプレート(ひな型)として用いて、平忠盛(あの有名な清盛の父)が作ったコピペ短歌が『新古今集』の中に収められているのですから ― **集きけむ昔の人は影絶えて宿守るものは有明の月**(すだきけむむかしのひとはかげたえてやどもるものはありあけのつき) ― 時間帯を「**夜**」から「**有明**=翌朝早く」に変えたのに加えて、「**只影する**=ただ影を投げかける」から「**宿守る**=館を守る」への修正も施しているあたり、皇居を警護する侍大将だった忠盛にはふさわしい感じですね。

—秋—

A tear-inducing scene of Autumn at the hands of "the master of the forlorn" 恵慶法師(Egyou houshi) at the same location (河原院:Kawara no inn) as he made "やへむぐらしげれるやど…(yae-mugura shigere-ru yado...)". Another example of Heianese plagiarism? Well, yes, in a reversed way: this TANKA became a convenient template for 平忠盛(Taira-no-Tadamori), father of the famous 平清盛 (Taira-no-Kiyomori), to copy and paste into the following song in 新古今集(Shin-Kokin shuu) — 集きけむ昔の人は影絶えて宿守るものは有明の月(sudaki-kemu mukashi no hito wa kage tae-te yado moru mono wa ariake-no-tsuki) — besides changing the hour from 夜(yo=the night) to 有明(ariake= early next morning), 忠盛(Tadamori) changed the phrase 只影する(tada kage-suru=just shines on) into 宿守る(yado moru=guards the house), a suitable alteration for the head of 侍(samurai) warriors who guarded the Imperial Palace.

★82★もろともにながめしひともわれもなき　やどにはひとりつきやすむらむ
諸共に眺めし人も我も無き宿には独り月やすむらむ

【秋】[溜息]『4)後拾遺集:856』藤原長家(ふじわらのながいえ)

かつて一緒に月を眺めたあの人もすでにもう亡くし、やがて私自身もこの世を去ったその後で、
二人の思い出だけが残る宿を、今も昔も変わることのない月だけがその澄み切った光で包み込み、
永遠の住人のように振る舞っているのだろうか。

Together we used to see it.
She has been gone now... I'll have been gone, too.
The deserted mansion of loneliness
To be only inhabited and illuminated
By the changeless moon we used to see together.

もろともに【諸共に】[副]＜一緒に｜(adv.)together＞／ながむ【眺む】[他マ下二]＜ぼんやりと見る｜(v.)vacantly watch＞(ながめ＝連用形)／き【き】[助動特殊型]過去＜〜[し]た｜(aux-v.)PAST＞(し＝連体形)／ひと【人】[名]＜あの人｜(n.)that [darling] one＞／も【も】[係助]＜〜もまた｜(adv.)also＞／われ【我】[代名]＜私｜(pron.)I, myself＞／も【も】[係助]＜〜もまた｜(adv.)also＞／なし【なし】[形ク]＜存在しない｜(v.)do not exist＞(なき＝連体形)／やど【宿】[名]＜家屋｜(n.)the house＞／に【に】[格助]＜場所｜(prep.)PLACE＞／は【は】[係助]＜｜(prep.)NO MEANING＞／ひとり【一人】[副]＜一人きり｜(adv.)alone＞／つき【月】[名]＜月｜(n.)the moon＞／や【や】[係助]＜疑問｜(adv.)INTERROGATIVE＞／**(A)すむ【澄む】[自マ四]**＜きれいに澄み渡る｜(v.)get serenely clean＞(すむ＝終止形)／**(B)すむ【住む】[自マ四]**＜住む｜(v.)live in＞(すむ＝終止形)／らむ【らむ】[助動ラ四型]現在推量＜〜だろう｜(aux-v.)SUPPOSITION＞(らむ＝連体形係り結び)

[morotomoni nagame-shi hito mo ware mo naki yado ni-wa hitori tsuki ya sumu-ramu]

この歌人はつい最近愛する人を亡くして、今は死者の供養のためにお寺に籠もっているところ…かつて愛の営みのために足繁く通った彼女のお部屋を、彼はもう二度と訪れることはないけれど、いつも変わらぬ夜の月だけは今後も訪れ続けるのだろうな、と想像を巡らしているのです…というわけで、「**我も無き宿**」の理由は「この歌人の恋人が死んでしまったから」というのが実際のところなのだけれど、「この歌人も遠い昔に死んでしまって今はもういないから」という風に「時」の空想を未来へと膨らませると、この短歌はぐっと劇的に悲しい響きで胸に迫ってきます。私達がみんな逝ってしまったその後も、月は、花は、星々は、そしてこの地球は、我々抜きでもみんな変わらず今まで通りであり続けるのでしょう ― 我々人間はそれを知っています；彼らはたぶん知らないでしょう…その知識をせめてもの慰めと感じるか、何も知らぬまま あり続ける彼らを羨ましく思うかは、微妙なところですが。

—秋—

The poet has just lost his loved one and is now locking himself up in a temple to mourn the dead, thinking about her room where he used to spend many nights to love her but will never be visited by him again, only to be visited by the ever-constant moon in the sky. The reason for 我も無き宿(ware mo naki yado=the house where I'll be no more) is actually because the sweetheart of the poet has been dead, but the sad impact of this TANKA should dramatically increase by imagining a time when the poet himself will have long been gone. After we have all been gone, the moon, the flowers, the stars and the earth will all go on without us the way they always did — we know it; they perhaps don't... a comforting knowledge for us, or an envious ignorance of theirs?

━━

●83● はるはただはなのひとへにさくばかり もののあはれはあきぞまされる

　　　春は只花の一重に咲くばかり物の哀れは秋ぞ勝れる

【秋】[機知]『3)拾遺集:511』詠み人知らず

「春」はただ辺り一面に花が咲くばかり・・・しみじみとした哀感を催す季節としては「秋」の方が上。

Spring scenery is simply flooded with flowers.
Sentiments permeate more than ever in Autumn.

はる【春】〔名〕＜春＞(n.)Spring＞／は【は】〔係助〕＜～に関しては｜(adv.)as for ～＞／ただ【只】〔副〕＜ただ単に｜(adv.)only＞／はな【花】〔名〕＜花｜(n.)flowers＞／の【の】〔格助〕＜主格｜(prep.)SUBJECT＞／ひとへに【偏に】〔副〕＜ただ単に｜(adv.)only＞／さく【咲く】〔自カ四〕＜咲く｜(v.)bloom＞(さく＝終止形)／ばかり【ばかり】〔副助〕＜～なだけ｜(adv.)just＞／もののあはれ【物の哀れ】〔名〕＜哀感｜(n.)pathos＞／は【は】〔係助〕＜～に関しては｜(adv.)as for ～＞／あき【秋】〔名〕＜秋｜(n.)Autumn＞／ぞ【ぞ】〔係助〕＜強調｜(adv.)EMPHASIS＞／まさる【勝る】〔自ラ四〕＜より上だ｜(v.)exceed＞(まされ＝已然形・命令形)／り【り】〔助動ラ変形〕存続＜～[し]ている｜(aux-v.)PERFECT TENSE＞(る＝連体形係り結び)

　　　[haru wa tada hana no hitoeni saku bakari mono no aware wa aki zo masare-ru]

「春と秋とはいずれか勝れる？」という問い掛けに対する返答の歌。この作者の言い分は統計的に見て正解 ― 八代集約9500首に詠まれた数で四季の順位を付けると、1)＜秋＝1300超＞2)＜春＝1100超＞3)＜夏・冬＝500台＞なのだから。

An answer to the question "Which is better, Spring or Autumn?" This author is statistically correct, for the order of appearance of the 4 seasons in some 9,500 poems in 八代集(Hachidai shuu＝8 great Imperial TANKA anthologies) is 1)Autumn(over 1,300), 2)Spring(over 1,100), and 3)Summer/Winter (each in the order of 500).

・・・・・・・・・・・・・・・・・・・・・・・・・・

《「かたき」どち仲良く遊ぶ「品定め」》

暇を持て余した金持ち連中の御多分に漏れず、平安時代の京都の高貴な面々もやはり「決闘」好き ― 体力や勇気を競い合うのではなく、機知や芸の嗜みを友好的な雰囲気の中で競い合わせて遊ぶのである。ここに紹介した短歌のような「競合する物事どうしを比べ合わせる遊び＝品定め」も大流行したし、同じお題で別々の歌人どうしに歌を作らせてどちらが優れているか判定を下す「歌合せ」も定期的に開催された。「かたき(敵＝競合者の片方)」という語はそうした平安調仲良し一対一決戦の中から生まれたもので、当時のこの語には今日の「かたき(仇)」のような怨恨の含みはなかった。

http//zubaraie.com　　　-91-　　　—Autumn—

—秋—

《品定め(shina-sadame＝weighing rivals) ― a joyful appraisal popular among Heianese nobles》
As with all the idle-rich, the noble folks in 京都(Kyoto) in the Heian era were fond of duels ― not the contest of their brawn or courage, but their wit and skill in artistic accomplishment were often put to test in a mood of joyful competition. A poetic comparison of rivaling things like this one ― 品定め (shina-sadame) ― was much in vogue, and the appraisal of several pairs of rivaling poets on the same theme to decide which side wins ― 歌合せ(uta awase＝duels of verse) ― was regularly held. The term かたき(敵:kataki＝one side of the pair... not "敵:teki＝an enemy" in this context) was born out of such Heianese friendly duels, which originally embraced no animosity as it does today.

●84●むらさきにうつろひにしをおくしもの　なほしらぎくとみするなりけり
　　　　紫に移ろひにしを置く霜の猶白菊と見するなりけり

【秋】[機知]『4)後拾遺集:358』藤原資綱(ふじわらのさねつな)
花の色はもう「紫」に変わっていた菊をなお「白菊」に見せていたのは、夜の間に降りた白い露だったのか。

**Although already purple in floral color
Still white-chrysanthemum frost made it appear.**

むらさき【紫】〔名〕＜紫色｜(n.)purple＞／に【に】〔格助〕＜補語｜(prep.)COMPLEMENT＞／うつろふ【移ろふ】〔自ハ四〕＜移り変わる｜(v.)shift＞(うつろひ＝連用形)／ぬ【ぬ】〔助動ナ変型〕完了＜すでに～[し]た｜(aux-v.)PERFECT TENSE＞(に＝連用形)／き【き】〔助動特殊型〕過去＜～[し]た｜(aux-v.)PAST＞(し＝連体形)／を【を】〔格助〕＜目的格｜(prep.)OBJECT＞／おく【置く】〔自カ四〕＜霜が降りる｜(v.)get frosty＞(おく＝連体形)／しも【霜】〔名〕＜霜｜(n.)frost＞／の【の】〔格助〕＜主格｜(prep.)SUBJECT＞／なほ【猶】〔副〕＜今なお｜(adv.)still＞／しらぎく【白菊】〔名〕＜白い菊｜(n.)a white chrysanthemum＞／と【と】〔格助〕＜資格｜(prep.)as＞／みす【見す】〔他サ下二〕＜見せる｜(v.)make something look like something else＞(みする＝連体形)／なり【なり】〔助動ナリ型〕断定＜～である｜(aux-v.)be＞(なり＝連用形)／けり【けり】〔助動ラ変型〕詠嘆＜～だったのだなぁ｜(interj.)REALIZATION＞(けり＝終止形)

[murasaki ni utsuroi-ni-shi wo oku shimo no nao sira-giku to misuru nari-keri]

「菊」は後鳥羽院のお気に入りの花。平安の世のラストエンペラーとして『新古今集』の編纂を命じ鎌倉幕府に反旗を翻した(そして敗れて失脚した)あの後鳥羽上皇が菊を愛したことから、その後「菊の御紋」は皇室並びに日本を象徴する絵柄となりました。八代集約9500首の中には「菊」絡みの短歌が70首ありますが、それに先立つ奈良時代に編まれた『万葉集』には菊の花は全く登場しません。当時も野生の菊は存在したものの、観賞用の花の栽培が始まったのはどうやら平安時代の初め頃だったようです。宮廷では毎年九月九日(新暦では十月九日)に菊花鑑賞の宴が催されました。変わりゆく色と霜の露を(葉ではなく)花びらの上に宿しながら、菊は咲きます ― 年の内に愛でることのできる最後の花として。

菊(kiku＝chrysanthemum) was the favorite flower of 後鳥羽院(Go-Toba inn), the last Emperor of the Heian era who ordered the compilation of 新古今集(Shin-Kokin shuu) and revolted against *and got defeated by* 鎌倉(Kamakura) shogunate ― so much did he love chrysanthemum that it later became the official symbol of the royal family and the nation of Japan. There are 70 chrysanthemum-related TANKA appearing in some 9,500 poems of 八代集(Hachidai shuu＝8 great Imperial TANKA anthologies), while there is none in 万葉集(mannyou shuu) compiled in the preceding Nara(奈良) era: though there had been wild chrysanthemum around, cultivation of this flower seems to have started in the early Heian era. The annual chrysanthemum viewing banquet was held at the Imperial Palace on 9/9 (October 9 on the solar calendar). Housing changing colors and frosty dew on the flower (not on the leaf), chrysanthemum blooms as the last flower to be cherished for the year.

―秋―

●85● あきくれどいろもかはらぬときはやま よそのもみぢをかぜぞかしける
秋来れど色も変はらぬ常磐山余所の紅葉を風ぞ貸しける

【秋】[機知]『1)古今集:362』坂上是則(さかのうえのこれのり)

永遠に変わることがない、というその名の通り、「常磐山」の木々の色は常に緑、秋が来ても紅葉しない…
その単調さに彩りを添えてやろうとして、余所の山で散った木の葉が、
風に舞い飛んで常磐山を紅葉に染めているよ。

The mountain of Tokiwa, worthy of the name
Changes no colors, immune to Autumnal fade
Looks clad in leaves on colorful whirling wind
Blown from other mountains as beauty lease of Fall.

あき【秋】[名]＜秋｜(n.)Autumn＞／く【来】[自力変]＜来る｜(v.)come＞(くれ＝已然形)／ど【ど】[接助]＜～だけれども｜(conj.)although＞／いろ【色】[名]＜色｜(n.)color＞／も【も】[係助]＜意味なし｜(adv.)NO MEANING＞／かはる【変はる】[自ラ四]＜変わる｜(v.)change＞(かはら＝未然形)／ず【ず】[助動特殊型]打消＜～[し]ない｜(adv.)not ～＞(ぬ＝連体形)／**(A1)とき【時】[名]**＜時｜(n.)the time＞／**(A2)は【は】[係助]**＜～に関しては｜(adv.)as for ～＞／**(B)ときはやま【常磐山】[名]**＜[架空の]常緑樹の山｜(n.)[an imaginary] evergreen mountain＞／よそ【余所】[名]＜どこか別の場所｜(n.)somewhere else＞／の【の】[格助]＜の｜(prep.)'s＞／もみぢ【紅葉】[名]＜もみじ｜(n.)varicolored leaves＞／を【を】[格助]＜目的格｜(prep.)OBJECT＞／かぜ【風】[名]＜風｜(n.)wind＞／ぞ【ぞ】[係助]＜強調｜(adv.)EMPHASIS＞／かす【貸す】[他サ四]＜貸す｜(v.)lend＞(かし＝連用形)／けり【けり】[助動ラ変型]詠嘆＜～だったのだなぁ｜(interj.)REALIZATION＞(ける＝連体形係り結び)

[aki kure-do iro mo kawara-nu Tokiwa-yama yoso no momiji wo kaze zo kashi-keru]

この短歌の中の「**常磐山**」は、京都あたりに実在する固有名称ではなく、「一年中色の変わることがない緑一色の山」を意味する架空の存在。それでもなおこの常緑樹の山が緑以外の色々に染まって見えるのは、余所の山から舞い飛んできた幾多の**紅葉**がこの単調な山肌に色彩を貸してくれているから…写実主義の提唱者正岡子規ならその大胆な虚構に激怒しそうな、作り物度数100％の『古今集』短歌。

常磐山(Tokiwa-yama) in this TANKA is not a proper name actually in existence somewhere around 京都(Kyoto) but an imaginary mountain where trees are always green without changing colors. Still, that evergreen mountain looks tinged with colors other than green because lots of **紅葉**(momiji= varicolored leaves) from other mountains are flying in the air to lend colors to the monotonous mountain. A 100% fictional poem in 古今集(Kokin shuu) that would infuriate the photo-realism advocate 正岡子規(Masaoka Shiki) with its blatant falsehood.

《歌詠みの名と技上げし「屏風歌」》

平安調短歌(とりわけ勅撰和歌集第一弾『古今集』)が、まじめに取り合うにはあまりにも突飛すぎる虚構歌だらけである理由の一つは、貴人の邸宅内の屏風に描かれた空想的情景に添えるための注釈的な歌(いわゆる「屏風歌」)として詠まれたものが多かったから。平安時代初期の著名な歌人のほとんどは、社会的地位が低すぎて本来なら宮廷の高位高官たちとの接点もないような平役人、そんな彼らが高い地位の人々の目に留まったのは、上流社会の雅びな生活を彩るにふさわしい空想的(あるいは奇想天外)な詩歌を即興で詠み上げるその技能ゆえのこと…そういうわけだから、平安調短歌(特に「恋歌」)を額面通りに受け取るようなマネは厳禁。その殆どは作り物であって、作り手の実生活を反映したものではまるでないのだから…恋愛だらけの生涯を送った人物として[悪]名高い在原業平だって、幾多の恋歌で彩られた彼

—秋—

のエセ人生録である『伊勢物語』が描くほど、呆れるまでにふしだらな性生活を送ったはずは、ないのである。詩歌は詩歌、人生は人生、程良く分けて味わいましょう・・・「ウソだ！インチキだ！」なんて言わないでね正岡子規センセ。私たちが本当に見たいのは、「自分語り」に必死な誰かさんのつまらぬ実話なんかじゃなく、他の人達に向けて訴えかけること(そして、しっかり楽しませること)目指して作られた「面白い作り話」の方なんだから。

《屏風歌(byoubu-uta＝accompanying rhymes to a pictorial screen) ― a great booster to Heianese poets' skill and fame》

One reason why Heianese TANKA ― especially the first Imperial TANKA anthology 古今集(Kokin shuu) ― are teeming with fictional songs too fantastic to be taken seriously is that many of them were made as explanatory verse to be added to some imaginary scene drawn on 屏風(byoubu＝screens for spatial division) in the residences of noblemen. Most of the famous TANKA poets in the early Heian era were too low in their social status to mingle among higher ranking officers at the Imperial Court. What brought these petty officials to the attention of dignitaries was their skill at improvising fantastic rhymes to decorate the elegant way of the high society. Such being the case, you must *never* take Heianese TANKA ― especially 恋歌(koi-uta＝love songs) ― at their face value: most of them were fictional, not at all reflecting the actual lives of their authors. The infamously amorous life of 在原業平(Ariwara-no-Narihira) must never have been so scandalously loose as 伊勢物語(Ise monogatari) ― the fake life-story of 業平(Narihira) decorated with lots of love poems ― made him out to be. Rhymes are rhymes, lives are lives, keep them apart to keep them alive... never say *LIES! LIES!* please, 正岡子規(Masaoka Shiki). What we want to see is not so much uninteresting true stories of someone intent on talking about himself, as interesting fables intended to appeal to others... and to fill them with joy.

―――――――――――――――――――――――――

●86●さほやまのははそのもみぢちりぬべみ　よるさへみよとてらすつきかげ
佐保山の柞の紅葉散りぬべみ夜さへ見よと照らす月影

【秋】［機知］『1)古今集:281』詠み人知らず

佐保山で、緑から茶への色の移ろいを終えつつあるハハソの葉たちは、もう明日にはきっと散ってしまうだろう・・・だから、「今夜は夜通し見るがいい、紅葉の最後の散り際を」とばかり、月が明るく照らし出してくれていることだよ。

Colors of leaves on the mountain of Saho

At the end of transition from green to yellow.

The night is bright for us to view in the dark

The moon-lit trees we'll see bare tomorrow.

さほやま【佐保山】〔名］＜［固有名詞]佐保山｜(n.)the mountain of Saho＞／の【の】〔格助］＜の｜(prep.)'s＞／ははそ【柞】〔名］＜ハハソ｜(n.)an oak＞／の【の】〔格助］＜の｜(prep.)'s＞／もみぢ【紅葉】〔名］＜もみじ｜(n.)varicolored leaves＞／ちる【散る】〔自ラ四］＜散る｜(v.)fall＞(ちり＝連用形)／ぬ【ぬ】〔助動ナ変型］確述＜きっと～する｜(adv.)EMPHASIS＞(ぬ＝終止形)／べし【べし】〔助動ク型］推量＜～にちがいない｜(aux-v.)CONVICTION＞(べ＝語幹)／み【み】〔接尾］＜理由｜(conj.)REASON＞／よる【夜】〔名］＜夜｜(n.)the night＞／さへ【さへ】〔副助］＜さえ｜(adv.)even＞／みる【見る】〔他マ上一］＜見る｜(v.)view＞(みよ＝命令形)／と【と】〔格助］＜内容提示｜(conj.)that ～＞／てらす【照らす】〔他サ四］＜照らす｜(v.)illuminate＞(てらす＝連体形)／つきかげ【月影】〔名］＜月明かり｜(n.)the moonlight＞

—秋—

[Saho-yama no hahaso no momiji chiri-nu-be-mi yoru sae miyo to terasu tsuki-kage]

晩秋の最後の紅葉を見物できるように、と夜間のライトアップを行なうのは、現代ではよくあること‥‥だけど『古今集』当時には現実的にあり得ないこと‥‥そう、この歌もまた空想物語として詠まれた短歌、ひょっとしたら(奈良に実在する)佐保山の麓で詠んだものですらなくて、紅葉に彩られた山に月影が照っているさまを描いた屏風に添える詩歌として詠まれたもの、かもしれません。

Nightly illumination for viewers to enjoy the last 紅葉(momiji=changing colors of leaves) in late Autumn is a usual custom nowadays, but no reality at the time of 古今集(Kokin shuu) — this is just another fantasy TANKA, maybe not even made at the foot of 佐保山(Saho-yama=an actual mountain in 奈良:Nara) but as an accompanying verse to a drawing on a 屏風(byoubu)-screen where the moon is shining on the varicolored mountain.

●87●ものごとにあきぞかなしきもみぢつつ うつろひゆくをかぎりとおもへば

物毎に秋ぞ悲しき紅葉ぢつつ移ろひ行くを限りと思へば

【秋】[溜息]『1)古今集:187』詠み人知らず

あぁ秋は、いちいち何もかもみな悲しいなぁ‥‥木々の葉っぱの色の移ろいも、いつまでも続くわけじゃなく、最後には散って終わりが来る‥‥それがわかっちゃった目で見つめる秋の切なさといったらもう‥‥

Everything in Autumn feels sad to me,
From green to yellow, red... and bare,
Leaves change colors and leave me alone in Winter.

もの【物】〔名〕<あれこれいろいろ | (n.)one thing or another>/ごと【毎】〔接尾〕<それぞれに | (adv.)each>/に【に】〔格助〕<時 | (prep.)TIME>/あき【秋】〔名〕<秋 | (n.)Autumn>/ぞ【ぞ】〔係助〕<強調 | (adv.)EMPHASIS>/かなし【哀し】〔形シク〕<悲しい | (adj.)sad>/(かなしき=連体形係り結び)/もみづ【紅葉づ】〔自ダ上二〕<葉の色が変わる | (v.)leaves change colors>(もみぢ=連用形)/つつ【つつ】〔接助〕<〜[し]ながら | (conj.)as>/うつろふ【移ろふ】〔自ハ四〕<移り変わる | (v.)shift>(うつろひ=連用形)/ゆく【行く】〔自カ四〕<次第に〜になる | (v.)come to 〜>(ゆく=連体形)/を【を】〔格助〕<目的格 | (prep.)OBJECT>/かぎり【限り】〔名〕<おしまい | (n.)the end>/と【と】〔格助〕<内容提示 | (conj.)that 〜>/おもふ【思ふ】〔他ハ四〕<思う | (v.)think>(おもへ=已然形)/ば【ば】〔接助〕<理由 | (conj.)REASON>

[mono-goto-ni aki zo kanashiki momiji-tsutsu utsuroi-yuku wo kagiri to omoe-ba]

春の花々は見るからに美しい‥‥まだ人生のつぼみの段階の子供たちの目で見てさえも、美しい‥‥が、秋の紅葉の美しさは、そこそこ年行った人にしかわからない:紅葉を美しく染めるものは落ち葉から搾り取られた最後の血の雫であること、落ちた後はひたすら荒涼として寂しい季節が来ることを告げる悲しい序曲であることを知っている者だけに、紅葉は美しく映えるのだ‥‥このように、ある種の感覚や行動へと見る者を誘う自然の(そして社会の)合図が、日本の国には満ちている‥‥日本人になるということは、この種の「キュー!」が出たらすぐに然るべき(決して「予想外の」とか「独自の」とかじゃない)反応を返せるようになるということ‥‥あまり西欧流じゃないし今風ですらないけれど、こうした「御約束大好き」感覚は今なお全ての日本人の根底にあるもの。

Flowers in Spring are beautiful to see, even in the eyes of kids in bud of their lives; 紅葉(momiji= varicolored leaves) in Fall are only beautiful to those old enough to know that beauty is the last drop of lifeblood squeezed out of falling leaves, a sad prologue to the season of total bleak and solitude. Japanese Nature (and society) is full of such staple cues to tell you to feel and act in certain ways... growing up to be a Japanese is to be able to respond with suitable (*NOT unexpected* or *unique*) actions to such cues... not quite Western or even modern, but such love of ruts is still at the root of all Japanese.

—秋—

●88● あきはきぬもみぢはやどにふりしきぬ　みちふみわけてとふひとはなし

秋は来ぬ紅葉は宿に降り敷きぬ道踏み分けて訪ふ人は無し

【秋】[溜息]『1)古今集:287』詠み人知らず

もう秋がやって来た・・・木々の紅葉も散って我が家の庭に降り敷いた・・・なのに、その紅葉の絨毯を踏み分けて私を訪ねてくれる人は、いない。

Fall has come. Leaves fell on my garden.
No one comes to tread on the thick carpet of leaves.

あき【秋】[名]＜秋｜(n.)Autumn＞／は【は】[係助]＜〜に関しては｜(adv.)as for 〜＞／く【来】[自カ変]＜来る｜(v.)come＞(き＝連用形)／ぬ【ぬ】[助動ナ変型]完了＜すでに〜[し]た｜(aux-v.)PERFECT TENSE＞(ぬ＝終止形)／もみぢ【紅葉】[名]＜もみぢ｜(n.)varicolored leaves＞／は【は】[係助]＜〜に関しては｜(adv.)as for 〜＞／やど【宿】[名]＜家屋｜(n.)the house＞／に【に】[格助]＜場所｜(prep.)PLACE＞／ふりしく【降り敷く】[自カ四]＜降り積もる｜(v.)fall thickly＞(ふりしき＝連用形)／ぬ【ぬ】[助動ナ変型]完了＜すでに〜[し]た｜(aux-v.)PERFECT TENSE＞(ぬ＝終止形)／みち【道】[名]＜道｜(n.)the path＞／ふみわく【踏み分く】[他カ下二]＜踏み分ける｜(v.)tread＞(ふみわけ＝連用形)／て【て】[接助]＜順接｜(conj.)and＞／とふ【訪ふ】[他ハ四]＜訪れる｜(v.)visit＞(とふ＝連体形)／ひと【人】[名]＜客人｜(n.)a visitor＞／は【は】[係助]＜〜に関しては｜(adv.)as for 〜＞／なし【なし】[形ク]＜存在しない｜(v.)do not exist＞(なし＝終止形)

[aki wa ki-nu momiji wa yado ni furi-shiki-nu michi fumi-wake-te tou hito wa nashi]

紅葉の色の移り変わりは晩秋最大の見物の一つ・・・ただしそれも、木々の上にあればこそ。この短歌の中の落ち葉は二重の意味で悲しい — 地べたに落ちた紅葉ではもう誰もお客さんは見に来てくれないだろうし、もし来てくれる客人がいれば踏みしめる一歩ごとに聞こえるはずの足音も、散り敷いた分厚い落ち葉のどこからもまるで響いて来ないのだから。

Changing colors of leaves — 紅葉(momiji) — are one of the highlights of late Autumn... so long as they feast our eyes on the trees. The fallen leaves in this TANKA are dually sad because they no longer interest any visitors who, if they came, would give out sound of their approach at each footstep they would make on the thick layers of dry leaves.

★89★ さびしさにやどをたちいでてながむれば　いづこもおなじあきのゆふぐれ

寂しさに宿を立ち出でて眺むれば何処も同じ秋の夕暮れ

【秋】[溜息]『4)後拾遺集:333』良暹(りょうぜん)

一人で家の中にいると、寂しくて淋しくていたたまれなくなって、何かを求めて外に出る・・・けれど、どこを見渡しても結局は同じ・・・寂しさだけが一面に広がる、秋の夕暮れがあるばかり。

Sadness filled me up out of this solitary hut,
What did I see but lonely dusk of Fall for all?

さびしさ【寂しさ】[名]＜さびしさ｜(n.)loneliness＞／に【に】[格助]＜原因｜(prep.)REASON＞／やど【宿】[名]＜家屋｜(n.)the house＞／を【を】[格助]＜目的格｜(prep.)OBJECT＞／たちいづ【立ち出づ】[他ダ下二]＜出て来る｜(v.)come out＞(たちいで＝連用形)／て【て】[接助]＜順接｜(conj.)and＞／ながむ【眺む】[他マ下二]＜ぼんやりと見る｜(v.)vacantly watch＞(ながむれ＝已然形)／ば【ば】[接助]＜〜したところ｜(conj.)when＞／いづこ【何処】[代名]＜どこ｜(adv.)wherever＞／も【も】[係助]＜意味なし｜(adv.)NO MEANING＞／おなじ【同じ】[形シク]＜同じ｜(adj.)the same＞(おなじ[き]＝連体形)／あき【秋】[名]＜秋｜(n.)Autumn＞／の【の】[格助]＜の｜(prep.)'s＞／ゆふぐれ【夕暮れ】[名]＜夕暮れ｜(n.)evening＞

—秋—

[sabishi-sa ni yado wo tachi-ide-te nagamure-ba izuko mo onaji aki no yuu-gure]

家の中で一人きりで耐え忍ぶにはあんまりすぎる寂しさも、夏の街に出れば何かしらはけ口が見つかるかもしれない・・・けど、寂しい世捨て人だけが住む秋の野山なら、どうしたらいい？・・・この詩人に出来ることはただ、孤独を歌に込めて、誰にともなく吐き出すだけでした（・・・ひょっとしたら、あなたに向けて）

Loneliness too much to bear alone indoors might be given some outlet if you go out into Summer town; but what if it's Autumn mountains where only lonely hermits live? All this poet could do was to rhyme out his sorrow for only God knows whom... maybe for you.

★90★さびしさはそのいろとしもなかりけり まきたつやまのあきのゆふぐれ
寂しさは其の色としもなかりけり槙立つ山の秋の夕暮れ

【秋】[悟り]『8)新古今集:361』寂蓮（じゃくれん）

秋になると寂しい思いが募るのは、緑色だった木の葉の色が、黄色く赤く変わり果て、やがてはみんな散ってしまうその色の移り変わりに、見る者の心が揺れるから、木々の移ろいに我が身の無常を重ね合わせて哀れを催すのが人情だから・・・だとばかり思っていたが、どうもそうではなかったようだ・・・色も変わらぬ常緑樹の檜のすっきりとした木立を前に佇むこの秋の夕暮れにさえも、私の心は、えも言われぬ寂寥感にこうして染まっているのだから。

> Greenery turning yellow, red and bare,
> Autumnal sorrow increases with color:
> I thought so till today I found my heart still tinged with sorrow
> At the sight of cypress trees changeless for ever in green...
> What then has made me blue on this sorrowful Autumnal eve?

さびしさ【寂しさ】[名]＜さびしさ｜(n.)loneliness＞／は【は】[係助]＜～に関しては｜(adv.)as for ～＞／そ【其】[代名]＜それ｜(pron.)that＞／の【の】[格助]＜の｜(prep.)'s＞／いろ【色】[名]＜色｜(n.)color＞／と【と】[格助]＜内容提示｜(conj.)that ～＞／しも【しも】[副助]＜意味なし｜(adv.)NO MEANING＞／なし【なし】[形ク]＜～というわけではない｜(v.)not that ～＞（なかり＝連用形）／けり【けり】[助動ラ変型]詠嘆＜～だったのだなぁ｜(interj.)REALIZATION＞（けり＝終止形）／まき【槙】[名]＜[スギ・ヒノキ等の]建築用良材｜(n.)cypress trees＞／たつ【立つ】[自タ四]＜立つ｜(v.)stand＞（たつ＝連体形）／やま【山】[名]＜山｜(n.)the mountain＞／の【の】[格助]＜の｜(prep.)'s＞／あき【秋】[名]＜秋｜(n.)Autumn＞／の【の】[格助]＜の｜(prep.)'s＞／ゆふぐれ【夕暮れ】[名]＜夕暮れ｜(n.)evening＞

[sabishi-sa wa so-no iro to-shimo nakari-keri maki tatsu yama no aki no yuu-gure]

秋の寂しさは紅葉の色の移ろいと共に深まるもの ― それは確かにそうだけど、「現象」は「原因」とは違うもの ― 色も変わらぬ常緑樹の「槙」の山の光景が、詩人にそれを教えている・・・色も変えずに、それでも彼を寂しくさせるその景色が、「**その色としもなかりけり**」と証明している。秋の哀愁は色もなく、名状し難く、あるいは何の原因もなく沸いてくるもの。

Autumnal sorrow deepens with the transition of colors on the leaves, it is true: but the phenomenon is not the cause ― the sight of an Autumnal mountain with evergreen leaves of 槙(maki＝cypress trees) is in front of the poet to prove it... without changing colors, this sight still leaves him sad. Autumnal sorrow is colorless, nameless, and maybe groundless.

—秋—

●91● むらさめのつゆもまだひぬまきのはに きりたちのぼるあきのゆふぐれ
　　　村雨の露も未だ干ぬ槇の葉に霧立ち昇る秋の夕暮れ

【秋】[叙景]『8)新古今集:491』寂蓮(じゃくれん)

空から出し抜けに落ちて来た通り雨が上がり、樹々の木の葉に溜まった雨粒もまだ乾かぬ先から、今度は木の葉の間を縫うようにして霧が空へと立ち昇り、周囲をぼーっと霞ませて行く、そんな秋の夕暮れ時。

Abrupt rain from the sky still wetting leaves in the form of dew,
Rising mist filling dusk of Fall hiding trees in thick white vell.

むらさめ【叢雨】[名]＜夕立｜(n.)showers of rain＞／の【の】[格助]＜の｜(prep.)'s＞／つゆ【露】[名]＜露｜(n.)dew＞／も【も】[係助]＜意味なし｜(adv.)NO MEANING＞／まだ【未だ】[副]＜まだ｜(adv.)yet＞／ひる【干る】[自ハ上一]＜乾く｜(v.)dry up＞(ひ＝未然形)／ず【ず】[助動特殊型]打消＜〜[し]ない｜(adv.)not 〜＞(ぬ＝連体形)／まき【槇】[名]＜スギ・ヒノキ等の]建築用良材｜(n.)cypress trees＞／の【の】[格助]＜の｜(prep.)'s＞／は【葉】[名]＜葉｜(n.)leaves＞／に【に】[格助]＜場所｜(prep.)PLACE＞／きり【霧】[名]＜霧｜(n.)fog＞／たちのぼる【立ち昇る】[自タ四]＜発生する｜(v.)rise＞(たちのぼる＝連体形)／あき【秋】[名]＜秋｜(n.)Autumn＞／の【の】[格助]＜の｜(prep.)'s＞／ゆふぐれ【夕暮れ】[名]＜夕暮れ｜(n.)evening＞

[mura-same no tsuyu mo mada hi-nu maki no ha ni kiri tachi-noboru aki no yuu-gure]

「未だ干ぬ」の表現は、1)雨の前;2)雨の最中;3)雨の直後の3つの場面を内包・・・木々の葉の上にまだ雨の露が残る中、木々の隙間には霧が立ち昇り、秋の夕暮れを白く霞ませ始める。幾つもの「時」と「情景」が精緻に凝縮された三十一文字の小宇宙 ― 『新古今集』の最も美味なる精髄ながら、最も味わわれずに眠っている短歌の一つ・・・何故そうも無視されるのか？そういうショートムービーはビデオカメラで撮るもの／言葉で表わせるはずがない、と現代日本人が思い込んでるから。

The term 未だ干ぬ (mada hinu＝not yet dried up) embraces the following 3 scenes: 1)before the rain; 2)during the rain; 3)immediately after the rain... with the dew still remaining on the leaves, mist is rising between the trees and starts to blur the Autumnal evening. Multiple time and scenes exquisitely condensed into a 31-letter/syllable universe ― the most delicious yet the least cherished essence of 新古今 (Shin-Kokin) TANKA... Why so ignored? The modern Japanese believe such short movies are only possible with videocams, never in *words*.

●92● みわたせばはなももみぢもなかりけり うらのとまやのあきのゆふぐれ
　　　見渡せば花も紅葉も無かりけり浦の苫屋の秋の夕暮れ

【秋】[謎掛]『8)新古今集:363』藤原定家(ふじわらのていか(さだいえ))

今、私は、平安中期の『源氏物語』の中で都落ちした光源氏が流れた先の、須磨の浜辺に立っている・・・が、どこを見渡しても、作中で「春・秋の花、紅葉の盛りなるよりも、ただそこはかとなう繁れる陰どもなまめかし」などと書かれたような風情ある景色は見当たらず、
さびれた小屋の上に、寂しげな秋の夕陽が影を落としているばかりである。

I look around and find there's no flower or beautifully tinged leaves.
There's just a shabby hut on the beach in the Autumnal evening.

みわたす【見渡す】[他サ四]＜見渡す｜(v.)look over＞(みわたせ＝已然形)／ば【ば】[接助]＜〜したところ｜(conj.)when＞／はな【花】[名]＜花｜(n.)flowers＞／も【も】[係助]＜列挙｜(conj.)or＞／もみぢ【紅葉】[名]＜もみじ｜(n.)varicolored leaves＞／も【も】[係助]＜列挙｜(conj.)or＞／なし【なし】[形ク

―秋―

＜存在しない｜(v.)do not exist＞(なかり＝連用形)／けり【けり】〔助動ラ変型〕詠嘆＜～だったのだなぁ｜(interj.)REALIZATION＞(けり＝終止形)／うら【浦】〔名〕＜浜辺｜(n.)the beachside＞／の【の】〔格助〕＜の｜(prep.)'s＞／とまや【苫屋】〔名〕＜粗末な草ぶきの小屋｜(n.)a thatched hut＞／の【の】〔格助〕＜の｜(prep.)'s＞／あき【秋】〔名〕＜秋｜(n.)Autumn＞／の【の】〔格助〕＜の｜(prep.)'s＞／ゆふぐれ【夕暮れ】〔名〕＜夕暮れ｜(n.)evening＞

[miwatase-ba hana mo momiji mo nakari-keri ura no toma-ya no aki no yuu-gure]

この詩は、二百年前の『源氏物語』に描かれた「明石」の美しい風景描写に対する詩的反論である、という前提知識なしには到底理解不能・・・これほど「常軌を逸した」短歌も珍しいが、同時にまたこの上なく「新古今歌」そのものとも言える・・・部外者を寄せ付けぬ内輪だけに通じる深遠さを追い求めつつ、十一世紀末の平安貴族たちの胸中に共通する「世紀末感覚」を痛ましいまでに代表する歌・・・藤原定家以外誰にも作れない「死に行く平安時代」に手向けた大胆な哀歌である。

An impossible TANKA to interpret without the knowledge that it's a poetic opposition to the beautiful description of 明石(Akashi)'s scenery in 源氏物語(Genji monogatari) 200 years before, saying 遙々と物の滞りなき海面なるに春・秋の花、紅葉の盛りなるよりも只そこはかとなう繁れる陰ども艶めかし (harubaru to mono no todokoori naki umizura naruni, haru aki no hana, momiji no sakari naru yori mo, tada sokohakatonou shigereru kage domo namamekashi＝the sea of Akashi spreads far and wide without any interruption; even more than the flowers of Spring and Autumn or the beautifully tinged leaves at their reddest, the shadowy accents here and there of the scene thick with nameless yet not charmless plants feel more than enticing) One of the most "*insane*" yet one of the most 新古今 *(Shin-Kokin)istic* TANKA, too esoteric but painfully representative of the bleak "fin de siècle" sentiment of the Heianese nobles at the end of the 11th century ― an audacious requiem to the dying Heian era only possible at the hands of 藤原定家(Fujiwara-no-Teika).

・・・・・・・・・・・・・・・・・・・・・・・・・・

《「ののの攻め＆体言止め」の「新古今」》

和泉式部や西行法師のような天才詩人は別にして、平安の世の歌人たちは概して「詩的韻律」に無頓着、五・七・五・七・七の字数の枠組みの中に言葉をはめ込むことにばかり頭が行ってしまい、流れるように心地良い音楽的台詞の躍動感の創出などほとんど全く考えてもいなかった・・・が、その歴史も終わりを告げようという頃になって、平安調短歌はようやく、独自な音響効果を生み出す手法を発見するに至った・・・助詞の「の」の一見バカっちぃ繰り返し(「**AのBのCの**」三連符で、*この筆者*(＝之人冗悟:のと・じゃうご呼ぶところの「**ののの攻め**」)や、詩歌の最後を名詞で締めくくることで生じる唐突ながら示唆に富む余韻効果(一般に「**体言止め**」と呼ばれるもの)もその一つである・・・『新古今集』にはその種の技巧の実例を(笑っちゃうほど)豊富に見ることができる。

《ののの攻め(no-no-no bombardment) and 体言止(taigen dome＝substantive stop) ―
typical technique of 新古今(Shin-Kokin)》

With the exception of such poetic geniuses as 和泉式部(Izumi shikibu) or 西行法師(Saigyou houshi), Heianese poets were generally nonchalant to poetic rhythm, with their mind fixed on making their words fit into the 5-7-5-7-7 letter/syllable framework, with little or no thought to creating a musically comforting stream of phrases. Towards the end of its history, however, Heianese TANKA found ways to achieve unique sound effects. The apparently absurd repetition of the 助詞(joshi＝postpositional particle) "**の**(no)" ― **A-no B-no C-no** triplet *which this author (之人冗悟:Jaugo Noto) personally calls "****ののの攻め***(no-no-no zeme)"* and the abrupt yet suggestive conclusion of a poem by ending the last phrase with a noun, generally known as 体言止(taigen dome＝substantive stop) are one of them, both of which you may find in amusing abundance in the works of 新古今集(Shin-Kokin shuu).

—秋—

●93●きりぎりすよざむにあきのなるままに　よわるかこゑのとほざかりゆく

蟋蟀夜寒に秋のなる儘に弱るか声の遠ざかり行く

【秋】[自然]『(8)新古今集:472』西行(さいぎょう)

あぁ、コオロギよ、秋も深まり夜が寒くなるにつれて、弱って行くのか、次第にその声が遠ざかって行く。

O, crickets, as the nights get colder
As Autumn becomes deeper, are you getting weaker?
I hear you cry further and further away.

きりぎりす【蟋蟀】〔名〕＜コオロギ｜(n.)crickets＞／よざむ【夜寒】〔名〕＜夜寒｜(n.)the nights getting colder＞／に【に】〔格助〕＜補語｜(prep.)COMPLEMENT＞／あき【秋】〔名〕＜秋｜(n.)Autumn＞／の【の】〔格助〕＜主格｜(prep.)SUBJECT＞／なる【成る】〔自ラ四〕＜〜になる｜(v.)become＞（なる＝連体形）／まま【儘】〔名〕＜そのままの状況｜(n.)the state being 〜＞／に【に】〔格助〕＜時｜(prep.)TIME＞／よわる【弱る】〔自ラ四〕＜弱る｜(v.)get weaker＞（よわる＝連体形）／か【か】〔終助〕＜疑問｜(adv.)INTERROGATIVE＞／こゑ【声】〔名〕＜声｜(n.)the voice＞／の【の】〔格助〕＜主格｜(prep.)SUBJECT＞／とほざかる【遠ざかる】〔自ラ四〕＜遠ざかる｜(v.)get far away＞（とほざかり＝連用形）／ゆく【行く】〔自カ四〕＜行く｜(v.)go＞（ゆく＝終止形）

[kirigirisu yo-zamu ni aki no naru mama-ni yowaru-ka koe no toozakari-yuku]

古歌の中での**きりぎりす**:蟋蟀は、現代の「(チョンギース って鳴く)キリギリス」ではなく「(キリキリ、コロコロ、の)こおろぎ」‥‥現代人にとってはこの歌、自然の当たり前の姿を詠んでるだけで特に注意を引くものじゃないけど、こういうちっぽけな生き物の置かれた苦境にこうして自然な共感を注ぐ歌というのも、平安時代の詩歌の中では本当に珍しい ─ 西行や和泉式部みたいな「感情移入の詩人」なればこそ詠めた歌です。

きりぎりす(kirigirisu) in ancient TANKA is not what it is today (a katydid) but what the modern Japanese call こおろぎ(kourogi=a cricket). This TANKA sounds too natural a truism for the modern reader to heed, but few poems were found in the Heian era to so naturally sympathize with the predicament of these petty creatures ─ a song only possible with such poets of empathy as 西行 (Saigyou) or 和泉式部(Izumi shikibu).

★94★おくやまにもみぢふみわけなくしかの　こゑきくときぞあきはかなしき

奥山に紅葉踏み分け鳴く鹿の声聞く時ぞ秋は悲しき

【秋】[溜息]『1)古今集:215』詠み人知らず

秋の山は紅葉の絨毯敷き詰め、踏みしめるごとにふぁさふぁさと音がして、奥深く分け入る我が身にも、人里離れた物寂しさを感じさせずにはおかない‥‥そこにまた聞こえる鹿の声‥‥愛しい女鹿を恋しむ男鹿のものだろうか‥‥あぁ、彼も独り、我も一人‥‥自らの心の郷愁が彼方にこだまして、何とも切ない秋の風情であることよ。

Feet deep in Autumnal leaves' carpets in the mountains,
Away from crowds along with distant voice,
Heart deep in sorrow with deer crying in solo.

おくやま【奥山】〔名〕＜山奥｜(n.)deep in the mountain＞／に【に】〔格助〕＜場所｜(prep.)PLACE＞／もみぢ【紅葉】〔名〕＜もみぢ｜(n.)varicolored leaves＞／ふみわく【踏み分く】〔他カ下二〕＜踏み分ける｜(v.)tread＞（ふみわけ＝連用形）／なく【鳴く】〔自カ四〕＜鳴く｜(v.)cry＞（なく＝連体形）／しか【鹿】〔名〕＜鹿｜(n.)a deer＞／の【の】〔格助〕＜の｜(prep.)'s＞／こゑ【声】〔名〕＜声｜(n.)the voice＞／きく【聞く】〔他カ四〕＜聞く｜(v.)hear＞（きく＝連体形）／とき【時】〔名〕＜時｜(n.)the time＞／ぞ【ぞ】〔係助〕＜強調

―秋―

| (adv.)EMPHASIS＞／あき【秋】〔名〕＜秋 | (n.)Autumn＞／は【は】〔係助〕＜主格 | (prep.)SUBJECT＞／かなし【悲し】〔形シク〕＜悲しい | (adj.)sad＞ (かなしき＝連体形係り結び)

[oku-yama ni momiji fumi-wake naku shika no koe kiku toki zo aki wa kanashiki]

「秋の悲しさ」の題詠歌、つまり実際には真実ならざる歌だけど、心情的にはとっても真実味のある歌だと感じませんか？この歌人がこの鹿の声(雌を恋い慕う雄の泣き声)を聞いている場所は、自宅の暖かい部屋の中ではありません。山奥深く自ら足を踏み入れ、一人ぼっちで、頭を垂れて、どこまでも続く落ち葉の絨毯をぼんやり眺めながら、地面に分厚く積もった紅葉の上を踏みしめるごとに聞こえる自分の足音を、自らの心の立てる孤独の音として聞いている･･･と、そこへ突然、遠くに聞こえる鹿の泣き声に、詩人は、孤独の伴侶を見出すのです･･･作り物の歌、と言われればその通りですが、ただそれだけで(あの厚顔無恥な正岡子規みたいに)切り捨ててしまえるような歌でしょうか？･･･ちなみに、この『古今集』の中の詠み人知らず歌を、藤原定家は彼の『小倉百人一首』の中で、伝説の(と言っても実在しない)「猿丸大夫」の作、としています･･･むろんこちらは「ウソこけ！」の一言で片付けちゃっていい話ですが、まぁどうでもいい話ですね。誰が作った歌だろうが、どうやって作られた歌だろうが、この歌の本質は変わらない ―「傑作」です！

A fictional poem on the theme of "Autumnal sorrow": yes, it's factually *not* true but mentally too true, don't you feel? This poet does not hear the voice of a deer (male one yearning for a female) in a warm room inside his house, but he is stepping out into the deep mountain himself, all alone, with his head low down, vacantly looking at an endless carpet of fallen leaves, hearing the sound of his sorrow with each step he makes deep down into the thick layers of 紅葉(momiji＝varicolored leaves), when suddenly he finds his solitary companion in the distant voice of 鹿(shika＝a deer) crying alone... fictional, yes it is, but is that reason enough to dismiss it as falsehood as 正岡子規(Masaoka Shiki) would shamelessly do? Incidentally, this anonymous TANKA in 古今集(Kokin shuu) is attributed by 藤原定家(Fujiwara-no-Teika) in his 小倉百人一首(Ogura hyakunin isshu) to a legendary *though fictional* poet 猿丸大夫(Sarumaru dayuu)... you have every reason to dismiss it as *bullshit*, of course, but what's the difference? Whoever made it, however it was made, it is just what it is ― a masterpiece!

●95●あきかぜにあへずちりぬるもみちばの　ゆくへさだめぬわれぞかなしき

秋風に敢へず散りぬるもみち葉の行く方定めぬ我ぞ悲しき

【秋】[序詞]『1)古今集:286』詠み人知らず

色もすっかり移ろい果てて、それでも必死に木々の梢にしがみついている頼りなげな葉っぱたちが、秋風に耐え切れず、舞い散って宙を漂う･･･そんな紅葉の運命にも似た、前途の当てもない我が身が、悲しい。

Old fading leaves barely sticking to trees
Blown by Autumn wind to go astray in the air...
Likewise will I go only God knows where.

あきかぜ【秋風】〔名〕＜秋風 | (n.)Autumnal wind＞／に【に】〔格助〕＜原因 | (prep.)REASON＞／あふ【敢ふ】〔自ハ下二〕＜耐える | (v.)endure＞(あへ＝未然形)／ず【ず】〔助動特殊型〕打消＜～[し]ない | (adv.)not ～＞(ず＝終止形)／ちる【散る】〔自ラ四〕＜散る | (v.)fall＞(ちり＝連用形)／ぬ【ぬ】〔助動ナ変型〕完了＜すでに～[し]た | (aux-v.)PERFECT TENSE＞(ぬる＝連体形)／もみぢば【紅葉葉】〔名〕＜モミジ | (n.)varicolored leaves＞／の【の】〔格助〕＜の | (prep.)'s＞／ゆくへ【行方】〔名〕＜行く先 | (n.)the destination＞／さだむ【定む】〔他マ下二〕＜決める | (v.)decide＞(さだめ＝未然形)／ず【ず】〔助動特殊型〕打消＜～[し]ない | (adv.)not ～＞(ぬ＝連体形)／われ【我】〔代名〕＜私 | (pron.)I, myself＞／ぞ【ぞ】〔係助〕＜強調 | (adv.)EMPHASIS＞／かなし【哀し】〔形シク〕＜哀れだ | (adj.)pathetic＞ (かなしき＝連体形係り結び)

—秋—

[aki-kaze ni ae-zu chiri-nuru momiji-ba no yukue sadame-nu ware zo kanashiki]

自然界の落ち葉の頼りなげな情景描写から、詩人自身のやるせない吐息へと、継ぎ目なしに移行して行く・・・絵画的イメージを駆使した前哨戦の「序詞」が、「恋愛場面」以外に用いられた稀有な例。

Helpless image of falling leaves in Nature seamlessly gradating into a hopeless sigh of the poet ― a very rare example of 序詞(jo-kotoba＝pictorial overture) outside the field of "love".

・・・・・・・・・・・・・・・・・・・

《「序詞」は「絵」から「本音」の橋渡し》

この短歌、かなりヘンテコだと感じませんでしたか？五分の四まで読んだ時点では「これは秋の落ち葉を詠んだ自然描写の歌に違いない」と思えたのに、結句に至って出し抜けにこの作者、「風に吹かれる葉っぱ」を描いた先行パートに「自分自身の運命」を重ね合わせているのだから。そう、実は、この歌の前半の「叙景部」は、結びの**我ぞ悲しき**のための絵画的導入部、この作者の内面に渦巻く感情の象徴的描写として働いているのです。詩の大部分をこうした冗長な導入部に用いる手法 ― 「序詞(じょことば・・・じょし、とは読みません：それだと助詞っぽいので)」と呼ばれる技巧 ― は、窮屈な17文字の「俳句」では実現不可能、平安後期の短歌にも滅多に見られない芸当です。序詞を用いた短歌は奈良時代の『万葉集』にも既に見られ、『古今集』の中でも幾多の優れた歌人たちが洗練の度を加えた「序詞歌」作りに挑みました。しかしその後、序詞の技巧は次第に「懸詞(・・・要するに、ダジャレ)」頼みの浮ついた言葉遊びへの転落の道を辿り、本来持っていた「象徴的イメージ・パート」としての美を失ってしまいました。いずれにせよ序詞歌というものは、大部分の字数を「冗長なイメージ作り」に費やしてしまう構造的制約からして、何か意味のある内容を表現するのには不向きです・・・ので、用いられる先は「恋歌」とほぼ相場が決まっています ― だって、恋の歌のキモなんて、煎じ詰めれば「**君ぞ恋しき！**」の一言だけで事足りますからね。

《序詞(jo-kotoba) ― pictorial overture to semantic essence》

You might have found this TANKA rather strange: while you are reading four-fifths of it, you are sure it's a Natural scene about fallen leaves in Autumn, until you come to the last phrase and find the author overlapping his own fate with the preceding description of the wind-blown leaves. Yes, the former scenery part is a pictorial overture to the final phrase 我ぞ悲しき(ware zo kanashiki＝how sad I am), working as a symbolic representation of the author's inner feelings. Spending the greater part of the poem in such redundant introduction ― a technique called 序詞(jo-kotoba) ― is an impossibility with a cramp 17-syllabled 俳句(HAIKU); it's also quite a rarity in the later years of the Heian era. TANKA with 序詞(jo-kotoba) were already found in 万葉集(mannyou shuu) in the Nara(奈良) era, and many a great poet attempted at its refined production in 古今集(Kokin shuu). In later years, however, this technique degraded into frivolous word play hinging on 懸詞(kake-kotoba＝puns) and lost its original beauty as symbolic image part. Anyway, 序詞(jo-kotoba) TANKA, with its structural limitation of using up most of the letters/syllables in redundant image-creation, was not fit for expressing anything meaningful, almost exclusively used in songs of *love*, whose essence can be summed up in a single phrase **君ぞ恋しき**(kimi zo koishiki＝*loving you!*).

—冬:Winter—

●96● あきのうちはあはれしらせしかぜのおとの はげしさそふるふゆはきにけり
秋の内は哀れ知らせし風の音の烈しさ添ふる冬は来にけり

【冬】[転季]『7)千載集:393』藤原教長(ふじわらののりなが)

まだ秋だった頃は哀感漂う風情だった風の音が、今や烈風の凄まじさで耳を刺す、厳しい季節の冬がやって来たのだなぁ。

While in Autumn, it used to sound forlorn
Now the wind is wild, coldly declaring Winter.

あき【秋】[名]<秋|(n.)Autumn>/の【の】[格助]<の|(prep.)'s>/うち【内】[名]<期間|(n.)the period>/は【は】[係助]<〜に関しては|(adv.)as for 〜>/あはれ【あはれ】[名]<哀感|(n.)pathos>/しる【知る】[他ラ四]<知|(v.)know>(しら=未然形)/す【す】[助動サ下二型]使役<〜[さ]せる|(aux-v.)CAUSATIVE>(せ=連用形)/き【き】[助動特殊型]過去<〜[し]た|(aux-v.)PAST>(し=連体形)/かぜ【風】[名]<風|(n.)wind>/の【の】[格助]<の|(prep.)'s>/おと【音】[名]<音|(n.)the sound>/の【の】[格助]<主格|(prep.)SUBJECT>/はげしさ【烈しさ】[名]<烈しさ|(n.)violent feel>/そふ【添ふ】[他ハ下二]<添える|(v.)add>(そふる=連体形)/ふゆ【冬】[名]<冬|(n.)Winter>/は【は】[係助]<主格|(prep.)SUBJECT>/く【来】[自カ変]<来る|(v.)come>(き=連用形)/ぬ【ぬ】[助動ナ変型]完了<すでに〜[し]た|(aux-v.)PERFECT TENSE>(に=連用形)/けり【けり】[助動ラ変型]詠嘆<〜たのだなぁ|(interj.)REALIZATION>(けり=終止形)

[aki no uchi wa aware shira-se-shi kaze no oto no hageshi-sa souru fuyu wa ki-ni-keri]

「風」の中の季節の変化は、「夏から秋」には肌合いで感じるもの。「秋から冬」には音色の違いで聞き分けるもの・・・暖かい家の中から、カタコト鳴る障子越しに、寒さで自然と人を隔てる(そして人と人をも隔てる)外の世界の遠い物音として。

The seasonal change in the wind from Summer to Autumn is felt on the skin; from Autumn to Winter, heard in its tone... inside the warmth of the house through the rattling 障子(shouji=paper screen) in the world outside that alienates people from Nature and from each other with its coldness.

●97● このはちるやどはききわくことぞなき しぐれするよもしぐれせぬよも
木の葉散る宿は聞き分く事ぞ無き時雨する夜も時雨せぬ夜も

【冬】[謎掛]『4)後拾遺集:382』源頼実(みなもとのよりざね)

屋根に木の葉の散り懸かる宿の冬場の夜の音は、落ち葉と思えば時雨だったり、時雨と思えば落ち葉だったり、どっちが降るやら、よくわかりません。

An inn under falling leaves makes it hard to find
Whether it's scattered rain at night
Or leaves rustling on the roof.

このは【木の葉】[名]<木の葉|(n.)leaves of the trees>/ちる【散る】[自ラ四]<散る|(v.)fall>(ちる=連体形)/やど【宿】[名]<家屋|(n.)the house>/は【は】[係助]<〜に関しては|(adv.)as for 〜>/ききわく【聞き分く】[他カ四]<聞き分ける|(v.)discern the sound>(わく=連体形)/こと【事】[名]<〜という事|(n.)the act of 〜ing>/ぞ【ぞ】[係助]<強調|(adv.)EMPHASIS>/なし【なし】[形]<

―冬―

存在しない｜(v.)do not exist＞ (なき＝連体形係り結び)／しぐれ【時雨る】〔自ラ下二〕＜[秋・冬に]通り雨が降る｜(v.)it rains in passing [in Autumn and Winter]＞(しぐれ＝連用形、転じて名詞)／す【為】〔補動サ変〕＜する｜(v.)do＞(する＝連体形)／よ【夜】〔名〕＜夜｜(n.)the night＞／も【係助】＜～もまた｜(adv.)also＞／しぐる【時雨る】〔自ラ下二〕＜[秋・冬に]通り雨が降る｜(v.)it rains in passing [in Autumn and Winter]＞(しぐれ＝連用形、転じて名詞)／す【為】〔補動サ変〕＜する｜(v.)do＞(せ＝未然形)／ず【ず】〔助動特殊型〕打消＜～し]ない｜(adv.)not ～＞(ぬ＝連体形)／よ【夜】〔名〕＜夜｜(n.)the night＞／も【係助】＜～もまた｜(adv.)also＞

[ko-no-ha chiru yado wa kiki-waku koto zo naki shigure-suru yo mo shigure-se-nu yo mo]

屋根を叩く「**時雨**」の音が、落ち葉が屋根に舞い落ちたり風にカリコソ鳴る音と聞き分けがつかない点を突いた機転の歌。この種の「箱の中の感受性」は、晩秋から初冬にかけての平安調短歌の一特徴。

A witty TANKA about the sound of **時雨**(shigure＝scattered rain) on the roof indistinguishable from the sound of leaves falling down to the roof or rustling in the wind. This type of "sensitivity in the box" is the hallmark of Heianese TANKA from late Autumn to early Winter.

・・・・・・・・・・・・・・・・・・・・・・・・

《秋去ぎてひた屋籠もりの「時雨」かな》

日本の「冬」は詩歌に乏しい季節で、「秋」や「春」の半数にも満たぬ数の短歌しか詠まれていない。「夏」の短歌も少ないが、それは人々が外に出てあれこれやることが山ほどあるからこそ。「冬」は(昔の人は)家の中にひたすら籠もって「春」の到来と寒い牢獄からの解放を待つより他に、仕方がなかった。「**時雨**」が屋根を叩く音は、この侘びしい閉じ籠もりの季節の到来を告げる悲しい音だったのである。

《時雨(shigure＝scattered rain) ― harbinger of shut-in season after Fall》

Japanese Winter is a poor season for poetry, with much less than half the number of TANKA about Autumn and Spring. Summer is also poor in TANKA because people have lots of things to do outside; in Winter, ancient people had nothing to do but stay indoors waiting for Spring to save them from the cold prison. The sound of **時雨**(shigure) on the roof is a sad announcement of this bleak season of imprisonment.

●98● たつたがはにしきおりかくかむなづき しぐれのあめをたてぬきにして
竜田川錦織り懸く神無月時雨の雨を経緯にして

【冬】[機知]『1)古今集:314』詠み人知らず

紅葉で名高い竜田山、麓を流れる竜田川、水面に散り敷く落ち葉の色に、空から注ぐ白い雨、冬の自然が縦横に織り成す、目にも綾なる錦織。

Water colorfully tinged with leaves fallen from mountains

Along with strings of rain down from Wintry sky

The river Tatsuta is clad in brocade of graceful Nature.

たつたがは【竜田川】〔名〕＜[固有名詞]竜田川｜(n.)the river of Tatsuta＞／にしき【錦】〔名〕＜錦｜(n.)brocade＞／おる【織る】〔自ラ下二〕＜織る｜(v.)weave＞(おり＝連用形)／かく【懸く】〔他カ四〕＜掛け渡す｜(v.)span＞(かく＝連体形)／かむなづき【神無月】〔名〕＜陰暦十月(＝新暦十一月)｜the luner October(=the solar November)＞／しぐれ【時雨】〔名〕＜[晩秋から初冬の]通り雨｜(n.)scattered rain[from late Autumn to early Winter]＞／の【の】〔格助〕＜の｜(prep.)'s＞／あめ【雨】〔名〕＜雨｜(n.)rain＞／を【を】〔格助〕＜目的格｜(prep.)OBJECT＞／たてぬき【経緯】〔名〕＜縦横｜(n.)the vertical and horizontal lines＞／に【に】〔格助〕＜補語｜(prep.)COMPLEMENT＞／す【為】〔他サ変〕＜～とする｜(v.)make＞(し＝連用形)／て【て】〔接助〕＜状態｜(conj.)while＞

―冬―

[Tatsuta-gawa nishiki ori-kaku kamunazuki shigure no ame wo tate-nuki-ni-shi-te]

山の木々からどっと流れ寄せた落ち葉の波が、川の水面を色取り取りの絨毯で覆い尽くし、垂直に降り注ぐ雨の糸と絡んで、目を見張るような自然の綾錦を織り上げる・・・この短歌をはじめとする(多くは虚構の)歌たちのおかげで、竜田川は「秋から冬に流れる紅葉の綾錦」の「歌枕」となりました。

Floods of leaves fallen from the mountain trees covering the whole surface of the river as a varicolored carpet, with vertical string of rain weaving up wonderful brocade of Nature... songs like this ― most of them fictional ― established the image of 竜田川(Tatsuta-gawa＝the river Tatsuta) as 歌枕 (uta-makura＝place or name famed for something) for flowing brocade of 紅葉(momiji＝varicolored leaves) from Autumn to Winter.

―――――――――――――――――――――――――

●99●あさぼらけうぢのかはぎりたえだえに　あらはれわたるせぜのあじろぎ
　　　朝朗け宇治の川霧絶え絶えに顕はれ渡る瀬々の網代木

【冬】[叙景]『7)千載集:420』藤原定頼(ふじわらのさだより)

夜の闇の底から朝がほろほろと顔を出す頃、宇治川の水面を覆っていた霧の白いヴェールが、あちこちで少しずつすーっと上がって行き、浅瀬に組んだ漁獲用の網代の木の棒が、川一面に点々と顔を出す・・・どこにそんなに隠れていたか、と思えるほどに、次々と・・・宇治川の広さと、それを包んでいた夜の深さを感じさせながら・・・新しい朝の幕開けである。

As the white veil of morning over the Uji River
Lifts itself up here and there in the shallows,
Piles after piles appear to greet the new day.

あさぼらけ【朝朗け】[名]＜早朝、あたりが明るくなり始める時間帯｜(n.)the earliest hour of the morning＞／うぢ【宇治】[名]＜[固有名詞]宇治｜(n.)Uji＞／の【の】[格助]＜の｜(prep.)'s＞／かはぎり【川霧】[名]＜川を覆う霧｜(n.)mist on the river＞／たえだえなり【絶え絶えなり】[形動ナリ]＜所々で途切れて｜(adv.)breaking here and there＞(たえだえに＝連用形)／あらはる【現はる】[自下二]＜出現する｜(v.)make one's appearance＞(あらはれ＝連用形)／わたる【渡る】[自ラ四]＜あたり一面～になる｜(adv.)all over＞(わたる＝連体形)／せぜ【瀬瀬】[名]＜あちらこちらの浅瀬｜(n.)shallows here and there＞／の【の】[格助]＜の｜(prep.)'s＞／あじろぎ【網代木】[名]＜漁獲用の仕掛けを結び付けて水中に立てた木｜(n.)poles of wood or bamboo with fish-catching device attached＞

[asaborake Uji no kawa-giri taedaeni araware-wataru seze no ajiro-gi]

「網代」は小魚を捕らえるための仕掛けで、川の片側に突き立てた木や竹の棒の間に網を張り、もう片側には魚獲りの罠を仕掛けておくもの。冬の宇治川にはこの種の仕掛けがいっぱい・・・その姿は、最初は夜の暗闇に隠れ、次に夜明けの白いヴェールに覆い隠され、最後に霧が上がるにつれて、次々そこかしこに網代が出現して、この詩人と新たな冬の朝にごあいさつする・・・「時の推移」と「場面転換」という『新古今集』の大好物のこの短歌は、『拾遺集』の時代に作られ、『千載集』に採録されたもの。

網代(ajiro) is a device to catch small fish, spreading a net between a pair of vertical wood or bamboo stuck in the river on one side, fish-catching traps on the other. 宇治川(Uji-gawa＝the Uji river) in Winter is full of such scheme, hidden first by the darkness of the night, then concealed in a white veil of dawn, and finally appearing as the mist rises, one after another, here and there, to greet this poet and the new Winter morning: a poem of time-shift and scene-change so much favored by 新古今集 (Shin-Kokin shuu) made around the year of 拾遺集(Shuui shuu) adopted by 千載集(Senzai shuu).

―冬―

●100● おきあかすしもとともにやけさはみな ふゆのよふかきつみもけぬらむ

おき明かす霜と共にや今朝は皆冬の夜深き罪も消ぬらむ

【冬】[季題]『3)拾遺集:257』大中臣能宣(おおなかとみのよしのぶ)

夜通し起きて御仏の名を唱え、今年一年の間に積み重なった自らの罪業を思い返し、御仏の赦免を祈る仏名会の夜・・・この冬の夜が明けたら、霜が消えると共に、悔い改めた我々の深い罪もまた消えてくれることだろう・・・か？

All through the dark night into the white dawn
Chanting names of Buddha praying for absolution
As this Wintry frost melts in the morn
So will our sins in the light of heavenly boon.

(A)おく【置く】[自カ四]＜霜が降りる｜(v.)get frosty＞(おき＝連用形)／**(B)おく【起く】[自カ上二]**＜寝ずに起きている｜(v.)keep awake＞(おき＝連用形)／あかす【明かす】[他サ四]＜夜明けまで過ごす｜(v.)stay up all night＞(あかす＝連体形)／しも【霜】[名]＜霜｜(n.)frost＞／と[と][格助]＜列挙｜(conj.)and＞／ともに【共に】[副]＜一緒に｜(prep.)along with＞／や[や][係助]＜疑問｜(adv.)INTERROGATIVE＞／けさ【今朝】[名]＜今朝｜(n.)this morning＞／は[は][係助]＜～に関しては｜(adv.)as for～＞／みな[皆][副]＜みんな｜(adv.)all＞／ふゆ【冬】[名]＜冬｜(n.)Winter＞／の【の】[格助]＜の｜(prep.)'s＞／よ【夜】[名]＜夜｜(n.)the night＞／**ふかし【深し】[形]**＜夜深い／罪が深い｜(adj.)late at night／deep in sin＞(ふかき＝連体形)／つみ【罪】[名]＜罪業｜(n.)sins＞／も[も][係助]＜意味なし｜(adv.)NO MEANING＞／きゆ[消ゆ][自ヤ下二]＜消える｜(v.)disappear＞(け(きえ)＝未然形)／ぬ[ぬ][助動ナ変型]確述＜きっと～する｜(adv.)EMPHASIS＞(ぬ＝終止形)／らむ[らむ][助動ラ四型]現在推量＜～だろう｜(aux-v.)SUPPOSITION＞(らむ＝連体形係り結び)

[oki-akasu shimo to tomo-ni ya kesa wa mina fuyu no yo fukaki tsumi mo kenu-ramu]

陰暦最後の月(陽暦では一月)の半ばは「仏名会」の季節、貴人たちは一堂に会して一晩中仏教の経典を唱和し、一年かけて積もった自らの罪業の消滅を祈りました。この短歌はそうした場面がとある貴族の邸宅の屏風に描かれているのを捉えて詠まれたものです。

The middle of the last lunar month (solar January) was an occasion for 仏名会(butsu-myou-e), when noble folks gathered to chant the Buddhist sutra all through the night, praying for the disappearance of their sin accumulated during the year. This TANKA rhymes out such an occasion drawn on a screen at some noble's residence.

・・・・・・・・・・・・・・・・・・・・

《「仏名」に罪消ち急ぐ師走かな》

大方の日本人の「罪」の意識は(まともな宗教観を持った世界中の人々と比べて) 奇妙なもので、自らが犯した罪を償うには、「罪滅ぼしに効き目がある」と一般に信じられている何らかの形式的行事に参加しさえすればそれでOK、と信じている・・・真面目な宗教を真面目に信仰している人々の目には「けしからん！」と映るかもしれないが、それが日本人全般の「信心」の姿・・・なればこそ日本では、汚職政治屋どもは辞職と再選を繰り返しつつしぶとく生き残る(政治関係者の間ではこれを「みそぎ＝禊ぎ＝身削ぎ＝ケガレを落としてキレイになって出直す」と呼ぶ；仮に「政治家としてあるまじき不祥事」を引き起こしてクビになろうとも、次の選挙で一定以上の得票を ― どんなケガレた手を用いてでも ― 掻き集めて「有権者の信任」を得た形を整えさえすれば、全ての罪は帳消しになり、幾度でもまた罪を犯す資格を回復できる、という論理である)し、旧暦の十二月が「師走」と呼ばれる理由もそこにある ― この月の半ばには、平安時代の貴族たちが「仏名会＝仏教の経典を唱える会合」を催し、一年間積もった自らの罪を綺麗に帳消しにした上で、汚れなき身で新年を迎えようとしたので、「仏師が町中を走り回る月＝師走」というわけである。

—冬—

《仏名(butsu-myou)　—　bonzes ran around for the atonement of the nobles' sin》
Most Japanese have a queer sense of sin or guilt – compared with sensibly religious people of the world – that they can be atoned for what they have done by engaging in some formal occasion publicly held to be a valid sin-purifier... however scandalous in the eyes of true believers in any serious religion. That's the reason for the resiliency of corrupted politicians in Japan vacated and reelected countless times (political mafias call this revival process みそぎ＝禊ぎ＝身削ぎ＝depriving themselves of filth and starting over pure and clean; even after having been expelled from their former positions for having committed something totally unbecoming to a politician, if they gain sufficient votes in the next election — by however filthy measures — to formally declare themselves backed up by the trust of their voters, all their past guilts and sins will be canceled to entitle them to commit any guilt again!), and also for the name of 師走(shiwasu＝Buddhist bonzes running around) for the lunar December, in the middle of which Heianese nobles held 仏名会(butsu-myou-e＝Buddhist sutra chanting meeting) to purify them of their year-thick sin to greet a guilt-free new year.

●101●なにごとをまつとはなしにあけくれて　ことしもけふになりにけるかな
何事を待つとは無しに明け暮れて今年も今日に成りにけるかな
【冬】[季題]『5)金葉集:(異本)』源国信(みなもとのくにざね)
特に何かを待つでもなく、ただ何となく日々を過ごしているうちに、気付けば今年も今日で終わり･･･
平穏無事な一年に感謝すべきか、平凡無地のまま流れ去る我が人生に溜息(ためいき)つくべきか･･･
いやはや、月日の巡(めぐ)りは早いもの。

Without waiting for anything in particular,
This year has come to this day already.

なにごと【何事】〔代名〕＜特に何か｜(n.)something in particular＞／を【を】〔格助〕＜目的格｜(prep.)OBJECT＞／まつ【待つ】〔他夕四〕＜待つ｜(v.)wait＞(まつ＝連体形)／と【と】〔格助〕＜内容提示｜(conj.)that ～＞／は【は】〔係助〕＜意味なし｜(adv.)NO MEANING＞／なし【なし】〔形ク〕＜～というわけではない｜(v.)not that ～＞(なし＝終止形)／に【に】〔格助〕＜様態｜(prep.)like＞／あけくる【明け暮る】〔自ラ下二〕＜日々が過ぎる｜(v.)days go by＞(あけくれ＝連用形)／て【て】〔接助〕＜順接｜(conj.)and＞／ことし【今年】〔名〕＜今年｜(n.)this year＞／も【も】〔係助〕＜～もまた｜(adv.)also＞／けふ【今日】〔名〕＜今日｜(n.)today＞／に【に】〔格助〕＜補語｜(prep.)COMPLEMENT＞／なる【成る】〔自ラ四〕＜～になる｜(v.)become＞(なり＝連用形)／ぬ【ぬ】〔助動ナ変型〕完了＜すでに～[し]た｜(aux-v.)PERFECT TENSE＞(に＝連用形)／けり【けり】〔助動ラ変型〕詠嘆＜～だったのだなぁ｜(interj.)REALIZATION＞(ける＝連体形)／かな【かな】〔終助〕＜詠嘆｜(interj.)EXCLAMATION＞

[nani-goto wo matsu to-wa nashi-ni ake-kure-te kotoshi mo kyou ni nari-ni-keru kana]

自分の人生に(必ずしも満足ではないにせよ)ひどい不満を抱(いだ)いてはいない人だからこそつぶやける年の瀬の歌･･･ちなみに、この歌の作者は堀河(ほりかわ)天皇の親戚、43歳で急死するまで順調な出世街道(しゅっせかいどう)を駆(か)け抜けた人です･･･と聞いたからって、この歌嫌いにならないでね･･･この歌にイラっと来ちゃった人は、来年の終わりにはニコっと笑って「うんうん、まったくだね」とこの歌に同感できちゃうように期待しましょう。
A year-end TANKA that can only come out of the mouths of those not massively unhappy, if not quite satisfied with their lives. Incidentally, the author of this TANKA led his life on the freeway of smooth promotion as a relative of Emperor 堀河(Horikawa) until his sudden death at the age of 43... don't let that knowledge make you hate this song. Should you find it irritating, let's hope you can smile at it in agreement at the end of next year.

—冬—

●102●けふごとにけふやかぎりとをしめども　またもことしにあひにけるかな
今日毎に今日や限りと惜しめども又も今年に会ひにけるかな

【冬】[季題]『8)新古今集:706』藤原俊成(ふじわらのしゅんぜい(としなり))

毎年この日が来るたびに、「あぁ、これが人生最後、来年の今日にはもう、会えまいなぁ」と思って名残りを惜しんできたけれど、今年もまた巡り会うことになったのだなぁ、一年最後の、大晦日。

Every year I've thought "This is it."
Again I met this day at the very end of this year.

けふ【今日】[名]＜今日｜(n.)today＞／ごと【毎】[接尾]＜それぞれに｜(adv.)each＞／に【に】[格助]＜時｜(prep.)TIME＞／けふ【今日】[名]＜今日｜(n.)today＞／や【や】[係助]＜疑問｜(adv.)INTERROGATIVE＞／かぎり【限り】[名]＜おしまい｜(n.)the end＞／と【と】[格助]＜内容提示｜(conj.)that ～＞／をしむ【惜しむ】[他マ四]＜惜しく思う｜(v.)miss＞(をしめ＝已然形)／ども【ども】[接助]＜～ではあるが｜(conj.)although＞／また【又】[副]＜再び｜(adv.)once again＞／も【も】[係助]＜～もまた｜(adv.)also＞／ことし【今年】[名]＜今年｜(n.)this year＞／に【に】[格助]＜対象｜(prep.)OBJECT＞／あふ【会ふ】[自ハ四]＜出会う｜(v.)meet＞(あひ＝運用形)／ぬ【ぬ】[助動ナ変型]完了＜すでに～[し]た｜(aux-v.)PERFECT TENSE＞(に＝連用形)／けり【けり】[助動ラ変型]詠嘆＜～だったのだなぁ｜(interj.)REALIZATION＞(ける＝連体形)／かな【かな】[終助]＜詠嘆｜(interj.)EXCLAMATION＞

[kyou-goto-ni kyou ya kagiri to oshime-domo mata-mo kotoshi ni ai-ni-keru kana]

人は年齢を重ねると、たとえどんなにありふれた日常的な出来事でも「今回限り」の感を催すもの — この感覚が、人生のもっと早い時期から持っていたならもっと良いもの — 「是や限り(‥‥これで最後？)」と思ったなら、人生で出会う物事の全てが、かけがえのない貴重なものに感じるはずだから‥‥この歌は、伝説の「千五百番歌合」の一首で、この史上最大の歌合の「判者＝勝敗判定人」の一人でもあった藤原俊成の作‥‥この行事の最中に、彼の「九〇歳(今から800年も昔の90歳です！)」の誕生祝いも催されています。

As one advances in years, every occasion, however routine, feels like "one-off"... it would be better to have this consciousness earlier in life, for it would make everything in life look all the more precious for thinking "是や限り(kore ya kagiri＝this may be the last time I meet it)". One of the songs of the legendary 千五百番歌合(sen-gohyaku-ban uta-awase＝1,500 TANKA duels) by 藤原俊成(Fujiwara-no-Shunzei, who was one of the official judges of this largest TANKA duels, during which occasion a celebration was held for his **90th** birthday... 800 years ago!

‥‥‥‥‥‥‥‥‥‥‥‥‥‥‥‥‥‥‥‥‥
《後の代に「歌の徳」説く嘘説話》

この短歌の詠み手の藤原俊成は、第七勅撰和歌集『千載集』の単独編者でもあったが、日本文学に多大な貢献をしたにもかかわらずその報いの少なること呆れ返るばかり、という点に於いて、平安期の偉大な歌詠みたちの御多分に漏れぬ人であった。最後の『新古今集』の編者連には当時の政界の大物数名が名を連ねていたから例外として、それ以外の八代集に関しては、その編者に全く何の世俗的栄達をももたらしはしなかったのである。文芸の世界で名を上げて自分の惨めな社会的境遇を向上させようと必死に足搔いた歌人達は大勢いたけれど、「歌は身を助ける」式の成功談は後の鎌倉時代の民間伝説の類であって、平安の世の貴人世界の現実からは遠いものだったのである。

《歌徳説話(katoku setsuwa＝promotion by virtue of poetic talents) — fabricated *bullshit* of post-Heianese years》

藤原俊成(Fujiwara-no-Shunzei), the author of this TANKA and the sole editor of the 7th Imperial TANKA anthology 千載集(Senzai shuu), is no exception to the really great TANKA masters of the

Heian era in that he was scandalously unrewarded for his great contribution to Japanese literature. Except for the last 新古今集(Shin-Kokin shuu) which included several political big shots as its editors, the rest of 八代集(Hachidai shuu＝8 great Imperial TANKA anthologies) contributed absolutely nothing to the worldly promotion of their editors. Although so many desperate poets attempted to raise their miserable social positions by virtue of literary fame, such a success story was more a stuff of later-year folklore in the Kamakura(鎌倉) era than actual reality of the Heianese nobles.

●103●ひとりみるいけのこほりにすむつきの やがてそでにもうつりぬるかな
一人見る池の氷にすむ月のやがて袖にもうつりぬるかな

【冬】[溜息]『8)新古今集:640』藤原俊成(ふじわらのしゅんぜい(としなり))

一人きり、庭の池に張った氷の鏡に映る月を見る･･･寂しさに顔を覆い隠せば、
袖の上に凍った涙の鏡にまた映る空の月･･･お前だけだよ、私を慰めてくれるのは。

Wintry moon in the icy mirror of the pond
Shines on me alone in this solitary mansion.
Tears wiped off forming a weepy mirror on the sleeve
Reflects again the moon as my sole constant companion.

ひとり【一人】[名]＜一人きり｜(adv.)all alone＞／みる【見る】[他マ上一]＜見る｜(v.)view＞(みる＝連体形)／いけ【池】[名]＜池｜(n.)a pond＞／の【の】[格助]＜の｜(prep.)'s＞／こほり【氷】[名]＜氷｜(n.)ice＞／に【に】[格助]＜場所｜(prep.)PLACE＞／***(A)すむ【澄む】[自マ四]***＜きれいに澄み渡る｜(v.)get serenely clean＞(すむ＝連体形)／***(B)すむ【住む】[自マ四]***＜住む｜(v.)live in＞(すむ＝連体形)／つき【月】[名]＜月｜(n.)the moon＞／の【の】[格助]＜主格｜(prep.)SUBJECT＞／やがて【やがて】[副]＜そのまま｜(adv.)just the way it is＞／そで【袖】[名]＜袖｜(n.)the sleeve＞／に【に】[格助]＜場所｜(prep.)PLACE＞／も【も】[係助]＜～もまた｜(adv.)also＞／うつる【映る】[自四]＜映る｜(v.)be reflected＞(うつり＝連用形)／ぬ【ぬ】[助動ナ変型]完了＜すでに～[し]た｜(aux-v.)PERFECT TENSE＞(ぬる＝連体形)／かな【かな】[終助]＜詠嘆｜(interj.)EXCLAMATION＞

[hitori miru ike no koori ni sumu tsuki no yagate sode ni-mo utsuri-nuru kana]

波打たぬ穏やかな水の表面に映る月の光･･･これは世界中どこの詩の世界にも見られる情景かもしれません･･･が、平安時代の貴人たちは、「月」を自然の鏡としての「氷」の上に見たがったのでした･･･だって、波打たぬ水よりよほど安定した鏡でしょう？「あり得ない！どれほど表面ツルツルな氷なんだよ？」って言うそこのあなた、思い出してください ― これは平安調詩歌の世界、「あ、それ、いいね！」と人々が思えば何でもアリの想像世界の話なんですから･･･それどころか、この歌人（哀しく孤独な老人の藤原俊成)が「月」を見ているのは、彼の着物の「袖」に出来たもう一つの鏡の中 ― 凍り付いた涙の上に反射する優美な月の光を彼は見ているのです！

The moonlight reflected on the calm surface of water may be a universal scene of the world's poetry. Heianese nobles liked to see the moon on 氷(koori＝the ice) as a Natural mirror... it's far more stable than calm water, don't you think? *"Impossible! How smooth could it be?"* you might say, but remember ― it's a world of Heianese poetry where anything goes wherever they thought it good to go. In fact, this poet ― the sad and lonely old 藤原俊成(Fujiwara-no-Shunzei) ― is looking at the moon in another mirror on his 袖(sode＝sleeve), *tears frozen solid* to reflect the gracious beam!

—冬—

●104●ふゆながらそらよりはなのちりくるは　くものあなたははるにやあるらむ

冬ながら空より花の散り来るは雲の彼方は春にやあるらむ

【冬】［機知］『1)古今集:330』清原深養父(きよはらのふかやぶ)

寒さの極みの空の上から、舞い散る白い冬の花・・・
雪に染まった地上を余所に、雲の彼方は春なのだろうか。

Even in Winter, flowers fall down from the sky.
Is it already Spring up above in the white heavens?

ふゆ【冬】〔名〕＜冬｜(n.)Winter＞／ながら【ながら】〔接助〕＜～ではあるが｜(conj.)although＞／そら【空】〔名〕＜空｜(n.)the sky＞／より【より】〔格助〕＜～から｜(prep.)from＞／はな【花】〔名〕＜花｜(n.)flowers＞／の【の】〔格助〕＜主格｜(prep.)SUBJECT＞／ちりくる【散り来】〔自力変〕＜舞い散り落ちる｜(v.)come falling＞(ちりくる＝連体形)／は【は】〔係助〕＜ということは｜(conj.)judging from it＞／くも【雲】〔名〕＜雲｜(n.)clouds＞／の【の】〔格助〕＜の｜(prep.)'s＞／あなた【彼方】〔名〕＜向こう側｜(prep.)beyond＞／は【は】〔係助〕＜～に関しては｜(adv.)as for ～＞／はる【春】〔名〕＜春｜(n.)Spring＞／なり【なり】〔助動ナリ型〕断定＜～である｜(aux-v.)be＞(に＝連用形)／や【や】〔係助〕＜疑問｜(adv.)INTERROGATIVE＞／あり【あり】〔補動ラ変〕＜～である｜(aux-v.)be＞(ある＝連体形)／らむ【らむ】〔助動ラ四型〕現在推量＜～だろう｜(aux-v.)SUPPOSITION＞(らむ＝連体形係り結び)

[fuyu nagara sora yori hana no chiri-kuru wa kumo no anata wa haru ni-ya-aru-ramu]

「雪」を「空から舞い降りる花」に見立てただけでは陳腐すぎて引き合いに出すにも値しないけど、「空の上は春なのかもね」というのは、冬の寒さに震える人々にとっては心温まる空想ですね。こうしたウィット(機知)は、この歌人清原深養父と、その孫の清原元輔と、更には曾孫の清少納言のお家芸・・・もっとも、彼女の機知が花開いたのは詩歌というより『枕草子』に見る通り)散文世界の話でしたが。

Snow as seen as flowers falling down from the sky is too hackneyed to recite: to imagine it may be Spring up above is a heart-warming fantasy for people shuddering with Wintry cold. A witticism like this was the stock of trade of this poet 清原深養父(Kiyohara-no-Fukayabu), his grandson 清原元輔(Kiyohara-no-Motosuke), and his great-granddaughter 清少納言(Sei shou-nagon), although her wit flourished not in verse but in prose as you can see in 枕草子(Makura no soushi).

●105●あさぼらけありあけのつきとみるまでに　よしののさとにふれるしらゆき

朝ぼらけ有明の月と見る迄に吉野の里に降れる白雪

【冬】［叙景］『1)古今集:332』坂上是則(さかのうえのこれのり)

朝がほろほろと明けて行く中、夜の名残りの有明の月がまだ照り映えているのか、と錯覚するほどに、地にも空にも白い光を投げていたのは、名高き吉野の白雪だったのだなあ。

Faintly white in hazy morning air...
Is it remaining moon shining on the village of Yoshino?
... No... oh yeah, I know – it's snow that's falling down!

あさぼらけ【朝朗け】〔名〕＜早朝、あたりが明るくなり始める時間帯｜(n.)the earliest hour of the morning＞／ありあけ【有明】〔名〕＜夜が明けて後も空に残る月｜(n.)the remaining moon from the previous night＞／の【の】〔格助〕＜の｜(prep.)'s＞／つき【月】〔名〕＜月｜(n.)the moon＞／と【と】〔格助〕＜内容提示｜(conj.)that ～＞／みる【見る】〔他マ上一〕＜見る｜(v.)view＞(みる＝連体形)／まで【迄】〔副助〕＜～な程に｜(adv.)to ～ extent＞／に【に】〔格助〕＜様態｜(prep.)like＞／よしの【吉野】〔名〕＜[固有

名詞]吉野｜(n.)Yoshino＞／の【の】〔格助〕＜の｜(prep.)'s＞／さと【里】〔名〕＜田舎の村｜(n.)a village＞／に【に】〔格助〕＜場所｜(prep.)PLACE＞／ふる【降る】〔自ラ四〕＜降る｜(v.)fall＞（ふれ＝已然形）／り【り】〔助動ラ変型〕存続＜～[し]ている｜(aux-v.)PERFECT TENSE＞（る＝連体形）／しらゆき【白雪】〔名〕＜白い雪｜(n.)white snow＞

[asaborake ariake-no-tsuki to miru made-ni Yoshino-no-sato ni fure-ru shira-yuki]

雪の白い色が明け方の月のまばゆい光と見分けが付かない･･･もしかしたらこれは大袈裟な趣向に過ぎないかもしれない･･･ひょっとしたらそれは名高き「雪と桜の歌枕」吉野の圧倒的な現実描写かもしれない･･･世の中には、実際自分の目で見ないことには到底信じられない物事もあるから、真相を知りたくば、雪と桜が奇跡のコラボレーションで見る者の目を幻惑する春の初めの吉野山を訪れて、自分の目でご確認あれ。

The whiteness of snow being confused with radiant moonlight towards dawn... maybe it's just a stylish exaggeration... possibly it's the overwhelming reality of all-consuming snow in 吉野(Yoshino), the famous 歌枕(uta-makura) of 雪(yuki＝snow) and 桜(sakura＝cherry blossom). There are some things in this world that just have to be seen to be believed: if you want to find out, come and visit 吉野(Yoshino) in early Spring when snow and cherry flowers magically feast your eyes side by side.

●106●まつひとのいまもきたらばいかがせむ ふままくをしきにはのゆきかな
待つ人の今も来たらば如何せむ踏ままく惜しき庭の雪かな

【冬】[願望]『5)金葉集:284』和泉式部(いずみしきぶ)

庭一面に積もった雪は、下り立って足跡を付けるのももったいない･･･
美しい銀世界を綺麗なままにしておきたいから？･･･ううん、そうじゃなくって、大事なあの人が訪ねて来た時に、他の誰かの足跡なんて、愛する女の庭に残っているのを見たがるはずがないでしょ？

My garden is covered with snow... tread on, *no*, I never would:
My darling may see it and wonder "*Who touched on my love?*"

まつ【待つ】〔他タ四〕＜待つ｜(v.)wait＞（まつ＝連体形）／ひと【人】〔名〕＜あの人｜(n.)that [darling] one＞／の【の】〔格助〕＜主格｜(prep.)SUBJECT＞／いま【今】〔副〕＜今｜(adv.)now＞／も【も】〔係助〕＜意味なし｜(adv.)NO MEANING＞／きたる【来到る】〔自ラ四〕＜やって来る｜(v.)come over＞（きたら＝未然形）／ば【ば】〔接助〕＜仮定｜(conj.)if＞／いかが【如何】〔副〕＜どのように｜(adv.)how＞／す【為】〔自サ変〕＜～する｜(v.)do＞（せ＝未然形）／む【む】〔助動マ四型〕意志＜～するつもりだ｜(aux-v.)be going to ～＞（む＝連体形係り結び）／ふむ【踏む】〔他マ四〕＜踏む｜(v.)tread＞（ふま＝未然形）／む【む】〔助動マ四型〕婉曲＜意味なし｜(adv.)NO MEANING＞（ま＝未然形）／く【く】〔接尾〕＜名詞化成分｜(suffix)[to make n. out of v.]＞／をし【惜し】〔形シク〕＜～したくない｜(v.)hate to ～＞（をしき＝連体形）／には【庭】〔名〕＜庭｜(n.)the garden＞／の【の】〔格助〕＜の｜(prep.)'s＞／ゆき【雪】〔名〕＜雪｜(n.)snow＞／かな【かな】〔終助〕＜詠嘆｜(interj.)EXCLAMATION＞

[matsu hito no ima mo kitara-ba ikaga semu fuma-ma-ku oshiki niwa no yuki kana]

雪が降れば、チビっ子や犬たちはそこいらじゅう駆け回って白いカンバスに自らの歓喜の跡を描くもの･･･
恋人の来訪を待つ大人の女は、庭の処女雪の純白性をけなげに守って、大事なあの人一人だけに触れて愛してもらいたがるもの･･･とっても女っぽいこの短歌の作者は、伝説の愛の歌人和泉式部。

When it snows, small kids and dogs run around to make their joy printed on the white canvas... an adult woman waiting for her lover to come will try faithfully to keep the virgin snow intact in her garden for him alone to touch and cherish. Quite a womanly TANKA by the legendary love poet 和泉式部 (Izumi shikibu).

―冬― ―恋愛―

● 107 ● さびしさにけぶりをだにもたたじとて しばをりくぶるふゆのやまざと
　　　　寂しさに煙をだにも絶たじとて柴折り焼ぶる冬の山里

【冬】[溜息]『4)後拾遺集:390』和泉式部(いずみしきぶ)

ここに居るのは自分だけ、周囲はひたすら雪だらけ…白い孤独を打ち消すために、
黒い煙は絶やさぬように、やたらと燃やす薪(まき)の火は、寂しい心の裏返し…傍目(はため)に沁みる冬の山里。

Buried in snow with nothing but loneliness
Smokes keep rising from chimneys of mountain huts
As if burning firewood is the only proof of their existence.

さびしさ【寂しさ】[名]＜さびしさ｜(n.)loneliness＞/に【に】[格助]＜原因｜(prep.)REASON＞/けぶり【煙】[名]＜煙｜(n.)smoke＞/を【を】[格助]＜目的格｜(prep.)OBJECT＞/だに【だに】[副助]＜せめて～だけでも｜(adv.)at least＞/も【も】[係助]＜意味なし｜(adv.)NO MEANING＞/たつ【絶つ】[他タ四]＜途切れさせる｜(v.)discontinue＞(たた＝未然形)/じ【じ】[助動特殊型]打消意志＜～ないつもりだ｜(aux-v.)be not going to ～＞(じ＝終止形)/とて【とて】[格助]＜～と思って｜(adv.)with ～ in mind＞/しば【柴】[名]＜たきぎ｜(n.)firewood＞/をる【折る】[他ラ四]＜折る｜(v.)snap＞(をり＝連用形)/くぶ【焼ぶ】[他バ下二]＜燃やす｜(v.)burn＞(くぶる＝連体形)/ふゆ【冬】[名]＜冬｜(n.)Winter＞/の【の】[格助]＜の｜(prep.)'s＞/やまざと【山里】[名]＜山里｜(n.)the countryside＞

[sabishi-sa ni keburi wo dani-mo tata-ji tote shiba ori-kuburu fuyu no yama-zato]

辺(あた)り一面、雪・雪・雪の情景の中にも、和泉式部は微かな煙の跡を見逃しません ― それは、人並み外れた人への共感力を持つ人だけに向けられた、寂しい山里の住人からの心の遭難信号だから。
Where nothing but snow is to be seen around, 和泉式部(Izumi shikibu) does not miss the faint smoke as an emotional *SOS* from lonely inhabitants solely appealing to the exceptionally empathic.

―恋愛：Love―

● 108 ● こひしともいはばこころのゆくべきに くるしやひとめつつむおもひは
　　　　恋しとも言はば心の行くべきに苦しや人目包む思ひは

【恋愛】[溜息]『8)新古今集:1090』近衛院(このえいん)

一言「好きです」と言えばもうそれだけで心もす～っと晴れるだろうに、人目を気にしてそうもできぬ身は、苦しいなぁ。

How relieved would I be to say "I love you!"
How painful it is to keep it all to myself!

こひし【恋し】[形シク]＜恋しい｜(v.)feel attached to＞(こひし＝終止形)/と【と】[格助]＜内容提示｜(conj.)that ～＞/も【も】[係助]＜意味なし｜(adv.)NO MEANING＞/いふ【言ふ】[他ハ四]＜告白する｜(v.)confess＞(いは＝未然形)/ば【ば】[接助]＜仮定｜(conj.)if＞/こころ【心】[名]＜心｜(n.)heart＞/の【の】[格助]＜主格｜(prep.)SUBJECT＞/ゆく【行く】[自カ四]＜納得が行く｜(v.)be satisfied＞(ゆく＝終止形)/べし【べし】[助動ク型]推量＜～にちがいない｜(aux-v.)CONVICTION＞(べき＝連体形)/に【に】[接助]＜逆接｜(conj.)although＞/くるし【苦し】[形シク]＜苦しい｜(v.)feel painful＞(くるし＝終止形)/や【や】[終助]＜詠嘆｜(interj.)EXCLAMATION＞/ひとめ【人目】[名]＜他人の目｜(n.)the eyes of others＞/つつむ【包む】[他マ四]＜気遣う｜(v.)care about＞(つつむ＝連体形)/おもひ【想ひ】[名]＜恋心｜(n.)loving feeling＞/は【は】[係助]＜～に関しては｜(adv.)as for ～＞

[koishi to-mo iwa-ba kokoro no yuku-beki-ni kurushi-ya hitome tsutsumu omoi wa]

この詩人、臆病すぎて告白できないのでしょうか？そうかもしれません、なにせまだ十代の若者ですから。あるいは社会的な立場上、軽々しい振る舞いを慎まざるを得ないのでしょうか？それはもうそうでしょう、なにせ彼はわずか三歳の時からずっと「日本の天皇」を務めている人ですから・・・そう、これは「忍ぶ恋」の題で詠まれた近衛天皇の歌・・・この若き帝は十七歳でこの世を去り、その突然の死が引き金となって「保元の乱（1156年）」が勃発、貴族の時代の崩壊が始まったのでした。

Is the poet too timid to confess? Possibly, because he is still in his teens. Or does his social position demand prudence? Definitely, because he has been the Emperor of Japan since he was just 3 years old. This is a poem by Emperor 近衛(Konoe) on the theme of "secretly cherished love"... this young Emperor died at the age of 17, whose sudden demise triggered the civil war (保元の乱：Hougen no ran, A.D. 1156) to initiate the collapse of the age of the nobles.

●109●たまのをよたえなばたえねながらへば しのぶることのよわりもぞする
玉の緒よ絶えなば絶えね永らへば忍ぶることの弱りもぞする

【恋愛】[溜息]『8)新古今集:1034』式子内親王(しきしないしんのう)

人の生命力をつなぎ止めるという命の糸よ、切れるならいっそ切れてしまっておくれ。切れもせずにこのまま生き続けていれば、今のところ隠しおおせている私の恋心も、隠す力が弱ってしまい、人に知られたその先に、どんな困った人生が待っていることか、わかったものではないのだから。

Frail string of life that keeps me alive,

Snap if you will, for, live long if I should,

My love might come out... hold out how long could I?

たまのを【玉の緒】[名]＜人の命をつなぎ止める魂の糸＞(n.)the string of one's life＞／よ【よ】[間投助]＜呼び掛け｜(interj.)APOSTROPHE＞／たゆ【絶ゆ】[自ヤ下二]＜断ち切れる｜(v.)snap＞(たえ＝連用形)／ぬ【ぬ】[助動ナ変型]確述＜きっと～する｜(adv.)EMPHASIS＞(な＝未然形)／ば【ば】[接助]＜仮定｜(conj.)if＞／たゆ【絶ゆ】[自ヤ下二]＜断ち切れる｜(v.)snap＞(たえ＝連用形)／ぬ【ぬ】[助動ナ変型]確述＜きっと～する｜(adv.)EMPHASIS＞(ね＝命令形)／ながらふ【長らふ】[自ハ下二]＜長生きする｜(v.)live long＞(ながらへ＝已然形)／ば【ば】[接助]＜仮定｜(conj.)if＞／しのぶ【忍ぶ】[他バ上二]＜耐え忍ぶ｜(v.)endure＞(しのぶる＝連体形)／こと【事】[名]＜～という事｜(n.)the act of ～ing＞／の【の】[格助]＜主格｜(prep.)SUBJECT＞／よわる【弱る】[自ラ四]＜弱る｜(v.)get weaker＞(よわり＝連用形)／も【も】[係助]＜意味なし｜(adv.)NO MEANING＞／ぞ【ぞ】[係助]＜強調｜(adv.)EMPHASIS＞／す【為】[自サ変]＜～する｜(v.)do＞(する＝連体形係り結び)

[tama-no-wo yo tae-na-ba tae-ne nagarae-ba shinoburu koto no yowari-mozo-suru]

これまた皇室関係者が詠んだ「忍ぶ恋」の題詠歌。作者の式子内親王はかつて賀茂神社にお仕えする(処女の)皇女の「斎院」として「男性との恋愛禁止」の立場に身を置いたことのある女性。彼女の家に藤原定家が二十年間も御奉公していたということで、二人は恋仲にあったらしい、などとする後代の卑俗な伝説もありますが、そうした根も葉もない噂はさておくとして、式子内親王が崇徳院・後鳥羽院と並ぶ皇室で最も優れた歌人の一人だったことは間違いありません。

Another TANKA on the theme of "secretly cherished love" also made by someone in the Imperial circle — 式子内親王(Shikishi naisinnou) who had once played the role of 斎院(sai inn＝sacred princess) — a maiden princess devoted to 賀茂神社(Kamo jinja＝the Kamo shrine) who was never allowed to fall in love with any man. Vulgar legends of later years made her romantically associated with 藤原定家(Fujiwara-no-Teika) because he served for 20 years in her residence. Such rootless rumors aside, she was definitely among the most talented royal TANKA poets along with 崇徳院(Sutoku inn) and 後鳥羽院(Gotoba inn).

―恋愛―

★110★しのぶれどいろにいでにけりわがこひは ものやおもふとひとのとふまで
忍ぶれど色に出でにけり我が恋は物や思ふと人の問ふ迄

【恋愛】[溜息]『3)拾遺集:622』平兼盛(たいらのかねもり)

素振りには出すまいとしてこれまで忍んできたけれど、とうとう顔色にはっきりと表われてしまったのだなあ、私の恋心は。「物思い、ですか？」と怪しまれてしまうほどに。

Stealthy love for you has tinged my heart so much
As to be readable in colors of love-hued face.

しのぶ【忍ぶ】〔他バ上二〕＜耐え忍ぶ｜(v.)endure＞(しのぶれ＝已然形)／ど【ど】[接助]＜～だけれども｜(conj.)although＞／いろ【色】[名]＜色｜(n.)color＞／に【に】[格助]＜結末｜(prep.)RESULT＞／いづ【出づ】〔自ダ下二〕＜出る｜(v.)come out＞(いで＝連用形)／ぬ【ぬ】[助動ナ変型]完了＜すでに～[し]た｜(aux-v.)PERFECT TENSE＞(に＝連用形)／けり【けり】[助動ラ変型]詠嘆＜～だったのだなぁ｜(interj.)REALIZATION＞(けり＝終止形)／わ【我】[代名]＜私｜(pron.)I, myself＞／が【が】[格助]＜の｜(prep.)'s＞／こひ【恋】[名]＜恋心｜(n.)love＞／は【は】[係助]＜主格｜(prep.)SUBJECT＞／もの【物】[名]＜あれこれいろいろ｜(n.)one thing or another＞／や【や】[係助]＜疑問｜(adv.)INTERROGATIVE＞／おもふ【思ふ】〔他ハ四〕＜思う｜(v.)think＞(おもふ＝連体形係り結び)／と【と】[格助]＜内容提示｜(conj.)that ～＞／ひと【人】[名]＜あの人｜(n.)that [darling] one＞／の【の】[格助]＜主格｜(prep.)SUBJECT＞／とふ【問ふ】〔他ハ四〕＜質問する｜(v.)ask＞(とふ＝連体形)／まで【迄】[副助]＜～な程に｜(adv.)to ～ extent＞

[shinobure-do iro ni ide-ni-keri wa-ga koi wa mono ya omou to hito no tou made]

「忍ぶ恋」の題で詠まれた数ある短歌の中でも、おそらく最も有名な歌がこれ・・・歌の中の「**人**」は、ひょっとしたら、この歌人が密かに恋しているまさにその人なのかもしれません。

Arguably the most famous TANKA on the theme of "silently cherished love"... the 人(hito=one) in this poem may even be the very one the poet is secretly in love with.

●111●いかでかとおもふこころのあるときは おぼめくさへぞうれしかりける
如何でかと思ふ心の有る時はおぼめくさへぞ嬉しかりける

【恋愛】[願望]『3)拾遺集:693』詠み人知らず

(この人と何としても仲良くなりたいなぁ)と思いを寄せる相手がいる時には、意中の人の何気ない素振りに(ぁ、これって、もしかして「好き」のサイン？)とか一人で勝手に舞い上がるだけでも嬉しかったりする。

When living, loving someone I'm dying to go steady with,
My heart leaps with joy at the slightest sign of acceptance.

いかで【如何で】〔副〕＜なんとかして｜(adv.)somehow or other＞／か【か】[係助]＜疑問｜(adv.)INTERROGATIVE＞／と【と】[格助]＜内容提示｜(conj.)that ～＞／おもふ【思ふ】〔他ハ四〕＜思う｜(v.)think＞(おもふ＝連体形)／こころ【心】[名]＜心｜(n.)heart＞／の【の】[格助]＜主格｜(prep.)SUBJECT＞／あり【あり】〔自ラ変〕＜存在する｜(v.)exist＞(ある＝連体形)／とき【時】[名]＜時｜(n.)the time＞／は【は】[係助]＜～に関しては｜(adv.)as for ～＞／おぼめく【おぼめく】〔自力四〕＜何となくそんな感じがする｜(v.)feel somehow like that＞(おぼめく＝連体形)／さへ【さへ】[副助]＜さえ｜(adv.)even＞／ぞ【ぞ】[係助]＜強調｜(adv.)EMPHASIS＞／うれし【嬉し】[形シク]＜嬉しい｜(adj.)happy＞(うれしかり＝連用形)／けり【けり】[助動ラ変型]詠嘆＜～だったのだなぁ｜(interj.)REALIZATION＞(ける＝連体形係り結び)

[ikade-ka to omou kokoro no aru toki wa obomeku sae-zo ureshikari-keru]

―恋愛―

「始まりの予感」は恋の喜びの最も甘美なエッセンス(・・・「終わりの予感」が愛の苦味のキモなのと同じく)
Imagined beginning is the sweetest part of loving joy, much as imagined ending is the bitterest part of love affairs.

★112★おもひつつぬればやひとのみえつらむ　ゆめとしりせばさめざらましを
思ひつつ寝ればや人の見えつらむ夢と知りせば覚めざらましを

【恋愛】[溜息]『1)古今集:552』小野小町(おののこまち)

恋しい、恋しい、と思いながら寝入ったせいかしら、あの人が夢に出てきたのは・・・
ああ、夢だとわかっていたならば、目覚めて再び一人ぼっちの現実に戻るようなまねはしなかったのに。

　　　　My passionate love toward you brought you into my dream, it seems.
　　　　Had I known it was a dream, I shouldn't have woken up again
　　　　Into this solitary life I spend without you in sight.

おもふ【想ふ】[他ハ四]＜愛しく思う｜(v.)love＞(おもひ＝連用形)／つつ【つつ】[接助]＜～[し]ながら｜(conj.)as＞／ぬ【寝】[自ナ下二]＜寝る｜(v.)sleep＞(ぬれ＝已然形)／ば【ば】[接助]＜理由｜(conj.)REASON＞／や【や】[係助]＜疑問｜(adv.)INTERROGATIVE＞／ひと【人】[名]＜あの人｜(n.)that [darling] one＞／の【の】[格助]＜主格｜(prep.)SUBJECT＞／みゆ【見ゆ】[自ヤ下二]＜見える｜(v.)appear＞(みえ＝連用形)／つ【つ】[助動タ下二型]完了＜すでに～した｜(aux-v.)PERFECT TENSE＞(つ＝終止形)／らむ【らむ】[助動ラ四型]現在推量＜～だろう｜(aux-v.)SUPPOSITION＞(らむ＝連体形係り結び)／ゆめ【夢】[名]＜夢｜(n.)a dream＞／と【と】[格助]＜内容提示｜(conj.)that ～＞／しる【知る】[他ラ四]＜知る｜(v.)know＞(しり＝連用形)／き【き】[助動特殊型]過去＜～[し]た｜(aux-v.)PAST＞(せ＝未然形)／ば【ば】[接助]＜仮定｜(conj.)if＞／さむ【覚む】[自マ下二]＜目覚める｜(v.)wake up＞(さめ＝連用形)／ず【ず】[助動特殊型]打消＜～[し]ない｜(adv.)not ～＞(ざら＝連用形)／まし【まし】[助動特殊型]推量＜～だろうに｜(aux-v.)should＞(まし＝終止形)／を【を】[間投助]＜～だというのに｜(interj.)EXCLAMATION＞

　　　　[omoi-tsutsu nure-ba-ya hito no mie-tsu-ramu yume to shiri-se-ba same-zara-mashi-wo]

「日中に底想っていれば、夢での逢瀬が待っている」というのは当時の俗信としては一般的なもので、「伝説の小野小町」の独創の産物では、ありません。

Sincere affection in waking life resulting in a dreamy rendezvous was a popular superstition in those days, not the original creation of the legendary 小野小町(Ono-no-Komachi).

●113●うたたねにこひしきひとをみてしより　ゆめてふものはたのみそめてき
うたた寝に恋しき人を見てしより夢と言ふものは頼み初めてき

【恋愛】[願望]『1)古今集:553』小野小町(おののこまち)

うたた寝の夢の中で恋しいあの人に出会って以来、「夢」というものに期待をかけるようになってしまった私。

　　　　Since I saw the man of my fancy in my beautifully brief nap,
　　　　I came to rely more on a dream than on this sad solitary reality.

うたたね【転寝】[名]＜短い眠り｜(n.)a nap＞／に【に】[格助]＜時｜(prep.)TIME＞／こひし【恋し】[形シク]＜恋しい｜(v.)feel attached to＞(こひしき＝連体形)／ひと【人】[名]＜あの人｜(n.)that [darling] one＞／を【を】[格助]＜目的格｜(prep.)OBJECT＞／みる【見】[他マ上一]＜見る｜(v.)view＞(み＝連用形)／つ【つ】[助動タ下二型]完了＜すでに～した｜(aux-v.)PERFECT TENSE＞(て＝連用形)／

http//zubaraie.com　　　　　-115-　　　　　―Love―

—恋愛—

き【き】〔助動特殊型〕過去＜〜[し]た｜(aux-v.)PAST＞(し＝連体形)／より【より】〔格助〕＜〜から｜(prep.)since＞／ゆめ【夢】〔名〕＜夢｜(n.)a dream＞と【と】〔格助〕＜内容提示｜(conj.)that 〜＞／いふ【言ふ】〔自ハ四〕＜〜という名の｜(prep.)with the name of 〜＞(いふ＝連体形)／もの【物】〔名〕＜物事｜(n.)a thing＞／は【は】〔係助〕＜目的格｜(prep.)OBJECT＞／たのむ【頼む】〔他マ四〕＜当てにする｜(v.)expect＞(たのみ＝連用形)／そむ【初む】〔補動マ下二〕＜〜し始める｜(v.)start to 〜＞(そめ＝連用形)／つ【つ】〔助動タ下二型〕完了＜すでに〜した｜(aux-v.)PERFECT TENSE＞(て＝連用形)／き【き】〔助動特殊型〕過去＜〜[し]た｜(aux-v.)PAST＞(き＝終止形)

[utata-ne ni koishiki hito wo mite-shi yori yume chuu mono wa tanomi-some-te-ki]

夢を頼むということは、現実生活にあまり期待が持てないことの裏返し。「夢見る小町」は、見た目の美しさほど幸せじゃない。

Dependence on a dream is the flip side of little hope in actual life. 小町(Komachi) the dreamer is not as happy as she appears beautiful in a poem.

———————————————————————————————

●114●ゆめよゆめこひしきひとにあひみすな　さめてののちはわびしかりけり
　　　　夢よ努恋しき人に逢ひ見すな覚めての後は侘びしかりけり

【恋愛】[溜息]『3)拾遺集:709』詠み人知らず

夢よ、夢・夢・夜の魔法、恋しい人は出さないで･･･夢中で愛して、目覚めて泣いて、
あまりの落差にメゲるから･･･絶対イヤだから、どうかお願い、あの人の夢は、見せないで。

**My dream, or dear, I pray you — never let my dear one appear!
Imagine how sad I will be to wake up to find myself alone.**

ゆめ【夢】〔名〕＜夢｜(n.)a dream＞／よ【よ】〔間投助〕＜呼び掛け｜(interj.)APOSTROPHE＞／ゆめ【努】〔副〕＜絶対に〜するな｜(adv.)never 〜＞／こひし【恋し】〔形シク〕＜恋しい｜(v.)feel attached to＞(こひしき＝連体形)／ひと【人】〔名〕＜あの人｜(n.)that [darling] one＞／に【に】〔格助〕＜対象｜(prep.)OBJECT＞／あひみる【逢ひ見る】〔他マ上一〕＜[恋人と]逢い引きする｜(v.)have a date＞(あひみ＝未然形)／す【す】〔助動サ下二型〕使役＜〜[さ]せる｜(aux-v.)CAUSATIVE＞(す＝終止形)／な【な】〔終助〕＜〜するな｜(adv.)don't 〜＞／さむ【覚む】〔自マ下二〕＜目覚める｜(v.)wake up＞(さめ＝連用形)／て【て】〔接助〕＜状態｜(conj.)while＞／の【の】〔格助〕＜の｜(prep.)'s＞／のち【後】〔名〕＜後｜(conj.)after＞／は【は】〔係助〕＜〜に関しては｜(adv.)as for 〜＞／わびし【侘びし】〔形シク〕＜わびしい｜(adj.)lonesome＞(わびしかり＝連用形)／けり【けり】〔助動ラ変型〕詠嘆＜〜だったのだなぁ｜(interj.)REALIZATION＞(けり＝終止形)

[yume yo yume koishiki hito ni ai-misu-na same-te no nochi wa wabishikari-keri]

恋しすぎて、夢見れば必ず出て来る誰かさん･･･その人に、現実の中では逢える見込みもないとしたら、それでもあなたは、せめてもの夢の逢瀬を、望みますか？

Someone you love so much that you can't dream without meeting the one... if you can't hope to meet the one in real life, will you still prefer a vicarious rendezvous in a dream?

———————————————————————————————

●115●ゆらのとをわたるふなびとかぢをたえ　ゆくへもしらぬこひのみちかも
　　　　由良の門を渡る舟人梶を絶え行く方も知らぬ恋の道かも

【恋愛】[序詞]『8)新古今集:1071』曾禰好忠(そねのよしただ)

由良川が若狭湾に注ぐ海峡で舟漕ぐ人が舵を失ったら、そこから先はもう、どこへ流れ着くか知れたものではない･･･そんな舵なき舟のさまに似て、この先どうなることか、まるでわからぬ我が恋の行方であることよ。

—恋愛—

**As a ship whose helm is lost at the Straits of Yura goes adrift,
Helplessly lost in love, what shore I'd reach, I'm not sure.**

ゆら【由良】〔名〕<[固有名詞]由良｜(n.)Yura>／の【の】〔格助〕<の｜(prep.)'s>／と【門】〔名〕<海峡｜(n.)the strait>／を【を】〔格助〕<目的格｜(prep.)OBJECT>／わたる【渡る】〔他ラ四〕<渡る｜(v.)navigate through>(わたる＝連体形)／ふなびと【舟人】〔名〕<漁師｜(n.)a fisherman>／***(A)かぢ【操舵】〔名〕***<操舵装置をくくりつける縄｜(n.)a rope fixing a rudder to a ship>／***(B1)かぢ【舵】〔名〕***<操舵装置｜a rudder>／***(B2)を【を】〔間投助〕***<主格｜(prep.)SUBJECT>／たゆ【絶ゆ】〔自ヤ下二〕<断ち切れる｜(v.)snap>(たえ＝連用形)／ゆくへ【行方】〔名〕<行く先｜(n.)the destination>／も【も】〔係助〕<意味なし｜(adv.)NO MEANING>／しる【知る】〔他ラ四〕<知る｜(v.)know>(しら＝未然形)／ず【ず】〔助動特殊型〕打消<～[し]ない｜(adv.)not ～>(ぬ＝連体形)／こひ【恋】〔名〕<恋心｜(n.)love>／の【の】〔格助〕<の｜(prep.)'s>／みち【道】〔名〕<道｜(n.)the way>／かな【かな】〔終助〕<詠嘆｜(interj.)EXCLAMATION>

[Yura-no-to wo wataru funa-bito kaji wo tae yukue mo shira-nu koi no michi kamo]

この歌(と、この後に続く三つの短歌)は、「序詞」の絵画的導入部が、結びの主意部へと流れるようにつながる構図・・・まぁ、主意といっても「好きです」って言ってるだけなんだけど・・・この短歌の前半部「**由良の門を渡る舟人梶を絶え**」のイメージ・スケッチは、自分で自分の感情のコントロールもままならぬ「恋の漂流者」の内面世界を生き生きと描き出しています。

This song (as well as the following three) includes 序詞(jo-kotoba) as a pictorial overture to the meaningful closing part: the meaning, though, is simpy "*I love you*". The image sketch in the former part of this TANKA — 由良の門を渡る舟人梶を絶え(Yura-no-to wo wataru funa-bito kaji wo tae) — vividly represents the inner world of a love-drifter totally out of control of his/her own emotion.

●116● かぜをいたみいはうつなみのおのれのみ くだけてものをおもふころかな
風を甚み岩打つ波の己れのみ砕けて物を思ふ頃かな

【恋愛】[序詞]『6)詞花集:211』源重之(みなもとのしげゆき)

吹き荒れる強風に煽られて、岩に当たって砕け散る波のように、激しい恋情に胸の中が波打つ・・・のは、この私だけ・・・あなたの気持ちはわからない・・・こんな激しい想い、あなたにぶつける訳にも行かない・・・そんな物思いの高波に千々に心乱れ、悩ましき日々を過ごす今日この頃の私です。

**As wind-driven waves dash against rocks,
Love-driven heart gets wilder within me.
Inside me alone: if known to you as such,
It'll frighten you off... what a powerlessly powerful passion!**

かぜ【風】〔名〕<風｜(n.)wind>／を【を】〔格助〕<主格｜(prep.)SUBJECT>／いたし【甚し】〔形ク〕<はげしい｜(adj.)violent>(いた＝語幹)／み【み】〔接尾〕<理由｜(conj.)REASON>／いは【岩】〔名〕<岩｜(n.)a rock>／うつ【打つ】〔他タ四〕<打ちつける｜(v.)dash against>(うつ＝連体形)／なみ【波】〔名〕<波｜(n.)waves>／の【の】〔格助〕<主格｜(prep.)SUBJECT>／おのれ【己】〔代名〕<自分｜(pron.)I, myself>／のみ【のみ】〔副助〕<ただ～だけ｜(adv.)only>／くだく【砕く】〔自力下二〕<砕ける｜(v.)be broken into pieces>(くだけ＝連用形)／て【て】〔接助〕<状態｜(conj.)while>／もの【物】〔名〕<あれこれいろいろ｜(n.)one thing or another>／を【を】〔格助〕<目的格｜(prep.)OBJECT>／おもふ【思ふ】〔他ハ四〕<思う｜(v.)think>(おもふ＝連体形)／ころ【頃】〔名〕<頃｜(n.)a time when ～>／かな【かな】〔終助〕<詠嘆｜(interj.)EXCLAMATION>

[kaze wo ita-mi iwa utsu nami no onore nomi kudake-te mono wo omou koro kana]

―恋愛―

これも「序詞」含みの短歌。まだ告白できずにいる臆病な男性(というのは平安時代の話で、現代なら性別不問)の胸中に怒濤のように沸き上がってはまた消える、おどおどとした恋情の起伏を、目にも鮮やかに描いています。「序詞」の最終部「波の／**砕けて**」の間には「**己れのみ**」が割り込んで真っ二つに裂けています・・・砕けた波のように「**よしっ、告白するぞぉ！**」と「**もし断わられたら、どうしよう？**」の間で千々に乱れる詠み手の心境の、実に巧みな表現です。

Another 序詞(jo-kotoba) TANKA which visually represents the timid affection surging up and down within the heart of a man (in the Heian era; nowadays, ignore sexes) who is in love but is too shy to make confession. The final part of the 序詞(jo-kotoba) 波の／**砕けて**(nami no/kudake-te＝the waves/dashed apart) is broken into two by the insertion of 己れのみ(onore nomi＝me alone), cleverly showing how turbulent is the poet's heart like the split waves ― **Oh yes, I WILL confess!**/*What if [s]he refused?*

●117● せをはやみいはにせかるるたきがはの われてもすゑにあはむとぞおもふ
　　　　瀬を早み岩に堰かるる滝川の分れても末に逢はむとぞ思ふ

【恋愛】[序詞]『6)詞花集:229』崇徳院(すとくいん)

滝を下ってほとばしる水は、浅瀬の流れの速さゆえ、岩に邪魔され分かれても、
下れば一つの流れに戻る・・・そんな激しい滝川のように、一時は別れて暮らしていても、
いずれはあなたとまた逢おう、このまま一人でいるものか、と、強く念じている私です。

**Current down so steep at rocks may depart
Soon to meet in the same flow downstream.
We two will meet in the same heart again.**

せ【瀬】〔名〕＜浅瀬｜(n.)shallows＞／を【を】〔格助〕＜主格｜(prep.)SUBJECT＞／はやし【速し】〔形ク〕＜速い｜(adj.)fast＞(はや＝語幹)／み【み】〔接尾〕＜理由｜(conj.)REASON＞／いは【岩】〔名〕＜岩｜(n.)a rock＞／に【に】〔格助〕＜行為主｜(prep.)by＞／せく【堰く】＜他カ四｜(v.)block off＞(せか＝未然形)／る【る】〔助動ラ下二型〕受身＜～[さ]れる｜(aux-v.)PASSIVE VOICE＞(るる＝連体形)／たきがは【滝川】〔名〕＜滝を流れる水｜(n.)water running down a cascade＞／の【の】〔格助〕＜主格｜(prep.)SUBJECT＞／わる【分る】〔自ラ下二〕＜二つに別れる｜(v.)be split apart＞(われ＝連用形)／て【て】〔接助〕＜仮定｜(conj.)if＞／も【も】〔係助〕＜～[で]さえも｜(adv.)even＞／する【末】〔名〕＜最後｜(n.)the end＞／に【に】〔格助〕＜時｜(prep.)TIME＞／あふ【逢ふ】＜他ハ四＞＜(恋人として)結ばれる｜(v.)be mutually in love＞(あは＝未然形)／む【む】〔助動マ四型〕意志＜～するつもりだ｜(aux-v.)be going to ～＞(む＝終止形)／と【と】〔格助〕＜内容提示｜(conj.)that ～＞／ぞ【ぞ】〔係助〕＜強調｜(adv.)EMPHASIS＞／おもふ【思ふ】＜他ハ四＞＜思う｜(v.)think＞ (おもふ＝連体形係り結び)

[se wo haya-mi iwa ni seka-ruru taki-gawa no ware-te-mo sue ni awa-mu to-zo omou]

これまた「序詞歌」で、その意味上の中核は最後の「**末に逢はむとぞ思ふ**(＝最後の最後には思いを遂げるつもり)」に凝縮されています・・・どうして「**末に**」なのか？・・・それは「**瀬を早み岩に堰かるる滝川の分れて**(＝厳しい時流が邪魔をして今は一緒にいられないから)」・・・別れ別れのカップルすべてに捧げる歌と言えそうですが、それも二人の距離が愛の炎を掻き消していない限りは、そしてまたこの歌の作者の崇徳院が辿った悲劇の運命を気にしないなら、の条件付き・・・平安末の政争に敗れて流罪に処せられた末に悪鬼となって京都の町に祟りを為した、と言われているのが「**崇徳院**」なのです・・・しかし実際には、この悲劇の元天皇こそ、日本の皇室関係者の中では群を抜く最高の詩人(あの有名な後鳥羽院さえ凌ぐ歌才の持ち主)なのでした。そんな崇徳院の優美な短歌の数々が、然るべき評価も受けずにかくも徹底的に無視され続けてきたという事実もまた、日本という国には真の芸術の目利きなど存在せず、良かれ悪しかれ「名ばかり」の影響力がどれほどの猛威を揮っているかを示す証拠品。

―Love―　　　　　　　　　-118-　　　　　　　　http//zubaraie.com

—恋愛—

Yet another 序詞(jo-kotoba) TANKA whose semantic essence is summed up at the end in the phrase 末に逢はむとぞ思ふ(sue ni awa-mu to-zo omou＝I'm going to come and get you in the end). Why *in the end*? Because the couple is being split apart by circumstances where 瀬を早み岩に堰かるる滝川の分れて(se wo haya-mi iwa ni seka-ruru taki-gawa no ware-te＝the tide is too harsh for them to go together). A song dedicatable to any departed couples, so long as their affectionate candles have not been extinguished by the distance — and only so long as they do not mind the tragic fate of this author 崇徳院(Sutoku inn), who got exiled as a loser in a political conflict at the end of the Heian era and *is said to have become a demon to haunt the city of* 京都*(Kyoto)*. In fact, this tragic ex-Emperor was definitely the greatest poet — even more talented than the famous 後鳥羽院(Go-Toba inn) — in the Japanese royal circle. The fact that the elegant TANKA by 崇徳院(Sutoku inn) should have been so completely ignored without due respect is just another proof of the lack of connoisseurship and the rampant dominance of mere names, good or *bad*, in Japan.

●118●みかきもりゑじのたくひのよるはもえ　ひるはきえつつものをこそおもへ
御垣守衛士の焚く火の夜は燃え昼は消えつつ物をこそ思へ

【恋愛】[序詞]『6)詞花集:225』大中臣能宣(おおなかとみのよしのぶ)

皇室の身辺をお守りする衛兵の焚くかがり火は、夜は激しく燃え盛り、昼間はひっそり消えているでしょう？···あれと同じなんです、私の恋心も。一人過ごす夜には狂おしいまでにあなたを想い、明けてはただもう抜け殻のように消沈した心を抱えて日中を過ごす···
それほど強く、己れの身を焼き尽くすほどに、あなたをお慕いしている私です。

Imperial guards burn fire in the Palace

Blazing by night, invisible by day.

As stealthy in the day is my love for you,

Burns up my heart at solitary nights,

Leaving me alone in silently yearning days.

みかきもり【御垣守】〔名〕＜御所の警備｜(n.)royal guards＞／ゑじ【衛士】〔名〕＜衛兵｜(n.)guardsmen＞／の【の】〔格助〕＜主格｜(prep.)SUBJECT＞／たく【焚く】〔他カ四〕＜火を燃やす｜(v.)burn＞(たく＝連体形)／ひ【火】〔名〕＜火｜(n.)fire＞／の【の】〔格助〕＜主格｜(prep.)SUBJECT＞／よる【夜】〔名〕＜夜｜(n.)the night＞／は【は】〔係助〕＜～に関しては｜(adv.)as for ～＞／もゆ【燃ゆ】〔自ヤ二〕＜燃える｜(v.)be on fire＞(もえ＝連用形)／ひる【昼】〔名〕＜昼間｜(n.)the daytime＞／は【は】〔係助〕＜～に関しては｜(adv.)as for ～＞／きゆ【消ゆ】〔自ヤ二〕＜消える｜(v.)disappear＞(きえ＝連用形)／つつ【つつ】〔接助〕＜～[し]ながら｜(conj.)as＞／もの【物】〔名〕＜あれこれいろいろ｜(n.)one thing or another＞／を【を】〔格助〕＜目的格｜(prep.)OBJECT＞／こそ【こそ】〔係助〕＜強調｜(adv.)EMPHASIS＞／おもふ【思ふ】〔他ハ四〕＜思う｜(v.)think＞(おもへ＝已然形係り結び)

[mi-kaki-mori eji no taku hi no yoru wa moe hiru wa kie-tsutsu mono wo-koso omoe]

これも「序詞」歌で、前半部「御垣守衛士の焚く火の夜は燃え昼は消えつつ」が、愛すれど満たされぬ想いに一晩中悶々としている詩人の心を絵画的な鮮やかさで描き出している···恋人と一緒に夜通しギンギンに燃えて疲れ果てちゃったから昼間は半ば居眠りしてるんだろう、なんて想像はしないように — その場合なら、この歌の結句は「＜君＞をこそ想へ(＝想うのはただあなたのことばかり)」であって「＜物＞をこそ思へ(＝物思いに沈むばかり)」にはなってないはずだから。

—恋愛—

Another 序詞(jo-kotoba) TANKA, with the former part — 御垣守衛士の焚く火の夜は燃え昼は消えつつ(mi-kaki-mori eji no taku hi no yoru wa moe hiru wa kie-tsutsu) — graphically symbolizing the wistful mind of the poet occupied all night with unsatisfied yearning for the love... don't imagine *he is half asleep by the day because he has burnt himself up physically along with his woman all night* — if that was the case, the final phrase must be <君>をこそ想へ(kimi wo koso omoe＝I'm thinking about <**you**>) instead of <物>をこそ思へ(mono wo koso omoe＝I'm lost in <**thought**>).

●119●いのちやはなにぞはつゆのあだものを　あふにしかへばをしからなくに
命やは何ぞは露の徒物を逢ふにし替へば惜しからなくに

【恋愛】[願望]『1)古今集:615』紀友則(きのとものり)

人の命はまるで露のようなもの、吹けば飛ぶような頼りなげな存在・・・なら、そんな命と引き替えにしてでも、恋しい人との逢瀬が叶えばもうそれだけで本望、たとえ死んでも悔いはない。

Life is fleeting as dew, soon to pass away,
Who am I to spare it for meeting you as a lover;
I'm dying to see you in exchange for my life!

いのち【命】〔名〕＜生命｜(n.)my life＞／やは【やは】〔係助〕＜～だろうか？否、そうではあるまい｜(prep.)RHETORICAL QUESTION＞／なに【何】〔副〕＜どうして｜(adv.)why＞／ぞ【ぞ】〔係助〕＜強調｜(adv.)EMPHASIS＞／は【は】〔係助〕＜は｜(prep.)NO MEANING＞／つゆ【露】〔名〕＜露｜(n.)dew＞／の【の】〔格助〕＜のような｜(prep.)just like＞／あだもの【徒物】〔名〕＜はかないもの｜(n.)fleeting existence＞／を【を】〔格助〕＜目的格｜(prep.)OBJECT＞／あふ【逢ふ】〔自ハ四〕＜[恋人どうしとして]逢う｜(v.)have a date＞(あふ＝連体形)／に【に】〔格助〕＜対象｜(prep.)OBJECT＞／し【し】〔副助〕＜意味なし｜(adv.)NO MEANING＞／かふ【交ふ】〔他ハ下二〕＜交換する｜(v.)exchange＞(かへ＝已然形)／ば【ば】〔接helm〕＜仮定｜(conj.)if＞／をし【惜し】〔形シク〕＜なくなるのを残念に思う｜(v.)be sorry to lose＞(をしから＝未然形)／ず【ず】〔助動特殊型〕打消＜～[し]ない｜(adv.)not～＞(な＝未然形)／く【く】〔接尾〕＜名詞化成分｜(suffix)[to make n. out of v.]＞／に【に】〔終助〕＜詠嘆｜(interj.)EXCLAMATION＞

[inochi yawa nani-zo-wa tsuyu no ada-mono wo au ni-shi kae-ba oshikara-na-ku-ni]

「こんなはかない人生なんて、君と深い仲になれるなら喜んで差し出すよ！」 — 平安の世の貴人よりむしろイタリアの色男の口に乗せるのがお似合いっぽい、死に物狂いの情熱的な台詞ですね。実際には、京都の殿方はこの種の考えを無責任なくらい大胆な詩の中で弄びはしたものの、実際の色事で燃え上がるほどの情熱を発揮することはありませんでした。そんな中でも、この「逢ふにし替へば(＝あなたの恋人になれるなら、この命と引き替えにしても惜しくない)」というのは、平安調恋文の最も熱愛する陳腐な定型句の一つとなりました・・・その結果、幾多の男たちが歌の中で虚しく討ち死にを遂げつつも、いくら死んでも名折れにもならず、ましてや実際に落命することも、ありませんでした。

"Life is so fragile that I won't mind exchanging it for getting intimate with you!" — a desperately passionate phrase more becoming on the lips of Italian playboys than to Heianese nobles. As a matter of fact, males in 京都(Kyoto) were not as flamboyant in their amorous behavior as they flirted with such ideas in irresponsibly audacious poems; among them, this 逢ふにし替へば(au ni-shi kae-ba＝if only I could exchange my life for your love!) became one of the most beloved clichés in Heianese love letters, making so many men vainly die in poems without losing any face, let alone, life.

●120●あひみてはしにせぬみとぞなりぬべき たのむるにだにのぶるいのちは
逢ひ見ては死にせぬ身とぞ成りぬべき頼むるにだに延ぶる命は

【恋愛】[俳諧]『3)拾遺集:692』詠み人知らず

逢瀬も叶わぬあの人に、それでも逢える日が来ることだけを頼みに生きているこの私・・・
こんな儚い期待だけでも露の命が延びるのだから、あの人と相思相愛の仲にでもなった日には、
きっと私は不死身になってしまうことだろう。

        Could I fall mutually in love with you,
        Immortal would I be, for ever happy together;
        For now, I survive this lonely life
        In the faint hope of dating with you.

あひみる【逢ひ見る】〔他マ上一〕<[恋人と]逢い引きする|(v.)have a date>(あひみ=連用形)/て【て】〔接助〕<仮定|(conj.)if>/は【は】〔係助〕<～に関しては|(adv.)as for ～>/しぬ【死ぬ】〔自ナ変〕<死ぬ|(v.)die>(しに=連用形)/す【為】〔補動サ変〕<する|(v.)do>(せ=未然形)/ず【ず】〔助動特殊型〕打消<～[し]ない|(adv.)not ～>(ぬ=連体形)/み【身】〔名〕<存在|(n.)an entity>/と【と】〔格助〕<結末|(prep.)RESULT>/ぞ【ぞ】〔係助〕<強調|(adv.)EMPHASIS>/なる【成る】〔自ラ四〕<～になる|(v.)become>(なり=連用形)/ぬ【ぬ】〔助動ナ変型〕確認<きっと～する|(adv.)EMPHASIS>(ぬ=終止形)/べし【べし】〔助動ク型〕推量<～にちがいない|(aux-v.)CONVICTION>(べき=連体形係り結び)/たのむ【頼む】〔他マ下二〕<期待する|(v.)hope>(たのむる=連体形)/に【に】〔格助〕<原因|(prep.)REASON>/だに【だに】〔副助〕<～さえ|(adv.)even>/のぶ【延ぶ】〔自バ上二〕<延びる|(v.)be prolonged>(のぶる=連体形)/いのち【命】〔名〕<生命|(n.)my life>/は【は】〔格助〕<は|(prep.)SUBJECT>

[ai-mi-te-wa shini-se-nu mi to-zo nari-nu-beki tanomuru ni-dani noboru inochi wa]

あまりの軽薄さにマジに取るわけには行かない(それどころかこの人ホントに恋してるのかなぁと疑われるほどの)冗談っぽい恋歌。これとか一つ前の歌とかが歴然と証明しているように、「死」みたいな不吉な「忌み言葉」も、平安調短歌の中では軽口めかして山ほど出て来たのです・・・無論これは当時の日常会話の中では決してあり得ない短歌世界ならではの放縦ですが。

A joking love song too frivolous to take seriously, or even to imagine the poet is really in love. A song like this or the previous one will be eloquent proof to show that such ominous words as 死(shi=death) ― 忌み言葉(imi kotoba=taboo words) ― were jestingly abundant in Heianese TANKA... which was never the case with everyday conversation of the day, of course.

●121●おもふひとおもはぬひとのおもふひと おもはざらなむおもひしるべく
思ふ人思はぬ人の思ふ人思はざらなむ思ひ知るべく

【恋愛】[俳諧]『2)後撰集:572』詠み人知らず

自分のことを恋い慕っている誰かさんのことを、冷たく袖にして何とも思わぬつれない誰かさん・・・
その冷淡な誰かさんが胸焦がして他の誰かさんを恋い慕った時には、その恋慕の相手の誰かさんが
冷淡な誰かさんのことを、何とも思わずフッちゃいますように・・・そうすれば、
自分を恋い慕う相手につれなく振る舞うことの罪深さ、身に滲みて思い知ることだろうから。

—恋愛—

One who doesn't care for someone who one knows is madly in love
May well also fall in love, but then, God, be hard on the one,
Let the loved one ignore the loving one to remind the one of the original sin:
Icy heart hard on someone comes back to haunt it with delayed echo.

おもふ【想ふ】〔他ハ四〕<愛しく思う|(v.)love>(おもふ＝連体形)／ひと【人】〔名〕<人間|(n.)a human being>／おもふ【想ふ】〔他ハ四〕<愛しく思う|(v.)love>(おもは＝未然形)／ず【ず】〔助動特殊型〕打消<～[し]ない|(adv.)not ～>(ぬ＝連体形)／ひと【人】〔名〕<人間|(n.)a human being>／の【の】〔格助〕<主格|(prep.)SUBJECT>／おもふ【想ふ】〔他ハ四〕<愛しく思う|(v.)love>(おもふ＝連体形)／ひと【人】〔名〕<その思い人|(n.)that [darling] one>／おもふ【想ふ】〔他ハ四〕<愛しく思う|(v.)love>(おもは＝未然形)／ず【ず】〔助動特殊型〕打消<～[し]ない|(adv.)not ～>(ざら＝連用形)／なむ【なむ】〔終助〕<～ならいいのになぁ|(v.)I hope>／おもひしる【思ひ知る】〔他ラ四〕<痛感する|(v.)bitterly feel>(おもひしる＝終止形)／べし【べし】〔助動ク型〕妥当<～するべき|(aux-v.)should>(べく＝連用形)

[omou hito omowa-nu hito no omou hito omowa-zara-namu omoi-shiru-beku]

自分を愛してくれない誰かさんを妬って恨んで詠んだ歌‥‥なのに陰湿さはまるでなく、失恋を明るく忘れて立ち直る役にすら立ちそうな響きあり。

A jealous grudge against someone who doesn't love the poet, which sounds anything but gloomy and may even serve the purpose of happy oblivion and recovery from the lost love.

★122★あひみてののちのこころにくらぶれば　むかしはものをおもはざりけり
逢ひ見ての後の心に比ぶれば昔は物を思はざりけり

【恋愛】[後朝]『3)拾遺集:710』藤原敦忠(ふじわらのあつただ)

あなたと恋人どうしとしてお逢いするようになってから、私もいろいろと物を思うようになりました。
それを思えば、あなたとのお付き合いが始まる前の私は、何も考えずに生きていたような気がします。

Compared with myself after I met you,
My heart used to be rather passionless,
Which is now burning so hot because of you.

あひみる【逢ひ見る】〔他マ上一〕<[恋人と]逢い引きする|(v.)have a date>(あひみ＝連用形)／つ【つ】〔助動ダ下二型〕完了<すでに～した|(aux-v.)PERFECT TENSE>(て＝連用形)／の【の】〔格助〕<の|(prep.)'s>／のち【後】〔名〕<後|(conj.)after>／の【の】〔格助〕<の|(prep.)'s>／こころ【心】〔名〕<心|(n.)heart>／に【に】〔格助〕<比較|(prep.)COMPARISON>／くらぶ【比ぶ】〔他バ下二〕<くらべる|(v.)compare>(くらぶれ＝已然形)／ば【ば】〔接助〕<仮定|(conj.)if>／むかし【昔】〔名〕<昔|(n.)the past>／は【は】〔係助〕<～に関しては|(adv.)as for ～>／もの【物】〔名〕<あれこれいろいろ|(n.)one thing or another>／を【を】〔格助〕<目的格|(prep.)OBJECT>／おもふ【思ふ】〔他ハ四〕<思う|(v.)think>(おもは＝未然形)／ず【ず】〔助動特殊型〕打消<～[し]ない|(adv.)not ～>(ざり＝連用形)／けり【けり】〔助動ラ変型〕詠嘆<～だったのだなぁ|(interj.)REALIZATION>(けり＝終止形)

[ai-mi-te no nochi no kokoro ni kurabure-ba mukashi wa mono wo omowa-zari-keri]

前夜を共に過ごした女性へと男性が送った恋の歌で、一般に「後朝の文」と呼ばれるもの。気取った言葉も趣向もない分、この恋の詩の魅力は詩人自身の情熱の一点にかかっている‥‥で、実際成功している‥‥でしょう？

A love poem sent from a man to the woman he had spent the previous night together, which was generally called 後朝の文(kinu-ginu no fumi＝a morning-after lover letter). Without any affected

—恋愛—

rhetoric or style, the appeal of this love poem solely depends on the poet's passion... and it does succeed, don't you feel?

《「きぬ／こぬ」に千々に乱るる姫心》

平安の世の恋愛は男性主導型。最初にまず男が女の噂を聞く(直に彼女を「見る」わけではない);男は愛情たっぷりの恋文を送って女を口説く;ひとたび女に「いいわ」と許されたなら、男は彼女の部屋を初訪問 ─ もし生身の彼女が魅力的なら、男はその場で(たぶん)彼女と肉体関係を結び、帰宅後数日以内に逢瀬(と味見)を許してくれた彼女にお礼の手紙を送ると共に、彼らの関係をもう一歩進めるための「又の逢瀬」を求めてくる。そうした初々しい逢瀬が二～三回ほども続いたなら、お互いを「夫婦」と認めた証し。そうして結婚生活が始まっても、夫婦は同じ家に住んで生活を共にするわけではない。女はただ自分の部屋でじぃ〜っと待つだけ ─ 男にヒマが出来て、夜空の月が彼を連れて来てくれそうなくらい明るく輝いていて、「今夜は可愛がってあげようかな」という気分が彼の胸中に満ちて来ることを期待しつつ、ひたすら待つのが平安女性の宿命・・・しかしながら、大抵の男たちは初逢瀬にすら辿り着くことなく砕け散る ─ 自分が口説いてる女性が実際どういう顔してるのかも知らぬまま・・・現代人には奇異に思えても、それが平安の世の恋愛の現実。彼らの世界での「逢ふ」はただ単に「会う」だけではない ─ お互い出逢って「お肉の味見」までする含みを持つのである・・・とはいえ中には、あまりに見た目がマズそうなので噛む気も起きない「お肉」もある ─ 初めて男を部屋に招いたものの、当たり障りのない話をしただけで、自分には指一本触れずに去り行く男を見送ることになる女性もいる・・・お礼の手紙が来ないのは言うまでもない・・・「後朝の文」が来るか来ないかは、肌と肌での本格的なやりとりの始まりを告げるか、紙の上だけの空想恋愛の終わりを告げるかの、大事な分かれ目だったのだ。

《後朝(kinuginu) ─ if it comes, love will go on; if not...》

Heianese love affair is male-dominated. In the beginning, a man hears about (*not SEES*) a woman, woos her by sending amorous love poems and, once accepted, sees her for the first time in her room — if she is attractive in the flesh, he will (perhaps) have carnal knowledge of her on the spot; within a couple of days after the first date, he will send her a letter of thanks for allowing him to meet (and taste) her, also asking for another date to make their relationship one step further. A series — a couple of times — of such initial rendezvous means mutually accepted marriage. After they get married, however, they don't live in the same house to spend life together: the woman just waits in her room for the man to come to love her whenever he has free time, bright moon in the sky to show him the way, and enough inclination to go out and love her for the night. Most men, however, would be dashed to pieces before they could even know what the woman they were wooing really looked like — odd as it seems to us, that was the Heianese reality of love: in their vocabulary, 逢ふ(au=to meet) was more than just "meet" — they would "meet" to taste the "meat" of each other. But the test of some meat was surely not in the biting — some women would invite a man for the first time, have a small talk, only to see him leave without touching her, let alone a follow-up letter of thanks... 後朝の文(kinuginu no fumi=a morning-after love letter), its arrival or absence, marked either the beginning of a substantial relationship in the flesh or the end of fanciful relation purely on paper.

―恋愛―

★123★あはざりしときいかなりしものとてか ただいまのまもみねばこひしき
逢はざりし時如何なりしものとてか只今の間も見ねば恋しき

【恋愛】[後朝]『2)後撰集:564』詠み人知らず

あなたと出会って恋をして、そうなる前だって私は生きていたわけだけど、いったいその頃は
どうやって生きていたんだろう、と不思議に思えるくらいに、今の私はもう、
一人で過ごす一瞬一瞬が耐え難いほどに、あなたのことが恋しくて逢いたくてたまらないのです。

I can't imagine my life alone before I fell in love.
Now a moment without you near is too painful for me to bear.

あふ【逢ふ】[自ハ四]<[恋人どうしとして]逢う│(v.)have a date>(あは=未然形)／ず【ず】[助動特殊型]
打消<～[し]ない│(adv.)not ～>(ざり=連用形)／き【き】[助動特殊型]過去<～[し]た│
(aux-v.)PAST>(し=連体形)／とき【時】[名]<時│(n.)the time>／いかなり【如何なり】[形動ナリ]<ど
んな具合だ│(adj.)how is it>(いかなり=連用形)／き【き】[助動特殊型]過去<～[し]た│(aux-v.)PAST
>(し=連体形)／もの【物】[名]<状態│(n.)state of things>／とて【とて】[格助]<～と思って│
(adv.)with ～ in mind>／か【か】[係助]<疑問│(adv.)INTERROGATIVE>／ただ【只】[副]<ただ
単に│(adv.)only>／いま【今】[名]<今│(n.)now>／の【の】[格助]<の│(prep.)'s>／ま【間】[名]<
間│(n.)while>／も【も】[係助]<～[で]さえも│(adv.)even>／みる【見る】<[恋人と]逢う│(v.)meet
[one's sweetheart]>(み=未然形)／ず【ず】[助動特殊型]打消<～[し]ない│(adv.)not ～>(ね=已
然形)／ば【ば】[接助]<仮定│(conj.)if>／こひし【恋し】[形シク]<恋しい│(v.)feel attached to>(こひ
しき=連体形係り結び)

[awa-zari-shi toki ikanari-shi mono tote-ka tada-ima no ma mo mi-ne-ba koishiki]

こんな「後朝の文:きぬぎぬのふみ=逢瀬直後のお礼の恋文」もらったら、どんな女性もきっと喜んで彼に
又の逢瀬を約束するだろう、ってぐらいの見事な歌・・・これをそっくりそのまま丸写しにしたような短歌がそれ
はもう沢山作られましたが、いくらコピーを繰り返してもその魔法の力が失われることはなかったようです。
恋愛に関しては、自前であれこれ考えるより、効果実証済みのテンプレート(ひな型)に頼る方が得策。

A 後朝の文(kinuginu no fumi=morning-after love letter) which will never fail to make the woman
happily grant him another date. There were many carbon-copy love songs made in the image of this
TANKA, but the magic didn't seem to fade through duplication. As for love, turn to an assured template
rather than contemplate on your own.

―――――――――――――――――――――――――――――――

★124★おもひやるこころにたぐふみなりせば ひとひにちたびきみはみてまし
思ひ遣る心に比ふ身なりせば一日に千度君は見てまし

【恋愛】[後朝]『2)後撰集:679』大江千古(おおえのちふる)

あなたへ寄せる私のこの思いに、この身がぴたりと寄り添うものならば、
一日に一千回はあなたにお逢いしていることでしょうに。

I will always send out my heart to you.
If my body could also be sent out to you,
A thousand times a day I would surely come and see you.

おもひやる【思ひ遣る】[他ラ四]<恋しい相手に心を寄せる│(v.)send one's heart to someone dear>(お
もひやる=連体形)／こころ【心】[名]<心│(n.)heart>／に【に】[格助]<比較│(prep.)COMPARISON
>／たぐふ【比ふ】[自ハ四]<相当する│(v.)be equal to>(たぐふ=連体形)／み【身】[名]<身体
│(n.)the body>／なり【なり】[助動ナリ型]断定<～である│(aux-v.)be>(なり=連用形)／き【き】[助動特

—恋愛—

殊型]過去＜〜[し]た｜(aux-v.)PAST＞(せ＝未然形)／ば【ば】〔接助〕＜仮定｜(conj.)if＞／ひと【一】〔接頭〕＜一｜(prefix)each＞／ひ【日】〔名〕＜日｜(n.)a day＞／に【に】〔格助〕＜比率｜(prep.)per 〜＞／ち【千】〔接頭〕＜千｜(prefix)a thousand＞／たび【度】〔名〕＜回｜(n.)times＞／きみ【君】〔代名〕＜あなた｜(pron.)you＞／は【は】〔係助〕＜目的格｜(prep.)OBJECT＞／みる【見る】〔他マ上一〕＜[恋人として]逢う｜(v.)meet [as lovers]＞(み＝連用形)／つ【つ】〔助動サ下二型〕確述＜きっと〜する｜(adv.)EMPHASIS＞(て＝連用形)／まし【まし】〔助動特殊型〕推量＜〜だろうに｜(aux-v.)should＞(まし＝終止形)

[omoi-yaru kokoro ni taguu mi nari-se-ba hito-hi ni chi-tabi kimi wa mi-te-mashi]

あまりにストレートに幸せすぎて、読むと思わず笑っちゃう・・・もらった彼女としては「もぅ、またなの？しょーもない人ね・・・」と受け入れざるを得なくなる歌。そんなことばっかしてたら恋愛以外の何も出来やしないじゃないか、なんて心配はご無用・・・どうせそう長くは続かないんだから(おっと、失言！)。
Too straightly happy for readers to refrain from a smile... for the receiver, to refrain from accepting him. Don't worry he'll be too busy to do anything else than love... it won't last forever (OOPS!).

●125● またもなくただひとすぢにきみおもふ　こひぢにまどふわれやなになる
又も無く只一筋に君思ふ恋路に惑ふ我や何なる

【恋愛】[俳諧]『7)千載集:674』藤原伊通(ふじわらのこれみち)

ただ一目散にあなたのことだけを思い続けるひたむきな恋の一本道を突っ走っているというのに、恋路に迷って何がなんだかわけがわからぬ無茶苦茶な心持ちに戸惑うばかりのこの私は、一体、どういう方向音痴なのでしょうか？

Straightly up to you, my mind is set on you,
Why, then, am I thus lost in endless loop of love?

また【又】〔副〕＜他に｜(adv.)something else＞／も【も】〔係助〕＜意味なし｜(adv.)NO MEANING＞／なし【なし】〔形ク〕＜存在しない｜(v.)do not exist＞(なく＝連用形)／ただ【只】〔副〕＜ただ単に｜(adv.)only＞／ひとすぢ【一筋】〔名〕＜一直線｜(adv.)straightforward＞／に【に】〔格助〕＜様態｜(prep.)like＞／きみ【君】〔代名〕＜あなた｜(pron.)you＞／おもふ【想ふ】〔他ハ四〕＜愛しく思う｜(v.)love＞(おもふ＝連体形)／こひぢ【恋路】〔名〕＜恋の道｜(n.)the freeway of love＞／に【に】〔格助〕＜場所｜(prep.)PLACE＞／まどふ【惑ふ】〔自ハ四〕＜迷う｜(v.)get lost＞(まどふ＝連体形)／われ【我】〔代名〕＜私｜(pron.)I, myself＞／や【や】〔係助〕＜疑問｜(adv.)INTERROGATIVE＞／なに【何】〔代名〕＜何｜(pron.)what＞／なり【なり】〔助動ナリ型〕断定＜〜である｜(aux-v.)be＞(なる＝連体形係り結び)

[mata-mo-naku tada hito-suji-ni kimi omou koi-ji ni madou ware ya nani-naru]

「あなたに向かって一直線の恋の高速道路上で不思議に道に迷っている私。どうしてこんなことが起こるのでしょうか？」――それは、気の利いたユーモアこそが人を引き付ける決め手になる平安調恋歌の世界だから。
In a straight highway of love to you, I'm strangely getting lost... how could it be possible? Because it's a Heianese love TANKA where witty humor wins the day.

《誰そ知らむ嘘か真か恋の歌》

この短歌みたいな恋の歌を受け取ったなら、(この男、口で言うほど誠実に私のこと愛してるようには思えないり)と感じるかもしれません。同様に、平安調短歌世界の恋歌なんて、そのほとんどが「作り物」だということを覚えておいたほうがいいでしょう ― 作り物じゃない本物の恋歌だとしたら、そんな個人的通信文が「深い仲でもない一般読者」のことをこうして面白がらせたり感動させたりしてるのは、おかしいでしょう？現代の消費者の多くは、大衆音楽の市場に並んだラブソングの虚構性について、十分認識しているはず・・・

http://zubaraie.com　　　　　　　　　　　　　　　　　　　　　　　　—Love—

―恋愛―

それと同じ想像力を、恋愛であれ哀悼(あいとう)であれ賛歌であれ自然であれ、平安調短歌の全領域に対して巡らしてください・・・そこは、事実に基づく現実性なんて、空想に基づく美の前に何の価値も持たない世界、目指すのは「口ずさんだ時に美しい詩」であって「誰か個人のウソのない作文」ではないのです。詩的面白味(おもしろみ)のかけらもない他の誰かの私生活の実話が聞きたければ、ツイッターかブログ(Twitter blogs)の世界へどうぞ。それ以外の人達だけ、ここで「空言の世界の優雅な愉悦(そらごと)」を一緒に楽しみましょう。

《be cautious of the sincerity of Heianese love TANKA》

If you receive a love song like this, you may not believe him so sincerely in love with you as he says. You should also remember that most of Heianese love poems were fictional — otherwise, why should such personal correspondences amuse or move someone those authors are not at all intimate with? Most modern consumers are well-aware of the fictional nature of love songs on the pop-music market: just extend that imagination to all the realms of Heianese TANKA, be it about love, lamentation, adulation, or Nature. Factual reality is nothing to fanciful beauty there: it is made to be beautifully recited, not to be personally trusted. If you want to hear someone else's personally true but poetically flat gibberish, go to the world of Twitter or blogs: the rest of you, come and join us in this elegant joy of falsehood.

────────────────────────────

●126●あかでこそおもはむなかははなれなめ そをだにのちのわすれがたみに
　　　　飽かでこそ思はむ仲は離れなめ其をだに後の忘れがたみに

【恋愛】[悟り]『1)古今集:717』詠み人知らず

相思相愛の恋人どうしは「まだ飽き足りない、もっと一緒に居たい」と感じている間に
「さよなら」言うのが良いでしょう ― その心引かれる感じを忘れられずに、また逢う時までの思い出にして。

    Men and women mutually in love,

    Be parted while your hearts resist,

    Anchor yourselves by insatiable memories,

    Unfailing desire for ever fresh affairs.

あく【飽く】〔自カ四〕＜飽きる｜(v.)have had enough of＞(あか＝未然形)／で【で】〔接助〕＜～することなしに｜(prep.)without ～ing＞／こそ【こそ】〔係助〕＜強調｜(adv.)EMPHASIS＞／おもふ【想ふ】〔他ハ四〕＜愛しく思う｜(v.)love＞(おもは＝未然形)／む【む】〔助動マ四型〕婉曲＜意味なし｜(adv.)NO MEANING＞(む＝連体形)／なか【仲】〔名〕＜関係｜(n.)relationship＞／は【は】〔係助〕＜主格｜(prep.)SUBJECT＞／はなる【離る】〔自ラ下二〕＜離れる｜(v.)part from each other＞(はなれ＝未然形)／ぬ【ぬ】〔助動ナ変型〕確述＜きっと～する｜(adv.)EMPHASIS＞(な＝未然形)／む【む】〔助動マ四型〕妥当＜～がよいだろう｜(aux-v.)had better＞(め＝已然形係り結び)／そ【其】〔代名〕＜それ｜(pron.)that＞／を【を】〔格助〕＜目的格｜(prep.)OBJECT＞／だに【だに】〔副助〕＜～さえ｜(adv.)even＞／のち【後】〔名〕＜後｜(adv.)afterwards＞／の【の】〔格助〕＜の｜(prep.)'s＞／**(A)わすれがたみ【忘れ形見】【名】**＜忘れないようにするための印｜(n.)a keepsake＞／**(B1)わすれがたし【忘れ難し】【形】**＜忘れられない｜(adj.)hard to forget＞(わすれがた＝語幹)／**(B2)み【み】【接助】**＜理由｜(conj.)REASON＞／に【に】〔格助〕＜様態｜(prep.)like＞

[aka-de koso omowa-mu naka wa hanare-na-me so wo-dani nochi no wasure-gatami ni]

「チーズケーキは半分だけかじって後は残しておきなさい、残りの半分が恋しくなって、再び手を付けずにはいられなくなるように」というアドバイスだけど、あまりに素面(しらふ)なその響き、本当の恋に酔(よ)ってるカップル(こいびとたち)には効き目なさそう ― お互いどうし貪(むさぼ)り尽くすまで、恋する男女は止まらない。

Leave the cheese cake half-bitten so that you'll miss the better half so much that you can't wait to touch it again. A piece of advice too sober for real lovers to accept — they won't stop until they devour each other up.

●127● つらかりしこころならひにあひみても　なほゆめかとぞうたがはれける
辛かりし心馴らひに逢ひ見ても猶夢かとぞ疑はれける

【恋愛】[後朝『5)金葉集:397』源行宗(みなもとのゆきむね)

恋しても恋してもつれない態度で私の求愛を拒み続けたあなた、その薄情さにすっかり馴らされてしまい、念願叶ってこうして生身でお逢いしてもなお(これは夢の中の出来事なのではないか)と、信じられない気分の私です。

So long have I endured not being allowed to meet you
That this morning I still wonder if I saw you only in my dream.

つらし【辛し】[形ク]＜冷淡だ｜(adj.)cold-hearted＞(つらかり＝連用形)／き【き】[助動特殊型]過去＜〜[し]た｜(aux-v.)PAST＞(し＝連体形)／こころならひ【心馴らひ】[名]＜精神的惰性｜(n.)emotion of inertia＞／に【に】[格助]＜原因｜(prep.)REASON＞／あひみる【逢ひ見る】[他マ上一]＜[恋人と]逢い引きする｜(v.)have a date＞(あひみ＝連用形)／ても【ても】[接助]＜〜[し]ても｜(conj.)although＞／なほ【猶】[副]＜それでもなお｜(adv.)still＞／ゆめ【夢】[名]＜夢｜(n.)a dream＞／か【か】[助助]＜疑問｜(adv.)INTERROGATIVE＞／と【と】[格助]＜内容提示｜(conj.)that 〜＞／ぞ【ぞ】[係助]＜強調｜(adv.)EMPHASIS＞／うたがふ【疑ふ】[他ハ四]＜疑｜(v.)doubt＞(うたがは＝未然形)／る【る】[助動ラ下二型]自発＜[思わず知らず]そうなる｜(adv.)naturally＞(れ＝連用形)／けり【けり】[助動ラ変型]過去＜〜[し]た｜(aux-v.)PAST＞(ける＝連体形係り結び)

[tsurakari-shi kokoro-narai ni ai-mi-te-mo nao yume ka-to-zo utagawa-re-keru]

男から女への「後朝の文」の体裁で作られた虚構歌。恨み言かましつつ夢見心地で語ってる雰囲気が面白い‥‥一夜限りの夢舞台に終わらなければいいけれど‥‥でもまぁ、もしこの心持ちが男の側で長持ちするならば(＝一度寝ただけでもう「彼女は俺のもの！」みたいに馴れ馴れしくならずにいられるならば)、彼女の側から絶縁状叩き付けられることは(当面)ないでしょう。夢を悪夢に変えないために必要なことは、延々だらだら長続けないこと‥‥悪夢の最悪の特性は「終わりの見えない堂々巡り」‥‥一緒に寝て起きてを繰り返す関係になっても、毎日毎日違う何かを見られる夢があれば、「馴れ馴れ死に」は避けられるはず(‥‥たぶん‥‥)

A fictional TANKA on the theme of 後朝の文(kinuginu no fumi＝a morning-after love letter from a man to a woman), amusing song at once complaining and dreaming... hope it won't turn out to have been a one-night-stand. But if that state of mind should persist on the side of the man, without taking it for granted that a single night with a woman entitles him to be her master, then, she shouldn't give him flat refusal for the time being. So as not to make a nightmare out of a dream, it should not be continued without a break... the most nightmarish trait of a nightmare is its endless continuation... countless nights and mornings together with your loved one would not (hopefully) make you tied up and tired to death from nauseating inertia, with a bit of dream different from day to day.

—恋愛—

★128★きみがためをしからざりしいのちさへ ながくもがなとおもひけるかな
君が為惜しからざりし命さへ永くもがなと思ひけるかな

【恋愛】[後朝]『4)後拾遺集:669』藤原義孝(ふじわらのよしたか)

「あなたの恋人になれるなら命を投げ出してもかわまない」と思っていた私でしたが、あなたと相思相愛の仲になった今では「この命が、あなたと二人、出来るかぎり長く続いたらいいなぁ」と思うようになりました。

I had thought I could give up my life for you, if only I could be your lover...
Now that you and I are in love with each other,
I hope we can live our happy life together as long as we can.

きみ【君】[代名]<あなた｜(pron.)you>／が【が】[格助]<の｜(prep.)'s>／ため【為】[名]<ため｜(n.)sake>／をし【惜】[形シク]<なくなるのを残念に思う｜(v.)be sorry to lose>[をしから=未然形]／ず【ず】[助動特殊型]打消<~[し]ない｜(adv.)not ~>[ざり=連用形]／き【き】[助動特殊型]過去<~[し]た｜(aux-v.)PAST>[し=連体形]／いのち【命】[名]<生命｜(n.)my life>／さへ【さへ】[副助]<さえ｜(adv.)even>／ながし【永し】[形ク]<長い｜(adj.)long>[ながく=連用形]／もがな【もがな】[終助]<~があってほしいな｜(adv.)hopefully>／と【と】[格助]<内容提示｜(conj.)that ~>／おもふ【思ふ】[他ハ四]<思う｜(v.)think>[おもひ=連用形]／けり【けり】[助動ラ変型]詠嘆<~だったのだなぁ｜(interj.)REALIZATION>[ける=連体形]／かな【かな】[終助]<詠嘆｜(interj.)EXCLAMATION>

[kimi-ga tame oshikara-zari-shi inochi sae nagaku-mogana to omoi-keru kana]

「惜しからざりし命」の辿った冒険物語···第一幕)彼は一人ぼっちで惨めな人生にうんざりして「こんな命、捨ててもいいや」と思っていました;第二幕)彼はある女性に燃えるような恋をして「この女性とたとえ一度きりでも逢瀬が叶うなら、引き換えにこの惨めな命を捨ててもいい」と思いました;第三幕)彼女は彼の愛情とその「惨めな人生」を受け入れて、それはもう幸せで実のあるものに変えてくれました:だから今、彼はこう思っています ── この命が、彼女の人生ともども、できるだけ長く続いたらいいなぁ···何ともドラマチックな「後朝の文」···二十歳でその人生を閉じることになる一人の薄幸の歌人の物語です。

The adventure story of 惜しからざりし命(oshikara-zari-shi inochi＝my life that I didn't hesitate to give up)... ACT-1) He felt his miserably solitary life was such that *he didn't mind giving it up in desperation*; ACT-2) He fell so much in love with a woman that *he felt he could gladly give up his miserable life in exchange for meeting her, if only once!*; ACT-3) She accepted his love along with his miserable life, which she made so happily substantial that, now, *he hopes his life ── along with hers ── will last as long as it can*... A dramatic 後朝の文(kinuginu no fumi＝morning-after love letter) by an unhappy poet who was to end his life at the age of 20.

★129★わすれじのゆくすゑまではかたければ けふをかぎりのいのちともがな
忘れじの行く末迄は難ければ今日を限りの命ともがな

【恋愛】[願望]『8)新古今集:1149』藤原伊周母高階貴子(ふじわらのこれちかのははたかしなのきし)

「君のことを忘れはしない」と誓ってくれたあなた···だけどその誓いがこの先ずっと変わらず続くのは難しい···だから、私の命も今日この日限り、あなたに愛されていることを確信したままで、いっそこのまま尽きてしまえばいいのに。

I wish you'd never forget your words "Never would I forget you."
Who am I to ask for better days than today you love me so much?
Would that my life, on this happiest day, came to a close so close to you.

わする【忘る】〔他ラ下二〕＜忘れる｜(v.)forget＞(わすれ＝未然形)／じ【じ】〔助動特殊型〕打消意志＜〜ないつもりだ｜(aux-v.)be not going to 〜＞(じ＝終止形)／の【の】〔格助〕＜主格｜(prep.)SUBJECT＞／ゆくすゑ【行く末】〔名〕＜最後の最後｜(n.)the very end＞／まで【迄】〔副助〕＜〜まで｜(prep.)until 〜＞／は【は】〔係助〕＜〜に関しては｜(adv.)as for 〜＞／かたし【難し】〔形ク〕＜難しい｜(adj.)difficult＞(かたけれ＝已然形)／ば【ば】〔接助〕＜理由｜(conj.)REASON＞／けふ【今日】〔名〕＜今日｜(n.)today＞／を【を】〔格助〕＜主格｜(prep.)SUBJECT＞／かぎり【限り】〔名〕＜おしまい｜(n.)the end＞／の【の】〔格助〕＜の｜(prep.)'s＞／いのち【命】〔名〕＜生命｜(n.)my life＞／と【と】〔格助〕＜結末｜(prep.)RESULT＞／もがな【もがな】〔終助〕＜〜があってほしいな｜(adv.)hopefully＞

[wasure-ji no yuku-sue made wa katakere-ba kyou wo kagiri no inochi to-mogana]

「真実の愛」の誓いの有効期限なんて、あっけないくらい短いもの；ならばいっそこの私の命の方が、その誓いが真に真実であることを信じられる今日この日のうちに、尽きてしまえばいいのに・・・と、こんなふうに「生・死」を軽々しくもてあそんでも、平安調短歌の中では不謹慎のそしりは受けませんでした・・・実際には、この歌を詠んだ女性、相手の男性から死ぬまでずっと本当に愛されて、三男四女を産むことになります。そして彼らはあの有名な清少納言の随筆『枕草子』の主人公たちになるのです。

An oath of true love will expire only too soon; if so, I wish my life would expire today while the oath is truly true... flirting with life and death like this was no blasphemy in Heianese TANKA. In actuality, the woman who rhymed it out had herself truly loved by the man until his death, giving rise to 3 boys and 4 girls, who would become the key players in the famous essay 枕草子(Makura no soushi) by 清少納言(Sei shou-nagon).

●130●まつよひにふけゆくかねのこゑきけば あかぬわかれのとりはものかは
待つ宵に更け行く鐘の声聞けば飽かぬ別れの鳥はものかは

【恋愛】[謎掛]『8)新古今集:1191』石清水別当光清女(いわしみずのべっとうみつきよのむすめ)

「あぁ、もう日が暮れる(・・・あなた、早く、来て！)」と祈る思いで聞く夕方の鐘の音の切なさに比べたら、「えぇっ、もう朝なの？(・・・まだ物足りない、もう少し一緒にこの夜を過ごしたい！)」という気持ちに水を差す明け方の 鶏 の鳴き声の悲しさなんて、物の数にも入りません。

When waiting for you to come, the sound of church-bell sounds sad.
The more dings I hear at night, the less likely you are to come.
When spending a night with you, *cock-a-doodle-doos* sound nasty.
Prompted by the morning bird, you feel like leaving me soon.
If asked which is worse, I say birds are nothing to bells.
I could bear him soon going; can't bear him *not coming*!

まつ【待つ】〔他夕四〕＜待つ｜(v.)wait＞(まつ＝連体形)／よひ【宵】〔名〕＜夜の早い時間｜(n.)early evening＞／に【に】〔格助〕＜時｜(prep.)TIME＞／ふく【更く】〔自カ下二〕＜夜遅くなる｜(v.)get late＞(ふけ＝連用形)／ゆく【行く】〔自カ四〕＜次第に〜になる｜(v.)come to 〜＞(ゆく＝連体形)／かね【鐘】〔名〕＜時刻を告げる鐘｜(n.)the toll to tell the hour＞／の【の】〔格助〕＜の｜(prep.)'s＞／こゑ【声】〔名〕＜音｜(n.)the sound＞／きく【聞く】〔他力四〕＜聞く｜(v.)hear＞(きけ＝已然形)／ば【ば】〔接助〕＜仮定｜(conj.)if＞／あく【飽く】〔自カ四〕＜飽きる｜(v.)have had enough of＞(あか＝未然形)／ず【ず】〔助動特殊型〕打消＜〜[し]ない｜(adv.)not 〜＞(ぬ＝連体形)／わかれ【別れ】〔名〕＜別れ｜(n.)parting＞／の【の】〔格助〕＜の｜(prep.)'s＞／とり【鳥】〔名〕＜朝鳴くニワトリ｜(n.)a cock crying early in the morning＞／は【は】〔係助〕＜主格｜(prep.)SUBJECT＞／ものかは【物かは】〔終助〕＜物の数ではない｜(v.)count for nothing＞

—恋愛—

[matsu yoi ni fuke-yuku kane no koe kike-ba aka-nu-wakare no tori wa mono-kawa]
「来ぬ人を空しく待ちつつ深夜を告げる寺の鐘の音を聞く」のと「愛する人と寝床の運動会に燃え上がってる最中に水を差すような早朝の鳥の声を聞く」のと、どっちが悲しい？という「品定め」の短歌。

This is a 品定め(shina sadame＝appraisal) TANKA on the theme of "Which is sadder, waiting in vain for a lover with the bell in the temple announcing midnight in the background, or hearing the early-morning bird announcing dawn while hotly engaged in physical exercise in bed with a lover?"

●131●ありあけのつれなくみえしわかれより　あかつきばかりうきものはなし
有明のつれなく見えし別れより暁ばかり憂き物は無し

【恋愛】[謎掛]『1)古今集:625』壬生忠岑(みぶのただみね)

夜が終わっても、明け方の空に、名残惜しげに残る月···あなたと一緒に過ごした素晴らしい夜が早くも明けてしまったその朝のせっかちさが薄情に感じられた、あなたとのお別れのあの時以来、私にとって、夜明け時ほど心に辛く感じるものは、他にありません
(···この辛さから私を救い出せるのはあなたただ一人 ― どうかもう一度、私と逢ってください！)

> Moon in the morn as vacant as my heart,
> Gone was the night, so was my love.
> Nothing since then gives me so much grief
> As downhearted dawn I greet without you.
> (...*You are the only one to save me from this pain: please meet me again!*)

ありあけ【有明】[名]＜夜が明けて後も空に残る月｜(n.)the remaining moon from the previous night＞／の【の】[格助]＜主格｜(prep.)SUBJECT＞／つれなし【つれなし】[形ク]＜薄情だ｜(adj.)cold-hearted＞(つれなく＝連用形)／みゆ【見ゆ】[自ヤ下二]＜見える｜(v.)appear＞(みえ＝連用形)／き【き】[助動特殊型]過去＜～[し]た｜(aux-v.)PAST＞(し＝連体形)／わかれ【別れ】[名]＜別れ｜(n.)parting＞／より【より】[格助]＜～から｜(prep.)since＞／あかつき【暁】[名]＜夜明け時｜(n.)the dawn＞／ばかり【ばかり】[副助]＜～と同じくらいに｜(adv.)as much as ～＞／うし【憂し】[形ク]＜憂鬱だ｜(adj.)melancholy＞(うき＝連体形)／もの【物】[名]＜物｜(n.)a thing＞／は【は】[係助]＜主格｜(prep.)SUBJECT＞／なし【なし】[形ク]＜存在しない｜(v.)do not exist＞(なし＝終止形)

[ariake no tsurenaku mie-shi wakare yori akatsuki bakari uki mono wa nashi]

「難解の巨匠」壬生忠岑の手になる、おそらくは短歌の全歴史を通じて最も誤解されている歌。短歌通を気取る日本人の大部分がこの歌のことを単なる「明け方にかけてこの詩人に惨めな思いをさせた恋人に対する恨み言」と思い込んでる ― もしそうだとしたらこれは救いようがないほど醜悪な歌···だけど実際にはこの歌は、持って回った「どうもありがとう」の宣言であると同時に「もう一度逢いたくてあいたくて死にそうです」の含みを持たせた短歌。普通の人なら「**あの夜はあなたと一緒**でもう**最高**でした！」と言うところ、この詩人は「**あれ以来、一人ぼっち**の明け方はもう**最悪**です」と言いつつ、優しい助けの手が伸びるのを期待しているのです···理解した末に救いの手を差し伸べるか、誤解したままこの歌[人]を毛嫌いして終わるか、あなたの反応は、どっちでしょうか？

Arguably the most misunderstood TANKA of all time by "the master of complication" 壬生忠岑 (Mibu-no-Tadamine). Most would-be connoisseurs in Japan believe this TANKA to be a mere grievance against a cruel man/woman who made the poet miserable towards dawn — how hopelessly ugly it would be if that was the case! In fact, it's a complicated declaration of gratitude and implication that [s]he is dying for another date. When ordinary folks would say "What a ***wonderful*** night we had *together*!", this poet says "What ***miserable*** dawns I've had *alone* since", hoping for graceful rescue... which would come out of you, an understanding salvage, or a misunderstood despise?

―恋愛―

●132● かずかずにおもひおもはずとひがたみ みをしるあめはふりぞまされる
数々に思ひ思はず問ひ難み身を知る雨は降りぞ増される

【恋愛】[謎掛]『1)古今集:705』在原業平(ありわらのなりひら)

「私のこと、愛してくれてます？」などとあなたにしつこくお尋ねすることもできない私は、「愛してくれてれば雨は降らないから、あの人はきっと訪ねて来る」/「愛されてないなら雨降りで、あの人は私のことなど忘れてしまう」と、空模様であなたの気持ちを占っています・・・けど、今、私は知りました、愛されてない自分の悲しい境遇を・・・外は雨、それもますます、ひどい雨 ― 私のこと、もう、愛してくれてないんですね。

"Do you or do you not love me?"
— That's not the kind of question I can ask you too many times.
Instead of asking you, I'll just ask the sky if you really love me or not.
It seems the answer is in the negative
— Rain keeps falling down ever more heavily,
Preventing you from coming,
Drowning me alone in the raging river of tears.

かずかずなり【数数】〔形動ナリ〕<あまりしつこく│(adv.)too persistently>(かずかずに=連用形)/おもふ【想ふ】〔他ハ四〕<愛しく思う│(v.)love>(おもひ=連用形)/おもふ【想ふ】〔他ハ四〕<愛しく思う│(v.)love>(おもは=未然形)/ず【ず】〔助動特殊型〕打消<〜[し]ない│(adv.)not 〜>(ず=終止形)/とふ【問ふ】〔他ハ四〕<質問する│(v.)ask>(とひ=連用形)/かたし【難し】〔形ク〕<難しい│(adj.)difficult>(がた=語幹)/み【み】〔接尾〕<理由│(conj.)REASON>/み【身】〔名〕<自分の立場│(n.)my situation>/を【を】〔格助〕<目的格│(prep.)OBJECT>/しる【知る】〔他ラ四〕<知る│(v.)know>(しる=連体形)/あめ【雨】〔名〕<雨│(n.)rain>/は【は】〔係助〕<主格│(prep.)SUBJECT>/ふる【降る】〔自ラ四〕<降る│(v.)fall>(ふり=連用形)/ぞ【ぞ】〔係助〕<強調│(adv.)EMPHASIS>/まさる【増さる】〔自ラ四〕<より一層〜になる│(adv.)increasingly>(まされ=已然形・命令形)/り【り】〔助動ラ変型〕存続<〜[し]ている│(aux-v.)PERFECT TENSE>(る=連体形係り結び)

[kazukazuni omoi omowa-zu toi-gata-mi mi wo shiru ame wa furi-zo-masare-ru]

ある男が付き合ってる女性に向かってこんなメッセージを送りました ―「空模様が怪しいです。もし雨が降って愛するあなたのところへ行けなくなったりしたら、残念です」― これに対して彼女は(実際には彼女の代筆者の在原業平ですが)この短歌を返答として送りました・・・その後はどうなったか？・・・土砂降りの雨の中、彼は大慌てで飛んで来ました ― 傘もささず、蓑笠もまとわず、雨にも消えぬ恋心を燃え上がらせて、一目散に彼女のもとへ！・・・『伊勢物語』に収められた恋物語の中でもとびきりハッピーなお話で、ここでの「男」は藤原敏行、いつもは主人公役の業平は、ここでは優しい恋のキューピッドとして活躍しています。

A man sends a message to the woman he is going steady with ― "The sky looks threatening. I'll be so sorry if the rain falls and prevents me from coming to love you" ― to which the woman, in actual fact, her ghostwriter 在原業平(Ariwara-no-Narihira), replies with this TANKA... What happened afterwards? The man who received this song came rushing in the torrential rain, without an umbrella, without wearing a raincoat, with nothing but his burning heart unquenched by the rain! No other story is happier than this one in 伊勢物語(Ise monogatari), in which the man in question is 藤原敏行 (Fujiwara-no-Toshiyuki), while the usual hero 業平(Narihira) plays the role of a benign Cupid.

http//zubaraie.com ―131― ―Love―

—恋愛— —悲恋—

●133●きみをおきてあだしごゝろをわがもたば すゑのまつやまなみもこえなむ
君を置きて徒し心を我が持たば末の松山波も越えなむ

【恋愛】[謎掛]『1)古今集:1093』詠み人知らず

大事なあなたを差し置いて浮気心(うわきごころ)をもし私が持つようなことがあれば、
「どんな津波(つなみ)も決してここまでは到達しない」と言われるあの末の松山を津波が越えることになるでしょう…
天地がひっくり返ってもそんなこと絶対あり得ません！

If I should have my mind wander off from you to someone else,
Waves from the sea would come beyond Sue-no-matsuyama to drown me.

きみ【君】〔代名〕<あなた│(pron.)you>／を【を】〔格助〕<目的格│(prep.)OBJECT>／おく【置く】〔他カ四〕<さしおく│(v.)put ~ aside>（おき＝連用形）／て【て】〔接助〕<順接│(conj.)and>／あだしごころ【徒し心】〔名〕<浮気心│(n.)unfaithful heart>／を【を】〔格助〕<目的格│(prep.)OBJECT>／わ【我】〔代名〕<私│(pron.)I, myself>／が【が】〔格助〕<主格│(prep.)SUBJECT>／もつ【持つ】〔他タ四〕<持つ│(v.)have>（もた＝未然形）／ば【ば】〔接助〕<仮定│(conj.)if>／すゑのまつやま【末の松山】〔名〕<[固有名詞]末の松山│(n.)the small hill of Sue-no-Matsuyama>／なみ【波】〔名〕<津波│(n.)tidal waves>／も【も】〔係助〕<～もまた│(adv.)also>／こゆ【越ゆ】〔自ヤ下二〕<超える│(v.)go beyond>（こえ＝連用形）／ぬ【ぬ】〔助動ナ変型〕確述<きっと～する│(adv.)EMPHASIS>（な＝未然形）／む【む】〔助動マ四型〕推量<だろう│(aux-v.)SUPPOSITION>（む＝連体形）

[kimi wo oki-te adashi-gokoro wo wa-ga mota-ba Sue-no-matsuyama nami mo koe-na-mu]

905年の『古今集』発刊に先立つことほぼ半世紀の紀元869年、「貞観地震(じょうがん)」と呼ばれる壊滅的大地震が東日本を直撃しました。地震の余波で沿岸一帯は津波に襲われましたが、その波は「末の松山」と呼ばれる小高い丘(こだか)にまでは達しませんでした…千年以上経(た)った2011年にも同じ事が起こっています。この「末の松山までは津波も来ない」という防災上の教訓は、その後「末の松山越す波」という形で「あり得ない事」の隠喩となり、やがては（ここに紹介した短歌のおかげで）「決して変わることなき愛情の誓(ちか)い」へと姿を変えて行くことになります。この隠喩的な愛の誓約(せいやく)としての「末の松山」を含む短歌は、八代集約9500首のうちの20首に上ります。

Prior by about a half-century to the publication of 古今集 (Kokin shuu) in A.D. 905, a disastrous earthquake hit the eastern part of Japan in A.D. 869 — 貞観地震 (Jougan earthquake). In the aftermath of the quake, waves of tsunami hit the coastal region, but a small hill called 末の松山(Sue-no-matsuyama) was safe from the waves... the same thing happened more than a millennium later in 2011. The anti-disaster lesson of this tsunami-immune hill of 末の松山(Sue-no-matsuyama) came to transform itself into 末の松山越す波(Sue-no-matsuyama kosu nami＝waves beyond the tsunami-immune hill) as a metaphor for something impossible, then into an oath of never-changing affection (thanks to this particular TANKA). This metaphoric hill of changeless affection appears in 20 poems among some 9,500 TANKA of 八代集(Hachidai shuu＝8 great Imperial TANKA anthologies).

—悲恋:Sad Love—

●134●いつはりのなきよなりせばいかばかり ひとのことのはうれしからまし
偽りの無き世なりせば如何ばかり人の言の葉嬉しからまし

【悲恋】[謎掛]『1)古今集:712』詠み人知らず

―悲恋―

もしもこの世に嘘・偽りというものがなければ、あなたの口から出る優しい言葉、
どれほど嬉しく感じることでしょう（・・・実際には、あまり当てにならなそうなのが悲しいのだけれど）。

How glad I would be to be greeted with your gentle words
If only there were no lies in this untrustworthy world!

いつはり【偽り】［名］＜ウソ｜(n.)falsehood＞／の【の】［格助］＜主格｜(prep.)SUBJECT＞／なし【なし】［形ク］＜存在しない｜(v.)do not exist＞（なき＝連体形）／よ【世】［名］＜世間｜(n.)the world＞／なり【なり】［助動ナリ型］断定＜～である｜(aux-v.)be＞（なり＝連用形）／き【き】［助動特殊型］過去＜～[し]た｜(aux-v.)PAST＞（せ＝未然形）／ば【ば】［接助］＜仮定｜(conj.)if＞／いかばかり【如何ばかり】［副］＜どれほど｜(adv.)just how much＞／ひと【人】［名］＜あの人｜(n.)that [darling] one＞／の【の】［格助］＜の｜(prep.)'s＞／ことのは【言の葉】［名］＜言葉｜(n.)words＞／うれし【嬉し】［形シク］＜嬉しい｜(adj.)happy＞（うれしから＝未然形）／まし【まし】［助動特殊型］推量＜～だろうに｜(aux-v.)should＞（まし＝連体形係り結び）

[itsuwari no naki yo nari-se-ba ika-bakari hito no koto-no-ha ureshikara-mashi]

恋の前哨戦で甘い言葉投げ込んで来る相手に向けて投げ返したちょっぴり皮肉な切り返し。警戒八分／陶酔二分の響きあり。恋愛場面以外でも、無し意味に脹れ上がったＳＮＳ（Social Network System「あなたに注目してます」の野次馬さんたち）フォロワー連や、何ということもないコメント巡って延々鳴り響く虚ろな賛辞へのお礼の歌にも使えそう。

A cynical counter-punch to someone who throws in sweet words in amorous overture. Sounds mostly cautious yet partly rapturous. Might as well be applied to meaninglessly swollen numbers of SNS followers and the resounding echoes of hollow praises regarding your casual comments.

●135●いつはりとおもふものからいまさらに　たがまことをかわれはたのまむ
偽りと思ふものから今更に誰が誠をか我は頼まむ

【悲恋】［溜息］『1)古今集:713』詠み人知らず

(どうせ今回もまた嘘なんでしょ・・・)と思うのだけれど、
さりとて今更あなた以外の誰の誠実を、私は信じたらよいのでしょう？(もう、あなたしかいないんです、私)

What fool would I be to trust your words again?
Who else should I trust? How inured to your lies am I!

いつはり【偽り】［名］＜ウソ｜(n.)falsehood＞／と【と】［格助］＜内容提示｜(conj.)that ～＞／おもふ【思ふ】［他ハ四］＜思う｜(v.)think＞（おもふ＝終止形）／ものから【ものから】［接助］＜～ではあるものの｜(conj.)although＞／いまさらなり【今更なり】［形動ナリ］＜今さら｜(adv.)after all this time＞（いまさらに＝連用形）／た【誰】［代名］＜誰｜(pron.)who＞／が【が】［格助］＜の｜(prep.)'s＞／まこと【誠】［名］＜誠実｜(n.)faith＞／を【を】［格助］＜目的格｜(prep.)OBJECT＞／か【か】［係助］＜疑問｜(adv.)INTERROGATIVE＞／われ【我】［代名］＜私｜(pron.)I, myself＞／は【は】［係助］＜主格｜(prep.)SUBJECT＞／たのむ【頼む】［他マ四］＜当てにする｜(v.)expect＞（たのま＝未然形）／む【む】［助動マ四型］意志＜～するつもりだ｜(aux-v.)be going to ～＞（む＝連体形係り結び）

[itsuwari to omou monokara imasarani ta-ga makoto wo-ka ware wa tanoma-mu]

愛しすぎて疑えない、というか、貸しが大きすぎて御破算にできない関係。借方があくまで嘘付き続ければ、普通、人生は破滅だけど、恋仲の場合は大方丸く収まる。恋嘘の罠に落ちたなら、毒喰らわば皿まで。

Too much in love to doubt, or too much in credit to dissolve partnership. Should the debtor keep lying, everything will be ruined in normal life, but most will be fine in love affairs. Once in doubtful love, in for a penny, in for a pound.

―悲恋―

★136★ちぎりおきしひともこずゑのこのまより　たのめしつきのかげぞもりくる
契り置きし人もこずゑの木の間より頼めし月の影ぞ漏り来る

【悲恋】[溜息]『5)金葉集:464』摂政家堀河（せっしょうけのほりかわ）

「今夜、君を訪ねて行くからね」と約束したはずのあの人はやって来ぬままに、夜道のあの人を我が家に導いてくれるはずの月影だけが、木の間を透かして律儀にも私の部屋まで入ってくる。

The night you promised to come has come, but you have not; I'm alone.

Only the moon has come through the trees to show you the way... in vain, it seems.

ちぎりおく【契り置く】[自カ四]＜約束する｜(v.)promise＞(ちぎりおき＝連用形)／き【き】[助動特殊型]過去＜〜[し]た｜(aux-v.)PAST＞(し＝連体形)／ひと【人】[名]＜あの人｜(n.)that [darling] one＞／も【も】[係助]＜意味なし｜(adv.)NO MEANING＞／**(A1)く【来】[自カ変]**＜来る｜(v.)come＞(こ＝未然形)／**(A2)ず【ず】[助動特殊型]打消**＜〜[し]ない｜(adv.)not 〜＞(ず＝終止形)／**(B)こずゑ【梢】[名]**＜こずゑ｜(n.)the end of a branch＞／の【の】[格助]＜の｜(prep.)'s＞／こ【木】[名]＜木｜(n.)a tree＞／の【の】[格助]＜の｜(prep.)'s＞／ま【間】[名]＜隙間｜(n.)a space＞／より【より】[格助]＜〜から｜(prep.)from＞／たのむ【頼む】[他マ四]＜当てにする｜(v.)expect＞(たのめ＝連用形)／き【き】[助動特殊型]過去＜〜[し]た｜(aux-v.)PAST＞(し＝連体形)／つき【月】[名]＜月｜(n.)the moon＞／の【の】[格助]＜の｜(prep.)'s＞／かげ【影】[名]＜光｜(n.)the light＞／ぞ【ぞ】[係助]＜強調｜(adv.)EMPHASIS＞／もりく【漏り来】[自カ変]＜漏れて来る｜(v.)leak＞(もりくる＝連体形係り結び)

[chigiri-oki-shi hito mo kozu...e no ko-no-ma yori tanome-shi tsuki no kage zo mori-kuru]

平安の世の女性たちが数限りなく味わってきた残念な場面を、説得力ある情景描写で見事に表現した短歌で、「こずゑ」という語が「来ず」と「梢」とにまたがる懸詞として巧みに用いられています。

A disappointing scene suffered by countless Heianese women perfectly represented with visual persuasion, in which the clever use of the term こずゑ(kozue) shines brilliantly working as 懸詞(kake-kotoba＝puns) between 来ず(kozu＝does not come) and 梢(kozue＝the end of a branch).

★137★よもすがらものおもふころはあけやらで　ねやのひまさへつれなかりけり
夜もすがら物思ふ頃は明けやらで閨の隙さへつれなかりけり

【悲恋】[溜息]『7)千載集:766』俊恵（しゅんえ）

更け行く夜の中、来てもくれないあの人のことを想いつつ、一人、為すこともない寝室で持て余す長い夜は、(もう早く終わって、朝になってしまって！)とジリジリする思いで過ごすのに、なかなか夜明けは来てくれなくて(もちろんあの人も来てくれなくて)板戸の隙間から漏れ来るはずの朝の光さえ、(いつになったら来てくれるのかしら)と、その薄情さに文句を言いたい気分になるもの。

Sleepless night without you in sight

Spent alone along with wistful sighs

Scarcely breaks into merciful morn...

Should I have to mourn for its desertion, too?

よもすがら【夜もすがら】[副]＜夜通し｜(adv.)all through the night＞／もの【物】[名]＜あれこれ色々｜(n.)one thing or another＞／おもふ【思ふ】[他ハ四]＜思う｜(v.)think＞(おもふ＝連体形)／ころ【頃】[名]＜頃｜(n.)a time when 〜＞／は【は】[係助]＜主格｜(prep.)SUBJECT＞／あく【明く】[自カ下二]＜夜が明ける｜(v.)break into the morning＞(あけ＝連用形)／やる【やる】[自ラ四]＜すっかり〜する｜(adv.)completely 〜＞(やら＝未然形)／で【で】[接助]＜〜することなしに｜(prep.)without 〜ing＞

ねや【寝屋】[名]＜寝室｜(n.)a bedroom＞／の【の】[格助]＜の｜(prep.)'s＞／**(A)ひま【暇】[名]**＜透き間｜(n.)an opening space＞／**(B)ひま【暇】[名]**＜何もする事のない時間｜(n.)leisure＞／さへ【さへ】[副助]＜さえ｜(adv.)even＞／つれなし【つれなし】[形ク]＜薄情だ｜(adj.)cold-hearted＞（つれなかり＝連用形）／けり【けり】[助動ラ変型]詠嘆＜だったのだなぁ｜(interj.)REALIZATION＞（けり＝終止形）
[yo-mo-sugara mono-omou koro wa ake-yara-de ne-ya no hima sae tsurenakari-keri]
これまた一人寂しい平安女性の哀歌、ただしこちらは男性の歌僧の詠んだ想像上の歌…とはいえ、あまりに見事に創られているので、その「ニセモノ性」を批判するのもナンセンス、と言えるほどの上出来歌。
Another elegy of a forlorn Heianese woman, only this time an imaginary poem made by a male 歌僧 (kasou＝singing bonze), so exquisitely created as to make it meaningless to criticize the fake identity.

★138★よにふるはくるしきものをまきのやに　やすくもすぐるはつしぐれかな
よに経るは苦しきものを槙の屋に安くも過ぐる初時雨かな

【悲恋】[謎掛]『8)新古今集:590』二条院讃岐（にじょういんのさぬき）
何となく煮え切らない思いにじいじいしている間に、私の花の色ももう移ろってしまったのかしら…この頃、あの人、私に会いに来てくれない…えっ？あら、なに、戸口を叩くこの音は、もしかして彼、来てくれたの？…あらやだ、なぁーんだ、時雨が屋根を叩く音か…いやだわ、もう、紛らわしいったらありゃしない…どうせなら昼間のうちに降って。夜はやめて。あの人の足がますます遠のくじゃないの…でも、まぁ、降っても降らなくても同じかな、どのみち今の私はもう「世に旧る花の色」、色褪せた昔の恋人なんて、あの人は最初から訪ねて来る気もなさそうだから…そうよ、いっそ、盛大に降ってよね、時雨さん、「これだけ降られれば、もう絶対無理、あの人が来てくれるはずがない」と諦めがつくぐらい、土砂降りの雨、降らせて頂戴…え、何、もう終わりなの？もう降らないの？…そう、それなら、もしかしてあの人、来てくれるかしら？時雨さんみたいに軽くさーっと来て、さっさとまた去って行くだけでも私としては嬉しいんだけど…無理かなやっぱり…はぁ…苦しい。来てくれるんだか来ないんだか、愛してくれるんだかくれないんだか、待っていいんだか諦めて忘れるべきなんだか、何が何だかもう、わかんなくなってきちゃった……それもこれもみんな、そもそもあなたが悪いのよ、時雨さん、どうせなら夜通し激しく降り続けてくれれば、こんな宙ぶらりんな気持ち抱えて悶々と過ごす夜もないはずなのに…そうよ、あの人だってそう、激しく愛し続けてくれないなら、いっそきっぱり忘れさせてくれればいいのに…ああもう嫌い、あの人も、時雨も…はっきりさせて、お願い、この恋に未来はあるの、それともないの？　今はまだ秋なの、それとももう冬なの？これからずっとこんな調子で煮え切らない時雨模様、続いちゃうの？…

> Rainfall at night prevents my love from visiting
> This crestfallen flower sadly aware of its wane.
> Suddenly I hear it coming, *I hear him knock on the door...*
> *Oh no*, not on the door... on the roof taps the mischievous rain.
> Scatter as much as you may so as to drown my hope,
> And get me down to sleep this reasonably mateless night...
> But *alas*, it seems it's gone... *you too, this fleeting rain?*
> Rain gone, will he come, shall I hope once more?
> Is it still Fall... or lonely Winter already?

(A1)よ【夜】[名]＜夜｜(n.)the night＞／**(A2)に【に】[格助]**＜時｜(prep.)TIME＞／**(A3)ふる【降る】[自ラ四]**＜降る｜(v.)fall＞（ふる＝連体形）／**(B1)よ【世】[名]**＜世間｜(n.)the world＞／**(B2)に【に】[格助]**＜場所｜(prep.)PLACE＞／**(B3)ふ【経】[自ハ下二]**＜経る｜(v.)grow old＞（ふる＝連体形）／は【は】[係助]＜主格｜(prep.)SUBJECT＞／くるし【苦し】[形シク]＜苦しい｜(v.)feel painful＞（くるし

―悲恋―

＝連体形〕／ものを【ものを】〔接助〕＜〜[だ]というのに｜(conj.)although＞／まき【槇】〔名〕＜[スギ・ヒノキ等の]建築用良材｜(n.)cypress trees＞／の【の】〔格助〕＜の｜(prep.)'s＞／や【屋】〔名〕＜屋根｜(n.)the roof＞／に【に】〔格助〕＜場所｜(prep.)PLACE＞／やすし【易し】〔形ク〕＜やすやすと｜(adv.)easily＞(やすく＝連用形)／も【も】〔係助〕＜意味なし｜(adv.)NO MEANING＞／すぐ【過ぐ】〔自ガ上二〕＜過ぎる｜(v.)go away＞(すぐる＝連体形)／はつしぐれ【初時雨】〔名〕＜[晩秋から初冬に]初めて降る通り雨｜(n.)the first scattered rain towards the end of Autumn＞／かな【かな】〔終助〕＜詠嘆｜(interj.)EXCLAMATION＞

[yo ni furu wa kurushiki mono-wo maki no ya ni yasuku-mo suguru hatsu-shigure kana]

これは、平安調短歌の中でも最高に精緻な示唆に満ちた短歌と言ってよい作品、これを正しく解釈できる日本人は現代にはまず一人もいないだろう･･･『古今集』から『新古今集』まで300年にわたって蓄積された文化の伝統を完璧に知り尽くした人以外には到底理解できない歌である。なぜ**時雨**が「**苦しきもの**」なのか？「秋はおしまい、侘びしい冬に備えよ」の宣言だから？ ― よろしい、出だしは好調･･･だけどこの詩人、どうして**安くも過ぐる**などと文句を言っているのか？この歌詠み(女性である)は「雨が降り続く」のを望むのか？それと**よにふるは苦し**とはどういう意味か？また**槇の屋**でなきゃならない理由がわからない･･･よし、ではまず簡単な疑問から最初に片付けよう ― **時雨**が「苫屋(＝草葺き屋根)」に降ったら何が起こるだろうか？ ― 答えは「(スポンジ状の屋根に雨が吸収されるので)何の音も聞こえない」･･･つまり**槇の屋**(＝板葺き屋根)は、冬の夜の家の中から屋根を叩く雨の音を詩人が聞くのに必要な「舞台装置」なのである･･･あるいは「冬」ではなく「**晩秋から初冬**」と言い換えるべきかもしれない：詩人は**初時雨**と言っているのだから。さて最初の疑問点に戻ろうか ― 雨が**苦しきもの**である理由は何か？**よにふる**雨の音を屋根に聞くのが**苦しきもの**なのは何故か？その雨に「降り続いてほしい」とこの詩人が願う理由は？これらの疑問点は、解決を見ぬまま終わりのない堂々巡りへとあなたを誘うことだろう ― 迷宮を抜け出したければ、まずはこの歌の詠み手の「性別」「年齢」と「置かれた状況」を突き止めることである。すでに指摘した通り、この詩人は「女性」である。『新古今集』にそう書いてあるから、というだけの理由ではなく、判断根拠はちゃんと歌の中にある･･･男性ではなく女性の歌だとどうして言い切れるのか？彼女の年齢は？彼女は今どんな状況にある？最初の手掛かりは初句の中にある―**よにふる**･･･この言い回しを見て、平安朝短歌の中で最も有名なあの小野小町の短歌**花の色は移りにけりな徒らに我が身＜世にふる＞ながめせし間に**を思い出せないとしたらその人は「詩的文盲」である ― 我が身の美しさの盛りが、その女の魅力を喜んでくれる恋人もいないままに、空しく過ぎ去ろうとしているのを意識する女性の、悲しい孤独な溜息の聞こえてくるあの歌を思い起こせばわかるはず ― この歌を詠んだのは「独り身を続けるにはいささか年齢が行き過ぎた女性」、平安時代なら「十代後半から二十代前半」(現代に置き換えるならお好みの年齢分だけ積み増ししてください)･･･そしてこれまた**世に経るは苦し**の意味もわかったはず：一緒に年を取ってくれる男性もなしに、女が一人で年齢を重ねるのは、実に苦しいもの、という意味である。だが、ちょっと待て、**よにふる**の意味は本当にそれだけか？「**夜に降る**」の意味もあるのではないのか？･･･当然ありそうである：なにしろこれは**時雨**の歌なのだから。だが**夜に降るは苦し**とはどういう意味か？･･･ここで、もう一つ別の短歌(当時としては先程の小町歌と同じくらい有名だったやつ)を思い出して見よう：『**数々に思ひ思はず問ひ難み身を知る雨は降りぞ増される**』― 雨が降れば、男から女への「愛の訪問」は不可能になる。そう考えると、なるほど、雨が屋根を叩いて「諦めなさい、今夜は彼は来ないから」と告げる音を聞くのは**苦しきもの**となる･･･だが、待て待て、だとすると、この女性、どうして**安くも過ぐる**などと文句を言っているのか？雨がすぐに上がってくれれば、彼が夜に逢いに来てくれる可能性も上がるはずではないか？**安くも過ぐる**だなどと、喜びよりも文句を言っているのは何故なのか？「雨が降り続けばいいのに」と思う理由が彼女にはあるのか？･･･そう、実際、あるのである･･･ここでさらにまた別の短歌を思い起こしてみよう ― 『**同ならば闇にぞあらまし秋の夜の何ぞ月影の人頼めなる**』･･･夜に男が来てくれるのを空しく待ち続ける女性は、夜道の彼を導いてくれる「月」がなければ、その空しい期待を捨て去れるのである：同様に、「**烈しい雨**」が彼の来訪を邪魔してくれれば、女性は、意地悪な期待など捨て去って心安く眠りに就けるのだ･･･さぁこれでわかったろう、「これならもしかしたら(彼、来てくれるかも)」という宙ぶらりんの空しい期待

―Sad Love― http//zubaraie.com

―悲恋―

に女性を閉じ込める「安くも過ぐる」雨の意地悪さが・・・だが、待て待て待て、「男」の側では本当に彼女に「今夜、逢いに行くよ」と約束していたのか？もしそうだとしたら、雨が「安くも過ぐる」のは良いことだろうに。雨に「降り続いてほしい」と願うような彼女の口ぶりから判断するに、彼女の恋人の男は「今夜、逢いに行くよ」と彼女に約束していたとは思えない。そこからまた別の疑問が生じる ― 仮に「雨降り」ではなく「月」が明るかったなら夜に彼女を訪ねてくれる「恋人」が、そもそも彼女にはいたのだろうか？・・・「いなかった」と想像するのは馬鹿げているだろう。明らかにこの歌の空想世界のベースになっている先程の三つの短歌を思い起こしてみても、「男女の恋情」抜きには成立しない話なのだから・・・だが、たぶん、その「恋人」は彼女のことをあまり強く愛してはいないようだ。この短歌の全体的雰囲気は、荒涼としていて「熱愛」を感じさせないからである。では、何が男の愛の情熱を失わせたのか？おそらく、彼女は彼にとっていささか退屈な（あるいは、少々老けた）存在になってしまった、ということだろう・・・「初時雨」はただ単に「晩秋から初冬」の季節を示唆するのみならず、この女性が「女としての最終段階」にあることをも暗示しているのである ― それでも「晩秋」ならまだいいだろうが、もう「初冬」だとしたら、どうしたらいい？・・・彼女に出来ることは、恋人が来て愛して救ってくれるのを、ただ待つだけ・・・それもおそらくは、空しく待ち続けるだけ・・・と、これはそういう信じられないほど難解な一人の女性の悲劇なのである。今の世の中でこれを正しく理解できるのはおそらく、この解説を読んでくれた人たちだけ・・・おわかりいただけたであろうか、真に優れた短歌が創出し得る想像世界の可能性の、この驚くべき深遠さ！

Arguably the most exquisitely significant Heianese TANKA too difficult for practically every modern Japanese to correctly interpret... without perfect knowledge of the cultural tradition accumulated over 300 years since 古今集(Kokin shuu) to 新古今集(Shin-Kokin shuu). Why is 時雨(shigure＝scattered rain) 苦しきもの(kurushiki mono＝something painful)? Because it's the announcement "Autumn is over: get ready for bleak Winter" ― OK, so far so good. But why does the poet grumble 安くも過ぐる(yasuku mo suguru＝come and go so easily)? Does the poet ― a woman ― want the rain to keep falling? And what's the meaning of よにふるは苦し(yo ni furu wa kurushi)? ― scattered rain falling at night is painful? And why does it have to be 槙の屋(maki no ya＝a cypress roof)? OK, easy things first: think what would 時雨(shigure＝scattered rain) make on 苫屋(tomaya＝a thatched roof)? ― no sound at all, because the rain is absorbed in the spongy roof without a sound: 槙の屋(maki no ya＝a wooden rooftop) is a necessary stage for the poet to hear the rain tapping the roof of her house at night in Winter... or late Autumn to early Winter, since the poet says 初時雨(hatsu shigure＝the first scattered rain). Now, let's come back to the initial questions ― why is the rain painful? Or why is it painful to hear the rain tap the roof at night? Or why does the poet wish the rain would keep falling? All these questions will keep you wander in wonder through an endless labyrinth, until you decide on the sex, age and circumstances of the poet ― a female, as I've already pointed out, but not jut because 新古今集(Shin-Kokin shuu) tells us so... what makes you sure that the poet is not a "he", how old she is likely to be, and in what situation she finds herself now? The first clue lies in the first phrase ― よにふる(yo ni furu)... you are poetically illiterate if this doesn't remind you of the most famed of all Heianese TANKA by 小野小町(Ono-no-Komachi): 花の色は移りにけりな徒らに我が身＜世にふる＞ながめながめせしまに(hana no iro wa utsuri-ni-keri-na itazura-ni wa-ga mi ＜yo ni furu＞ nagame se-shi ma ni), a sad and lonely sigh of a woman who is conscious of the passing of her prime of beauty without having her womanly charm cherished by any particular man... now you see, the poet (she) is a woman a little too old to remain single ― in her late teens to early twenties in the Heian era... add as many years as you see fit to put her in the present day; now you also know the meaning of 世に経るは苦し(yo ni furu wa kurushi) ― it's really tough going past her prime without a man who will grow old beside her. But wait, is that all there is to よにふる(yo ni furu)? Doesn't it also mean "夜に降る：rain at night"? It seems it does, since it's a song about 時雨(shigure＝scattered rain); but why 夜に降るは苦し(yo ni furu wa kurushi＝it is painful for the rain to fall at night)? Well, remember another TANKA as famous as 小町

—悲恋—

(koomachi)'s in those days: 数々に思ひ思はず問ひ難み身を知る雨は降りぞ増される(kazu-kazu-ni omoi omowa-zu toi-gata-mi mi wo shiru ame wa furi-zo-masare-ru) — rain will prevent a man from paying an amorous visit to a woman: it certainly is painful to hear the rain tap on her rooftop, telling her "Give it up, he won't come tonight"... but wait, wait, if so, why does she grumble 安くも過ぐる(yasuku mo suguru＝the rain just goes away so easily)? The sooner the rain goes, the more likely he is to come to love her for the night, don't you think? Why does she grumble, instead of feeling glad, that the scattered rain just goes away so easily? Is there any reason for her to hope that the rain should keep falling?... well, in fact, there is: remember another TANKA — 同ならば闇にぞあらまし秋の夜の何ぞ月影の人頻めなる (koto-nara-ba yami ni-zo ara-mashi aki no yo no na-zo tsuki-kage no hito-danome-naru): a woman waiting for a man to come for the night in vain could give up her vain hope if only there was no moon to show him the way... likewise, if there was heavy rain to prevent him from coming, the woman could give up her nasty hope and get down to sleep peacefully. Now you can see how nasty for the rain to come and go so easily, leaving the woman in vainly hopeful suspense. But wait, wait, wait: did the man actually promise her to come for the night? If so, it would be good for the rain to stop quickly. Since she sounds as if she wished it would keep raining, it is unlikely that her lover promised her to come for the night. It also raises another question — does she have any lover at all who would come to love her for the night if there was a bright moon and no rain? It would be foolish not to imagine so, in view of the three TANKA the imaginary world of this one is apparently based upon. But more likely than not, her lover is not so hotly in love with her: the ambient atmosphere of this TANKA is too bleak to suggest any passionate love affair. What made him lose his passion? As likely as not, she is getting a little too tame (or maybe, too old) for him... 初時雨(tatsu-shigure＝the first scattered rain) is not just suggestive of late Autumn to early Winter: it also suggests that the woman is in the final stage of her womanhood — late Autumn would still be fine; what if it's already early Winter?... All she could do was to wait for her lover to come and love and save her... in vain, maybe... an incredibly intricate tragedy of a woman no one but who has read this explanation would correctly understand nowadays... Now you know what imaginative kingdom a really great TANKA is capable of creating!

・・・・・・・・・・・・・・・・・・・・・・・・・・・

《パクらずに作り替へてぞ「本歌取り」》
この傑作短歌の中に見られる想像世界の広がりは、小野小町の有名な短歌から借りた「**よにふる**」の文言によって可能になっている。この種の文言拝借を「本歌取り」と呼び、その原典となる歌(小町の『花の色は移りにけりな徒らに我が身＜世にふる＞ながめせし間に』)のことを「本歌」と呼ぶ。この歌の場合、単に「**よにふる**」の文言を借りているだけでない点に注目してほしい：季節の設定が、元になった小町歌の場合は「春の終わり」なのに対し、こちらの歌では「晩秋から初冬」に変わっている — こうした独自の改変を施すことこそ「本歌取り」の理想なのである。「本歌取り」は三十一文字の短歌世界の物理的限界を超えた想像的拡張の可能性を秘めているが、この技巧が効力を発揮するには、作者だけでなく読者もまたその「本歌」の意味とそれを取り巻く雰囲気まで認識している必要がある・・・さもないと、読者は何の感慨も催さず途方に暮れるだけである・・・実際問題として、平安時代の終わり、とりわけ『新古今集』の頃には、余りにも多くの短歌が余りにも安易に過去の偉大な作品からの文言拝借イタダキに走りすぎた結果、それが何を意味するものやらさっぱりわからぬ読者が続出することになってしまったのだった・・・うまく使えば絶大な効力を発揮するはずの技巧をこうして乱用する態度もまた、短歌が爛熟から没落への道を辿る残念な原因の一つとなったことは間違いない。

《本歌取り(honka dori＝borrowed phrases) — should be no plagiarism but reinvention》
The extension of imagination you have seen in this masterpiece was made possible by the phrase **よにふる**(yo ni furu) it borrows from 小野小町(Ono-no-komachi)'s famous TANKA. A borrowed phrase

like this is called 本歌取り(honka dori), in which 小町(komachi)'s original TANKA 花の色は移りにけり な徒らに我が身＜世にふる＞ながめせしまに(hana no iro wa utsuri-ni-keri-na itazura-ni wa-ga mi ＜yo ni furu＞ nagame se-shi ma ni) is called 本歌(honka＝the original verse). Note that this TANKA just doesn't simply borrow the phrase よにふる(yo ni furu); the seasonal setting of the new poem is "from late Autumn to early Winter", as opposed to "the end of Spring" in 小町(komachi)'s original TANKA — such original alteration is the ideal way of 本歌取り(honka dori). This technique can expand the imaginary possibility of TANKA beyond the physical boundary of 31 letters/syllables, but in order for it to be effective, the reader as well as the author must be aware of the meaning and atmosphere of 本歌(honka＝the original); otherwise, it will simply leave the reader cold and bewildered. In fact, towards the end of the Heian era, especially in the years of 新古今集(Shin-Kokin shuu), too many TANKA too easily resorted to this borrowing from their great ancestors for so many readers to imagine what they were supposed to mean. This abusive attitude of potentially great technique was certainly one of the regrettable causes of the downfall of TANKA in its overgrown years.

★139★くろかみのみだれもしらずうちふせば まづかきやりしひとぞこひしき
黒髪の乱れも知らず打ち臥せば先づ掻き遣りし人ぞ恋しき

【悲恋】[懐旧]『4)後拾遺集:755』和泉式部(いずみしきぶ)

束ね髪も解けて、心ゆくまで乱れ合った夜の果て、乱れ髪もそのままに横たわる寝床で、一人物思いに沈む私・・・その黒髪を生まれて初めて優しく掻き撫でてくれた、懐かしいあの人の思い出に抱かれながら。

Jet-black hair in sensual tousle after a night of wild abandon with a man
Brings back the feel of the one that ran his fingers through my hair...
Throughout my freshly timorous flesh... for the first time in my life.

くろかみ【黒髪】［名］＜黒髪＞(n.)jet black hair＞／の【の】［格助］＜の｜(prep.)'s＞／みだれ【乱れ】［名］＜乱れ｜(n.)untidiness＞／も【も】［係助］＜～[で]さえも｜(adv.)even＞／しる【知る】[他ラ四]＜知る｜(v.)know＞(しら＝未然形)／ず【ず】［助動特殊型］打消＜～[し]ない｜(adv.)not ～＞(ず＝終止形)／うちふす【打ち臥す】[自サ四]＜寝転ぶ｜(v.)lie down＞(うちふせ＝已然形)／ば【ば】［接助］＜～したところ｜(conj.)when＞／まづ【先づ】［副］＜最初に｜(adv.)first＞／かきやる【掻き遣る】[他ラ四]＜指で掻き撫でる｜(v.)run the fingers through the hair＞(かきやり＝連用形)／き【き】［助動特殊型］過去＜～[し]た｜(aux-v.)PAST＞(し＝連体形)／ひと【人】［名］＜あの人｜(n.)that [darling] one＞／ぞ【ぞ】［係助］＜強調｜(adv.)EMPHASIS＞／こひし【恋し】［形シク］＜恋しい｜(v.)feel attached to＞(こひしき＝連体形係り結び)

[kuro-kami no midare mo shira-zu uchi-fuse-ba mazu kaki-yari-shi hito zo koishiki]

何とまぁ生々しく官能的なこと！・・・平安時代にこんな詩を詠める人、和泉式部以外誰がいません！
How vividly voluptuous! Who but 和泉式部(Izumi shikibu) could ever rhyme it out in the Heian era?

★140★ながからむこころもしらずくろかみの みだれてけさはものをこそおもへ
長からむ心も知らず黒髪の乱れて今朝は物をこそ思へ

【悲恋】[溜息]『7)千載集:802』待賢門院堀河(たいけんもんいんのほりかわ)

ゆうべはあんなにも激しく愛し合った私たち・・・でも、こんな燃える思いが、長続きするのかしら・・・
遠い先のことはわからないけれど、乱れ髪もそのままに、ゆうべの愛の余韻に身を任せている
今朝の私の心は、あなたへの想いに、こうして乱れ続けているのです。

―悲恋―

Long may you love me as hot as you did last night,
As densely long as my hair untidy still in bed...
Brooding over our future, possibly not so bright,
This morn I'll sleep on along with remnants of love.

ながし【長し】[形]＜長い｜(adj.)long＞（ながから＝未然形）／む【む】[助動マ四型]婉曲＜意味なし｜(adv.)NO MEANING＞（む＝連体形）／こころ【心】[名]＜心｜(n.)heart＞／も【も】[係助]＜意味なし｜(adv.)NO MEANING＞／しる【知る】[他ラ四]＜知る｜(v.)know＞（しら＝未然形）／ず【ず】[助動特殊型]打消＜～[し]ない｜(adv.)not ～＞（ず＝連用形）／くろかみ【黒髪】[名]＜黒髪｜(n.)jet black hair＞／の【の】[格助]＜主格｜(prep.)SUBJECT＞／*みだる*【乱る】[自ラ下二]＜乱れる｜(v.)get wild＞（みだれ＝連用形）／て【て】[接助]＜順接｜(conj.)and＞／けさ【今朝】[名]＜今朝｜(n.)this morning＞／は【は】[係助]＜～に関しては｜(adv.)as for ～＞／もの【物】[名]＜あれこれいろいろ｜(n.)one thing or another＞／を【を】[格助]＜目的格｜(prep.)OBJECT＞／こそ【こそ】[係助]＜強調｜(adv.)EMPHASIS＞／おもふ【思ふ】[他ハ四]＜思う｜(v.)think＞（おもへ＝已然形係り結び）

[nagakara-mu kokoro mo shira-zu kuro-kami no midare-te kesa wa mono wo koso omoe]

さっきの和泉式部の歌の二百年後の子孫みたいな歌･･･そのさらに七百年後の1901年、もう一人、与謝野晶子という女性が、『みだれ髪』という名の自作短歌集を出版することになります。「(付き合い／髪の)**長さ**」と「(毛髪／心の)**乱れ**」は異質の文脈を介して絡み合う「**縁語**」です。

A 200-year later offspring of 和泉式部(Izumi shikibu)'s previous song... Still 700 years later in 1901, another woman, 与謝野晶子(Yosano Akiko), published her personal TANKA anthology named "みだれ髪(midare gami)". **長さ**(nagasa＝either of her relationship with the man or of her hair) and **乱れ**(midare＝either of her hair or of her peace of mind) are 縁語(engo＝associated words) tangled with each other in apparently irrelevant contexts.

●141●こひすればわがみはかげとなりにけり　さりとてひとにそはぬものゆゑ
　　　恋すれば我が身は影と成りにけり然りとて人に添はぬ物故

【悲恋】[俳諧]『1)古今集:528』詠み人知らず

あなたに恋い焦がれる日々が続いたばっかりに、私のこの身はまるで影のようにやつれてしまいました･･･そうして影になったとて、愛しいあなたの身に寄り添うことは出来ないのだけれど。

A ghastly shadow I've become due to my love for you
Is no use at all without access to coveted substance.

こひ【恋】[名]＜恋｜(n.)love＞／す【為】[自サ変]＜～する｜(v.)do＞（すれ＝已然形）／ば【ば】[接助]＜理由｜(conj.)REASON＞／わ【我】[代名]＜私｜(pron.)I, myself＞／が【が】[格助]＜の｜(prep.)'s＞／み【身】[名]＜自身｜(n.)[one]self＞／は【は】[係助]＜主格｜(prep.)SUBJECT＞／かげ【影】[名]＜影のようにやつれた状態｜(n.)a ghastly figure like a shadow＞／と【と】[格助]＜結末｜(prep.)RESULT＞／なる【成る】[自ラ四]＜～になる｜(v.)become＞（なり＝連用形）／ぬ【ぬ】[助動ナ変型]完了＜すでに～[し]た｜(aux-v.)PERFECT TENSE＞（に＝連用形）／けり【けり】[助動ラ変型]過去＜～[し]た｜(aux-v.)PAST＞（けり＝終止形）／さりとて【然りとて】[接続]＜とは言っても｜(adv.)all the same＞／ひと【人】[名]＜あの人｜(n.)that [darling] one＞／に【に】[格助]＜対象｜(prep.)OBJECT＞／そふ【添ふ】[自ハ四]＜寄り添う｜(v.)get close to＞（そは＝未然形）／ず【ず】[助動特殊型]打消＜～[し]ない｜(adv.)not ～＞（ぬ＝連体形）／ものゆゑ【物ゆゑ】[接助]＜ではあるものの｜(conj.)although＞

[koi-sure-ba wa-ga mi wa kage to nari-ni-keri sari-tote hito ni sowa-nu monoyue]

―悲恋―

「物故(ものゆゑ)」は誤解を招きやすい語で、現代日本語だと「順接:であるから」になるのに、平安時代は「逆接:であるにもかかわらず」になるという困った代物(しろもの)…頓智(とんち)の利いたこの短歌で、その種の誤解に備えましょう。
ものゆゑ(物故:monoyue) is a misleading term which means "because (であるから:de aru kara)" in modern Japanese while meaning "although (であるにもかかわらず:de aru nimo kakawarazu)" in the Heian era — prepare against such misunderstanding with this witty TANKA.

●142●あしひきのやまどりのをのしだりをを ながながしよをひとりかもねむ
足引の山鳥の尾のしだり尾の長々し夜を一人かも寝む

【悲恋】[序詞]『3)拾遺集:778』柿本人麻呂(かきのもとのひとまろ)

雉科(きじか)の山鳥の雄(おす)・雌(めす)は、夜は別れて寝るという…止まり木の下、ひとり虚(むな)しくぶら下がるその長い尾のように、この長い夜を、私も、愛する人と寄り添うこともない独り寝のまま過ごすことに、なるのかなぁ。

> Long, long tails of birds sleeping alone,
> Away from mates to have separate nights.
> Long way from home alone in a mountain cot,
> Long, wrong nights without my wife in sight.

あしひきの【あしひきの】[枕詞]<意味なし|(adj.)NO MEANING>/やまどり[山鳥][名]<山に住む[夫婦仲良しの]鳥|(n.)lovebirds in the mountain>/の【の】[格助]<の|(prep.)'s>/を[尾][名]<尻尾|(n.)tails>/の【の】[格助]<主格|(prep.)SUBJECT>/しだりを[垂り尾][名]<垂れた尻尾|(n.)tails dangling>/の【の】[格助]<主格|(prep.)SUBJECT>/ながながし[長長し][形ク]<とても長い|(adj.)very long>(ながながし[き]=連体形)/よ[夜][名]<夜|(n.)the night>/を【を】[格助]<目的格|(prep.)OBJECT>/ひとり【一人】[名]<一人きり|(adv.)all alone>/か【か】[係助]<疑問|(adv.)INTERROGATIVE>/も【も】[係助]<意味なし|(adv.)NO MEANING>/ぬ[寝][自ナ下二]<寝る|(v.)sleep>(ね=未然形)/む【む】[助動マ四型]推量<だろう|(aux-v.)SUPPOSITION>(む=連体形係り結び)

[ashihiki-no yama-dori no o no shidari-o no naganagashi yo wo hitori ka-mo ne-mu]

「**あしひきの**」は後続の「山」という語を導く以外何の意味も持たない形式的(あるいは神秘的)な「枕詞(まくらことば)」。初句から第三句の「**足引<の>山鳥の<を><の>しだり<を><の>**」までは、独特の抑揚と視覚効果を伴いつつ「**長々し**」へとつながる導入部の「**序詞**」として、「**山鳥**」の尻尾の長さを表すと共に「**夜**」の長さをも表現している。「**山鳥**」の夫婦は夜は別々の木の枝の上に寝ると言われているが、この詩人もまた見知らぬ旅先で妻(か)もなく寂しい独り寝を託つことになるようだ。伝説の「旅する歌人」柿本人麻呂の手になるとても古い歌。意味上の整合性をきっちり保ちつつギュッと詰め込まれた詩でありながら、「**お(o)**」音の繰り返しによるその魅惑(みわく)的な音楽性にも注目したい。

あしひきの(ashihiki-no) is 枕詞(makura-kotoba=a pillow phrase) with no meaning at all except as the formal (or mysterious) introduction to the following term 山(yama=a mountain). From the opening phrase to the third — **足引の山鳥の尾のしだり尾の**(ashihiki-no yama-dori no o no shidari-o no) — forms a rhythmically visual introductory part called 序詞(jo-kotoba) to lead to **長々し**(naganagashi= very long), which both means the length of the tail of 山鳥(yama-dori=a bird in the mountain) and the duration of 夜(yo=the night). A couple of 山鳥(yama-dori) is said to sleep on separate branches; likewise, the poet will sleep alone without his wife away on a journey in a strange place. A very ancient poem made by the legendary traveling poet 柿本人麻呂(Kakinomoto-no-Hitomaro). See how compactly consistent in meaning while enchantingly musical in its repetition of "**お(o)**" sound.

—悲恋—

●143● すみのえのきしによるなみよるさへや　ゆめのかよひぢひとめよくらむ
住江の岸に寄る波夜さへや夢のかよひぢ人目避くらむ

【悲恋】[序詞]『1)古今集:559』藤原敏行(ふぢわらのとしゆき)

住吉の岸辺に打ち寄せる波…寄せては返す波のごとく、私の心も揺れています ― どうしてあなたに逢えないのだろう、と…目覚めて過ごす時間は会えなくとも、せめて夜の夢の中ぐらいは逢ってくれてもいいでしょうに、その通い路さえも閉ざされているなんて…辛すぎます。

Shoal of Suminoe is approached by waves after waves,
While my precious one, inapproachable in waking hours
Shuns me even in dreams... What makes you so coldly shy?

すみのえ【住之江】[名]＜[固有名詞]住吉｜(n.)Sumiyoshi＞／の【の】[格助]＜の｜(prep.)'s＞／きし【岸】[名]＜岸辺｜(n.)the shoal＞／に【に】[格助]＜場所｜(prep.)PLACE＞／よる【寄る】[自ラ四]＜近寄る｜(v.)come near＞(よる＝連体形)／なみ【波】[名]＜波｜(n.)waves＞／よる【夜】[名]＜夜｜(n.)the night＞／さへ【さへ】[副助]＜さえ｜(adv.)even＞／や【や】[係助]＜疑問｜(adv.)INTERROGATIVE＞／ゆめ【夢】[名]＜夢｜(n.)a dream＞／の【の】[格助]＜の｜(prep.)'s＞／かよひぢ【通ひ路】[名]＜通り道｜(n.)the passage＞／ひとめ【人目】[名]＜他人の目｜(n.)the eyes of others＞／よく【避く】[他カ上二]＜避ける｜(v.)avoid＞(よく＝終止形)／らむ【らむ】[助動ラ四型]現在推量＜～だろう｜(aux-v.)SUPPOSITION＞(らむ＝連体形係り結び)

[Suminoe no kishi ni yoru nami yoru sae-ya yume no kayoi-ji hito-me yoku-ramu]

「誰かが夢に出て来なくなったってことは、その人の愛情が消えた証し」― 夢を巡る俗信の裏側から生まれた哀しき詩の宝玉…波は来ては去る…が、この詩人は愛する人に夢の中でさえ近付くことはできない…そしてまた**学生注目** ― この詩の最後の助動詞「らむ」は、省略されている疑問副詞「**などか**」=何故」と組み合わないと意味が取れません…知らずにいると試験で点数取れません！

The disappearance of someone from a dream is the sign of failing affection on the part of that someone — the other side of the popular dream-myth culminating in a sad poetic gem, in which waves come and go but the poet is not allowed to come to the one he loves, even in a dream. Beware, students — the auxiliary verb らむ(ramu) at the end of the verse only makes sense when combined with the *omitted* adverb of question **などか**(nado[ka])=why, the ignorance of which will lead to your loss in exams.

《「序詞」の「蹈鞴」踏まぬは「霞懸け」》

この短歌の出だし部分 ― 住江の岸に＜よる(寄る)＞波 ― は、同音の＜よる(夜)＞で始まる後半の主意部への絵画的導入部となっている。この種の「同音異義語(ダジャレ)依存型」はふつう「序詞」としては最も安直にして(文芸的に見れば)最悪の事例(この筆者之人冗悟はこれを個人的に「蹈鞴踏み」と呼んでいる)…なのだが、この短歌に関しては、同一音の冗長な繰り返しに安直に依存することなく、印象的な絵画的訴求力を保ち続けている(この種の「絵柄的に美しい序詞」は冗悟語緑的に言えば「霞懸け」)…平安調短歌も年月が進むにつれて、序詞の真の美(それは「霞懸け」によってのみ実現可能なもの)は殆ど全く見失われてしまい、軽佻浮薄な「たたら踏み」ダジャレ歌の無意味な洪水へと流れ着いた…平安時代の最後も最後、藤原定家が「霞懸け」の持つ絵画的含意を再発見して自らもその再発明を試みるまでは…それもいささか遅きに失した感があるが。

《two types of 序詞(jo-kotoba) ― たたら踏み(tatara-bumi) hinging on 懸詞(kake-kotoba=puns) and 霞懸け(kasumi-gake) working as pictorial overture》

The opening part of this TANKA ― すみのえのきしに＜よる＞なみ(Suminoe no kishi ni **<yoru>** nami =the waves **coming to** the shoal of Suminoe) ― is a pictorial overture to the meaningful latter

—Sad Love—

part which begins with the same sound ー 懸詞(kake-kotoba＝a pun)ー ＜よる(yoru)＝**the night**)＞. Normally, such pun-based ones are the easiest and shabbiest examples of 序詞(jo-kotoba) from artistic point of view ー which *this author(之人冗悟:Jaugo Noto) personally calls* たたら踏み(tatara-bumi＝same-sound stomping) ー but this particular TANKA never relies easily on the redundancy of sound but retains its impressive visual appeal ー 霞懸け(kasumi-gake＝seamless visual transition) *according to* 冗悟*'s lexicon*. As years went on, Heianese poets practically lost sight of the true beauty of 序詞(jo-kotoba) which can solely be realized by 霞懸け(kasumi-gake), only to end up in the meaningless floods of frivolous たたら踏み(tatara-bumi)... until 藤原定家(Fujiwara-no-Teika) rediscovered the pictorial implication of 霞懸け(kasumi-gake) and tried to re-invent it himself towards the very end of the Heian era... a little too late, perhaps.

― ―

●144● きみこふるなみだのとこにみちぬれば　みをつくしとぞわれはなりぬる
君恋ふる涙の床に満ちぬればみをつくしとぞ我は成りぬる

【悲恋】[失恋]『1)古今集:567』藤原興風(ふぢわらのおきかぜ)

あなたに恋い焦がれて泣き続けて、私の寝床はもう涙の川、その川にぽつりと一人寂しく横たわるこの私は、まるで難波(なにわ)の水に浮かぶ航路標識の澪標･･･烈しい思いに身(み)を焼き尽くしつつ、あなたに逢(あ)えるのを待っているのです。

Alone in the sea of lonely tears cried over you in bed,
A watermark pole burnt in love — that's what I've become.

きみ【君】〔代名〕＜あなた｜(pron.)you＞／こふ【恋ふ】〔他ハ上二〕＜恋しく思う｜(v.)long for＞(こふる＝連体形)／なみだ【涙】〔名〕＜涙｜(n.)tears＞／の【の】〔格助〕＜主格｜(prep.)SUBJECT＞／とこ【床】〔名〕＜寝床｜(n.)the bed＞／に【に】〔格助〕＜場所｜(prep.)PLACE＞／みつ【満つ】〔自タ四〕＜満ちる｜(v.)overflow＞(みち＝連用形)／ぬ【ぬ】〔助動マ変型〕完了＜すでに～[し]た｜(aux-v.)PERFECT TENSE＞(ぬれ＝已然形)／ば【ば】〔接助〕＜理由｜(conj.)REASON＞／***(A)みをつくし【澪標】*〔名〕**＜水中に刺さった航路標識の棒｜(n.)a watermark pole＞／***(B1)み【身】*〔名〕**＜生命｜(n.)my life＞／***(B2)を【を】*〔格助〕**＜目的格｜(prep.)OBJECT＞／***(B3)つくす【尽くす】*〔他サ四〕**＜果てさせる｜(v.)consume＞(つくし＝連用形)／と【と】〔格助〕＜結末｜(prep.)RESULT＞／ぞ【ぞ】〔係助〕＜強調｜(adv.)EMPHASIS＞／われ【我】〔代名〕＜私｜(pron.)I, myself＞／は【は】〔係助〕＜主格｜(prep.)SUBJECT＞／なる【成る】〔自ラ四〕＜～になる｜(v.)become＞(なり＝連用形)／ぬ【ぬ】〔助動ナ変型〕完了＜すでに～[し]た｜(aux-v.)PERFECT TENSE＞(ぬる＝連体形係り結び)

[kimi kouru namida no toko ni michi-nure-ba mi-wo-tsukushi to-zo ware wa nari-nuru]

冷たい恋人を思って流す苦(にが)い涙に、寝床は洪水(こうずい)、あわれ詩人は溺(おぼ)れ死(じ)に･･･という冗談めかした誇張で綴(つづ)った悲劇的状況の物語。平安時代にこの種の「涙川」で自ら好きこのんで溺死(できし)した歌人の数は、数え切れるものではありません･･･ちなみに八代集9500首中の溺死者数は、45名。

A jokingly exaggerated tragic situation where bitter tears cried over a cruel sweetheart floods the bed to drown the poet. Countless poets in the Heian era had themselves drowned in such 涙川(namida-gawa＝rivers of tears)... the death toll among 9,500 poems in 八代集(Hachidai shuu＝8 great Imperial TANKA anthologies) amounts to 45.

― ―

—悲恋—

●145● わびぬればいまはたおなじなにはなる みをつくしてもあはむとぞおもふ
侘びぬれば今将同じ難波なるみをつくしても逢はむとぞ思ふ

【悲恋】[序詞]『2)後撰集:961』元良親王(もとよししんのう)

難波潟の水先案内の澪標、水に沈んで動かないあの杭のように、この身を捨ててでもあなたに逢いたい・・・逢えれば死んでも悔いはない・・・逢えずにただただ思いに沈む、今の私はもう死んだも同然の身なのですから。

> Downhearted as deep as a watermark pole in the mud of the sea of Naniwa,
> As good as dead am I dying to see you again in vain.
> Drowned in love I dread no death, why should I miss a life without you?

わぶ【侘ぶ】[自バ上二]<意気消沈する│(v.)be dejected>（わび＝連用形)／ぬ【ぬ】[助動ナ変型]完了<すでに～[し]た│(aux-v.)PERFECT TENSE>（ぬれ＝已然形)／ば【ば】[接助]<理由│(conj.)REASON>／いま【今】[名]<今│(n.)now>／はた【将】[副]<そりゃもう│(adv.)just>／おなじ【同じ】[形シク]<同じ事│(adj.)the same thing>（おなじ＝終止形)／なには【難波】[名]<[固有名詞]大阪湾│(n.)the bay of Osaka>／なり【なり】[助動ナリ型]所在地<～に存在する│(prep.)PLACE>（なる＝連体形)／*(A)みをつくし【澪標】[名]*<水中に刺さった航路標識の棒│(n.)a watermark pole>／*(B1)み【身】[名]*<生命│(n.)my life>／*(B2)を【を】[格助]*<目的格│(prep.)OBJECT>／*(B3)つくす【尽くす】[他サ四]*<果てさせる│(v.)consume>（つくし＝連用形)／て【て】[接助]<状態│(conj.)while>／も【も】[係助]<～[で]さえも│(adv.)even>／あふ【会ふ】[他ハ四]<会う│(v.)meet>（あは＝未然形)／む【む】[助動マ四型]意志<～するつもりか│(aux-v.)be going to ～>（む＝終止形)／と【と】[格助]<内容提示│(conj.)that ～>／ぞ【ぞ】[係助]<強調│(adv.)EMPHASIS>／おもふ【思ふ】[他ハ四]<思う│(v.)think>（おもふ＝連体形係り結び)

[wabi-nure-ba ima hata onaji Naniwa naru mi-wo-tsukushi-te-mo awa-mu to-zo omou]

これまた「涙で溺死」の歌ながら、真の悲劇の響きあり。この短歌の作者は(本来なら逢うことを許されない)とある女性と密かな逢瀬を重ねており、彼らの密通が明るみに出て彼女が彼に逢うことを禁じられた後で、彼女への伝言として送られたのがこの悲劇的な歌だったのである。「今はた同じ」の語順の転倒に要注意 ―「何」が「何」と「同じ」なのか、と言えば、「あなたと逢えずに一人きりで生きる」のは「難波なるみをつくし＝1)難波の海路標識として水中にぽつんと立った木の棒＝澪標;2)自らの流す涙の川で溺れ死にする寂しい男＝身を尽くし」に成り下がるのと「同じこと」・・・「航路標識」と「涙川溺死者」双方のイメージとしての「みをつくし＝澪標／身を尽くし」が、視覚的にも意味の上でも見事な効果を上げている点に注目 ―「意味部」につながる「叙景部」からの橋渡し役というその機能から見て、この「難波なる」は「みをつくし＝悲しい涙に我が身を滅ぼす男」を導く「序詞」と解釈し得るもの・・・もっとも、この種の「序詞」は、1)歌の冒頭部に置かれていない;2)たった一句で構成されているという理由で、従来「序詞」としては認められずにきたこともまた事実・・・しかしながら、思い出してほしい ― この歌は、「短歌」の最初期の『古今集』時代に生まれたものであり、当時は「序詞」もまだあれこれ様々な形態を模索する「実験段階」にあったのだということを・・・そしてまた、この「序詞」という技巧はその後年月を重ねるにつれて次第に廃れて行き、視覚的に洗練されたその効用に対する評価も、実際の用法に関する理解も、年月を追うごとにどんどん劣化して行ったという事実をも思い起こしてもらいたい・・・理解力に劣る後代の批評家連中が何と言おうとも、これは間違いなく「序詞歌」なのである。

Another "tear-drowned" poem but with authentic tone of tragedy. The author of this TANKA had a covert love affair with a woman he was not supposed to meet. This tragic poem was a message sent to her after their secret affairs came to light and she was forbidden to meet him again. Pay attention to the inverted word order 今はた同じ(ima hata onaji＝it's just the same) — what is the same with what? Living alone without meeting you is the same as 難波なるみをつくし(Naniwa naru miotsukushi＝a watermark pole stuck in the mud of the sea of Naniwa＝the poet drowned in the river of his own tears)... see how visually and semantically effective is the image of みをつくし(miotsukushi) both as a watermark pole(澪標) and as a tear-drowned man(身を尽くし) — in its function as a pictorial bridge to the semantic part, this 難波なる(Naniwa naru) can be interpreted as 序詞(jo-kotoba) introducing みをつくし(miotsukushi), someone who is drowned in floods of sad tears... although 序詞(jo-kotoba) like this has not been generally recognized as such, both because it is not placed at the head of the poem and because it only consists of a single phrase... but remember — this TANKA was born in the years of 古今集(Kokin shuu) when TANKA poetry was still in its infancy and the technique of 序詞(jo-kotoba) was still in its experimental stage... and be it also remembered that this particular technique gradually came into disuse as years went on, with less and less appreciation of its visual sophistication and actual usage... whatever critics of later years and lesser understanding would say, this is definitely a 序詞歌(jo-kotoba uta).

●146● いまはただおもひたえなむとばかりを ひとづてならでいふよしもがな
今は只思ひ絶えなむとばかりを人伝てならで言ふ由もがな

【悲恋】【願望】『4)後拾遺集:750』藤原道雅(ふじわらのみちまさ)

今となってはもう逢うことすらも許されないあなた・・・そんなあなたへの想いを、私は断ち切ることにします・・・あぁ、せめてその「もう忘れます。さようなら」の別れの言葉だけでも、人づてでなく、直接あなたに言わせてもらえる機会があればいいのに・・・それすらも私には許されてはいないのです。

After all these days of yearning for you,
All I want now is a chance to tell you in person:
"I'll give you up."... that much isn't given to me.

いま【今】〔名〕＜今｜(n.)now＞／は【は】〔係助〕＜〜に関しては｜(adv.)as for 〜＞／ただ【只】〔副〕＜ただ単に｜(adv.)only＞／おもふ【想ふ】〔他ハ四〕＜愛しく思う｜(v.)love＞（おもひ＝連用形）／たゆ【絶ゆ】〔自ヤ下二〕＜〜するのをやめる｜(v.)stop 〜ing＞（たえ＝連用形）／ぬ【ぬ】〔助動ナ変型〕確述＜きっと〜する｜(adv.)EMPHASIS＞（な＝未然形）／む【む】〔助動マ四型〕意志＜〜するつもりだ｜(aux-v.)be going to 〜＞（む＝終止形）／と【と】〔格助〕＜内容提示｜(conj.)that 〜＞／ばかり【ばかり】〔副助〕＜〜だけ｜(adv.)only＞／を【を】〔格助〕＜目的格｜(prep.)OBJECT＞／ひとづて【人伝て】〔名〕＜第三者を通しての伝言｜(n.)an indirect message＞／なり【なり】〔助動ナリ型〕断定＜〜である｜(aux-v.)be＞（なら＝未然形）／で【で】〔接助〕＜〜することなしに｜(prep.)without 〜ing＞／いふ【言ふ】〔他ハ四〕＜言う｜(v.)say＞（いふ＝連体形）／よし【由】〔名〕＜手段｜(n.)means＞／もがな【もがな】〔終助〕＜〜があってほしいな｜(adv.)hopefully＞

[ima-wa tada omoi-tae-na-mu to-bakari-wo hito-zute-nara-de yuu yoshi mogana]

これもまた実際にあった悲劇を詠んだ歌で、作者(男性)は密かな(禁じられた)恋の相手の女性と口を利くことも許されない・・・問題の女性は伊勢神宮に仕える聖なる女性の「斎院」で、男の手も触れぬ「処女性」を当然のごとく求められる立場・・・この密通事件発覚後、彼女は隠遁生活を強いられ、寂しい尼僧として余生を過ごすことになった・・・現代読者には信じられない悲しい歌ながら、これに似た状況 — 別れたばかりの誰かに向かって「さようなら」を言うこともままならぬ立場になってしまうこと — は、実際にはそう珍しいことではない・・・あなたがそういう立場にならないといいけれど、もしなっちゃった場合にはこの詩を思い出すといい —「あぁ、自分だけじゃない、他にもいたんだ、こういう人が」ってわかるだけでも、せめてもの悲しい慰めになるはずだから。

―悲恋―

Another TANKA of a real tragedy, in which the author (man) is prevented from talking with a woman he has been in stealthy (and forbidden) love with. The woman in question was 伊勢神宮(Ise jinguu)'s 斎院(sai-inn＝a sacred woman devoted to the shrine), who was naturally supposed to be a virgin untouched by any man... she was later forcibly retired into seclusion and lived the rest of her life as a lonely nun. A song too sad to be true to modern readers, but a situation like this ― where you can't even say "Good bye" to someone you've just parted from ― is actually not quite rare... hope you won't find yourself in it, but if you do, just remember this poem as a sad comfort that *you are not the only one*.

●**147**● よそながらあはれといはむことよりも　ひとづてならでいとへとぞおもふ
　　　　余所ながら哀れと言はむ言よりも人伝てならで厭へとぞ思ふ

【悲恋】[願望]『6)詞花集:196』藤原成通(ふじわらのなりみち)

私の知らないところで、誰かさんに向かって「あの人もまぁ、お気の毒に」などと私への見せかけの同情心見せびらかしたりしないで、人づてじゃなく、私の目の前で、きっぱりと「あなたとはお付き合いできません」と言い放ってもらえたら、どれだけ救われることか！

Please stop pitying me in front of others
But just tell me "I don't like you, SORRY!"

よそ【余所】[名]＜どこか別の場所｜(n.)somewhere else＞／ながら【ながら】[接助]＜〜のままで｜(conj.)while＞／あはれ【あはれ】[感]＜あぁ残念｜(n.)a pity＞／と【と】[格助]＜内容提示｜(conj.)that 〜＞／いふ【言ふ】[他ハ四]＜言う｜(v.)say＞(いは＝未然形)／む【む】[助動マ四型]婉曲＜意味なし｜(adv.)NO MEANING＞(む＝連体形)／こと【言】[名]＜発言｜(n.)a comment＞／より【より】[格助]＜より｜(prep.)COMPARISON＞／も【も】[係助]＜意味なし｜(adv.)NO MEANING＞／ひとづて【人伝て】[名]＜伝言｜(n.)an indirect message＞／なり【なり】[助動ナリ型]断定＜〜である｜(aux-v.)be＞(なら＝未然形)／で【で】[接助]＜〜することなしに｜(prep.)without 〜ing＞／いとふ【厭ふ】[他ハ四]＜嫌う｜(v.)hate＞(いとへ＝命令文)／と【と】[格助]＜内容提示｜(conj.)that 〜＞／ぞ【ぞ】[係助]＜強調｜(adv.)EMPHASIS＞／おもふ【思ふ】[他ハ四]＜思う｜(v.)think＞(おもふ＝連体形係り結び)

[yoso-nagara aware to iwa-mu koto yori-mo hito-zute-nara-de itoe to-zo omou]

愛する誰かに嫌(きら)われるのは嫌(いや)なこと・・・だけどそれよりもっとヒドいのは、その誰かさんが他の誰かさんの目の前で(自分はいない余所(よそ)の場で)フラれた自分への憐(あわ)れみを示して見せること。形ばかりの哀れみは、心ない残虐(ざんぎゃく)行為の最(さい)たるもの。愛してはやれない誰かに対し、真のいたわりを示すつもりなら、ただ一言「愛してません！」と面(めん)と向かって言ってやることだ ― 言い寄って来る相手を拒絶する「とどめの一撃」は、その哀れな相手への「高貴なる慈悲(じひ)」であるとともに、ヘタすればストーカー(stalker)として自分に付きまといかねない相手にきっぱりとクギを刺す「最高の予防措置(よぼうそち)」でもあるのだから。

It's hateful to have yourself hated by someone you love... but it's still more hateful to have that someone pity you before someone else somewhere without you in sight. Superficial pity is the most heartless cruelty: should you really feel for someone you don't love, just say so to his/her face ― a "coup de grâce" is the noble mercy to a rejected wooer and the surest safeguard against a potential stalker.

●148● おもひやるかたなきままにわすれゆく ひとのこころぞうらやまれける
思ひ遣る方無き儘に忘れ行く人の心ぞ羨まれける

【悲恋】[失恋]『4)後拾遺集:787』中原頼成妻(なかはらのよりしげのつま)

あなたに忘れ去られた悲しみのやり場もなくてひどく打ちひしがれている私には、
かつて愛した相手のことをあっさり忘れてしまえるあなたの薄情な心が、うらやましい限りです。

Where and how shall I desert our memories?
How I envy you... how did you forget me?

おもひやる【思ひ遣る】〔他ラ四〕＜内心のモヤモヤを晴らす｜(v.)let out steam＞(おもひやる＝連体形)／かた【方】[名]＜方法｜(n.)means＞／なし【なし】〔形〕＜存在しない｜(v.)do not exist＞(なき＝連体形)／まま【儘】[名]＜そのままの状況｜(n.)the state being ～＞／に【に】[格助]＜様態｜(prep.)like＞／わする【忘る】〔他ラ下二〕＜忘れ｜(v.)forget＞(わすれ＝連用形)／ゆく【行く】〔自カ四〕＜次第に～になる｜(v.)come to ～＞(ゆく＝連体形)／ひと【人】[名]＜あの人｜(n.)that (darling) one＞／の【の】[格助]＜の｜(prep.)'s＞／こころ【心】[名]＜心｜(n.)heart＞／ぞ【ぞ】[係助]＜強調｜(adv.)EMPHASIS＞／うらやむ【羨む】〔他マ四〕＜うらやむ｜(v.)envy＞(うらやま＝未然形)／る【る】[助動ラ下二型]自発＜[思わず知らず]そうなる｜(adv.)naturally＞(れ＝連用形)／けり【けり】[助動ラ変型]過去＜～[し]た｜(aux-v.)PAST＞(ける＝連体形係り結び)

[omoi-yaru kata naki mama-ni wasure-yuku hito no kokoro zo urayama-re-keru]

古語の「思ひやる」は、大抵の場合、現代の「他者の気持ちを慮(おもんぱか)る」とは違う意味を持つ・・・この歌の作者の場合、冷たい恋人に忘れ去られた後で、「胸に溜まった思いを吐き出す(すべ)」術もないままに途方に暮れている・・・長いこと自分を訪問してくれない男へのメッセージとして送られたこの短歌は、悪意を込めた「さようなら」の縁切り状とも取れるけれど、同時にまた「優しい訪問」を求めるおねだりとも取れないではない。

Ancient 思ひやる(omoi-yaru) usually means different things from its modern use "feeling for someone"; this author simply doesn't know how to "let off steam" after being forgotten by the cruel sweetheart. A message sent from a woman to a man who has been absent for quite some time, this TANKA may still as well be interpreted as a request for a graceful visit as a spiteful good-bye.

●149● いまよりはとへともいはじわれぞただ ひとをわするることをしるべき
今よりは訪へとも言はじ我ぞ只人を忘るる事を知るべき

【悲恋】[願望]『6)詞花集:266』詠み人知らず

もう今となっては「来て、私のところへ」なんて、言いません・・・
今の私が望むことはたった一つ ― 薄情なあなたをきっぱりと忘れ去ること、それだけです。

Never more will I ask you to come to love me.
All I want with you is that I'll forget about you.

いま【今】[名]＜今｜(n.)now＞／より【より】[格助]＜～から｜(prep.)from＞／は【は】[係助]＜～に関しては｜(adv.)as for ～＞／とふ【訪ふ】〔他ハ四〕＜訪れる｜(v.)visit＞(とへ＝命令形)／と【と】[格助]＜内容提示｜(conj.)that ～＞／も【も】[係助]＜意味なし｜(adv.)NO MEANING＞／いふ【言ふ】〔他ハ四〕＜言う｜(v.)say＞(いは＝未然形)／じ【じ】[助動特殊型]打消意志＜～ないつもりだ｜(aux-v.)be not going to ～＞(じ＝終止形)／われ【我】[代名]＜私｜(pron.)I, myself＞／ぞ【ぞ】[係助]＜強調｜(adv.)EMPHASIS＞／ただ【只】[副]＜ただ単に｜(adv.)only＞／ひと【人】[名]＜あの人｜(n.)that [darling] one＞／を【を】[格助]＜目的格｜(prep.)OBJECT＞／わする【忘る】〔他ラ下二〕＜忘れる｜(v.)forget＞(わするる＝連体形)／こと【事】[名]＜～という事｜(n.)the act of ～ing＞／を【を】[格助]＜

―悲恋―

目的格｜(prep.)OBJECT＞／しる【知る】〔他ラ四〕＜学ぶ｜(v.)learn＞（しる＝連体形）／べし【べし】〔助動ク型〕妥当＜～するべき｜(aux-v.)should＞（べき＝連体形係り結び）

[ima yori-wa toe to-mo iwa-ji ware zo tada hito wo wasururu koto wo shiru-beki]

一つ前の短歌に似た「不実な欠席者」宛てのメッセージながら、前のやつより切羽詰まった響きあり・・・問題の「男」に向けてというよりむしろ、魔法の忘却をもたらしてくれる恵み深い「神様」に向けて祈っている感じ。

A similar message to the previous TANKA sent to a faithless absentee, only with a more desperate tone as if prayed not so much to the man as to some graceful god who would grant her magical oblivion.

――――――――――――――――――――――――――――――

★150★ちぎりしももろともにこそちぎりしか　わすればわれもわすれましかば
契りしも諸共にこそ契りしか　忘れば我も忘れましかば

【悲恋】[願望]『7)千載集:864』藤原為通（ふじわらのためみち）

変わらぬ愛を誓った時も、二人一緒にそう誓ったのだから、その誓いを忘れて愛情が冷める時だって、相手一人じゃなく自分も同じように忘れてしまいたいのに・・・いまだに忘れられないこの身が、辛い。

It was at the same time that we made our vow to love and please each other.
It should also be at the same time that we should cease to love and forget each other
— It's unfair, why should I be still bound by the vow alone?

ちぎる【契る】〔他ラ四〕＜約束する｜(v.)promise＞（ちぎり＝連用形）／き【き】〔助動特殊型〕過去＜～[し]た｜(aux-v.)PAST＞（し＝連体形）／も【も】〔係助〕＜～もまた｜(adv.)also＞／もろともに【諸共に】〔副〕＜一緒に｜(adv.)together＞／こそ【こそ】〔係助〕＜強調｜(adv.)EMPHASIS＞／ちぎる【契る】〔他ラ四〕＜約束する｜(v.)promise＞（ちぎり＝連用形）／き【き】〔助動特殊型〕過去＜～[し]た｜(aux-v.)PAST＞（しか＝已然形係り結び）／わする【忘る】〔他ラ下二〕＜忘れる｜(v.)forget＞（わすれ＝已然形）／ば【ば】〔接助〕＜仮定｜(conj.)if＞／われ【我】〔代名〕＜私｜(pron.)I, myself＞／も【も】〔係助〕＜～もまた｜(adv.)also＞／わする【忘る】〔他ラ下二〕＜忘れる｜(v.)forget＞（わすれ＝未然形）／まし【まし】〔助動特殊型〕願望＜～だったらいいのに｜(aux-v.)would rather ～＞（ましか＝未然形）／ば【ば】〔接助〕＜仮定｜(conj.)if＞

[chigiri-shi mo morotomoni koso chigiri-shika wasure-ba ware mo wasure-mashika-ba]

「契り」とは「誓約」のこと。平安調短歌の中では大抵「永遠の愛の誓い」の意味になるが、必ずしも「神前での誓い」とは限らず、「愛し合う二人の間でのみ有効」な約束事・・・あるいは「どちらか一方がひどく色褪せてせてしまうまで有効」な空約束というべきか。恋人はみな「恋の始まり」に向けては一緒に踏み出すものの、「恋の一抜け」で足並みが揃うことは滅多にない・・・相方が抜けて関わり合いを放棄した「まだ終わってない共同事業」を清算するのは、一苦労。

契り (chigiri) means an oath, usually meaning "a pledge to love for ever" in Heianese TANKA, not necessarily sworn before some god but just valid between each other... well, *valid* until one of them gets *pallid*. Although all lovers start out on love at the same time, few of them will finish together... it's tough liquidating an unfinished joint-venture from which your partner has gone and has nothing to do with any more.

――――――――――――――――――――――――――――――

―悲恋―

●151● おもふことなすこそかみのかたからめ　しばしわするるこころつけなむ
　　　　思ふ事成すこそ神の難からめ暫し忘るる心付けなむ

【悲恋】[願望]『3)拾遺集:997』詠み人知らず

神様、もうこうなっては今更「あの人が私のこと好きになってくれますように」なんて無理難題は言いません…ほんの少しでいいから、あの人のこと、思い浮かべずにいられる心安らかな時間を私にください！

Oh God, if it's difficult for you to make me beloved,
Make me forget this painful love only for a while.

おもふ【思ふ】[他ハ四]＜期待する｜(v.)hope for＞(おもふ＝連体形)／こと【事】[名]＜物事｜(n.)a thing＞／なす【為す】[他サ四]＜実現する｜(v.)realize＞(なす＝連体形)／こそ【こそ】[係助]＜逆接｜(conj.)although＞／かみ【神】[名]＜神｜(n.)a god＞／の【の】[格助]＜主格｜(prep.)SUBJECT＞／かたし【難し】[形ク]＜難しい｜(adj.)difficult＞(かたから＝未然形)／む【む】[助動マ四型]推量＜だろう｜(aux-v.)SUPPOSITION＞(め＝已然形係り結び)／しばし【暫し】[副]＜しばらくの間｜(adv.)for the time being＞／わする【忘る】[他ラ下二]＜忘れる｜(v.)forget＞(わするる＝連体形)／こころ【心】[名]＜心｜(n.)heart＞／つく【付く】[他カ下二]＜植え付ける｜(v.)implant＞(つけ＝連用形)／なむ【なむ】[終助]＜～ならいいのになぁ｜(v.)I hope＞

[omou koto nasu koso kami no katakara-me shibashi wasururu kokoro tsuke-namu]

どうやらこの詩人は神さま(日本じゃ西欧のように神様は一人だけとは限らない)に向かって「恋がうまく行きますように」と祈っていた模様…その恋の成就のお祈りを神様が聞き入れてくれなかったので、今度は、満たされぬ心を絶えず苦しめ続ける恋心からの解放(ほんの一時でもいいから！)をお祈りしています。

It seems this poet has prayed to some god (in Japan, not a single God as in the West) for successful development of his or her love affair. Now that the prayer has proved to have been unattended, this poet prays for liberation – *however temporary* – from his/her passion which is a constant torture to the unsatisfied heart.

―――――――――――――――――――――――――――

●152● いのちをしかけてちぎりしなかなれば　たゆるはしぬるここちこそすれ
　　　　命をし懸けて契りし仲なれば絶ゆるは死ぬる心地こそすれ

【悲恋】[失恋]『5)金葉集:413』実源(じつげん)

命懸けで愛し続ける約束だったあなたと私だけに、お別れするのは私にとって死ぬも同然の気分です…(…誓いを破った以上、私たちの命も、そうそう長くはないでしょうし…)

To love as long as we live we swore in the name of God.
For me to be deserted by you feels like being dead.
(...*For us to break a divine oath may soon result in our deaths*...)

いのち【命】[名]＜生命｜(n.)our lives＞／を【を】[格助]＜目的格｜(prep.)OBJECT＞／し【し】[副助]＜意味なし｜(adv.)NO MEANING＞／かく【懸く】[他カ四]＜懸ける｜(v.)pawn＞(かけ＝連用形)／て【て】[接助]＜状態｜(conj.)while＞／ちぎる【契る】[他ラ四]＜約束する｜(v.)promise＞(ちぎり＝連用形)／き【き】[助動特殊型]過去＜～[し]た｜(aux-v.)PAST＞(し＝連体形)／なか【仲】[名]＜関係｜(n.)relationship＞／なり【なり】[助動ナリ型]断定＜～である｜(aux-v.)be＞(なれ＝已然形)／ば【ば】[接助]＜理由｜(conj.)REASON＞／たゆ【絶ゆ】[自ヤ下二]＜終わる｜(v.)end＞(たゆる＝連体形)／は【は】[係助]＜主格｜(prep.)SUBJECT＞／しぬ【死ぬ】[自ナ変]＜死ぬ｜(v.)die＞(しぬる＝連体形)／ここち【心地】[名]＜気持ち｜(n.)feeling＞／こそ【こそ】[係助]＜強調｜(adv.)EMPHASIS＞／す【為】[自サ変]＜～な感じがする｜(v.)feel＞(すれ＝已然形係り結び)

—悲恋—
[inochi wo-shi kake-te chigiri-shi naka nare-ba tayuru wa shinuru kokochi koso sure]
この虚構歌もまた「不実な相手が愛の誓いを破ったことからくる傷心」がテーマだが、今回にこの詩人が「死ぬる心地」なのは、ただ単に「恋に破れたから」のみならず、「神聖なるべき誓い」の当事者として「神前でウソをついた罰で、死罪」になっても不思議はないと感じているから・・・もっともその「嘘」の犠牲者となったのは、この傷心の詩人の方なのだけれど。

This fictional TANKA is also about a heartbreak due to the breach of a love oath by a faithless partner. This time, however, the poet feels as though dead not only because he or she has been lost in love but also because he/she, as a party to the sacred pledge, might as well be punished by death for "having lied before a god"... although this broken-hearted poet is the victim of the lie.

●153● わすらるるみをばおもはずちかひてし　ひとのいのちのをしくもあるかな
忘らるる身をば思はず誓ひてし人の命の惜しくもあるかな
【悲恋】[謎掛]『3)拾遺集:870』藤原季縄女(ふじわらのすえなわのむすめ)

忘れ去られる日が来ようとは、思いもしないで誓った永遠の愛・・・私はあなたを忘れはしないけど、あなたは私を忘れてしまった・・・そんなあなたの身の上が心配です(忘れ去られる我が身の辛さよりも)・・・だって、神さまの前で立てた誓いを、破った罰は、重いのよ・・・。

How was I to know I'd be deserted like this
When we two swore before God we'd never be apart?
What should I care now but the dear life of yours
That would soon be lost by divine punishment?

わする【忘る】〔他ラ四〕<忘れる｜(v.)forget＞(わすら＝未然形)/る【る】[助動ラ下二型]受身<～[さ]れる｜(aux-v.)PASSIVE VOICE＞(るる=連体形)/み【身】[名]<この私｜(pron.)I, myself＞/を【を】[格助]<目的格｜(prep.)OBJECT＞/ば[ば][格助]<強調｜(adv.)EMPHASIS＞/おもふ【思ふ】[他ハ四]<思う｜(v.)think＞(おもは＝未然形)/**(A)ず【ず】**[助動特殊型]打消<～[し]ない｜(adv.)not ～＞(ず=終止形・・・ここで切れる:stops here)/**(B)ず【ず】**[助動特殊型]打消<～[し]ない｜(adv.)not ～＞(ず=連体形・・・「ちかひてし」に懸かる:negating the next verb "vow")/ちかふ【誓ふ】[他ハ四]<誓う｜(v.)vow＞(ちかひ＝連用形)/つ【つ】[助動タ下二型]完了<すでに～した｜(aux-v.)PERFECT TENSE＞(て＝連用形)/き【き】[助動特殊型]過去<～[し]た｜(aux-v.)PAST＞(し=連体形)/ひと【人】[名]<あの人｜(n.)that [darling] one＞/の【の】[格助]<の｜(prep.)'s＞/いのち【命】[名]<生命｜(n.)the life＞/の【の】[格助]<主格｜(prep.)SUBJECT＞/をし【惜し】[形シク]<なくなるのを残念に思う｜(v.)be sorry to lose＞(をしく=連用形)/も【も】[係助]<意味なし｜(adv.)NO MEANING＞/あり【あり】〔自ラ変〕<感じる｜(v.)feel＞(ある＝連体形)/かな【かな】[終助]<詠嘆｜(interj.)EXCLAMATION＞

[wasura-ruru mi wo-ba omowa-zu chikai-te-shi hito no inochi no oshiku-mo aru kana]
巧妙に構築された冗長構造を持つ「二重性」短歌で、共通の軸線としての「忘らるる身をば思はず」の言い回しが、次の二つの意味へと分岐する — 1)今はもうあなたに忘れ去られた我が身のことを＜私は＞残念に思ったりしません;2)私があなたに忘れ去られることになるなんて＜あなたは＞思ってもいなかったんですよね、二人で「神前の誓い」をした(「誓ひてし」)あの時には — どうして彼女は「男に忘れ去られた我が身を残念に思ったりしない」のか？それは「もはや彼のことなど思わない」(というか、思わぬように努力している)からである。どうして彼女は「人の命の惜しくもあるかな」と言っているのか？それは、彼女を裏切ることでこの男が「神聖なる誓い」を破る罪を犯したから — その罪の行き着く果ては「天罰による男の死」・・・早くもお悔やみを申し上げることで、この女性は(実のところ)「私を裏切ったあなたに、どうかひどい罰が当たりますように」と願っているのである・・・どうです、オッソロしい詩でしょう？

—Sad Love—

―悲恋―

A duality TANKA with cleverly structured redundancy centering around a single phrase 忘らるる身をば思はず(wasura-ruru mi wo-ba omowa-zu), which both means 1)now, I don't feel sorry for myself who have been forgotten by you, and 2)you didn't imagine me forgotten by you... when you made your sacred oath(誓ひてし:chikai-te-shi). Why does she "not feel sorry for herself who has been forgotten by him"? Because she has ceased to (or *trying not to*) think about him. Why does she say 人の命の惜しくもあるかな(hito no inochi no oshiku-mo aru kana=I feel sorry for your life that will be lost)? Because he is to blame for having broken the sacred oath by betraying her ― the ultimate result of which is his death by divine punishment... by extending her premature condolences, she is actually *hoping for some disastrous fate of her betrayer*... a terrific poem, don't you think?

《祈りても恐るに足らぬ「大和神」》

「唯一の神たる我以外のものを神として崇めるべからず」／「唯一の神以外の崇拝対象としての偶像を勝手に作るべからず」／「お前たちの主たる神の名をみだりに唱えるべからず」／「道徳的に正しくない恋愛にふけるべからず」・・・「十戒」のうちのこれら四つの戒めを、平安時代の貴人たちはいとも簡単に無視した・・・現代日本人のほとんども相変わらずそうである。「偶像（アイドル）」と「道徳的に正しくない恋愛」の二つについては、その定義も昔と今では明らかに違っているのでさておくとして、他の二つの聖なる戒めに関しては、西欧人の多くは今日でもなおしっかり守っている・・・自分の信じる宗教以外の異教徒に対して西欧人は（*最近は以前にもまして*）嫌悪感をあらわにするし、「God!（神よ！）」や「Jesus Christ!（キリスト様よ！）」などとずけずけ叫ぶのは「神に対する冒瀆」と今日でもなお多くの人々が感じている。これとは対照的に、日本人は、呆き返るほどに「神」を乱用する ― それどころか「神の粗製濫造」までやってのける ―「神頼み」したい時や、生身の人間をベタ褒めして「神様扱い」したくなった時にはいつでも、「神・かみ・カミカミ」のオンパレードである。日本人にとっては、昔も今も、自分にとって都合の良い人や物なら何でも「神」であり、「冒瀆」を理由に自分を罰するような厳しい相手は「神じゃない」し「使えないヤツ」として見向きもされない。「冒瀆」なんてものは、日本人の心の成り立ちを考えれば、構造的に理解できっこない概念なのだ（他にもその種の構造理解不能概念は日本には色々あるけどね）・・・「嘘だろ？」と思うなら（いや、マトモな西欧人なら誰もが「そんなの嘘にちがいない」と思って当然だけど）、第二次世界大戦中の日本の軍艦やドイツの戦車や古代の日本や中国の武将や自分の能力と予測をちょっとばかり上回る誰かさんや、そういうものを材料に、日本人がどんな「アイドル」や「神」をデッチ上げているか、チェックしてみるといい・・・心底「ゲゲェーッ！」と驚くこと請け合いだから。

《Japanese gods are too easy on folks》

You shall have no other gods before me. / You shall not make for yourself an idol. / You shall not make wrongful use of the name of the Lord your God. / You shall not commit adultery... These four of the **Ten Commandments** were lightly ignored by the Heianese Japanese nobles... and they still *are* by most modern Japanese. Aside from idols and adultery, the definitions of which have apparently changed nowadays from what they used to be, most Western folks still abide by the other two sacred orders: they have (*increasing*) abhorrence of those who believe in any other religion than their own, and the direct reference to "*God!*" or "*Jesus Christ!*" is still considered by many as *blasphemy*. In contrast, the Japanese are shockingly abusive in their use ― indeed *creation* ― of "gods" whenever they feel inclined to turn to them or to exalt mortals into them. To the Japanese, now as of old, anyone or anything that is good to them is "a god"; those that will punish them for blasphemy are "no gods" and no good. Blasphemy is just another notion the Japanese are structurally ignorant of. If you doubt me ― as all sane Westerners should reasonably do ― just examine what kinds of "idols" or "gods" the Japanese make of such things as the WWII Japanese warships or German battle tanks or ancient warlords of Japan and China or someone who does something just a little beyond their ability or expectation... you are in for a real weird surprise!

http//zubaraie.com　　　　　―Sad Love―

—悲恋—

●154● ひたすらにうらみしもせじさきのよに あふまでこそはちぎらざりけめ
只管に恨みしもせじ前の世に逢ふ迄こそは契らざりけめ

【悲恋】【悟り】『7)千載集:775』藤原家通(ふじわらのいえみち)

いくら恋しく思ってもつれないあなたのことを一方的に恨んだりするのはやめましょう･･･あなたと私の前世には、今のこの世で相思相愛になるほどの強い縁なんて無かった、ただそれだけのことなのでしょうから。

**No grudge will I bear against you for denying me love in this world.
In life preceding this one, we didn't promise to meet as lovers here.**

ひたすら【一向】〔形動ナリ〕<ひたすらに|(adv.)entirely>(ひたすらに=連用形)/うらむ【恨む】〔他マ上二〕<恨む|(v.)hold a grudge against>(うらみ=連用形)/しも【しも】〔副助〕<意味なし|(adv.)NO MEANING>/す【為】〔補動サ変〕<する|(v.)do>(せ=未然形)/じ【じ】〔助動特殊型〕打消意志<～ないつもりだ|(aux-v.)be not going to ～>(じ=終止形)/さきのよ【前の世】〔名〕<前世(=この世に生まれる前に存在していた別世界)|(n.)our former lives>/に【に】〔格助〕<時|(prep.)TIME>/あふ【逢ふ】〔自ハ四〕<[恋人どうしとして]逢う|(v.)have a date>(あふ=連体形)/まで【まで】〔副助〕<～の程度まで|(adv.)to ～ extent>/こそ【こそ】〔係助〕<強調|(adv.)EMPHASIS>/は【は】〔係助〕<～に関しては|(adv.)as for ～>/ちぎる【契る】〔他ラ四〕<約束する|(v.)promise>(ちぎら=未然形)/ず【ず】〔助動特殊型〕打消<～[し]ない|(adv.)not ～>(ざり=連用形)/けむ【けむ】〔助動マ四型〕過去推量<～[し]たのだろう|(aux-v.)PAST SUPPOSITION>(けめ=已然形係り結び)

[hitasurani urami-shimo-se-ji saki-no-yo ni au made koso-wa chigira-zari-keme]

失くした恋の忘れ方／受け入れ方の作法は様々だけど、平安時代の日本人がひどい悲劇に見舞われた場合、「これは運命なのだ」と受け止めるのが習わしでした。彼らの「現世」の運命は、これまでに彼らが積み重ねて来た数々の「前世」での善行・悪行の「積もり」によって、この世に生まれる前からすでにもう決まっているものとみなされたのでした。

There can be so many ways for broken-hearted persons to forget or accept their lost love; Japanese people in the Heian era were in the habit of attributing gross tragedies to fate, which they believed had been predetermined by the accumulated deeds of theirs – good and bad – in their "former lives".

《あるはありなきはなしとて耐ふる民》

驚くべきことに、この歌に見るような運命観は、現代日本人の中に今なお(幸／不幸の幾多の場面ごとに)見られたりします。いやしくも文明国の市民としての自負ある者がこの国に来てそこそこの期間暮らすことになったなら、誰もが必ずや「それは違うだろう？！」と異議申し立てをせずにはおられぬほどの明らかな社会的不正義の数々を、日本人がまるで気にせぬかのごとくじっと耐えている(あるいは面倒くさがって全然変えようともせずにいる)そのさまには、びっくりさせられるはずです･･･「文明的市民」の意味するところは、西欧では「文明の発展をもたらすに好適な学識ある人間としての態度」を意味するのに対し、日本では「既存の体制の保全に都合の良い自主性なき従属的態度」という風に、日本と西欧とでは全く違うのです･･･その種の「奴隷根性倭人」は、その口癖から容易に見分けることができます･･･彼らは二言目にはこう言うのです ―「しょうがない」― こうした日本人の諦めの良い運命観は、西欧人(そして日本人自身)が思っているよりもずーっと根の深いものです。2011年、超巨大地震が引き起こした災厄の真っ只中で、恐慌を来たすこともなく辛抱強く秩序を保っていた東北の民の不屈の姿を見て、日本人の誰もが「日本人であることを誇りに思う」と感じたものでした ―「しょうがない:起こったことは、今更なしには出来ないんだから」の哲学が最高の輝きを放っていた日々でした･･･あれから5年経った今、その堅忍の姿勢が、荒廃した東北の地に一体いかなる進歩をもたらしたでしょうか？古いものが何もなくなった所には、新たな何かが生まれていて然るべきでしょう ― それが西欧での物事のありようですが、日本では全然そうではないのです･･･

—Sad Love—   http//zubaraie.com

―悲恋―

「しょうがない(あれこれ言っても始まらない)」と「**しょうもない**(何を言っても意味がない、何一つ意味あることも始まらない)」は、西欧では似て非なるものなのに、日本ではほとんどいつも同じもの・・・残念、と言えば実に残念なことです・・・「しょうがないよ、そういうものなんだから」？・・・いいえ、**断じてそういうものであっては、いけません！**「忍耐」は「しんどいけど前向きな歩み」に黙々と従う「従僕(じゅうぼく)」としてこき使うべきものであって、「冷酷な現状(げんじょう)」を維持するための「奴隷(どれい)」として使いつぶしてはなりません。

《accept ― whatever *is* is, whatever *isn't* is not ― that's the way it is in Japan》
Surprisingly, such fatalism as seen in this TANKA ― good and bad ― is still to be seen among the modern Japanese in quite a few numbers of cases. No self-respecting citizen from any civilized world who really lived in this country for reasonable amount of time could help being astonished at the patience or indolence of the Japanese people who apparently never mind so much social injustice which would never be left unchallenged by any other civilized citizens of the world... the meaning of "civilized" totally differs in Japan from the West: in the latter, it means educated attitude suitable for the progress of civilization: in Japan, servile attitude convenient for the preservation of the status quo... you can easily identify such slavish Japanese by their pet phrase ― しょうがない(shouganai=it cannot be helped)... the Japanese fatalism is much more deep-rooted than most Westerners (and the Japanese) think. Practically all the Japanese were proud of being Japanese, rightly, when they witnessed the fortitude of folks in 東北(touhoku=the north eastern region of Japan) who didn't cause panic and patiently kept order in the middle of the disaster caused by the mega-quake in 2011 ― those were the days when the philosophy of しょうがない(shouganai=what's happened cannot be undone) shone at its best... <u>5 years later, what progress did their patience bring to the devastated region of 東北(touhoku)?</u>
Where there was nothing old, there ought to have been built something new ― that's the way it is in the West; *not at all so in Japan*... しょうがない(shouganai=it cannot be helped) and **しょうもない**(shoumonai=you're simply *IMPOSSIBLE*!) are two different things in the West; almost always identical in Japan... regrettable, yes it is: it cannot be helped? ― **NO**! it **MUST** be helped! <u>Patience must be a servant of grueling progress, never let patience be a slave to the cruel status quo.</u>

━━━━━━━━━━━━━━━━━━━━━━━━━━━━━━━━━━

●155●うとくなるひとをなにとてうらむらむ しられずしらぬをりもありしに
　　　疎く成る人を何とて恨むらむ知られず知らぬ折も有りしに

【悲恋】[悟り]『8)新古今集:1297』西行(さいぎょう)
愛の情熱が次第(しだい)に冷めて疎遠(そえん)になって行く相手のことを、恨んだりするのは筋違い。お互いそうまで親密になる前には、見ず知らずの他人同士だった頃もあったのだから・・・元の振り出しに戻っただけ。

If someone grows weaker in affection, there's no sense in holding a grudge.
Before getting so mutually intimate, they didn't even know each other.

うとし【疎し】[形ク]<疎遠だ｜(adj.)be estranged>(うとく=連用形)／なる【成る】[自ラ四]<～になる｜(v.)become>(なる=連体形)／ひと【人】[名]<あの人｜(n.)that [darling] one>／を【を】[格助]<目的格｜(prep.)OBJECT>／なに【何】[副]<どうして｜(adv.)why>／とて【とて】[格助]<～と思って｜(adv.)with ～ in mind>／うらむ【恨む】[他マ上二]<恨む｜(v.)hold a grudge>(うらむ=終止形)／らむ【らむ】[助動ラ四型]現在推量<～だろう｜(aux-v.)SUPPOSITION>(らむ=連体形係り結び)／しる【知る】[他ラ四]<知る｜(v.)know>(しら=未然形)／る【る】[助動ラ下二型]受身<～[さ]れる｜(aux-v.)PASSIVE VOICE>(れ=連用形)／ず【ず】[助動特殊型]打消<～[し]ない｜(adv.)not ～>(ず=終止形)／しる【知る】[他ラ四]<知る｜(v.)know>(しら=未然形)／ず【ず】[助動特殊型]打消<

―悲恋―

〜[し]ない｜(adv.)not 〜＞(ぬ＝連体形)／をり【折】【名】＜〜な頃｜(n.)a time when 〜＞／も【も】〔係助〕＜〜もまた｜(adv.)also＞／あり【あり】〔自ラ変〕＜存在する｜(v.)exist＞(あり＝連用形)／き【き】〔助動特殊型〕過去＜〜[し]た｜(aux-v.)PAST＞(し＝連体形)／に【に】〔終助〕＜詠嘆｜(interj.)EXCLAMATION＞

[utoku-naru hito wo nani-tote uramu-ramu shira-re-zu shira-nu ori mo ari-shi ni]

かつては二人とも見知らぬ同士だった頃もある‥‥だったらどうして、お互い別れて別の道を歩むことになったからといって、それを悔やんだり深刻に思い詰めたりする必要があるだろうか？ ― というこの論法、自分で自分を納得させるには何とも無理のある代物で、「かつてこの世に我々が生まれていなかった時もあったのだから、死んでこの世から出て行く時も、心配には及ばないよ」と言っているようなもの。何かを失うことを残念に思うのは、その何かを所有してしまったからこそであって、自分がそれを手にせぬ限りは失う愁いなど生じようもない。喪失の引き起こす心の動揺は、所有する前の心の安らかさを引き合いに出して合理化できるものではない‥‥こんな筋の通らぬ理屈で自分自身を納得させようとしているあたり、もしかしたらそれほどまでにこの詩人が必死になって（筋が通ろうがバカげていようがどんな手を使ってでも！）自分が失ったものを忘れようとしている、何よりの証拠なのかもしれない‥‥だって、この歌人（西行法師）はそんなバカなことするには賢すぎるし、同時にまたそうした必死の手段に頼ってでも忘れたいほどに不幸な人生を歩んだ人でもあったから。

There used to be a time when we didn't know each other, why, then, should we regret and take it so seriously that you and I should part from each other and go our separate ways?... This is quite a strange way of persuading oneself, just like saying that we need not worry about dying and getting out of this life because there used to be a time when we weren't born and didn't exist at all. We are sorry to lose something because we have come into possession of that something. We don't worry about losing anything so long as we don't own it. The mental disturbance caused by loss can never be rationalized by its absence before possession. Such illogicality may only go to show the desperate effort of the poet to forget about his loss by any means, logical or stupid... for, this poet, 西行法師(Saigyou houshi), was too clever to fall into such absurdity, and yet unhappy enough to resort to such desperate measures.

―――――――――――――――――――――――――――――――――――

●156●うらみわびほさぬそでだにあるものを こひにくちなむなこそをしけれ
　　　　恨み侘び干さぬ袖だに有るものを恋に朽ちなむ名こそ惜しけれ

【悲恋】[失恋]『4)後拾遺集:815』相模(さがみ)

つれないあなたの仕打ちを恨み、心寂しく過ごす私の着物の袖は、涙に濡れて乾く暇もない‥‥
というのに、そんなあなたとの恋の噂だけは、今なお世間に流れ続け、
もはや抜け殻のような虚しい浮き名に、私の評判も朽ち果ててしまうのでしょうか‥‥
だとすれば、それは残念なことでしょうね‥‥生身の恋の果てになら、名など惜しまぬ私だけれど。

　　　　　　My sleeves are sodden in tears cried over you,
　　　　　　With a bodiless rumor as your love still in the air.
　　　　　　Will my name decay too along with fruitless love?
　　　　　　Rotten fame would just be fine after substantial affairs...

うらむ【怨む】〔他マ上二〕＜恨む｜(v.)hold a grudge＞(うらみ＝連用形)／わぶ【侘ぶ】〔自バ上二〕＜意気消沈する｜(v.)be dejected＞(わび＝連用形)／ほす【干す】〔他サ四〕＜乾かす｜(v.)dry up＞(ほさ＝未然形)／ず【ず】〔助動特殊型〕打消＜〜[し]ない｜(adv.)not 〜＞(ぬ＝連体形)／そで【袖】【名】＜袖｜(n.)the sleeve＞／だに【だに】〔副助〕＜〜さえ｜(adv.)even＞／あり【あり】〔自ラ変〕＜存在する｜(v.)exist＞(ある＝連体形)／ものを【ものを】〔接助〕＜〜[だ]というのに｜(conj.)although＞／こひ【恋】【名】＜恋

—Sad Love—

―悲恋―

｜(n.)love＞／に【に】〔格助〕＜原因｜(prep.)REASON＞／くつ【朽つ】〔自夕上二〕＜腐食する｜(v.)rot＞(くち＝連用形)／ぬ【ぬ】〔助動ナ変型〕確述＜きっと～する｜(adv.)EMPHASIS＞(な＝未然形)／む【む】〔助動マ四型〕推量＜だろう｜(aux-v.)SUPPOSITION＞(む＝連体形)／な【名】〔名〕＜評判｜(n.)reputation＞／こそ【こそ】〔係助〕＜強調｜(adv.)EMPHASIS＞／をし【惜し】〔形シク〕＜なくなるのを残念に思う｜(v.)be sorry to lose＞(をしけれ＝已然形係り結び)

　　　　[urami-wabi hosa-nu sode dani aru mono-wo koi ni kuchi-na-mu na koso oshikere]

根も葉もない噂に朽ち果てる「＜名＞こそ惜しけれ」は、実のある恋愛の果てになら「＜身＞やは惜しまむ＝我が身を誰が惜しむものですか」の裏返し。色恋の真相は当事者二人にしかわからない・・・にもかかわらず、外野の連中は彼らの個人的悲劇を酒の肴に無責任な冗談で盛り上がる。昔も今も変わらない(否、ネット上で爆発的に増殖する不純な情報のせいで平安時代よりはるかにひどくなってる)全人類の非人間的営みを、この平安歌人は嘆いて見せる・・・ついでに言えば、この歌人、まさにこの歌一つの評判をもって、後代の日本人には「恋多き女流歌人」として知られることになるのである。

＜名＞こそ惜しけれ(＜na＞ koso oshi-kere＝I regret ＜my name＞ rotten by groundless rumors) is the flip side of the poet's emotion of ＜身＞やは惜しまむ(＜mi＞ yawa oshima-mu＝why should I regret ＜myself＞ ruined after substantial affairs?). The truth of any love affair is only known to the two... but the third party makes party jokes of their personal tragedies. The same old inhumanity of all humanity still prevalent (or still more prevalent due to the explosion of defiled info on the Net) today deplored by a Heianese poet... who, incidentally, came to be known later as "an amorous poet" by virtue of this particular TANKA.

― ―

●157●よのなかのうきもつらきもしのぶれば　おもひしらずとひとやみるらむ
　　　世の中の憂きも辛きも忍ぶれば思ひ知らずと人や見るらむ

　　　　　　　　　　　　　【悲恋】〔溜息〕『3)拾遺集:933』詠み人知らず

世の中悲しいことだらけ。辛い思いの連続に、じぃーっと耐えているうちに、世間は私をどう見ることか・・・(あの人は、人を愛する喜びも、愛を失う悲しみも、ロクに知らないつまらない人)と、心ならずもそう思われてしまうのだろうか。

　　　　　　This world, full of hardships and sorrow,
　　　　　　When inured after so much painful endurance,
　　　　　　May make others see me too dull to feel anything,
　　　　　　Without knowing how much I'm capable of feeling.
　　　　　　How much I've felt and suppressed would surprise them.

よのなか【世の中】〔名〕＜世の中｜(n.)the world＞／の【の】〔格助〕＜主格｜(prep.)SUBJECT＞／うし【憂し】〔形ク〕＜憂鬱だ｜(adj.)melancholy＞(うき＝連体形)／も【も】〔係助〕＜～もまた｜(adv.)also＞／つらし【辛し】〔形ク〕＜冷淡だ｜(adj.)cold-hearted＞(つらき＝連体形)／も【も】〔係助〕＜～もまた｜(adv.)also＞／しのぶ【忍ぶ】〔他バ上二〕＜耐え忍ぶ｜(v.)endure＞(しのぶれ＝已然形)／ば【ば】〔接助〕＜仮定｜(conj.)if＞／おもひ【想ひ】〔名〕＜恋心｜(n.)loving feeling＞／しる【知る】〔他ラ四〕＜知る｜(v.)know＞(しら＝未然形)／ず【ず】〔助動特殊型〕打消＜～[し]ない｜(adv.)not ～＞(ず＝終止形)／と【と】〔格助〕＜内容提示｜(conj.)that ～＞／ひと【人】〔名〕＜他人｜(n.)others＞／や【や】〔係助〕＜疑問｜(adv.)INTERROGATIVE＞／みる【見る】〔他マ上一〕＜見る｜(v.)view＞(みる＝終止形)／らむ【らむ】〔助動ラ四型〕現在推量＜～だろう｜(aux-v.)SUPPOSITION＞(らむ＝連体形係り結び)

　　　　[yo-no-naka no uki mo tsuraki mo shinobure-ba omoi shira-zu to hito ya miru-ramu]

―悲恋―

水量多ければ水面は静か。声が大きければ心は浅はか。目立つ奴らにゃ目もくれず、静かなる者に注目せよ。感情の刺激は、進入角度が浅ければ心の上っ面で跳ね返り、深すぎれば心の奥底に吸い込まれて表面的には何の反応も起こらない・・・心の奥底の潜在的反応が、繊細な言葉の衣をまとって表出する時、人はそれを「詩」と呼ぶ。

Still waters run deep. The louder a shout, the shallower the mind. Ignore the salient and heed the silent. Emotional stimulus is instantly reflected off on the mind's surface at a shallow angle; if too steep, it's absorbed deep inside without apparent reaction... when the latent reaction comes to the surface delicately wrapped in sensitive words, we call it "poetry".

●158● いでていにしあとだにいまだかはらぬに　たがかよひぢといまはなるらむ
　　　出でて住にし跡だに未だ変はらぬに誰が通ひ路と今は成るらむ

【悲恋】[失恋]『8)新古今集:1409』在原業平(ありわらのなりひら)
あなたと最後に愛し合ったあの夜に部屋を後にした時とまるで変わらぬ様子なのに、
今ではその同じ道を、誰があなたの元へと通っているのでしょうか？

It seems as if my footsteps were still fresh
Upon the old familiar path to your room.
Who treads it now, I wonder,
To replace my old footsteps?

いづ【出づ】〔自ダ下二〕<出る｜(v.)come out>(いで=連用形)／て【て】〔接助〕<順接｜(conj.)and>／いぬ【往ぬ】〔自ナ変〕<行く｜(v.)go away>(いに=連用形)／き【き】〔助動特殊型〕過去<～[し]た｜(aux-v.)PAST>(し=連体形)／あと【跡】〔名〕<足跡｜(n.)a trace>／だに【だに】〔副助〕<～さえ｜(adv.)even>／いまだ【未だ】〔副〕<まだ｜(adv.)yet>／かはる【変はる】〔自ラ四〕<変わる｜(v.)change>(かはら=未然形)／ず【ず】〔助動特殊型〕打消<～[し]ない｜(adv.)not ～>(ぬ=連体形)／に【に】〔接助〕<逆接｜(conj.)although>／た【誰】〔代名〕<誰｜(pron.)who>／が【が】〔格助〕<の｜(prep.)'s>／かよひぢ【通ひ路】〔名〕<誰かのもとへと通う道｜(n.)the beaten path to someone's house>／と【と】〔格助〕<結末｜(prep.)RESULT>／いま【今】〔副〕<今｜(adv.)now>／は【は】〔係助〕<～に関しては｜(adv.)as for ～>／なる【成る】〔自ラ四〕<～になる｜(v.)become>(なる=終止形)／らむ【らむ】〔助動ラ四型〕現在推量<～だろう｜(aux-v.)SUPPOSITION>(らむ=連体形係り結び)

[ide-te ini-shi ato dani imada kawara-nu-ni ta-ga kayoi-ji to ima-wa naru-ramu]
「この道はもう、私の通い路ではない」・・・この切ない感じ、「昔の恋人の家へと続く道」のみならず、「かつて通った懐かしの母校への通学路」にも通じそうですね。「その心余りて言葉足らず(・・・心情が有り余り過ぎて、表現がうまく追いついていない)」と紀貫之が評した在原業平らしい、ストレートな感情表現の詩です。
This is no longer the way for me to go... this sad feeling might just as well be true to one's old school as to old darling's home. A straightforward emotional expression typical of 在原業平(Ariwara-no-Narihira), about whom 紀貫之(Ki-no-Tsurayuki) said その心余りて言葉足らず(so-no kokoro amari-te kotoba tara-zu＝too much emotion overflows deficient expression).

★159★ こひてしねこひてしねとやわぎもこが　わがやのかどをすぎてゆくらむ
　　　恋ひて死ね恋ひて死ねとや吾妹子が我が家の門を過ぎて行くらむ

【悲恋】[失恋]『3)拾遺集:936』柿本人麻呂(かきのもとのひとまろ)
つれないあの人を乗せた牛車が、ぎっし・ぎっしと音を立てて、私の家の前を素通りして行く・・・「私に焦がれて死になさい、恋煩いで死になさい」と言わんばかりの残酷な足音だけを残して。

―Sad Love―　　　　　　　　　　　　　　http://zubaraie.com

―悲恋―

"I wanna see you die, I wanna see you die..."
I hear the cart singing past my front door
With my old love in I'm dying to see in vain.

こふ【恋ふ】〔他ハ上二〕＜恋しく思う｜(v.)long for＞(こひ＝連用形)／て【て】〔接助〕＜順接｜(conj.)and＞／しぬ【死ぬ】〔自ナ変〕＜死ぬ｜(v.)die＞(しね＝命令形)／こふ【恋ふ】〔他ハ上二〕＜恋しく思う｜(v.)long for＞(こひ＝連用形)／て【て】〔接助〕＜順接｜(conj.)and＞／しぬ【死ぬ】〔自ナ変〕＜死ぬ｜(v.)die＞(しね＝命令形)／と【と】〔格助〕＜内容提示｜(conj.)that ～＞／や【や】〔係助〕＜疑問｜(adv.)INTERROGATIVE＞／わぎもこ【吾妹子】〔名〕＜我が愛しの女性｜(n.)my sweet girl＞／が【が】〔格助〕＜主格｜(prep.)SUBJECT＞／わ【我】〔代名〕＜私｜(pron.)I, myself＞／が【が】〔格助〕＜の｜(prep.)'s＞／や【家】〔名〕＜家｜(n.)house＞／の【の】〔格助〕＜の｜(prep.)'s＞／かど【門】〔名〕＜門｜(n.)the gate＞／を【を】〔格助〕＜目的格｜(prep.)OBJECT＞／すぐ【過ぐ】〔自ガ上二〕＜通り過ぎる｜(v.)pass by＞(すぎ＝連用形)／て【て】〔接助〕＜順接｜(conj.)and＞／ゆく【行く】〔自力四〕＜行く｜(v.)go away＞(ゆく＝終止形)／らむ【らむ】〔助動ラ四型〕現在推量＜～だろう｜(aux-v.)SUPPOSITION＞(らむ＝連体形係り結び)

[koi-te shine koi-te shine to-ya wa-gimo-ko ga wa-ga-ya no kado wo sugi-te yuku-ramu]

平安貴族は自分の足では歩かず、牛に引かせた車(牛車)に乗り、大勢の従者を伴って移動するのが通例、その車輪のけたたましい音で、その接近は誰の耳にも明らか･･･その大音響はこの詩人にはまるで拷問の歯車の軋る音･･･牛車の中には彼の愛しい人がいて、彼の家の門前の手が届きそうな距離を ― しかし社会的には手も触れられぬ遠い人として ― 聞こえよがしに通り過ぎて行く･･･この悲喜劇の作者とされるのは、『古今集』前代の伝説の歌人柿本人麻呂。この作品もそうだが、人麻呂の恋歌のかなりの部分は(大方の人々の思い込みに反して)平安時代のそれと同じく「作り話」であって彼の実人生の感慨ではない。後代になると、奈良時代の「詠み人知らず」の歌をいいかげんな編者が「素晴らしい！」と感じたなら無責任にそれを「伝(一説によれば)人麻呂」としたり、中には大胆にも自作歌に「人麻呂」のラベルを貼る連中さえいたりしたので、どれが本当の人麻呂作でどれがニセモノか、今となっては判別するのは至難の業･･･この作品は(筆者 之人冗悟の耳には)あまり人麻呂っぽく聞こえないのだけれど、それはそれとしてこの歌はとても面白い響きを持っている･･･悲劇的状況が放つ喜劇的訴求力、本当に良い歌の偉大さがこの歌には備わっているのだ：その意味で、これは「歌聖」の手になる短歌と呼んでも構わない歌だろう。

Heianese nobles didn't walk around on foot; they usually rode on ox-driven carts with many attendants, making their approach felt by the roaring of the wheels... it sounds like wheels of torture to the ears of this poet who knows there is someone so dear inside the cart outside his gate painfully within hearing but socially out of reach. A tragicomedy attributed to the legendary pre-古今集(Kokin shuu) poet 柿本人麻呂(Kakinomoto-no-Hitomaro). Contrary to popular belief, quite a lot of 人麻呂(Hitomaro)'s love poems, including this one, were as fictional as their Heianese counterparts. In later years, quite a few anonymous poems in the Nara(奈良) era which sounded superb to the ears of sloppy editors were irresponsibly ascribed to 人麻呂(Hitomaro)... some would even venture to label their own works as 人麻呂(Hitomaro)'s... which makes it hard for us to discern which is really his and which is not... this one sounds not quite like 人麻呂(Hitomaro) *to this author (之人冗悟:Jaugo Noto)*, but it *does* sound funny... comical appeal of a tragic situation, that's what's great about a really good poem: in that sense, this one can be rightly attributed to the 歌聖(kasei＝the sacred poet), I agree.

―――――――――――――――――――――

―悲恋―

★160★あふことのたえてしなくばなかなかに　ひとをもみをもうらみざらまし

会ふ事の絶えてし無くば中中に人をも身をも恨みざらまし

【悲恋】[失恋]『3)拾遺集:678』藤原朝忠(ふじわらのあさただ)

今となってはもう叶わぬ想い‥‥その相手のあなたに、今でもこうして会わねばならぬなんて、なんて残酷な仕打ちでしょうか。いっそ全く会わずにいれば、つれないあなたや、我が身の不幸を、こんなに恨むこともないでしょうに。

If I were never allowed to see her again,
Would it be a reason for me to hold a grudge against her? *NO!*
My opportunity to see her even when I can't meet her in her room
Is all the more reason for me to hold a grudge against her,
And a scourge on me who can still see yet can never touch her.

あふ【会ふ】〔他ハ四〕＜[視覚的に、チラと]目に入る｜(v.)have a glimpse＞(あふ＝連体形)／こと【事】〔名〕＜～という事｜(n.)the act of ～ing＞／の【の】〔格助〕＜主格｜(prep.)SUBJECT＞／たえて【絶えて】〔副〕＜全く～ない｜(adv.)not at all＞／し【し】〔副助〕＜意味なし｜(adv.)NO MEANING＞／なし【なし】〔形ク〕＜存在しない｜(v.)do not exist＞(なく＝連用形)／は【は】〔係助〕＜仮定｜(conj.)if＞／なかなかなり【中中なり】〔形動ナリ〕＜かえって逆に｜(adv.)on the contrary＞(なかなかに＝連用形)／ひと【人】〔名〕＜あの人｜(n.)that [darling] one＞／を【を】〔格助〕＜目的格｜(prep.)OBJECT＞／も【も】〔係助〕＜～もまた｜(adv.)also＞／み【身】〔名〕＜私自身｜(n.)I, myself＞／を【を】〔格助〕＜目的格｜(prep.)OBJECT＞／も【も】〔係助〕＜～もまた｜(adv.)also＞／うらむ【怨む】〔他マ上二〕＜恨む｜(v.)hold a grudge＞(うらみ＝未然形)／ず【ず】〔助動特殊型〕打消＜～しない｜(adv.)not ～＞(ざら＝未然形)／まし【まし】〔助動特殊型〕推量＜～だろうに｜(aux-v.)should＞(まし＝終止形)

[au koto no taete-shi naku-ba nakanakani hito wo-mo mi wo-mo urami-zara-mashi]

普通なら「あふ(逢ふ)」は平安時代の貴人男性にとっては幸福な特権を意味する語。愛のリクエストを受け入れてもらえた男性だけが「(生身の女性と)逢ふ」ことを許されるわけで、その「逢ふ」は通例「肉体関係を持つ」の意味まで含むのだから‥‥それならどうしてこの歌人は「できれば彼女に＜あふ＞ことがなければいいのに」などと文句を言っているのか？それは彼が「平安的な意味」で彼女と「あふ」(即ち、夫婦として愛し合う)状態にはなく、ただ単に自分の職場で彼女の姿を「見る」だけだからである。具体的には、彼らの職場は「日本の朝廷」、彼が恋しながら「逢ふ」ことを許されなかった彼女は、住み込みの「女房(現代的な＜奥様＞の意味ではない)」として朝廷に勤務しているのだ‥‥古歌なのに、不思議と現代の(同じクラブや学校や会社やご近所の相手に失恋しちゃった)似たような状況の男女にも当てはまる歌である。

"あふ(au＝to meet)" is usually a happy privilege of noble men in the Heian era: only men who have had their loving request accepted will be allowed to 逢ふ(au＝meet the woman in the flesh), which normally means "to have carnal knowledge of each other". Why then should this poet grumble that he would rather not meet her? Because he is not "meeting her" in the Heianese sense ("mating with her", that is), but he is just "*seeing* her" at the place where she is working ― more specifically, in the Imperial Palace of Japan, where the woman he fell in love with but was not allowed to love is living as a worker called 女房(nyoubou＝Court attendant lady; not "*wife*" as in the modern sense). An ancient song strangely applicable to modern men and women lost in love with some other member of the same club, school, company or neighborhood.

《逢ふべくもあらぬ人見る「宮仕へ」》

平安の世の女性たちはふつう世間からは隠されており、彼女が(というか彼女の両親が)その恋人・夫として

―悲恋―

認めた特別な男性以外の目に触れることはなかった。唯一の例外は、宮廷に住み込み奉公する「女房」と呼ばれる女性達で、彼女らだけは、朝廷の役人として勤務する男たちが日々目にすることのできる(そしてちょっかい出すこともできる)例外的に近しい存在なのだった。女房は、権勢を誇る家柄の娘達の中から選ばれるのが通例だったが、特に知識があり文芸的嗜みに優れた女性もまた選ばれて、より身分の高い女性の御側近くに仕えることがあった。このような身分の低い女房たちは(多少さげすみを込めて)「受領の娘(＝中の上程度の貴族の娘)」と呼ばれたが、彼女たちこそ平安期の日本文学に対する最大の貢献者なのだった。和泉式部、赤染衛門、紫式部、清少納言といった大物たちも、この階層に属する女性たちである。

《宮仕へ(miya-zukae) ― where men could daily see normally invisible women》
Heianese women were usually kept out of sight from anyone other than special men whom she ― or rather her parents ― admitted as her lover or husband. The only exception to this rule were Court-serving ladies called 女房(nyoubou) who were living in the Imperial Palace within daily sight and reach of noble men who served as Imperial officials. These ladies were normally chosen from the daughters of politically powerful families, but women with exceptional knowledge or cultural accomplishment were also chosen to wait on higher-ranking ladies. Such lower-class 女房(nyoubou) were somewhat spitefully called 受領の娘(juryou no musume＝daughters of upper-middle class nobles), who were the greatest contributors to Heianese Japanese literature, among whom were such big names as 和泉式部(Izumi shikibu), 赤染衛門(Akazome emon), 紫式部(Murasaki shikibu) and 清少納言(Sei shou-nagon).

― ―

●161● きみこふとかつはきえつつほどふるを かくてもいけるみとやみるらむ
君恋ふと且つは消えつつ程経るを斯くても生ける身とや見るらむ

【悲恋】[謎掛]『4)後拾遺集:807』藤原元真(ふじわらのもとざね)
あなたに恋を打ち明けて「イヤ！」と言われて、消え入るようにすごすごと退散したこの私…あれから随分時は経ちましたが、恋する男としての私は死んでも、一人の人間としては今なおこうして生きいます…そんな私を、あなたはどう見ているのでしょうか？…(私に拒絶されたら死んでしまう、とか、大袈裟なこと言ってたわりには、今ものうのうと生きてるわね、あの人)と、そういう目で見ているのでしょうか。

 I used to love you so much,
 So much so that I felt I would die if I failed to be in mutual love with you;
 I begged you to love me to save me from dying of love;
 You refused to love me, to save me from dying of love;
 What could I do but live alone this lifeless life without you?...
 It's been a long time since I lost you even before I had you.
 How do I look in your eyes?
 ― A living dead surviving ridiculously too long?
 A foolish man dying as many times as he falls in and out of love?

きみ【君】[代名]＜あなた｜(pron.)you＞／こふ【恋ふ】[他ハ上二]＜恋しく思う｜(v.)long for＞(こふ＝終止形)／と【と】[格助]＜内容提示｜(conj.)that ～＞／かつ【且つ】[副]＜一方で｜(adv.)on one hand＞／は【は】[係助]＜～に関しては｜(adv.)as for ～＞／きゆ【消ゆ】[自ヤ下二]＜消える｜(v.)disappear＞(きえ＝連用形)／つつ【つつ】[接助]＜～し]ながら｜(conj.)as＞／ほど【程】[名]＜時間｜(n.)time＞／ふ【経】[自ハ下二]＜経る｜(v.)[time] go by＞(ふる＝連体形)／を【を】[格助]＜目的格｜(prep.)OBJECT＞／かくて【斯くて】[副]＜こんな有り様｜(adv.)like this＞／も【も】[係助]＜～[で]さえも｜(adv.)even＞／いく【生く】[自カ四]＜死なずにいる｜(v.)still survive＞(いけ＝已然形・命令形)／

http://zubaraie.com   -159-   ―Sad Love―

―悲恋―

り【り】〔助動ラ変型〕存続<~[し]ている｜(aux-v.)PERFECT TENSE>(る=連体形)／み【身】〔名〕<存在｜(n.)an entity>／と【と】〔格助〕<内容提示｜(conj.)that ~>／や【や】〔係助〕<疑問｜(adv.)INTERROGATIVE>／みる【見る】〔他マ上一〕<見る｜(v.)view>(みる=終止形)／らむ【らむ】〔助動ラ四型〕現在推量<~だろう｜(aux-v.)SUPPOSITION>(らむ=連体形係り結び)

[kimi kou to katsu-wa kie-tsutsu hodo-furu wo kakute-mo ike-ru mi to-ya miru-ramu]

平安時代の日本の宮廷の中でしか生まれない歌で、そこでの当時の人間模様を知らぬ人には絶対解釈できない歌でもある。「**且つは消えつつ程経る**=もう消え入ってしまいたい、と思いつつ、これまでの年月を過ごしてきました」という心情の背後には一体どんな理由があるのだろう？初句「**君恋ふと**=あなたが好きです、と告白しつつ」がその答え・・・ということは、彼、失恋したのか？それはもちろんそうだろう、さもなくば「消え入りたい気分」になるはずもあるまい？この男が彼女を口説いたその様子まで手に取るようにわかる――彼は、彼女にこう言って脅したのだ――「もしあなたが私の愛を受け入れてくれないなら、私は死んでしまい[たいと思い]ます！」・・・このありきたりな脅迫は、しかし、相手の女性にとってはあまりにも陳腐すぎて効き目もないままに、彼女は彼の愛のリクエストを拒絶してしまったのだ。さらに悪いことには、彼をフッたこの彼女、(社会的にはともかく)物理的には手を伸ばせば届く宮廷内のすぐそばで、彼の視界の中に常に(女房として)いるのである・・・この哀れな歌人がいま彼女に望むことはただ一つ――「約束通り自らの命を絶つだけの勇気もない、臆病な嘘吐き男だことよ)」とか、俺のこと、思ってないといいんだけどなぁ・・・

A poem that can only be born in the Imperial Palace of Japan in the Heian era, which can never be understood by those ignorant of the way it was then and there. What's the reason for **且つは消えつつ程経る**(katsu-wa kie-tsutsu hodo-furu=going through these years while feeling like fading away)? See the first phrase **君恋ふと**(kimi kou to=while I made my confession that I loved you)... was he lost in love, then? Yes, he sure was, otherwise, why should he "feel like fading away"? We can even see how he wooed her: he threatened her by saying "I would [*rather*] die if you wouldn't accept my love!"... this stereotyped threat, however, seems to have been so tame for her that she rejected his love request. What is worse still, she is still within sight and physical (though not social) reach of him in the Imperial Court as 女房(nyoubou=Court attendant lady)... all this poor poet wants from her is that she wouldn't see him *a coward liar who didn't have the nerve to terminate his life as he promised he would*!

★162★かたみこそいまはあたなれこれなくば　わするるときもあらましものを
形見こそ今は仇なれ是無くば忘るる時も有らましものを

【悲恋】［失恋］『1)古今集:746』詠み人知らず

今となっては、あなたが残して行った形見の品が、私にとっては仇敵のようなものです。これさえなければ、あなたのことを忘れる時もあるでしょうに、これがあるばかりにどうしてもあなたのことが忘れられないのです・・・それなのに、捨てられないのです、この形見も、あなたとの切ない思い出の数々も・・・

**The memento of broken love that she left behind
Has turned out to be the archenemy of my heart.
Forget her I could without it...
But how could I ever desert it?**

かたみ【形見】〔名〕<思い出の品｜(n.)a memento>／こそ【こそ】〔係助〕<強調｜(adv.)EMPHASIS>／いま【今】〔名〕<今｜(n.)now>／は【は】〔係助〕<~に関しては｜(adv.)as for ~>／あた【仇】〔名〕<仇敵｜(n.)the nemesis>／なり【なり】〔助動ナリ型〕断定<~である｜(aux-v.)be>(なれ=已然形係り結び)／これ【是】〔代名〕<これ｜(pron.)this>／なし【なし】〔形〕<存在しない｜(v.)do not exist>(なく=已然形)／ば【ば】〔接助〕<仮定｜(conj.)if>／わする【忘る】〔他ラ下二〕<忘れる｜(v.)forget>(わす

るる＝連体形）／とき【時】〔名〕＜時｜(n.)the time＞／も【も】〔係助〕＜意味なし｜(adv.)NO MEANING＞／あり【あり】〔自ラ変〕＜存在する｜(v.)exist＞（あら＝未然形）／まし【まし】〔助動特殊型〕推量＜～だろうに｜(aux-v.)should＞（まし＝連体形）／ものを【ものを】〔終助〕＜～だろうになぁ｜(interj.)EXCLAMATION＞

[katami koso ima-wa ata nare kore naku-ba wasururu toki mo ara-mashi-mono-wo]
恋愛の記憶を心の中から消し去るのは容易ではない・・・では、「心の外」では、どうか？この歌人にとってはそれもやっぱり難しいようで、昔の恋人が残した「形見＝物理的な思い出の品」をつかまえてブツブツ文句を言っている・・・その気になれば捨て去れるだろうに・・・恋を失った後で、この上さらに別の何かを失うことにはもう耐えられない、ということかもしれない。
Memories of lost love are hard to do away with within your heart: but what about outside it? This poet finds it equally difficult; he/she holds a grudge against 形見(katami＝a physical souvenir she/he left behind). The poet could throw it away if [s]he would... maybe [s]he cannot bear to think of any more loss other than the love that's gone.

●163●わびぬればしひてわすれむとおもへども　ゆめてふものぞひとだのめなる
　　侘びぬれば強ひて忘れむと思へども夢と言ふ物ぞ人頼めなる

【悲恋】〔溜息〕『1)古今集:569』藤原興風（ふじわらのおきかぜ）

いくら恋しく思ってもつれないあなたに、私の心はすっかりくたびれ果ててしまい、
あなたのことはもう忘れてしまおうと思ったのですが、それでも夢には出てくるあなた・・・
儚い逢瀬の嬉しさに、まだひょっとして、現実の中でも逢えるのでは、などと期待してしまう・・・
あぁ、何と思わせぶりで罪作りなものなのでしょう、夢というやつは。

Love-exhaustion unworthy of its pain
Had me decide to stop thinking about you
My dream, however, derides my resolution
By making you appear to keep me still hopeful.

わぶ【侘ぶ】〔自バ上二〕＜意気消沈する｜(v.)be dejected＞（わび＝連用形）／ぬ【ぬ】〔助動ナ変型〕完了＜すでに～［し］た｜(aux-v.)PERFECT TENSE＞（ぬれ＝已然形）／ば【ば】〔接助〕＜理由｜(conj.)REASON＞／しひて【強ひて】〔副〕＜無理にでも｜(adv.)forcibly＞／わする【忘る】〔他ラ下二〕＜忘れる｜(v.)forget＞（わすれ＝未然形）／む【む】〔助動マ四型〕意志＜～するつもりだ｜(aux-v.)be going to ～＞（む＝終止形）／と【と】〔格助〕＜内容提示｜(conj.)that ～＞／おもふ【思ふ】〔他ハ四〕＜思う｜(v.)think＞（おもへ＝已然形）／ども【ども】〔接助〕＜～ではあるが｜(conj.)although＞／ゆめ【夢】〔名〕＜夢｜(n.)a dream＞／と【と】〔格助〕＜内容提示｜(conj.)that ～＞／いふ【言ふ】〔自ハ四〕＜～という名の｜(prep.)with the name of ～＞（いふ＝連体形）／もの【物】〔名〕＜物事｜(n.)a thing＞／ぞ【ぞ】〔係助〕＜強調｜(adv.)EMPHASIS＞／ひとだのめなり【人頼めなり】〔形動ナリ〕＜思わせぶりだ｜(adj.)promising＞（ひとだのめなる＝連体形係り結び）

[wabi-nure-ba shiite wasure-mu to omoe-domo yume chuu mono zo hito-danome-naru]
現実の中で別れてしまった誰かがいまだに夢に現れるとなれば、その失恋のことを忘れるのは今日でさえ容易なことではないだろうけど、平安時代はもっと大変・・・なにせ「夢の中に現れるってことは、その登場人物が実際あなたに好意を抱いていることを示す吉祥」と思われていた時代なんだから。
Someone you've lost in real life still appearing in your dream makes it hard for you to forget about your lost love even today, but still more so in the Heian era when appearance in a dream was thought to be a positive sign that the dramatis personae is actually fond of you.

—悲恋—

●164● わすれなむとおもふこころのつくからに ありしよりけにまづぞこひしき
忘れなむと思ふ心の付くからに有りしより異に先づぞ恋ひしき

【悲恋】[失恋]『1)古今集:718』詠み人知らず

(もう忘れてしまおう、あの人のことは)と思う心が芽生えてからというもの、
以前にも増して(あの人が恋しい)という思いが、心に真っ先に浮かぶようになってしまいました。

Ever since I began to hope to forget
More than ever I grew impatient to meet again.

わする【忘る】〔他ラ下二〕＜忘れる｜(v.)forget＞(わすれ＝未然形)／ぬ【ぬ】〔助動ナ変型〕確述＜きっと〜する｜(adv.)EMPHASIS＞(な＝未然形)／む【む】〔助動マ四型〕意志＜〜するつもりだ｜(aux-v.)be going to 〜＞(む＝終止形)／と【と】〔格助〕＜内容提示｜(conj.)that 〜＞／おもふ【思ふ】〔他ハ四〕＜思う｜(v.)think＞(おもふ＝連体形)／こころ【心】〔名〕＜心｜(n.)heart＞／の【の】〔格助〕＜主格｜(prep.)SUBJECT＞／つく【付く】〔自カ四〕＜沸き上がる｜(v.)rise up＞(つく＝連体形)／からに【からに】〔接助〕＜〜したばっかりに｜(conj.)just because＞／あり【有り】〔自ラ変〕＜[状況が]ある｜(v.)things stand＞(あり＝連用形)／き【き】〔助動特殊型〕過去＜〜[し]た｜(aux-v.)PAST＞(し＝連体形)／より【より】〔格助〕＜比較対象｜(prep.)than＞／けに【異に】〔副〕＜より一層｜(adv.)still more＞／まづ【先づ】〔副〕＜何よりもまず｜(adv.)more than any＞／ぞ【ぞ】〔係助〕＜強調｜(adv.)EMPHASIS＞／こひし【恋し】〔形シク〕＜恋しい｜(v.)feel attached to＞(こひしき＝連体形係り結び)

[wasure-na-mu to omou kokoro no tsuku-kara-ni ari-shi-yori-keni mazu-zo koishiki]

失くした恋を忘れようとすればするほど、かえってそれに恋着する自分がいる・・・この歌が詠まれてから1100年も経つのに、いまだに人類が答えを見つけられずにいる逆説的恋愛感情の謎。
The more you try to forget about your lost love, the more deeply attached to it you find yourself. A riddle of paradoxical affection still left unsolved after 1,100 years of human experience.

《今昔で蒟蒻ほども違う歌》

この『古今集』の短歌は、三世紀後の『新古今集』に、形も意味も全く違う短歌に変えて収録されている ― 『忘くるらむ＞と思ふ心の＜疑ひ＞に有りしより異に＜物＞ぞ＜悲しき＞』・・・「あの人は私のこと、たぶん、忘れてる」との疑念が生じてからというもの、以前にもまして寂しく悲しい思いです・・・西欧の古典作品では絶対に考えられない大胆な書き換え、原典のみわけも付かぬほどの修正を意識的に(あるいは思わず知らず)行なうことで「伝統の価値」を全く無視する、という日本の「残念な伝統」の一例。書き残された文物であれ日本語の語形や語義であれ(ひょっとしたら「憲法」でさえ)好き勝手にいじくられることもなく本来の姿のまま今日まで残っている物事なんて、この日本にはとても、とっても、とぉーーーーっても少ないのです。

《the same song now and old ― swaying to and fro as a devil's tongue》
This TANKA in 古今集(Kokin shuu) is converted 3 centuries later in 新古今集(Shin-Kokin shuu) into another form with totally different meaning ― 忘くるらむ＞と思ふ心の＜疑ひ＞に有りしより異に＜物＞ぞ＜悲しき＞(*wasuru-ramu* to omou kokoro no utagai ni ari-shi-yori-ke-ni mazu-zo kanashiki＝ since I started to **suspect that you would forget about me**, I became more sad and lonely than ever)... an audacious alteration never possible in the world of Western classics, which goes to show the deplorable Japanese tradition of paying no homage to the value of tradition by consciously (or even *subconsciously*) altering the original out of recognition. There are very, very, *veeeeerrrrrryyy* few things in Japan which have existed in their original forms without being tampered with, whether in literary documents or in the forms and meanings of Japanese language (or even CONSTITUTION I'm afraid).

★165★かくばかりうしとおもふにこひしきは われさへこころふたつありけり
斯くばかり憂しと思ふに恋しきは我さへ心二つ有りけり

【悲恋】[失恋]『3)拾遺集:989』詠み人知らず

あなたに冷たくされて、こうまで辛く悲しい思いをしておきながら、それでも今なおあなたのことが恋しくて恋しくてたまらないなんて…私を裏切ったあなたに二心あるように、私自身の心もまた、二つに割れてこの私を苦しめようとしているみたいです。

At once so painfully pensive and still so deep in love
With such a faithless one once kind but now so cold
— *You* too betray me again? —
***My heart* that's broken in two!**

かく【斯く】[副]<こんなに│(adv.)thus>／ばかり【ばかり】[副助]<〜なほど│(adv.)to 〜 exent>／うし【憂し】[形ク]<憂鬱だ│(adj.)melancholy>(うし＝終止形)／と【と】[格助]<内容提示│(conj.)that 〜>／おもふ【思ふ】[他ハ四]<思う│(v.)think>(おもふ＝終止形)／に【に】[接助]<逆接│(conj.)although>／こひし【恋し】[形シク]<恋しい│(v.)feel attached to>(こひしき＝連体形)／は【は】[係助]<ということは│(conj.)judging from it>／われ【我】[代名]<私│(pron.)I, myself>／さへ【さへ】[副助]<さえ│(adv.)even>／こころ【心】[名]<心│(n.)heart>／ふたつ【二つ】[名]<二つ│(n.)two>／あり【有】[自ラ変]<存在する│(v.)exist>(あり＝連用形)／けり【けり】[助動ラ変型]詠嘆<〜だったのだなぁ│(interj.)REALIZATION>(けり＝終止形)

[kaku-bakari ushi to omou-ni kohishiki wa ware sae kokoro futatsu ari-keri]

「我さへ心二つ有りけり」という一節が、この詩人は不実な恋人に裏切られたことを示唆しています。そうして裏切られた後もなお残る愛情…剣の達人にあまりにも見事に斬られたせいで自分がもう死んでいることに気付かずにいる漫画の中の悪党みたいな気分…だけど、実際、こういうことって(恋愛に関しては)起こるんです。生ける死人の復活には、長い時間が必要…あるいは新たな恋(の予感)が必要。

The phrase 我<さへ>心二つ有りけり(ware <sae> kokoro futatsu ari-keri=<even> my own mind is not faithful to me) implies this poet has been double-crossed by an unfaithful sweetheart. Lingering affection after betrayal like the consciousness of a cartoon villain cut into two by a master swordsman so admirably that he doesn't yet know he's dead already... these things happen actually in love, though. To revive the living dead, it takes considerable amount of time... or a new [hope of] love.

●166●よのうきもひとのつらきもしのぶるに こひしきにこそおもひわびぬれ
世の憂きも人の辛きも忍ぶるに恋しきにこそ思ひ侘びぬれ

【悲恋】[溜息]『8)新古今集:1424』藤原元真(ふじわらのもとざね)

世の中の苦しさも、あの人の薄情さも、その気になれば何とか我慢できる私なのですが、世の中やあの人からではなく、私自身の胸中から沸き上がる「恋しいっ！」の思いだけは抑え難くて、どうにもならずに途方に暮れてしまいます。

The harshness of this world or the cruel attitude of you
I could forbear and forget.
But this urge for love surging up from within
I can't stop or endure, I simply can't help myself.

―悲恋―

よ【世】〔名〕<世間│(n.)the world>／の【の】〔格助〕<主格│(prep.)SUBJECT>／うし【憂し】〔形ク〕<憂鬱だ│(adj.)melancholy>(うき=連体形)／も【も】〔係助〕<～もまた│(adv.)also>／ひと【人】〔名〕<あの人│(n.)that [darling] one>／の【の】〔格助〕<主格│(prep.)SUBJECT>／つらし【辛し】〔形ク〕<冷淡だ│(adj.)cold-hearted>(つらき=連体形)／も【も】〔係助〕<～もまた│(adv.)also>／しのぶ【忍ぶ】〔他バ上二〕<耐え忍ぶ│(v.)endure>(しのぶる=連体形)／に【に】〔接助〕<逆接│(conj.)although>／こひし【恋し】〔形シク〕<恋しい│(v.)feel attached to>(こひしき=連体形)／に【に】〔接助〕<理由│(conj.)REASON>／こそ【こそ】〔係助〕<強調│(adv.)EMPHASIS>／おもひわぶ【思ひ侘ぶ】〔自バ上二〕<物思いに沈む│(v.)feel gloomy>(おもひわび=連用形)／ぬ【ぬ】〔助動ナ変型〕完了<すでに～した│(aux-v.)PERFECT TENSE>(ぬれ=已然形係り結び)

[yo no uki mo hito no tsuraki mo shinoburu ni koishiki ni-koso omoi-wabi-nure]

自らの心の内なる敵は、外なる敵よりずっと打倒・対処が困難な強敵・・・「内にも外にも敵なんていない」状態は理想だけど、純真無垢な子供ならともかく、そんな完璧な心の平安なんて誰も手に出来るものではない・・・内なる敵に打ち勝つには、外に出て友に会うなり堂々敵と渡り合うなりして、外界との対応に忙殺される我が身を作り出すといい。自分自身の弱い心をいくら覗き込んだところで、心が強くなることはない・・・どうせ覗き込むなら、この本とかをペラペラめくって、他の人達が(自分同様)彼らなりの(しかし誰もが似たり寄ったりの)個人的な悲しみや苦しみとどのように向き合ってきたか、見せてもらうといい ― 「*君だけ特別!なわけじゃない*」 ― この魔法の言葉に、ある者は不思議と元気付けられて難局を乗り越え、またある者は不機嫌になって「*誰にもわからない自分の不幸の特別な値打ち*」を主張したがる・・・そういう人には悪いけど、自分自身の不幸をいくら理解したところで、それでいくらかでも幸せになれるかと言えば、そんなことは全然ないんだな、これが。

Enemies within are much tougher to beat or manage than enemies without... being without enemies inside or out would be desirable, but none but innocent children could ever achieve such perfect peace of mind. To overcome enemies within, come over to your friends or boldly face your enemies to make yourself busy with the business of dealing with the world outside; weak heart will never get stronger by looking inside... if you look into something at all, just browse through books like this to know how others, like yourself, have faced their own personal — yet universal — sorrow or trouble. "*You are not the only one*" is the magic word that will help some miraculously get over their hardship, and will make others resentfully assert *the unique value of their own unhappiness never to be understood by others*... unfortunately, understanding your own unhappiness doesn't make you any happier.

―――――――――――――――――――――――

●167●うきみをばわれだにいとふいとへただ そをだにおなじこころとおもはむ
憂き身をば我だに厭ふ厭へ只其をだに同じ心と思はむ。

【悲恋】[失恋]『8)新古今集:1143』藤原俊成(ふじわらのしゅんぜい(としなり))

何とも残念なこの私のことを、あなたもどうぞ嫌ってください ― 私自身でさえ大嫌いなのですから ― 「好き」の気持ちで結ばれることはなかったあなたと、
「キライ」の気分だけでも共有できれば、それが私にとってせめてもの慰めです。

This detestable personage I hate so much
I hope you also hate as much as I do.
Feeling of affection I couldn't share with you.
I'd love to be with you at least in hatred of me.

うし【憂し】〔形ク〕＜みじめだ｜(adj.)miserable＞(うき＝連体形)／み【身】〔名〕＜私｜(pron.)I, myself＞／を【を】〔格助〕＜目的格｜(prep.)OBJECT＞／ば【ば】〔格助〕＜強調｜(adv.)EMPHASIS＞／われ【我】〔代名〕＜私｜(pron.)I, myself＞／だに【だに】〔副助〕＜‥さえも｜(adv.)even＞／いとふ【厭ふ】〔他ハ四〕＜嫌う｜(v.)hate＞(いとふ＝終止形)／いとふ【厭ふ】〔他ハ四〕＜嫌う｜(v.)hate＞(いとへ＝命令形)／ただ【只】〔副〕＜ただ単に｜(adv.)only＞／そ【其】〔代名〕＜それ｜(pron.)that＞/を【を】〔格助〕＜目的格｜(prep.)OBJECT＞／だに【だに】〔副助〕＜せめて～だけでも｜(adv.)at least＞／おなじ【同じ】〔形シク〕＜同じ｜(adj.)the same＞(おなじ[き]＝連体形)／こころ【心】〔名〕＜心｜(n.)heart＞／と【と】〔格助〕＜内容提示｜(conj.)that ～＞／おもふ【思ふ】〔他ハ四〕＜思う｜(v.)think＞(おもは＝未然形)／む【む】〔助動マ四型〕意志＜～するつもりだ｜(aux-v.)be going to ～＞(む＝終止形)

[uki mi wo-ba ware dani itou itoe tada so wo dani onaji kokoro to omowa-mu]

「恋人どうし」とは、同じ時と所と*(ある程度まで似た)* 経験とを共有する二人のこと。この詩人の場合、自分が愛した相手との「時と所の共有」は許されなかったので、ヤケ気味に、せめて「同種の感覚」ぐらいあの人と共有したいと望みます ― それは「彼への嫌悪感」！‥‥ちょっと見「何をバカなこと言ってるんだか、くだらない歌」と思うかもしれないけど、実は、こういう不思議な感情、幸せ者が思ってるほどの珍事なんかじゃ、ないんですよ‥‥恋が(まだ始まりもしないうちに)終わっちゃった時、「*ごめんなさい*」と言ってきた相手の*申し訳なさそう*な表情と同じくらい自分で自分を*可哀想*に思い込んじゃう人もいれば、本当は自分が愛したかった相手に*嫌われちゃった*その分だけ激しい*自己嫌悪*に陥る人もいるものです‥‥「愛」って不思議な相互同調作用、たとえ「恋人になり損ねた他人どうし」の間でさえ、お互いの気持ち、伝染しちゃうんです。

Lovers are a pair of people who share the same time, place and ― *more or less similar* ― experience. This poet is not allowed to share the same time and same place with the one he loves; in his desperation, he desires to share at least the same kind of feeling ― the *hatred* of himself. An apparently crazy and frivolous song, but, trust me, such a strange feeling is not as rare as happy people believe it is. When lost in love that didn't even start, some will feel as **sorry for themselves** as they made their refusers feel **sorry to them**, while others **hate themselves** as much as the ones they liked to have loved **hated them**. Love is a strange act of mutual synchronization even between a pair of strangers.

―――――――――――――――――――――――――――――――

—悲恋—

●168● おもひきやあひみしよはのうれしさに のちのつらさのまさるべしとは
思ひきや逢ひ見し夜半の嬉しさに後の辛さの勝るべしとは

【悲恋】[慨嘆]『5』金葉集:439『徳大寺実能(とくだいじさねよし)

あなたとの初の逢瀬(おうせ)に胸ときめかせたあの夜の嬉しさよりも、あなたの心変わりに傷付いた後の心の辛さの方が強烈だなんて、この恋が始まる前には、思ってもみないことでした。

So exulted was I to meet you in the flesh that night.
How was I to expect any greater feelings later?
The bitter sorrow of losing you is more than I can take.

おもふ【思ふ】〔他ハ四〕＜予想する｜(v.)expect＞(おもひ＝連用形)／き【き】〔助動特殊型〕過去＜〜[し]た｜(aux-v.)PAST＞(き＝終止形)／や【や】〔終助〕＜〜だろうか？否、そうではあるまい｜(prep.)RHETORICAL QUESTION＞／あひみる【逢ひ見る】〔他マ上一〕＜[恋人と]逢い引きする｜(v.)have a date＞(あひみ＝連用形)／き【き】〔助動特殊型〕過去＜〜[し]た｜(aux-v.)PAST＞(し＝連体形)／よは【夜半】〔名〕＜夜間｜(n.)the night-time＞／の【の】〔格助〕＜の｜(prep.)'s＞／うれしさ【嬉しさ】〔名〕＜嬉しさ｜(n.)happiness＞／に【に】〔格助〕＜比較｜(prep.)COMPARISON＞／のち【後】〔名〕＜後｜(adv.)afterwards＞／の【の】〔格助〕＜の｜(prep.)'s＞／つらさ【辛さ】〔名〕＜辛さ｜(n.)bitterness＞／の【の】〔格助〕＜主格｜(prep.)SUBJECT＞／まさる【勝る】〔自ラ四〕＜より上だ｜(v.)exceed＞(まさる＝終止形)／べし【べし】〔助動ク型〕可能性＜〜ということがありうる｜(aux-v.)POSSIBILITY＞(べし＝終止形)／と【と】〔格助〕＜内容提示｜(conj.)that 〜＞／は【は】〔格助〕＜目的格｜(prep.)OBJECT＞

[omoi-ki-ya ai-mi-shi yowa no ureshi-sa ni nochi no tsura-sa no masaru-beshi to-wa]

最初の歓喜を最後の悲嘆が上回る — これは事実上すべての恋愛が行き着く運命・・・結局最後にはあの停滞状態「*結婚*」に落ち着いてしまう関係まで含めて、恋愛なんてみんな「初めはいいけど、終わりがねぇ・・・」なわけだが、この歌の状況は「結婚後の倦怠」を嘆くものとは明らかに違う・・・これは「出逢うや否や終わりになってしまった恋愛」のお題で詠まれた虚構短歌なのである・・・どちらがどちらをフッたのか、男と女、どっちがフラれたのか、それは我々の知るところではない。わかっているのは、この種の「初逢瀬(はつおうせ)」までは行った；けど、それでおしまい」という恋愛が、平安時代には実際頻発(ひんぱつ)したということだけ・・・なにせ当時は「女性のお部屋の中での初対面(しょたいめん)」までお互い実際どんな姿の男・女なのかはわからない、という時代だったのだから・・・うーん、なんたるスリル！

The initial exultation exceeded by final lamentation – the destiny of practically all love affairs... including those ending up in the stale state of life called *"marriage"*, which this one obviously isn't: it's a fictional TANKA on the theme of "a love affair which ended as soon as it started"... who refused whom, the man or the woman, we don't know: what we know is that it *did* happen quite often in the Heian era when the couple didn't know what they actually looked like until they met for the first time in the woman's room... oh, what a thrill!

●169● あひみしをうれしきこととおもひしは かへりてのちのなげきなりけり
逢ひ見しを嬉しき事と思ひしは却りて後の嘆きなりけり

【悲恋】[謎掛]『4』後拾遺集:772『道命(どうみょう)

あなたとお互い気持ちが通じ合い、深いお付き合いができるようになった頃は、それはもう幸せだった私ですが・・・そしてまた今日はそんな懐(なつ)かしいあなたに久々に再会できて嬉しく思った私ですが・・・それもこれもみな、今にして思えば、お別れした後の嘆きの辛(つ)さを増すばかりだったようです

(・・・またの出逢いがあれば、そして二度とお別れがなければ、話はまったく違ってくるんですが・・・)

—Sad Love— -166- http//zubaraie.com

―悲恋―

The days I began to spend with you
Brought me up to the top of the world
Drag me down to the depth of sorrow
All the more deadly for the sorely missed joy.
(... *I wish I could meet you again and never miss you again...*)

あひみる【逢ひ見る】〔他マ上一〕<[恋人と]逢い引きする│(v.)have a date>(あひみ＝運用形)／き【き】〔助動特殊型〕過去<〜[し]た│(aux-v.)PAST>(し＝連体形)／を【を】〔格助〕<目的格│(prep.)OBJECT>／うれし【嬉し】〔形シク〕<嬉しい│(adj.)happy>(うれしき＝連体形)／こと【事】〔名〕<事│(n.)a thing>／と【と】〔格助〕<内容提示│(conj.)that 〜>／おもふ【思ふ】〔他ハ四〕<思う│(v.)think>(おもひ＝運用形)／き【き】〔助動特殊型〕過去<〜[し]た│(aux-v.)PAST>(し＝連体形)／は【は】〔係助〕<主格│(prep.)SUBJECT>／かへりて【却りて】〔副〕<かえって逆に│(adv.)on the contrary>／のち【後】〔名〕<後│(adv.)afterwards>／の【の】〔格助〕<の│(prep.)'s>／なげき【嘆き】〔名〕<嘆き│(n.)grief>／なり【なり】〔助動ナリ型〕断定<〜である│(aux-v.)be>(なり＝運用形)／けり【けり】〔助動ラ変型〕詠嘆<〜だったのだなぁ│(interj.)REALIZATION>(けり＝終止形)

[ai-mi-shi wo ureshiki koto to omoi-shi wa kaeri-te nochi no nageki nari-keri]

この短歌、一つ前のやっと何も変わらないように見えるものの、「かつての恋人だった女性と偶然ばったり出逢った直後に、彼女に実際送ったメッセージ」という点が違ってる･･･この状況、あなたならどう解釈しますか？「あんな女になんて会わなきゃよかった、って言ってるの？彼女には最初から出会わぬ運命だった方がマシだったってこと？そんなこと昔の恋人に言うなんて、なんてイヤな男なんだろう！」って思いますか？･･･それとも、「もう一度逢って、長らく休眠中の愛の第二幕を始めるチャンスを与えることで、この自分を苦しみから救ってほしい！」という持って回ったおねだりのメッセージとしてこの歌を解釈できるほど、あなたは繊細な人でしょうか？･･･うーん、まぁ現代の日本じゃ（男も女も）そんな共感的解釈が可能な人はほとんどいないだろうけど、平安時代の詩人の中には、自分の大事な人にはそれくらいの繊細な感性を求める人が、少なからずいたんです･･･少なくとも壬生忠岑とこの短歌の作者の道命法師が自らの短歌の中でそれを実演している場面を、この本の中で、あなたは目撃しているわけですからね･･･ちなみに、道命はあの有名な「藤原道綱母」（＝藤原兼家（道長の父）のトンデモ行状録暴露本としてそのドロドロな内容と難解な古文で今なお日本の高校生を悩ませ続ける『蜻蛉日記』作者）の孫にあたります。

This TANKA seems to be no different from the previous one, except that it was a message actually sent from a man to a woman whom he accidentally met, who used to be a true love of his... What do you make of that? Do you feel "Is he saying he shouldn't have met the woman? Was he better off *not* to have met her at all? How nasty of the man to say such a thing to his old love!"?... Or are you sensitive enough to take the message as a roundabout request asking you to relieve him of the pain by giving him another chance to "meet her again to start ACT-2 of their long-dormant love"?... Well, few modern Japanese — men or women — would be capable of that sympathetic interpretation; but not a few Heianese poets expected their darlings to be that much sensitive, at least 壬生忠岑(Mibu-no-Tadamine) and this author 道命法師(Doumyou houshi) did that in their TANKA as you have witnessed in this book. Incidentally, this 道命(Doumyou) was a grandson of that famous 藤原道綱母(Fujiwara-no-Michitsuna-no-haha＝mother of 道綱:Michitsuna) who wrote 蜻蛉日記(Kagerou nikki), the gossipy diary revealing the scandalous private life of 藤原兼家(Fujiwara-no-Kaneie, father of 道長:Michinaga) which keeps troubling the mind of modern Japanese high school students with its sickly thick confession and simply complicated writing style.

—悲恋—

●170● いまはただそよそのこととおもひいでて わするばかりのうきこともがな

今は只其よ其の事と思ひ出でて忘るばかりの憂き事もがな

【悲恋】[願望]『4)後拾遺集:573』和泉式部(いずみしきぶ)

「あぁそうそう、そうだったわ、こんなことしてる場合じゃなかったんだわ！」とばかり(ハッ！)と我に返って、失ってしまった過去の悲しみが消え去るほどのとてつもなく辛い出来事が、我が身を見舞ってくれないものかしら。眼前に展開する巨大な悲劇に翻弄されて、悲しい過去のことなんて「あぁ、そう言えば、そんなこともあったわね」程度の思い出話になるほどの、ひどい災難こそが、今の私の望み。

Happiness gone away I wouldn't want back any more.

Overwhelming misery — that's what I want now.

Break me away from sad memories, wake me up to reality.

Keep me busy for some time... to remember only later.

いま【今】〔名〕< 今 | (n.)now >／は【は】〔係助〕< 〜に関しては | (adv.)as for 〜 >／ただ【只】〔副〕< ただ単に | (adv.)only >／そよ【そよ】〔副〕< あぁ、そうだった | (interj.)oh yeah >／そ【其】〔代名〕< それ | (pron.)that >／の【の】〔格助〕< の | (prep.)'s >／こと【事】〔名〕< 件 | (n.)a matter >／と【と】〔格助〕< 内容提示 | (conj.)that 〜 >／おもひいづ【思ひ出づ】〔他ダ下二〕< 思い出す | (v.)remember >(おもひいで=連用形)／て【て】〔接助〕< 順接 | (conj.)and >／わする【忘る】〔他ラ四〕< 忘れる | (v.)forget >(わする=連体形)／ばかり【ばかり】〔副助〕< 〜なほど | (adv.)to 〜 exent >／の【の】〔格助〕< の | (prep.)'s >／うし【憂し】〔形ク〕< 辛い | (adj.)harsh >(うき=連体形)／こと【事】〔名〕< 件 | (n.)a matter >／もがな【もがな】〔終助〕< 〜があってほしいな | (adv.)hopefully >

[ima-wa tada so-yo so-no koto to omoi-ide-te wasuru-bakari-no uki koto mogana]

この詩人(和泉式部)は、自分個人の悲劇がもっと巨大な悲劇によって洗い流されることを望んでいます・・・イカれてる、って思いますか？でも、個人的に不幸な人々は、圧倒的に悲惨な周囲の状況に取り巻かれると、どこかホッとするのも事実、それも世の中の人たち全員と一緒に悲惨な目に遭うのであればなおさら理想的・・・第二次大戦のまっただ中に作られた伝説の映画『カサブランカ(Casablanca)』の中のハンフリー・ボガート(Humphrey Bogart)の台詞、思い出してください ―『俺達三人のちっぽけなゴタゴタなんて、このイカれた世界の中じゃ、物の数にもなりゃしない』・・・作り物じゃない現実の話がお望みなら、『カサブランカ』や『風と共に去りぬ(Gone with the Wind)』がアメリカで作られたのと同じ頃、日本では太宰治(だざいおさむ)がどれほど幸福にして多作な時期を送っていたことか、思い出すといいでしょう・・・その太宰は、戦後わずか三年にして自ら命を絶っています。憂鬱(ゆううつ)な青に染まった心は、黒い世界でこそ最も輝くものの、幸せげな白い世界ではほとんど息もできないのです。

This poet — 和泉式部(Izumi shikibu) — wants to drown her personal tragedy away by some even bigger tragedy... Sounds *crazy*? But it is true that personally unhappy people will find some comfort in being surrounded by overwhelming misery, preferably along with all the people in the world... just listen to Humphrey Bogart say in the legendary film "Casablanca" made right in the middle of World War II — **"it doesn't take much to see that the problems of three little people don't amount to a hill of beans in this crazy world"**... if you prefer truth to fiction, just remember how happily prolific 太宰治(Dazai Osamu) was in Japan in the same years as they were making "Casablanca" or "Gone With the Wind" in America... it was only three years after the war was over that 太宰(Dazai) killed himself. A blue heart will shine best in a black world but can hardly breathe in a happily white one.

—悲恋—

●171●よもすがらちぎりしことをわすれずば こひむなみだのいろぞゆかしき

夜もすがら契りし事を忘れずば恋ひむ涙の色ぞゆかしき

【悲恋】[慨嘆]『4)後拾遺集:536』藤原道隆女定子(ふじわらのみちたかのむすめていし)
夜通し愛し合い、「何があってもずっと一緒だからね」と誓い合ったことを今でも忘れず
覚えていてくれるなら、泣き別れの苦しさに流すあなたの涙の色、この目で見てみたい‥‥
あまりの辛さに、血の涙で真っ赤に染まっているのでしょうか、この私みたいに。

We loved all through the night bound by mutual oath
That we'd love each other until the end of time.
If you still remember, I'd like to see you cry
With tears of blood as red as mine.

よもすがら【夜もすがら】[副]<夜通し｜(adv.)all through the night>／ちぎる【契る】[他ラ四]<[永遠の愛を]誓う｜(v.)make a vow [of eternal love]>(ちぎり＝連体形)／き【き】[助動特殊型]過去<～[し]た｜(aux-v.)PAST>(し＝連体形)／こと【事】[名]<～という事｜(n.)the act of ～ing>／を【を】[格助]<目的格｜(prep.)OBJECT>／わする【忘る】[他ラ下二]<忘れる｜(v.)forget>(わすれ＝未然形)／ず【ず】[助動特殊型]打消<～[し]ない｜(adv.)not ～>(ず＝終止形)／ば【ば】[接助]<仮定｜(conj.)if>／こふ【恋ふ】[他ハ上二]<懐かしく思い出す｜(v.)sorely miss>(こひ＝未然形)／む【む】[助動マ四型]推量<だろう｜(aux-v.)SUPPOSITION>(む＝連体形)／なみだ【涙】[名]<涙｜(n.)tears>／の【の】[格助]<の｜(prep.)'s>／いろ【色】[名]<色｜(n.)color>／ぞ【ぞ】[係助]<強調｜(adv.)EMPHASIS>／ゆかし【ゆかし】[形シク]<ぜひとも知りたい｜(v.)I'm dying to see>(ゆかしき＝連体形係り結び)

[yo-mo-sugara chigiri-shi koto wo wasure-zu-ba koi-mu namida no iro zo yukashiki]

この短歌は、一条天皇の第一皇妃だった中宮定子の悲しい辞世の歌。兄弟二人が藤原道長(もう一人の皇妃彰子の父)との政争に敗れたため、定子は皇居の中でも寂しい片隅へと追いやられてしまい、二人目の娘を産んだ直後に、この涙まみれの死に際のメッセージを残して、24歳で命を落としてしまいます‥‥清少納言が(主として)優美なご主人さまの思い出を書き残すために世に出した『枕草子』の中で生き生きと愛着を込めて語られていたあの中宮定子の人生の最期としては、あまりに悲しすぎるエンディングでした。
This TANKA is a sad swan song of 中宮定子(chuuguu Teishi), first Princess of 一条天皇(Ichijou tennnou＝Emperor Ichijou). Her two brothers lost a political war against 藤原道長(Fujiwara-no-Michinaga), father of another Princess 彰子(Shoushi), forcing 定子(Teishi) into a forlorn secluded life in a remote corner of the Imperial Palace. She died at the age of 24 immediately after she gave birth to her second daughter, along with this tearful dying message. Too sad an ending to her life, which is vividly and affectionately recounted in 枕草子(Makura no soushi) that 清少納言(Sei shou-nagon) published largely in memory of her graceful master 定子(Teishi).

‥‥‥‥‥‥‥‥‥‥‥‥‥‥‥‥‥‥
《血の涙氷の鏡涙川》

ここで、平安調短歌世界の中で「涙」が演じる離れ業の数々をまとめておこう:1)「涙川」の中にぽつんと立った航路標識の「澪標:みをつくし‥‥身を尽くし」のイメージで、涙は一人寂しく過ごす寝床を水浸しにしてその独り者を溺死させる;2)寂しい人が涙を拭い去るハンカチ代わりの着物の袖は、びしょ濡れになり、朽ち果て、果ては凍り付いた鏡となって空に浮かぶ侘びしい月影を映し出す;3)どうしようもなく悲しく寂しい人の流す涙は血の色に染まって着物の袖を赤く染め、ウルトラマンのカラータイマーみたいに非常事態を告げるシグナルと化す‥‥こうしたイメージはどれもこれもあまりに漫画っぽくて現代読者には訴えるところがないばかりか嘲笑すら誘うことが多いだろう‥‥が、ここに紹介した「中宮定子の死に際の短歌」は数少ない例外 ─ 涙なしには見られない現実の悲劇の重みで読者に訴えてくる。

―悲恋― ―哀感―

《tears in many colors and forms》

Let us sum up the fanciful stunts 涙(namida＝tears) perform in the world of Heianese TANKA: 1)tears flood the beds of lonely persons to drown them in the image of 澪標(miotsukushi＝a watermark pole standing alone in a bay) of 涙川(namida-gawa＝a river of tears); 2)tears will be wiped off with the sleeves of lonely persons' KIMONO, making them sodden, rotten, or even frozen solid to form mirrors to reflect the image of a forlorn moon; 3)desperately sad and lonely persons' tears will turn red to dye their sleeves as signals for emergency like ウルトラマン(the Ultraman)'s color-timer... These images are all too cartoonish to appeal to the modern reader and will often invite scornful laughter ― this particular TANKA by dying 中宮定子(chuuguu Teishi) is a rare exception by the power of reality too sad to see without tears.

―哀感：Pathos―

★172★よのなかのうきもつらきもつげなくに まづしるものはなみだなりけり
世の中のうきも辛きも告げなくに先づ知る物は涙なりけり

【哀感】[悟り]『1)古今集:941』詠み人知らず

悲しいことや辛いことがあるたびに、「私は悲しい」・「私は辛い」と特に教えられたわけでもないのに、真っ先に出て来てはそうした気持ちをこの私に教えてくれる、不思議な先触れ役が、この涙。

**Even before I know how sad or painful it can be,
Tears will let me know it's time to sigh and weep.**

よのなか【世の中】[名]＜世の中｜(n.)the world＞／の【の】[格助]＜主格｜(prep.)SUBJECT＞／**(A)うし【憂し】**[形ク]＜憂鬱だ｜(adj.)melancholy＞(うき＝連体形)／**(B)うく【浮く】[自カ四]**＜浮く｜(v.)float＞(うき＝連用形)／も【も】[係助]＜〜もまた｜(adv.)also＞／つらし【辛し】[形ク]＜冷淡だ｜(adj.)cold-hearted＞(つらき＝連体形)／も【も】[係助]＜〜もまた｜(adv.)also＞／つぐ【告ぐ】[他ガ下二]＜告げる｜(v.)tell＞(つげ＝未然形)／ず【ず】[助動特殊型]打消＜〜[し]ない｜(adv.)not 〜＞(な＝未然形)／く【く】[接尾]＜名詞化成分｜(suffix)[to make n. out of v.]＞／に【に】[接助]＜逆接｜(conj.)although＞／まづ【先づ】[副]＜最初に｜(adv.)first＞／しる【知る】[他ラ四]＜知る｜(v.)know＞(しる＝連体形)／もの【物】[名]＜物事｜(n.)a thing＞／は【は】[係助]＜主格｜(prep.)SUBJECT＞／なみだ【涙】[名]＜涙｜(n.)tears＞／なり【なり】[助動ナリ型]断定＜〜である｜(aux-v.)be＞(なり＝連用形)／けり【けり】[助動ラ変型]詠嘆＜〜だったのだなぁ｜(interj.)REALIZATION＞(けり＝終止形)

[yo-no-naka no uki mo tsuraki mo tsuge-na-ku-ni mazu shiru mono wa namida nari-keri]

悲しいから泣くのか、涙が出るから悲しいのか？・・・人の心を巡る「鶏が先か／卵が先か」問答。**憂き**が「浮き」に化けて**涙**とさりげなく結び付くあっち向いてホイ！の意外なお仲間関係は、「縁語」。

Do we cry because we are sad, or are we sad because we cry? An emotional version of chicken-or-egg question. 憂き(uki＝feeling blue) changes into 浮き(uki＝float) through the same sound "**uki**" to be associated with 涙(namida＝tears) in apparently irrelevant context ― a technique called 縁語(engo).

—哀感—

★173★おもひわびさてもいのちはあるものを うきにたへぬはなみだなりけり

思ひ侘び然ても命はあるものをうきに堪へぬは涙なりけり

【哀感】[悟り]『7)千載集:818』道因(藤原敦頼)(どういん(ふじわらのあつより))

思い悩んで苦しんで、これでは命も尽きてしまうと、かつては恐れたこともある・・・それでも、こうして生きている。生命は、存外、しぶといもの・・・それにひきかえ、涙ってやつは、悲しくなればすぐ落ちる。耐えに耐えても命は絶えず、湛える涙の絶え間もない。辛抱強い命と、堪え性のない涙・・・干上がることなき涙の川を、今日も明日も懲りずに渡る・・・死ぬまでずっと・・・それが人生。

    Thoughts apparently so deadly didn't kill after all in sadness.
    Tears appear too readily to blur the world with blues.
    Life is as bleak as it feels, won't break with grief and sighs.

おもひわぶ【思ひ侘ぶ】〔自バ上二〕<物思いに沈む>|(v.)feel gloomy>(おもひわび=連用形)／さても【然ても】〔副〕<それでもなお>|(adv.)even then>／いのち【命】〔名〕<生命>|(n.)my life>／は【は】〔係助〕<～に関しては>|(adv.)as for ～>／あり【あり】〔自ラ変〕<消えずに残る>|(v.)survive>(ある=連体形)／ものを【ものを】〔接助〕<～[だ]というのに>|(conj.)although>／(A)うし【憂し】[形ク]<憂鬱だ|(adj.)melancholy>(うき=連体形)／(B)うく【浮く】[自カ四]<浮く>|(v.)float>(うき=連用形)／に【に】〔格助〕<対象>|(prep.)OBJECT>／たふ【堪ふ】[他ハ下二]<持ちこたえる>|(v.)resist>(たへ=未然形)／ず【ず】〔助動特殊型〕打消<～[し]ない>|(adv.)not ～>(ぬ=連体形)／は【は】〔係助〕<主格>|(prep.)SUBJECT>／なみだ【涙】〔名〕<涙>|(n.)tears>／なり【なり】〔助動ナリ型〕断定<～である>|(aux-v.)be>(なり=連用形)／けり【けり】〔助動ラ変型〕詠嘆<～だったのだなぁ>|(interj.)REALIZATION>(けり=終止形)

    [omoi-wabi sate-mo inochi wa aru mono-wo uki ni tae-nu wa namida nari-keri]

ウィリアム・シェイクスピアが自らの想像で再構築した『ジュリアス・シーザー』の芝居の中で彼に語らせた有名な台詞がある ― 『臆病者どもは実際に死ぬ前に「死ぬ！もう死ぬ！」と何度も繰り返し死んで見せるが、勇者が死ぬのは一度きり』・・・こういう毅然とした不屈の精神は、昔の日本の百戦錬磨の侍たちの間でも見られ、讃えられ、奨励されたものである。侍たちの(口に出しては語らない)無言の心得は『弱音を吐くな！無意味に泣くな！』・・・これに対し、平安の世の御公家さんたちは、自分の内心を劇的に表現して他人を自分優位に動かすための小道具として、溢れんばかりの「涙」をこれでもかとばかり乱用した・・・TVやネットに溢れ返る安直な涙や怒りや笑いの洪水のせいもあって、今日の日本人は「涙川で溺れ死に」する御公家さんの直系子孫・・・「日本には武士道がある」と信じ込んでいる外国人諸君、御用心あれ ―「武士道」なんてものは(平安朝短歌の中の「涙の色」と同じく)今の日本では実在しない作話。

In his dramatic re-imagination, William Shakespeare famously had **Julius Caesar** say "**Cowards die many times before their deaths. The brave experience death only once.**" Such fortitude is also to be seen, admired and recommended among battle-hardened 侍(samurai=warrior) class of ancient Japan, whose tacit motto was "Never say *DIE*! Never vainly *CRY*!" Heianese nobles, on the other hand, abused profuse 涙(namida=tears) as dramatic representation of their emotions to move others to their favor. The present-day Japanese are direct descendants of tear-drowned nobles — thanks partly to the floods of easy tears, anger and laughter that drown them on TV or Net. Foreign believers in Japanese 武士道(bushidou=the way of samurai warriors), beware ― in today's Japan, it is as fictional as the colors of tears in Heianese TANKA.

―哀感―

●174● とまりゐてまつべきみこそおいにけれ あはれわかれはひとのためかは
留まり居て待つべき身こそ老いにけれ哀れ別れは人の為かは

【哀感】[別離]『5)金葉集:344』菅原資忠(すがわらのすけただ)

今日のこのお別れは、旅立つあなたが主役のはずなのに、後に残った私の方こそもう年老いてしまって、あなたの帰る頃には帰らぬ客になってしまっているかもしれません。そう考えると、あぁ情けなや、このお別れの主役は、あなたでしょうか？むしろ私のためのお別れ会のような気がしてきます。

Staying here waiting for you to come back,
I myself have grown too old to expect to meet you again when you are back.
How piteous! Is this farewell meant for you who are going away from me,
Or are you bidding farewell to me who will soon pass away from this world?

とまる【留まり】〔自ラ四〕＜残る｜(v.)remain＞(とまり＝連用形)／ゐる【居る】〔自ワ上一〕＜居る｜(v.)stay＞(ゐ＝連用形)／て【て】〔接助〕＜順接｜(conj.)and＞／まつ【待つ】〔他夕四〕＜待つ｜(v.)wait＞(まつ＝連体形)／べし【べし】〔助動ク型〕妥当＜～するべき｜aux-v.)should＞(べき＝連体形)／み【身】〔名〕＜私自身｜(n.)I, myself＞／こそ【こそ】〔係助〕＜強調｜(adv.)EMPHASIS＞／おゆ【老ゆ】〔自ヤ上二〕＜老いる｜(v.)get old＞(おい＝連用形)／ぬ【ぬ】〔助動ナ変型〕完了＜すでに～[し]た｜(aux-v.)PERFECT TENSE＞(に＝連用形)／けり【けり】〔助動ラ変型〕過去＜～[し]た｜(aux-v.)PAST＞(けれ＝已然形係り結び)／あはれ【あはれ】〔感〕＜あぁ残念｜(n.)a pity＞／わかれ【別れ】〔名〕＜別れ｜(n.)parting＞／は【は】〔係助〕＜主格｜(prep.)SUBJECT＞／ひと【人】〔名〕＜他人｜(n.)others＞／の【の】〔格助〕＜の｜(prep.)'s＞／ため【為】〔名〕＜ため｜(n.)sake＞／かは【かは】〔終助〕＜～だろうか？否、そうではあるまい｜(prep.)RHETORICAL QUESTION＞

[tomari-i-te matsu-beki mi koso oi-ni-kere aware wakare wa hito no tame kawa]

この短歌は、京都から遠く離れた地方へと(四年の任期で)旅立つ友人に送ったメッセージ。すでに老境にあったこの歌人は、戦争の最前線へと出征して恐らくは二度と戻って来ない息子を見送る母親のような気分だったのでしょう。当時の旅は現在よりずっと危険なものだったことも忘れてはいけません。昔日(せきじつ)の別れの歌には、今日の我々の目に映る以上の重い意味が込められていたのです。

This is a message to a friend going for 4 years on his official trip to a distant region away from 京都(Kyoto). This old poet must have felt like a mother seeing his son going to a battlefront, perhaps never to return again. Also remember, traveling in those days was much more hazardous than today. There is much more to old songs of departure than meets the present eye.

●175● これやこのゆくもかへるもわかれつつ しるもしらぬもあふさかのせき
是や此の行くも帰るも別れつつ知るも知らぬも逢坂の関

【哀感】[別離]『2)後撰集:1090』蝉丸(せみまる)

都を離れて行く人も地方から帰って来る人も、出立(しゅったつ)する旅人もそれを見送る人達も、みんなこの場所を通って行く…見知った人も見知らぬ他人も、これを限りのお別れかもしれないけれども、とにかくみんなここに出逢い、そしてまた散り散りに消えて行く…ここは「大坂(逢う坂)の関」、出会いと別れの交差点。

Whoever comes in and out, friends and strangers alike,
It's here that everyone departs ― for once or once and for all ―
Ausaka ― slope of encounter.

―Pathos―   http//zubaraie.com

—哀感—

これ【是】〔代名〕＜これ｜(pron.)this＞／や【や】〔間投助〕＜やがな｜(interj.)yeah＞／こ【此】〔代名〕＜これ｜(pron.)this＞／の【の】〔格助〕＜の｜(prep.)'s＞／ゆく【行く】〔自カ四〕＜行く｜(v.)go away＞（ゆく＝連体形）／も【も】〔係助〕＜〜もまた｜(adv.)also＞／かへる【帰る】〔自ラ四〕＜帰る｜(v.)go back＞（かへる＝連体形）／も【も】〔係助〕＜〜もまた｜(adv.)also＞／わかる【別る】〔自下二〕＜別れる｜(v.)be parted＞（わかれ＝連用形）／つつ【つつ】〔接助〕＜〜[し]ながら｜(conj.)as＞／しる【知る】〔他ラ四〕＜知る｜(v.)know＞（しる＝連体形）／も【も】〔係助〕＜〜もまた｜(adv.)also＞／しる【知る】〔他ラ四〕＜知る｜(v.)know＞（しら＝未然形）／ず【ず】〔助動特殊型〕打消＜〜[し]ない｜(adv.)not 〜＞（ぬ＝連体形）／も【も】〔係助〕＜〜もまた｜(adv.)also＞／**(A1)あふ【逢ふ】〔自ハ四〕**＜出会う｜(v.)meet＞（あふ＝連体形）／**(A2)さか【坂】〔名〕**＜坂｜(n.)the slope＞／**(B)あふさか【逢坂】〔名〕**＜[固有名詞]大阪｜(n.)Osaka＞／の【の】〔格助〕＜の｜(prep.)'s＞／せき【関】〔名〕＜関所｜(n.)the checkpoint＞

[kore-ya-ko-no yuku mo kaeru mo wakare-tsutsu shiru mo shira-nu mo Ausaka-no-seki]

一見「**行くも帰るも／知るも知らぬも**」の調子の良いリズムのみが取り柄の歌に見えますが、実は意味深長な短歌です。「**知るも知らぬも**」は「知り合いも見知らぬ人も」の意を表わすのみならず、「再び会えると知っている（つもりの）人々も、そんな確信は抱けずにいる人々も」の意味まで含むもの･･･かもしれないから。
A significant TANKA seemingly relying solely on its rhythmical redundancy — **行くも帰るも**(yuku mo kaeru mo＝both going and coming) / **知るも知らぬも**(shiru mo shira-nu mo＝both knowing and not knowing) — but the latter part may not only mean "both friends and strangers" but also signify "both those who know – or *think* they know – they are going to meet again and those who are not so sure".

●**176**●たちわかれいなばのやまのみねにおふる　まつとしきかばいまかへりこむ
立ち別れ因幡の山の峰に生ふるまつとし聞かば今帰り来む

【哀感】[別離]『1)古今集:365』在原行平（ありわらのゆきひら）

あなたと別れて遠い因幡の国へと旅立つ自分ですが･･･往く先の稲葉山の峰にも「松」の樹が生い茂っていることでしょうねえ･･･でも、あなたが私を「待つ」と、風の噂にでも聞いたなら、すぐにも帰って来ますよ。ええ、そうそういつまでも別れ別れでいるものですか。

I bid farewell to you to depart for Mount Inaba,
Like mountains of pinewoods if you pine to see me then,
It won't be long before I come back again.

たちわかる【立ち別る】〔他ラ下二〕＜別れ別れになる｜(v.)part from each other＞（たちわかれ＝連用形）／**(A1)いぬ【往ぬ】〔自力変〕**＜行く｜(v.)go away＞（いな＝未然形）／**(A2)ば【ば】〔接助〕**＜仮定｜(conj.)if＞／**(B)いなば【因幡】〔名〕**＜[固有名詞]因幡｜(n.)Inaba＞／の【の】〔格助〕＜の｜(prep.)'s＞／やま【山】〔名〕＜山｜(n.)the mountain＞／の【の】〔格助〕＜の｜(prep.)'s＞／みね【峰】〔名〕＜山の頂｜(n.)the ridge＞／に【に】〔格助〕＜場所｜(prep.)PLACE＞／おふ【生ふ】〔自ハ上二〕＜生える｜(v.)thrive＞（おふる＝連体形）／**(A)まつ【松】〔名〕**＜松｜(n.)pine trees＞／**(B)まつ【待つ】〔他タ四〕**＜待つ｜(v.)wait＞（まつ＝終止形）／と【と】〔格助〕＜内容提示｜(conj.)that 〜＞／し【し】〔副助〕＜意味なし｜(adv.)NO MEANING＞／きく【聞く】〔他カ四〕＜風の噂に]聞く｜(v.)hear the rumor of＞（きか＝未然形）／ば【ば】〔接助〕＜仮定｜(conj.)if＞／いま【今】〔名〕＜今すぐにでも｜(adv.)very soon＞／かへり【帰り来】〔自力変〕＜戻って来る｜(v.)come back＞（かへりこ＝未然形）／む【む】〔助動マ四型〕意志＜〜するつもりだ｜(aux-v.)be going to 〜＞（む＝終止形）

[tachi-wakare Inaba no yama no mine ni ouru matsu to-shi kika-ba ima kaeri-ko-mu]

この歌人(在原行平)は、公用で京都を離れ因幡の国へと向かうところ。この短歌の出だしの部分は、その因幡の所柄の視覚的イメージであると同時に、後続の「**まつ**」の語(「松」と同時に「**待つ**」の意味)を導く

http://zubaraie.com　　　　　　　　　　　—Pathos—

―哀感―

絵画的導入部の「序詞(じょことば)」にもなっています・・・この別れの歌を贈った友人たちのもとへ、約束通りこの歌人は無事戻って来ました・・・その逸話のおかげで、この短歌は後々、迷子の猫(のらのこ)に向けて「戻っておいで、おまえのいるべき場所(ばしょ)に」と呼び掛けるおまじないとして知られるようになりました。

This poet, 在原行平(Ariwara-no-Yukihira), is leaving 京都(Kyoto) for the region of 因幡(Inaba) on an official trip. The opening part of this song rhymes out the graphical image of that region, at the same time functioning as the pictorial introductory ― 序詞(jo-kotoba) ― to the succeeding term まつ(matsu), which can both mean 1)松(matsu＝pinewoods) and 2)待つ(matsu＝waiting). As promised, this poet safely returned to the friends for whom he made this parting message... thanks to this episode, this TANKA later came to be known as a magical incantation calling out to a stray cat to "Come back to where you belong!"

―――――――――――――――――――――――――――――

●177●わたのはらやそしまかけてこぎいでぬと ひとにはつげよあまのつりぶね
　　海の原八十島懸けて漕ぎ出でぬと人には告げよ蜑の釣舟
　　　　　　　　　　　　【哀感】[別離]『1)古今集:407』小野篁(おののたかむら)
本当は失意の旅ではあるけれど、「大海原(おおうなばら)に広がる無数の島々を目指して、あの人は元気そうに船出(ふなで)したよ」と、折あらば、そして心あらば、船漕(ふなこ)ぐ漁師のお兄さんよ、私の愛(いと)しい人にはそう伝えておくれ。
　　　　　　　　For myriads of isles scattered in vast ocean
　　　　　　　　Set sail I did ― or, so you should say
　　　　　　　　If, by any chance, you met my dearest one.
わたのはら【海の原】〔名〕＜広い海｜(n.)the vast ocean＞／やそしま【八十島】〔名〕＜無数の島々｜(n.)countless islands＞／かく【懸く】〔他カ下二〕＜目指す｜(prep.)for＞（かけ＝運用形）／て【て】〔接助〕＜順接｜(conj.)and＞／こぐ【漕ぐ】〔他ガ四〕＜漕ぐ｜(v.)row＞（こぎ＝連用形）／いづ【出づ】〔自ダ下二〕＜出立する｜(v.)start on a journey＞（いで＝連用形）／ぬ【ぬ】〔助動ナ変型〕完了＜すでに～[し]た｜(aux-v.)PERFECT TENSE＞（ぬ＝終止形）／と【と】〔格助〕＜内容提示｜(conj.)that ～＞／ひと【人】〔名〕＜あの人｜(n.)that [darling] one＞／に【に】〔格助〕＜対象｜(prep.)OBJECT＞／は【は】〔係助〕＜～に関しては｜(adv.)as for ～＞／つぐ【告ぐ】〔他ガ下二〕＜告げる｜(v.)tell＞（つげよ＝命令形）／あま【海人】〔名〕＜漁師｜(n.)a fisherman＞／の【の】〔格助〕＜の｜(prep.)'s＞／つりぶね【釣り舟】〔名〕＜漁船｜(n.)a fishing boat＞

　　　　　[wata-no-hara yaso-shima kake-te kogi-ide-nu to hito ni-wa tsugeyo ama no tsuri-bune]

この詩人は小野篁、中央の朝廷への大胆すぎる批判をやらかしたせいで、嵯峨院(さがいん)(退位した嵯峨天皇)を激怒させ、隠岐(おき)の島(しま)への流刑(るけい)となったのでした。内心ではひどく打ちひしがれていたはずなのに、この(おそらくは京都に取り残された彼の妻に向けての)メッセージ(ことづて)には不思議と前向きな響きがあります・・・強がりと、愛する人へのせめてものいたわりが入り交じった響き・・・史実としては、篁は赦免(しゃめん)されてじきに戻って来ました。一つ前の在原行平(ありわらのゆきひら)のやつと同様、これまた「戻っておいで」のおまじないに使えそうな可能性を秘めた歌です。

This poet, 小野篁(Ono-no-Takamura), did something audaciously critical about the Imperial Court and infuriated the retired Emperor 嵯峨院(Saga inn), resulting in exile to the island of 隠岐島(Oki-no-shima). Though he must have been totally devastated inside, this message, probably to his wife left alone in 京都(Kyoto), sounds strangely promising... bravado in part, partly caring consolation to his loved one. In fact, 篁(Takamura) was granted pardon and came back soon. Just another poem that has the potential of come-back incantation like the previous one by 在原行平(Ariwara-no-Yukihira).

―哀感―

●178●からころもきつつなれにしつましあれば　はるばるきぬるたびをしぞおもふ
唐衣着つつなれにしつまし有ればはるばるきぬる旅をしぞ思ふ

【哀感】[懐旧]『1)古今集:410』在原業平(ありわらのなりひら)

絢爛豪華な中国衣裳、それを着るのが当たり前、そばに居るのも当たり前･･･
そうまで慣れ親しんだ妻がありながら、彼女を都に一人残して、遙々来てしまったこの旅の、
寂しい長さをつくづく思う･･･恋しい彼女をしみじみ想ふ。

Beautiful clothes I purchased for my wife
No match for her beauty I cherished every day
Both left behind far away in a lonely home
Now feel so near in my sad fondest memories.

『か』ころも【唐衣】[名]＜中華風衣裳＞(n.)Chinese clothes＞／『き』る【着る】[他カ上一]＜着る｜(v.)be clad in＞(き＝連用形)／つつ【つつ】[接助]＜～[し]ながら｜(conj.)as＞／(A)なる【馴る】[自ラ下二]＜慣れ親しむ｜(v.)be accustomed to＞(なれ＝連用形)／(B)なる【萎る】[自ラ下二]＜シワが寄る｜(v.)wrinkle＞(なれ＝連用形)／ぬ【ぬ】[助動ナ変型]完了＜すでに～[し]た｜(aux-v.)PERFECT TENSE＞(に＝連用形)／き【き】[助動特殊型]過去＜～[し]た｜(aux-v.)PAST＞(し＝連体形)／(A)『つ』ま【妻】[名]＜妻｜(n.)a wife＞／(B)『つ』ま【棲】[名]＜端の部分｜(n.)the end＞／し【し】[副助]＜意味なし｜(adv.)NO MEANING＞／あり【あり】[自ラ変]＜存在する｜(v.)exist＞(あれ＝已然形)／ば【ば】[接助]＜理由｜(conj.)REASON＞／(A)『は』るばる【遙々】[副]＜はるばる｜(adv.)all the way＞／(B1)『は』る【張る】[他ラ四]＜引っ張る｜(v.)pull＞(はる＝終止形)／(B2)『は』る【張る】[他ラ四]＜引っ張る｜(v.)pull＞(はる＝終止形)／(A)く【来】[自カ変]＜来る｜(v.)come＞(き＝連用形)／(B)きる【着る】[他カ上一]＜着る｜(v.)be clad in＞(き＝連用形)／ぬ【ぬ】[助動ナ変型]完了＜すでに～[し]た｜(aux-v.)PERFECT TENSE＞(ぬる＝連体形)／『た』び【旅】[名]＜旅｜(n.)the journey＞／を【を】[格助]＜目的格｜(prep.)OBJECT＞／し【し】[副助]＜意味なし｜(adv.)NO MEANING＞／ぞ【ぞ】[係助]／強調｜(adv.)EMPHASIS＞／おもふ【思ふ】[他ハ四]＜思う｜(v.)think＞(おもふ＝連体形係り結び)

[kara-koromo ki-tsutsu nare-ni-shi tsuma shi are-ba harubaru ki-nuru tabi wo-shi-zo omou]

『伊勢物語』にも登場する有名な短歌で、在原業平が京都から遠く離れた地への政治的追放状態にあった時に詠まれたもの、とされています。しかしながら、業平の実際の経歴を振り返って見ると、幾多の伝説から受ける彼のイメージほど政治的に不遇だったわけではありません。ましていわんや、『伊勢物語』のせいで幾多の日本人が信じ込むようになったほど見境のない性生活を、実際の業平が送っていたはずも、ありません。

A famous TANKA appearing also in 伊勢物語(Ise monogatari), supposedly made by 在原業平 (Ariwara-no-Narihira) when he was on political exile away from 京都(Kyoto). If we look back on the real history of 業平(Narihira), however, he was not so politically miserable as lots of legends made him out to be. Needless to say, he couldn't have been as promiscuous a lover as his episodes in 伊勢物語(Ise monogatari) had many Japanese believe him to be.

･･････････････････
《「あいうえお作文」の父祖「折り句」歌》

この短歌の五つの句の冒頭の文字を組み合わせると、隠れていた「か・き・つ・ば・た:燕子花･･･花の名」が浮かび上がる。このように短歌の冒頭文字を使って遊ぶかくれんぼを「折り句」と呼ぶ･･･最近では、短歌を知らない日本人の多くはこれを「あいうえお作文」と呼んでいたりもする。

—哀感—

《折り句(ori-ku) — acronymous TANKA with a hidden term spelled by the headers》
Combine the initial letters of the whole five phrases of this TANKA, and you will see a hidden term かきつばた(燕子花=iris laevigata). This type of "hide and seek" played with headers of TANKA phrases is called 折り句(ori-ku), which is currently called あいうえお作文(aiueo composition) by quite a few TANKA illiterate Japanese.

●179●あまのはらふりさけみればかすがなる　みかさのやまにいでしつきかも
　　天の原振り放け見れば春日なる三笠の山に出でし月かも

【哀感】[懐旧]『1)古今集:406』安部仲麿(あべのなかまろ)
あぁ帰りたい、懐かしい‥‥遙かなる故郷に思いを馳せて、夜空の彼方を眺めれば、
大和の国の三笠山の端に懸かっていたあの月が、遠い異国のこの空にも、変わらず浮かんでいる。

　　　　Among friends I made with people on this land
　　　　Coming out on shore to see me off back home
　　　　I look up at the sky to find the same old moon
　　　　I saw on Mt. Mikasa shining as bright as ever.

あまのはら【天の原】〔名〕＜果てしない大空｜(n.)the endless sky＞／ふりさく【振り放く】〔自力下二〕＜振り返る｜(v.)look back＞(ふりさけ＝連用形)／みる【見る】〔他マ上一〕＜見る｜(v.)view＞(みれ＝連用形)／ば【ば】〔接助〕＜～したところ｜(conj.)when＞／かすが【春日】〔名〕＜[固有名詞]春日｜(n.)Kasuga＞／なり【なり】〔助動ナリ型〕所在地＜～に存在する｜(prep.)PLACE＞(なる＝連体形)／みかさ【三笠】〔名〕＜[固有名詞]三笠｜(n.)Mikasa＞／の【の】〔格助〕＜の｜(prep.)'s＞／やま【山】〔名〕＜山｜(n.)the mountain＞／に【に】〔格助〕＜場所｜(prep.)PLACE＞／いづ【出づ】〔自ダ下二〕＜出る｜(v.)come out＞(いで＝連用形)／き【き】〔助動特殊型〕過去＜～[し]た｜(aux-v.)PAST＞(し＝連体形)／つき【月】〔名〕＜月｜(n.)the moon＞／かも【かも】〔終助〕＜～だなぁ｜(interj.)EXCLAMATION＞
　　　　[ama-no-hara furi-sake-mire-ba Kasuga naru Mikasa no yama ni ide-shi tsuki kamo]

望郷の歌としては最も有名なものの一つで、阿倍仲麻呂が官僚制度を学ぶために渡った(そして中華皇帝のお側近くで高級官僚として仕えるにまで至った)中国から、今まさに旅立とうとする時に詠まれたものとされています。25年に及ぶ中国での生活の末に、仲麻呂は日本行きの船に乗り込みますが、その船は難破してしまいます‥‥日本からは彼を連れ帰るために別の船が派遣されますが、運の悪いことに中国で内乱(安禄山の乱)が勃発、彼はまたも帰国の道を阻まれてしまいます‥‥結局、その15年後に73歳で仲麻呂は中国の地で没しています(時に西暦770年)。遣唐使廃止(894年)からすでに十年経った『古今集』の頃には(そして21世紀初頭の今なお極端な内弁慶状態の日本にとっては)どこか遠い異国の物語のような、老いたる留学生の悲しい人生のお話でした。

One of the most famous of nostalgic songs longing for home, this one was made by 阿倍仲麻呂 (Abe-no-Nakamaro) when he was about to leave China, where he had been sent to study the country's bureaucratic system and even served as a high-ranking officer at the Imperial Court of China quite near the Chinese Emperor. After a quarter of a century's stay there, 仲麻呂(Nakamaro) got aboard a ship to Japan... which got wrecked; another ship came from Japan to bring him back home, but as ill luck would have it, a civil war broke out in China and prevented him from coming back again... 仲麻呂 (Nakamaro) ended up dying in China fifteen years later at the age of 73 in A.D.770. In 905, ten years after the abolition of 遣唐使(kentoushi=envoy to the Tang Dynasty) in 894, 古今集(Kokin shuu) recounted this tragedy of an old overseas student as a somewhat exotic story abroad... maybe as much so to the still less-than-international Japanese at the beginning of the 21st century.

—哀感—

●180● このよにはすむべきほどやつきぬらむ よのつねならずもののかなしき
此の世には住むべき程や尽きぬらむ世の常ならず物の悲しき

【哀感】[慨嘆]『7) 千載集:1094』藤原道信(ふじわらのみちのぶ)

こんなにも尋常(じんじょう)一様(いちよう)じゃなく物悲しい気持ちで胸が一杯になるなんて、もうこの世での私の滞在期間も終わろうとしているのかもしれない。

Is my earthly sojourn overdue?
Why am I so unearthly sad?

こ【此】〔代名〕＜これ｜(pron.)this＞／の【の】〔格助〕＜の｜(prep.)'s＞／よ【世】〔名〕＜世界｜(n.)the world＞／に【に】〔格助〕＜場所｜(prep.)PLACE＞／は【は】〔係助〕＜～に関しては｜(adv.)as for ～＞／すむ【住む】〔自マ四〕＜住む｜(v.)live in＞(すむ＝終止形)／べし【べし】〔助動ク型〕可能＜～できる｜(aux-v.)can＞(べき＝連体形)／ほど【程】〔名〕＜時間｜(n.)time＞／や【や】〔係助〕＜疑問｜(adv.)INTERROGATIVE＞／つく【尽く】〔自カ上二〕＜終わりになる｜(v.)come to the end＞(つき＝連用形)／ぬ【ぬ】〔助動ナ変型〕完了＜すでに～[し]た｜(aux-v.)PERFECT TENSE＞(ぬ＝終止形)／らむ【らむ】〔助動ラ四型〕現在推量＜～だろう｜(aux-v.)SUPPOSITION＞(らむ＝連体形係り結び)／よのつねなり【世の常なり】〔形動ナリ〕＜ごく普通だ｜(adj.)as usual＞(よのつねなら＝未然形)／ず【ず】〔助動特殊型〕打消＜～[し]ない｜(adv.)not ～＞(ず＝終止形)／もの【物】〔名〕＜あれこれいろいろ｜(n.)one thing or another＞／の【の】〔格助〕＜主格｜(prep.)SUBJECT＞／かなし【哀し】〔形シク〕＜悲しい｜(adj.)sad＞(かなしき＝連体形)

[ko-no-yo ni-wa sumu-beki hodo ya tsuki-nu-ramu yo-no-tsune-nara-zu mono no kanashiki]

悲しさのあまり「この世には自分の居場所なんてないんだ」とか感じたこと、ありません？・・・この短歌は、世の中に自分の居場所がちゃんとある、と自信持って言えないほどのお年寄りだけの感覚だろう、とか思いますか？・・・実はこの歌人、当時京都の町で猛威をふるっていた天然痘(てんねんとう)にかかってしまい、23歳で命を落としています・・・そう聞くと、「虫の知らせだったのか」って思いますか？・・・まぁ、そうやって単純な因果のお話で片付けたがる日本人は多いけど、この場合、「結果」の方がむしろ「原因」だったのかもしれません。当時の京都では疫病(えきびょう)での感染死がひどく多かったので、都の住人ならたいてい自分に近しい大事な人々に先立(さきだ)たれる体験をしていたのです・・・そんな世界の中でなら、あなたもこの歌の作者みたいに感じて(いよいよ自分の順番が来たか)と怯えたとしても、不思議はありません・・・良い人生を送るため、結果と原因の取り違えは、避けましょう。後知恵(あとぢえ)は愚か者の英知。注釈は想像の敵。明らかな間違いに陥(おちい)らぬ限り、詩の解釈はあなたの感じるままにすればよいし、人生の生き方もあなたの思う通りにすればよいのです。外から飛び込むどうでもいい情報のあれこれに、自らの感じ方・生き方をあまり左右されないようにしましょう。

Haven't you ever felt so sad as to feel yourself totally out of place in this world? Do you feel this TANKA belongs only to those too old to feel positive about their position in society? In fact, this poet ended up dying of smallpox rampant in 京都(Kyoto) in those days at the age of 23... *Presentiment*, you say?... Well, lots of Japanese like that kind of simplified cause-and-effect story, but the *effect* may have been the *cause* of his pessimistic mood in this case: death by epidemic was so prevalent in 京都(Kyoto) in those days that most of its inhabitants had someone near and dear die on them... in a world like that, you may well feel like this poet and may fear *your turn has come*... To live well, don't confuse an effect with a cause. Hindsight is the wisdom of fools. Annotation can be the enemy of imagination. Except in obvious mistakes, you have your right to make out poetry the way you feel, much as you have your right to live your life the way you want: don't let extraneous info unduly influence the way you feel and live.

----

http//zubaraie.com

—哀感—

●181● よをすててやまにいるひとやまにてても　なほうきときはいづちゆくらむ

世を捨てて山に入る人山にても　猶憂き時は何方行くらむ

【哀感】［溜息］『1)古今集:956』凡河内躬恒(おうしこうちのみつね)

俗世を捨てて山に入って仏の道を歩もうとする人は、
俗世間とは別世界の山の中でもなお憂愁(ゆうしゅう)に苦しんだ時には、今度は一体どこへ行けばよいのだろうか？

Those who leave behind crowds to seek peace of mind in mountains,
Will they still have anywhere to stay away from solitary sorrow there?

よ【世】〔名〕＜世間｜(n.)the world＞／を【を】〔格助〕＜目的格｜(prep.)OBJECT＞／すつ【捨つ】〔他タ下二〕＜捨てる｜(v.)desert＞(すて＝連用形)／て【て】〔接助〕＜順接｜(conj.)and＞／やま【山】〔名〕＜山｜(n.)the mountain＞／に【に】〔格助〕＜場所｜(prep.)PLACE＞／いる【入る】〔自ラ四〕＜入る｜(v.)go into＞(いる＝連体形)／ひと【人】〔名〕＜人間｜(n.)a human being＞／やま【山】〔名〕＜山｜(n.)the mountain＞／にて【にて】〔格助〕＜場所｜(prep.)PLACE＞／も【も】〔係助〕＜～もまた｜(adv.)also＞／なほ【猶】〔副〕＜それでもなお｜(adv.)still＞／うし【憂し】〔形ク〕＜憂鬱だ｜(adj.)melancholy＞(うき＝連体形)／とき【時】〔名〕＜時｜(n.)when＞／は【は】〔係助〕＜～に関しては｜(adv.)as for ～＞／いづち【何処】〔代名〕＜どこ｜(adv.)where＞／ゆく【行く】〔自カ四〕＜行く｜(v.)go＞(ゆく＝終止形)／らむ【らむ】〔助動ラ四型〕現在推量＜～だろう｜(aux-v.)SUPPOSITION＞(らむ＝連体形係り結び)

［yo wo sute-te yama ni iru hito yama nite-mo nao uki toki wa izuchi yuku-ramu］

俗世に暮らす人から俗世を捨てて山＝仏教的悟りの追究に入った人に向けての、素朴(そぼく)にして深刻な疑問。
A naive but serious question from someone living in the secular world addressed to someone who has deserted it to seek his way in　山(yama＝the mountains,) that is, in search of Buddhist enlightenment.

●182● よのなかよみちこそなけれおもひいる　やまのおくにもしかぞなくなる

世の中よ道こそ無けれ思ひ入る山の奥にも鹿ぞ鳴くなる

【哀感】［溜息］『7)千載集:1151』藤原俊成(ふじわらのしゅんぜい(としなり))

とかくままならぬ世の中と、どう決着を付けてよいかわからずに、それでも思い詰めた末に、
俗世を離れて分け入った山奥の隠遁(いんとん)生活…人の暮らしを離れれば、俗世の辛(つら)さも忘れるだろうと、思って入った山の中…なのに、ふと聞こえてくる鹿の声…雌鹿(めじか)を求めて鳴く牡鹿(おじか)の心の叫びか…
あぁ、どこへどう逃れても、結局、この世の悩み・苦しみは、付いて回るのだなあ。

Turning my back on the ruthless world
Searching my soul deep in routeless mountains...
Forlorn cries of mateless deer from nowhere
Wake me up to the nature of limitless sorrow.

よのなか【世の中】〔名〕＜世の中｜(n.)the world＞／よ【よ】〔間投助〕＜呼び掛け｜(interj.)APOSTROPHE＞／みち【道】〔名〕＜道｜(n.)the way＞／こそ【こそ】〔係助〕＜逆接｜(conj.)although＞／なし【なし】〔形ク〕＜存在しない｜(v.)do not exist＞(なけれ＝已然形係り結び)／**(A)おもひいる【思ひ入る】〔自ラ四〕**＜思い悩む｜(v.)dwell upon＞(おもひいる＝連体形)／**(B)いる【入る】〔自ラ四〕**＜入る｜(v.)go into＞(いる＝連体形)／やま【山】〔名〕＜山｜(n.)the mountain＞／の【の】〔格助〕＜の｜(prep.)'s＞／おく【奥】〔名〕＜奥｜(n.)the remote part＞／に【に】〔格助〕＜場所｜(prep.)PLACE＞／も【も】〔係助〕＜～もまた｜(adv.)also＞／しか【鹿】〔名〕＜鹿｜(n.)a deer＞／ぞ【ぞ】〔係助〕＜強調｜(adv.)EMPHASIS＞／なく【鳴く】〔自カ四〕＜鳴く｜(v.)cry＞(なく＝連体形)／なり【なり】〔助動ラ変型〕伝聞推量＜～のようだ｜(aux-v.)I hear＞(なる＝連体形係り結び)

―哀感―

[yo-no-naka yo michi koso nakere omoi-iru yama no oku ni-mo shika zo naku-naru]
俗世に背を向け山に入ってはみたけれど、そこでもやはり外の世界同様、寂しさは常について回ることを知った誰かさんの姿を、象徴的に描いた短歌。「世の中」と対照的に用いた場合の「山」は「仏の道に帰依する人の住むところ」の意味になる点に注意。この歌の作者の藤原俊成は、62歳の時、朝廷の職を辞した直後に仏教僧となり、「釈阿」の名でその後30年の余生を短歌世界の主導者として送った末に、当時としては珍しい91歳という高齢で没しています・・・山の中ではなく、京都の町で、貴族の時代の最終崩壊段階をその目で見届けながら、世を去ったのでした。

A symbolic TANKA of someone turning his back upon the secular world to find his way into mountains, only to find loneliness as inevitable in the wild as anywhere else. Note that "山(yama＝a mountain)" means "a place for someone devoted to the way of the Buddha" as opposed to "世の中(yo-no-naka＝the [secular] world)". The author, 藤原俊成(Fujiwara-no-Shunzei), became a bonze at the age of 62 immediately after he retired from the Imperial Court and spent the remaining 30 years as the leading figure of Heianese TANKA in the Buddhist name of 釈阿(Shakua) until he died at the then unusually old age of 91... not in the mountains but in 京都(Kyoto), witnessing the final collapse of the age of the nobility.

●183● よをそむくところとかきくおくやまは ものおもひにぞいるべかりける
世を背く所とか聞く奥山は物思ひにぞ入るべかりける

【哀感】[悟り]『8)新古今集:1639』道命(どうみょう)
世間では、俗世を捨て去って仏道の精進に心澄ませるべく分け入る先が山奥だ、と言われているようですが、実際こうして入ってみて悟りました ― 俗世に居た頃にも増して物思いを深めるために分け入る先が、奥山だったのですね・・・

When people turn their back on the secular world,
They go deep into mountains for the salvation of their soul.
That's what I'd heard before I actually went into mountains.
Now I find the contrary truth ―
The further away from town, the deeper into mountains,
The more people turn their minds into the deepest sorrow of their souls.

よ【世】〔名〕＜世間｜(n.)the world＞／を【を】〔格助〕＜目的格｜(prep.)OBJECT＞／そむく【背く】〔自カ四〕＜背を向ける｜(v.)turn one's back on＞(そむく＝連体形)／ところ【所】〔名〕＜所｜(n.)the place＞／と【と】〔格助〕＜内容提示｜(conj.)that ～＞／か【か】〔係助〕＜とか何とか｜(adv.)or something＞／きく【聞く】〔他カ四〕＜聞く｜(v.)hear＞(きく＝連体形)／おくやま【奥山】〔名〕＜山奥｜(n.)deep in the mountain＞／は【は】〔係助〕＜目的格｜(prep.)OBJECT＞／ものおもひ【物思ひ】〔名〕＜物思い｜(n.)a pensive mood＞／に【に】〔格助〕＜目的｜(prep.)for the purpose of＞／ぞ【ぞ】〔係助〕＜強調｜(adv.)EMPHASIS＞／いる【入る】〔自ラ四〕＜入る｜(v.)go into＞(いる＝終止形)／べし【べし】〔助動ク型〕妥当＜～するべき｜(aux-v.)should＞(べかり＝連用形)／けり【けり】〔助動ラ変型〕詠嘆＜～だったのだなぁ｜(interj.)REALIZATION＞(ける＝連体形係り結び)

[yo wo somuku tokoro to-ka kiku oku-yama wa mono-omoi ni-zo iru-bekari-keru]
実際に世を捨てた遁世者のとっても正直な告白・・・と言ってこの作者(道綱母の孫の道命さん)、名のある歌僧だったので、仏教的な「涅槃」の境地から程遠かったのも、うなずけます。

A quite sincere confession of an actual recluse, though a famous singing bonze 道命, 道綱母(Michitsuna's Mom)'s grandson understandably far from the Buddhist state of 涅槃(nehan＝nirvana).

―哀感―

●184●たらちめはかかれとてしもむばたまの　わがくろかみをなでずやありけむ
垂乳女はかかれとてしも鳥羽玉の我が黒髪を撫でずやありけむ

【哀感】[懐旧]『2)後撰集:1241』遍昭（良岑宗貞）（へんじょう(よしみねのむねさだ)）

我が母は、幼い頃の私の黒髪を、どういう思いで撫でてくれたのだろう・・・今日こうして髪を下ろして
俗世を捨て去ることになる未来の私の姿を不憫に思いながら撫でていた、なんてことはないだろうになぁ。

When my dear mother ran her fingers through my jet hair
Did she caress it imagining me like this today?

たらちめ【垂乳女】[名]＜我が母｜(n.)my mother＞／は【は】[係助]＜～に関しては｜(adv.)as for ～＞／かかり【斯かり】[自ラ変]＜このような｜(v.)be like this＞(かかれ＝命令形)／とて【とて】[格助]＜～と思って｜(adv.)with ～ in mind＞／しも【しも】[副助]＜意味なし｜(adv.)NO MEANING＞／**むばたまの【むばたまの】[枕詞]**＜意味なし｜(adj.)NO MEANING＞／わ【我】[代名]＜私｜(pron.)I, myself＞／が【が】[格助]＜の｜(prep.)'s＞／くろかみ【黒髪】[名]＜黒髪｜(n.)jet black hair＞／を【を】[格助]＜目的格｜(prep.)OBJECT＞／なづ【撫づ】[他ダ下二]＜なでる｜(v.)fondle＞(なで＝未然形)／ず【ず】[助動特殊型]打消＜～[し]ない｜(adv.)not ～＞(ず＝終止形)／や【や】[係助]＜疑問｜(adv.)INTERROGATIVE＞／あり【あり】[補動ラ変]＜意味なし｜(adv.)NO MEANING＞(あり＝連用形)／けむ【けむ】[助動マ四型]過去推量＜～[し]たのだろう｜(aux-v.)PAST SUPPOSITION＞(けむ＝連体形係り結び)

[tarachime wa kakare tote-shimo mubatama-no wa-ga kuro-kami wo nade-zu ya ari-kemu]

母親と一緒に過ごした世界から、母親なら絶対に大事な我が子を送りたくない別世界へと入ろうとしている誰かさんの脳裏に浮かんだ、悲しい母の回想イメージ。

A sad nostalgic image of the mother flashing in the mind of someone going out of the world shared with her into somewhere she would never have wanted to see her darling child in.

・・・・・・・・・・・・・・・・・・・・・・・・・

《上代の「枕詞」の成れの果て》

この短歌には二つの「枕詞」が含まれている。そのうちの一つ「**うばたまの**」は後続の「**黒髪**」を導くという本来の用法に忠実に用いられているが、もう一方の「**たらちめ**[の]」は、本来ならその直後にあるべき「母」を導く役割を果たしておらず、ここでは「**たらちめ**」という「枕詞」そのものが「母」の同義語として用いられている。この例にも見られる通り、平安調短歌は、その発展過程の最初期の段階にしてすでにもう「枕詞」の正しい用法を見失い、かなりいい加減な形で用いていたのである。

《枕詞(makura-kotoba) of olden times in a state of chaos in the Heian era》

This TANKA includes two 枕詞(makura-kotoba＝pillow words), one of which — **うばたまの** (ubatama-no) — is true to its original usage of introducing the succeeding term **黒髪**(kuro-kami＝black hair), while the other — **たらちめ**[の](tarachime[no]) — is not used as an introduction to 母(haha＝mother) theoretically placed immediately after it; in this case, **たらちめ**(tarachime) itself is used as a synonym for 母(haha＝mother). This only goes to show that the correct usage of 枕詞(makura-kotoba) had already been lost sight of and quite loosely used in the earliest years of Heianese TANKA's development.

―哀感―

●185● いとひてもなほをしまるるわがみかな ふたたびくべきこのよならねば

厭ひても猶惜しまるる我が身かな二度来べき此の世ならねば

【哀感】[悟り]『6)詞花集:346』藤原季通(ふじわらのすえみち)

所詮この世は儚いもの、束の間の幻のような現世でしかない‥‥と、そうは思ってもやはり、未練がましく大事に思えて仕方ない我が身‥‥だって、仮初めだろうが幻だろうが、今のこの世には二度と再び生まれ落ちることなどないのだから。

Hatefully tainted with worldly avarice, yes, I know:
Still, my existence in this world is something I feel so dear:
When else should I come here to love this life of mine again?

いとふ【厭ふ】〔他ハ四〕<嫌う｜(v.)hate>（いとひ＝連用形）／ても【ても】〔接助〕<～[し]ても｜(conj.)although>／なほ【猶】〔副〕<それでもなお｜(adv.)still>／をしむ【惜しむ】〔他マ四〕<惜しく思う｜(v.)miss>（をしま＝未然形）／る【る】〔助動ラ下二型〕自発<[思わず知らず]そうなる｜(adv.)naturally>（るる＝連体形）／わ【我】〔代名〕<私｜(pron.)I, myself>／が【が】〔格助〕<の｜(prep.)'s>／み【身】〔名〕<自身｜(n.)[one]self>／かな【かな】〔終助〕<詠嘆｜(interj.)EXCLAMATION>／ふたたび【再び】〔副〕<もう一度｜(adv.)once again>／く【来】〔自力変〕<来る｜(v.)come>（く＝終止形）／べし【べし】〔助動ク型〕可能<～できる｜(aux-v.)can>（べき＝連体形）／こ【此】〔代名〕<これ｜(pron.)this>／の【の】〔格助〕<の｜(prep.)'s>／よ【世】〔名〕<世間｜(n.)the world>／なり【なり】〔助動ナリ型〕断定<～である｜(aux-v.)be>（なら＝未然形）／ず【ず】〔助動特殊型〕打消<～[し]ない｜(adv.)not ～>（ね＝已然形）／ば【ば】〔接助〕<理由｜(conj.)REASON>

[itoi-te-mo nao oshima-ruru wa-ga mi kana futatabi ku-beki ko-no-yo nara-ne-ba]

平安時代の日本仏教の悲観的な(あるいは嘲笑的な)世界観によれば、「現世」に執着する者は「無意味な影」の価値を信じる愚か者であり、「真の道」と呼ばれる本質的世界は「御仏への帰依」の中にのみ見出し得るものであって、「影」にも等しいこの世での儚い宿りが終わった後で向かう先の「来世」に於ける自分の立場をより良いものにするために、人々は仏道に帰依せねばならない、というのである‥‥が、実のところ、この珍妙な「修行期間」の考え方は、社会的不正義を正当化するための呆れ果てた言い訳に過ぎない‥‥世の中で栄えている人は、幾多の前世を通じて重ねて来た善行の蓄積によって栄えているのだから、その繁栄は当然のことである一方、貧しく惨めな連中は、前世での仏道修行者としての義務を怠った結果そうなったのだから、同情など一切無用、というわけである‥‥こんな狂った決定論は、マトモな西欧人なら誰一人受け入れないが、当時の(**そして今なお**)日本人の不合理に対する適応力・受容力は(周りの連中もそれに合わせて受け入れている限りは)信じ難いほど高いのだ‥‥そうした平安時代のイカレ仏教の矛盾は、当時の歌人たちの「正直な戸惑いの声」の中に見出すことができる。

In the strangely pessimistic (or scornful) world view of the Heianese Japanese Buddhism, those who stuck to the secular world were foolish believers in worthless shadows; the substance — 真の道 (makoto no michi＝the correct way) — was only to be found in the Buddhist devotion, which would prepare people for better positions in the next world they would go after their shadowy existence in this world came to its end. This strange idea of "apprenticeship" was, in fact, a scandalous excuse for justifying the gross social injustice, where the successful were deservedly so by virtue of their total score of good deeds accumulated through their former lives, while the poor and miserable were never pitied because they had neglected their Buddhist duties in their former lives. No sane Western people would ever accept such crazy determinism, but the Japanese were (and still *are*) an incredibly adaptive and receptive people to anomaly, *so long as those around them would adapt and receive...* we can witness the inconsistencies of such crazy Heianese Buddhism in the sincere bewilderment of poets of the day.

―哀感―

●186● ときしもあれあきやはひとのわかるべき あるをみるだにこひしきものを
時しもあれ秋やは人の別るべき在るを見るだに恋ひしきものを

【哀感】[慨嘆]『1)古今集:839』壬生忠岑(みぶのただみね)

よりによって「秋」にこの世を去りますか？･･･まだ生きてる人たちにだって無性に会いたくなる
この切ない季節に逝ってしまって二度と会えないなんて･･･あんまりですょ。

Of all the seasons, in Autumn you passed away
When we can't even bear not seeing those living!

とき【時】[名]＜場合｜(n.)an occasion＞／しも【しも】[副助]＜意味なし｜(adv.)NO MEANING＞／あり【あり】[補動ラ変]＜意味なし｜NO MEANING＞(あれ＝已然形)／あき【秋】[名]＜秋｜(n.)Autumn＞／やは【やは】[係助]＜～だろうか？否、そうではあるまい｜(prep.)RHETORICAL QUESTION＞／ひと【人】[名]＜あの人｜(n.)that one＞／の【の】[格助]＜主格｜(prep.)SUBJECT＞／わかる【別】[自ラ下二]＜別れる｜(v.)be parted＞(わかる＝終止形)／べし【べし】[助動ク型]妥当＜～するべき｜(aux-v.)should＞(べき＝連体形係り結び)／あり【あり】[自ラ変]＜存在する｜(v.)exist＞(ある＝連体形)／を【を】[格助]＜目的格｜(prep.)OBJECT＞／みる【見る】[他マ上一]＜見る｜(v.)view＞(みる＝終止形)／だに【だに】[副助]＜‥さえも｜(adv.)even＞／こひし【恋し】[形シク]＜恋しい｜(v.)feel attached to＞(こひしき＝連体形)／ものを【ものを】[接助]＜～[だ]というのに｜(conj.)although＞

[toki-shimo-are aki yawa hito no wakaru-beki aru wo miru dani koishiki mono-wo]

「難解の巨匠」壬生忠岑から紀友則に捧げた挽歌。友則は自分が編んだ『古今集』が世に出るのを見届けることなく亡くなってしまいました。他の人達なら単に「死者を哀悼」するところを、忠岑の場合は(さすがというべきか)「一番寂しい季節である秋に自分を置き去りにした」と言って友則を(責めることで)悼んでいます。
An elegy by "the master of complication" 壬生忠岑(Mibu-no-Tadamine) for 紀友則(Ki-no-Tomonori), co-editor of 古今集(Kokin shuu) who died before he could see it published. Where others would simply *mourn* the dead, 忠岑(Tadamine) ― characteristically ―laments *by blaming* 友則(Tomonori) 's untimely departure in Autumn, the saddest of all seasons.

●187● ひとのよのおもひにかなふものならば わがみはきみにおくれましやは
人の世の思ひに適ふものならば我が身は君に後れましやは

【哀感】[慨嘆]『2)後撰集:1399』藤原兼輔(ふじわらのかねすけ)

この世が人の望み通りになるものだとしたら、私の大事なあの人に先立たれて
一人この世に取り残される憂き目を見ることなど、ないはずなのに。

If this world should grant me my wishes
Why should I miss you, left behind alone?

ひと【人】[名]＜人間｜(n.)a human being＞／の【の】[格助]＜の｜(prep.)'s＞／よ【世】[名]＜世間｜(n.)the world＞／の【の】[格助]＜主格｜(prep.)SUBJECT＞／おもひ【思ひ】[名]＜願い｜(n.)wishes＞／に【に】[格助]＜対象｜(prep.)OBJECT＞／かなふ【適ふ】[自ハ四]＜～通りになる｜(v.)fit＞(かなふ＝連体形)／もの【物】[名]＜物事｜(n.)a thing＞／なり【なり】[助動ナリ型]断定＜～である｜(aux-v.)be＞(なら＝未然形)／ば【ば】[接助]＜仮定｜(conj.)if＞／わ【我】[代名]＜私｜(pron.)I, myself＞／が【が】[格助]＜の｜(prep.)'s＞／み【身】[名]＜自身｜(n.)[one]self＞／は【は】[係助]＜主格｜(prep.)SUBJECT＞／きみ【君】[代名]＜あなた｜(pron.)you＞／に【に】[格助]＜対象｜(prep.)OBJECT＞／おくる【後る】[自ラ下二]＜死に後れる｜(v.)outlive＞(おくれ＝未然形)／まし【まし】[助動特殊型]推量＜～だろうに｜(aux-v.)should＞(まし＝終止形)／やは【やは】[終助]＜～だろうか？否、そうではあるまい｜(prep.)RHETORICAL QUESTION＞

―哀感―

[hito no yo no omoi ni kanau mono nara-ba wa-ga mi wa kimi ni okure-mashi-yawa]
先帝崩御後、同じ主君に仕えた友人に向けて送られた「先帝への頌歌＝特定人物に呼び掛ける抒情歌」。
An ode to the late Emperor sent to a friend who also served under the same master.

★188★みなひとのむかしがたりになりゆくを いつまでよそにきかむとすらむ
皆人の昔語りに成り行くを何時迄余所に聞かむとすらむ

【哀感】[懐旧]『6)詞花集:359』清昭(せいしょう)

私の古い知り合いはあの人もこの人もみな「そういえば、そんな人もいましたっけねぇ」という形で人の口に乗るばかりの昔語りの登場人物になってしまって、もうこの世では二度と会えない人たちばかり⋯
そういう三人称の昔話を、この先どこまで私は他人事として聞くことになるのだろう⋯
私自身が「昔話の登場人物」として人の口に乗ることになる日も、そう遠くはないのだろうなぁ⋯

People I once knew I hear about only in stories.
In person never could I see them...
All gone leaving me behind.
From hearing about to being talked about...
Just how many years away for me?

みな【皆】〔副〕＜みんな｜(adv.)all＞／ひと【人】〔名〕＜他人｜(n.)others＞／の【の】〔格助〕＜主格｜(prep.)SUBJECT＞／むかしがたり【昔語り】〔名〕＜昔話｜(n.)an old story＞／に【に】〔格助〕＜補語｜(prep.)COMPLEMENT＞／なる【成る】〔自ラ四〕＜～になる｜(v.)become＞(なり＝連用形)／ゆく【行く】〔自力四〕＜次第に～になる｜(v.)come to ～＞(ゆく＝連体形)／を【を】〔格助〕＜目的格｜(prep.)OBJECT＞／いつ【何時】〔名〕＜いつ｜(adv.)when＞／まで【まで】〔副助〕＜～まで｜(conj.)until＞／よそ【他所】〔名〕＜自分とは関係ない話｜(adv.)someone else's business＞／に【に】〔格助〕＜様態｜(prep.)like＞／きく【聞く】〔他力四〕＜聞く｜(v.)hear＞(きか＝未然形)／む【む】〔助動マ四型〕推量＜だろう｜(aux-v.)SUPPOSITION＞(む＝連体形)／と【と】〔格助〕＜結末｜(prep.)RESULT＞／す【為】〔自サ変〕＜～する｜(v.)do＞(す＝終止形)／らむ【らむ】〔助動ラ四型〕現在推量＜～だろう｜(aux-v.)SUPPOSITION＞(らむ＝連体形係り結び)

[mina-hito no mukashi-gatari ni nari-yuku wo itsu-made yoso-ni kika-mu-to-su-ramu]
古い友人たちのほとんどに先立たれて自分一人この世に取り残された寂しい老人が、自分もまた「昔の人」リストに加わる順番がもうじき来るんだろうなぁと恐れている(ある程度、望んでもいる)という悲しい短歌⋯と、確実にそう見える歌ですね⋯しかし実際にはこれ、伝染病が京都の町で荒れ狂い、あまりにも多くの住人たちが亡くなったので、自分だけは「物故者名簿」に載らないだろう、なんて誰一人安心できなかった頃に詠まれた数多くの短歌のうちの一つなのでした⋯もしあなたが戦争や疫病大流行の最中にこの詩を読むなら、後者の解釈をどうぞ⋯筆者としては、前者の解釈の方に個人的真実の響きを感じ取れるくらい熟した老境に至るまで長生きしてから、あなたがこの詩に再会できるようお祈り申し上げます。

A sad song of a sad old man left behind in this world by most of his old friends and fears – or partly desires – that his turn may soon come to join the list of "who used to be"... so it probably seems to you. In fact, this is one of those many poems made when epidemic was rampant in 京都(Kyoto) and claimed too many lives of its inhabitants for anyone to feel themselves exempt from being talked about as the have-been. Should you read this poem in times of war or pandemic, take the latter interpretation... I'd rather you grew up into a ripe old age to find your personal truth in the former interpretation.

―哀感―

●189●たれをかもしるひとにせむたかさごの　まつもむかしのとものならなくに
　　　　誰をかも知る人にせむ高砂の松も昔の友ならなくに

【哀感】[懐旧]『1)古今集:909』藤原興風(ふじわらのおきかぜ)

私の親しかった人たちは、もう、みんな逝ってしまった。私が誰か、どんな人か、知ってくれている人はもう誰も、どこにも、いない・・・長寿ゆえの孤独・・・あぁ、そうだ、高砂神社の松の老木なら、私の気持ちをわかってくれるかもしれない・・・が、やっぱり駄目だ。往時を共に過ごしてきた旧友でもないのだから、昔話のしようもないもの。

What friends have I left who know my olden days?
The longer I live, the lonelier I grow.
Willfully alone I am not: a sole old survivor.
The pine of Takasago, famous for its age,
Wouldn't know me either as his dear old friend.

たれ【誰】〔代名〕＜誰｜(pron.)who＞／を【を】〔格助〕＜目的格｜(prep.)OBJECT＞／か【か】〔係助〕＜疑問｜(adv.)INTERROGATIVE＞／も【も】〔係助〕＜意味なし｜(adv.)NO MEANING＞／しる【知る】〔他ラ四〕＜知る｜(v.)know＞(しる＝連体形)／ひと【人】〔名〕＜友人｜(n.)a friend＞／に【に】〔格助〕＜補語｜(prep.)COMPLEMENT＞／す【為】〔他サ変〕＜～とする｜(v.)make＞(せ＝未然形)／む【む】〔助動マ四型〕意志＜～するつもりだ｜(aux-v.)be going to ～＞(む＝連体形係り結び)／たかさご【高砂】〔名〕＜[固有名詞]高砂｜(n.)Takasago＞／の【の】〔格助〕＜の｜(prep.)'s＞／まつ【松】〔名〕＜松｜(n.)pine trees＞／も【も】〔係助〕＜～もまた｜(adv.)also＞／むかし【昔】〔名〕＜昔｜(n.)the past＞／の【の】〔格助〕＜の｜(prep.)'s＞／とも【友】〔名〕＜友人｜(n.)a friend＞／なり【なり】〔助動ナリ型〕断定＜～である｜(aux-v.)be＞(なら＝未然形)／ず【ず】〔助動特殊型〕打消＜～[し]ない｜(adv.)not ～＞(な＝未然形)／く【く】〔接尾〕＜名詞化成分｜(suffix)[to make n. out of v.]＞／に【に】〔格助〕＜詠嘆｜(interj.)EXCLAMATION＞

[tare wo-ka-mo shiru hito ni se-mu Takasago no matsu mo mukashi no tomo nara-na-ku-ni]

実際老境にある人の本物の哀歌で、周りにはもう昔の仲間もいなくなってしまった後で、名のある古木を友としようかな、と思った彼は、気付くのです ― 自分は相手を知ってはいても、相手は自分のことなど知りはしない、と・・・「高砂の松」は「太古の昔からずっと存在し続ける何か」を象徴する「歌枕」・・・最近では(同じ根から生えているように見える)「相生の松＝永遠の愛情のシンボル」で有名ですが、このイメージは平安調短歌の脈絡には当てはまりません。

A truly sad song of an actual old man, who has no old friend left around him and seeks friendship in a famous old tree, only to find he knows it but it doesn't know him. 高砂の松(Takasago no matsu＝a pine tree at Takasago) is a famous 歌枕(uta-makura) signifying something old that has been in existence since time immemorial; although it is nowadays famed for 相生の松(ai-oi no matsu＝a couple of pine trees apparently coming out from the same root), a symbol of eternal affection, such is not the case in the context of Heianese TANKA.

────────────────────────

●190●すてはてむとおもふさへこそかなしけれ　きみになれにしわがみとおもへば
　　　　捨て果てむと思ふさへこそ悲しけれ君に馴れにし我が身と思へば

【哀感】[懐旧]『4)後拾遺集:574』和泉式部(いずみしきぶ)

あまりの悲しさにもうこの身を捨ててしまおう、尼になって仏門に入ろう、と、そう思うことさえ悲しい・・・
あんなにも愛してくれた彼の「形見」のこの身体、あの人の思い出ともども捨て去るなんて、できない。

―哀感―

The very notion of completely deserting my life as a woman to become a nun,
It would be too much for me to bear.
My life, my body, is too deeply tinged with memories of you, my dear.
How could I desert my secularity, my flesh that you loved so much,
Along with my fondest memory of you?

すてはつ【捨て果つ】〔自タ下二〕＜すっかり捨ててしまう＞(v.)give up completely＞(すてはて＝未然形)／む【む】〔助動マ四型〕意志＜～するつもりだ｜(aux-v.)be going to ～＞(む＝終止形)／と【と】〔格助〕＜内容提示｜(conj.)that ～＞／おもふ【思ふ】〔他ハ四〕＜思う｜(v.)think＞(おもふ＝連体形)／さへ【さへ】〔副助〕＜さえ｜(adv.)even＞／こそ【こそ】〔係助〕＜強調｜(adv.)EMPHASIS＞／かなし【哀し】〔形シク〕＜悲しい｜(adj.)sad＞(かなしけれ＝已然形係り結び)／きみ【君】〔代名〕＜あなた｜(pron.)you＞／に【に】〔格助〕＜対象｜(prep.)OBJECT＞／なる【馴る】〔自ラ下二〕＜慣れ親しむ｜(v.)be accustomed to＞(なれ＝連用形)／ぬ【ぬ】〔助動ナ変型〕完了＜すでに～[し]た｜(aux-v.)PERFECT TENSE＞(に＝連用形)／き【き】〔助動特殊型〕過去＜～[し]た｜(aux-v.)PAST＞(し＝連体形)／わ【我】〔代名〕＜私｜(pron.)I, myself＞／が【が】〔格助〕＜の｜(prep.)'s＞／み【身】〔名〕＜身体｜(n.)the body＞／と【と】〔格助〕＜内容提示｜(conj.)that ～＞／おもふ【思ふ】〔他ハ四〕＜思う｜(v.)think＞(おもへ＝已然形)／ば【ば】〔接助〕＜理由｜(conj.)REASON＞

[sute-hate-mu to omou sae-koso kanashikere kimi ni nare-ni-shi wa-ga mi to omoe-ba]

夫と死別すると、平安時代の女性の多くは世を捨てて尼となりました・・・が、この詩人には「我が身＝肉体を持った存在」を捨て去るのは難しいのです；今となってはそれが唯一の「彼から彼女への熱愛の形見」なのだから・・・これまた和泉式部が作った女心の真実の歌、平安時代にこんな短歌詠める女性は彼女を置いて他に存在しません。

When bereaved by the husband, many a woman in the Heian era renounced the world to announce herself a nun. This poet, however, finds it hard to discard her 身(mi=carnal existence) which she feels to be the sole memento of his passionate love for her. Just another piece of womanly truth no one but 和泉式部(Izumi shikibu) could ever have made in the Heian era.

《ほぼ生身和泉捨て身の詩小説》

平安時代の短歌のほとんどは虚構であり、歌人当人の実体験や感情に基づくものではありませんでした。特に「恋歌」は最も「作り物」感が強い分野でした・・・が、和泉式部はその奇跡的例外と呼べる女流歌人。彼女の実人生は劇的な出来事(大部分、色事)の連続で、最初の夫と離婚した後、愛してくれた二人の高貴な皇子とは死別、最後には宮廷に出仕して藤原道長の長女の中宮彰子に仕えつつ、宮廷で幾多の高貴な人々(男・女双方)との交流を持ちました。彼女の作品は、類い希なる才能と感受性を持ち波瀾万丈の人生を送った(おそらく見た目も魅力的だった)一人の女性のセミドキュメンタリー作品(少なくとも我々にはそう感じられる迫真の作品群)・・・和泉式部は、人生を素材として芸術を生み出すことを意志的に求めて生きた芸術家だったのです。

《和泉式部(Izumi shikibu) ― a woman who made virtual life story by fictionally actual life of herself》
Most Heianese poems were mere fiction and not based on actual experience or emotion of the poet, love poems least of all... to which 和泉式部(Izumi shikibu) was a miraculous exception. Her real life was a series of dramatic adventures ― mostly of an amorous kind ― starting from a divorce from the first husband, through bereavement by two royal princes, ending up in association with quite a number of noble folks, men and women, at the Imperial Court as she served under Princess 彰子(Shoushi), eldest daughter of 藤原道長(Fujiwara-no-Michinaga). Her works are ― at least seem to us to be ― a semi-documentary of an exceptionally talented, sensitive, adventurous (and perhaps physically attractive) woman who was consciously determined to make art out of her own life.

—哀感—

★191★とどめおきてたれをあはれとおもふらむ こはまさるらむこはまさりけり
留め置きて誰を哀れと思ふらむ子は勝るらむ子は勝りけり

【哀感】[悟り]『4)後拾遺集:568』和泉式部(いずみしきぶ)

自分一人だけ先立ってしまって、この世に置き去りにした人たちのうち、あの娘は今、一体誰のことを一番悲しく思っているかしら？・・・子供たち、でしょうね、きっと・・・私だってそう、別れた男たちよりも誰よりも、母である私を残して旅立ってしまったあなたのことを思うと、やり切れない気持ちでいっぱいだもの。

Who do you sorely miss of all those you left behind?
— Children... yes *you* will.
My child... yes *I* do.

とどむ【留む】〔他マ上二〕＜この世に残す｜(v.)leave in this world＞(とどめ＝連用形)／おく【置く】〔補動カ四〕＜〜のままにしておく｜(adv.)behind＞(おき＝連用形)／て【て】〔接助〕＜順接｜(conj.)and＞／たれ【誰】【代名】＜誰｜(pron.)who＞／を【を】〔格助〕＜目的格｜(prep.)OBJECT＞／あはれ【あはれ】〔感〕＜あぁ残念｜(n.)a pity＞／と【と】〔格助〕＜内容提示｜(conj.)that 〜＞／おもふ【思ふ】〔他ハ四〕＜思う｜(v.)think＞(おもふ＝終止形)／らむ【らむ】〔助動ラ四型〕現在推量＜〜だろう｜(aux-v.)SUPPOSITION＞(らむ＝連体形係り結び)／こ【子】〔名〕＜子供たち｜(n.)children＞／は【は】〔係助〕＜主格｜(prep.)SUBJECT＞／まさる【勝る】〔自ラ四〕＜より上だ｜(v.)exceed＞(まさる＝終止形)／らむ【らむ】〔助動ラ四型〕現在推量＜〜だろう｜(aux-v.)SUPPOSITION＞(らむ＝終止形)／こ【子】〔名〕＜我が子｜(n.)the child＞／は【は】〔係助〕＜主格｜(prep.)SUBJECT＞／まさる【勝る】〔自ラ四〕＜より上だ｜(v.)exceed＞(まさる＝終止形)／けり【けり】〔助動ラ変型〕詠嘆＜〜だったのだなぁ｜(interj.)REALIZATION＞(けり＝終止形)

[todome-oki-te tare wo aware to omou-ramu ko wa masaru-ramu ko wa masari-keri]

痛々しく悲しい想像の中で、娘の小式部内侍と向き合う和泉式部の歌・・・小式部は、三人の幼い子(父親は三人とも別人)を残し、母の和泉より先に逝ってしまったのでした・・・「恋多き女」として共に有名だったこの母娘の仮想対話の中での「*男なんて、子供にくらべれば物の数にも入らない*」という気付きの迫真の響き、他の誰にも真似できません。この悲しき真実が、「**らむ**＝*彼女はきっとこう感じていることでしょう*」という形で娘の心情を代弁する母の声と、「**けり**＝*あぁ私、今、ようやくわかったわ*」という形で自らの個人的発見を告白する母親との間の、美しい音楽の響きのような対話の中へと織り込まれているこの詩・・・これほどまでの珠玉の詩は、ただの天才だけで生み出せるものではありません。個人的体験(否、犠牲！)もまたこの詩に欠くべからざる必須要素・・・確かに悲しい物語;だけど偉大な物語・・・それが成立し得たのは、日本に和泉式部が ― そして和歌が ― あったればこそ。

In her painfully sad imagination, 和泉式部(Izumi shikibu) finds herself face to face with her daughter 小式部内侍(Ko-shikibu no naishi), who died on her leaving behind three small children she gave birth to with three different fathers... the realization that "*men are nothing to children*" could never sound more true than in this imaginary dialogue between the mother and the daughter both legendary for their amorous adventures. This painfully sad truth is woven into a musically beautiful conversation between the daughter who speaks in the vicarious voice (らむ:ramu=*perhaps she should feel*) and the mother who announces her personal discovery (けり:keri=*now I found out*). Mere genius could never have given birth to this superb gem of poetry: personal experience, no, *sacrifice*, is another essential ingredient of this masterpiece. It's a sad story, to be sure; but also a great story, made possible only because there was 和泉式部 ― and 和歌(WAKA) ― in Japan.

―哀感―

●192●うたたねのこのよのゆめのはかなきに さめぬやがてのいのちともがな
うたた寝のこのよの夢の儚きに覚めぬやがての命ともがな

【哀感】[慨嘆]『4)後拾遺集:564』藤原実方(ふじわらのさねかた)

ふっと眠りに落ちたその夢の中で、今は亡き我が子に出会った…けれども目覚めてみればそれは夢…考えてみれば、目覚めて戻ったこっちの現実だって、まるで夢のごとく儚いもの…どうせなら、こんな夢みたいに頼りない現実なんていらないから、さっきのあの夢の中でずっと、そのまま醒めずに一生を過ごすことができたなら、どんなにかいいだろうに。

My child I surely had... in a dream that instantly passed.
In life I don't any more... in the past, did I?... I'm not sure.
Life is as fleeting as a dream... O that I'd never wake again!

うたたね【転寝】〔名〕<短い眠り｜(n.)a nap>／の【の】〔格助〕<の｜(prep.)'s>／**(A1)こ【子】[名]**<子供｜(n.)a child>／**(A2)の【の】[格助]**<の｜(prep.)'s>／**(A3)よ【夜】[名]**<夜｜(n.)the night>／**(B1)こ【此】[代名]**<これ｜(pron.)this>／**(B2)の【の】[格助]**<の｜(prep.)'s>／**(B3)よ【世】[名]**<世間｜(n.)the world>／の【の】〔格助〕<の｜(prep.)'s>／ゆめ【夢】〔名〕<夢｜(n.)a dream>／の【の】〔格助〕<主格｜(prep.)SUBJECT>／はかなし【儚し】〔形〕<はかない｜(adj.)evanescent>(はかなき＝連体形)／に【に】〔接助〕<理由｜(conj.)REASON>／さむ【醒む】〔自マ下二〕<目覚める｜(v.)wake up>(さめ＝未然形)／ず【ず】〔助動特殊型〕打消<〜[し]ない｜(adv.)not 〜>(ぬ＝連体形)／やがて【やがて】〔副〕<そのまま｜(adv.)just the way it is>／の【の】〔格助〕<の｜(prep.)'s>／いの ち【命】〔名〕<生命｜(n.)my life>／と【と】〔格助〕<結末｜(prep.)RESULT>／もがな【もがな】〔終助〕<〜があってほしいな｜(adv.)hopefully>

[utata-ne no ko-no-yo no yume no hakanaki ni same-nu yagate-no inochi to-mogana]

「伝説の色男」藤原実方が作ったニセモノ歌。「詞書」では「子供(7人とも9人ともいわれる実方の子供達のうちの誰のことを指すのかはわからないけど、とにかくその子)を最近亡くしてその子の夢を見た時に詠んだ歌」ということになっているけれど、全然本物の響きがないのは次の理由による…1)当時あまりに乱発されまくった陳腐な決まり文句の「命ともがな＝あぁ、この命がたった今終わってしまえばいいのに！」なんか使っちゃってる;2)「子の夜の夢」にも「此の世の夢」にもどちらにも取れる「このよの夢」という二股膏薬っぽい言い回しをわざと使ってる;3)「うたた寝の此の世の夢」という言い回しから更に有名な中国の伝説「邯鄲の枕＝それに頭を乗せて寝ると冒険の連続の人生の夢を見るけど、寝覚めて気付いてみればそれは邯鄲の宿屋での午後の短い**うたた寝**の間に見た幻に過ぎなかった」への連想をも意図的に誘ってる…そんな感じでウソっぽさ満載なんですが、それでもその色んな含みを持たせた気取った趣向のおかげで、多くの人々の訴える力を持った歌であることは確かでしょう:あなた個人にとって真実の響きを持った素晴らしいものであると感じるなら、短歌が「事実、あったこと」である必要なんて、ない、ってことをお忘れなく。

A phony poem by the legendary playboy 藤原実方(Fujiwara-no-Sanekata); though the annotation to this TANKA says he made it after a dream of the child he had just lost (*nobody knows exactly which of his 7 or 9 children*), it just doesn't sound true at all, due to the use of the most overused cliché of the day 命ともがな(inochi tomogana＝I wish my life came to an end now!) and the consciously equivocal term of このよの夢(ko-no yo no yume) diverging both into 1)my dream at night about the child I lost and 2)my dream of this life as fleeting as a dream — apparently intending to refer to the famous Chinese legend of 邯鄲の枕(Kantan no makura＝a magical pillow which makes the sleeper dream of a life full of adventures, only to be found to have been just a fantasy dreamt in a short nap in the afternoon in an inn at Kantan, China)... such as it is, it certainly will appeal to many with its stylish implications. Remember — TANKA just doesn't have to be factually true to be personally true and great to you.

―観念―

―観念：Finding Out―

●193● ひとのおやのこころはやみにあらねども　こをおもふみちにまどひぬるかな
人の親の心は闇に非ねども子を思ふ道に惑ひぬるかな

【観念】[悟り]『2)後撰集:1103』藤原兼輔(ふじわらのかねすけ)

子を持つ親の心は、理不尽な闇に包まれているわけではないけれど、
我が子を思う余りに分別を失って、愚かな脇道に逸れてしまったりもするものなのですよねぇ。

Parental mind otherwise rarely illogical
Goes strangely astray when it comes to worrying about children.

ひと【人】[名]＜人間｜(n.)a human being＞／の【の】[格助]＜の｜(prep.)'s＞／おや＜親｜(n.)a parent＞／の【の】[格助]＜の｜(prep.)'s＞／こころ【心】[名]＜心｜(n.)heart＞／は【は】[係助]＜主格｜(prep.)SUBJECT＞／やみ【闇】[名]＜無知蒙昧｜(n.)darkness without enlightenment＞／なり【なり】[助動ナリ型]断定＜～である｜(aux-v.)be＞(に=連用形)／あり【あり】[補動ラ変]＜～である｜(aux-v.)be＞(あら=未然形)／ず【ず】[助動特殊型]打消＜～[し]ない｜(adv.)not ～＞(ね=已然形)／ども【ども】[接助]＜～ではあるが｜(conj.)although＞／こ【子】[名]＜子供｜(n.)a child＞／を【を】[格助]＜目的格｜(prep.)OBJECT＞／おもふ【思ふ】[他ハ四]＜思う｜(v.)think＞(おもふ=連体形)／みち【道】[名]＜道｜(n.)the way＞／に【に】[格助]＜原因｜(prep.)REASON＞／まどふ【惑ふ】[自ハ四]＜迷う｜(v.)get lost＞(まどひ=連用形)／ぬ【ぬ】[助動ナ変型]完了＜すでに～[し]た｜(aux-v.)PERFECT TENSE＞(ぬる=連体形)／かな【かな】[終助]＜詠嘆｜(interj.)EXCLAMATION＞

[hito no oya no kokoro wa yami ni ara-ne-domo ko wo omou michi ni madoi-nuru kana]

子供を思う親心を、本物の親が詠んだ歌で、何の技巧も凝らさぬその詠いぶりが、詩的とは呼び難いが素晴らしいこの詩の真直な魅力になっている。この歌が有名になったおかげで、「心の闇」の言い回しは「我が子のことが心配でならない親心」の意味で広く用いられるようになった。「闇に惑ふ」というのは「宗教の開明の光に当たっていない俗人が＜煩悩＝世俗的欲望＞のなすがままになっている精神状態」を指すものとして仏教徒が好んで用いる言い回し…ということで想像が付くと思うが、＜子煩悩＞や＜心の闇＞といった言い回しは、「わかるわぁ、その感じ。まぁ仕方ないよね」の感じを伴って用いられたものであって、否定的な響きもなければ困りものを指す表現でもなかったのだ…が、近頃では文化的素養のない日本人が増えてきて、これらの表現を「テメェのガキに入れ込み過ぎて回りの迷惑かえりみる余裕もねぇバカ親」とか「人間心理の邪悪な面」とかの意味に間違って解釈されている、という驚愕すべき暗黒の事実もあったりする…少子高齢化街道まっしぐらの今の日本の潮流を思えば、この種の錯誤も当然と言うべきか。

A true feeling of a true parent caring for the child, without any technique whatsoever, which contributes to the sincere charm of this prosaic piece of superb poem. Due to its popularity, the term 心の闇 (kokoro no yami=darkness of the mind) was popularly used in the sense of excessive worries of parents about their children. 闇に惑ふ(yami ni madou=lost in the dark) is the Buddhist's favorite expression for the mental state of those without religious enlightenment totally at the mercy of worldly desires ― 煩悩(bonnou). You could imagine the term 子煩悩(ko-bonnou=at the mercy of parental love and worries of children) and the expression 心の闇(kokoro no yami=lack of logicality when it comes to children) were used with indulgent compassion, never meaning anything negative or troublesome... an alarmingly dark fact about the current Japanese society is that these terms are mistakenly interpreted as "*crazy parents too much indulgent in their kids to care about the nuisance to others*" and "*the evil side of the human mentality*" by increasing numbers of culturally illiterate Japanese... natural fallacy in view of the ever-decreasing number of children in this nation, perhaps.

—観念—

●194● よもすがらむかしのことをみつるかな かたるやうつつありしよやゆめ
夜もすがら昔の事を見つるかな語るや現有りし世や夢

【観念】[懐旧]『8)新古今集:824』大江匡衡(おおえのまさひら)

ゆうべは一晩中、昔の夢を見ちゃったなぁ…懐かしい人々とも夢の中で語り合ったなぁ…
あの語らいこそ本物、現実のつもりで過ごして来た時間のほうは幻 ― なんか、そんな気もするなぁ。

I dreamed all through the night about things of the past.
Was our dreamy conversation reality, the rest of my life a dream?

よもすがら【夜もすがら】〔副〕＜夜通し｜(adv.)all through the night＞／むかし【昔】〔名〕＜昔｜(n.)the past＞／の【の】〔格助〕＜の｜(prep.)'s＞／こと【事】〔名〕＜出来事｜(n.)the event＞／を【を】〔格助〕＜目的格｜(prep.)OBJECT＞／みる【見る】〔他マ上一〕＜見る｜(v.)view＞(み＝連用形)／つ【つ】〔助動タ下二型〕完了＜すでに～した｜(aux-v.)PERFECT TENSE＞(つる＝連体形)／かな【かな】〔終助〕＜詠嘆｜(interj.)EXCLAMATION＞／かたる【語る】〔他ラ四〕＜語り合う｜(v.)engage in conversation＞(かたる＝連体形)／や【や】〔係助〕＜疑問｜(adv.)INTERROGATIVE＞／うつつ【現】〔名〕＜現実｜(n.)the reality＞／あり【あり】〔自ラ変〕＜存在する｜(v.)exist＞(あり＝連用形)／き【き】〔助動特殊型〕過去＜～[し]た｜(aux-v.)PAST＞(し＝連体形)／よ【世】〔名〕＜世間｜(n.)the world＞／や【や】〔係助〕＜疑問｜(adv.)INTERROGATIVE＞／ゆめ【夢】〔名〕＜夢｜(n.)a dream＞

[yo-mo-sugara mukashi no koto wo mi-tsuru kana kataru ya utsutsu ari-shi yo ya yume]

古代中国の有名な哲学問答に、荘子(「道教」の祖の一人)が「人生の本質は夢なのではないか？」と疑うものがあります…彼は一羽の蝶となって空を飛び回る夢から覚めたばかりなのですが、自分は実は自分がそうだと思い込んでいるもの(蝶の夢から覚めたばかりの人間)ではなくて、自分のことを夢の中で「自分は人間だ」と思い込んでいる蝶なのではないかと疑い始めるのです…この短歌の作者は中国の古典に精通した著名な学者の大江匡衡ですから、おそらくこの古代中国の伝説に触発されて作った歌なのでしょう…彼はまた著名な歌人(で、藤原道長と彼を取り巻く人々を美しく飾り立てて書いた『栄花物語』の作者でもある)赤染衛門の夫としても知られています。

There is a famous philosophical argument in ancient China by 荘子(Zhuangzi), one of the founders of 道教(Taoism), suspecting the essence of this life to be a dream: he just wakes up from a dream in which he has been flying in the air as a butterfly, and comes to doubt if he is really what he believes himself to be — a human being who just woke up from a butterfly dream — and suspects that he may really be a butterfly dreaming itself to be a human being in its dream. That story must have been the inspiration to this author, 大江匡衡(Oue-no-Masahira), famous scholar well-read in Chinese classics; he is also known as the husband of the famous poet 赤染衛門(Akazome emon) who also wrote 栄花物語(Eiga monogatari), beautifully decorated stories of 藤原道長(Fujiwara-no-Michinaga) and his company.

―――――――――――――――――――――――――――――

—観念—

★195★みるほどはゆめもゆめともしられねば うつつもいまはうつつとおもはじ
見る程は夢も夢とも知られねば現も今は現と思はじ

【観念】[慨嘆]『7)千載集:1234』藤原資隆(ふじわらのすけたか)

夢の中にいる時は、それが夢であるとは知らずに過ごしているもの･･･であれば、現実の中に身を置いてはいても、それを現実だとは思わずに過ごしていれば、それは「夢」も同じこと･･･だから、これから先はもう、こんな 儚(はかな) い世の出来事は「現実」とは思わず、所詮(しょせん)は「夢」だと思うことにしよう。

A dream is never a dream while I'm in it it's nothing but real.
What's real would never be real so long as I believe it unreal.
This world I'll deem as unreal... for it's already too much to be real.

みる【見る】[他マ上一]＜見る｜(v.)view＞(みる＝連体形)／ほど【ほど】[副助]＜間｜(conj.)while＞／は【は】[係助]＜～に関しては｜(adv.)as for ～＞／ゆめ【夢】[名]＜夢｜(n.)a dream＞／も【も】[係助]＜～もまた｜(adv.)also＞／ゆめ【夢】[名]＜夢｜(n.)a dream＞／と【と】[格助]＜内容提示｜(conj.)that ～＞／も【も】[係助]＜意味なし｜(adv.)NO MEANING＞／しる【知る】[他ラ四]＜知る｜(v.)know＞(しら＝未然形)／る【る】[助動ラ下二型]受身＜～[さ]れる｜(aux-v.)PASSIVE VOICE＞(れ＝未然形)／ず【ず】[助動特殊型]打消＜～[し]ない｜(adv.)not ～＞(ね＝已然形)／ば【ば】[接助]＜理由｜(conj.)REASON＞／うつつ【現】[名]＜現実｜(n.)the reality＞／も【も】[係助]＜～もまた｜(adv.)also＞／いま【今】[名]＜今｜(n.)now＞／は【は】[係助]＜～に関しては｜(adv.)as for ～＞／うつつ【現】[名]＜現実｜(n.)the reality＞／と【と】[格助]＜内容提示｜(conj.)that ～＞／おもふ【思ふ】[他ハ四]＜思う｜(v.)think＞(おもは＝未然形)／じ【じ】[助動特殊型]打消意志＜～ないつもりだ｜(aux-v.)be not going to ～＞(じ＝終止形)

[miru hodo wa yume mo yume to-mo shira-re-ne-ba utsutsu mo ima-wa utsutsu to omowa-ji]

一つ前のと似た感じの短歌ですが、こちらは「現世での我々の存在は夢のようなもの」という仏教の経典(きょうてん)の教えを下敷きにしたものです。もう一つ情報を加えるなら、この短歌の作者の後半生は、福原への遷都や源平合戦(げんぺいかっせん)で古い京都の町並みが荒廃して行く平安時代の最末期(さいまっき)と重なります･･･「これは現実じゃない、夢だ！」と思いたがったのも、無理からぬことですね。

A similar TANKA to the previous one, except that this one has its basis on a Buddhist sutra telling us "our existence in this world is just like a dream". As an additional piece of info, the later life of the author of this TANKA corresponded to the very last days of the Heian era, when such catastrophic events as 福原遷都(Fukuhara sento＝relocation of the capital to Fukuhara) and 源平合戦(Gen-Pei gassen＝the civil war between the clans of Minamotos and Tairas) devastated the old city of 京都(Kyoto)... no wonder he'd rather think "*this can't be real but a dream!*"

──────────────────────

●196●よのなかをなににたとへむあさぼらけ こぎゆくふねのあとのしらなみ
世の中を何に例へむ朝朗け漕ぎ行く舟の跡の白波

【観念】[悟り]『3)拾遺集:1327』沙弥満誓(さみまんせい)

この世の中を何に例えようか？･･･
暗い夜が明けていよいよ朝になった、とばかり希望に満ちて船出(ふなで)してはみたけれど、前途洋々(ぜんとようよう)のはずだったその船旅の航跡(こうせき)もあっという間に波の彼方(かなた)に掻き消され、後には何も残らない無常の舞台･･･
さしずめそんなところか。

—Finding Out—　　　　　　　　http//zubaraie.com

—観念—

What should this life be likened to?
Going out in a boat early in the morn,
Full of hopes what awaits in the day.
But, alas, the wake is gone as the boat rows on.
Where will it go... will we know at the end of the day?

よのなか【世の中】〔名〕＜世の中｜(n.)the world＞／を【を】〔格助〕＜目的格｜(prep.)OBJECT＞／なに【何】〔代名〕＜何｜(pron.)what＞／に【に】〔格助〕＜比較｜(prep.)COMPARISON＞／たとふ【喩ふ】〔他ハ下二〕＜たとえる｜(v.)liken＞(たとへ＝未然形)／む【む】〔助動マ四型〕意志＜～するつもりだ｜(aux-v.)be going to ～＞(む＝連体形係り結び)／あさぼらけ【朝朗け】〔名〕＜早朝、あたりが明るくなり始める時間帯｜(n.)the earliest hour of the morning＞／こぐ【漕ぐ】〔他カ四〕＜漕ぐ｜(v.)row＞(こぎ＝連用形)／ゆく【行く】〔自カ四〕＜行く｜(v.)go＞(ゆく＝連体形)／ふね【舟】〔名〕＜船｜(n.)a ship＞／の【の】〔格助〕＜の｜(prep.)'s＞／あと【跡】〔名〕＜航跡｜(n.)a wake＞／の【の】〔格助〕＜の｜(prep.)'s＞／しらなみ【白波】〔名〕＜白い波｜(n.)white waves＞

[yo-no-naka wo nani ni tatoe-mu asaborake kogi-yuku fune no ato no shira-nami]

奈良時代の僧が作った有名な例え歌。
A famous analogy TANKA made by a Buddhist bonze in the Nara(奈良) era.

●197●すめばみゆにごれぱかくるさだめなき このみやみづにやどるつきかげ
澄めば見ゆ濁れば隠る定め無き此の身や水に宿る月影

【観念】[悟り]『7)千載集:1224』藤原永範(ふじわらのながのり)

心澄まして眺めればその姿が見えるが、濁った心にはまるで見えぬもの ―
人間存在の本質は、さしずめ、水面に映る月影のようなものか。

With calm and peace of mind, it appears.
Dirty turbulent mind makes it disappear:
Is human entity like the moon in the water?

すむ【澄む】〔自マ四〕＜きれいに澄み渡る｜(v.)get serenely clean＞(すめ＝已然形)／ば【ば】〔接助〕＜仮定｜(conj.)if＞／みゆ【見ゆ】〔自ヤ下二〕＜見える｜(v.)appear＞(みゆ＝終止形)／にごる【濁る】〔自ラ四〕＜濁る｜(v.)get dirty＞(にごれ＝已然形)／ば【ば】〔接助〕＜仮定｜(conj.)if＞／かくる【隠る】〔自ラ下二〕＜隠れる｜(v.)hide＞(かくる＝終止形)／さだめ【定め】〔名〕＜確かな宿命｜(n.)a guaranteed destiny＞／なし【なし】〔形ク〕＜存在しない｜(v.)do not exist＞(なき＝連体形)／こ【此】〔代名〕＜これ｜(pron.)this＞／の【の】〔格助〕＜の｜(prep.)'s＞／み【身】〔名〕＜自身｜(n.)[one]self＞／や【や】〔係助〕＜疑問｜(adv.)INTERROGATIVE＞／みづ【水】〔名〕＜水｜(n.)water＞／に【に】〔格助〕＜場所｜(prep.)PLACE＞／やどる【宿る】〔自ラ四〕＜宿る｜(v.)stay＞(やどる＝連体形)／つきかげ【月影】〔名〕＜月明かり｜(n.)the moonlight＞

[sume-ba miyu nigore-ba kakuru sadame-naki ko-no mi ya mizu ni yadoru tsuki-kage]

これもまた例え話の短歌で、作られたのは平安末期。「この世のすべては、それを見る者の心次第で、いかようにも映るもの」というのが当時の貴族の基本的態度・・・こうした態度の証拠品は、これまでに紹介してきた彼らの詩歌の中でふんだんに見てきた通りです。
Another TANKA of analogy made in the end of the Heian era. *Everything in life is what the mind of its viewer makes it appear to be* – this is the fundamental attitude of nobles of the day, the proof of which you have seen in abundance in their poems.

―観念―

●198●ながらへばまたこのごろやしのばれむ うしとみしよぞいまはこひしき
永らへば又此の頃や偲ばれむ憂しと見し世ぞ今は恋しき

【観念】【悟り】『8)新古今集:1843』藤原清輔(ふじわらのきよすけ)

私が長生きしたとすれば、この頃の私のあまり幸せとは言えないあれこれもまた、
懐かしく思い出すことになるのだろうなぁ、ちょうど、辛くて仕方ないと感じていたあの当時のことが、
今では恋しく思い出されるのと同じように。

If I were to live long, would I also miss these days?
I now miss the cruel world that used to treat me so bad
That I thought "*I've had enough!*"... good memories now.

ながらふ【長らふ】〔自ハ下二〕<長生きする│(v.)live long＞(ながらへ＝未然形)/ば【ば】〔接助〕<仮定│(conj.)if＞/また【亦】〔副〕<また│(adv.)also＞/こ【此】〔代名〕<これ│(pron.)this＞/の【の】〔格助〕<の│(prep.)'s＞/ごろ【頃】〔名〕<頃│(n.)a time when ～＞/や【や】〔係助〕<疑問│(adv.)INTERROGATIVE＞/しのぶ【偲ぶ】〔他バ四〕〔他バ上二〕<懐かしく思い出す│(v.)fondly remember＞(しのば＝未然形)/る【る】〔助動ラ下二型〕自発<思わず知らずそうなる│(adv.)naturally＞(れ＝未然形)/む【む】〔助動マ四型〕推量<だろう│(aux-v.)SUPPOSITION＞(む＝連体形係り結び)/うし【憂し】〔形ク〕<憂鬱だ│(adj.)melancholy＞(うし＝終止形)/と【と】〔格助〕<内容提示│(conj.)that ～＞/みる【見る】〔他マ上一〕<見る│(v.)view＞(み＝連用形)/き【き】〔助動特殊型〕過去<～[し]た│(aux-v.)PAST＞(し＝連体形)/よ【世】〔名〕<世間│(n.)the world＞/ぞ【ぞ】〔係助〕<強調│(adv.)EMPHASIS＞/いま【今】〔名〕<今│(n.)now＞/は【は】〔係助〕<～に関しては│(adv.)as for ～＞/こひし【恋し】〔形シク〕<恋しい│(v.)feel attached to＞(こひしき＝連体形係り結び)

[nagarae-ba mata ko-no-goro ya shinoba-re-mu ushi to mi-shi yo zo ima-wa koishiki]

自分自身のあまり幸せとは言えない若き日々を振り返りながら、詩人は我々にこう教えてくれます ―
思い出のフィルターで濾過して、時の鏡に映して見れば、美しくないものなんて、なにもない。
This poet looks back upon his not so happy younger days and tells us ― *everything looks beautiful in the mirror of time through the filter of memories.*

★199★うきままにいとひしみこそをしまるれ あればぞみつるあきのよのつき
憂き儘に厭ひし身こそ惜しまるれ在ればぞ見つる秋の夜の月

【観念】【悟り】『4)後拾遺集:263』藤原隆成(ふじわらのたかしげ)

満たされぬ思いに耐えかねて、思わず俗世を捨て去ってしまった私だったが、今となってはそのことも
悔やまれる…この眼前に展開する見事な秋の夜の月景色も、この世に生きていればこそ見られたもの…
諦めて投げ出してしまえばそれっきり、耐え忍んでこそ出会える素晴らしいものだって、きっとある…
この世の真理とはそういうもの ― それを知るのは、めげずに歩み続ける生者のみ。

I deserted the world that treated me so bad.
How I regret it now in the radiant grace of the moon.
This Autumn I hold so dear... all because I am still here.

うし【憂し】〔形ク〕<憂鬱だ│(adj.)melancholy＞(うき＝連体形)/まま【儘】〔名〕<そのままの状況│(n.)the state being ～＞/に【に】〔格助〕<原因│(prep.)REASON＞/いとふ【厭ふ】〔他ハ四〕<俗世を嫌って出家する│(v.)desert the filthy world and become a recluse＞(いとひ＝連用形)/き【き】〔助動特殊型〕過去<～[し]た│(aux-v.)PAST＞(し＝連体形)/み【身】〔名〕<境遇│(n.)circumstances＞/こそ

—観念—

【こそ】〔係助〕＜強調│(adv.)EMPHASIS＞／をしむ【惜しむ】〔他マ四〕＜後悔する│(v.)regret＞(をしま＝未然形)／る【る】〔助動ラ下二型〕自発＜[思わず知らず]そうなる│(adv.)naturally＞(るれ＝已然形係り結び)／あり【あり】〔自ラ変〕＜存在する│(v.)exist＞(あれ＝已然形)／ば【ば】〔接助〕＜理由│(conj.)REASON＞／ぞ【ぞ】〔係助〕＜強調│(adv.)EMPHASIS＞／**(A1)みる【見る】**〔他マ上一〕＜見る│(v.)view＞／**(A2)つ【つ】**〔助動タ下二型〕完了＜すでに～した│(aux-v.)PERFECT TENSE＞(つる＝連体形係り結び)／**(B)みつ【満つ】**〔自タ上二〕＜満たされる│get fulfilled＞(みつる＝連体形)／あき【秋】〔名〕＜秋│(n.)Autumn＞／の【の】〔格助〕＜の│(prep.)'s＞／よ【夜】〔名〕＜夜│(n.)the night＞／の【の】〔格助〕＜の│(prep.)'s＞／つき【月】〔名〕＜月│(n.)the moon＞

[uki-mama-ni itoi-shi mi koso oshima-rure are-ba-zo mi-tsuru aki no yo no tsuki]

「厭ひし身＝嫌い遠ざけた我が身」には現代人向けの注釈が必要で、単なる「自己嫌悪」ではなく「俗世を捨てて仏教僧になる」と解釈するのが「厭ふ」の正しい平安調解釈。しかしこの歌人は、「憂し＝憂鬱・惨め・不機嫌」の感情に身を任せて世捨て人になった自分の所業を、悔いている・・・何故？・・・だって、月があぁも美しく輝いているのを見て「美しい！」と言えるのは、この世に生きて在る者だけの特権。この歌人が捨て去ってしまった世の中の喜びも悲しみも、背を向けずに全て向き合ってさえいれば、愛着を込めて満喫する(満つる)ことができたかもしれない(否、できたに違いない！)ものなのだから・・・たった今、苦しんでいる人たちに向けての良い助言になる歌 ― 空を見上げて思ってごらん、自暴自棄に走れば失うことになる、大事なあれこれのことを。

厭ひし身(itoi-shi mi＝myself that I found hateful) needs explaining to modern readers: it does not mean mere self-hate — deserting the secular world to become a Buddhist bonze — that's the correct Heianese version of 厭ふ(itou＝hate, renounce). This poet, however, regrets having renounced the world just because he felt 憂し(ushi＝blue, miserable, melancholy)... why? — because the moon is so beautiful to see only for those alive in this world to cherish it. The worldly joy and sorrow he has left behind might (no, **MUST**!) have been there for him to fondly <u>taste to the full</u> (満つる：mitsuru)... if only he had not turned his back upon them all. A good advice for those currently in trouble – *look up at the sky to imagine what you'll miss in desperation.*

―――――――――――――――――――――――――――

投げずに歩み　生き忍べ／偲べ　　　　Don't give up, just walk on to look back and smile

いとひても(厭ひても)　　　　　　　　**A** life ever so hateful
きとまたいきよ(きと又生きよ)　　　　**L**ived long with courage
しなざれば(死なざれば)　　　　　　　**I**n retrospect will revive
のちのたからの(後の宝の)　　　　　　**V**ery precious memories of
へりゆきのひび(経/減り行きの日々)　　**E**ver-decreasing days of yours.

死ねば終りの人の感慨　　　　　　　　Human emotions *only valid while alive*
猶も斯く見す歌の尊さ　　　　　　　　*Still* so vivid in precious songs of the dead

・・・と、のと・じゃうご　　　　　　　...thus spoke *Jaugo Noto*

http//zubaraie.com　　　　-193-　　　　—Finding Out—

—観念—

★200★つくづくとおもへばやすきよのなかを こころとなげくわがみなりけり

つくづくと思へば安き世の中を心と歎く我が身なりけり

【観念】【悟り】『8)新古今集:1774』荒木田長延(あらきだながのぶ)

「あぁ、なんてひどい世の中だ、これではとても生きて行けない」と嘆き続けて生きて来た私・・・だけど、結局、こうして今なお生きている・・・よくよく考えてみれば、生きて行くのはさほど難しいことじゃない・・・この世を生き辛くさせるものは、嘆きに沈みたがる私自身の心だったのだ。

    In a world that used to feel too harsh for me to bear
    I've lived so far... long enough to come to realize ―
   ― Life is rather easy to accept, nothing too tough to take
    Only if I tame my heart that wants to think the worst of it.

つくづくと【熟くと】〔副〕<じっくりと｜(adv.)deeply>／おもふ【思ふ】〔他ハ四〕<思う｜(v.)think>（おもへ＝已然形)／ば【ば】〔接助〕<～したところ｜(conj.)when>／やすし【安し】〔形〕<容易だ｜(adj.)easy>（やすき＝連体形)／よのなか【世の中】〔名〕<世の中｜(n.)the world>／を【を】〔格助〕<目的格｜(prep.)OBJECT>／こころ【心】〔名〕<自分自身の心｜(n.)my own state of emotion>／と【と】〔格助〕<～に発して｜(prep.)out of>／なげく【嘆く】〔自カ四〕<嘆く｜(v.)grieve>（なげく＝連体形)／わ【我】〔代名〕<私｜(pron.)I, myself>／が【が】〔格助〕<の｜(prep.)'s>／み【身】〔名〕<自身｜(n.)[one]self>／なり【なり】〔助動ナリ型〕断定<～である｜(aux-v.)be>（なり＝連用形)／けり【けり】〔助動ラ変型〕詠嘆<～だったのだなぁ｜(interj.)REALIZATION>（けり＝終止形)

  [tsukuzukuto omoe-ba yasuki yo-no-naka wo kokoro-to nageku wa-ga mi nari-keri]

八代集の最後を飾る『新古今集』に収められた、悟りの（あるいは、諦めの）短歌 ― 結局のところ、人生は、頭で考えるほど、心で感じるほど、自分の望みのモノサシで測るほど、ヒドい代物ではなかったなぁ ― ハッと気付いたこの悟り(諦め？)が、誰もにあればいいのだろうけど・・・残念ながら『新古今集』撰進を命じた後鳥羽院には、それはなかったようです。鎌倉幕府打倒に失敗して隠岐島へと流されて後、院は、約2000首の『新古今集』の短歌の中から最良の精髄を選び出すべく、彼の気に食わぬ約350首を除外しました ― ここに紹介した短歌もそうした「除棄歌」の一つです・・・後鳥羽院は結局、その侘びしい島でその悔恨に満ちた人生を閉じることになります ― おそらくは、自らの頭・心・望みと、折り合いを付けることもできぬままに。「あるべき人生」の実現に躍起になりすぎれば「あり得る人生」の姿を見逃しがち。自分の人生を最高のものに仕上げるのは素晴らしいことだけど、日々の暮らしの中に転がっている良いもの探しはあなたにも友達全員にももっと素晴らしいこと。幸せは、達成するものじゃなく、*発見するもの*なのかも・・・

みなさんに、どうぞすばらしい発見がありますように！

A TANKA of enlightenment ― or resignation ― in 新古今集(Shin-Kokin shuu), the last of the eight great Imperial TANKA anthologies. "*After all, life was not so tough as my head, heart, and hopes wanted to make it out to be*"... it would be nice if we all came to this glimmer of realization... unfortunately, 後鳥羽院(Go-Toba inn), the ex-Emperor who ordered the compilation of 新古今集 (Shin-Kokin shuu), didn't: after he failed in his revolt against 鎌倉幕府(the Kamakura shogunate) and was exiled to the island of 隠岐島(Oki-no-shima), he tried to extract the very best essence of some 2,000 新古今 TANKA by filtering out about 350 poems he didn't like ― this particular poem was one of those omitted: he ended his remorseful life on that forlorn island... perhaps without coming to terms with his head, heart and hopes. Those too keen on realizing what life *should* be are often dull in finding what life *can* be. Making the best of your life is good for you; finding the good of everyday life is finer still for you and all those around you. Happiness , possibly, is not to be achieved but *discovered*.

    Happy discovery for all of you!
     ― **F I N** ―

—Finding Out—   http//zubaraie.com

《一・二・三・四・五 各句ページ索引》
— あ —

あかつきばかり[歌 131:四]壬生忠岑(集 1:古今) 130
あかでこそ[歌 126:一]詠み人知らず(集 1:古今) 126
あかねくに[歌 56:一]在原業平(集 1:古今) 67
あかぬこころは[歌 22:四]藤原元真(集 6:詞花) 38
あかぬわかれの[歌130:四]石清水別当光清女(集 8:新古今) 129
あきかぜに[歌75:一]藤原顕輔(集 8:新古今) 85
あきかぜに[歌 95:一]詠み人知らず(集 1:古今) 101
あきぎぬと[歌 65:一]藤原敏行(集 1:古今) 76
あきくれど[歌 85:一]坂上是則(集 1:古今) 93
あきぞかなしき[歌 87:二]詠み人知らず(集 1:古今) 95
あきぞまされる[歌 83:五]詠み人知らず(集 3:拾遺) 91
あきちかき[歌 60:一]藤原(九条)良経(集 8:新古今) 71
あきとつげつる[歌 68:四]詠み人知らず(集 2:後撰) 78
あきにはあらねど[歌 74:五]大江千里(集 1:古今) 83
あきにまた[歌 80:一]三条院(集 6:詞花) 88
あきのうちは[歌 96:一]藤原教長(集 7:千載) 103
あきのゆふぐれ[歌89:五]良暹(集4:後拾遺) 96
あきのゆふぐれ[歌 90:五]寂蓮(集8:新古今) 97
あきのゆふぐれ[歌 91:五]寂蓮(集8:新古今) 98
あきのゆふぐれ[歌 92:五]藤原定家(集 8:新古今) 98
あきのゆふべは[歌 70:四]詠み人知らず(集1:古今) 80
あきのよの[歌 72:三]詠み人知らず(集 3:拾遺) 81
あきのよの[歌78:三]藤原家成(集 6:詞花) 87
あきのよのつき[歌 199:五]藤原隆成(集 4:後拾遺) 192
あきのよのつき[歌 71:五]藤原基光(集 5:金葉) 80
あきのよのつき[歌 76:三]詠み人知らず(集 1:古今) 85
あきのよのつき[歌 81:五]恵慶(集 4:後拾遺) 89
あきはかなしき[歌 94:五]詠み人知らず(集 1:古今) 100

あきはきにけり[歌 66:五]詠み人知らず(集1:古今) 76
あきはきにけり[歌 67:五]恵慶(集 3:拾遺) 77
あきはきぬ[歌 88:一]詠み人知らず(集 1:古今) 96
あきやはひとの[歌 186:二]壬生忠岑(集 1:古今) 182
あくがれいづる[歌 52:四]和泉式部(集 4:後拾遺) 64
あけくれて[歌 101:三]源国信(集 5:金葉) 107
あけぬるを[歌 57:三]清原深養父(集 1:古今) 67
あけやらで[歌137:三]俊恵(集 7:千載) 134
あさがほを[歌 61:一]藤原道信(集 3:拾遺) 72
あさちはら[歌 35:一]恵慶(集 3:拾遺) 50
あさぼらけ[歌105:一]坂上是則(集1:古今) 110
あさぼらけ[歌 196:三]沙弥満誓(集 3:拾遺) 190
あさぼらけ[歌 99:一]藤原定頼(集 7:千載) 105
あしひきの[歌 142:一]柿本人麻呂(集3:拾遺) 141
あだしごころを[歌 133:二]詠み人知らず(集 1:古今) 132
あだものを[歌 119:二]紀友則(集 1:古今) 120
あつめしものを[歌 49:二]藤原季通(集 7:千載) 62
あとだにいまだ[歌158:二]在原業平(集 8:新古今) 156
あとのしらなみ[歌 196:三]沙弥満誓(集 3:拾遺) 190
あともなし[歌 34:三]藤原定家(集 8:新古今) 47
あなざりし[歌 123:一]詠み人知らず(集 2:後撰) 124
あはでもなげく[歌 58:二]詠み人知らず(集 3:拾遺) 68
あはむあはじも[歌80:二]三条院(集 6:詞花) 87
あはむとぞおもふ[歌 117:五]崇徳院(集 6:詞花) 118
あはむとぞおもふ[歌 145:五]元良親王(集 2:後撰) 144
あはれしらせし[歌 96:二]藤原教長(集 7:千載) 103
あはれといはむ[歌 147:二]藤原成通(集 6:詞花) 146
あはれとおもへ[歌 24:二]行尊(集 5:金葉) 39
あはれわかれの[歌 15:四]赤染衛門(集 6:詞花) 32

あはれわかれは[歌 174:四]菅原資忠(集 5:金葉) 172
あひにけるかな[歌 102:五]藤原俊成(集8:新古今) 108
あひぬらむ[歌 40:三]藤原定成(集 5:金葉) 56
あひみしよはの[歌 168:二]徳大寺実能(集 5:金葉) 166
あひみしを[歌 169:一]道命(集 4:後拾遺) 166
あひみすな[歌 114:三]詠み人知らず(集 3:拾遺) 116
あひみての[歌 122:一]藤原敦忠(集 3:拾遺) 122
あひみては[歌 120:一]詠み人知らず(集 3:拾遺) 121
あひみても[歌 127:三]源行宗(集 5:金葉) 127
あひみても[歌 58:一]詠み人知らず(集 3:拾遺) 68
あひみむことは[歌 26:四]詠み人知らず(集 1:古今) 40
あふことの[歌 160:一]藤原朝忠(集 3:拾遺) 158
あふことの[歌 47:一]藤原永相女(集 5:金葉) 60
あふさかのせき[歌 175:五]蝉丸(集 2:後撰) 172
あふにしかへば[歌 119:四]紀友則(集 1:古今) 120
あふまでこそは[歌154:四]藤原家通(集 7:千載) 152
あへずちりぬる[歌95:一]詠み人知らず(集 1:古今) 101
あまのつりぶね[歌177:五]小野篁(集1:古今) 174
あまのはら[歌179:一]安部仲麿(集1:古今) 176
あめはふりきぬ[歌23:一]詠み人知らず(集 3:拾遺) 39
あやしかりけり[歌 70:五]詠み人知らず(集 1:古今) 80
あやめぐさ[歌 47:三]藤原永相女(集 5:金葉) 60
あらでうきよに[歌 79:二]三条院(集 4:後拾遺) 87
あらねども[歌 193:三]藤原兼輔(集 2:後撰) 188
あらねども[歌 70:三]詠み人知らず(集 1:古今) 80
あらはれわたる[歌 99:四]藤原定頼(集 7:千載) 105
あらましものを[歌 162:五]詠み人知らず(集 1:古今) 160
ありあけの[歌 131:一]壬生忠岑(集 1:古今) 130
ありあけのつきと[歌 105:二]坂上是則(集 1:古今) 110

各句索引 —あ— —い— —う—

ありしよやゆめ[歌 194：五]大江匡衡(集 8：新古今) 189

ありしよりけに[歌 164：四]詠み人知らず(集 1：古今) 162

ありとやここに[歌 3：一]詠み人知らず(集 1：古今) 18

ありなめど[歌 26：三]詠み人知らず(集 1：古今) 40

あるじなしとて[歌 5：四]菅原道真(集 3：拾遺) 21

あるじなりけれ[歌 13：五]藤原公任(集 3：拾遺) 30

あるときは[歌 111：三]詠み人知らず(集 3：拾遺) 114

あるものを[歌 156：三]相模(集 4：後拾遺) 154

あるものを[歌 173：三]道因(藤原敦頼)(集 7：千載) 171

あるをみるだに[歌186：四]壬生忠岑(集 1：古今) 182

あればぞみつる[歌 199：四]藤原隆実(集 4：後拾遺) 192

—い—

いかがせむ[歌 106：三]和泉式部(集 5：金葉) 111

いかがみるらむ[歌 18：五]藤原基長(集 7：千載) 35

いかでかと[歌 111：一]詠み人知らず(集 3：拾遺) 114

いきばかり[歌 134：三]詠み人知らず(集 1：古今) 132

いくかへり[歌 40：一]藤原定成(集 5：金葉) 54

いけのこほりに[歌 103：二]藤原俊成(集 8：新古今) 109

いたづらに[歌28：三]小野小町(集1：古今) 42

いつかこころの[歌 58：三]詠み人知らず(集 3：拾遺) 68

いづくにも[歌 77：二]藤原忠教(集 5：金葉) 86

いづこもおなじ[歌 89：四]良暹(集 4：後拾遺) 96

いぢゆくらむ[歌 181：五]凡河内躬恒(集 1：古今) 178

いつとても[歌 70：一]詠み人知らず(集 1：古今) 80

いつはりと[歌 135：一]詠み人知らず(集 1：古今) 133

いつはりの[歌 134：一]詠み人知らず(集 1：古今) 132

いつまでよそに[歌 188：四]清昭(集 6：詞花) 183

いづれをもめと[歌 1：四]紀友則(集 1：古今) 16

いでしつきかも[歌 179：五]安部仲麿(集 1：古今) 176

いでていにし[歌 158：一]在原業平(集 8：新古今) 156

いとどしく[歌 68：一]詠み人知らず(集 2：後撰) 78

いとひしまこそ[歌 199：二]藤原隆信(集 4：後拾遺) 192

いとひても[歌 185：一]藤原季通(集 6：詞花) 181

いとへただ[歌 167：三]藤原俊成(集 8：新古今) 164

いとへとぞおもふ[歌 147：五]藤原成通(集 6：詞花) 146

いなばのやまの[歌 176：二]在原行平(集 1：古今) 173

いにしへに[歌18：一]藤原基長(集 7：千載) 35

いにしへは[歌 36：一]藤原伊尹(集 3：拾遺) 50

いのちさへ[歌 128：三]藤原義孝(集 4：後拾遺) 128

いのちともがな[歌 129：五]藤原(伊周母)高階貴子(集 8：新古今) 128

いのちともがな[歌 192：五]藤原実方(集 4：後拾遺) 187

いのちなりけり[歌 26：五]詠み人知らず(集 1：古今) 40

いのちやは[歌 119：一]紀友則(集 1：古今) 120

いのちをし[歌 152：一]実源(集 5：金葉) 149

いはうつなみの[歌 116：二]源重之(集 6：詞花) 117

いはたたく[歌 53：一]藤原教長(集 7：千載) 65

いはにせかるる[歌 117：二]崇徳院(集 6：詞花) 118

いはばこころの[歌 108：二]近衛院(集 5：金葉) 112

いはもるしみづ[歌 54：二]慈円(集 7：千載) 65

いふばかりにや[歌 8：二]壬生忠岑(集 3：拾遺) 23

いふよしもがな[歌 146：五]藤原道雅(集 4：後拾遺) 145

いまかへりこむ[歌 176：五]在原行平(集 1：古今) 173

いまさらに[歌 135：三]詠み人知らず(集 1：古今) 133

いまはあたなれ[歌 162：二]詠み人知らず[集 1：古今) 160

いまはこひしき[歌 198：五]藤原清輔(集 8：新古今) 192

いまはたおなじ[歌 145：二]元良親王(集 2：後撰) 144

いまはただ[歌 146：二]藤原道雅(集 4：後拾遺) 145

いまはただ[歌 170：一]和泉式部(集 4：後拾遺) 168

いまはなるらむ[歌 158：五]在原業平(集 8：新古今) 156

いまもきたらば[歌 106：二]和泉式部(集 5：金葉) 111

いまよりは[歌 149：一]詠み人知らず(集 6：詞花) 147

いるべかりける[歌183：五]道命(集 8：新古今) 179

いれずもあらなむ[歌 56：五]在原業平(集 1：古今) 67

いろぞゆかしき[歌 171：五]藤原道隆女定子(集 4：後拾遺) 169

いろにいでにけり[歌 110：二]平兼盛(集 3：拾遺) 114

いろもかはらず[歌 17：二]秦兼方(集 5：金葉) 34

いろもかはらぬ[歌 85：二]坂上是則(集 1：古今) 93

—う—

うきこともがな[歌 170：五]和泉式部(集 4：後拾遺) 168

うきにたへぬは[歌173：四]道因(藤原敦頼)(集7：千載) 171

うきままに[歌199：一]藤原隆信(集 4：後拾遺) 192

うきみをば[歌 167：一]藤原俊成(集 8：新古今) 164

うきもつらきも[歌 157：二]詠み人知らず(集 3：拾遺) 155

うきもつらきも[歌 172：一]詠み人知らず(集 1：古今) 170

うきものはなし[歌 131：五]壬生忠岑(集 1：古今) 130

うぐひすのなく[歌 3：五]詠み人知らず(集 1：古今) 18

うしとおもふに[歌 165：二]詠み人知らず(集 3：拾遺) 163

うしとみしよぞ[歌 198：四]藤原清輔(集 8：新古今) 192

うたがはれける[歌127：五]源行宗(集5：金葉) 127

うたたねに[歌113：一]小野小町(集1：古今) 115

うたたねの[歌 192：一]藤原実方(集 4：後拾遺) 187

うぢのかはぎり[歌 99：二]藤原定頼(集 7：千載) 105

うちふせば[歌 139：三]和泉式部(集 4：後拾遺) 139

うつつとおもはじ[歌 195：五]藤原資隆(集 7：千載) 190

うつつもいまは[歌 195：四]藤原資隆(集 7：千載) 190

うつりにけりな[歌28：二]小野小町(集1：古今) 42

うつりぬるかな[歌 103：五]藤原俊成(集 8：新古今) 109

うつろひにしを[歌 84：二]藤原資綱(集 4：後拾遺) 92

うつろひゆくを[歌 87：四]詠み人知らず(集 1：古今) 95

うとくなる[歌155：一]西行(集8：新古今) 153

うのはなの[歌44：三]藤原(三条) 実房(集7：千載) 58

うめのはな[歌2：三]藤原頼通(集8：新古今) 17

うめのはな[歌3：三]詠み人知らず(集1：古今) 18

うめのはな[歌5：三]菅原道真(集3：拾遺) 21

うらのとまやの[歌92：四]藤原定家(集8：新古今) 133

うらみざらまし[歌160：五]藤原朝忠(集3：拾遺) 158

うらみしもせじ[歌154：二]藤原家通(集7：千載) 152

うらみわび[歌156：一]相模(集4：後拾遺) 154

うらむらむ[歌155：三]西行(集8：新古今) 153

うらやまれける[歌148：五]中原頼成妻(集4：後拾遺) 147

うれしからまし[歌134：五]詠み人知らず(集1：古今) 132

うれしかりける[歌111：二]詠み人知らず(集3：拾遺) 114

うれしきことと[歌169：二]道命(集4：後拾遺) 166

うれしさに[歌168：三]徳大寺実能(集5：金葉) 166

— お —

おいにけれ[歌174：三]菅原資忠(集5：金葉) 172

おきあかす[歌100：一]大中臣能宣(集3：拾遺) 106

おくしもの[歌84：三]藤原資綱(集4：後拾遺) 92

おくやまに[歌94：一]詠み人知らず(集1：古今) 100

おくやまは[歌183：二]道命(集8：新古今) 179

おくれましやは[歌187：五]藤原兼輔(集2：後撰) 182

おしみけむ[歌36：三]藤原伊尹(集3：拾遺) 50

おとさえて[歌54：三]慈円(集7：千載) 65

おとづれて[歌53：三]藤原教長(集7：千載) 65

おどろかれぬる[歌65：三]藤原敏行(集1：古今) 76

おなじくは[歌23：三]詠み人知らず(集3：拾遺) 39

おなじさくらの[歌21：二]藤原公時(集7：千載) 37

おのれのみ[歌116：三]源重之(集6：詞花) 117

おぼろくさへぞ[歌111：四]詠み人知らず(集3：拾遺) 114

おぼろづきよに[歌43：四]大江千里(集8：新古今) 57

おもはざらなむ[歌121：四]詠み人知らず(集2：後撰) 121

おもはざりけり[歌122：五]藤原敦忠(集3：拾遺) 122

おもはざりけれ[歌17：五]秦兼方(集5：金葉) 34

おもはする[歌73：三]西行(集7：千載) 82

おもはぬひとの[歌121：二]詠み人知らず(集2：後撰) 121

おもはむなかは[歌126：二]詠み人知らず(集1：古今) 126

おもひいでて[歌170：三]和泉式部(集4：後拾遺) 168

おもひいでて[歌49：三]藤原季通(集7：千載) 62

おもひいる[歌182：三]藤原俊成(集7：千載) 178

おもひおもはず[歌132：二]在原業平(集1：古今) 131

おもひきや[歌168：一]徳大寺実能(集5：金葉) 166

おもひける[歌61：三]藤原道信(集3：拾遺) 72

おもひけるかな[歌128：五]藤原義孝(集4：後拾遺) 128

おもひしは[歌169：二]道命(集4：後拾遺) 166

おもひしらずと[歌157：四]詠み人知らず(集3：拾遺) 155

おもひしるべく[歌121：二]詠み人知らず(集2：後撰) 121

おもひすててし[歌19：二]能因(橘永愷)(集4：後拾遺) 36

おもひたえせぬ[歌25：四]敦慶親王女(集3：拾遺) 40

おもひたえなむ[歌146：二]藤原道雅(集4：後拾遺) 145

おもひつつ[歌112：一]小野小町(集1：古今) 115

おもひなりけり[歌50：五]詠み人知らず(集2：後撰) 62

おもひにかなふ[歌187：二]藤原兼輔(集2：後撰) 182

おもひやる[歌124：一]大江千古(集2：後撰) 124

おもひやる[歌148：一]中原頼成妻(集4：後拾遺) 147

おもひわび[歌173：一]道因(藤原敦頼)(集4：後拾遺) 171

おもひわびぬれ[歌166：五]藤原元真(集8：新古今) 163

おもふこころの[歌111：二]詠み人知らず(集3：拾遺) 114

おもふこころの[歌164：二]詠み人知らず(集1：古今) 162

おもふこと[歌151：一]詠み人知らず(集3：拾遺) 149

おもふこころかな[歌116：五]源重之(集6：詞花) 117

おもふさこそを[歌190：二]和泉式部(集4：後拾遺) 184

おもふひと[歌121：三]詠み人知らず(集2：後撰) 121

おもふひと[歌121：三]詠み人知らず(集2：後撰) 121

おもふものから[歌135：二]詠み人知らず(集1：古今) 133

おもふらむ[歌191：三]和泉式部(集4：後拾遺) 186

おもへども[歌163：三]藤原興風(集1：古今) 161

おもへばやすき[歌200：二]荒木田長延(集8：新古今) 194

おもへばやまの[歌62：四]詠み人知らず(集1：古今) 72

— か —

かからましかば[歌15：五]赤染衛門(集6：詞花) 32

かかれとてしも[歌184：二]遍昭(良岑宗貞)(集2：後撰) 180

かぎりとおもへば[歌87：五]詠み人知らず(集1：古今) 95

かぎりならまし[歌38：五]源俊頼(集5：金葉) 52

かくてもいける[歌161：四]藤原元真(集4：後拾遺) 159

かくばかり[歌165：一]詠み人知らず(集3：拾遺) 163

かくるるか[歌56：三]在原業平(集1：古今) 67

かくれぬものは[歌50：二]詠み人知らず(集2：後撰) 62

かぞもりくる[歌136：五]摂政家堀河(集5：金葉) 134

かけてちぎりし[歌152：二]実原(集5：金葉) 149

かげにかくれん[歌23：五]詠み人知らず(集3：拾遺) 39

かげにぞありける[歌62：五]詠み人知らず(集1：古今) 72

かげのさやけさ[歌75：五]藤原顕輔(集8：新古今) 85

かげみれば[歌66：三]詠み人知らず(集1：古今) 76

かげろひて[歌59：三]西行(集8：新古今) 70

かこちがほなる[歌73：四]西行(集7：千載) 82

かずかずに[歌132：一]在原業平(集1：古今) 131

かすがなる[歌179：三]安部仲麿(集1：古今) 176

かずきへみゆる[歌76：四]詠み人知らず(集1：古今) 85

かすみにこめて[歌 11：二]遍昭（良岑宗貞）（集1：古今）28
かぜぞかしける[歌 85：五]坂上是則（集1：古今）93
かぜにちるらむ[歌 35：五]恵慶（集3：拾遺）50
かぜのおとにぞ[歌 65：四]藤原敏行（集1：古今）76
かぜのおとの[歌 96：三]藤原教長（集7：千載）103
かぜのわびしさ[歌 68：五]詠み人知らず（集2：後撰）78
かぜやとくらむ[歌 7：五]紀貫之（集1：古今）22
かぜやふくらむ[歌 64：五]凡河内躬恒（集1：古今）73
かぜをいたみ[歌 116：一]源重之（集6：詞花）117
かたからめ[歌 151：三]詠み人知らず（集3：拾遺）149
かたければ[歌 129：三]藤原（伊周母高階貴子（集8：新古今）128
かたなきままに[歌 148：二]中原頼成妻（集4：後撰）147
かたへすずしき[歌 64：四]凡河内躬恒（集1：古今）73
かたみこそ[歌 162：一]詠み人知らず（集1：古今）160
かたらふこゑに[歌 41：四]証凞（集5：金葉）54
かたるやうつつ[歌194：四]大江匡衡（集8：新古今）189
かぢをたえ[歌 115：二]曾禰好忠（集8：新古今）116
かつはきえつつ[歌 161：二]藤原元真（集4：後撰）159
かなしきは[歌 51：三]藤原高遠（集6：詞花）63
かなしけれ[歌 190：三]和泉式部（集4：後拾遺）184
かなしけれ[歌 74：三]大江千里（集1：古今）83
かににほひける[歌 4：三]紀貫之（集1：古今）20
かはらざりけり[歌 18：二]藤原基長（集7：千載）35
かはらぬに[歌 158：三]在原業平（集8：新古今）156
かへりてのちの[歌 169：四]道命（集4：後拾遺）166
かへるかり[歌 12：三]詠み人知らず（集3：拾遺）29
かむなづき[歌 98：三]藤原基光（集1：古今）104
かよひぢは[歌 64：三]凡河内躬恒（集1：古今）73
からころも[歌 178：一]在原業平（集1：古今）175

かをかげば[歌 46：三]詠み人知らず（集1：古今）59
かをだににぬすめ[歌 11：四]遍昭（良岑宗貞）（集1：古今）28
かをなつかしみ[歌 6：二]源時綱（集6：詞花）22

— き —

きえがてにする[歌 32：五]承均（集1：古今）46
きかむとすらむ[歌 188：五]清胤（集6：詞花）183
きこえぬは[歌69：三]和泉式部（集6：詞花）79
きこえぬものの[歌 51：二]藤原高遠（集6：詞花）63
きごとにはなぞ[歌 1：二]紀友則（集1：古今）16
きしによるなみ[歌 143：三]藤原敏行（集1：古今）142
きつつなれにし[歌 178：二]在原業平（集1：古今）175
きみおもふ[歌 125：三]藤原伊通（集7：千載）125
きみがため[歌 128：一]藤原義孝（集4：後拾遺）128
きみこふと[歌161：一]藤原元真（集4：後拾遺）159
きみふる[歌 144：一]藤原興風（集1：古今）143
きみになれにし[歌 190：四]和泉式部（集4：後拾遺）184
きみはみてまし[歌124：五]大江千古（集2：後撰）124
きみをおきて[歌 133：一]詠み人知らず（集1：古今）132
きりぎりす[歌93：一]西行（集8：新古今）100
きりたちのぼる[歌 91：五]寂蓮（集 8：新古今）98

— く —

くだかなむ[歌 37：三]藤原定頼（集4：後撰）52
くだけてものを[歌 116：四]源重之（集6：詞花）117
くものあなたは[歌 104：四]清原深養父（集1：古今）110
くものいづこに[歌 57：四]清原深養父（集1：古今）67
くものなみたち[歌 55：二]柿本人麻呂（集3：拾遺）66
くもらばくもれ[歌 71：四]藤原基光（集 5：金葉）80
くもりもはてぬ[歌 43：二]大江千里（集8：新古今）57
くらぶれば[歌 122：三]藤原敦忠（集3：拾遺）122
くるしきものを[歌 138：二]二条院讃岐（集8：新古今）135

くるしやひとめ[歌108：四]近衛院（集8：新古今）112
くるほたるかな[歌 49：五]藤原季通（集7：千載）62
くれなゐにほふ[歌 2：二]藤原頼通（集8：新古今）17
くろかみの[歌 139：一]和泉式部（集 4：後拾遺）139
くろかみの[歌 140：三]待賢門院堀河（集7：千載）139

— け —

けさしろたへに[歌 2：四]藤原頼通（集8：新古今）17
けさはみな[歌 100：三]大中臣能宣（集3：拾遺）106
けさはみゆらむ[歌 8：五]壬生忠岑（集3：拾遺）23
けさみれば[歌 33：一]徳大寺実能（集5：金葉）47
けしきのもりに[歌 60：二]藤原（九条）良経（集8：新古今）71
けふごとに[歌 102：一]藤原俊成（集 8：新古今）108
けふにわがみの[歌 40：四]藤原定成（集5：金葉）54
けふのみと[歌39：一]凡河内躬恒（集1：古今）53
けふやかぎりと[歌 102：二]藤原俊成（集 8：新古今）108
けふやわがみの[歌 38：四]源俊頼（集5：金葉）52
けぶりをだにも[歌 107：二]和泉式部（集4：後拾遺）112
けふをかぎりの[歌 129：四]藤原（伊周母高階貴子（集8：新古今）128

— こ —

こぎいでぬと[歌177：三]小野篁（集1：古今）174
こぎかくるみゆ[歌 55：五]柿本人麻呂（集3：拾遺）66
こきまぜて[歌 10：三]素性（集 1：古今）27
こぎゆくふねの[歌196：四]沙弥満誓（集3：拾遺）190
ここちこそすれ[歌152：五]実源（集5：金葉）149
こころごころに[歌 69：二]和泉式部（集6：詞花）79
こころづくしの[歌 66：四]詠み人知らず（集1：古今）76
こころつけなむ[歌 151：五]詠み人知らず（集3：拾遺）149
こころとおもはば[歌 167：五]藤原俊成（集 8：新古今）164
こころとなげく[歌 200：四]荒木田長延（集 8：新古今）194
こころならひに[歌127：二]源行宗（集5：金葉）127

こころなりけり[歌21：五]藤原公時(集7：千載) 37
こころにたぐふ[歌124：二]大江千古(集2：後撰) 124
こころにも[歌79：一]三条院(集4：後拾遺) 87
こころはやみに[歌193：二]藤原兼輔(集2：後撰) 188
こころもしらず[歌140：二]待賢門院堀河(集7：千載) 139
こころもしらず[歌4：二]紀貫之(集1：古今) 20
こころやおなじ[歌77：四]藤原忠教(集5：金葉) 86
こころやすくや[歌35：四]恵慶(集3：拾遺) 50
こころよわしと[歌19：二]能因(橘永愷)(集4：後拾遺) 36
こぞのはる[歌15：三]赤染衛門(集6：詞花) 32
こぞみしに[歌17：一]秦兼方(集5：金葉) 34
こちふかば[歌5：二]菅原道真(集3：拾遺) 21
ことしもけふに[歌101：四]源国信(集5：金葉) 107
ことぞなき[歌97：三]源頼実(集4：後拾遺) 103
ことならば[歌72：一]詠み人知らず(集3：拾遺) 81
ことよりも[歌147：三]藤原成通(集6：詞花) 146
ことをしるべき[歌149：五]詠み人知らず(集6：詞花) 147
このしたかぜは[歌30：二]紀貫之(集3：拾遺) 45
このはちる[歌97：一]源頼実(集4：後拾遺) 103
このまより[歌136：三]摂政家堀河(集5：金葉) 134
このまより[歌66：一]詠み人知らず(集1：古今) 76
このみやみうに[歌197：四]藤原永範(集7：千載) 191
このもとに[歌45：三]慈円(集8：新古今) 58
このよならねば[歌185：五]藤原季通(集6：詞花) 181
このよには[歌180：一]藤原道信(集7：千載) 177
このよのゆめを[歌192：二]藤原実方(集4：後拾遺) 187
こはさりけり[歌191：五]和泉式部(集4：後拾遺) 186
こはまさるらむ[歌191：四]和泉式部(集4：後拾遺) 186
こひしからずと[歌70：二]詠み人知らず(集1：古今) 80

こひしかるべき[歌79：四]三条院(集4：後拾遺) 87
こひしきに[歌71：三]藤原基光(集5：金葉) 80
こひしきにこそ[歌166：四]藤原元真(集8：新古今) 163
こひしきひとに[歌165：三]詠み人知らず(集3：拾遺) 163
こひしきひとに[歌114：二]詠み人知らず(集3：拾遺) 116
こひしきひとの[歌71：二]藤原基光(集5：金葉) 80
こひしきひとを[歌113：二]小野小町(集1：古今) 115
こひしきものを[歌186：五]壬生忠岑(集1：古今) 182
こひしくて[歌16：三]詠み人知らず(集3：拾遺) 34
こひしとも[歌108：一]近衛院(集8：新古今) 112
こひすれば[歌141：一]詠み人知らず(集1：古今) 140
こひちにまどふ[歌125：四]藤原伊通(集7：千載) 125
こひてしね[歌159：一]柿本人麻呂(集3：拾遺) 156
こひてしねとや[歌159：二]柿本人麻呂(集3：拾遺) 156
こひにくちなむ[歌156：四]相模(集4：後拾遺) 154
こひのみちかも[歌115：五]曾禰好忠(集8：新古今) 116
こひむなみだの[歌171：四]藤原道隆女定子(集4：後拾遺) 169
こほれるを[歌7：三]紀貫之(集1：古今) 22
こよひのつきを[歌77：四]藤原忠教(集5：金葉) 86
こよひばかりの[歌80：四]三条院(集6：詞花) 88
これなくば[歌162：五]詠み人知らず(集1：古今) 160
これやこの[歌175：一]蝉丸(集2：後撰) 172
こゑきくときぞ[歌94：四]詠み人知らず(集1：古今) 100
こゑきけば[歌130：三]石清水別当光清女(集8：新古今) 129
こをおもふみちに[歌193：四]藤原兼輔(集2：後撰) 188

— さ —

さかねばこひし[歌25：二]敦慶親王女(集3：拾遺) 40
さかりなりけれ[歌33：五]徳大寺実能(集5：金葉) 47
さきにけり[歌15：三]赤染衛門(集6：詞花) 32
さきにけり[歌17：三]秦兼方(集5：金葉) 34

さきにける[歌1：三]紀友則(集1：古今) 16
さきのよに[歌154：三]藤原家通(集7：千載) 152
さくばかり[歌83：三]詠み人知らず(集3：拾遺) 91
さくらいろの[歌34：一]藤原定家(集8：新古今) 47
さくらがえだに[歌9：二]西行(集8：新古今) 25
さくらがり[歌23：二]詠み人知らず(集3：拾遺) 39
さくらちる[歌30：一]紀貫之(集3：拾遺) 45
さくらちる[歌32：一]承均(集1：古今) 46
さくらばな[歌22：一]藤原元真(集6：詞花) 38
さくらばな[歌31：二]紀貫之(集1：古今) 46
さくらばな[歌35：三]恵慶(集3：拾遺) 50
さけばちる[歌25：一]敦慶親王女(集3：拾遺) 40
さけるわたりは[歌44：四]藤原(三条)実房(集7：千載) 58
さこそみるらめ[歌61：五]藤原道信(集3：拾遺) 72
さだめなき[歌197：三]藤原永範(集7：千載) 191
さつきまつ[歌46：一]詠み人知らず(集1：古今) 59
さてもありやと[歌22：五]藤原元真(集6：詞花) 38
さてもいのちは[歌173：二]道因(藤原敦頼)(集7：千載) 171
さほのほたるも[歌52：二]和泉式部(集4：後拾遺) 64
さびしきに[歌67：三]恵慶(集3：拾遺) 77
さびしさに[歌107：一]和泉式部(集4：後拾遺) 112
さびしさに[歌89：一]良暹(集4：後拾遺) 96
さびしさに[歌90：一]寂蓮(集8：新古今) 97
さほやまの[歌86：一]詠み人知らず(集1：古今) 94
さむからで[歌30：三]紀貫之(集3：拾遺) 45
さめざらましを[歌112：五]小野小町(集1：古今) 115
さめてののちは[歌114：四]詠み人知らず(集3：拾遺) 116
さめぬやがての[歌192：四]藤原実方(集4：後拾遺) 187
さやけかりけり[歌44：五]藤原(三条)実房(集7：千載) 58

さりとてひとに[歌 141:四]詠み人知らず(集1:古今) 140

— し —

しかぞなくなる[歌 182:五]藤原俊成(集7:千載) 178
しくものぞなき[歌 43:五]大江千里(集8:新古今) 57
しぐれするよも[歌 97:四]源頼実(集 4:後拾遺) 103
しぐれせぬよも[歌 97:五]源頼実(集 4:後拾遺) 103
しぐれのあめも[歌98:四]詠み人知らず(集1:古今) 104
しげれるやどの[歌 67:二]恵慶(集 3:拾遺) 77
したばそむらむ[歌 60:五]藤原(九条)良経(集8:新古今) 71
しどりをの[歌142:三]柿本人麻呂(集 3:拾遺) 141
しつこころなく[歌29:四]紀友則(集1:古今) 43
しにせぬみとぞ[歌 120:二]詠み人知らず(集 3:拾遺) 121
しのばれむ[歌 198:三]藤原清輔(集 8:新古今) 192
しのびにもゆる[歌 51:四]藤原高遠(集 6:詞花) 63
しのぶることの[歌 109:四]式子内親王(集8:新古今) 113
しのぶるに[歌 166:三]藤原元真(集 8:新古今) 163
しのぶれど[歌 110:一]平兼盛(集 3:拾遺) 114
しのぶれば[歌 157:五]詠み人知らず(集3:拾遺) 155
しばしわするる[歌 151:二]詠み人知らず(集 3:拾遺) 149
しばをりくぶる[歌 107:四]和泉式部(集 4:後拾遺) 112
しひてわすれむと[歌 163:二]藤原興風(集 1:古今) 161
しもとともにや[歌 100:二]大中臣能宣(集 3:拾遺) 106
しらくもに[歌76:一]詠み人知らず(集1:古今) 85
しらぬみに[歌 80:三]三条院(集 6:詞花) 88
しられずしらぬ[歌155:五]西行(集8:新古今) 153
しられねば[歌 195:三]藤原資隆(集 7:千載) 190
しるしにせむ[歌189:二]藤原興風(集1:古今) 184
しるひともなし[歌 24:五]行尊(集 5:金葉) 39
しるもしらぬも[歌 175:四]蝉丸(集 2:後撰) 172

— す —

すぎてゆくらむ[歌 159:五]柿本人麻呂(集3:拾遺) 156
すぐるのみかは[歌 40:五]藤原定成(集5:金葉) 54
すずしくくもる[歌 59:四]西行(集 8:新古今) 70
すだきけむ[歌 81:一]恵慶(集 4:後拾遺) 89
すてはてむと[歌 190:一]和泉式部(集 4:後拾遺) 184
すみのえの[歌 143:一]藤原敏行(集 1:古今) 142
すむつきの[歌 103:三]藤原俊成(集 8:新古今) 109
すむべきほどな[歌 180:二]藤原道信(集7:千載) 177
すめばみゆ[歌197:一]藤原永範(集7:千載) 191
するのまつやま[歌 133:四]詠み人知らず(集1:古今) 132

— せ —

せぜのあじろぎ[歌 99:五]藤原定頼(集7:千載) 105
せをはやみ[歌 117:一]崇徳院(集 6:詞花) 118

— そ —

そこにうつれば[歌 48:四]凡河内躬恒(集 3:拾遺) 61
そでこそにほへ[歌 3:二]詠み人知らず(集 1:古今) 18
そでのかぞする[歌 46:五]詠み人知らず(集1:古今) 59
そでひぢて[歌7:一]紀貫之(集1:古今) 22
そのいろともに[歌 90:二]寂蓮(集 8:新古今) 97
そはぬものゆる[歌 141:五]詠み人知らず(集1:古今) 140
そめますものは[歌 21:四]藤原公時(集7:千載) 37
そのこととと[歌 170:二]和泉式部(集 4:後拾遺) 168
そらにしられね[歌 30:四]紀貫之(集 3:拾遺) 45
そらにすむらむ[歌 77:五]藤原忠教(集 5:金葉) 86
そらのうみに[歌 55:一]柿本人麻呂(集 3:拾遺) 66
そらやはかはる[歌 78:五]藤原家成(集 6:詞花) 87
そらよりはなの[歌 104:二]清原深養父(集 1:古今) 110
そをだにおなじ[歌 167:四]藤原俊成(集 8:新古今) 164
そをだにのちの[歌 126:四]詠み人知らず(集1:古今) 126

— た —

たえだえに[歌99:三]藤原定頼(集7:千載) 105
たえてさくらの[歌 20:二]在原業平(集1:古今) 37
たえてしなくば[歌 160:二]藤原朝忠(集3:拾遺) 158
たえなばたえね[歌 109:二]式子内親王(集8:新古今) 113
たえまより[歌 75:三]藤原顕輔(集 8:新古今) 85
たがかよひぢと[歌158:四]在原業平(集8:新古今) 156
たかさごの[歌 189:三]藤原興風(集 1:古今) 184
たがまことをか[歌 135:四]詠み人知らず(集1:古今) 133
たきがはの[歌 117:三]崇徳院(集 6:詞花) 118
ただいまのまも[歌 123:四]詠み人知らず(集2:後撰) 124
ただかげするは[歌81:四]恵慶(集4:後拾遺) 89
ただかりそめの[歌 47:四]藤原永相女(集5:金葉) 60
たたじとて[歌107:三]和泉式部(集4:後拾遺) 112
ただひとすぢに[歌 125:二]藤原伊通(集 7:千載) 125
たちやとまると[歌 41:五]証観(集 5:金葉) 54
たちよらぬかな[歌 14:五]詠み人知らず(集2:後撰) 31
たちわかれ[歌 176:一]在原行平(集 1:古今) 173
たつことやすき[歌 39:四]凡河内躬恒(集1:古今) 53
たつことやすき[歌 45:四]慈円(集8:新古今) 58
たつたがは[歌98:一]詠み人知らず(集1:古今) 104
たてぬきにして[歌98:五]詠み人知らず(集1:古今) 104
たなばたは[歌 58:三]詠み人知らず(集 3:拾遺) 68
たなびくもの[歌 75:二]藤原顕輔(集 8:新古今) 85
たにのみづの[歌 53:二]藤原教長(集7:千載) 65
たのみそめてき[歌113:五]小野小町(集1:古今) 115
たのむるにだに[歌 120:四]詠み人知らず(集 3:拾遺) 121
たのめしつきの[歌 136:四]摂政家堀河(集 7:千載) 134
たびしぞおもふ[歌 178:五]在原業平(集1:古今) 175
たまかとぞみる[歌 52:五]和泉式部(集 4:後拾遺) 64
たまのをよ[歌 109:二]式子内親王(集8:新古今) 113

たゆるはしぬる[歌152:四]実源(集5:金葉) 149
たらちめは[歌184:一]遍昭(良岑宗貞)(集2:後撰) 180
たれとはなくて[歌27:四]源道済(集4:後拾遺) 41
たれをあはれと[歌191:二]和泉式部(集4:後拾遺) 186
たれをかも[歌189:一]藤原興風(集1:古今) 184

— ち —

ちかひてし[歌153:三]藤原季縄女(集3:拾遺) 150
ちぎらざりけめ[歌154:五]藤原家通(集7:千載) 152
ちぎりおきし[歌136:一]摂政家堀河(集5:金葉) 134
ちぎりしか[歌150:三]藤原為通(集7:千載) 148
ちぎりしことを[歌171:二]藤原道隆女定子(集4:後拾遺) 169
ちぎりしも[歌150:一]藤原為通(集7:千載) 148
ちちにものこそ[歌74:二]大江千里(集1:古今) 83
ちらさでちよも[歌22:二]藤原元真(集6:詞花) 38
ちらさぬほどの[歌6:四]源時綱(集6:詞花) 22
ちりくるは[歌104:三]清原深養父(集1:古今) 110
ちりにしはなも[歌15:二]赤染衛門(集6:詞花) 32
ちりぬべみ[歌86:二]詠み人知らず(集6:詞花) 96
ちりぬるかぜの[歌31:二]紀貫之(集1:古今) 46
ちりはてて[歌33:三]徳大寺実能(集5:金葉) 47
ちりはてて[歌45:一]慈円(集8:新古今) 58
ちりはてぬべき[歌27:四]源道済(集4:後拾遺) 41
ちるやひとの[歌36:二]藤原伊尹(集3:拾遺) 50

— つ —

つきしもいかで[歌78:四]藤原家成(集6:詞花) 87
つきぬらむ[歌180:二]藤原道信(集7:千載) 177
つきのふね[歌55:三]柿本人麻呂(集3:拾遺) 66
つきみれば[歌74:二]大江千里(集1:古今) 83
つきやすむらむ[歌82:五]藤原長家(集4:後拾遺) 90
つきやどるらむ[歌57:五]清原深養父(集1:古今) 67
つきやはものを[歌73:二]西行(集7:千載) 82
つきをだにみむ[歌80:五]三条院(集6:詞花) 88
つくからに[歌164:三]詠み人知らず(集1:古今) 162
つくぐと[歌200:一]荒木田長延(集8:新古今) 194
つげなくに[歌172:三]詠み人知らず(集1:古今) 170
つつむおもひは[歌108:五]近衛院(集8:新古今) 113
つつめども[歌50:一]詠み人知らず(集2:後撰) 62
つましあれば[歌178:三]在原業平(集1:古今) 175
つまとこそみれ[歌47:五]藤原永相女(集5:金葉) 60
つみもけぬらむ[歌100:五]大中臣能宣(集3:拾遺) 106
つゆもまだひぬ[歌91:二]寂蓮(集8:新古今) 98
つらかりし[歌127:一]源行宗(集5:金葉) 127
つれなかりけり[歌137:五]俊恵(集7:千載) 134
つれなくみえし[歌131:二]壬生忠岑(集1:古今) 130

— て —

てもふれで[歌48:一]凡河内躬恒(集3:拾遺) 61
てらすつきかげ[歌86:五]詠み人知らず(集1:古今) 94
てりまさるらむ[歌78:五]藤原家成(集6:詞花) 87
てりもせず[歌43:一]大江千里(集8:新古今) 57

— と —

ときいかなりせ[歌123:二]詠み人知らず(集2:後撰) 124
ときしもあれ[歌186:一]壬生忠岑(集1:古今) 182
ときだにも[歌39:三]凡河内躬恒(集1:古今) 53
ときはやま[歌85:三]坂上是則(集1:古今) 93
ところとかきく[歌183:二]道命(集8:新古今) 179
としにもあるかな[歌9:五]西行(集8:新古今) 25
としをへて[歌21:一]藤原公時(集7:千載) 37
としをへて[歌37:三]藤原定頼(集4:後拾遺) 52
とどめおきて[歌191:一]和泉式部(集4:後拾遺) 186
とばかりに[歌146:三]藤原道雅(集4:後拾遺) 145
とはばぞひとの[歌34:四]藤原定家(集8:新古今) 47
とひがたみ[歌132:三]在原業平(集1:古今) 131
とぶかりの[歌76:三]詠み人知らず(集1:古今) 85
とふにうからめ[歌14:二]詠み人知らず(集2:後撰) 31
とふひとはなし[歌88:五]詠み人知らず(集1:古今) 96
とへともいはじ[歌149:一]詠み人知らず(集6:詞花) 147
とほざかりゆく[歌93:五]西行(集8:新古今) 100
とまりゐて[歌174:一]菅原資忠(集5:金葉) 172
ともならなくに[歌189:五]藤原興風(集1:古今) 184
とりはものかは[歌130:五]石清水別当光清女(集8:新古今) 129

— な —

ながからむ[歌140:一]待賢門院堀河(集7:千載) 139
ながくもがなと[歌128:四]藤原義孝(集4:後拾遺) 128
ながながしよを[歌142:四]柿本人麻呂(集3:拾遺) 141
なかなかに[歌160:三]藤原朝忠(集3:拾遺) 158
なかなれば[歌152:三]実源(集5:金葉) 149
ながむれば[歌71:一]藤原基光(集5:金葉) 80
ながむれば[歌89:三]良暹(集4:後拾遺) 96
ながめしひとも[歌82:二]藤原長家(集4:後拾遺) 90
ながめせしまに[歌28:五]小野小町(集1:古今) 42
ながらへば[歌109:三]式子内親王(集8:新古今) 113
ながらへば[歌198:一]藤原清輔(集8:新古今) 192
ながらへば[歌79:三]三条院(集4:後拾遺) 87
なかりけり[歌90:三]寂蓮(集8:新古今) 97
なかりけり[歌92:三]藤原定家(集8:新古今) 98
なかりせば[歌20:三]在原業平(集1:古今) 37
なきつるなへに[歌62:二]詠み人知らず(集1:古今) 72
なきやどに[歌81:三]恵慶(集4:後拾遺) 89
なきよなりせば[歌134:二]詠み人知らず(集1:古今) 132
なくこゑも[歌51:一]藤原高遠(集6:詞花) 63

―な―

なくしかの[歌 94:三]詠み人知らず(集1:古今) 100

なくせみの[歌 60:三]藤原(九条)良経(集8:新古今) 71

なくむしの[歌 69:一]和泉式部(集6:詞花) 79

なげきなりけり[歌169:五]道命(集4:後拾遺) 166

なげけとて[歌 73:一]西行(集 7:千載) 82

なこそをしけれ[歌156:五]相模(集4:後拾遺) 154

なごりには[歌31:三]紀貫之(集1:古今) 46

なすこそかみの[歌 151:二]詠み人知らず(集3:拾遺) 149

なぞつきかげの[歌 72:四]詠み人知らず(集3:拾遺) 81

なつごろもかなし[歌45:五]慈円(集8:新古今) 58

なっとあきと[歌 64:一]凡河内躬恒(集1:古今) 73

なつにしられぬ[歌 53:二]藤原教長(集7:千載) 65

なつのほかなる[歌54:四]慈円(集7:千載) 65

なつのよは[歌 57:一]清原深養父(集1:古今) 67

なつむしの[歌 50:三]詠み人知らず(集2:後撰) 61

なでずやありけむ[歌 184:五]遍昭(良岑宗貞) (集2:後撰) 180

なにおもひけむ[歌 42:五]後鳥羽院(集8:新古今) 56

なにごとを[歌 101:一]源国信(集 5:金葉) 107

なにぞはつゆの[歌 119:二]紀友則(集1:古今) 120

なににたとへむ[歌 196:二]沙弥満誓(集3:拾遺) 190

なにはかなしと[歌 61:二]藤原道信(集3:拾遺) 70

なにはなる[歌 145:三]元良親王(集 2:後撰) 144

なにめでて[歌 163:一]遍昭(良岑宗貞) (集1:古今) 74

なほうきときけば[歌 181:四]凡河内躬恒(集1:古今) 178

なほしらぎくと[歌 184:四]藤原資綱(集4:後拾遺) 92

なほふるさとの[歌 12:三]詠み人知らず(集3:拾遺) 12

なほゆめみかとぞ[歌 127:四]源行宗(集5:金葉) 127

なほをしまるる[歌 185:二]藤原季通(集6:詞花) 181

なみぞたちける[歌 31:五]紀貫之(集1:古今) 46

―に―

なみぞをりける[歌 48:五]凡河内躬恒(集3:拾遺) 61

なみだなりけり[歌172:五]詠み人知らず(集1:古今) 170

なみだなりけり[歌 173:五]道因(藤原敦頼) (集7:千載) 171

なみだのつゆや[歌 60:二]藤原(九条)良経(集8:新古今) 71

なみだのとこに[歌144:二]藤原興風(集1:古今) 143

なみもこえなむ[歌 133:五]詠み人知らず(集1:古今) 132

なりにけり[歌 141:三]詠み人知らず(集1:古今) 140

なりにけるかな[歌101:五]源国信(集5:金葉) 107

なりぬべき[歌120:三]詠み人知らず(集3:拾遺) 121

なりゆくを[歌 188:三]清昭(集 6:詞花) 183

なるままに[歌 93:三]西行(集 8:新古今) 100

―に―

にごればかくる[歌197:二]藤原永範(集7:千載) 191

にしきおりかく[歌 98:二]詠み人知らず(集1:古今) 104

にしきなりける[歌 10:五]素性(集 1:古今) 27

にはこそはなの[歌 33:四]徳大寺実能(集5:金葉) 47

にはのはるかぜ[歌34:二]藤原定家(集8:新古今) 47

にはのゆきかな[歌 106:五]和泉式部(集5:金葉) 111

にほひおこせよ[歌 5:二]菅原道真(集3:拾遺) 21

―ぬ―

ぬしなきやどの[歌35:二]恵慶(集3:拾遺) 50

ぬるともはなの[歌 23:四]詠み人知らず(集3:拾遺) 39

ぬればやひとの[歌 112:二]小野小町(集1:古今) 115

―ね―

ねやのひまさへ[歌137:四]俊恵(集7:千載) 134

―の―

のちのこころに[歌 122:二]藤原敦忠(集3:拾遺) 122

のちのつらさの[歌 168:四]徳大寺実能(集5:金葉) 166

のどけからまし[歌 20:五]在原業平(集1:古今) 37

のどけかるべき[歌 58:二]藤原定家(集3:拾遺) 68

のぶるいのちは[歌 120:五]詠み人知らず(集3:拾遺) 121

のもせのくさの[歌 59:二]西行(集 8:新古今) 70

―は―

はかなきに[歌 192:三]藤原実方(集 4:後拾遺) 187

はぎのはに[歌 68:三]詠み人知らず(集2:後撰) 78

はげしさそふる[歌 96:四]藤原教長(集7:千載) 103

はつしぐれかな[歌 138:五]二条院讃岐(集8:新古今) 135

はなおそげなる[歌 9:四]西行(集 8:新古今) 25

はなこそいまは[歌 36:四]藤原伊尹(集3:拾遺) 50

はなこそものは[歌 17:四]秦兼方(集5:金葉) 34

はなこそやどの[歌 13:四]藤原公任(集3:拾遺) 30

はなざかりかな[歌 16:五]詠み人知らず(集3:拾遺) 34

はなぞむかしの[歌 4:四]紀貫之(集1:古今) 20

はなたちばなの[歌 46:二]詠み人知らず(集1:古今) 59

はなならば[歌 38:三]源俊頼(集 5:金葉) 52

はなにこころを[歌 37:二]藤原定頼(集4:後拾遺) 52

はなにつけても[歌14:二]詠み人知らず(集2:後撰) 31

はなにみえける[歌 19:五]能因(橘永愷) (集4:後拾遺) 36

はなのいろは[歌 11:一]遍昭(良岑宗貞) (集1:古今) 28

はなのいろは[歌28:一]小野小町(集1:古今) 42

はなのいろを[歌 21:三]藤原公時(集7:千載) 37

はなのうへかな[歌 25:五]敦慶親王女(集3:拾遺) 40

はなのかげかな[歌 39:五]凡河内躬恒(集1:古今) 53

はなのかげなき[歌45:二]慈円(集8:新古今) 58

はなのさかりに[歌 12:二]詠み人知らず(集3:拾遺) 29

はなのさかりは[歌 26:二]詠み人知らず(集1:古今) 40

はなのちらるむ[歌 29:五]紀友則(集1:古今) 43

はなのところは[歌 32:二]承均(集 1:古今) 46

はなのひとへに[歌 83:二]詠み人知らず(集3:拾遺) 91

はなはわれをば[歌18:四]藤原基長(集7:千載) 35

はなももみぢも[歌 92:二]藤原定家(集8:新古今) 98

はなゆゑに[歌 27:三]源道済(集 4:後拾遺) 41
はなよりほかに[歌 24:四]行尊(集 5:金葉) 39
はなれなめ[歌 126:三]詠み人知らず(集 1:古今) 126
はゆらうかいはし[歌 76:二]詠み人知らず(集 1:古今) 85
ははそのみち[歌 86:二]詠み人知らず(集 1:古今) 94
はるがすみ[歌 14:三]詠み人知らず(集 2:後撰) 31
はるかぜもがな[歌 6:五]源時綱(集 6:詞花) 22
はるきてぞ[歌 13:一]藤原公任(集 3:拾遺) 30
はるごとに[歌 26:一]詠み人知らず(集 1:古今) 40
はるたつけふの[歌 7:四]紀貫之(集 1:古今) 22
はるたつと[歌 8:一]壬生忠岑(集 3:拾遺) 23
はるながら[歌 32:三]承均(集 1:古今) 46
はるなつに[歌 78:一]藤原家成(集 6:詞花) 87
はるにやあるらむ[歌 104:五]清原深養父(集 1:古今) 110
はるのこころは[歌 20:四]在原業平(集 1:古今) 37
はるのひに[歌 29:三]紀友則(集 1:古今) 43
はるのやまかぜ[歌 11:五]遍昭(良岑宗貞)(集 1:古今) 28
はるのゆく[歌 41:五]証観(集 5:金葉) 54
はるのよの[歌 43:三]大江千里(集 8:新古今) 57
はるはただ[歌 83:一]詠み人知らず(集 3:拾遺) 91
はるはなけれど[歌 37:五]藤原定頼(集 4:後拾遺) 52
はるばるきぬる[歌 178:四]在原業平(集 1:古今) 175
はるやこひしき[歌 12:五]詠み人知らず(集 3:拾遺) 29
はるははなは[歌 39:二]凡河内躬恒(集 1:古今) 53
はるをわするな[歌 5:五]菅原道真(集 3:拾遺) 21

— ひ —

ひかりのどけき[歌 29:二]紀友則(集 1:古今) 43
ひぐらしの[歌 62:一]詠み人知らず(集 1:古今) 72
ひぐらしのこゑ[歌 54:五]慈円(集 7:千載) 65
ひさかたの[歌 29:一]紀友則(集 1:古今) 43

ひさしにふける[歌 47:二]藤原永相女(集 5:金葉) 60
ひたすらに[歌 154:一]藤原家通(集 7:千載) 152
ひとこそみえね[歌 67:四]恵慶(集 3:拾遺) 77
ひとぞこひしき[歌 139:五]和泉式部(集 4:後拾遺) 139
ひとぞまたるる[歌 27:五]源道済(集 4:後拾遺) 41
ひとだのめなる[歌 163:五]藤原興風(集 1:古今) 161
ひとだのめなる[歌 72:五]詠み人知らず(集 3:拾遺) 81
ひとつこゑにも[歌 69:二]和泉式部(集 6:詞花) 79
ひとづてならで[歌 146:二]藤原道雅(集 4:後拾遺) 145
ひとづてならで[歌 147:二]藤原成通(集 6:詞花) 146
ひとにかたるな[歌 63:三]遍昭(良岑宗貞)(集 1:古今) 74
ひとにはつげよ[歌 177:四]小野篁(集 1:古今) 174
ひとのいのちの[歌 153:四]藤原季繩女(集 3:拾遺) 150
ひとのおやの[歌 193:二]藤原兼輔(集 2:後撰) 188
ひとのこころぞ[歌 148:四]中原頼成妻(集 4:後拾遺) 147
ひとのことのは[歌 134:四]詠み人知らず(集 1:古今) 132
ひとのためかは[歌 174:五]菅原資忠(集 5:金葉) 172
ひとのつらきも[歌 166:二]藤原元真(集 8:新古今) 163
ひとのとふまで[歌 110:五]平兼盛(集 3:拾遺) 114
ひとのよの[歌 187:一]藤原兼輔(集 2:後撰) 182
ひとはいさ[歌 4:一]紀貫之(集 1:古今) 20
ひとひにちたび[歌 124:四]大江千古(集 2:後撰) 124
ひとめよくらむ[歌 143:五]藤原敏行(集 1:古今) 142
ひともこずゑの[歌 136:二]摂政家堀河(集 5:金葉) 134
ひともとひける[歌 13:二]藤原公任(集 3:拾遺) 30
ひとやみるらむ[歌 157:五]詠み人知らず(集 3:拾遺) 155
ひとりかもねむ[歌 142:五]柿本人麻呂(集 3:拾遺) 141
ひとりみまうき[歌 16:二]詠み人知らず(集 3:拾遺) 34
ひとりみる[歌 103:一]藤原俊成(集 8:新古今) 109

ひとをなにとて[歌 155:二]西行(集 8:新古今) 153
ひとをもはなは[歌 61:四]藤原道信(集 3:拾遺) 72
ひとをもみをも[歌 160:四]藤原朝忠(集 3:拾遺) 158
ひとをするぞ[歌 149:四]詠み人知らず(集 6:詞花) 147
ひはくれぬと[歌 62:三]詠み人知らず(集 1:古今) 72
ひるはきえつつ[歌 118:四]大中臣能宣(集 6:詞花) 119

— ふ —

ふきくれば[歌 6:一]源時綱(集 6:詞花) 22
ふけゆくかねの[歌 130:二]石清水別当光清女(集 8:新古今) 129
ふたたびくべき[歌 185:四]藤原季通(集 6:詞花) 181
ふたつありけり[歌 165:五]詠み人知らず(集 3:拾遺) 163
ふぢのはな[歌 48:三]凡河内躬恒(集 3:拾遺) 61
ふままくをしき[歌 106:四]和泉式部(集 5:金葉) 111
ふゆながら[歌 104:一]清原深養父(集 1:古今) 110
ふゆのやまざと[歌 107:五]和泉式部(集 4:後拾遺) 112
ふゆのよふかき[歌 100:四]大中臣能宣(集 3:拾遺) 106
ふゆはきにけり[歌 96:五]藤原教長(集 7:千載) 103
ふりさけみれば[歌 179:二]安部仲麿(集 1:古今) 176
ふりしきぬ[歌 88:三]詠み人知らず(集 1:古今) 96
ふりぞまされる[歌 132:五]在原業平(集 1:古今) 131
ふるさとは[歌 4:三]紀貫之(集 1:古今) 20
ふれるしらゆき[歌 105:五]坂上是則(集 1:古今) 110

— ほ —

ほさぬそでだに[歌 156:二]相模(集 4:後拾遺) 154
ほしのはやしに[歌 55:四]柿本人麻呂(集 3:拾遺) 66
ほたるなりけり[歌 51:五]藤原高遠(集 6:詞花) 63
ほととぎす[歌 41:三]証観(集 5:金葉) 54
ほどふるを[歌 161:三]藤原元真(集 4:後拾遺) 159
ほのめくかげも[歌 44:二]藤原(三条)実房(集 7:千載) 58

— ま —

まきたつやまの[歌 90:四]寂蓮(集 8:新古今) 97

まきのはに[歌91:三]寂蓮(集8:新古今) 98

まきのやに[歌138:三]二条院讃岐(集8:新古今) 135

まさるべしとは[歌168:五]徳大寺実能(集5:金葉) 166

まだきもつらき[歌56:二]在原業平(集1:古今) 67

またこのごろや[歌198:二]藤原清輔(集8:新古今) 192

またもことしに[歌102:二]藤原俊成(集8:新古今) 108

またもなく[歌125:一]藤原伊通(集7:千載) 125

まだよひながら[歌57:二]清原深養父(集1:古今) 67

まづかきやりし[歌139:四]和泉式部(集4:後拾遺) 139

まづしるものは[歌172:四]詠み人知らず(集1:古今) 170

まづぞこひしき[歌164:五]詠み人知らず(集1:古今) 162

まつとしきかば[歌176:四]在原行平(集1:古今) 173

まつとはなしに[歌101:二]源国信(集5:金葉) 107

まつひとの[歌106:一]和泉式部(集5:金葉) 111

まつべきみこそ[歌174:三]皆吉資忠(集5:金葉) 172

まつもむかしの[歌189:四]藤原興風(集1:古今) 184

まつよひに[歌130:一]石清水別当光清女(集8:新古今) 129

まどひぬるかな[歌193:五]藤原兼輔(集2:後撰) 188

— み —

みえつらむ[歌112:三]小野小町(集1:古今) 115

みえねども[歌65:三]藤原敏行(集1:古今) 76

みかきもり[歌118:一]大中臣能宣(集6:詞花) 119

みかさのやまに[歌179:四]安倍仲麿(集1:古今) 176

みするなりけり[歌84:五]藤原資綱(集4:後拾遺) 92

みせずとも[歌11:三]遍昭(良岑宗貞)(集1:古今) 28

みだれてけさは[歌140:四]待賢門院堀河(集7:千載) 139

みだれもしらず[歌139:二]和泉式部(集4:後拾遺) 139

みちこそなけれ[歌182:二]藤原俊成(集7:千載) 178

みちにきむか〜[歌41:二]証観(集5:金葉) 54

みちぬれば[歌144:三]藤原興風(集1:古今) 143

みちふみわけて[歌88:四]詠み人知らず(集1:古今) 96

みづなきそらに[歌31:四]紀貫之(集1:古今) 46

みつるかな[歌194:三]大江匡衡(集8:新古今) 189

みてしがな[歌22:三]藤原元真(集6:詞花) 38

みてしより[歌113:三]小野小町(集1:古今) 115

みとやみもるらむ[歌161:五]藤原元真(集4:後拾遺) 159

みてば[歌42:三]後鳥羽院(集8:新古今) 56

みなひとの[歌188:一]清昭(集6:詞花) 183

みなりせば[歌124:三]大江千古(集2:後撰) 124

みなれがほにも[歌49:四]藤原季通(集7:千載) 62

みなれども[歌19:三]能因(橘永愷)(集4:後拾遺) 36

みにかへて[歌38:一]源俊頼(集5:金葉) 50

みねにおふる[歌176:三]在原行平(集1:古今) 173

みねばこひしき[歌123:五]詠み人知らず(集2:後撰) 124

みやこぞはるの[歌10:四]素性(集1:古今) 27

みやまべのさと[歌53:五]藤原教長(集7:千載) 65

みよしのの[歌8:三]壬生忠岑(集3:拾遺) 23

みよりあまれる[歌50:五]詠み人知らず(集2:後撰) 64

みるひとの[歌77:三]藤原忠教(集5:金葉) 86

みるほどは[歌195:一]藤原資隆(集7:千載) 190

みるまでに[歌105:三]坂上是則(集1:古今) 110

みれどあかぬ[歌12:一]詠み人知らず(集3:拾遺) 29

みわたせば[歌10:一]素性(集1:古今) 27

みわたせば[歌42:一]後鳥羽院(集8:新古今) 56

みわたせば[歌92:一]藤原定家(集8:新古今) 98

みをしるあめは[歌132:五]在原業平(集1:古今) 131

みをつくしても[歌145:四]元良親王(集2:後撰) 144

みをつくしとぞ[歌144:一]藤原興風(集1:古今) 143

みをばおもはず[歌153:二]藤原季縄女(集3:拾遺) 150

— む —

むかしがたりに[歌188:二]清昭(集6:詞花) 183

むかしこふらし[歌36:五]藤原伊尹(集3:拾遺) 50

むかしのことを[歌194:二]大江匡衡(集8:新古今) 189

むかしのひとの[歌46:四]詠み人知らず(集1:古今) 59

むかしのひとも[歌81:二]恵慶(集4:後拾遺) 89

むかしはものを[歌122:四]藤原敦忠(集3:拾遺) 122

むかしわが[歌49:一]藤原季通(集7:千載) 62

むすびしみづの[歌7:二]紀貫之(集1:古今) 22

むばたまの[歌184:三]遍昭(良岑宗貞)(集2:後撰) 180

むめのはな[歌6:三]源時綱(集6:詞花) 22

むらさきに[歌84:一]藤原資綱(集4:後拾遺) 92

むらさめの[歌91:一]寂蓮(集8:新古今) 98

— め —

めにはさやかに[歌65:二]藤原敏行(集1:古今) 76

— も —

ものおもひにぞ[歌183:四]道命(集8:新古今) 179

ものおもふころは[歌137:二]俊恵(集7:千載) 134

ものおもふやどの[歌68:二]詠み人知らず(集2:後撰) 78

ものおもへば[歌52:一]和泉式部(集4:後拾遺) 64

ものごとに[歌87:一]詠み人知らず(集1:古今) 95

ものとてか[歌123:三]詠み人知らず(集2:後撰) 124

ものならば[歌187:三]藤原兼輔(集2:後撰) 182

もののあはれは[歌83:四]詠み人知らず(集3:拾遺) 91

もののかなしき[歌180:五]藤原道信(集7:千載) 177

ものやおもふと[歌110:四]平兼盛(集3:拾遺) 114

ものやなしき[歌69:五]和泉式部(集6:詞花) 79

ものをこそおもへ[歌118:五]大中臣能宣(集6:詞花) 119

ものをこそおもへ[歌140:五]待賢門院堀河(集7:千載) 139

もみぢつつ[歌87:三]詠み人知らず(集1:古今) 95

もみぢばの[歌95:三]詠み人知らず(集1:古今) 101

各句索引 —も— —や— —ゆ— —よ— —わ—

もみぢはやどに[歌 88:二]詠み人知らず(集1:古今) 96
もみぢふみわけ[歌 94:二]詠み人知らず(集1:古今) 100
もりくるつきの[歌 66:二]詠み人知らず(集1:古今) 76
もれいづるつきの[歌 75:四]藤原顕輔(集8:新古今) 85
もろともに[歌 16:一]詠み人知らず(集3:拾遺) 34
もろともに[歌 24:一]行尊(集 5:金葉) 39
もろともに[歌 82:一]藤原長家(集 4:後拾遺) 90
もろともにこそ[歌 150:二]藤原為通(集7:千載) 148

— や —

やがてそでにも[歌 103:四]藤原俊成(集8:新古今) 109
やすくもすぐる[歌 138:四]二条院讃岐(集8:新古今) 135
やそしまかけて[歌177:二]小野篁(集1:古今) 174
やどにはひとり[歌 82:四]藤原長家(集 4:後拾遺) 90
やどはききわく[歌 97:二]源頼実(集 4:後拾遺) 103
やどるつきかげ[歌 197:五]藤原永範(集7:千載) 191
やどをたちいでて[歌89:二]良暹(集4:後拾遺) 70
やなぎざくらを[歌 10:二]素性(集 1:古今) 27
やへむぐらに[歌 67:一]恵慶(集 3:拾遺) 77
やまかげやに[歌 54:一]慈円(集 7:千載) 65
やまざくら[歌 18:三]藤原基俊(集 7:千載) 35
やまざくら[歌 24:三]行尊(集 5:金葉) 39
やまざくら[歌 25:三]敦慶親王女(集 3:拾遺) 40
やまざとに[歌 27:一]源道済(集 4:後拾遺) 41
やまざとは[歌 13:三]藤原公任(集 3:拾遺) 30
やまどりのをの[歌 142:二]柿本人麻呂(集 3:拾遺) 141
やまにいるひと[歌 181:二]凡河内躬恒(集 1:古今) 178
やまにても[歌181:三]凡河内躬恒(集1:古今) 178
やまのおくにも[歌 182:四]藤原俊成(集7:千載) 178
やまのはにげて[歌 56:四]在原業平(集 1:古今) 67
やまもかすみて[歌 8:二]壬生忠岑(集 3:拾遺) 23

やまもとかすむ[歌 42:二]後鳥羽院(集8:新古今) 56
やみにぞあらまし[歌 72:二]詠み人知らず(集 3:拾遺) 81

— ゆ —

ゆきかふそらの[歌 64:二]凡河内躬恒(集1:古今) 73
ゆきぞふりける[歌 30:五]紀貫之(集 3:拾遺) 45
ゆきぞふりつつ[歌 32:四]承均(集1:古今) 46
ゆきちりて[歌 9:三]西行(集 8:新古今) 25
ゆきとだにみむ[歌 34:五]藤原定家(集8:新古今) 47
ゆきはふれれど[歌 2:五]藤原頼通(集8:新古今) 17
ゆきふれば[歌1:一]紀友則(集1:古今) 16
ゆくするまでは[歌 129:二]藤原(伊周母)高階貴子(集8:新古今) 128
ゆくべきに[歌 108:三]近衛院(集 8:新古今) 112
ゆくへさだめぬ[歌 95:二]詠み人知らず(集1:古今) 101
ゆくへもしらぬ[歌 115:四]曾禰好忠(集8:新古今) 116
ゆくもかへるも[歌 175:二]蝉丸(集 2:後撰) 172
ゆふだちのそら[歌 59:五]西行(集8:新古今) 70
ゆふづくよ[歌 44:一]藤原(三条) 実房(集 7:千載) 58
ゆふべはあきと[歌 42:四]後鳥羽院(集8:新古今) 56
ゆめてふものぞ[歌 163:四]藤原興風(集1:古今) 161
ゆめてふものは[歌 113:四]小野小町(集1:古今) 115
ゆめとしりせば[歌 112:四]小野小町(集1:古今) 115
ゆめのかよひぢ[歌 143:四]藤原敏行(集 1:古今) 142
ゆめもゆめとも[歌 195:二]藤原資隆(集7:千載) 190
ゆめよゆめ[歌114:一]詠み人知らず(集 3:拾遺) 116
ゆらのとを[歌115:一]曾禰好忠(集8:新古今) 116

— よ —

よざむにあきて[歌 93:二]西行(集8:新古今) 100
よしののさとに[歌 105:四]坂上是則(集1:古今) 110
よしのやま[歌 9:三]西行(集 8:新古今) 25
よそながら[歌 147:一]藤原成通(集 6:詞花) 146

よそのもみぢを[歌 85:四]坂上是則(集1:古今) 93
よにふるは[歌 138:一]二条院讃岐(集8:新古今) 135
よのうきも[歌 166:一]藤原元真(集8:新古今) 163
よのつねならず[歌 180:四]藤原道信(集 7:千載) 177
よのなかに[歌 20:一]在原業平(集1:古今) 37
よのなかの[歌 157:一]詠み人知らず(集 3:拾遺) 155
よのなか172:一]詠み人知らず(集1:古今) 170
よのなかよ[歌 182:一]藤原俊成(集 7:千載) 178
よのなかを[歌19:一]能因(橘永愷) (集 4:後拾遺) 36
よのなかに[歌 196:一]沙弥満誓(集 3:拾遺) 190
よのなかを[歌 200:三]荒木田長延(集 8:新古今) 194
よはのつきかな[歌 79:五]三条院(集 4:後拾遺) 87
よもすがら[歌 137:一]俊恵(集 7:千載) 134
よもすがら[歌 171:一]藤原道隆女定子(集 4:後拾遺) 169
よもすがら[歌 194:一]大江匡衡(集 8:新古今) 189
よられつる[歌 59:一]西行(集 8:新古今) 70
よるさへよと[歌 86:四]詠み人知らず(集 1:古今) 94
よるさへや[歌143:三]藤原敏行(集1:古今) 142
よるのあらしに[歌 33:二]徳大寺実能(集 5:金葉) 47
よるはもえ[歌118:三]大中臣能宣(集 6:詞花) 119
よわりもぞする[歌 109:五]式子内親王(集 8:新古今) 113
よわるかごゑの[歌 93:四]西行(集 8:新古今) 100
よをすてて[歌 181:一]凡河内躬恒(集 1:古今) 178
よをそむく[歌 183:一]道命(集 8:新古今) 179

— わ —

わがくろかみを[歌184:四]遍昭(良岑宗貞) (集 2:後撰) 180
わがこひは[歌 110:三]平兼盛(集 3:拾遺) 114
わがなみだかな[歌73:五]西行(集7:千載) 82
わがみかな[歌 185:三]藤原季通(集 6:詞花) 181
わがみとおもへば[歌 190:五]和泉式部(集 4:後拾遺) 184

各句索引 —わ— —ゑ— —を—

わがみなりけり[歌 200：五]荒木田長延（集 8：新古今）194
わがみはかげと[歌 141：二]詠み人知らず（集 1：古今）140
わがみはきみに[歌 187：四]藤原兼輔（集 2：後撰）182
わがみひとつの[歌 74：四]大江千里（集 1：古今）83
わがみよにふる[歌 28：四]小野小町（集 1：古今）42
わがみより[歌 52：三]和泉式部（集 4：後拾遺）64
わがもたば[歌 133：三]詠み人知らず（集 1：古今）132
わがやのかどを[歌 159：四]柿本人麻呂（集 3：拾遺）156
わかるべき[歌 186：三]壬生忠岑（集 1：古今）182
わかれつつ[歌 175：三]蝉丸（集 2：後撰）172
わかれより[歌 131：三]壬生忠岑（集 1：古今）130
わきてをらまし[歌 1：五]紀友則（集 1：古今）16
わぎもこが[歌 159：三]柿本人麻呂（集 3：拾遺）156
わすらるる[歌 153：一]藤原季縄女（集 3：拾遺）150
わするばかりの[歌170：四]和泉式部（集 4：後拾遺）168
わするるときも[歌 162：四]詠み人知らず（集 1：古今）160
わすれがたみに[歌 126：五]詠み人知らず（集 1：古今）126
わすれじの[歌 129：一]藤原伊周母:高階貴子(集 8：新古今）128
わすれずば[歌 171：三]藤原道隆女定子（集 4：後拾遺）169
わすれなむと[歌 164：一]詠み人知らず（集 1：古今）162
わすればわれも[歌 150：四]藤原為通（集 7：千載）148
わすれましかば[歌 150：五]藤原為通（集 7：千載）148
わすれゆく[歌 148：五]中原頼成妻（集 4：後拾遺）147
わたのはら[歌 177：一]小野篁（集 1：古今）174
わたるふなびと[歌 115：二]曾禰好忠（集 8：新古今）116
わびしかりけり[歌 114：五]詠み人知らず（集 3：拾遺）116
わびぬれば[歌 145：一]元良親王（集 2：後撰）144
わびぬれば[歌 163：一]藤原興風（集 1：古今）161
われおちにきと[歌 63：四]遍昭（良岑宗貞）（集 1：古今）74

われさへこころ[歌 165：四]詠み人知らず（集 3：拾遺）163
われぞかなしき[歌 95：五]詠み人知らず（集 1：古今）101
われぞただ[歌 149：三]詠み人知らず（集 6：詞花）147
われだにいとふ[歌 167：二]藤原俊成（集 8：新古今）164
われてもすゑに[歌 117：四]崇徳院（集 6：詞花）118
われはたのまむ[歌 135：五]詠み人知らず（集 1：古今）133
われはなりぬる[歌144：五]藤原興風（集 1：古今）143
われもなき[歌 82：三]藤原長能（集 4：後拾遺）90
われやなにになる[歌 125：五]藤原伊通（集 7：千載）125
われをこそ[歌 14：一]詠み人知らず（集 2：後撰）31

— ゑ —

ゑじのたくひの[歌 118：二]大中臣能宣（集 6：詞花）119

— を —

をしからざりし[歌 128：二]藤原義孝（集 4：後拾遺）128
をしからなくに[歌 119：五]紀友則（集 1：古今）120
をしくもあるかな[歌 153：五]藤原季縄女（集 3：拾遺）150
をしまるれ[歌 199：三]藤原隆成（集 4：後拾遺）192
をしむかひなく[歌 48：二]凡河内躬恒（集 3：拾遺）61
をしむとまる[歌 37：四]藤原定頼（集 4：後拾遺）52
をしむとまる[歌 38：二]源俊頼（集 5：金葉）52
をしむははるの[歌 40：四]藤原定成（集 5：金葉）54
をしめども[歌 102：三]藤原俊成（集 8：新古今）108
をみなへし[歌 63：三]遍昭（良岑宗貞）（集 1：古今）74
をられけり[歌 2：一]藤原頼通（集 8：新古今）17
をりはしるのみ[歌 16：二]詠み人知らず（集 3：拾遺）34
をりつれば[歌 3：一]詠み人知らず（集 1：古今）18
をりもありしに[歌 155：五]西行（集 8：新古今）153
をれるばかりぞ[歌 63：二]遍昭（良岑宗貞）（集 1：古今）74

＝八代集 概説＝

・・・八代集の成立順に、その『名称』[成立時期]＜撰進を下命した天皇または元天皇(院)＞選者(同集内収載歌数):収載歌総数(異本収載歌数:同歌集または既存歌集収載歌との重複歌数)と、各勅撰集の特徴について記す。

・・・「重複歌数」は、一言一句に至るまで完全に同一のもの(134首)のほか、一部文言のみ微妙に異なるもの(94首)も含め、各種異本をまたいでの数を記す。

1)『**古今集**』[905年]＜醍醐天皇下命＞選者＝紀貫之(105)・凡河内躬恒(62)・紀友則(46)・壬生忠岑(37): 全1100首(異本歌29首:墨滅歌11首:重複2首)

・・・『万葉集』(奈良時代末)以降の短歌の集大成を目指したものの、和歌黎明期だけに選者達の考える理想の水準に達する作品が集まらず、苦肉の策として編入された**選者自作歌がなんと全体の四分の一近く**を占めている・・・が、そのおかげで「古今調」と呼ばれる理知的な詠みぶりが確立され、平安調短歌隆盛への道を開いたこの和歌集の全体的水準の高さは(勅撰集・私撰集を問わず)他の何物の追随をも許さない・・・本書を読んで平安調和歌に興味を持ったなら、まず読むべきは『古今集』、この一冊さえあれば他の七つには触れずともよし、何度読み返しても「素晴らしい!」の一言、短歌という文芸ジャンルは「初代が完璧な理想型」という点で世界の文芸史に希有なる足跡を印すものだったことを思い知らされる、奇跡のような珠玉の勅撰和歌集。

2)『**後撰集**』[950年代]＜村上天皇下命＞選者＝清原元輔(1)・大中臣能宣(0)・源 順(0)・紀時文(0)・坂上望城(0):全1426首(重複25首、うち『古今集』16首、9首は同じ『後撰集』内で重複)

・・・『古今集』から半世紀を経て和歌が貴族社会に完全に定着した時期に編まれた勅撰集だけに、選者達(通称「梨壺の五人」)の自作歌は皆無(元輔のダジャレ歌が一つ混入しているが、これは草稿段階でのイタズラで正規版では排除されていた可能性が高い)・・・内容的には当時の権門貴族の日常的贈答歌だらけの「有名人ツイート集」の趣があり、(秀歌の数は多いものの)凡歌・戯れ歌の混入比率があまりに高すぎて歌集としての品質は八代集中ドン底の最低水準。詞書の粗雑さや重複歌の多さから見ても「**正規版は960年の内裏火災で焼失、後代に流布したのは未完成段階の草稿でしかない**」という通説に間違いないものと思われる・・・正規版がどの程度の品質だったかとても気になる「とっても残念な勅撰和歌集」。

3)『**拾遺集**』[1000年代]＜花山院下命＞選者＝なし:全1351首(重複64首、うち31首が『古今集』、26首が『後撰集』、7首が同じ『拾遺集』内で重複、なお「公任秀歌選」には重複は一首もない)

・・・当代随一の文化人藤原公任の私的秀歌選(『拾遺抄』のほぼ全首と、『和漢朗詠集』『三十六人撰』『金玉集』『和歌九品』『深窓秘抄』『前十五番歌合』からの選歌)に、花山院(とその近臣)が選んだ歌をほぼ半々の比率で加えたもの・・・なので、八代集で唯一**短歌撰進用臨時部署＜和歌所＞が公式に設置されなかった**ばかりか「**選者未詳**」という変わり種。実質上の選者の公任(14首)と、花山院の近臣として選に加わったとされる藤原長能(7首)の歌が加わったことで、前作『後撰集』で確立されかかった「選者の自作歌は勅撰集に入れない」という約束事は崩れたが、前作でガタ落ちした勅撰和歌集の品質を立て直した公任の目利きの確かさと「恋歌」の秀歌の数々が光る短歌集。

―八代集 概説―

4)『後拾遺集』[1086年]＜白河天皇下命＞選者＝藤原通俊(5)：全1220首(重複8首、うち『後撰集』1首、『拾遺集』7首)
・・・選者の藤原通俊は白河天皇のお気に入りの近臣だが、和歌界では若輩者だったため、当然自分が選者に選ばれるものと自負していた当時の歌壇の重鎮源経信が『難後拾遺』を著してその内容を批判するなど色々波風の立った勅撰集・・・しかしながら、集められた歌の**対象年代が王朝文学最盛期の一条朝(和泉式部・赤染衛門らの活躍期)だったため**(特に女流歌人の)**華やかな秀歌も多く**、選者の未熟さ(詞書のクドさ等々)を救っている。その一方で、平安の世の陰りを感じさせるような哀感漂う短歌も目立つ・・・『古今集』『後撰集』『拾遺集』の所謂「三代集」の頃とは(短歌も貴族社会も)微妙に違う時代(日本史でいう「院政期」)に入りつつあったのである。

5)『金葉集』[1126年]＜白河院下命＞選者＝源俊頼(42)：(初度本＋二度本＋三奏本総合)865首(正規三奏本648首：異本歌5首：重複26首、うち『拾遺集』が23首、『後拾遺集』が3首)
・・・前作『後拾遺集』で撰進を任されずふてくされた源経信への弁済措置のごとく、その三男の俊頼を選者に選んだ白川院(法皇)だが、その**撰進内容に難色を示して二度も選者に突き返す**異例の過程を経て(初度本巻頭歌に白川院が毛嫌いしていた異母弟の輔仁親王の短歌があったせいで院がヘソを曲げてしまった、という説もある)、**正規版としてようやく認められた三奏本は白川院の寵愛する待賢門院**(崇徳・後白河両天皇の母)**が手元に秘蔵して世に出ず**、世間には「(ボツになったはずの)二度本」が流布、度重なる改撰過程で徐々に増してきた**前衛的歌風(当代歌人偏重、それまで戯れ歌扱いだった「連歌」を正規の部立に組み入れる等)も当時としては不評**で、八代集中最もややこしい来歴と散々の評判を背負う歌集になってしまった・・・が、そうしたゴシップの色眼鏡を外して見れば、超一級の歌人源俊頼の目利きの確かさが随所に光るなかなかの「トンガった歌集」と言える。

6)『詞花集』[1150年代]＜崇徳院下命＞選者＝藤原顕輔(6)：全420首(異本歌5首：重複66首、全て『金葉集』との重複)
・・・「前衛的失敗作」だった前作『金葉集』への反省からか、当代歌人よりも一条朝まで遡る古い秀歌に比重を移したおとなしい内容となっている。**通常の勅撰集の半数にも満たぬ収録歌数の極端な少なさから**も、正規三奏本が世に出回らなかった『金葉集』との重複歌の異常な多さからも、前作からわずか25年後という撰進間隔の短さからも、＜『金葉集』(二度本)を『詞花集』で補ってようやく一つの勅撰和歌集＞の感がある。当代歌人枠の少なさのせいで「勅撰和歌集に名を載せて自らの名を上げたい！」と望む俗っぽい貴人達から(歌の質ではなく、歌集の編集態度に対して)猛烈な批判が沸き上がったあたりいかにも「平安の世も末」の感を催させるが、**清明な叙景歌の秀作が際立つ「詩集」としてのその完成度は極めて高く**、「短歌」より「ポエム」が好きな読者向きの歌集と言えるだろう(・・・短歌初心者にお勧めの勅撰集としては『古今集＞詞花集＞拾遺集』の順でベスト3と言ってよい；間違っても『新古今集＞千載集＞金葉集』あたりの＜短歌通向け遭難路＞を歩ませてはいけない！)。

7)『千載集』[1188年]＜後白河院下命＞選者＝藤原俊成(36)：全1288首(異本歌2首：重複23首、うち『拾遺集』3首、『金葉集』15首、『詞花集』5首)
・・・選者が高倉帝に上奏して勅撰集として認めてもらうべく一条帝以降の十五代の治世に渡る秀歌を(15代＝3×5＝『三五代集』の名で)編んだ私撰集を元に、その後の安徳帝・後鳥羽帝の二代の歌も加えて練りに練り込まれた勅撰集・・・選者自身も認めている通り**「俊成色＝幽玄の体」が非常に色濃く**、「歌読み」

には評判が高い勅撰集だが、**歌人の内面世界を吐露した精緻な描写がこれでもかこれでもかと続く**（一気読みするには）少々息が詰まる感じの短歌集ではある（・・・『紫式部日記』を延々読み進めるような感じ、と言えば伝わる人には伝わるだろう）・・・前作『詞花集』とは対照的に、叙景より叙情に重きを置き、当代歌人が半数を占め、うち二割が俗世を捨てた「**歌僧**」であるあたりに、源平争乱で壊れつつあった平安末世の内省的雰囲気がずっしり重く伝わって来る勅撰和歌集である（・・・『平家物語』と併せ読むのに最もふさわしい短歌集、と言えば古典に疎い日本人にもその感じは伝わるだろう）

8)『**新古今集**』[1201～1216年]＜後鳥羽院下命＞選者＝藤原定家(47)・藤原家隆(43)・寂蓮(35)・藤原(飛鳥井)雅経(22)・藤原(六条)有家(19)・源(堀川)通具(17):全1978首(除棄歌20首:重複13首、うち『古今集』2首、『拾遺集』2首、『金葉集』7首、『詞花集』1首、同じ『新古今集』内での重複1首・・・後鳥羽院独自の「隠岐本除棄歌」344首)

・・・後鳥羽院の御所に「和歌所」が置かれたのが1201年、最終完成を見たのは1216年頃、この間には最終的に選者として名を連ねた6名以外にも更に8名の「寄人」として釈阿(＝藤原俊成)・慈円・藤原隆信・藤原秀能・藤原良経・源通親・源具親・鴨長明(そして他ならぬ後鳥羽院その人)も選に加わっている。『＜新＞古今』の名が示す通り、『古今集』以来の平安調短歌の集大成を目指しつつ、収載歌範囲を『万葉集』にまで広げており、前作『千載集』がどこまでも＜当代重視の藤原俊成お気に入り歌集＞だったのとは対照的に、**百花繚乱**のきらびやかさがある・・・ただ、古歌には編者独自の身勝手な改変を施し、「**小野小町(6)**」や「**蟬丸(2)**」といった(長らく顧みられなかった)「伝説の歌人」の名を勝手に騙って古歌めかした新作歌を作り散らし、当代歌では「**本歌取り**」「**本説取り**」が異常なまでに多用される(全体の約二割に及ぶ)など、良くも悪しくも強烈すぎるクセのあるその作風は「**新古今調**」と呼ばれ、好き嫌いが(当時もそうだったが、後代は特に)極端に分かれる(有り体に言えば、大方の日本人に毛嫌いされて「短歌」が衰亡する原因を作った)勅撰和歌集である・・・古典短歌世界によほど精通していない限り「何のこっちゃ？！」と途方に暮れるばかりの排他的難解さ満載の歌集だけに、現代読者が敢えて挑んだとしても軽々弾き返されてしまう点で、「新古今」と言えば「形而上学」や「Kantカント哲学」同様の「**門外漢殺し文物**」の代名詞たり得る代物と言っても決して過言ではない・・・まぁ、挑む現代人もそうそういるまいが、挑戦するなら『古今集』から『千載集』までの有名作品軒並み即座に脳裏に浮かぶほどの和歌の素養と瞬発的記憶力がないと — または八代集の全てを＜総ひらがな表記＞して自在に検索可能にしたコンピュータ・データベースが手元にないと — 無駄骨に終わるか、もっと悪いことには「本に付いてる学者の解説の受け売り」で「インテリ気取った新古今調エソテリ野郎(エセ・ウソ・インテリジェンス・エソテリシズム＝真の知性とは似て非なるインテリ気取った**排他的卓越主義者**)」となって門外漢の嫌悪と嘲笑と無視の対象となるばかり(・・・実はそれこそまさに「正調新古今隘路」ってアイロニーが待っているばかり)・・・

・・・結局、こうして自己閉塞的滅びの道を辿った平安調短歌だったが、その「**知る人ぞ知る;知らない人にはわかるまい**」的な「**部外者蔑視＆ひけらかし目的の排他性**」だけは、和歌と無縁の日本人の間にも各方面で**連綿と引き継がれて今日に至っている**・・・歌舞伎の演目から一般企業の不文律まで、日本の社会は「こんなことも知らんようじゃ、お前らまだまだだな」として余所者・新参者を嘲笑うことで己れのステータスを誇示しいびつな優越欲求を満たそうとする無意識的参入障壁だらけである。＜**部外者の目から見れば度し難きその排他的陰湿さ＆ウソ知識人**のエソテリシズム＆エセインテリ気取りの醜悪さ、それを思い知る目的のためだけにでも、古典に無知な現代日本人が『新古今集』でガツンとノックアウトされる反面教師体験は貴重かも＞とか皮肉の一つ

http://zubaraie.com　　-209-　　— 八代集(Hachidai shuu) Overview —

―八代集 概説―

も言いたくなるが、無意識のうちにも＜ヨソモノ・シロウト、お断わり！＞の壁ばかり作りたがる日本の「自称文化人／専門家」の囲い者として飼い殺しにしてしまうにはいささか惜しい短歌も（数少ないとはいえ）あることを知るこの筆者(之人冗悟)としては、その純粋な文学的愉悦に（世界中の「本物の文化人」と共に）耽る喜びを味わうための本を一冊作っておくのもよろしかろう、と思ってこの本を世に出す次第である。

＝八代集(Hachidai shuu) Overview ＝

・・・the following is an overview of 八代集(Hachidai shuu＝8 great Imperial TANKA anthologies) in order of appearance, with 『**TITLE**』[publication year]＜ at the order of what [ex]Emperor＞ editor[s](number of songs in the anthology in question) : total number of songs(number of songs in variant texts : number of redundant songs) and cursory review of the anthology's characteristics

・・・"redundant songs" embrace not only totally identical ones (134) but also songs with minor alterations in some phrase[s] (94), including those seen in variant texts

1)『**古今集**(Kokin shuu, meaning "Songs old and new")』[A.D.905]＜at the order of 醍醐天皇(Emperor Daigo)＞editors＝紀貫之(Ki-no-Tsurayuki:105)・凡河内躬恒(Oushikouchi-no-Mitsune:62)・紀友則(Ki-no-Tomonori:46)・壬生忠岑(Mibu-no-Tadamine:37): total 1100 songs (29 songs in variant texts : 墨滅歌(sumi-kechi-uta＝blotted out songs)11 : 2 redundant songs)

・・・This first Imperial TANKA anthology was intended to be the corpus of TANKA poetry since the time of 『万葉集(Mannyou shuu, meaning "Myriad leaves")』 at the end of the Nara(奈良) era. As it turned out, however, the world of Heianese(平安) poetry was still in its infancy with hardly enough numbers of sophisticated TANKA coming up to the expectations of the editors. In order to fill the gap between the reality and their ideals, the original songs of the four editors occupied as much as almost one-fourths of the total number of songs in this anthology. This quite abnormal intervention of the editors, however, perfectly established 古今調(Kokin chou) rhyming style noted for imaginative enhancement of the world outside, exquisitely balanced with personal emotions in sophisticated terminology. This anthology paved the way for the glorious prosperity of Heianese TANKA, whose overall level of poetic sophistication is absolutely unmatched by any other anthologies, Imperial or otherwise... Should you, readers, have real interest ignited by my book in the world of Heianese TANKA, the first thing you should get to read is 『古今集(Kokin shuu)』: if you get your hand on this one, the other 7 anthologies may just as well be left untouched. No matter how many times you come back to cherish it, you'll hear the same echo of your heart's exclamation "*WONDERFUL!*" A miraculous gem of an Imperial TANKA anthology, whose genre achieved the height of its ideal at its very first attempt at climbing... a uniquely giant step unthinkable anywhere else in the world's literary history.

2)『**後撰集**(Go-sen shuu, meaning "Selected works after Kokin shuu")』[in the 950s]＜at the order of 村上天皇(Emperor Murakami)＞editors＝清原元輔(Kiyohara-no-Motosuke:1)・大中臣能宣(Ounakatomi-no-Yoshinobu:0)・源順(Minamoto-no-Shitagau:0)・紀時文(Ki-no-Tokibumi:0)・坂上望城(Sakanoue-no-Mochiki:0): total 1426 songs (25 redundant songs, including 16 songs from 『古今集』 and 9 songs from the same 『後撰集』)

―八代集　概説―

…Half a century after the publication of 『古今集(Kokin shuu)』, when TANKA poetry had already been firmly established in the everyday life of the society of nobles in 京都(Kyoto), the editors of this second Imperial TANKA anthology ― known as 梨壺の五人(Nashi-tsubo no go nin＝five staff at the office of Nashitsubo) ― didn't have any of their original TANKA poems included in their final work... only a joking stuff of pun song by 元輔(Motosuke) is seen included among the prevalent version probably as a result of a small laugh in the drafting stage, which *MUST* have been excluded from the final official version. This second song book is very much alike "a hodgepodge of celebrities TWEETS" full of petty daily conversation in 31 letters between the thriving nobles of the day. There do exist lots of good poems in it, but the absurdly high proportion of rubbish and jesting songs makes it by far the worst of 八代集(Hachidai shuu) from qualitative point of view. Judging from the crudity of 詞書 (kotoba-gaki＝annotations) and the number of redundant songs, the popular legend must be right that the prevailing version of this anthology in later years was an unfinished draft, with the final official version burnt down in the fire at the Imperial Palace in A.D.960... such a sorry Imperial anthology is it that I'm more than curious about the quality of its final version lost for ever to taint its honor.

3)『**拾遺集**(Shuui shuu, meaning "Leftovers from Kokin and Go-sen shuu")』[in the 1000s]＜at the order of 花山院(ex-Emperor Kazan)＞editors＝NONE : total 1351 songs（64 redundant songs, including 31 songs from 『古今集(Kokin shuu)』, 26 songs from 『後撰集(Go-sen shuu)』 and 7 songs from the same 『拾遺集(Shuui shuu)』... no redundancy among "公任(Kintou)'s best selection"）

…The essential half of this anthology is composed of the personally selected great songs by the greatest cultural figure of the day 藤原公任(Fujiwara-no-Kintou) ― practically all the songs from 『拾遺抄(Shuui shou)』 and selected songs from 『和漢朗詠集(Wa-Kan rouei shuu)』『三十六人撰 (San-juu-roku nin sen)』『金玉集(Kingyoku shuu)』『和歌九品(Waka ku-bon)』『深窓秘抄(Shin-sou hishou)』『前十五番歌合(Saki-no juu-go ban uta-awase)』 ― the other half supplemented by favorite songs of 花山院(Kazan inn) and his nearest courtiers. Such being the case, this is the only Imperial TANKA anthology of 八代集(Hachidai shuu) with no 和歌所(waka-dokoro＝a temporary Imperial office for the sole purpose of TANKA anthology publication) and even no official editor. By embracing 14 songs of 公任(Kintou, virtually the main editor of the anthology) and 7 from 藤原長能(Fujiwara-no-Nagayoshi, who is said to have participated in song selection as the nearest courtier of Kazann inn), this anthology demolished the official rule of "never including editors' original songs" which seemed to have been established by the previous anthology 『後撰集(Go-sen shuu)』. From qualitative point of view, this anthology made a wonderful recovery from the downfall of its predecessor by virtue of the scrutinizing eye of the virtuoso 公任(Kintou) and the entrancing repertoires of superb 恋歌(koi uta＝songs of love).

http://zubaraie.com　　　-211-　　― 八代集(Hachidai shuu) Overview ―

—八代集 概説—

4)『**後拾遺集**(Go-Shuui shuu, meaning "Sequel to Shuui shuu")』[A.D.1086]＜at the order of 白河天皇(Emperor Shirakawa)＞editor＝藤原通俊(Fujiwara-no-Michitoshi:5)：total 1220 songs(8 redundant songs, including 1 song from 『後撰集(Go-sen shuu)』 and 7 songs from 『拾遺集(Shuui shuu)』)

…The editor of this anthology was a favorite courtier of Emperor 白河(Shirakawa), but he was considered too immature for the great honor of compiling an Imperial TANKA anthology. 源経信(Minamoto-no-Tsunenobu), dean of TANKA poetry of the day and proudly hopeful of the honorable duty of editing it, became understandably indignant and published 『難後拾遺(Nan Go-Shuui, meaning "Criticism of Go-Shuui")』. Despite so much scandalous repute, since the target age of this anthology was 一条朝(Ichijou-chou＝the reign of Emperor Ichijou), the prime of Heianese literature with such talents as 和泉式部(Izumi shikibu) and 赤染衛門(Akazome emon), the immaturity of the editor (the long, prosaic annotations wet-blanketing poetry, etc.) is somewhat relieved by the number of great songs of so many great poets (especially women). On the other hand, poems with pathos signaling the twilight of the Heian era began to appear in this anthology… tide was turning from the good old days of 三代集(Sandai shuu) — 『古今集(Kokin shuu)』, 『後撰集(Go-sen shuu)』 and 『拾遺集(Shuui shuu)』 — into something different — 院政期(inn-sei ki＝the period of wire-pulling politics)as Japanese historians call it — both in the world of TANKA and the Heianese nobles.

5)『**金葉集**(Kinnyou shuu, meaning "Golden leaves of words")』[A.D.1126]＜at the order of 白河院(ex-Emperor Shirakawa)＞editor＝源俊頼(Minamoto-no-Toshiyori:42)：(初度本:1st＋二度本:2nd＋三奏本:3rd editions)total 865 songs(the official 3rd edition alone＝648 songs:5 songs in variant texts：26 redundant songs, including 23 songs from 『拾遺集(Shuui shuu)』 and 3 songs from 『後拾遺集(Go-Shuui shuu)』)

…In the previous Imperial anthology 『後拾遺集(Go-Shuui shuu)』, the then Emperor Shirakawa didn't choose 源経信(Minamoto-no-Tsunenobu) as its editor and made him indignantly disappointed; this time, as if in compensation, 白川院(ex-Emperor Shirakawa) chose 経信(Tsunenobu)'s 3rd son 俊頼(Toshiyori) as the sole editor of a new Imperial TANKA anthology; but 白川院 was anything but kind to 俊頼(Toshiyori). Rumor has it that the 1st edition started with a song by 輔仁親王(Sukehito shinnou＝prince Sukehito), a brother-in-law of 白川院 whom he hated so much that he turned absolutely sour on what 俊頼(Toshiyori) offered afterwards: after having his compilation rejected TWICE (which was quite unusual), the third and official version of this anthology was cached away at the hand of 待賢門院(Taiken-mon inn), the beloved court lady of 白川院 who gave birth to two Emperors, 崇徳(Sutoku) and 後白河(Go-Shirakawa), never to circulate outside, only to be substituted publicly with the officially turned-down 2nd version. In such unhappily complicated circumstances, this anthology became more and more "*avant-garde*" — shifting heavily towards the works of contemporary poets, giving proper space for 連歌(renga＝linked verse rhymed out as a combination play between two different poets, which was generally dismissed as a party trick). Such *progressive* characteristics of this anthology were not to the taste of poets of the day; seen without any such gossipy prejudice, however, this "*far-out*" anthology strikes authentic poets as extraordinary (in a good sense) here and there by dint of the unique choice by 源俊頼(Minamoto-no-Toshiyori) whose poetic virtuosity was not lethally spoiled by such less than favorable circumstances unbearably heavy on him..

6)『詞花集(Shika shuu, meaning "Flowers of words")』[in the 1150s]＜at the order of 崇徳院(Sutoku inn)＞editor＝藤原顕輔(Fujiwara-no-Akisuke:6)：total 420 songs（5 songs in variant texts：66 redundant songs, all from 『金葉集(Kinnyou shuu)』）

・・・Perhaps in conscious contrast to the "*progressive failure*" of the previous 『金葉集(Kinnyou shuu)』, this anthology is a little too orthodox, weighing much more on old excellent TANKA back in the years of Emperor 一条(Ichijou) in preference to the contemporary poems. Its unusually small number of volume (with less than half the normal volume) along with its abnormal redundancy from the previous anthology which was published as recently as 25 years before makes it appear that 『金葉集(Kinnyou shuu)』's 2nd edition supplemented by 『詞花集(Shika shuu)』 composes a normal volume of a single Imperial anthology. Due to the small number of space for contemporary poets, those noble (but *ignoble*) ones who aspired for prestige through being listed among the Imperial TANKA anthology poets rebuked this anthology — not for its contents but for the editor's attitude in compilation... you can see how *deep in shit* the world of Heianese nobles already was. Aside from such turbulence outside, the poetic world of this anthology is extremely high in quality with lots of crystal clear depiction of Nature, which will be to the taste of those readers who prefer "poems" to "TANKA"... in fact, the best 3 Imperial anthologies for novice readers of TANKA should be 『古今集(Kokin shuu)＞詞花集(Shika shuu)＞拾遺集(Shuui shuu)』 in that order; never let them tread the distress course of 『新古今集(Shin-Kokin shuu)＞千載集(Senzai shuu)＞金葉集(Kinnyou shuu)』 meant solely for experts.

7)『千載集(Senzai shuu, meaning "A millennium of poems")』[A.D.1188]＜at the order of 後白河院(ex-Emperor Go-Shirakawa)＞editor＝藤原俊成(Fujiwara-no-Shunzei:36)：total 1288 songs（2 songs in variant texts：23 redundant songs, including 3 songs from 『拾遺集(Shuui shuu)』, 15 songs from 『金葉集(Kinnyou shuu)』 and 5 songs from 『詞花集(Shika shuu)』）

・・・Prior to this anthology, its editor 俊成(Shunzei) had prepared his personal selection of good poems over fifteen different reigns of Emperors starting from Emperor 一条(Ichijou) — called 『三五代集(San-juu-go dai shuu)』, meaning *poems from 3x5=15 different reigns* — which he had expected Emperor 高倉(Takakura) to admit as an Imperial TANKA anthology. The editor later added two more generations of TANKA from the reigns of Emperor 安徳(Antoku) and 後鳥羽(Go-Toba), culminating in this 『千載集(Senzai shuu)』 which, as he admits, is characteristically 俊成(Shunzei)istic — he personally called it 幽玄の体(yuugen no tei＝a style of poetry with much imaginary reverberation between the lines), so much so that professional readers of TANKA poetry think highly of this anthology, where you will find no end of exquisite depiction of the inner worlds of numberless TANKA poets, a little too choking to be read through in your casual lyrical spree... you'll know how it is if you have had the nerve-exhausting experience of rushing *nonstop* through 『紫式部日記(Murasaki shikibu nikki＝the diary of Lady Murasaki)』. In contrast to the previous anthology 『詞花集(Shika shuu)』, this anthology is much more lyric than descriptive, half of its poems were made by the contemporary, of which some 20% were the songs of 歌僧(kasou), singing bonzes who deserted the secular world that was being destroyed by the civil war between the 源(Minamoto)'s and 平(Taira)'s... pessimistic communion with oneself resounding as heavily as 祇園精舎の鐘の声(Gion shouja no kane no koe＝the toll ringing at the Jetavana-vihāra), this anthology will be the perfect choice for reading along with 『平家物語(Heike monogatari＝the tales of the rise and fall of the Tairas)』... now, even those Japanese who are totally ignorant of classics will have known what 『千載集(Senzai shuu)』 is like.

http//zubaraie.com

8)『新古今集』(Shin-Kokin shuu, meaning "Kokin shuu reinvented")』[A.D.1201〜1216]＜at the order of 後鳥羽院(ex-Emperor Go-Toba)＞editors＝藤原定家(Fujiwara-no-Teika:47)・藤原家隆(Fujiwara-no-Ietaka:43)・寂蓮(Jakuren:35)・藤原(飛鳥井)雅経(Fujiwara-no/Asukai Masatsune:22)・藤原(六条)有家(Fujiwara-no/Rokujou Ariie:19)・源(堀川)通具(Minamoto-no/Horikawa Michitomo:17)：total 1978 songs(除棄歌(nozoki uta＝blotted out songs) 20:13 redundant songs, including 2 songs from 『古今集(Kokin shuu)』, 2 songs from 『拾遺集(Shuui shuu)』, 7 songs from 『金葉集(Kinnyou shuu)』, 1 song from 『詞花集(Shika shuu)』and 1 song from the same 『新古今集(Shin-Kokin shuu)』・・・後鳥羽院(Go-Toba inn)'s original「隠岐本除棄歌(Oki-bon nozoki-uta＝blotted out songs in the books of Oki-no-shima)」344 songs)

・・・In 1201, 後鳥羽院(Go-Toba inn) established 和歌所(waka-dokoro＝a temporary office for Imperial TANKA anthology publication) in his own residence; around 1216, this extraordinarily lengthy project of Imperial anthology came to its conclusion... during which period, besides the 6 poets whose names finally appeared as its editors, there were 8 more poets who took part in song selection as 寄人(yori-udo＝participating experts) ── 釈阿(Shakua＝藤原俊成:Fujiwara-no-Shunzei)・慈円(Jien)・藤原隆信(Fujiwara-no-Takanobu)・藤原秀能(Fujiwara-no-Hideyoshi)・藤原良経(Fujiwara-no-Yoshitsune)・源通親(Minamoto-no-Michichika)・源具親(Minamoto-no-Tomochika)・鴨長明(Kamo-no-Choumei)... and none other than 後鳥羽院(Go-Toba inn). As its name 『＜新＞古今(**Shin=New**-Kokin)』implies, this anthology aspired to be the corpus of Heianese TANKA since 『古今集(Kokin shuu)』, extending its scope to the preceding years of 『万葉集(Mannyou shuu)』. In contrast to the previous anthology 『千載集(Senzai shuu)』which was too much contemporary and too much 俊成(Shunzei)istic, this final anthology of 八代集(Hachidai shuu) is brilliantly gorgeous in its variations. The songs of this anthology, however, are grossly characteristic for good or *evil* ── called 新古今調(Shin-Kokin chou) ── *arranging wordings of old poems according to the editors' own fancy, making "fake" old songs in the name of long-ignored legendary poets like* 小野小町(Ono-no-Komachi)(6) *or* 蝉丸(Semi-maru)(2), *borrowing terms and backgrounds from old songs as imaginary foundations of contemporary poems* (「本歌取り:honka-dori, word-borrowing」「本説取り:honsetsu-dori, background-borrowing」) *in abnormal frequency (amounting to some 20%!)*... Such eccentric traits made this 『新古今集(Shin-Kokin shuu)』the most *liked* and **disliked** of all TANKA anthologies, even in its day, much more so in later years; directly speaking, most Japanese of later years totally hated and negated such *Shin-Kokin*istic eccentricity, leading to the downfall of TANKA poetry along with the fate of the noble folks in 京都(Kyoto). Unless you are exceptionally well-versed in the world of classical TANKA poetry, you are in for endless bewilderment in the works of this anthology which were made intentionally difficult to understand for all but the erudite. Practically all the modern challengers will be simply and miserably spurned, making 新古今(Shin-Kokin) the equal of "*metaphysics*" and "philosophy of *Immanuel Kant*" ── *laymen-eliminator*... well, I guess few modern readers will venture to challenge it, but if they do, they'll simply go nowhere without adequate knowledge of Heianese TANKA from 『古今集(Kokin shuu)』to 『千載集(Senzai shuu)』, with all the famous poems instantly coming up to mind in their well-versed, quick-response brains... or without a perfect computer database with ひらがな(hiragana)-search capability of all the phrases appearing in 八代集

(Hachidai shuu) near at hand... otherwise, something much worse than lack of understanding will be in store for such daredevil challengers — they will end up reciting (without *understanding*) what scholars say in the books they happened to have their hands on!... thereby making themselves *hated*, **scorned** and **ignored** by all the laypersons, dismissed as would-be intellectuals, or 新古今調エソテリ野郎 (Shin-Kokin-chou *ESOTERI* yarou = self-styled super-intelligentsia empowered by something somewhat similar yet quite alien to authentic intelligence trying consciously to exclude others from their esoteric circles) of would-be pundits... which, ironically, is nothing but the actual narrow path opened up by 新古今集(Shin-Kokin shuu) to close the door of TANKA poetry to the general reading public...

···After all, Heianese TANKA ended up in the impasse of self-suffocation, with fewer and fewer followers of the intentionally narrowed path in later years. But **even those Japanese totally alien to the tradition of TANKA have inherited its negative heritage here and there in today's Japan — the exclusive consciousness to show off knowledge and drive away strangers as if silently asserting "those who know will know; those who don't simply won't"**... from repertoires of 歌舞伎(Kabuki) to unwritten rules of business companies, Japanese society is surrounded by *subconscious* walls against newcomers laughing away their ignorance of "what insiders should *NATURALLY* know" thereby taking pride in their established *insider status* and satisfying their *perverted superiority complex* over ignorantly bewildered outsiders... I cannot help being sarcastic about such Japanese exclusiveness, feeling inclined to say **"Classically illiterate Japanese folks should have their ignorant heads scornfully hit hard by 『新古今集(Shin-Kokin shuu)』, to learn a lot from this lethally bad example how intolerably ugly their esotericism and pseudo-intelligence appear in the eyes of outsiders and any objective observers"**... Yes, the self-styled men of culture or self-proclaimed professionals in Japan are in the *subconscious* habit of making walls around them to reject outsiders and laypersons: the world of Heianese TANKA has been tucked away behind such esoteric walls, somewhat deservedly, all these long while... but there *do* exist in this world some poems, if not many, too precious to be left gathering moss as pets of petty-minded seclusionists. This author 之人冗悟 (Noto Jaugo) regrets it as one who knows them too well, so he thought it better to save them out of such secluded obscurity and provide authentic men of culture all over the world with an opportunity to rejoice in their purely literary enjoyment by making this book available in **ENGLISH**/Japanese...

＝八代集と本書の関わりについて＝

勅撰和歌集「**八代集**」(「八大」集とは書かない)の「代」は「天皇の御代」の意だが、さりとて「代々の天皇の治世」のたびに朝廷で公式和歌集が編纂されたわけではないし、天皇の「御代」が終わって上皇になった後に勅撰和歌集撰進の下命を出す場合も多かったし、白河天皇／法皇のように在位中＋退位後に二度も勅撰集撰進命令を出した帝もあるから「八代集＝八人の天皇各代の和歌選集」というわけでもないし、『古今集』以外の勅撰集では「当代の＜有名人＞」であれば＜名人＞ならずともその凡歌を勅撰集に入集させて当人をいい気分にさせてやる社交辞礼的(ゴマスリ)慣行もあったのだから、「八代集＝各時代ごとの短歌名作選集」などという間違った前提でこれに向かえば、落胆を通り越して嘲笑・憤激を禁じ得ないので、「八**大**集」と呼ぶにもいささか抵抗がある‥‥という風に、何から何まで何とも微妙な呼び名ながら、日本文学史上「**八代集**」と言えば＜第60代醍醐帝から第82代後鳥羽帝までの「**23代**」、905年から1216年の約三百年間に「**7人**」の帝／院の勅命によって撰進された「**8つ**」の勅撰和歌集＞を指すものである。

およそ「短歌」ほど＜選別＞が死活的重要性を持つ文芸ジャンルはない‥‥優れた詩人の個人作品集ではない「勅撰和歌集」では特にそうである。五・七・五・七・七で字数を合わせさえすれば韻律も何も関係なしに日本人なら誰でも簡単に「詩歌めいた散文」が無尽蔵に作り散らされてしまうだけに、品質管理は極めて困難、「平安の世の雅びを今に伝える大和歌の集大成」などと美辞麗句で粉飾してみても、実際には残念な凡作の方が圧倒的に多い約千三百人の歌人の寄せ集め歌集(異本を含む八代集収載歌総数は9708首；重複除外すれば9480首)なのだから、その中から本当に良い歌だけを選りすぐって眼前に示さぬ限り、後代の読者としては「短歌って、クズだな！」で終わりなのである‥‥で、実際、「川柳・俳句はまだしも、短歌なんて、ねぇ‥‥」というのが大方の現代日本人の感覚のように思われる‥‥五・七・五の十七文字だけでボソッと言い切る「川柳(季語付きなら、俳句)」では(140文字の英文ツイッター同様)名句も凡句もなかなか生まれない(優劣差がさほど際立たず似たり寄ったりになる；ので、誰でも簡単に手を出せる)が、意気揚々の「五・七・五」(上の句)が「七・七」(下の句)段階でガクっと腰砕けで終わる「腰折れ歌」の惨めさが誰の目にも明らかな「短歌」の世界では、凡歌を排して秀歌のみに絞り込む「目利きの選別作業を少しでも怠れば、潜在的「歌読み」たちはたちまち逃げて行く‥‥「歌詠み」が育たぬのは言うまでもない‥‥そうした自己閉塞状況を、「短歌」は、少なくとも一世紀以上の長きに渡って託ち続けている‥‥と、この筆者(之人冗悟)の目には映る‥‥これが見立て違いであればそれに越したことはないのだが、「自分だけは熱心に短歌を読んで／詠んでいる！」と言い張る少数の好事家が何をどう主張しようとも、かつて「物語よりも随筆よりも、何をおいてもまず短歌」だった時代がこの国にあったことを思えば、そして「わずか三十一文字の小宇宙で凝縮的に物語を構築し得る短歌の潜在力」自体は今なお健在である(のに活かされているとは到底言い難い)ことを思えば、「**21世紀初頭の日本にあって、短歌文芸は(死んではいないにせよ)休眠状態にある**」と言い切るのに何のためらいもないこの筆者である‥‥がゆえに、その状況を打ち破るに十分な「良材」選びに一年間寝ても覚めても「八代集」まみれの生活の果てに、本書をこうして世に問う次第である。

<u>本書の生命線はズバリ、その＜選別＞の品質にある</u>。「八代集」9480首のうち、筆者の「古文教育者」としての目で見て「短歌(必ずしも詩歌ならず)」として敢えて現代の古文学習者の眼前に提示してもよいと思える作品は1000首足らず、現代の詩的・文芸的感性から見て鑑賞に堪え解説・対訳を付けてやるに値する短歌たるやわずか200首程度、その中でも特に「★＜詩＞として、あるいは＜箴言＞として、**特に優れている**★」と筆者が個人的に太鼓判を押せる作品はわずか50首に過ぎない‥‥その★**筆者の個人的お気に入りベスト50首**★に●**古典短歌として紹介したいもの150首**●を加えて膨らませたのが本書である。本書に収めた200首が必ずしも「八代集(9480首分の)ベスト200」というわけではない：「●**日本の伝統的季節・情緒を今に伝えるのに好適な短歌**●」であれば「凡歌」でも敢えて混入させてあるので(★筆者の個人

―八代集と本書の関わりについて―

的ベスト50★以外は)その純度をあまり当てにしてもらっても困るが、この一冊さえあれば「八代集」そのものには触れずとも、(「八代集って、何?」というような日本の人々にとっては)問題なしと言えるぐらいの「日本の古典的短歌の入門編&決定版」に仕上がっていることは保証しよう。あの有名な藤原定家の『小倉百人一首』が「一歌人一首のみの著名歌人の名刺入れ(しかも必ずしも各歌人ベスト集ならず)」だったのと異なり、本書の選別基準は「歌人」ではなく「歌の内容」のみなので、天才歌人の和泉式部や西行法師のようにやたら数多く登場する歌詠みもあれば、殆ど無名の人の歌も多く、半数近くは「詠み人知らず」である···名よりも実を重んじればこそのその変則性もまた本書の醍醐味の一つとして味わっていただければと思う。

　本書はあくまで「詩集」であって「和歌指南書」ではないので、「短歌の技法」「古典文法」「古文単語」の詳細で体系的な解説は期待しないでほしい ― そうした参考書としての役柄は、同じ筆者の既刊本『古文・和歌マスタリング・ウェポン』および『古文単語千五百マスタリング・ウェポン』の両書が完璧に演じてくれているし、両書に含まれる古文単語1500+古典助動詞37+古典助詞77を「生きた古文の文脈」で読解・暗記するための「之人冗悟自作の平安調擬古文で構成した22編の歌物語集」としての『扶桑語り』も併用してもらえば、日本の平安時代の散文/韻文の読み解き能力としては(読者の期待を確実に上回るほどの)超絶的水準に到達し得ることを約束しよう···だから、本書はあくまで「詩集」として愉しんでもらえばよし、本書を読んで古歌に興味が沸いたなら上記3冊で日本語と日本文学の源流に直接触れることで自らの日本人/日本文化愛好者としての精神的核心の再確認・再構築にいそしんでもらえればなおよしである。

　かつて「経済力」で世界にその名を轟かせた日本は、今、「高品質なハードウェア」だけでは勝ち残れぬ「無形文化時代」にあって、何でもかんでも手当たり次第「これぞまさしく日本が世界に誇る文化遺産!」と叫んでは「UNESCO世界遺産」みたいな「有形のお墨付き」による箔付けを求めるという(自信も実力もない人間が「資格マニア」に化けるのと同質の)唾棄・嘲笑を誘う惨めなまでの「他者からの高評価による自己肯定感の渇望充足行動」に終始している···真の文化とは最も遠い場所に生息するその種の精神的無脊椎生物どもが「そうだ!日本には、世界に誇る<和歌>があったじゃないか!」などと叫ぶ事態が(とりあえず今のところ)起こらずに済んでいるのは、ひとえに「現代日本人には<和歌>を解釈するのに必要な<古典文法力><古文単語力><短歌修辞法理解力><漢字同音異義語認識力(=懸詞・縁語理解力)><詩的共感力><虚構的想像力>の全てが致命的に欠落している」という不様な付帯状況の保護壁があるからこそである···こんな非文化的な連中が「<和歌>は日本が世界に誇る優れた短編詩!」と叫んでも、まぁとりあえずそこまでは(見当違いながら結果的には正しいので)許せるが、トチ狂って「だから<八代集>を読むべし!」などと叫ばれた日にゃあ「なんだ、短歌って、実はクズじゃん!」の惨めな結末が待っているだけ···なので、詩的・文化的素養なき倭人連の事実無根の自画自賛が「真に優れた短歌の名誉」を汚すことになる前に、先手を制して本書を世に問うことにしたこの筆者としては、「古典的和歌世界の実を伝えるに好適な良品選び」に尋常一様ならざる情熱を注ぐと共に、詩的・文化的には日本人より遙かに信頼の置ける「日本文化に興味関心を抱く海外の文化的人間たち」をこそ真のターゲットに見立てて本書を編むことにした ― であるがゆえに、本書の内容は(索引を除く)その全てにおいて「現代日本語/英語」対訳形式となっている···筆者の本業は「英語教育者」であって「古文教育者・擬古文作者・平安調歌詠み」は数多ある筆者の知的多重人格のうちの一つなのだ ― そんな本書であるから、日本人英語学習者の「文化&語学錬磨の一石二鳥教則本」として用いるもよし、外国の友人に「真に優れた短歌を通して日本古来の季節感と情緒を伝える至れり尽くせりの英語版ガイドブック」として使って(あるいは、贈って)もらえればなおよしである···が、日本人としての真の文化的核心も持ち合わせぬ連中が無根拠な自己陶酔に陥って叫ぶような「美しい日本、バンザイ!」的な虚飾本とは真逆の立ち位置の「良いものは良い/悪いものは悪い;それを見据えようとせぬ日本人は一番悪い!」という是々非々の日本文化紹介本なので、自らの知的・文化的

http//zubaraie.com　　　-217-　　　―How this book relates to 八代集―

―八代集と本書の関わりについて―
質量の乏しさゆえに「誇大妄想的自国(=代理自我)礼賛」以外受け付けぬ独善白痴的虚弱体質の(=自ら
の無根拠な自画自賛への批判に耐える甲斐性無しの)日本人にはお勧めしない・・・自らの文化的伝統を
真に誇るために「無意味な埃は払い落とす御祓(みそぎ=身削ぎ)」を望む真摯な知性と根性ある諸賢と
のみ、本書を通して「そうそう、これが日本の真の姿!」の発見の喜びの共有を切に望むこの筆者である。

2016年3月11日
・・・あの壊滅的大震災からすでに五年、「新たな道を切り開く」よりも「狭まり行く古い世界にすがりつく」道を
選んで自己閉塞的排他性隘路を転げ落ち続ける日本人への「温故知新の書」として、これを遺す

之人冗悟(のと・じゃうご:Noto Jaugo)

= How this book relates to Hachidai shuu =

八代集(Hachidai shuu), not 八"大"集, is a collective term for the 8 great Imperial TANKA anthologies, in which「代(dai)」stands for "the reign of an Emperor", which does not mean each and every reign of respective Japanese Emperor had its own TANKA anthology published as an official business at its Palace. Many Imperial TANKA anthologies were made at the order of ex-Emperors after his「御代 (miyo=holy reign)」was over; Emperor/ex-Emperor Shirakawa gave two orders to compile two different Imperial TANKA anthologies while he was at the throne and after he left the throne, which makes it impossible to define 八代集(Hachidai shuu) as 8 different anthologies in the reign of **8** different [ex-]Emperors. As for their contents, it was customary in those days to include songs of mere *celebrities* of the day — not at all *masters* of the way — in the Imperial anthologies to give them prestige as a way of social flattery; prevalence of such snobbery (except in『古今集:Kokin shuu』) makes totally absurd the false assumption that 八代集(Hachidai shuu) *is a collection of the greatest poems of respective periods of the Heian era...* those who face them (except『古今集:Kokin shuu』) on such a false imaginary premise will be disappointed, disillusioned, even feel inclined to deride, resent or destroy 八代集(Hachidai shuu), which makes me somewhat reluctant to term it 八"大"集(Eight "GREAT" Imperial TANKA anthologies)... Such being the case, the name does not quite do justice to the contents, but in the history of Japanese literature, the term 八代集(Hachidai shuu) stands for "**8**" Imperial TANKA anthologies compiled at the orders of "**7**" Emperors/ex-Emperors during "**23**" reigns from 醍醐(Daigo: 60th) to 後鳥羽(Go-Toba: 82nd) over "**3**" centuries from A.D.905 to A.D.1216.

Nowhere in the world of literature does SELECTION have more critical importance than in the field of 短歌:TANKA, especially in the introduction of Imperial TANKA anthologies totally different from a collection of good poems by a single good poet. Practically every Japanese can easily make no end of "lyrical prose" by saying anything disregarding rhythms in the comfortable mold of 5・7・5・7・7 letters/syllables, making it extremely difficult to keep up tolerable level of overall quality. "*The corpus of* 大和歌*(Yamato-uta) handing down the noble tradition of the Heian era*" is a shamelessly thin veneer of 八代集(Hachidai shuu) through which its true colors will be clear to see (for those who would try to peer) — *a hodgepodge of 9,708 songs (9,480 without redundancy) by some 1,300 poets the bulk of which leaves too much to be desired*. Unless someone picks out the very best essence of it to show to the reading public of later years, they will end up dismissing it saying "TANKA being noble and great? Bullshit!" As it turns out, most Japanese feel that way: "川柳(SENRYUU) *sounds fine,* 俳句(HAIKU) *is not bad, but* 短歌(TANKA) *is no good or no use to me.!*" Just like (English version of) TWITTER in

—八代集と本書の関わりについて—

140 cramped letters, 17 letter/syllabled stream of 5・7・5 川柳(SENRYUU) — 俳句(HAIKU) if rhymed out with some seasonal phrase in it — is a difficult platform on which to sound *too **great*** or *too **shabby***: disparity between the good and the bad is small enough for any ordinary person to try it. While, in the world of 短歌(TANKA or 和歌:WAKA), the hopefully ambitious opening phrase of 5・7・5 (上の句):kami no ku＝upper part) will so often fall miserably flat at the stage of 7・7 (下の句):shimo no ku ＝lower part) — 腰折れ歌(koshi-ore uta＝songs laid waste at the waist) they call it — whose deplorable downfall is plain to see for all... no one wants to see such waste; <u>unless some connoisseur meticulously gets rid of shabby songs and selects tolerably good ones only, *potential readers* of TANKA poetry are sure to go away</u>... needless to say, no *makers* of TANKA will ever grow. Such self-suffocating circumstances have been suffered by 短歌(TANKA) for at least as long as a century, as it seems to this author (之人冗悟... *how fortunate it would be if I were wrong!*)... there might, of course, be a small number of dilettantes who assert themselves ardent readers/makers of TANKA poetry, but however or whatever they assert, in a country where there used to be a time when TANKA reigned supreme above stories or essays in the world of literature, and in view of the fact that the potentiality of TANKA as a 31-letter/syllable microcosm embracing densely eloquent stories is still alive (*untapped*) today, this author does not hesitate to say "**the literary genre of TANKA is in the state of dormancy, if not total death, in Japan at the beginning of the 21st century**"... this book is the author's personal attempt at a breakthrough of such stale status quo of TANKA dormancy, on the strength of selected TANKA good enough to wake up the Japanese to its potential — an end result of a whole year of getting involved in the world of 八代集(Hachidai shuu) all through my waking (sometimes *dreaming*) hours in search of its best possible essence to be presented to you.

<u>The life force of this book springs from the quality of its **SELECTION**</u>. Of 9,480 (non-redundant) poems included in 八代集(Hachidai shuu), only about 1,000 ones are worthy of introduction before the eyes of learners of 古文(kobun＝ancient Japanese language) as TANKA(*not* necessarily as *poetry*) — that is what I feel inclined to say as an educator of 古文(kobun); as a person interested in poetry, literature and culture, no more than **200** TANKA will be found good enough for show with serious explanation and modern Japanese/English translation; of which as few as **50** poems are the personal favorites of this author recommendable as ★<u>**excellent pieces of poetry or aphorism**</u>★ — the very core of this book — supplemented with ●<u>150 recommendable as classical TANKA poems</u>● culminated into this book. *I don't mean to say that the 200 poems in this book constitute the very best of 9,480* 八代集*(Hachidai shuu) songs*: quite a few of not-so-good ●<u>TANKA poems instrumental in introducing Japanese seasonal and emotional tradition</u>● have been intentionally included without regard to poetic excellence, making it impossible for me to guarantee the overall quality of this book (except the ★**50 personal favorites of the author**★). I can guarantee, however, that this is the best possible book for *novice readers of TANKA* — those Japanese to whom the term 八代集 *(Hachidai shuu) is a total stranger* — as a decisive introduction to the essence of Japanese classical TANKA, which will make it practically unnecessary for amateur readers to actually touch any of 八代集 (Hachidai shuu). Unlike the legendary 『小倉百人一首(Ogura Hyakunin isshu)』which was the showcase of 100 different poets with respective (*not quite respectable*) poems, the criterion of this book is not "the <u>names</u> of poets" but "the <u>quality</u> of poems": with the result that some poets with authentic genius like 和泉式部(Izumi shikibu) or 西行法師(Saigyou houshi) will appear again and again, while

―八代集と本書の関わりについて―

you will find quite a lot of poets with no literary fame; poets with no names (詠み人知らず:yomi-bito shirazu＝anonymous) constitute half of it... this book (and its author) pays respect to the substance, not to the name ‒ please just join me in appreciating poetry, not appraising or applauding poets.

This book is "a collection of poems", no "和歌(WAKA) mastery guide": please don't expect it to be a comprehensive guide on "the technique of TANKA", "ancient Japanese grammar" or "ancient Japanese words" ― you can expect all those "reference book" functions to be perfectly played by 『古文・和歌マスタリング・ウェポン』 and 『古文単語千五百マスタリング・ウェポン』 ― written by the same author in Japanese (*not* in English) for students seriously considering taking full marks in Japanese college entrance exams of 古文(kobun); studied along with 『扶桑語り(Fusau gatari)』 ― 22 short stories centering around TANKA poems written by 之人冗悟 (Jaugo Noto) in the language of Japan 1,000 years ago ― you can read, understand and memorize the 1,500 important terms of ancient Japanese, all the detailed usage of classical 37 auxiliary verbs and 77 postpositional particles, in the living context of intriguing stories, which this author guarantees will lead you to the level of excellence in your understanding of Heianese Japanese prose and verse even beyond your greediest expectations!... That having been said, I recommend this particular book as **a collection of charming poems**: if it ignites your interest in ancient Japanese poetry, just resort to the 3 books above to have direct access to the original streams of Japanese language and literature, through which to reconfirm and reconstruct your own spiritual core as a Japanese/a lover of Japanese culture.

Japan, which used to reign supreme over the rest of the world as "an economic giant", is suffering in an age of "culture with no specific shape" where "mere quality in hardware" guarantees no excellence or even survival. Even in an age like this, Japan is doing nothing but resorting to "warrants with some specific shape or name" like *UNESCO's WORLD HERITAGE* by which to acquire prestige and satisfy its urge for positive self-image... high esteem by others hopefully supplementing the vacuum of self-confidence and substantial power desperately sought as if by those intent on chasing one empty qualification after another... detestably laughable act of those spiritually spineless creatures which place themselves at the furthest place from authentic culture has not (as yet) touched and tainted the world of TANKA by exclaiming "*Oh yes, Japan still has* 和歌*(WAKA), the world-class poetry!*" ― simply because the modern Japanese are lethally lacking in intellectual ability needed for TANKA appreciation ― understanding of ancient Japanese grammar, ancient Japanese words, poetic technique of TANKA, adequate vocabulary of 漢字(KANJI＝Chinese characters) enough to discern homonyms (needed for the appreciation of 懸詞:kake-kotoba＝puns and 縁語:engo＝associated words in apparently irrelevant contexts), poetic empathy, fictional imagination ― all these capacities are lethally absent, which miserable circumstances constitute the protective barrier for 和歌(WAKA) against the empty applause from cultural morons... when such miserable creatures cry out "和歌*(WAKA) as a proud world-class Japanese heritage*", that much is admissible (though *groundless*, it certainly *is true*): but when they go so far as to cry out crazily "*You must read* 八代集*(Hachidai shuu)!*", the result will be disastrous ― those who actually do will end up realizing "*the actual bulk of TANKA is bunk!*"... This author knows it only too well; so, he decided to publish this book in order to forestall those Japanese who will taint the honor of truly excellent TANKA poems by groundless self-praise as a result of their

―八代集と本書の関わりについて―

ignorance of authentic Japanese poetry and culture. That is why this author (之人冗悟) took unusual pains in selecting the really good poems instrumental in introducing the true substance of classical Japanese TANKA; he also composed this book in such a way as to be enjoyable by truly cultured people all over the world who have authentic interest in Japanese culture – who are much more to be trusted than ordinary Japanese when it comes to appreciating poetry and culture – that is the reason all the contents of this book (*except in index*) are written both in modern Japanese/English... **the main profession of this author is "a Japanese teacher of English", with whom "an educator of 古文(kobun=ancient Japanese language), writer of Heianese Japanese prose and verse" are mere facets of his multiple intellectual personalities**. As such, this book can be used by a Japanese learner of English as a dual-purpose textbook for cultural and linguistic accomplishment; you can make even better use of it as a guide (or a gift) for your foreign friends which will tell them (in English/Japanese) the seasonal and emotional makeup of traditional Japanese culture through really excellent pieces of TANKA. But I will tell you once thing – no other book could ever be further from such *vanity balloons* exclaiming "*this beautiful NIPPON, BANZAI!*" rapturously published and purchased by those Japanese who have no real cultural core substantial enough to see through such empty bravados – this book is meant to be the antithesis to such dangerously foolish self-praise of the Japanese, **which proudly declares the goodness of the really good while detecting and denouncing what is bad about Japan, not the least of which is the Japanese attitude to pretend ignorance of what is bad about their nation**... so much so that those Japanese should refrain from reading it who are so destitute of intellectual and cultural substance that they simply won't accept anything but megalomaniac accolade of BEAUTIFUL JAPAN as their *alter ego*, too much self-righteous and too mentally weak to stand any criticism against their groundless self-praise – this book is meant only for those who are earnestly intelligent and mentally tough enough to willingly go through the process of depriving themselves of groundless and meaningless vanity, so as to pride themselves upon their authentic cultural heritage – **only along with such cultured people would I really like to share the genuine discovery of Japan as it really is** through this humbly ambitious book of mine.

March 11, 2016
・・・5 long years after the devastating earthquake, most Japanese have simply refused to open up an unprecedented new way to a positive new world; instead, they chose to stick to ever-dwindling old world pushing away their old friends, driving themselves and all around them straight down to self-suffocating Hell through narrower and narrower exclusive path... I will leave this book as a means to know where they stand now in the light of their own past ― Hell-bound Japanese may make many discoveries in it ― *good* and *bad* ― if they dare to peer.

之人冗悟(のと・じゃうご:*Noto Jaugo*)

散らで猶世に経る花を　手折りてぞ如何で伝へむ香しの過去
unfailing fragrance millennium long　smell as you will in this book
　　　　　　　　... hope you enjoy the smell, sometimes bad, but mostly good

http//zubaraie.com　　　　-221-　　　―How this book relates to 八代集―

http://zubaraie.com ←合同会社ズバライエ(ZUBARAIE LLC.)ホームページ

— about **the author** of this book (本書の**著者**について) —

Jaugo Noto is a professional educator in linguistics, who makes it his business to enable students to see, do, or be what he's been through and what he can see through, in ways other humans have never imagined or even thought possible. His field of business activity ranges from modern English to ancient Japanese, developing not so much on paper or in the flesh as on the WEB currently.

之人冗悟(のと・じゃうご)は語学教育の専門家。彼本人の実践・予見の体験を、学生にも認識・実践・体得させること(それも、他者が想像もせず、不可能とさえ思っていた方法で可能ならしめること)を仕事とする彼の活動の幅は、現代英語から古典時代の日本語まで多岐に渡る。現在、紙本執筆や生身の授業よりインターネット上での事業展開が主力。

— about **ZUBARAIE** LLC. (Limited Liability Company 合同会社ズバライエについて) —

ZUBARAIE LLC. was established in Tokyo, Japan, on July 13th (Friday), 2012, as a legal vehicle for Jaugo Noto to perform such services as education, translation, publication and other activities to help enlighten people.

合同会社ズバライエ(ごうどうがいしゃZubaraie)は、2012年7月13日(金曜日)(おまけに仏滅)、日本国の東京にて、之人冗悟(のと・じゃうご)が教育・翻訳・出版その他の啓蒙(けいもう)活動を遂行(すいこう)するための法的枠組として設立された。

「歌型二百(うたかた にひゃく)(千代苔歌(ちよたいか)):UTA-KATA200(Millennium Moss)」

ISBN 978-4-9906908-5-4

Copyright © 2016 by Jaugo Noto
1st edition published from ZUBARAIE LLC. 2016/03/11

大学入試「古文」/「英文法」に完璧を期す受験生には理想的な**自学自習WEBレッスン**あり:

＊『**扶桑語り**(ふさうがたり)』(古典文法/古文単語/読解力総合講座)→**http://fusaugatari.com/**

＊『**英文法＋Q&A**』(体系的英文法学習講座)→**http://furu-house.com/**

= also from the same **author** 之人冗悟(*Jaugo Noto*) =

Beneath **U**mbrella of **Z**ubaraie *LLC.*

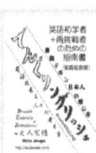

『**でんぐリングリッシュ**:英・和 対訳版』ISBN 978-4-9906908-0-9

日本の初学者&再挑戦者に贈る、英語を真にモノにするための心得(英文／和訳見開き対訳本)。
･･･本書一冊では効果半減:『英文解剖編』との併用により、真の英文解釈力の開眼を図るべし。

『**でんぐリングリッシュ**:英文 解剖編』ISBN 978-4-9906908-1-6

同書の全英文を、解剖学的解釈の詳細な構造図で「**可視化**」した古今未曾有の英文読解指南書。
英語がこの形で「見える」ようになることこそ、全学習者の理想形･･･よーく見て、マネぶべし。

『**古文・和歌**マスタリング・ウェポン』ISBN 978-4-9906908-2-3

大学入試で出題される古文と和歌の知識を完全網羅。暗記必須事項は抱腹絶倒の語呂合わせで、
重要事項の全ての暗記＋確認は巻末穴埋めテストで、調べ物は詳細な索引で、完全サポート。

『**古文単語千五百**マスタリング・ウェポン』ISBN 978-4-9906908-3-0

充実の語義解説で大学入試古文にも和歌・古文書解釈にも不自由を感じぬ完璧な古語力を養成。
入試得点力に直結する受験生の福音書にして、日本語・日本文化への目からウロコの知識の宝庫。

『**扶桑語り**(Fusau Tales):古文・英文・現代和文対釈』ISBN 978-4-9906908-4-7

『古文単語千五百』の**全見出語1500**(＋**平安助動詞37**＆**平安助詞77**全用法)で書かれた22編の
擬古文歌物語で『古文・和歌マスタリングウェポン』の説く古典読解法の実践を図る英和古対釈本。

http://zubaraie.com